# OUR BLUE PLANET

# OUR BLUE PLANET

## AN INTRODUCTION TO MARITIME AND UNDERWATER ARCHAEOLOGY

*Ben Ford*
*Jessi J. Halligan*
*Alexis Catsambis*

OXFORD
UNIVERSITY PRESS

Oxford University Press is a department of the University of Oxford. It furthers
the University's objective of excellence in research, scholarship, and education
by publishing worldwide. Oxford is a registered trade mark of Oxford University
Press in the UK and certain other countries.

Published in the United States of America by Oxford University Press
198 Madison Avenue, New York, NY 10016, United States of America.

CIP data is on file at the Library of Congress
ISBN 978–0–19–064993–7 (pbk.)
ISBN 978–0–19–064992–0 (hbk.)

1 3 5 7 9 8 6 4 2

Paperback printed by Sheridan Books, Inc., United States of America
Hardback printed by Bridgeport National Bindery, Inc., United States of America

*With gratitude to our families*

# CONTENTS

# LIST OF ILLUSTRATIONS

**FIGURES**

## TABLES

# PREFACE

Much of the academic literature in the field of maritime and underwater archaeology requires an existing understanding of archaeological concepts, nautical terms, and overarching research questions. It also assumes the reader already knows a significant amount of historic context. Conversely, numerous popular articles or volumes elicit a great deal of interest in the field, or are visually appealing, but are generally short on scholarly detail. This textbook is meant to fill the gap between these disparate sources. Our intent is to introduce basic archaeological terms and concepts, especially those applicable to maritime and underwater archaeology, while also offering an avenue into the professional literature through organizing the text around the major research themes pursued by modern maritime and underwater archaeologists. Though we anticipate that faculty who use this volume may wish to supplement the following chapters with more in-depth articles or books, this text is meant to provide the background to allow students to absorb the meaning within those scholarly works.

## ABOUT THE AUTHORS

Each of us came to this field through a very different path. Maritime and underwater archaeology is multifaceted, covering research underwater and on land and from many different times and places; as a result the routes through which scholars discover this field are rarely straightforward. Ben Ford chose maritime archaeology when it became apparent at the beginning of graduate school that he had to specialize in something. At the time, shipwrecks seemed like a much more exciting specialty than pots or sharp rocks. Just like he learned as an undergraduate that archaeology was more than what was shown in movies, he soon discovered that there was more to maritime archaeology than shipwrecks. In both cases, he was fortunate to find that the reality of archaeology was much more interesting than his preconceived notions. Ben ultimately gravitated to a form of maritime archaeology that draws from both terrestrial and underwater archae-ology to study how people interact with the water's edge. This approach allows him to ask broad questions about how people adapt the spaces around them and to employ techniques he learned working in heritage management.

Jessi Halligan became an underwater archaeologist somewhat obliquely. She was always most interested in the lifeways and archaeology of foraging (rather than food-producing) societies. While working on an actively eroding coastal site on Martha's Vineyard during her undergraduate field school, she became increasingly interested in how the geological processes of erosion, deposition, and soil formation determine if, and to what extent, an archaeological site will survive after people have abandoned it. She became especially drawn to how sea-level change impacts our understanding of how past people used the coasts during her undergraduate thesis research. So she learned to SCUBA dive, and, studied both geoarchaeology and underwater archaeology in graduate school. She combines both to study the inundated remains of the earliest sites in the Americas, as these sites are well-preserved in comparison to their terrestrial counterparts and contain information only discoverable by working underwater.

Alexis Catsambis came to maritime archaeology through his love for the sea. Before the end of secondary school he became an accredited diver and soon decided to pursue archaeology with a view toward graduate studies in nautical archaeology. His focus in the study of seafaring and maritime antiquity transitioned over the course of his doctoral studies to one concentrated on the management of maritime cultural heritage, which in turn broadened the time period and types of heritage sites in which he held an interest. The opportunity to work as a maritime archaeologist and heritage manager for the US Navy permitted him to consider the field through a new perspective—one that views heritage sites through the lens of a variety of stakeholders, and explores the relationship between humans and the marine environment through time and to the present day. The diversity of what can be learned through maritime and nautical archaeological research—technological advancement, environmental adaptation, intercultural exchange—as well as the way maritime heritage sites are perceived today, as repositories of knowledge, sites of cultural identity, economic drivers, sacred places of human loss, environmental communities or hazards, even obstacles, reinforced in him the belief that this field is truly the study of the human condition, past and present.

We each found our way to maritime archaeology through a different path. This diversity of experiences is reflected in this book. Together, we feel that we can accurately portray this broad and expanding field. This collaborative approach also reflects how maritime and underwater archaeology is conducted. Archaeology is a social science not just because it studies people but because one cannot do it alone. Every archaeological project involves collaboration and coordination between numerous experts and colleagues of all sorts, and methods, analyses, and interpretations are strengthened by this interaction. We hope you find that this book is no different.

# ACKNOWLEDGMENTS

First and foremost, we would like to thank our families, friends, and loved ones for their support while we wrote on this book. They bore countless extra burdens so that we could focus. Ivy Owens read a draft of this manuscript and offered innumerable insights and suggestions that helped focus and correct the text; the book was also strengthened in many important ways by a series of diligent reviewers of the proposal and manuscript, to whom we are grateful for providing challenging feedback. We would like to extend our sincere appreciation to all the colleagues, scholars, and artists who contributed sidebars, images, suggestions, and assistance. They gave selflessly of their time and talents to make this book better. We also wish to acknowledge our home institutions—Indiana University of Pennsylvania, Florida State University, and the Naval History and Heritage Command—along with the many archives, museums, and universities that permitted us use of images to illustrate this text. Stefan Vranka and his colleagues at Oxford University Press were instrumental in leading us through the publishing process. We each also owe a debt of gratitude to our respective academic advisors and the numerous teachers we have had along the way, formal and informal; we are especially grateful to the Department of Anthropology at Texas A&M University for the many opportunities it provided each of us, not least of which was the opportunity to work together. Finally, each author would like to acknowledge the hard work and collegiality of their co-authors. Honestly, none of us could have done something like this alone, and that we are still friends speaks to everyone's good nature.

# TIMELINE OF MAJOR EVENTS

**Ca. 3.3 million years ago** – oldest stone tools (ch. 7)

**Ca. 2.8 million years ago** – oldest fossil of genus *Homo* (ch. 7)

**Ca. 2.6 million years ago** – beginning of Pleistocene

**Ca. 840,000 years ago** – *Homo erectus* arrives by boat on Flores (ch. 2)

**Ca. 200,000 years ago** – *Homo sapiens sapiens* appears in fossil record (ch. 8)

**Ca. 165,000 years ago** – earliest evidence of seafood, shellfish in South Africa (ch. 2)

**Ca. 130,000 years ago** – humans arrive on Crete by boat (chs. 2 and 8)

**Ca. 100,000 years ago** – human ancestors begin to spread out of Africa (ch. 8)

**Ca. 60,000 years ago** – humans reach Australia (ch. 8)

**Ca. 20,000 years ago** – end of last glacial maximum, rising sea levels (ch. 2)

**Ca. 14,000 BCE (ca. 16,000 years ago)** – *Homo sapiens* arrives in the Americas (ch. 7)

**Ca. 10,000 BCE** – earliest drawing of a boat (ch. 9)

**Ca. 10,000 BCE** – people retrieving obsidian from island of Melos (ch. 1)

**Ca. 10,000 BCE** – people accessing California Channel islands (ch. 1)

**Ca. 9,450 BCE** – beginning of Holocene and end of Pleistocene (ch. 7)

**Ca. 8000 BCE** – earliest surviving boat (ch. 9)

**Ca. 7000–4300 BCE** – ages of canoes found from a single lake in Florida (ch. 9)

**Ca. 7300–6300 BCE** – Approximate date of Neolithic submerged sites in Israel (ch. 1)

**Ca. 4000 BCE** – seafarers begin leaving islands of Southeast Asia (ch. 9)

**Ca. 4000 BCE** – earliest archaeological evidence of tattooing (ch. 10)

**Ca. 3700 BCE** – earliest surviving dock (ch. 8)

**Ca. 3400 BCE** – earliest evidence of writing (ch. 3)

**3400–3200 BCE** – pre-Dynastic periods in Egypt (ch. 3)

**Ca. 3100 BCE** – Abydos boats buried (ch. 9)

**2566 BCE** – Khufu ship entombed (ch. 9)

Ca. 2500 BCE – Indian Ocean shipbuilders constructing sewn-plank, shell-first vessels (ch. 9)

Ca. 2500 BCE – Egypt begins trading with Punt (ch. 11)

Ca. 2300 BCE – first textual mention of shipping (ch. 9)

Ca. 2250 BCE – global sea levels stabilize at approximately modern levels (ch. 7)

2055 BCE – Egyptians begin utilizing harbor of Mersa Gawasis (ch. 11)

Ca. 2030-1680 BCE – Ferriby boats (ch. 8 and 9)

Ca. 2000 BCE – Dor founded (ch. 8)

Ca. 1800 BCE – Mesopotamian tablet describing huge vessel transporting pairs of animals (ch. 9)

Ca. 1500 BCE – spread of people in the Pacific Islands begins (ch. 9)

Ca. 1500-400 BCE – Olmec period in Central America (ch. 8)

Ca. 1320 BCE – Uluburun ship wrecks (chs. 9 and 11)

Ca. 1250 BCE – seafarers populate many of the Pacific Islands (ch. 9)

1210 BCE – first recorded naval battle, Hittites and Cypriots (ch. 2)

Ca. 1200 BCE – arrival of the Sea People in the Mediterranean (chs. 11 and 12)

Ca. 1200 BCE – San Lorenzo founded (ch. 8)

1176 BCE – earliest depiction of a naval battle involving galleys (ch. 12)

Ca. 1000 BCE – Egypt ceases trading with Punt (ch. 11)

800 BCE–100 CE – Iron Age (ch. 8)

Ca. 725 BCE – Tanit and Elissa ships wreck (ch. 11)

Ca. 700 BCE – *Odyssey* written (ch. 10)

Ca. 600 BCE – monsoon wind navigation discovered before this date. (ch. 10)

Ca. 600 BCE – Bajo de la Campana ship wrecks (ch. 11)

Ca. 500 BCE – adoption of mortise-and-tenon shipbuilding in the Mediterranean (ch. 9)

493 BCE – Athenians begin to fortify Piraeus (ch. 8)

480 BCE – decisive battle of the Persian Wars takes place in straits of Salamis (ch. 12)

440 BCE – Herodotus writes the *Histories* (ch. 11)

430 BCE – during Peloponnesian War sickness from Persia or Egypt arrives at Piraeus, resulting in massive loss of life (ch. 10)

404 BCE – Athens surrenders to Sparta (ch. 10)

4th century BCE – Antikythera ship wrecks (ch. 1)

Ca. 350 BCE – Hjortspring boat built (ch. 9)

331 BCE – city of Alexandria founded (ch. 2)

330 BCE – Pytheas of Massalia travels to Northern Europe (chs. 9 and 11)

Ca. 325 BCE – Kyrenia ship built (ch. 11)

323–31 BCE – Hellenistic period in Greece (ch. 8)

Ca. 300 BCE – Hasholme boat built (ch. 9)

Ca. 300 BCE – Kyrenia ship wrecks (chs. 9 and 12)

Ca. 300 BCE – fore-and-aft sail appears in Mediterranean (ch. 9)

241 BCE – First Punic War (ch. 12)

Ca. 100 BCE - Godavaya ship wrecks (ch. 11)

1st century BCE – Hydraulic concrete developed (ch. 8)

1st century BCE – Madrague de Giens merchantman ship (ch. 9)

31 BCE – Battle of Actium (ch. 12)

Ca. 20 BCE – Caesarea Maritima built (ch. 8)

42 CE – *Portus* built by Emperor Claudius (ch. 3 and 8)

50 CE – London founded (ch. 8 and 9)

Ca. 50 CE – *Periplus of the Erythean Sea* written (ch. 10

Ca. 50 CE – lodestone used to find directions (ch. 10)

1st century CE – rudder developed in China (chs. 6 and 9)

Ca. 100 CE – Earliest bottom-based vessels (ch. 9)

Ca. 200 CE – Nydam boat built (ch. 9)

Ca. 200 CE – Roman *uninatores* used to salvage wrecks and sabotage ships

295 CE – County Hall ship built (chs. 9 and 11)

414 CE – Arabian merchants established in Sri Lanka (ch. 11)

6th to 7th century CE – joggled ship construction popular in Northern Europe (ch. 9)

6th century CE – evidence of trade between Arabia and China (ch. 9)

Ca. 500 CE – Dhow introduced to Indian Ocean (ch. 9)

515 CE – Journey of Saint Brendan (ch. 11)

7th to 10th century CE – ages of ships found in Harbor of Theodosius in Yenikapı, Turkey (ch. 8)

7th century CE – introduction of Greek fire (ch. 12)

Ca. 600 CE – Sutton Hoo ship burial (ch. 9)

Ca. 600 CE – widespread use of bulkheads in Chinese shipbuilding (ch. 9)

Ca. 600 CE – large, open-decked galleys replace overlapping planks technology (ch. 12)

Ca. 600 CE – Hawaii settled (ch. 9)

650 CE – Vikings reach Faroes (ch. 11)

Ca. 700 CE – Easter Island (Rapa nui) settled (ch. 9)

Ca. 700 CE – transition from shell to skeleton construction in Mediterranean (chs. 2 and 9)

Ca. 750 CE – Arabian merchants regularly sailing to China (ch. 11)

771 CE – earliest recorded astrolabe (ch. 10)

Ca. 800 CE – Sinbad the Sailor's journeys said to have occurred (ch. 11)

Ca. 800 CE – beginning of the Viking Age (ch. 11)

830 CE – Belitung ship wrecks (chs. 9 and 11)

Ca. 850 CE – Gokstad ship built (ch. 12)

860 CE – Vikings reach Iceland (ch. 11)

Ca. 875 CE – *kamal* navigation instrument developed (ch. 10)

879 CE – *Portus* reaches greatest expansion (ch. 3)

Ca. 900 CE – *Landnámabók* written (ch. 10)

980 CE – Vikings reach Greenland (ch. 11)

**10th to 11th century CE** – Hedeby ships (ch. 9)

**Ca. 1000** CE – widespread use of iron in Chinese shipbuilding (ch. 9)

**Ca. 1000** CE – Vikings reach Newfoundland and settle at L'Anse aux Meadows (ch. 11)

**1025** CE – Serçe Limanı ship built (ch. 9)

**1025** CE – Roskilde 6 ship built (ch. 12)

**1040** CE – Vikings conquer Sicily (ch. 11)

**Ca. 1050** CE – Skuldelev ships sunk (ch. 9)

**1070** CE – Bryggen founded (ch. 8)

**12th century** CE – The Crusades (ch. 9)

**Ca. 1100** CE – development of the cog (ch. 9)

**Ca. 1180** CE – hybridization of Mediterranean and Northern European ships begins (ch. 9)

**13th century** CE – Nanhai No. 1 ship wrecks (ch.11)

**Ca. 1200** CE – nautical charts invented (ch. 10)

**Ca. 1250** CE – initial spread of people in the Pacific islands ends (ch. 9)

**Ca. 1250** CE – sand clock invented (ch. 10)

**1270** CE – Quanzhou ship wrecks (ch. 11)

**1271** CE – Marco Polo begins his journey (ch. 11)

**1274** CE – Khubilai Khan sends naval forces across Tsushima Strait (ch. 12)

**Ca. 1275** CE – modern compass developed (ch. 10)

**1281** CE – Khubilai Khan conquers Southern Song dynasty (ch. 12)

**1298** CE – Marco Polo's *The Description of the World* (ch. 12)

**1325** CE – Muhammad Ibn Battuta begins his journey (ch. 11)

**Ca. 1370** CE – development of the carrack (ch. 9)

**Ca. 1330** CE – Culip VI ship wrecks (ch. 9)

**Ca. 1380** CE – Bremen Cog wrecks (ch. 9)

**Ca. 15th century** CE – amateurs conduct breath-holding dives in Lake Nemi (ch. 2)

**1405** CE – Treasure Shipyard at Nanjing used (ch. 8)

**1405-1433** CE – voyages of Zheng He (ch. 11)

**13th-15th c.** CE – Tulum, Mexico (ch. 8)

**1409** CE – third mast added to ship design (ch. 9)

**1415** CE – Portuguese capture Ceuta in North Africa (ch. 11)

**1418** CE – *Grace Dieu* ship launched (ch. 12)

**1440** CE – *Mezza luna* first recorded (ch. 9)

**Ca. 1450** CE – Ozette buried in a landslide (ch. 3)

**1450** CE – Vikings withdraw from Greenland (ch. 11)

**1462** CE – Portuguese reach Sierra Leone (ch.11)

**Ca. 1480** CE – fully rigged ship developed (ch. 9)

**1482** CE – Portugese build Elmina Castle in Ghana (ch. 11)

**1488** CE – *Sovereign* built (ch. 9)

**1492** CE – Christopher Columbus arrives in the Americas (ch. 1 and 11)

1498 CE – Portuguese round southern tip of Africa (ch.11)

Ca. 1500 CE – oldest archaeological astrolabe (ch. 10)

1508 CE – Woolwich ship rebuilt (ch. 9)

1510 CE – *Mary Rose* built (ch. 1)

1511 CE – *Great Michael* making use of gunports (ch. 12)

1512 CE – Woolwich Royal Navy dockyard founded (ch. 8)

1519 CE – Ferdinand Magellan begins circumnavigation of the Earth (ch. 11)

1535 CE – Francesco De Marchi explores wrecks in Lake Nemi using a diving bell (ch. 2)

1545 CE – Battle of Solent (ch. 12)

1545 CE – *Mary Rose* sinks (ch. 12)

1564 CE – *Mars* lost during Nordic Seven Years' War (ch. 12)

1565 CE – *San Juan* sinks at Red Bay (ch. 7 and 11)

1571 CE – Ottoman fleet defeated by the Holy League (ch. 12)

1578 CE – Francis Drake begins attacking Spanish ships in the Pacific (ch. 11)

1588 CE – King Phillip II of Spain attempts to invade England with Spanish Armada (ch. 12)

Ca. 1590 CE – hammocks adopted for sleeping on sailing vessels (ch. 10)

17th century XX – Irish curachs utilized (ch. 9)

Ca. 1600 CE – Crossing the Line ceremony becomes widespread (ch. 10)

Ca. 1600 CE – use of log to gauge speed formalized (ch. 10)

1602 CE – Verenigde Oostindische Compagnie (VOC), or Dutch United East India Company, formed (chs. 11 and 12)

1628 CE – *Vasa* ship built and sank (ch. 12)

1628 CE – *Batavia* wrecks (chs. 11 and 12)

1660 CE – Oostenburg shipyard founded (ch. 8)

1684 CE – *La Belle* sails from La Rochelle (ch. 6)

1686 CE – *La Belle* wrecks in Matagorda Bay, TX (ch. 6, 10)

1692 CE – Port Royal suffers earthquake and sinks (ch. 7)

1696–1698 CE – siege of Fort São Jesus (ch. 12)

1696 CE – *Santo Antonio de Tanná* deployed (ch. 12)

18th century CE – development of ship design using line drawings (ch. 6)

1708 CE – *San Jose* leaves Spain (ch. 1)

1718 CE – Blackbeard purposefully grounds Queen Anne's Revenge (ch. 12)

1746 CE – *Traité du navire* written by Pierre Bougers (ch. 9)

1747 CE – James Lind demonstrates effectiveness of lime juice for curing scurvy (ch. 10)

1760 CE – John Harrison develops a chronometer to accurately measure longitude (ch. 10)

1768 CE – *Fredensborg* wrecks (ch. 11)

Ca. 1800 CE – tattooing becomes popular among sailors (ch. 10)

1805 CE – Battle of Trafalgar (ch. 12)

1807 CE – first economically-viable steamboat (ch. 9)

**1807** CE – British abolish slave trade (ch. 11)

**1814** CE – USS *Jefferson* built (ch. 4)

**1814** CE – Dutch abolish slave trade (ch. 11)

**1819** CE – first Atlantic passage by a steamship (ch. 9)

**1820** CE – Whaleship *Essex* sunk by a whale (ch. 11)

**1823** CE – *Two Brothers* **wrecks (ch. 11)**

**1827** CE – War of Greek Independence (ch. 12)

**Ca. 1830** CE – clipper ship developed (ch. 9 and 11)

**1831** CE – Charles Darwin begins voyage on the *Beagle* (ch. 11)

**1832** CE – *Heroine* built (ch. 9)

**1834** CE – Greece passes law on the preservation and use of antiquities (ch. 13)

**1836** CE – Deane brothers discover Mary Rose shipwreck in England (ch. 2)

**1837** CE – *Eric Nordewall* built (ch. 9)

**1838** CE – *Heroine* sinks in Red River, OK (ch. 3)

**1839** CE – First Opium War begins (ch. 11)

**1841** CE – whaleship *Charles W. Morgan* launched (ch. 11)

**1843** CE – SS *Great Britain* launched (ch. 9)

**1845** CE – Franklin Arctic exploration expedition begins (ch. 11)

**1847** CE – *Alvin Clark* built (ch. 5)

**1849** CE – massive expansion of San Francisco (ch. 8)

**1849** CE – *Nitantic* arrives in San Francisco (ch. 8)

**1851** CE – *Nitanic* destroyed by fire (ch. 8)

**1854–1856** CE – Crimean War (ch. 12)

**Mid 1800s** CE – discovery of stone tools in association with bones of extinct animals revises understanding about the age of the world (ch. 2)

**1862** CE – CSS *Virginia* and USS *Monitor* fight; first naval battle between iron-armored warships (ch. 12)

**1862** CE – USS *Monitor* sinks (ch. 12)

**1863** CE – *H. L. Hunley* completes successful test dive (ch. 2)

**1864** CE – *Snow Squall* runs aground on the Falkland Islands (ch. 9)

**1864** CE – *Alvin Clark* sinks in Green Bay (ch. 5)

**1865** CE – steamboat *Bertrand* sinks (ch. 11)

**1869** CE – *Cutty Sark* launched (ch. 12)

**1885** CE – earliest underwater archaeological survey conducted near Salamis, Greece (ch. 2)

**Late 18th**–early 20th century CE – archaeology as a field of study develops (ch. 2)

**1900** CE – Antikythera shipwreck discovered

**1906** CE – HMS *Dreadnought* sparks modern era of naval warships (ch. 12)

**1907–1913** CE – Mahdia shipwreck salvaged by Alfred Merlin (ch. 1)

**1911** CE – USS *Birmingham* launches first naval aircraft (ch. 12)

**1930s** CE – first prototypes for SCUBA developed (ch. 2)

**1930s** CE – underwater excavation at Wakulla Springs, Florida (ch. 2)

**1935** CE – recovery of Benedict Arnold's gunboat Philadelphia from Lake Champlain (ch. 2)

**1941** CE – *Bismarck* launched (ch. 12)

**1945** CE – USS *Indianapolis* sinks (ch. 12)

**1949** CE – John Goggin surveys bottom of Ichetucknee River, Florida for Spanish artifacts (ch. 2)

**1950s** CE – French and Italian divers use airlifts at archaeological sites in Mediterranean (ch. 2)

**1954** CE – UNESCO Convention for the Protection of Cultural Property in the Event of Armed Conflict (ch. 13)

**1954** CE – Khufu vessel excavated (ch. 9)

**1955** CE – fire reveals historic port of Bryggen (ch. 8)

**1956-1961** CE – *Vasa* shipwreck discovered in Stockholm harbor and raised (ch. 2)

**1960** CE – George Bass directs Cape Gelidonya excavations

**1969** CE – *Alvin Clark* raised by sport diver Frank Hoffman (ch. 5)

**1970** CE – UNESCO Convention on the Means of Prohibiting and Preventing the Illicit Import, Export and Transfer of Ownership of Cultural Property (ch. 13)

**1972** CE – UNESCO Convention concerning the Protection of the World Cultural and Natural Heritage (ch. 13)

**1982** CE – *Mary Rose* raised (ch. 5)

**1982** CE – Ronson ship discovered (ch. 8)

**1985** CE – *Titanic* discovered (ch. 1)

**1996** CE – International Charter on the Protection and Management of the Underwater Cultural Heritage passed by International Council of Monuments and Sites (ch. 13)

**2001** CE – UNESCO Convention on the Protection of the Underwater Cultural Heritage (ch. 13)

**2004** CE – crew of *H. L. Hunley* laid to rest (ch. 1)

**2004–2005** CE – excavation and documentation of Ormen Lange shipwreck using ROVs (chs. 2 and 5)

**2007** CE – excavation and documentation of Mardi Gras shipwreck using ROVs (ch. 1)

**2008** CE – Oranjemund shipwreck excavation in Namibia (ch. 11)

**2009** CE – USS *Hamilton* mapped in 3D (ch. 12)

**2009–2013** CE – *Nautilus* expedition to Aegean and Black seas (ch. 5)

**2011** CE – *Mars* shipwreck discovered (ch. 1, 10 and 12)

**2011** CE – Takashima No.1 Ship discovered (ch. 12)

**2012** CE – Royal Netherlands Navy submarine O 16 salvaged (ch. 12)

**2013** CE – UNESCO Manual for Activities directed at Underwater Cultural Heritage (ch. 13)

**2014** CE – HMS *Erebus* discovered (ch. 11)

**2014** CE – Italian submarine *Scirè* declared war grave and protected heritage site (ch. 7)

**2015** CE – Takashima No.2 Ship discovered (ch. 12)

**2015–2017** CE – Ironclad CSS *Georgia* excavated (ch. 12)

**2015–2017** CE – Black Sea Maritime Archaeology Project discoveres 60 historic shipwrecks (ch. 5)

**2016** CE – HMS *Terror* discovered (ch. 11)

**2016** CE – *La Belle* shipwreck placed on permanent display (ch. 6)

**2017** CE – USS *Indianapolis* discovered (ch. 12)

# A NOTE ABOUT NAMES

Throughout this book we have elected to refer to ships using the gender neutral pronoun "it." This is a break with tradition. Ships have long been referred to using the female pronouns "she" and "her." There is no agreement as to why this is the case, but it remains a beloved convention of many seafarers and is still prevalent within naval communities. The use of "it" is becoming more common and we adopted this terminology for two primary reasons: (1) most of the explanations for referring to ships as women have sexism, either overt or implicit, at their core; and (2) the use of a gendered pronoun implies that the ship has a soul. Given the complexity of ships and the intimate relationship that sailors have with ships, it is an understandable convention among seafarers. The ships that archaeologists engage with most often, however, are those that sank and are no longer intact vessels to be personified. It was also deemed important to maintain a consistent approach, and as archaeological sites are universally referred to by the gender neutral "it," so it is that, in this volume, we refer to an archaeological ship(wreck) using the neutral pronoun.

Readers may also notice that ship names are italicized, but the names of shipwrecks where the original vessel name is unknown are in plain type. This is because ship names are a title, just like the title of a book. Italicizing ship names also helps distinguish them in sentences where they might otherwise cause confusion because ships are often named after people (SS *Edmund Fitzgerald*), places (USS *Arizona*), animals (K-317 *Pantera*), and mythical figures (HMS *Charon*). Note that the prefixes, such as SS (steamship), USS (United States Ship), and HMS (Her Majesty's Ship) are not italicized. If the original name of the ship is unknown, archaeologists often name it based on a distinguishing feature (Horseshoe wreck), a nearby landmark (Belitung shipwreck), or the body of water where it was found (Tantura shipwreck). Sometimes these site names are replaced with ship names once the site, artifacts, and historical records are fully analyzed. For example, the Horseshoe wreck was later identified as the vessel named *Nuestra Señora de Encarnación*, in which case the archaeological site adopted the title of the original vessel and the accompanying conventions.

# INTRODUCTION

Two-thirds of the planet is covered by water. This textbook introduces and discusses the role that water—rivers, lakes, seas, and oceans—has played throughout human history and provides an overview of the field of maritime and underwater archaeology. We describe the history of seafaring and the nature of coastal communities. We examine the part that ships and watercraft have played in human discovery, colonization, warfare, trade, and everyday life. We investigate inundated terrestrial sites and the archaeology of great maritime centers. We also address how archaeologists discover, excavate, study, and preserve the material remains of past human culture and the professional ethics that guide the field.

We have chosen to use the term "maritime and underwater archaeology" throughout the text to refer to the totality of research conducted underwater and on land related to maritime peoples. Though the reader will note that some chapters of the book are focused on what would traditionally be called nautical archaeology, while others aim at discussing maritime cultural heritage or the geoarchaeology of inundated landscapes, we have found in our own practice of the field that most researchers move smoothly between the wet and the dry in the pursuit of knowledge. After all, what lies underwater is inextricably tied to the coast or hinterland, past or present.

This book is geared toward undergraduate students, students attending introductory graduate courses, and anyone interested in how our ancestors interacted with the water. Our aim in writing it is to enable readers to:

- understand the breadth of submerged and coastal heritage sites and how these sites form
- understand the primary methods archaeologists use to recover data from underwater and maritime sites

- discuss how archaeologists interpret and conserve these data and heritage sites in order to provide meaningful information about human history
- define and describe the key terms and concepts related to underwater archaeology
- understand the history of seafaring and the role that maritime environments have played in the development of the modern world
- understand how the changing underwater environment both preserves and destroys archaeological sites and critically discuss underwater site management principles and policies
- critically analyze how the past is valued and presented and how these notions affect public policies and perceptions.

## ORGANIZATION OF THE TEXT

Part I (chapters 1–3) introduces the field of maritime and underwater archaeology. Part II (chapters 4–6) describes the methods of conducting archaeology underwater, while part III (chapters 7–12) presents a thematic discussion of human adaptations to water with significant maritime archaeological sites discussed as examples. Part IV (chapters 13-14) concludes the volume by discussing the current state of heritage preservation and the future of maritime and underwater archaeology. This organization is intended to provide students a progressive and comparable reference through which to appreciate the formative role that the watery portion of our planet has had in the development of human history.

Several chapters feature personal reflections by maritime archaeologists aimed at further illustrating chapter themes and, highlighting the diverse paths maritime archaeologists can take in their careers. A number of chapters also include informational boxes that provide greater insight into how we know what we know.

We deliberately wrote this text in an accessible style, limiting technical terms to important archaeological concepts, which are marked in **bold** and referenced in the glossary. There is also a timeline of important historical events and important archaeological dates for reference at the beginning of the text, in order to illustrate how events discussed in different chapters fit together.

## THE BIG QUESTIONS FOR MARITIME ARCHAEOLOGY

To help you, the reader, better understand how maritime and underwater archaeology can increase our knowledge about the past, as well as the modern world around us, we put forward ten Big Questions. Each chapter will begin with several of these focus questions that point to the aims of the chapter and link the chapters together. As you read that chapter, try to connect the questions to what you are learning. These questions will be directly addressed in a summary at the end of the chapter with comprehension questions to help you solidify your new knowledge.

- When and how did maritime societies emerge?
- How have people interacted with seas, lakes, and rivers? How was this interaction shaped by their culture and environment? What are the similarities, differences, and outcomes of these interactions?
- What types of maritime archaeological sites are there, and how do they differ in what they can teach us about the past?
- How can the preservation of artifacts in submerged environments, which tends to be better than on land, improve our understanding of past cultures?
- What information can be gained from inundated landscapes and submerged terrestrial sites?
- What kind of information do ship and aircraft wrecks hold? What can their contents tell us about trade, colonization, warfare, and the people on board?
- What do maritime technological innovations tell us about broader trends in society, history, and culture? How does naval innovation shape the rise and fall of maritime societies?
- How did maritime people shape world history?
- How can we gather data in a precise and rigorous way while still maintaining archaeological sites and the data they contain for future societies?
- How do we balance the needs of modern societies with the preservation of cultural heritage sites?

You will see these questions repeated at the beginning of multiple chapters, but the way they will be answered within each chapter will vary greatly. This reflects the multitude of direct and indirect methods archaeologists employ to reconstruct human history. Maritime and underwater archaeology is multifaceted, covering research underwater and on land from many different times and places; therefore, the ways in which we can answer these questions is also exceptionally varied.

Finally, we hope you will find this volume thought-provoking and inspiring. Maritime and underwater archaeology is a possible source of employment or fulfilling volunteer service. Every archaeological project is a collaboration between the field and the lab, between various experts, and between friends and colleagues. Along with combining multiple work environments, it provides many benefits, including being intellectually stimulating, physically challenging, and diverse in research opportunities. By the end of this book, we hope you will understand why archaeologists put so much effort into studying our submerged and maritime past, and maybe even decide that it is something you may want to pursue yourself.

## CHAPTER 1

# WHAT WE CAN LEARN FROM MARITIME AND UNDERWATER ARCHAEOLOGY?

## FOCUS QUESTIONS

- When and how did maritime societies emerge?
- How have people interacted with seas, lakes, and rivers? How was this interaction shaped by their culture and environment? What are the similarities, differences, and outcomes of these interactions?
- What types of maritime archaeological sites are there, and how do they differ in what they can teach us about the past?
- How can the preservation of artifacts in submerged environments, which tends to be better than on land, improve our understanding of past cultures?
- What information can be gained from inundated landscapes and submerged terrestrial sites?
- What kind of information do ship and aircraft wrecks hold? What can their contents tell us about trade, colonization, warfare, and the people on board?
- What do maritime technological innovations tell us about broader trends in society, history, and culture? How does naval innovation shape the rise and fall of maritime societies?
- How did maritime people shape world history?

"It is probable that a greater number of monuments of the skill and industry of man will in the course of ages be collected together in the bed of the ocean, than will exist at any one time on the surface of the Continents." Charles Lyell, Principles of Geology (1832: 258)

## THE *NUESTRA SEÑORA DE LAS MERCEDES* (1786)—CULTURAL PATRIMONY AND HISTORICAL TREASURE

In 1804, a Spanish flotilla of four vessels left Montevideo, Uruguay en route to Cadiz, Spain carrying a treasure of silver, gold, cinnamon, and other goods. Although Spain and Britain had spent much of the preceding centuries at war with one another, in 1804 they were at peace. Therefore, when the flotilla was intercepted off the southern coast of Portugal on 5 October 1804 by a British Navy taskforce led by Graham Moore and ordered to come into a British port for inspection, the Spanish commanding officer, José de Bustamente y Guerra refused to comply and ordered his men to battle stations. A shot from HMS *Amphion* struck the magazine of *Nuestra Señora de las Mercedes*, a 36-gun frigate built in Cuba and launched in 1786. This single shot caused the vessel to explode and rapidly sink; approximately 250 lives were lost, while only 40 to 50 survivors were rescued. Thus ended the Battle of Cape Santa Maria and the last regular shipment of gold and silver coins from the New World colonies to Spain's coffers. The other three vessels were hauled into port in Gibraltar and then to England where they were refitted as Royal Navy vessels. Spain declared war on Britain on 14 December 1804, with this unprovoked attack as the ostensible reason; Spain's resounding defeat at the Battle of Trafalgar the following year led Spain to firmly ally itself with Napoleon, Emperor of France, against Britain. A long legal battle forced the British crown to repay Spain a small amount of the lost wealth aboard the four vessels—160,000 British pounds (more than $16,100,000 today), approximately 10 to 15 percent of the estimated value of the ships and cargo.[1]

In 2007, Odyssey Marine Exploration, an American marine salvage company, discovered a vessel near the approximate location of the Battle of Cape Santa Maria in nearly 1,100 meters (3,600 feet) of water and codenamed it the "Black Swan." The salvors removed approximately 600,000 silver and gold coins from the wreck and brought them to the United States; at this time, Odyssey Marine filed a salvor's claim to the wreck, with an estimated treasure of $500 million. A long court battle ensued as several countries tried to reclaim the treasure. As *Nuestra Señora de las Mercedes* was a government-owned vessel sunk as an act of war, Spain claimed the vessel and its contents; abandoned vessels could be claimed for salvage, but this vessel was not abandoned. Peru tried to claim the treasure as part of its possessions that were plundered by the Spanish during Spanish colonial rule; the coins were minted in Lima and had never touched Spanish soil. Odyssey Marine Exploration claimed the contents under the rights of salvage, arguing that a large percentage of the treasure aboard at the sinking was civil cargo, and not, in fact, Spain's property at all, so the coins should be salvageable even if the vessel was not. Odyssey further claimed that the vessel was not definitively *Nuestra Señora de las Mercedes*. In 2012, the US Eleventh Circuit Court of Appeals determined that the Peruvian government had no rights to the vessel because Peru was a colony of Spain at the time of wrecking. However, they also upheld the Spanish claim to the vessel and contents, as examination of a small sample of the coins demonstrated that they were the right sort, made from the right types of silver and gold, and clearly had suffered from an explosion. The Spanish government took control of the treasure in 2012 and has had the coins on display in a traveling exhibit. In 2015, the Spanish government conducted an archaeological expedition to the site to investigate and salvage more of the materials. The Odyssey Marine explorations had left large areas of very obvious damage to the vessel, severely limiting the research potential of the vessel.[2]

This case well illustrates the tensions between modern and historical governments, researchers, and marine salvors. Archaeologists and historians want to research the wreck, its cargo, and its construction, while others want to see, hold, and own portions of its wealth. Its cargo may be valuable enough to change the economy of an entire nation, making the stakes anything but small, but should it just be mined for its contents or studied? In short, a two-centuries-old shipwreck may just seem to be a bit of esoterica to most people, but the *Nuestra Señora de las Mercedes* carried valuables representing the wealth and power of the Spanish nation, and it was sunk by an enemy nation supposedly at peace, starting a war and costing 250 people their lives. Political power has waxed and waned since then, and the former colonies have become nations of their own, making their own claims. Laws of salvage and the sea also have a very long tradition, with the rules of "finders keepers" holding sway in many situations. We will return to all of these themes throughout this text.

## THE BLUE PLANET

Throughout time and space, humans have been drawn to the coasts and the waterways of our world. People, without exception, need reliable sources of fresh water for life and often for transport. The seas, rivers, and lakes provide food, routes to other lands, and fodder for myths and dreams. These waterways, however, are also perilous to humans, destroying our strongest vessels, drowning our cities, and erasing all traces of our passage. In a very real way, the story of humanity is tied to the rhythms of tide and wave, and to fully tell the story of humanity, which is the ultimate goal of **archaeology**, we have to understand humanity's complex interactions with our world's waterways.

This entire textbook is dedicated to maritime and underwater archaeology. This may seem far too ambitious to you at first glance. After all, how much can there be to learn from the underwater world? Humans have not yet built any cities under the sea, and there are so few shipwrecks in comparison to all of the ancient cities and towns, settlements and campsites, cemeteries and trash pits that archaeologists have recorded and excavated on land. Today, however, more than 70 percent of Earth's surface is covered by water, including freshwater lakes, rivers, and streams (although they only contribute 0.3 percent of the total water volume). Throughout human history, this percentage has varied as sea levels

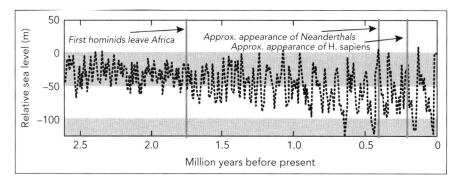

Figure 1.1 Sea-level fluctuations throughout the past 2.6 million years of the Pleistocene.

dropped during glacial periods and rose during warmer interglacials (figure 1.1). As the planet continues to warm and polar ice caps continue to melt, this percentage will increase. The rising and falling of sea levels, which we discuss in more detail in later chapters, has changed the configuration of coastlines and has submerged millions of square kilometers of land upon which people in the past lived, worked, and died. For instance, Neolithic water wells dating to ca. 7300-6300 BCE and now submerged off the coast of Israel in 8 to 12 meters (26 to 40 feet) of water clearly show when the surrounding village was abandoned as the wells became contaminated with salt water intruding from the Mediterranean, the result of rising sea levels.[3]

Submerged settlements are not the only reason we are interested in the underwater world. For perhaps as long as 800,000 years, humans have been moving upon the surface of the oceans. Some of these movements have been significant; people colonized Australia by more than 50,000 years ago, a landmass separated from others and surrounded by dozens of kilometers (10 to 20 miles) of open water even when the oceans were at their lowest. Boats were the only viable means for ancient peoples to access this island continent, although the route and exact timing of the first colonization are still relatively unknown. Elsewhere, humans were regularly retrieving obsidian for making tools from the island of Melos in the Greek archipelago by 10,000 BCE and accessing the California Channel islands, also only reachable by boat, at approximately the same time. People have always been attracted to water and developed technologies to use it whenever and however they could. At the same time, as marine biologist Gene Feldman has pointed out, we have better maps of the surface of the moon than we do of the oceans' floors.[4]

One hundred percent of the world's oceans have been mapped at a resolution of approximately 6 kilometers (3.7 miles). This means we can see features that are greater than 6 kilometers in size, but not smaller. This is pretty good, but 6 kilometers would completely encompass many towns and some small cities, and we cannot see any individual features within that 6-kilometer square. Less than 0.05 percent of the world's oceans have been mapped at a great enough resolution to see things like shipwrecks, small landscape features, or the remains of a missing aircraft. We will discuss why resolution is so important in later chapters, but for now, it is important to note that there is far more unknown than known about the submerged portions of our blue planet.[5]

This may seem to be a problem for marine biologists or geologists, cartographers or oceanographers, or maybe even for our militaries, but it is also important for all of us who study humanity and human history. Without understanding our relationship to the sea we cannot hope to have a complete view of human history. Materials from underwater sites are often better preserved than similar materials on land. Underwater sites often contain information not discoverable on land because the terrestrial counterparts have long since been destroyed or dismantled. They commonly show evidence of ways of life not observable on land. Underwater sites contain both direct and indirect evidence of migration, globalization, and cultural exchange. Archaeological sites can also contain repositories of information about the rate, timing, extent, and impacts of past climate change, which may well be relevant for planning for modern rates of change.

## WHY STUDY MARITIME AND UNDERWATER ARCHAEOLOGY? ANSWERS FROM THE DEPTHS

Part III goes into detail about many of the things that we can learn from maritime and underwater archaeology. Before we get to that and the methods of archaeology underwater (Part II), it is helpful to address the "why" of maritime and underwater archaeology. Much of this has to do with the amphibious nature of humans. We are cultural amphibians, rather than biological amphibians, as our species' ability to spend at least part of our lives on water comes from cultural and technological adaptations. In this global world, very few of us have not eaten seafood or purchased something made overseas. The same was true for much of the human past. We have been eating seafood for at least 165,000 years (and likely much, much longer) and traveling across open water for more than 800,000 years.[6] Nearshore and river travel goes back even further.

In addition to moving ourselves and our wares by water, humans also transport our cultures over the waves. We travel by water to inhabit new lands, and, more often, to colonize already-inhabited lands. Ships and boats have been one of the major vectors for human expansion across the globe, allowing people to spread to every continent, to remain in contact with their homelands, and to move raw materials, finished goods, and ideas back and forth over immense distances. With all of these goods and people moving on the water, we have also invested enormous amounts of time, energy, and resources into protecting ourselves and attacking our competitors by sea. The first recorded sea battle occurred in 1210 BCE when the Hittites defeated a fleet of ships from Cyprus, and the stakes have continued to increase into the modern era.[7] Humans have also invested heavily in our relationship with the water. We are notable in the animal kingdom for the scale of our ability to change our surrounding physical environment.

These changes are perhaps most profound along the coasts where intentional and unintended changes to both sea and land tend to aggregate. The sea also looms large in our social and spiritual environments. Cultures worldwide imbue water with symbolic power ranging the entire gamut from purification to threat. These numerous, tight, and long-standing connections with the water are why we study maritime and underwater archaeology. The following sections of this chapter introduce some of the major lessons that we can learn.

### SUBMERGED COASTLINES AND OUR ANCESTORS

Much of humanity's early maritime history is now underwater. Since glaciers started melting at the end of the last Ice Age, approximately 21,000 years ago, sea levels have risen nearly 130 meters (426 feet) across much of the globe. Today, roughly half of the human population lives within 60 kilometers (37 miles) of the coast, and there is little reason to believe that our ancestors were any less inclined to live near the sea.[8] It would seem that much of the evidence of past human, and, very likely, earlier hominin, activity has been drowned by sea level rise. Underwater archaeology offers us a way to understand the lives of these early coastal peoples and how changes in sea level might affect our own lives.

Ignoring the submerged landscapes of early people would be like trying to understand the modern world without acknowledging the existence of our coastal cities. This would be like attempting to explain modern economics and politics without reference to New York, Guangzhou, Singapore, Mumbai, London, Shanghai, New Orleans, Cape Town, Shenzen, Rotterdam, Osaka, Melbourne, or Rio de Janeiro. It is an incomplete story. People tend to cluster along the shore because the shore provides a wide variety of resource and transportation options, especially in locations where a river meets the sea. Terrestrial, open water, near-shore, brackish, and freshwater environments all support different animal and plant populations, allowing for a diverse and stable diet. These plants and animals also produce shells, hides, reeds, feathers, and many other materials that can be made into clothes, tools, ornaments, and all the other trappings of human culture.

Water also makes it easier to move these goods. A modern analogy is to compare backpacking to canoeing—you can move more quickly and bring more along in a canoe. If ancient peoples positioned themselves to take advantage of rivers as well as the coast, they were able to move relatively easily both along the shore and inland. Because of these advantages, past peoples tended to congregate along the coasts, just like people do today. Also like today, the places where people congregate tended to be the places where innovation occurred. Population density and diversity are why cities tend to be hotbeds of technological, design, and artistic development. It is very *likely* that this pattern extended into the deep past. Likely, as we do not know for sure, because all but the last few thousand years of coastal settlement has been submerged by rising sea levels everywhere but in the extreme latitudes. Until we more completely explore drowned coastal settlements, we cannot claim to understand the past.

The relationships between rising seas, changes in the earth's temperature, and human adaptation also hold important lessons. Rising sea levels are why global warming should make us all very nervous. Human ingenuity will hopefully allow us to adapt to incremental increase in global temperature and the associated changes in crop ranges. However, continued warming means continued melting of the ice caps, which means continued sea level rise, and there is currently little hope that we will be able to push back the sea. In all but the wealthiest and most proactive areas, these rising sea levels will displace the dense populations clustered along the coasts, forcing huge numbers of people to move into other, already occupied, regions. The potential for unrest and competition for increasingly-scarce resources is possibly the most concerning aspect of global warming.

On the other hand, our species has faced rising waters before, and we can learn from this past experience. We often think of the shore as a fixed boundary, but the truth is that the shore is constantly moving from day to day, year to year, and century to century. Underwater archaeology helps us understand what coastal environments survive inundation, and that helps us understand what modern settlements are most at risk for coastal erosion. We can also learn how earlier groups adapted to these changes. The ways that they altered their houses, settlements, diets, and daily routines could advise our own adaptations. It is unlikely that we will settle on exactly the same solutions—our technologies, population densities, and opportunities are different than those of our ancestors—but it would be unwise to turn our backs on evidence of groups that survived environmental changes of a scale unprecedented in our time.

Our understanding of both coastal settlements and adaptation to coastal change is influenced by the preservation of artifacts and sites underwater. Water is both wonderful and disastrous for the preservation of archaeological remains. Rising sea levels tend to destroy archaeological sites. The incessant pounding of waves, the liquefaction of sediments, and the movement of tides and currents all work to obliterate features and grind artifacts into oblivion, wiping coastal sites clean from the slate of history. However, in protected inlets, river mouths, behind barrier beaches, and in other specific environments, archaeological sites can be preserved. In these locations, the preservation can be spectacular. Once a site is submerged, inundation can act like a buffer, limiting the light, heat, oxygen, and activity that reach an artifact or feature, thereby greatly slowing the process of decay. This is why underwater archaeology often produces much more intact and better preserved artifacts than are found on land (chapter 3) (figure 1.2). We also often find much more organic material (wood, leather, etc.) on underwater sites than terrestrial sites, providing the potential to learn much more about earlier cultures and complement the terrestrial record.

Figure 1.2 Example of underwater preservation: A Neolithic flint axe that is still held within its wooden handle. (Courtesy of Museum Lolland-Falster)

## THE PEOPLE ON THE SHORE

Maritime and underwater archaeology also includes more recent coastal communities. In many past cultures, only a small fraction of the population was personally involved with seafaring. However, the power of ships, the mythology surrounding water, the imported goods, and the ideas brought home by sailors were wide-reaching. More directly, many maritime cultures had substantial infrastructure to support seafaring, such as shipyards, sail and rope makers, churches, boarding houses, brothels, taverns, warehouses, docks, aids-to-navigation, and fortifications. In addition to all of the people working in these and other facilities, pilots, porters, families of seafarers, and countless others lived in coastal settlements. These settlements and their inhabitants formed a bridge between the world afloat and the world ashore, linking the maritime and non-maritime aspects of the culture. The sites they left behind form a similar link between terrestrial and underwater archaeology. Ultimately, maritime and underwater archaeology is part of the larger field of archaeology, with the goal of understanding past peoples holistically. Maritime and underwater archaeology studies important aspects of those past cultures, which need to be integrated into our understanding of a past culture as a whole in order to truly make sense of it.

The sunken port city of Alexandria, Egypt is an example of what maritime and underwater archaeology can learn from coastal settlements. The waterfront portion of Alexandria slipped beneath the waves between 200 and 600 CE, possibly as a result of tsunamis, earthquakes, and subsidence. A large, and, by archaeological standards, nearly intact portion of the ancient city now holds vast amounts of information about everyday life in shallow water just off the modern shoreline.

Alexandria's story is closely tied to that of Egypt, Greece, and Rome. The city was founded in 331 BCE on the orders of Alexander the Great as a maritime link between Greece and Egypt. The more-than 40-story-tall Pharos lighthouse, one of the seven wonders of the ancient world, guided ships into the harbor. The port drew in goods from throughout the Mediterranean Sea, across the Indian Ocean, and along the length of the Nile. With these goods came ideas, which were enshrined in the city's library, perhaps the largest in the ancient world. The later rulers of ancient Egypt governed from a royal quarter fronting the harbor where Cleopatra courted Julius Caesar and Mark Antony. The royal palaces, lighthouse, and library, as well as evidence of daily commerce and life are now submerged (figure 1.3).[9] The submerged portions of Alexandria provide evidence of the interconnected nature of the Mediterranean. There we find information, cultures, and goods from throughout the region arriving by sea and intermixing before being exported to another port.

**Figure 1.3** Statuary being recorded at the submerged city of Alexandria. (Courtesy of Stéphane Compoint)

### SHIPS AS ARTIFACTS

Up until circa 4000 years ago, most of known underwater sites are drowned settlements, but in researching more recent societies, archaeological efforts have tended to concentrate on the remains of ships and boats. These shipwrecks form the primary, though by no means only, focus of what most people consider maritime and underwater archaeology. The same often-excellent preservation discussed above means that ships have much to teach us about the peoples and cultures that built them (figure 1.4).

The influential underwater archaeologist Keith Muckelroy claimed that "In any preindustrial society, from the Upper Paleolithic to the 19th century AD, a boat or (later) a ship was the largest and most complex machine produced."[10] Among our earliest ancestors, the ability to build successful boats is evidence of the creative and powerful mind that makes us human. These early vessels that required the sophisticated combination of multiple materials are evidenced by the progression of humans to islands farther and farther offshore. In more recent

**Figure 1.4** Diving on *Mars* (1564). (Courtesy of Kirill Egerov/Mars Project)

times, ships grew in size and complexity as humans continued to press into un-known waters, fight over the waters they knew of, and seek increased efficiency through larger vessels in the waters they could access. Ships were clearly impor-tant in terms of the amount of materials, effort, thought, and planning that went into them. As such, they are an important source of information for an archaeol-ogist wishing to understand past cultures.

Archaeologists often refer to the artifacts and features that we study as **mate-rial culture**. That is culture made physical. Much of human culture exists only as thoughts in our heads and words from our mouths, but every so often we make something based on those thoughts; that is material culture. Working backward from the physical object—an artifact, a house, a landscape, or a ship—an ar-chaeologist can begin to understand the ideas that lay behind it. We can work backward from multiple individual objects to understand a culture; in the case of maritime and underwater archaeology, using shipwrecks to understand how cultures adapted to the world around them and changed through time.

One of the most fundamental ways archaeologists treat ships and boats as material culture is to answer the technological question, "How did a past culture solve the problem of moving people and cargo from point *a* to point *b* across the water?" In order to answer this question, archaeologists must consider not only the technology available at the time and the environment where the people lived, but also available resources, knowledge, and cultural traits such as the group's penchant for innovation or risk and its goal in reaching point *b*.

The variation between Viking longships and the cargo ships known as cogs demonstrate this line of inquiry. Cogs and longships operated in the same environment, the North and Baltic seas, during approximately the same time; longships flourished during the 9th to 11th centuries and cogs had their heyday as cargo vessels during the 10th through 14th centuries. They also shared many technological characteristics, both being part of the Nordic shipbuilding tradition (chapter 9). To look at them side by side, however, these similarities might not be readily apparent. The longship is sleek (figure 1.5), while the cog is decidedly tubbier (figure 9.18), but both were an excellent fit for the needs of their owners. The Vikings built longships for raiding, and designed them to quickly move a substantial number of men across the sea and up a river to surprise an unsuspecting settlement and return with a small cargo of high value items.

**Figure 1.5** *Sea Stallion*, Skuldelev 2 reconstruction. (Courtesy of The Viking Ship Museum)

Speed, maneuverability, and the ability to work in shallow waters were valued more than reliability or cargo capacity. The cog, on the other hand, carried large cargos, ranging from cloth to grain and from furs to iron, between established harbors in sturdy and capacious **hulls**. By studying the shape and construction of archaeologically recorded longships and cogs such as the Skuldelev ships and the Bremen cog, archaeologists can better understand the priorities and needs of northern European maritime societies.[11]

Changes in ship design and construction can also be used to understand changes in culture that stretch beyond the coasts. During the mid-first millennium CE, the Mediterranean Sea witnessed a fundamental change in ship construction. Shipbuilders transitioned from building ships shell-first, with the vessel being sculpted one hull plank at a time, to skeleton-first, in which frames were used to define the shape of the hull and provide much of its strength (see chapter 9 for a fuller description of this change).[12] This transition has been recorded in more than a dozen shipwrecks and is one of the biggest changes in ship construction prior to the adoption of steam engines, but the ships are only part of the story. There also was a temporary decline in slavery during this period, partially related to the rise of Christianity. Whereas earlier shipyards could employ highly skilled slave shipbuilders relatively cheaply, the cost of skilled workmen increased during this period. This period also saw the decline of the Western Roman Empire, and with it a loss in shipbuilding infrastructure. Together with declining slavery, this would have led shipyards to embrace cost-saving measures such as skeleton-first construction where one trained shipbuilder could layout the frames and a crew of laborers could then assemble the ship. Iron for mundane objects like nails additionally increased during the first millennium CE. With relatively inexpensive nails, it was possible to spike the hull planks to the frames of a skeleton-first ship, which was a major change from the shell-first ships that were often built, like fine cabinetry, without nails. In summary, we can see the technological change in the artifact (ships), but that change is indicative of changes in culture that include religion, labor, economics, and the availability of resources. No culture exists in a vacuum, so changes in one aspect of a culture can almost always be linked to other changes in that culture and interactions with neighboring groups. In this case, the change from shell to skeleton ship construction is interesting, but for an archaeologist, understanding how the technological change relates to other changes in the culture and its environs is really the fundamental goal.

### SHIPS AS VECTORS: TRADE AND COLONIZATION

Things, people, and ideas have been moving by ships for thousands of years, making ships one of the major drivers for the divergence and convergence of human societies. If you want to understand how human culture formed and reformed, you have to understand how people moved across the water. During the first few hundred thousand years of human history, we spread across the globe, entering previously uninhabited areas. Some parts of the world, such as Australia, would have only been accessible by boat, but nearly all of human divergence would have benefitted from boatbuilding technology. This divergence provided for the wonderful variety of peoples that populate Earth, giving groups sufficient time and space to develop unique cultures. Then over perhaps the last 4,000 years we embarked on a much more rapid convergence, as increasingly longer and longer overseas voyages brought formerly disparate cultures into contact.[13]

North and South America are an example of this divergence and subsequent convergence of peoples. The Americas were one of the last places that humans colonized, likely sometime in the last 20,000 years. While some of the first inhabitants may have traveled on foot from northeast Asia to North America over the since-inundated Beringian landmass connecting Asia to Alaska (chapter 7), there is increasing evidence that others took a similar route but clung to the coasts. These coastal people likely traveled at least in part by boat, which helps explain the early settlement of coastal sites in South America at a time when much of North America seems to have been unoccupied. Whether by foot or boat, these first peoples had sufficient time on both continents to develop a wide range of societies before the largescale arrival of Europeans by ship starting in the in the 16th century. Since then, and until the early 20th century development of aviation, all immigrants to the Americas also came by ship.

Contact with new or already-inhabited lands by ship was rarely a one-time event as ships made it relatively easy to return time and again, carrying goods and raw materials back and forth. Nearly everything made by humans has been transported by ship, ranging from tiny obsidian blades to entire stone columns in antiquity, to the automobiles and electronics of today. As archaeologists, we can find the evidence of this trade in the objects people leave behind, but the ideas that flowed with the objects are as important as the objects themselves. Thus, the arrival of Europeans to the Americas was accompanied by a variety of new technologies in the New World and an influx of valuable materials to the Old World, as well as violence and the exchange of diseases and populations. The results of these seaborne exchanges have shaped the faces of all modern nations.

Shipwrecks and their cargos help us to understand the movement of peoples and goods. Identifying the shipwrecks of various nations and what they were carrying sheds new light on trade networks by creating a linkage between a group, a cargo, and a location. In the case of mixed cargos it is even possible to occasionally reconstruct the origin, route, and destination of the vessel. Shipwrecks also give us insight into illicit trade that we would not otherwise have. The careful excavation of a shipwreck can reveal evidence of personal or smuggled cargos that do not match the rest of what was being shipped. Though rarer than trading vessels, shipwrecks carrying settlers contain a wealth of information about the culture that sent the colonizers. When newly establishing themselves, it was not possible to run out to the nearest store to pick up a lamp or blanket, so people had to bring the store with them. These shipwrecks contain what you might expect (agricultural and industrial tools) but also less expected items (fine ceramics and smoking pipes). These goods let us know what was important to a society because the settlers were not moving just to make a living but also to replicate a culture.

### SHIPS AS SOCIETIES

By this point, we have hopefully established that ships were important in a wide variety of practical ways. If it is true that ships were important, it stands to reason that the people who operated them were also important. Sailors have been an identifiable subculture since the time when ships became large enough and complicated enough to require specialists to operate them. An important part of maritime and underwater archaeology is to better understand the culture of sailors and relate them to the larger groups of landsmen that they interacted with at home and abroad.

Social hierarchy, hygiene, food, entertainment, and beliefs, as well as many other aspects of sailing life, can all be studied through the investigation of a shipwreck. Ships formed floating villages, and, when they sank, all of the trappings of life aboard went down with them. Just as archaeologists excavate a terrestrial site to understand the activities that took place in a village, they can piece together what life was like afloat through the artifacts they find. Also like archaeology on land, the spatial relationships between artifacts are often as important, or more important, than the artifacts themselves for understanding who used the object and for what purpose. For example, since antiquity, common sailors have slept in the bow of the ship, while the stern, which tends to be drier and less tossed by waves, was reserved for the captain and other officers. These spatial associations are borne out again and again on shipwrecks with finer (or any) ceramics, more sophisticated or expensive personal goods, and better foods found in the stern.

Archaeologists are also able to compare the behaviors of sailors across cultures. Anthropology is a comparative science, making its arguments by comparing one culture to another and exploring similarities and differences. Maritime and underwater archaeology is no different. Just as we can compare shipwrecks through time to determine that the stern has long been the domain of the captain, we can compare other aspects of seafaring life to study how sailors have changed through time or how they vary among cultures. We can also compare sailors to their countrymen left behind on the shore to determine how sailors represent a distinct subculture. Interestingly, due to the particular challenges of living at sea and the mixing of nationalities on ships, sailors from different countries sometimes had more in common with each other than they did with landsmen of their own nationality or ethnic group.

Sailors also formed the cutting edge of intercultural contact. Since most long-distance contact was by sea, the sailors of exploratory vessels, first-wave merchant ships, or, occasionally, lost fishing vessels were the untrained ambassadors of their people. Their interactions with indigenous populations could flavor the subsequent contact. Sailors additionally formed a conduit for ideas, adopting words, concepts, and technology from the people they met and bringing those notions home with them. The modern proliferation of tattoos, for example, can be traced to their popularization among whalers who interacted with Pacific Islanders during the 19th century (chapter 10).

### SHIPS AND THE SEA AS SYMBOLS

Ships and the sea play important and varied roles as religious, cultural, and political symbols for many cultures. Many readers may think of the seas as a barrier, separating continents, countries, us, and them. For much of human history, however, water has been *the* highway, connecting disparate places across open water and linking people along rivers. Many people in the past, therefore, perceived water as a connector rather than a barrier, allowing them access to friends, family, trading partners, goods, and resources across immense spaces. This access was not without risk. For as long as people have been living along the shore and going to sea in boats there have been floods, other natural disasters, and shipwrecks. Maritime peoples must therefore balance the risks of traveling by water against the opportunities it brings. Across cultures, humans have attempted to mitigate risks through a variety of means, including superstition and religion. This tendency has resulted in a rich mythology around the seas, with all of the gods, monsters, prohibitions, and rituals that often populate dangerous places. The dangers of open water also likely explain why there is a less robust mythology around often-safer rivers and why fresh water was frequently seen as less morally, as well as less physically, dangerous than salt water.

The fact that ships sometimes just disappear at sea, shipwrecked without warning or evidence, has also led many cultures to perceive the oceans as boundless. The ancient Greeks, for example, believed the offshore Mediterranean to be a place of no return where items could be permanently deposited. A similar perception permeated many countries, including the United States through the 20th century; the United States dumped a wide range of things in the oceans, ranging from old subway cars to obsolete weapons to nuclear waste. In more recent years, the global view of the oceans has changed, and we have come to see oceans as finite, threatened, and physically, rather than morally, polluted. This change in belief has led to changes in public and personal policies around water.

As the primary instrument of overseas trade and as the only physical means of overcoming the risks of open water travel, boats and ships have also been important symbols for many cultures. Representing wealth and commerce, they are displayed prominently on the seals and arms of many cities, states, and families. They can also represent power, with famous warships such as *Vasa*, "Old Iron Sides," and the reconstructed Yongle ships of Zheng He figuring prominently in modern national identities (figure 1.6). Ships are also linked to notions of freedom in art and literature, and generally spark the imagination of seagoing and land-loving populations alike. As Michel Foucault wrote, "From the sixteenth century until present, [the ship has not only been] the great instrument of economic development . . . but has been simultaneously the greatest reserve of imagination. . . . In civilizations without boats dreams dry up. . . ."[14]

Since the goal of archaeology is to find out about people, not just to find things, it is important for archaeologists to understand how people perceived the waters around them. These perceptions shaped how they interacted with the water and often took physical form in ships, shoreline construction, and treatment of the water. As the descendants of these past groups, we have inherited not only some of their perceptions but also some of their changes to the coasts, oceans, and rivers. One of the most important lessons of archaeology is that, just as past actions affect us today, our actions will have long and unanticipated consequences for our descendants.

**Figure 1.6** Model of the elaborate carvings on the stern of the *Vasa*. (Courtesy of Peter Isotalo)

## George Bass, Professor Emeritus, Texas A&M University, USA

My most important contribution to underwater archaeology is my role in transforming it into a respected academic field from its earlier perceived state as an avocational undertaking limited to hardy scuba divers. It was certainly not something I aimed for as a doctoral candidate when I took diving lessons in 1960 to prepare me for directing the excavation of a Late Bronze Age shipwreck at Cape Gelidonya, Turkey. I undertook that enterprise solely because the site was from the Bronze Age, the period that most interested me, and of which I had firsthand archaeological experience from assisting in the terrestrial excavation of Lerna in Greece.

There were skilled diving archaeologists before me, so the contribution of the Cape Gelidonya excavation was simply that it was the first complete excavation of an ancient shipwreck on the Mediterranean seabed, and that it was directed by the diving archaeologist who researched and published it. I intended to return to terrestrial Bronze Age sites. I was, however, convinced by two of the volunteer divers at Cape Gelidonya that we had started something worthwhile and that we should continue together because as an archaeologist I had the credentials to obtain excavation permits, which they could not do alone.

Throughout the 1960s, therefore, I directed the excavation of Late Roman and Byzantine ships lost at Yassıada, Turkey. In so doing, my staff and I devised and improved methods of removing sediment, mapping, and searching for other wrecks. These included the launching in 1964, by the Electric Boat Division of General Dynamics, of the first commercially built American research submersible, *Asherah*. In 1967, largely funded by the U.S. Navy, we photogrammetrically mapped one of the shipwrecks at Yassıada with cameras and strobe lights attached to *Asherah*. The same summer we assembled experts for the first location of an ancient shipwreck by side-scan sonar.

By the end of the 1960s, I was burned out with fundraising, ordering and shipping equipment, and assembling staffs for what the head of U.S. Navy Diving and Salvage said was the largest diving operation in the world, with 20 to 30 excavators diving twice daily to 40 meters (130 feet) for up to three months at a time. I was doing it without assistants while also teaching at the University of Pennsylvania. In 1972, at the request

of the University Museum, I began excavating a Bronze Age terrestrial site in Italy. By then, archaeologists Michael Katzev and David Owen, who had apprenticed with me at Yassıada, had excavated classical Greek shipwrecks off Kyrenia, Cyprus, and in the Straits of Messina between Italy and Sicily.

At the end of the summer I realized that I had missed the unique offerings of shipwreck archaeology with extraordinarily well-preserved artifacts, both organic and inorganic, that could often be dated accurately. Further, underwater archaeology provided precious information about the ships that were so important to the ancients for transportation, colonization, commerce, warfare, and exploration. Rather than leave underwater archaeology, I decided to solve my earlier problems by having a permanent staff of assistants and by relinquishing teaching responsibilities so that I could devote myself full time to this blossoming field. With a year's notice, I resigned from a tenured associate professorship. Almost immediately, my wife, our tax lawyer, and I registered as the three essential members of a new corporation: American Institute of Nautical Archaeology (AINA). AINA's first board of directors met in early 1973 with various pledges of funds for various periods of time.

At the suggestion of Michael Katzev, who had moved to Cyprus to devote himself fully to the reassembly of the Kyrenia wreck's hull, and who had agreed to serve as the AINA's vice president, we decided to base ourselves on centrally located Cyprus where our still-slim funds would go further. I immediately conducted a survey in Turkey; three of the dozen shipwrecks located have since been excavated by the institute.

Within a year war broke out on Cyprus and we scattered as refugees, the Katzevs to Athens and the Basses, with J. Richard Steffy, to Steffy's hometown of Denver, Pennsylvania. Elizabeth Whitehead, an AINA director, seeing my commitment to the new institute, offered a suggestion: why not find a university with which we could affiliate in the same manner as a new medical institute, funded by her husband, had recently done with the Massachusetts Institute of Technology (MIT). Although

*(continued)*

the Whitehead Medical Institute shared facilities and personnel with MIT, it retained its independence, with its own board, its own administration, and its own funding, leaving its staff completely free to pursue research.

Through fortuitous circumstances, Texas A&M University (TAMU) heard of our availability and offered to create an independent graduate program in nautical archaeology if AINA would base itself there. Under the agreement, some of us would teach one term a year for the university and work for AINA one term, with summer salaries paid by the university since we would take students into the field. This worked ideally, although it meant a return to teaching part of every year, because we could staff our various projects with graduate students who had taken courses in every aspect of early seafaring, including detailed study of hull design and construction.

In 1979 AINA shortened its name to INA to represent foreign members of its board, staff, and projects. Since its humble beginnings, INA has conducted excavations in North America, Europe, Asia, Africa, and the Caribbean. It has a staffed research center in Turkey with library, dormitory, conservation laboratory, and an oceangoing research vessel designed for underwater archaeology and capable of tending INA's two-person submersible.

Having nautical archaeology accepted as a serious scholarly discipline was not initially easy. Two students who worked with me at Yassıada in the 1960s shortly thereafter applied unsuccessfully for faculty positions. In one case a member of the interviewing committee is reported to have blurted out "We want an historian, not a skin diver!" and in the other, the interview went well until the applicant revealed that his doctoral dissertation was his analysis of the hull construction of a sunken Byzantine ship. A third student who worked with them at Yassıada, fearing similar rejection, chose not to write his doctoral dissertation on his own superb excavation of an ancient shipwreck lest he be pegged as "an underwater archaeologist." Luckily, the first two did obtain positions and retired as respected full professors.

How different it is today! Academic programs and departments of nautical archaeology have emerged in countries around the globe, government agencies have maritime archaeologists on staff, international conferences are held specifically on the subject, peer-reviewed journals have been established, and a proliferation of museums devoted to shipwrecks, often reconstructed after being conserved, are increasingly popular throughout the world.

I have tried to describe my contributions to the global acceptance of nautical archaeology as a respected academic field. To reach that point required a willingness to gamble, perseverance, some luck, the ability to speak and write for the public as well as for other scholars, perhaps a certain naïveté about what was possible, but mainly the ability to put together cohesive staffs of people able to live together in remote camps for months at a time, people also skilled in photography, mechanics, illustration, medicine, diving, conservation, seamanship, and so on—often found among the archaeologists themselves.

## MY MOST IMPORTANT CONTRIBUTION TO MARITIME AND UNDERWATER ARCHAEOLOGY

### Pilar Luna Erreguerena, Archaeologist, Vice-Directorate of Underwater Archaeology, National Institute of Anthropology and History (INAH), Mexico

The most important thing that I have done in maritime and underwater archaeology is to convince Mexico's National Institute of Anthropology and History (INAH) to create an area devoted to the research, protection, conservation, and dissemination of information related to the underwater cultural heritage

This struggle began in 1971 when I heard a lecture about the removal of the temples of Abu Simbel in Egypt to protect them from the rising waters behind what would soon be the Aswan dam. For the first time in my life, I thought about what was happening with all the cultural vestiges lying in Mexican waters. As soon as the class ended, I ran to the library and discovered the only book on underwater archaeology available there: *Archaeology Under Water*, by George F. Bass. My excitement was immense. So, underwater archaeology existed and there was someone in the world already doing it!

But, who would believe in such a thing in Mexico? None of the authorities within INAH would pay any attention to my concern or my requests. Being a naive student, in 1978, I wrote Dr. Bass inviting him to give the central part of the first course on underwater archaeology ever offered in Mexico. To my surprise, he accepted and brought with him archaeologist Donald H. Keith. The course was a success and at the end Dr. Bass invited me to work with him and his team at the Serçe Limanı glass wreck in Turkey. To me, this was my golden opportunity to learn how true underwater archaeology was done.

In 1979, a formal proposal for the creation of an underwater archaeology area of study was presented to INAH's authorities, but nothing happened. In October of that same year, two North American sport divers reported, through Donald H. Keith, the finding of a very old cannon in one of the reefs in the Gulf of Mexico. After a complex process, INAH's director then accepted an invitation to attend to this case and asked if I was capable of organizing a recovery operation. This was in the middle of the north winds season, which made a recovery very challenging, but I said yes. A group of Mexican archaeologists, headed by Norberto González Crespo, Director of Centro INAH Yucatan, was selected. We also invited the two discoverers—Farley Sonnier and Edward Weeks—so they could help us to locate the cannon. Donald H. Keith, Roger C. Smith, and Donny Hamilton from the Institute of Nautical Archaeology (INA) were sent by Dr. Bass. The Mexican Navy provided a minesweeper.

We did find the cannon at a depth of 6 meters, but due to the strong winds, when we were about to place it on the deck of the ship, it fell back into the sea. We returned in May 1980 and found it at 40 meters (131 feet) depth. This time, we were successful. The 16th century bronze cannon, the only one of its type ever recovered in the Western Hemisphere, is now exhibited in a museum in the city of Campeche.

This was the missing element that convinced INAH's director to create the Department of Underwater Archaeology in February 1980, when even many of my colleagues laughed at the idea. However, once created and located in an "office" without even chairs, we wondered if there would really be something to do; we were starting from scratch. Since the beginning, we have realized that it was very important to investigate not only shipwrecks in marine waters, but also in inland, continental waters, where a rich prehistoric and pre-Hispanic legacy was waiting to be found and researched. We also decided at the beginning that all projects should be multidisciplinary, interinstitutional, and involve international participation. This has been the key to the consolidation of underwater archaeology in Mexico.

The Department was promoted to a Vice-Directorate in 1995. Besides recording finds across the country, currently we are carrying out inventories and projects in coastal, marine, and inland waters. We are also engaged in five additional program priorities: technical and legal protection, training in archaeology and other related disciplines, conservation of artifacts recovered from aquatic environments, dissemination of information through different forums and media, and promotion of interinstitutional and international collaboration agreements.

Another long-term, capacity-building goal that has been reached is the training of young archaeologists and collaborators such as historians, biologists, physical anthropologists, and cave divers, among others. This has been possible thanks to the invaluable support of colleagues mainly from the United States.

On the other hand, heading the struggle against pressure from looters and treasure hunters has been a real nightmare; we have been successful so far, however, through the engagement of INAH's Council of Archaeology, and with the support of the Vice-directorate of Underwater Archaeology. Mexico has not granted a single permit for these groups, and our role in the protection and defense of the national underwater cultural heritage is recognized here and abroad.

In this sense, my participation as Mexico's representative in the elaboration and the ratification of the 2001 UNESCO Convention on the Protection of the Underwater Cultural Heritage was at the same time a privilege, a challenge, and, in the end, an enriching experience. Discussions on almost each article and rule were exhausting, but fruitful.

Underwater archaeology and the protection of underwater cultural heritage have been my mission and my passion. I am now in the process of retiring, but I will remain involved in a very peculiar and significant project named Hoyo Negro, in the Yucatan Peninsula. There, the oldest (12,000 to 13,000 years old) complete human skeleton, of a 15 to 17-year-old female, was found, providing the missing link between ancient Paleoamericans and native Americans; both, it seems, descending from the same Beringian source.

**SUMMARY**

Maritime and underwater archaeology have the ability to answer a wide variety of questions that cannot be addressed by terrestrial archaeology or historical documents alone. A substantial number of formerly terrestrial sites are now submerged. These sites can provide new information about past lifeways and settlement patterns by expanding our knowledge of how and where people lived. Additionally, they contain organic materials that are not regularly preserved on land, leading to a better understanding of the technological and artistic achievements of ancient peoples. These sites also have valuable lessons to teach us about sea-level rise. Shipwrecks, the remains of the largest and most complicated machines built by many ancient cultures, provide a unique way to understand how those cultures solved technological problems. The cargos contained within shipwrecks are a matchless store of information about trade, commerce, and intercultural exchanges. Ships and the seas also figure prominently in the worldviews of past cultures, and maritime and underwater archaeology provides a way to study and interpret past religions and symbols. Maritime and underwater archaeology extends to shore communities that serve as a bridge between ships and land-based communities, as well as a linkage between maritime and terrestrial archaeology.

**DISCUSSION QUESTIONS**

1. This chapter describes humans as "amphibious." To what extent is that an accurate characterization of our species?
2. What can we learn about a society by studying its shipwrecks?
3. What is the role of coastal sites in maritime and underwater archaeology? How much do we know about these sites?
4. What is the connection between the things that archaeologists uncover and the cultures that created those things?

**FURTHER READING**

Anderson, A., J. Barrett, and K. Boyle, Eds. (2010). *The Global Origins and Development of Seafaring*. Oxbow Books, Oxford.

Empereur, J.-Y. (1998). *Alexandria Rediscovered*. George Braziller Publisher, New York.

Fernández-Armesto, F. (2007). *Pathfinders: A Global History of Exploration*. W.W. Norton, New York.

Gardiner, R., Ed. (1994). *Cogs, Caravels and Galleons*. Conway Maritime Press, London.

Pomey, P., Y. Kahanov, and E. Rieth (2012). Transition from Shell to Skeleton in Ancient Mediterranean Ship-Construction: Analysis, Problems, and Future Research. *International Journal of Nautical Archaeology* 41(2): 235–314.

Williams, G. (2014). *The Viking Ship*. British Museum Press, London.

## CHAPTER 2

# WHAT IS MARITIME AND UNDERWATER ARCHAEOLOGY?

## FOCUS QUESTIONS

- How have people interacted with seas, lakes, and rivers? How was this interaction shaped by their culture and environment? What are the similarities, differences, and outcomes of these interactions?
- What types of maritime archaeological sites are there, and how do they differ in what they can teach us about the past?
- How can the preservation of artifacts in submerged environments, which tends to be better than on land, improve our understanding of past cultures?
- What information can be gained from inundated landscapes and submerged terrestrial sites?
- What kind of information do ship and aircraft wrecks hold? What can their contents tell us about trade, colonization, warfare, and the people on board?

## WHAT IS MARITIME AND UNDERWATER ARCHAEOLOGY?

In 1995, Clive Cussler, bestselling author of novels featuring maritime explorer Dirk Pitt, announced that he and his team had discovered the wreck of the world's first combat submarine, the Confederate *H. L. Hunley* (figure 2.1). As will be discussed in chapter 12, *H. L. Hunley* was the first ever submersible to sink an enemy vessel, a move that forever changed naval combat, and its excavation, recovery, and conservation provide a dynamic example of how multiple groups can marshal resources for important sites. From the beginning of the American Civil War, the Confederacy was working on a secret weapon to break the Union Navy blockade choking Confederate ports. On its final voyage, under cover of darkness, the roughly 12-meter-long (40-foot-long) submarine rammed

**Figure 2.1** *H. L. Hunley* undergoing conservation. (Courtesy of Friends of the *Hunley*)

the USS *Housatonic*, causing the frigate—more than five times its size—to sink in a matter of minutes. *H. L. Hunley* itself also disappeared below the water for more than 130 years until the time of its discovery. After *H. L. Hunley's* discovery, it took another 5 years to determine who was ultimately responsible for the Confederate submarine (the U.S. Navy), how to raise it (with a truss system and foam cradle), where it would be conserved (in a purposefully refurbished laboratory in Charleston, South Carolina), and how to pay for it all (through private donations along with federal and state funds). Upon recovery, its crew was found to be still inside, all men at their stations. They were laid to rest in 2004 in a **historic** cemetery in Charleston with tens of thousands of people in attendance. Conservation of the hull and artifacts within is still ongoing, and new discoveries are still being made as the secret Confederate weapon was never documented with designs, and there are no inventories or crew lists to consult. The conservation plan will not have the boat fully stabilized for display until the mid-2020s.[1] This story of collaboration between governments, academics, and the general public is commonplace in the practice of maritime and underwater archaeology. Careful coordination and long-term planning are required to recover material culture from the watery world and to stabilize this material for study and display while ethically treating this material, especially any affiliated human remains.

Archaeology is the study of past human societies through the analysis of their material remains. This definition is fairly straightforward, but it contains some important details. First, without tangible remains, there cannot be archaeology. Humans are the only technology-dependent species on the planet, and much of our technology appears in material things, so studying these material items can be very informative about how past people dealt with the myriad of challenges they faced daily. Conversely, archaeology cannot address all aspects of life with equal ease. Think about how few of your daily activities actually leave any tangible traces. You probably discard a few dozen things every day, and archaeologists of the future could potentially find those, but some carry more meaning than others. Your clothing, home, possessions, and body are all tangible, but the dozens of conversations you have every day are not. Your thoughts are not. The routes you walk to class are tangible in the sense that they are probably along marked paths, but your traverse of them is not. In other words, archaeologists study the *remains* of past activities, not the activities themselves; we reconstruct those past activities by the contextual clues provided by the remains.

We look at what people leave behind, either on purpose or on accident. We find **artifacts** (portable objects made or modified by humans, such as tools), **features** (the nonportable objects made by people, such as houses and other structures, refuse dumps, burials, and docks), and **ecofacts** (natural materials used by humans, such as food refuse or large cobbles used in construction) at archaeological **sites** (a place where people left behind material remains that we can recover). Sites can be very simple, such as a scatter of stone tools left on the edge of an old lakeshore, eventually drowned by rising lake levels, or very complex, such as the Roman harbor at Caesarea Maritima discussed in chapter 8. Archaeologists use the relationship of these material remains to one another, the **context** in which we find them, to interpret what people were doing, how they were doing it, and what these activities meant to the past people. Getting from those things and the relationships between them to a reconstruction of past lifeways, therefore, can be extremely complex and difficult, and some sorts of activities (such as *what* types of items people were shipping from point *a* to point *b*) will always be a little easier to talk about than others (*why* people at point *b* wanted item *x* instead of item *y*). These material remains will only tell part of the story of the past, but through years of research, we have gotten better and better at finding new approaches to tease more information from scant evidence.

While archaeologists study the remains of past peoples, not all of those remains are ancient, despite common public perception. Some archaeologists study the material remains from modern landfills, for instance, and there are underwater archaeologists looking at sunken airplanes from World War II whose pilots might still be alive and whose families almost certainly are. For more recent times, there are more types of material culture available to study, including copious amounts of textual information, but archaeology can still reveal insights hidden from the written word. In most times and in most places, few people were literate, and those literate few were generally members of more privileged strata of the society. Even in literate societies, few people recorded the minutiae of daily life or addressed matters that were, at the time, common knowledge. Therefore, archaeological research can contribute much to our understanding of the strategies people of different social statuses and ethnicities used in a given time and place. In maritime archaeology, for instance, many of our records were written by clerks, accountants, and officers, and we know much less about the lives of the ordinary men and women involved in a maritime life: sailors, shipbuilders, fishermen, cooks, midwives, homemakers, seamstresses, waitresses, prostitutes, and many others. For cultures and eras with no written records, archaeology, sometimes called **prehistoric archaeology**, is the only way to learn about these lifeways.

Archaeology as a field sits on the confluence of the humanities and the sciences, and many consider archaeology to be "the most scientific of the humanities and the most humanistic of the sciences." Archaeologists study past cultures and their physical remains, so we have natural links with history. We study things found underground (and sometimes underwater), so we often borrow heavily from the earth sciences. We study past human cultures, so anthropological theory is extremely relevant to our research. Thus, whether we focus more upon scientific or humanistic approaches varies between person to person and from place to place, and with the material culture that is studied. In fact, the ability to be both scientific and humanistic in outlook is one of the great strengths of archaeology as a field, and there can be a great deal of crossover in the field of maritime archaeology. In most archaeology textbooks, a discussion of how archaeology fits within classics, history, or anthropology would follow, but for maritime and underwater archaeology, this varies based on the time period and location that are being studied.

Maritime and underwater archaeology is a worldwide field of study covering the instruments of global connection (ships) and the environment inhabited by 60 percent of the world's population (coasts) as well as all evidence of human history that is now underwater. **Maritime archaeology** focuses upon the study of human societies that were dependent upon waterways for their livelihoods. This includes researching material culture within the underwater environment, like shipwrecks, but also includes studying harbor towns, social and economic activities along the shoreline, or even the hinterland, where at times forests were carefully curated to serve as the raw material for ships' timbers. Therefore, maritime archaeology covers both sides of the shoreline and discusses life on land as well as life on the water. Some would make a further distinction between maritime archaeology and **nautical archaeology**, which more specifically focuses upon the study of shipwrecks, their contents, and shipbuilding technology. You will notice that this text adopts a more holistic approach, including nautical archaeology within the sphere of maritime archaeology. **Underwater archaeology**, on the other hand, is an environment-derived term, and pertains to the study of all cultural material found underwater. This includes shipwrecks but also things like sunken airplanes and landscapes submerged by sea level rise or seismic occurrences. By definition then, underwater archaeology stops at the shoreline (figure 2.2).

Obviously, there is much overlap between these categories, and few archaeologists have the luxury of working on just one type of site or answering just one type of question during their careers, so many archaeologists will draw their data from whatever sources are available and answer important questions as both maritime and underwater archaeologists. For this textbook, therefore, we have decided to use the combined term maritime and underwater archaeology, which we define as the totality of research conducted underwater and related to maritime peoples, to refer to all of these fields.

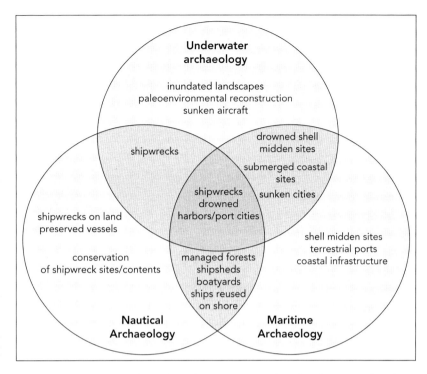

**Figure 2.2** Overlapping relationship of maritime, nautical, and underwater archaeology.

Archaeologists excavate or investigate a given site to answer specific research questions, and so conduct *knowledge-driven research*. Sometimes our research questions are as simple as "what is this collection of timbers on the seafloor?," or "are there any archaeological remains in this area?," but sometimes they are quite complex, along the lines of "how was the dissolution of the Roman Empire slowed or facilitated by the evolution of shipping technologies?" Occasionally our questions are related to modern-day problems, such as "how did the recent hurricane impact this recorded site?" Questions are developed based upon what is known about a given site and its greater context within its cultural period and area. Sometimes, questions are based upon previous research into the site or the cultural period. Occasionally, they come from historical records of a certain ship or battle. Somewhat often, they are the basis for **surveys** (systematic exploration for new sites), or they arise from discoveries made during the survey. In all cases, however, the archaeologist can tell you what he or she is hoping to learn from specific research.

## Brief history of the field

The beginnings of what would become archaeology arose during the scientific awakenings of the Renaissance, as scholars began to realize that there was a remote past that remained largely unknown. By the mid-1800s, Europeans had begun to discover stone tools in association with the bones of extinct animals and to mine sites in Egypt and in the classical world for antiquities. Public interest in the ancient past was ever-increasing, as was **antiquarianism** (collecting items of the ancient past in order to display them); by the early 20th century archaeology had begun to evolve as a separate and formal field of study. It had also developed subfields. For example, most archaeological research in the United States focused upon the origins and lifeways of Native American populations, who were also being studied by cultural anthropologists and linguists. Archaeology in the Americas thus became a part of the field of anthropology, where it remains today. In Europe, archaeologists focused upon excavation of classical sites and the remains of other great civilizations (classical archaeology, Near Eastern archaeology, and Egyptology), or focused upon excavating the sites of their ancient ancestors, rediscovering their nations' histories. Therefore, archaeology became part of history and classics departments. The field continued to develop, becoming increasingly scientific and increasingly rigorous and systematic in its methodologies, finding new ways of recovering information from new types of sites, and undergoing several major intellectual paradigm shifts over time. These intellectual trends have varied from country to country, so you are advised to consult an introductory archaeology textbook in your area of interest for a more detailed discussion of the field's development and current trends (e.g., Kelly and Thomas [2013] for North American archaeology, Renfrew and Bahn [2016] for a European perspective, or Trigger [2006] for a more global viewpoint; see Further Reading at the end of this chapter).

Maritime and underwater archaeology did not arise as a developed subfield of archaeology until the latter part of the 20th century, but people have always known that valuables and valuable information are contained beneath the waterline (figure 2.3). In fact, in the ancient world, the Romans had specially trained free divers from the city of Ostia called *urinatores* (possibly due to the side effects of pressure on their bladders caused by depth) who would recover materials from shipwrecks and who were also used to sabotage enemy ships, causing some of the wrecks they later salvaged. These divers, who regularly did not use any equipment to facilitate breathing underwater, would also sometimes use an ancient form of diving bell—upside down cauldrons filled with air—to allow them to spend more time underwater. In the 15th century, interested amateurs conducted breath-holding dives on enormous Roman vessels built by Emperor Caligula sunk in Lake Nemi (Italy), and in 1535 Franceso De Marchi further explored the same wrecks using a diving bell, removing a number of artifacts from the wrecks that he sold to visiting dignitaries. These wrecks were eventually raised in 1929 and displayed until their destruction during WWII (figure 2.4).

Diving bells (figure 2.5) were increasingly used to salvage material from wrecks in numerous locations after the 16th century, followed by helmeted divers in the 18th and 19th centuries.[2]

Most of this early exploration was done either in search of valuables or to remove harbor obstructions. Arguably, the first case of historically driven underwater research was undertaken by the Deane brothers in England; in 1836 they discovered the wreck of Henry VIII's flagship *Mary Rose* (built 1510), and salvaged a few objects of historical interest. A few years later, in 1885, the Greek state sponsored Ephore Christos Tsoundas to conduct an archaeological survey using helmeted divers near the site of the Battle of Salamis where in 479 BCE ancient Greeks defeated the Persian navy. One of the most notable early examples, the Antikythera wreck from the 4th century BCE, was discovered in 1900 by sponge divers. It contained the oldest known navigation instrument and numerous bronze and marble sculptures; it was excavated by some of these same divers over the next year under the supervision and direction of a non-diving professor at the University of Athens. In 1907 to 1913, the Mahdia shipwreck off the coast of Tunisia was salvaged by a nondiving French archaeologist, Alfred Merlin. The wreck contained Greek sculptures, decorative items, and elaborate furniture fittings.[3]

In fact, during the 1910s to 1920s, sponge divers recovered dozens of classical bronze statues from the Aegean and Mediterranean seas and sold them to museums all over Europe. This effort was applauded by most researchers because those on land had been melted down in antiquity. Examples of salvage under the direction of an archaeologist were rare. As terrestrial archaeology became more and more focused upon careful recording and stratigraphic excavation in the late 19th and early 20th century, the underwater world remained largely the purview of salvors and sponge divers, who collected valuables of historic or artistic interest, such as the 1935 recovery of Benedict Arnold's gunboat *Philadelphia* from the bottom of Lake Champlain, and rarely involved trained archaeologists.

Helmeted diving was not for most people, and especially not for those interested in scientific pursuits. This changed in the 1930s when people started using the first prototypes of SCUBA (self-contained underwater breathing apparatus)

| | |
|---|---|
| *ca. CE 200-* | Roman *urinatores* salvage wrecks |
| | occasional free diving salvage |
| *CE 1535-* | Francesco De Marchi explores wrecks in Lake Nemi using a diving bell |
| | diving bell used for salvage |
| 1885- | earliest underwater archaeological survey done near Salamis |
| | archaeology develops as field of study |
| 1900- | Antikythera shipwreck discovered |
| | non-archaeological divers salvage many wrecks, archaeologists oversee some salvage efforts |
| 1930s- | development of SCUBA |
| | continued exploration of underwater worlds, mostly by non-archaeologists |
| 1940s- | More archaeologists become interested in submerged heritage-Goggin surveys rivers |
| 1950s- | French and Italian divers begin using airlifts to excavate; First UNESCO |
| 1960s- | Diving archaeologists at Cape Gelidonya diving archaeology and cofferdam |
| 1970s- | excavations become increasingly common |
| | excavation and conservation methods develop; |
| 1980s- | underwater surveys mandated prior to development; shipwreck authropology |
| 1990s- | inundated landscape studies develop |
| | deepwater survey develops |
| 2000s- | maritime cultural landscape approach |
| | increasing interest in *in situ* preservation, |
| 2010s- | multidisciplinary approaches |

**Figure 2.3** Brief timeline of major developments in maritime and underwater archaeology.

**Figure 2.4** The Lake Nemi vessel after its raising. Note scale from figures in foreground. (Courtesy of Arcuivi Storici Museo Nazionale della Scienza e Tecnologia Leonardo da Vinci. Photograph by Guido Ucelli)

to explore our underwater worlds. With the development of Cousteau and Gagnan's Aqua-lung, the popularity of SCUBA exploded, and trained divers began to conduct increasingly careful investigations of underwater sites. In the 1930s a mastodon was excavated from the bottom of Wakulla Springs in central Florida, and in 1949 archaeologist John Goggin surveyed the bottom of the Ichetucknee River, also in Florida, for Spanish artifacts. In the 1950s, French and Italian divers, using what became known as airlifts, began research at numerous sites in the Mediterranean with archaeologists on the surface monitoring and directing their progress via televised feeds.[4]

The 1960s saw an expansion in the pervasiveness of maritime archaeology. Numerous sites in northern Europe, such as the Skuldelev Viking ships discussed in chapter 9, were excavated using cofferdams that allowed water to be removed from them so they could be treated like terrestrial sites. The Swedish warship *Vasa*, which sunk within moments of its initial launch in 1628, was discovered in 1956 and raised intact from Stockholm harbor using salvage techniques to be placed in the *Vasa* Museum where it can be seen today. Excavation occurred after the vessel was lifted. More importantly, archaeologists began to dive. Honor Frost, Frédéric Dumas, and Peter Throckmorton worked at several sites in the Mediterranean, verifying their finds first-hand. However, in 1960, a Bronze-age wreck off Cape Gelidonya, Turkey was the first shipwreck to be fully excavated by diving archaeologists actually working underwater, under the direction of George Bass, who is often called the father of nautical archaeology (figure 2.6). This excavation was proof positive that important historical information with correct contextual details could be recovered from underwater sites and that archaeology could be conducted to the same standards underwater as archaeology on land. By the mid-1960s, there were several nautical archaeology organizations and at least a few dozen diving archaeologists.[5]

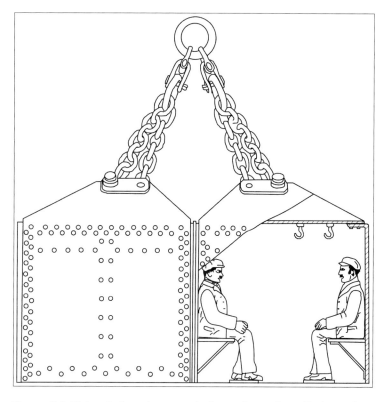

**Figure 2.5** Diving bell and setup of divers descending. (Redrawn from Encyclopædia Britannica, Volume 8, Slice 5)

Over the next 20 years, the field rapidly developed, with diving archaeologists inventing or borrowing numerous techniques for careful survey, mapping, and recording of shipwreck and other underwater sites. The application of these technologies will be discussed in detail in later chapters, but it soon became clear that excellent data could be safely recovered by archaeologists even though they were working in a foreign environment. Hundreds of excavations were conducted all over the globe; although the focus was mostly on shipwrecks, excavations at inundated Mesolithic villages in Scandinavia, Neolithic towns in Swiss lakes, and sinkhole cemeteries in central Florida demonstrated that the underwater world contained well-preserved organic materials (even human remains with brain tissue still intact) that could not preserve in terrestrial environments (figure 2.7). This work also established that there were many types of submerged cultural material that should be investigated.[6]

Through the end of the 20th century, underwater archaeology focused mostly on survey and excavation of sites within the limits of SCUBA diving (approximately 40 meters, or 130 feet, of water or less). However, many underwater sites have been discovered in deep waters well beyond human tolerance (100s of

**Figure 2.6** Excavations underway at Cape Gelidonya. (Courtesy of Institute of Nautical Archaeology. Photograph by Peter Throckmorton)

meters deep in some cases). In 1973, a survey of Lake Ontario discovered *Hamilton* and *Scourge*, two shipwrecks from the War of 1812, in 90 meters (300 feet) of water. These wrecks were so perfectly preserved in the cold waters that human remains could be observed off the bow of one during a photographic survey of the wrecks in 1982. Robert Ballard of the Woods Hole Oceanographic institute expanded ways to record these deep sites through the use of remotely operated vehicles (ROVs), most notably through his joint discovery of the *Titanic* in 1985 in 3,800 meters (12,500 feet) of water off the coast of Newfoundland. Further technological advances allowed video recording of the wreck and recovery of some small items during a return voyage in 2004.[7]

Formal archaeological investigations of these deep sites have remained rare due to effort and expense. However, many of these sites have been discovered via surveys for oil and gas development, and occasionally the oil companies are persuaded to investigate further. The first such excavation took place in 2004 to 2005 at a historic shipwreck in the Ormen Lange gas fields off the coast of Norway. The well-preserved wooden ship was located in approximately 170 meters (550 feet) of water, directly on the only possible route for a gas pipeline. A custom-built ROV was used to document the wreck using multiple sonar methods followed by a video camera survey of the whole site, followed by careful excavation using a custom frame and custom ROV with suction devices for artifact collection. In 2007 a Texas A&M University-led team was able to conduct a limited excavation and documentation of an early 19th century wreck (called the Mardi Gras wreck by the investigators) found in 1,200 meters (4,000 feet) of water. These investigations allowed for the recovery of information formerly inaccessible to archaeologists (figure 2.8).[8]

Underwater archaeology has often been accused by terrestrial archaeologists of focusing too much on the particulars of specific sites and not attempting to answer larger questions about the human condition.[9] It is true that the field is only a little over a half-century old, and we have spent much time developing methods for increasingly precise recovery of data from underwater sites. However, maritime archaeologists of today work underwater and on land to

**Figure 2.7** Excavations at Warm Mineral Springs, Florida, in 1973. (Courtesy of Florida Department of Historical Resources)

answer a wide variety of questions about human lifeways in numerous times and places. Maritime and underwater archaeology is integral to an understanding of the past because water has played such an essential role in the development of humankind. Many of the major connections between human societies occurred first and most frequently over waterways, and many parts of the world were first accessed by people via water. The scope of this research is the subject of the rest of this book.

## Core principles, ethics, and laws

As we discuss in the final chapters of this textbook, the field of maritime and underwater archaeology is subject to numerous ethical and legal considerations. These considerations are given different weights and values by different people and nations, so there is no single approach to the treatment of underwater cultural heritage. However, since the latter part of the 20th century, most developed nations have recognized the universal value of humanity's shared cultural heritage. Representing this acknowledgment, the United Nations Education Scientific and Cultural Organization (UNESCO) created agreements to institute World Heritage status for important archaeological sites both underwater and

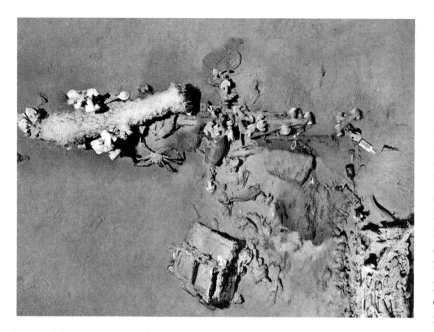

**Figure 2.8** Excavations underway at the deepwater Mardi Gras shipwreck. (Ford et al. 2008)

on land, and promotes care for these sites through multinational cooperation and by prohibiting the illegal antiquities trade.

One of the major principles of UNESCO and other similar organizations is that cultural heritage does not belong to any one person or culture. Instead, the knowledge to be gained from cultural heritage, including archaeological sites, belongs to all humanity, present and future, as part of the shared story of humankind. Therefore, we as archaeologists have a responsibility to share the results of our research with the general public, not simply because much of our research funding comes from public sources, but also because we are ethically bound to add to the human story. Whereas the archaeological process, as any scientific process, includes reporting on results to regulatory agencies, or presenting results in professional journals and conferences, archaeologists also carry a responsibility to engage directly with the interested public. Researchers approach this responsibility in different ways—through websites and social media, public talks, documentaries, novels, and so on—but many practitioners in the field find sharing their discoveries with the interested public among the most fulfilling elements of the profession.

The popularity of maritime archaeology in particular can serve to raise awareness of how fragile and threatened cultural heritage sites can be. As archaeologists, we have the ethical duty to advocate for cultural heritage and to serve as stewards of our maritime and underwater sites. This means not only protecting them from wanton destruction and looting, but also adhering to professional excavation and documentation standards when a site is to be scientifically disturbed. It also means that we should not needlessly excavate a site or a portion of a site. Archaeologists may try to obtain the data they need through nonintrusive means, or leave a portion of a site undisturbed for future research given the recognition that science, technology, and research questions all evolve over time. The latter is common practice in terrestrial sites, but can be difficult in marine environments as exposure of a wreck often destabilizes it, meaning that it may degrade more rapidly thenceforth. Further, the increased awareness of a site that comes along with archaeological research may lead to such sites being subsequently threatened by visitors who further destabilize them through anchoring, collecting, or disturbing what remains.

Archaeology is a destructive science in and of itself. We are one of the few fields that actively destroys much of what we are trying to learn about as we study it. One influential archaeologist once said that excavation is "like cutting pieces out of a hitherto unexamined manuscript, transcribing the fragments, and then destroying them."[10] Excavation destroys the layers at a site and removes all of the artifacts from their contexts of discovery. If one misses an important detail while excavating, it may be lost forever. Archaeologists are therefore obsessive about note-taking and documentation of excavated sites, features, and artifacts. The objective is to record the process of excavation so precisely that we can virtually recreate the site and its excavation during the subsequent analysis phase, as we will discuss later in this book.

In an underwater context, buried material has often reached an equilibrium with its surrounding environment to the point where degradation occurs at a very reduced pace. Once artifacts are uncovered, however, they start to break down as a result of being exposed to a new environment. How fast they degrade depends upon what their buried context was and what material they were originally made from. Once removed from the water, the deterioration is even more dramatic due to the abrupt change from being buried in an environment with little oxygen and light to being exposed to the atmosphere. As a result, almost all artifacts recovered from underwater sites need careful conservation. This can be very time-consuming and is concurrently expensive. Underwater projects, therefore, have the additional ethical consideration of not collecting things that cannot be completely conserved under the project budget. As a result, there is a trend toward the **in situ** (in place) conservation of underwater sites. This means that the shipwreck or material remains of the site are recorded in place and then reburied in place instead of being collected. The site may benefit from treatments aimed at reducing degradation rates underwater and is periodically monitored to make sure it remains stable. This form of conservation works on the principle that the site has survived for decades, centuries, or even millennia in its previous environment, and therefore, with proper reburial, may survive in place for additional generations.

A corollary of the last two points is that archaeologists do not excavate sites just because we know about them. Archaeology is driven by research questions and the drive to gain knowledge about the past. Therefore, archaeologists work to learn *about* and *from* the material things found during the excavations of sites, and we do not excavate unless we have specific things to learn or the site is in immediate danger of destruction.

This differs greatly from salvage and commercial exploitation, which are extremely detrimental to the preservation and understanding of submerged cultural heritage. Salvage companies seek to recover shipwrecks or cargoes in order to sell the material for profit. Often these companies are focused upon recoveries of and from ships that sank within recent weeks and months. However, salvage of historical wrecks, especially those thought to contain treasure, is, as our opening example of the *Nuestra Señora de las Mercedes* showed, a significant subfield. Salvors try to find old wrecks to collect and sell their cargos. This process is driven by potential profits from the sale of the items, and therefore is not oriented toward recovering historical information or recording the context of finds. Often they discover wrecks or recover materials from discovered wrecks using the fastest (and therefore, most cost-effective) means possible, blowing giant holes in sand covering the wrecks to expose artifacts, and utterly destroying any opportunity to learn about their context. They usually search for the most historically important wrecks because their cargoes will also be the most valuable, but not because they are interested in the historical information.

The ship itself is of little interest to the treasure hunters, so it may be ignored or only cursorily recorded. In the worst cases, it is torn apart in the search for more valuables. Further, the cargos are sold piecemeal to the highest bidders, usually private individuals, meaning that few are available for further study, and none are available as a whole collection. Therefore any information that could be gained from the items themselves is also lost or difficult to obtain, and monetarily worthless items usually are not recovered, even though they often contain the information most useful to archaeologists and other people looking to recreate the past. These historical salvors point out that they have the time and money to research individual vessels and collect materials at a scale that archaeologists do not. Some even hire archaeologists to record the materials they recover and raise, and conserve some items that are not worth much money. The profit motive, however, always underlies treasure hunting, meaning that methods and goals are inherently different than archaeological research and what research is done is rarely up to the standard of an archaeological excavation. George Bass has justly pointed out that there are a few examples of good research done by treasure hunters and examples of bad research conducted by archaeologists (especially the research that archaeologists do not publish), but the difference between question-driven research and profit-driven recovery remains and is unlikely to be resolved in the near future, as historical salvage very rarely allows for historically valuable research.[11]

The international recognition of the value of preserving and professionally researching underwater cultural heritage, defined as all traces of human existence that are at least partially underwater, is exemplified through the UNESCO Convention on the Protection of the Underwater Cultural Heritages (2001), which defined principles for providing underwater cultural heritage with protections similar to those extended to archaeological sites on land. This is discussed much more fully in chapter 13, but this Convention has now been signed by more than 50 nations who have agreed upon its definition of underwater cultural heritage and support its core principles that (1) underwater cultural heritage should be preserved, (2) in situ preservation should be the first option if possible, (3) commercial exploitation of this heritage needs to be prevented, and (4) information about underwater cultural heritage is to be shared cooperatively. These norms serve as excellent guidelines that are used by many nations, even those who have not signed the UNESCO Convention.

This transnational cooperation is especially important in regards to underwater cultural heritage because underwater sites of all types are often at the frontier of ethical and legal debates. For instance, ships were literally built to transcend boundaries. Merchant ships were themselves usually filled with multinational crews. Often they had one home port, but carried cargoes from multiple locations. They probably wrecked somewhere in between, in the waters of a different nation or in international waters. For instance, who is the rightful owner of the remains of a 13th-century vessel that was owned by a Venetian merchant, sailed by a Genoese captain, crewed by Sardinians and Sicilians, and sunk off of Malta? Does it belong to the people who found it? To the descendants of the Venetian merchant? To the country off whose waters it was discovered? Who has the responsibility of caring for it and conserving the finds?

In many nations, by long tradition, shipwrecks fall under the laws of abandoned property and come under the management of the state as a public asset, although military craft generally are considered to remain the property of the sovereign nation who owned them at the time of their sinking. This is not as clear as it might be. Naval vessels may have had crews that were loosely members of the same nation, but in the colonial world, this meant that many of the sailors were born in the colonies or picked up as needed in various ports. Most of these colonies are now separate nations, and some of the original countries no longer exist at all. Should, then, naval vessels belong to the government that inherited the rights and territory of the former country? Should they be the responsibility of the country in whose waters they are discovered? What if they are in international waters? Further, shipwrecks are also frequently graveyards, and this is especially true of military craft. What about the sailors who died as a vessel sank? Should these sites be treated with the respect we give battlegrounds and cemeteries? Finally, a great number of these sunken vessels may contain valuable materials, but many, especially those from the wars of the 20th century, also contain hazards such as leaking fossil fuels and unexploded ordnance. What rights do the nations impacted by these environmental hazards have? What responsibilities do nations have toward mitigating this hazards? (figure 2.9).

To return to the case study from the beginning of the book, the *Nuestra Señora de las Mercedes* became a political battleground not only because it contains valuable treasure, but also because it contains rare historic information about the colonial history of the New World that has not been preserved elsewhere. It was found in the waters of one nation, carrying materials that originally belonged to another, destroyed by yet another nation, and discovered by a private entity. Whose needs should be privileged and why in these cases? This case was decided

**Figure 2.9** SS *Richard Montgomery,* still filled with unexploded WWII ordnance at its place of sinking in the Thames estuary. (Courtesy of Clem Rutter)

in favor of Spain, but others have been ruled differently, as there are many ambiguities when dealing across national lines of past and present.

Further, few of the laws deal specifically with ancient sites that were fully inundated by subsidence and sea level rise before the invention of written records, so it is difficult to say what rules apply to the discovery, excavation, and collection of materials from these sites. For instance, hundreds of pounds of ancient terrestrial animal bones and the occasional artifact are dragged from the bottom of the North Sea every month by fishermen. These are roughly sorted by the fishermen and the more interesting pieces are sold online, including some artifacts. The rest are thrown in dumpsters, headed for landfills.[12] Should these materials be considered the spoils of the ocean like the fish themselves, and so the possession of the fishermen? Should they belong to the nation from whose waters they came? Should the trawling be stopped to protect the ecofacts, archaeology, and the marine environment? What, then, about the livelihood of living people? How do we balance the needs of modern living people with our interest in the lives of those dead for millennia? What balance do we strike? Who decides? The last chapter of this book will discuss this in much more detail, but these are issues that require input from many groups and cannot be decided by archaeologists alone.

**MY MOST IMPORTANT CONTRIBUTION TO MARITIME AND UNDERWATER ARCHAEOLOGY**

## Dolores Elkin, Director, Underwater Archaeology Program, National Institute of Anthropology, Argentina

I remember the moment vividly: I was sitting at my desk at the National Institute of Anthropology (Ministry of Culture) with the usual lot of animal bones on the desk; it was the early 1990s and I was working on my PhD research on Early Holocene human subsistence in the high deserts of the Andes. Suddenly a stranger walked through the door and introduced himself as an architect and diver who belonged to an International Council on Monuments and Sites (ICOMOS) working group, mostly formed by architects, specializing in underwater cultural heritage. They were surveying the wreck of an 18th century British sloop of war that had sunk in Patagonia and were looking for an archaeologist to join the team. After all, they thought, it was an archaeological site; it just happened to be lying on the seabed.

I listened to the fascinating story of the loss of the vessel, called HMS *Swift*, which sank during an exploratory mission that originated from Port Egmont, the British base in the Malvinas/Falkland Islands. The fatal accident occurred in March 1770, when the ship stranded on a rock hidden by the high tide very close to what later became Puerto Deseado, in Santa Cruz Province, southern Argentina. After a month of despair, the survivors were rescued, thanks to the outstanding accomplishment of five seamen and an officer who rowed back to Port Egmont, a distance of over 300 nautical miles (555 km).

To my knowledge, at the time there were no archaeologists who were also divers in Argentina. Moreover, the vast majority, like myself, were involved in prehistoric archaeology. Cultural remains such as lithic

tools, bones, and pottery used by sedentary groups prior to the arrival of the Spanish conquistadores were all very familiar, but an 18th century British shipwreck site submerged in Patagonia could not have been a more alien research topic. However, it seemed clear that somebody within our discipline had to get off the beaten path. So, I believe the most important thing I have done in my career was deciding to face the challenge of developing maritime archaeology in my country. To me, this could only be achieved with archaeologists actually working underwater and interacting directly with the sites, not expecting divers who were not trained in archaeology to do that.

After completing my PhD on my original topic, I followed the logical steps: learning to scuba dive, assembling an interdisciplinary maritime archaeology team formed of people who either were already divers or were willing to learn to dive, seeking advice from colleagues around the world, gathering a bibliography (pre Internet!), asking for institutional support, and getting financial aid to buy some equipment to get going: an inflatable boat, a compressor, and some regulators, cylinders, and so on.

Finally, yes, the moment of beginning to survey HMS *Swift* arrived! The site itself turned out to be fabulous,

*(continued)*

with excellent preservation conditions thanks to the cold temperature of the water and the anaerobic environment that surrounds most of the wreck: a thick layer of compact, fine-grained sediment. The artifact collection comprises a great variety of materials, from delicate glassware and porcelain to iron cannons and anchors; from food and condiments to hull timbers of all sorts; from clothing to pharmaceutical products. There was even a complete human skeleton! After many years of field, lab, and desk-based research we have learned a lot about life on board (including eating, drinking, and sanitary habits), the technology of the time, site-formation processes, and ship construction. The latter has been the research focus of the Cristian Murray, the architect who originally introduced me to the site, and still a key member of the National Institute of Anthropology team. As for the human remains, which were eventually ascribed to one of the marines who died in the sinking of the *Swift*, they allowed a series of bioanthropological studies plus a very positive collaboration between Argentina and the United Kingdom, not long after the Falklands War.

The HMS *Swift* also set the basis for the development of legislation to protect submerged archaeological remains. Thanks to the initiative of the local divers who discovered the site in 1982, shortly thereafter it was declared a Historical Heritage site. This was the first time a shipwreck was so designated, and the site even came to have its own museum in the town of Puerto Deseado. Some years later, taking into account the precedent of HMS *Swift*, Argentina passed a national law that automatically protects all submerged archaeological remains more than 100 years old. More recently, our country became a State Party of the UNESCO 2001 Convention for the Protection of Underwater Cultural Heritage. The current awareness of the nation's submerged archaeological remains is a natural outcome of the events surrounding the *Swift* in the 1980s and 1990s, reinforced by the growth of professional activities regarding research and management of underwater sites.

In sum, despite the deep satisfaction that every single project has given me throughout my whole career, that major decision of leaving my comfort zone on land archaeology and doing something for a shipwreck in need of a professional approach has been an unquestionable landmark. And an extremely rewarding one.

## SUMMARY

Archaeology is the study of past (sometimes the very recent past) human lifeways from their material remains. It can be a humanistic or scientific study, depending upon the research questions and interest of the researcher. Maritime and underwater archaeologists study the material remains of cultures focused upon marine lifeways and cultural material now underwater. These remains include shipwrecks and harbors, but also terrestrial components associated with maritime activities, sunken aircraft, and drowned landscapes. Maritime and underwater archaeology developed as its own subfield in the latter half of the 20th century but has its roots in antiquity. Maritime and underwater archaeology can help us to understand human history in a way that no other type of social science or humanity can because it provides access to and consideration of material culture that cannot otherwise be interpreted. Many legal and ethical complexities surround this research because of the often-international nature of the original material culture, the complicated tangle of ownership, and the shifting political boundaries from nations past to modern.

## DISCUSSION QUESTIONS

1. How does archaeology differ from other social sciences and humanities? Why is the study of material culture important?
2. What is context? Why does it matter? What could a future archaeologist learn about you by studying the context of finds in your room?
3. How did underwater and maritime archaeology develop?
4. What are some of the ethical constraints upon maritime archaeology? How do these differ from other sorts of archaeology?

## FURTHER READING

Adams, J. (2013). *A Maritime Archaeology of Ships.* Oxbow Books, Oxford.

Bass, G. (2011). The Development of Maritime Archaeology. In *Oxford Handbook of Maritime Archaeology*, A. Catsambis, B. Ford and D. L. Hamilton, eds. 3–22. Oxford University Press, New York.

Friends of the *Hunley* (2018). Hunley. Available at https://hunley.org/.

Horrell, C. and Borgens, A, Eds. (2017). The Mardi Gras Shipwreck: The Archaeology of an Early Nineteenth-Century Wooden-Hulled Sailing Ship. *Historical Archaeology* 51(3): 323–461.

Institute of Nautical Archaeology. (2018). Cape Gelidonya Late Bronze Age Shipwreck Excavation Site Report. Available at https://nauticalarch.org/cape-gelidonya-late-bronze-age-shipwreck-excavation-site-report/.

Kelly, R.L. and D.H. Thomas. (2013). *Archaeology: Down to Earth,* fifth edition, chapters 1-2. Wadsworth Publishing, New York.

Renfrew, C. and P. Bahn. (2016). *Archaeology: Theories, Methods, and Practice.* seventh edition. Thames and Hudson, New York.

Trigger, B. (2006). *A History of Archaeological Thought.* Cambridge University Press, New York.

## CHAPTER 3

# HOW DO WE LEARN
# FROM THINGS?

**FOCUS QUESTIONS**

- What types of maritime archaeological sites are there, and how do they differ in what they can teach us about the past?
- How can the preservation of artifacts in submerged environments, which tends to be better than on land, improve our understanding of past cultures?
- What information can be gained from inundated landscapes and submerged terrestrial sites?
- What kind of information do ship and aircraft wrecks hold? What can their contents tell us about trade, colonization, warfare and the people on board?
- What do maritime technological innovations tell us about broader trends in society, history, and culture? How does naval innovation shape the rise and fall of maritime societies?
- How can we gather data in a precise and rigorous way while still maintaining archaeological sites and the data they contain for future societies?

**TYPES OF ARCHAEOLOGICAL EVIDENCE**

The previous chapters have discussed what maritime and underwater archaeology is and what archaeologists attempt to learn from submerged and underwater sites. This chapter begins our discussion of how maritime and underwater research is done. Archaeologists straddle the line between the humanities and the sciences, and we often use methods and data from each in order to understand the material remains found at an archaeological site. An archaeologist excavating a classical Greek shipwreck, for instance, is quite likely to collaborate with a geologist, a material scientist, a botanist, an epigrapher, and an art historian in order to more completely interpret the site. However, sites differ greatly from one another for both cultural and natural reasons, and so do corresponding research methods that can provide the most insight. Therefore, the underwater archaeologist must be familiar with numerous categories of analyses and data. This chapter introduces these categories, providing terms that will be used throughout the rest of the text.

## What do we want to learn from maritime and underwater sites?

As will be repeatedly mentioned throughout this text, maritime and underwater archaeologists investigate sites in order to answer research questions. These questions can be very simple, such as "are there any archaeological remains in this area?," but when excavating a site, we tend to have more specific questions about the site as a whole, about each component, and about individual artifacts, ecofacts, and features. In general, all archaeologists always want to know how old a site is and what it was used for. We want to know how the site was created and what happened to it after people left it behind. We want to know how the artifacts were made, how the artifacts and ecofacts were used, and how they ended up where we found them. We want to know the significance of the various features at the site and what activities caused them to be created. We want to know what the whole tells us about the people who made this site. We then want to expand that analysis to put the site into a broader regional context, comparing this site to as many sites from the same time period as possible or comparing it to similarly functioning sites from numerous times, or possibly both. In other words, when possible, we want to compare sites to discuss variation through time or over space. Nearly all archaeological research questions are variations on these themes, and there are a number of methods developed or borrowed over the years in order to help answer these questions.

For maritime and underwater archaeology, there are some more precise questions archaeologists tend to ask of specific site types. For instance, when working on ships and shipwrecks, we want to know the original purpose of the vessel, its route during its voyage, the technology used to create, sail, and maintain it, the cultural connections that the ship represents, the reasons it sank, and its age (both in terms of how long it was in service and its historical date), among other things. When discussing coastal facilities, archaeologists ask slightly different questions. We want to know where the water was when the site was occupied and if that had any impact on the people who created it such as where the site was situated, how it was created, and how it was modified over time. If the site is underwater, we want to know when and how it was submerged and whether that submergence was deliberate or accidental. As you read the remainder of this text, you will see that a great deal of the research we present addresses some of the above questions. It should be noted, however, that an introductory text such as this one tends to present more refined case studies. Many (perhaps even most) sites are small, ephemeral, and poorly preserved, and so do not contain information that allows us to answer as many of these questions as we would like.

## Sites

As a reminder, archaeological sites are places where the material remains of past human activities have preserved. Maritime and underwater archaeology encompasses a broad range of human activities and variety of archaeological remains, settings, and types of material culture, ranging from a lighthouse perched high on a rocky cliff, to docks located in the intertidal zone, to submerged cities in shallow water, to a nearly intact Roman ship 300 meters deep in the Black Sea. The numerous case studies in this text will provide a sense of this range, which typically spans three major categories of sites: (1) sites created by loss while using the water or over the water (shipwrecks and aircraft remains); (2) sites created on the margins of the water (or within shallow water), such as harbor installations or the Neolithic "pile dwelling" villages of the alps and; (3) sites that when created were far inland but are now submerged.[1]

Many people think that underwater archaeologists focus solely on the first type of site, and individual ships and aircraft are, indeed, important to underwater and maritime archaeology. The investigation of a shipwreck or downed aircraft may consist of a brief survey to note its location, or may result in a large, multiyear excavation. Plans and reconstructions of these wrecks are used to compare vessels and their contents to each other and to learn more about the development of seafaring and shipbuilding, much of which is poorly documented in the written record.

In order to fully understand a maritime culture, it also is important to reconstruct how its members were tied to the land and how they used the water. Ships were made for shipping and traveled to and from ports in order to transport their valuable cargos. These ports, some of them sites of the second type above, are equally relevant to maritime and underwater archaeology, serving as anchors for a culture, and as nodes for exchange. As discussed in chapter 1, port cities served not only as homes for the sailors, their families, and the myriad of services that are needed to support and outfit ships, but also as loci of contact between people and cultures. They became places where ideas as well as goods were exchanged, where new ways of thinking were explored and spread. This often led to port cities becoming wealthy, granting them significant political power.

The coastal infrastructure of a culture, the bridge between land and sea, sometimes consists of nothing more than relatively ephemeral habitation sites, informal landing sites, or small dock structures. At the same time, many of our world's largest cities started as (and often still function as) port towns with major harbor installations. Often, coastal infrastructure at these sites is reused, repurposed, and buried over the course of generations as the city changes and develops. The archaeological evidence of these past structures is often discovered accidentally during harbor improvements or new building projects—such as the repeated discovery of Gold Rush ships that had been abandoned and reused as buildings in San Francisco.[2]

Coastal infrastructure of the past may now be found far inland, as in the case of silted-in harbors, however, there are also numerous examples of former terrestrial sites that are now far underwater, which is the third category of maritime and underwater sites. In fact, much of the coastal landscape available to our ancestors has been inundated by the natural process of sea-level and lake-level rise due to glaciers melting at the end of the Pleistocene, also known as the Ice Age. This will be discussed in more detail in ensuing chapters, but remember that millions of hectares were drowned from about 21,000 to 5,000 years ago by more than 130 meters (426 feet) of sea level rise. Usually the process of inundation is somewhat slow, but this is not always the case. Some landscapes, cities, and towns have been drowned almost instantaneously. The pirate city of Port Royal in Jamaica sank in a day due to an earthquake (see chapter 7). Hundreds of other towns and archaeological sites have been drowned by the worldwide construction of hydro-electric and flood-control dams, such as the Aswan, Hoover, Three Gorges, and Oahe. When these dams were closed, the rivers running through them backed up, creating large reservoirs and flooding the lands adjacent to the former river channels. Permanent inundation of the river valleys was nearly instantaneous, drowning archaeological sites and active settlements, and dislocating thousands of people, who left behind homes and possessions in many cases. Although little formal scientific investigation of these drowned settlements has yet occurred, they are underwater cultural heritage as well.[3]

## Site formation processes and context

As evident through the discussion above on the diversity of archaeological sites, they are each the result of a distinct combination of cultural and natural **site formation** processes. People live and work, creating and using artifacts and features, and using ecofacts as part of daily life. Material culture is then functioning within its social system (or **systemic context**). As things are lost or discarded, they enter the archaeological context, in which they become subject to natural site formation processes. Organic materials begin to decay or be eaten, buried things get moved around by burrowing animals, sea grasses grow through the abandoned items, waves bury items in sand, and so on. For maritime and underwater sites, these can be broken into "extracting filters" which lead to the loss of materials such as currents that float timbers away and "scrambling filters" which rearrange, mix, or alter material culture, such as fish burrowing or sand deposition and removal.[4] Archaeologists need to pay very close attention to sites when excavating because we need to determine how "intact" a site is. The patterns associated with the material culture at a site are documented and analyzed in order to recreate past human activity. Therefore, the most informative sites are those in which the relationships between objects has been undisturbed since they entered the archaeological context. When natural processes cause cultural material to be moved around, the relationship between the articles is telling us about what animals, plants, currents, or sand dunes did in the past, but not about people. Resources are best aimed at sites and portions of sites where relatively little happened to destroy the original associations between artifacts, ecofacts, and features. This is discerned by careful excavation and by paying very close attention to the stratigraphy at the site, which will be discussed further in chapter 4.

No matter what type of site an archaeologist investigates, he or she will carefully analyze the archaeological **context** of all the associated material culture. Context is the time and space setting of an artifact, feature, culture, or site. An *artifact's* context is made of its immediate **matrix** (the material surrounding it), its **provenience** (horizontal and vertical position within the site's grid), and its **association** (co-occurrence) with other material culture or non-cultural items. For instance, a stone spear point found in the hip joint of a human burial tells a different story than one found on the seafloor next to a shipwreck than one found within a trash pit adjacent to whale bones. A *site's* context is similarly made of its immediate position on the landscape, such as near a river or on a coral reef; its provenience, or the location of the entire artifact **assemblage** within the stratigraphy, such as within the ship's hold or scattered on the reef; and its association with other archaeological sites from the same time period or in the same region. When artifacts are excavated from undisturbed settings, this material is considered to be found in **primary context**, while material excavated from disturbed portions of a site is found in **secondary context**. Material in undisturbed context tells the most about past people because patterns and associations were created by human action rather than natural processes.

Archaeological sites contain **components**, or bounded periods for which we have evidence of site occupation or use. Single component sites only contain evidence for a single period of occupation or use, though people may have reused the area many times but did not leave any tangible remains behind. Multiple component sites, on the other hand, contain cultural material indicating the site was (re)used more than once in the past. Shipwrecks are commonly considered single component sites, even if the ship was rebuilt during its use-life, because the act of becoming a wreck and settling onto the ocean floor is something that only happens once, even though the site formation processes of a shipwreck breaking down occur over a long period of time. In the rare case where a younger shipwreck settles on top of an older one, the location would also be a multiple component site (figure 3.1).

Though all archaeologists are concerned with context, provenience, and associations, **geoarchaeologists** focus on determining how natural processes have impacted the cultural material since it entered the archaeological context, defining how and where the site has been disturbed and where the site is more intact. They often do this by analyzing the stratigraphy at a site. Stratigraphy is the study of the spatial and temporal relationships between the layers (strata) at a site. A site or landscape, whether presently above or below water, can be affected by three major processes: deposition (or aggradation), during which sediments are deposited and materials are accumulating on the surface; stability, during which soils form and the surface is relatively stable; and erosion (or degradation), when previously deposited materials are worn away. Though it is impossible to see the material that has been eroded away, erosion can be apparent through gaps in dates at sites or through obvious discontinuities in the stratigraphy. Geoarchaeologists spend at least as much time looking at the sediments and ecofacts at a site as at the material culture, as these can be very informative about the natural processes that have impacted the

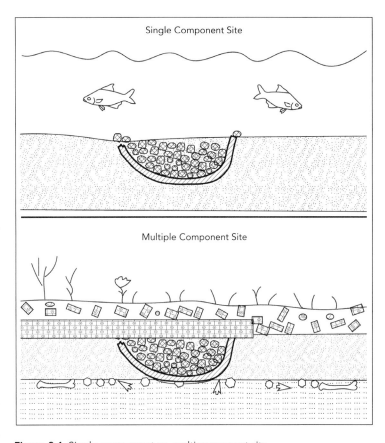

**Figure 3.1** Single-component vs. multicomponent site.

site. They are also commonly responsible for figuring out how old a site is and it if it contains multiple components or not.

## Features

Artifacts can be carried back to a lab to be conserved, weighed, and studied. Features, however, as non-portable material culture, are destroyed by excavation and, thus, can only be studied in situ prior to and during excavation. Features can range from dark stains that represent where a long-rotted post once held up a dock, to hearths, to the enormous concrete structure that is the Roman Emperor Trajan's harbor at Portus (chapter 7). Features are created by people either accidentally or on purpose whenever they conduct an activity that leaves a tangible mark on the earth's surface, such as constructing a building, installing a dock, or sinking a ship to serve as the base of a lighthouse. Some features are created by excavation, some are created by adding things to the earth's surface, and many contain elements of both, such as a dredged channel bounded by seawalls.

Features can be very obvious: sometimes they are large stone structures or deep holes, or stained areas that looks very different from the surrounding dirt; other times, though, we know we have discovered a feature only because the sediment is a little softer or harder, a little more or less sandy, or it contains artifacts that the surrounding sediment did not. Many large features are made up of series of smaller features. Thus, archaeologists often have to figure out if the features are distributed in such a way that they can be linked into meaningful patterns. A house floor could consist of a number of post features, a hearth, and wall fragments. Cities and towns are composed of hundreds or thousands of overlapping features that are the remains of numerous structures. **Structures** can be defined as composite features that were probably used for containing things and are large enough for humans to enter. The term structure implies that the function is unknown. For instance, we would describe a feature as a house floor if we knew that the original building served as a residence, but would refer to it as a structure floor if not certain of the original building's purpose.

Features often contain artifacts and ecofacts. They can be very informative about people in the past because features reflect the tangible ways in which people modified their environments. Features thus contain important information about site age, function, and social history. Artifacts and ecofacts are informative whether they are found in features or not, but the associations between them if they are found in undisturbed context in a feature are much more revealing than the items in isolation.

## Artifacts

Whether a site is thousands of years old, decades old, or only a few weeks old, it must contain definite evidence of human activity for it to be considered a site. Artifacts, portable human-made objects, are the most common items found at most archaeological sites. These might consist of ca. 250,000-year-old Neanderthal tools discovered in 2009 in the North Sea off the United Kingdom[5] or bottles thrown off a modern dock. Prior to the Industrial Revolution, nearly all artifacts were made by hand, and prior to the invention of plastic and synthetic materials, nearly all artifacts were made of some combination of metal, stone, ceramic, and/or organic materials. People tend to use things until they are lost, taken, or discarded intentionally. Discarded items are often used until they are worn out, meaning that archaeologists very rarely find pristine items. Instead, archaeologists tend to find the broken remnants of things that were no longer useful. Answering questions about the individual artifacts at a site and about the entire artifact assemblage requires us to piece together (sometimes literally) the fragments that were left behind. We want to know what the artifacts were; what they were used for; how, when and from what they were made; where they came from; what their life histories were before they were lost or discarded; and how and why they ended up in their final location. Archaeologists also want to explicate the relationships between the artifacts, ecofacts, and features at the site.

Maritime and underwater archaeologists have an occasional advantage in the types of artifacts we discover. Some submerged sites, such as shipwrecks, were created rapidly and unintentionally, and are therefore filled with items that people still valued. These artifacts can demonstrate what was considered valuable enough to risk transporting on the open waters, based on the contents of cargo holds; what ports were connected with one another, based on the source of the artifacts; information about the crew and passengers aboard, based on identifiable personal items; or details about how people organized their spaces, based on where things are found.

Not all artifacts are equally likely to be discovered at archaeological sites. Oftentimes what survives depends on site formation processes and what was commonly available at the time of use, but the material of which an artifact was made also plays a determinative role. Stone, ceramic fragments, brick, and glass are common as few processes destroy stone, glass, or pottery. Even though the artifacts made of them may be breakable and fragile, and they can be broken into smaller and smaller pieces, the materials themselves are rather resilient. Iron artifacts, on the other hand, are commonly found at some sites but rare at others given the material's propensity to rust. Metals such as lead fare better, while others typically fare worse.

**Organic** artifacts, such as those made of wood, bone, cotton, and leather, contain carbon and derive from once-living organisms. They rarely survive in the archaeological record, even though they were extremely common in past societies. As soon as people abandoned a site, nature began to take its toll, and in most cases, organics were either eaten by animals or bacteria or broke down through exposure to the sun, rain, wind, erosion, or chemical weathering. However, sometimes archaeologists are lucky enough to find portions of sites that contain well-preserved organic artifacts. What allows this preservation? Microorganisms require warmth, oxygen, and water to cause decomposition. Remove one (or better yet, two) of these, and excellent organic preservation is possible. There are a few types of environments that are more likely to have good organic preservation. In arid dry environments, such as caves and rockshelters, artifacts have never been exposed to the elements and humidity is very low. Mersa Gawasis in Egypt is one such site, in which Middle Kingdom Egyptian ship supplies were stored for later use. In sites that have been buried very rapidly, there is no oxygen to break down organics, so material can be extremely well-preserved, such as the maritime site of Ozette, buried in a landslide around 1450 CE on the northwestern coast of the United States. Organic artifacts can also survive in arid, cold environments, such as mountains, glaciers, and in the Arctic, because they become frozen and/or dried, as exemplified by the **midden** (trash pit) remains from the Viking-age site in Newfoundland, L'anse Aux Meadows.[6]

The preceding are all rare examples of well-preserved terrestrial maritime sites; a much more common combination favoring organic preservation occurs when a site is submerged. Waterlogged settings, especially dark, muddy environments and oxygen-free (anaerobic) environments, prevent the decay of organics. Not all underwater environments preserve equally well. Shipwrecks in the low-oxygen waters of the Black Sea, or the cold, dark, fresh waters of the Great Lakes are almost perfectly preserved after hundreds or even thousands of years. At the same time, portions of shipwrecks exposed in shallow warm Caribbean waters may be nearly consumed by organisms, especially the wood-eating teredo worm (*Teredo navalis*) in a matter of decades, leaving behind only portions of the shipwreck buried in the seafloor.

The potential for excellent organic preservation is one of the main reasons to conduct underwater excavations. Some of the things that can be found underwater cannot be discovered in any other environment. Ships were rarely stored on land for posterity, so the *only* place shipping technology is systematically preserved is underwater. Other types of sites may be discoverable on land but terrestrial counterparts often have poor organic preservation.

While well-preserved organic artifacts from underwater environments can provide a wealth of information about past lifeways, abruptly altering their surroundings through excavation and recovery risks compromising their integrity. As soon as they are exposed to air, light, oxygen, and warmth, they begin to decompose and therefore require special care and conservation postrecovery. The excavation itself is also conducted at a more measured pace in order to care for these rare finds and to recover them responsibly. It may take years or even decades

## SITE, ARTIFACT, OR FEATURE: WHAT IS A SHIP?

What is a ship? Is it a site, a feature, or an artifact? Ships are literally created for the purpose of portability, and definitely are manmade. They can (with great effort) be moved to a lab. They can be weighed and measured. They also can be taken apart and put back together. All of this would indicate that they are artifacts. However, sites are locations from which we can recover evidence of human activity. A ship is a place where people live and work and from which we can recover tangible evidence of this. It may also be a matter of scale. A ship contains features (the galley or mast step, for instance), but it could potentially be considered a very complex composite feature. It is, after all, definitely a structure, as its entire purpose is to hold people and contents inside and water outside. This debate is worth considering for the still-floating portion of our maritime cultural heritage, but, luckily, a shipwreck is more clearcut. A shipwreck is a site, containing any hull remains and any preserved contents. The distribution of these remains in and outside of the hull determine the extent of the site. The hull contents consist of artifacts, ecofacts, such as preserved provisions or ballast stones, and features that made up parts of the original ship, such as the mast step. The relationship between these things tells us about natural site formation processes during and after the time of wrecking or about how a particular ship served in its systemic context. Some aspects, such as the relationship between the hull features, are more likely to inform on the latter, while some, such as the distribution of all material on the seabed, are more likely to inform on the former, although sometimes this distribution can tell us why the vessel wrecked in the first place, which can be due to either human or natural processes.

before they are properly conserved and stable, which cost time and money. Therefore, it is especially important for maritime and underwater archaeologists to budget for these potential expenses from the outset, as discussed more fully in chapter 5.

## Human remains

While archaeologists excavating at maritime and underwater sites only infrequently encounter human remains, human skeletal material can be extremely informative. Because accessing much of this information precisely and ethically requires specialized analysis by people trained specifically in this work, forensic anthropologists or **bioarchaeologists** are usually consulted. Bioarchaeologists focus on analyzing human skeletons from archaeological contexts in order to further our understanding of past lifeways. Depending upon how well-preserved the skeletal material is, bioarchaeologists generally will be able to determine how old the person was, what his or her sex was, and something about his or her general health during life. For example, isotopic studies of human teeth recovered concreted to a cannon from CSS *Alabama* helped determine elements of the unfortunate sailor's diet, and, as a consequence, where the person likely was born and grew up (chapter 13). Sometimes it is possible to observe signs of illness or determine the cause of death as well. When there are numerous remains recovered from a cemetery, it is possible to ask more general questions about cultural norms and status differences between different segments of the burial population.

For example, excavation at the Windover site in northeastern Florida revealed the remains of more than a hundred individuals who had been buried in a shallow pond (known as a charnel pond) over the course of several centuries, from approximately 6500 to 5500 BCE. Because of the excellent preservation in this bog-like cemetery, many of the skeletons and their effects survived to be excavated by archaeologists when the burials became exposed in the pond during a modern building project. People were buried with fiber mats, clothing and other perishable goods, and many were staked in place by mats placed around their bodies (table 3.1). However, there were fewer than two dozen stone artifacts in the entire site. If the pond had not remained wet for several millennia, almost everything at this site would have decomposed. Because of its excellent preservation, Windover challenged many assumptions about hunting and gathering societies. Theoretical models suggested that people in Florida at this time were very mobile. Given that most people were buried within days of death, it appears communities were much more sedentary than previously thought. Archaeologists also thought that foraging societies did not generally have the resources to maintain persons in poor health, but several skeletons showed severe and crippling pathologies that meant they would have needed years of attentive care before death. Thus, this one site completely changed much of what we

TABLE 3.1 **SOME KEY DATA GAINED FROM THE WINDOVER CHARNEL POND EXCAVATIONS**

| 168 Individuals | Count |
| --- | --- |
| Female | 47 |
| Male | 47 |
| Undetermined (subadults, disarticulated, indeterminate) | 74 |
| Adults | 101 |
| Subadults | 67 |
| Grave goods | 68 |
| No goods | 100 (42 known burials, 58 individuals from disturbed contexts, so unknown) |

Technology Recovered; items in italics are organic and are extremely rare in archaeological contexts

| *Antler tools: punches, awls, shaft straighteners, pressure flakers* | *Spearthrowers (atlatls) and components* |
| --- | --- |
| *Bone projectile points* | Stone knife |
| *Bone tools: awls, gouges, needles,* | Stone projectile point |
| *Bone tubes* | *Textiles (clothing and mats wrapping many bodies)* |
| *Canine tooth gravers* | *Turtle shell containers* |
| *Food remains* | *Unmodified bone* |
| *Shark tooth drills* | *Unmodified shell* |
| *Shark tooth scraper* | *Wooden bowls* |
| *Shell beads* | *Wooden pestles* |
| *Snares made from fibers* | *Wooden stakes for holding bodies in place* |

thought we knew about early societies in the southeastern United States because of the large burial population the researchers were able to examine.[7]

Human remains have special status in most cultures and most countries by law or custom, and there are important legal and ethical frameworks that must be considered before disturbing, removing, or investigating human bodies, although these vary greatly from country to country. These studies must be undertaken by specialists in order to make certain they are conducted with proper care and respect. This is particularly relevant for maritime and underwater archaeologists. Many shipwrecks caused the sudden and tragic deaths of numerous individuals. In the case of naval vessels that sank due to military actions, the wreck site may be considered a war grave and special rules could apply to any actions that might disturb it; again, these vary by country. If it were an inundated cemetery, human remains would fall under unmarked graves laws or cemetery laws. In many countries, the excavation of graves is only undertaken when absolutely necessary by law, by ethical and moral imperative, and by custom. Further, as we consider more-recent sites, such as WWII vessels, the needs of living family members regarding these graves outweighs archaeological considerations, sometimes leading to recovery of the remains and sometimes leading to in situ preservation of the site.

## Floral and faunal remains

Many of the floral and faunal (plant and animal) remains at an archaeological site can be considered ecofacts. An ecofact is an element found in an archaeological context that was deposited by human activity but that was not made by a human being, such as burned wood, butchered animal bone, pebbles used to create a walkway, or shellfish remains. Ecofacts can arrive at site intentionally (such as stone used as ballast in a ship) or unintentionally (such as the pollen found within the bilges of a shipwreck). Ecofacts often are recovered from features and can be used to help understand past subsistence strategies, past environments, and past construction schemes. The analysis of inorganic ecofacts such as stones used for construction can be very informative at some sites, even pointing to the quarry from which a stone artifact was carved. These studies tend to be very site-specific, however, so the remainder of this section will focus on general things archaeologists can learn from the plants and animals found at archaeological sites.

Floral and faunal analyses require years of training and are undertaken by specialists. **Zooarchaeologists** specialize in studying the faunal remains from sites, while **paleoethnobotanists** or **archaeobotanists** focus on plant remains from sites. As organic preservation at archaeological sites is nearly always incomplete and sometimes nonexistent, these studies cannot be conducted at all sites or in all locations. These sorts of studies are usually aimed at reconstructing past environments, past **foodways**, or both. What a culture considers "food" can vary greatly, and the rules for what should be eaten, by whom, when, and how can provide very important insights into past cultures. In the case of shipwrecks, these studies are also occasionally undertaken to determine cargo provenience or vessel voyaging routes.

Both types of researchers follow a similar process. First, they must determine if they are looking at remains that arrived at the site due to cultural or natural processes. Next, they assess how **taphonomic** processes may have affected the site's preservation to determine how representative the recovered materials are of what was once at the site. The researchers may collect **control samples** to help with these determinations. The control samples and the archaeological samples will then be compared to modern **biomes** to help reconstruct what the world at the archaeological site was like and to determine what was brought to the site due to human agency.

Wood, especially charcoal, preserves a bit better than more fragile remains like seeds, leaves, and fruit. Ship timbers, because they can be very large and thick, may be the primary organic material preserved at a site. These larger botanical remains can be used to date the site via radiocarbon analyses, and wood remains can also sometimes be used for dendrochronology (see below). When there is botanical preservation, it is also possible to conduct species analysis to see what types of plants were being used and, from context, what they were used for—such as the residues from pottery vessels in shipwrecks being used to recreate past beer recipes.[8]

At many sites, microfossils not visible to the naked eye can preserve even when all of the larger organics have decomposed. The most common remains of this kind are pollen, phytoliths, and diatoms. **Palynology**, the study of pollen grains, can be used to understand past environments, and, because pollen gets trapped on and in almost everything, it can be used to indicate such things as what was buried in a feature, where a ship had been prior to sinking, and what types of foods were stored in a ceramic vessel. Phytoliths, literally "plant stones," can be left behind wherever a plant decomposes. These form from silica that is absorbed by a plant during its life, and so are exact casts of the inside of the plant in which they formed. Based on context (within a barrel, on the deck of a ship, or within a pit feature, for instance), phytoliths indicate the plant was likely harvested and stored for food, was used for packing, or is a weed that grew and died after a site was abandoned. Pollen, because many types are windborne, can be somewhat inaccurate in representing local environments; phytoliths, on the other hand, can only inform upon extremely local environments or upon very local human choices, so these two analyses work best in tandem.

Some microfossil remains only serve as environmental proxies because they are not directly used by people. Diatoms, a type of algae, are found in lake and shore environments. Many of the species have very narrow environmental constraints, so examination of the types of diatoms in underwater sediments (including those trapped in shipwrecks) can inform upon past water temperatures, salinities, nutrients, and so on. This can be useful for broad environmental reconstructions, and can also tell about nearshore environments and sea level rise to help reconstruct maritime lifeways. Other microfossils such as ostracods (tiny crustaceans) can also help with sea level reconstructions. These are only found in marine and nearshore environments. Insects, snails, and occasional rodent remains at sites are often other good indicators of past environments, as all of these are very sensitive to local environmental change. Some pests and parasites, such as rodents and lice, can be found at sites and used to learn about human social environments.

Larger fauna are more likely to be at a site due to human agency. Animals may be pets, draft beasts, or food, for instance. Most of the time faunal analyses are focused on the animals that can tell us about foodways, so what species an analyst examines varies with the site. Some cultures, in fact, love to eat snails and shellfish. Others have taboos about certain types of seafood. A faunal analyst trying to understand these past food strategies will determine the species of as many remains as possible, as well as the age and sex of the individuals, what season they were killed, whenever possible, and if the animals were domesticated or wild. They will try to determine which portion of larger animals the people were interested in and examine the remains for any evidence of butchery marks. If there is a large enough faunal assemblage from the site (or from the larger culture as a whole), comparisons can be made to determine what kind of diet people had, which has implications for their health and social status. It can be determined, with large enough samples and the right sorts of spatial data, if some foods were considered to be high or low status, and if some things were rare or prized.

These sorts of investigations can be especially interesting in maritime and underwater archaeology, as humans must pack most of their food for voyages over water. Analyses of the floral and faunal remains can tell us about provisioning strategies, the logistics of transportation for long and unpredictable voyages, food preservation strategies, and how and where people traveled and reprovisioned. Further, foodstuffs are regularly included in the cargos of vessels. Sometimes they are even the purpose of the vessel's voyage, such as the numerous ships involved in the Roman grain trade focused on bringing supplies from Egypt to feed the burgeoning capital city, or the steamship *Heroine*, which sank in the Red River of Oklahoma in 1838 on its way to resupply soldiers at the nearby Fort Towson. *Heroine's* cargo contained a large store of flour and salt pork, and due to its hull filling immediately with sand upon its rapid sinking, this cargo was extraordinarily well-preserved. In fact, it was so well-preserved that a detailed analysis conducted upon three of the intact pork barrels (figure 3.2) allowed researchers to learn about how early 19th century frontier forts were provisioned.[9]

### HOW TO GET ANSWERS FROM WHAT WE FIND: FROM *THINGS* TO *BEHAVIOR*

The preceding section has provided the basic categories of data that archaeologists might recover from a maritime or underwater site. Finding these artifacts, features, and ecofacts, however, is only the initial step in reconstructing the past. While it may seem that the material culture discovered by archaeologists "speaks for itself," it should soon become very apparent that the past is only accessible through interpretation. As noted in chapter 2, archaeologists find things, not "the past," and our interpretations of those things are made based upon our analyses of them. Interpretations are generally the strongest when they are supported by multiple lines of evidence and precise evaluations. Thus, all good archaeological

**Figure 3.2** Well-preserved pork barrel from *Heroine* being removed from site. (Courtesy of INA/TAMU and the Oklahoma Historical Society)

research begins with accurate documentation, followed by detailed analyses and comparisons with previously acquired knowledge, in order to draw the best-supported conclusions possible.

## Documentation

Because archaeology is a destructive science, archaeologists only get one chance to do it right. If careless excavation destroys the association between two artifacts, ecofacts, or features, we have permanently lost that knowledge, many times without even realizing it. If we fail to take a measurement between two points on a sunken vessel and fail to realize it until back ashore from the project, we may never be able to definitively recreate an accurate site plan. If we raise something too hastily, or conserve it incorrectly, crucial details that would have allowed us to properly place a site, artifact, or feature within its broader cultural context may be destroyed. In short, we must think before excavation and try to plan for all possible contingencies in order to make sure that our scientific destruction recovers all possibly important information.

Archaeologists take copious notes of everything done and observed while searching for sites, excavating them, and conserving them. This documentation includes notebooks full of impressions from before, during, and after dives. Polyester drafting film and pencils can be used underwater to take notes and make sketches that can be turned into professional drawings for later publication or just to note important aspects about the site (figure 3.3). We also take photographs and videos of everything possible. Though there are some underwater sites where visibility is too poor to obtain any meaningful footage, the emergence of inexpensive, waterproof action cameras that can be mounted to the head of an excavator helps ensure that any visible information is recorded, even in very dark water or water full of particulates. These photographs and videos can then often be seamed together to create a representation of an entire site, something that the excavators themselves were unable to directly observe. This

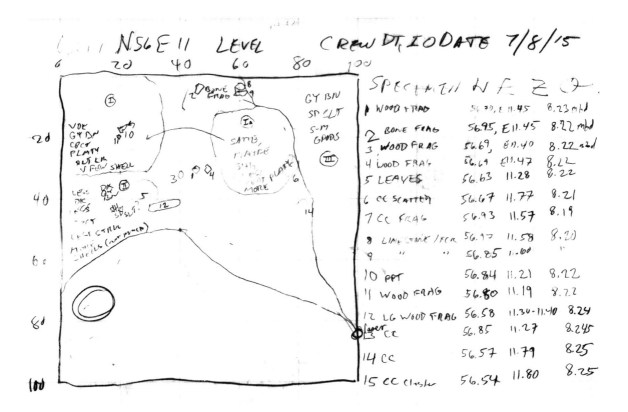

**Figure 3.3** Example of underwater field notes recorded on a data table: in this case, a map of the location of artifacts in an excavation unit at an inundated landscape site.

extensive documentation continues throughout the analysis and conservation processes, as discussed in chapters 5 and 6.

## How old is it? Dating methods

Before, during, and after excavation, archaeologists will be looking for materials that help to determine and confirm the age of a site, artifact, ecofact, or feature. Nearly any research question can be answered more completely and our discussions of past people are much richer if we know when a site was created or used. Therefore, it should not be surprising that archaeologists have invested a great deal of time in creating or borrowing various dating methods (table 3.2). In many introductory archaeology texts, dating methods compose one or two entire chapters, highlighting their importance to our understanding of the past. The discussion in this text is much briefer, focusing only on the methods most relevant to maritime and underwater archaeology and only providing an overview to the topic.

Dating methods can be broken into two main categories, **absolute dating** and **relative dating**. Absolute dating methods provide a calendar date for an item of interest, while relative dating methods only let you know if something is older than or younger than something else. Absolute dating methods typically work in one of four main ways: through historical chronologies, annual cycles, charged particles, or radioactive decay. Relative dating methods use **diagnostic artifacts**, artifacts that were made in a distinctive way for a limited period of time, in combination with stratigraphy, to assign relative chronologies. Archaeologists will frequently cross-check various dating methods with one another and will obtain as many dates as possible, so it is common for both relative and absolute dating methods to be used in tandem. Further, all dating methods have their drawbacks and limitations, which is another reason archaeologists strive to confirm ages from multiple lines of evidence.

### Absolute dating methods

One of the most common dating methods used in maritime and underwater archaeology is the historical record. Much of maritime life is focused on economic pursuits of various kinds, and in societies with writing systems, economic transactions were usually important enough to write down and store. In most times and places, the loss of a ship was important enough to be noted in public records of various kinds, including more recently in newspapers. Harbors recorded the comings and goings of vessels. Port city construction is often found in tax records. Alehouses and brothels may be found in tax records and in the records of court proceedings. Shipyards, garrisons, and other places of employment will have accounting books, and so on. In other words, when possible, archaeologists use the written record to help interpret the archaeological data. However, the written record is often incomplete, inaccurate, or nonexistent. Further, writing is a relatively recent invention—dating to only about 3400 BCE at

**TABLE 3.2 SUMMARY OF MOST COMMON DATING METHODS UTILIZED FOR MARITIME AND UNDERWATER ARCHAEOLOGY**

| Technique | Range of Accuracy | Method | Limitations |
|---|---|---|---|
| Association | Any time | Cultural material associated with material of known ages is assumed to be contemporaneous | The associations between cultural material and dated item may not be correct |
| Dendrochronology | Now–ca. 13,000 BCE | Comparing tree ring section from a site to a master sequence for that species to determine when archaeological tree was cut. | Not all tree species work, master sequence must exist, potential for "old wood" problem |
| Historical Chronology | Varies greatly by region, but up to about 3500 BCE | Read the written record | Historical records need calibration to our calendar and often are spotty |
| Optically Stimulated Luminescence | Now–300,000 BCE (theoretically) | Need to collect sand sample. Lab exposes sample to light, measures released radiation. Calculates how long sand was buried by amount of radiation released | Large standard deviations, expensive, sampling is difficult; most useful for landscapes; need to know background radiation |
| Thermoluminescence | Now–300,000 BCE (theoretically) | Need to collect burnt sample. Lab exposes sample to heat, measures released radiation. Calculates how long ago last melting occurred by amount of radiation released | Large standard deviations; need to know burning is associated with cultural activity; need to know background radiation |
| Radiocarbon | 1950 CE–ca. 48,000 BCE | Need an organic item from site. Radioactive carbon isotope 14 degrades predictably in an organism after it dies. By measuring ratio of $^{14}$C to $^{12}$C, can estimate how long item has been dead. | Need to have organic materials preserved at site; potential "old wood" problem. Need to calibrate ages. Only good until ca. 48,000 BCE |
| Seriation | Any time for which we have a large enough artifact assemblage | Ordering artifacts by changing styles (using attribute analysis). Master seriation diagrams and frequency seriation can be used to relatively date sites. | Not all artifact classes change regularly. Cannot know which types are older or younger without stratigraphy. |
| Stratigraphy | Any time | Law of superposition: the deeper you are at a site, the older. Analyzing the layers at the site. | Can't know how much older deeper layers are without absolute dating method. Stratigraphy can be disturbed |
| *Terminus post quem* | Any time | List all of the known ages for a stratum or feature. Stratum or feature is younger than most recent age. (everything must exist in order for it to be discarded) | Not all strata can be dated; Cannot know how much younger layer is without other dating methods. |
| *Terminus ante quem* | Any time | Works with stratigraphy-the stratum or feature (or artifact) you are interested in MUST be older than oldest date in the overlying layers if strata are undisturbed. | Not all strata can be dated. Cannot know how much older underlying layer is without other dating methods. |

the oldest[10]—and not universal, so there are many instances in which there is no accompanying written record.

For the many sites that do not appear in written records, or for corollary empirical dating purposes, archaeologists turn to other dating methods. These dating methods all need to be **calibrated** to our calendar because they usually tell the researcher that *X* happened approximately *Y* years ago. Scientists chose 1950 CE, the approximate date radiocarbon dating was implemented, to represent the year "0" for dating methods that provide dates of "before present." Accordingly, it is important to remember to account for the years that have elapsed since 1950 for precise dating (table 3.3).

TABLE 3.3 **HOW TO CONVERT DATES BETWEEN THE MAJOR RECORDING SYSTEMS**

| If you have the age in: | and you want it to be in: | You: | Example from | Example to |
|---|---|---|---|---|
| BC | BCE | Just change the ending | 100 BC | 100 BCE |
| BCE | BC | Just change the ending | 1250 BCE | 1250 BC |
| AD | CE | Just change the ending | AD 1492 | 1492 CE |
| CE | AD | Just change the ending | 1900 CE | AD 1900 |
| BP | BC/AD | You subtract the age from 1950 | 1950 – 1000 BP = 950 | AD 950 |
| | | | 1950 – 2000 BP = –50 | 50 BC |
| BP | BCE/CE | You subtract the age from 1950 | 1950 – 1000 BP = 950 | 950 CE |
| | | | 1950 – 2000 BP = –50 | 50 BCE |
| BC/AD | BP | You subtract the age from 1950 (and make the answer positive—you can't have negative years before present)** | 1000BC (– 1000) – 1950 = –2950 | 2950 BP |
| | | | AD 1000 (+1000) –1950 = –950 | 950 BP |
| BCE/CE | BP | You subtract the age from 1950 (and make the answer positive—you can't have negative years before present)** | 1000BCE (– 1000) –1950 = –2950 | 2950 BP |
| | | | AD 1000 (+1000) – 1950 = –950 | 950 BP |

** Remember, BC/BCE ages are negative (i.e., before the birth of Christ)! Also remember that the "0" age for radiocarbon is 1950.

Radiocarbon dating is the most commonly used radioactive decay method. It works like this: every living thing is made up of carbon (among other things). Some of this carbon—approximately one in every trillion carbon atoms—is in the form of Carbon-14, an unstable isotope that carries two extra neutrons in its nucleus. While the organism is alive, Carbon-14 to Carbon-12 ratios remain the same as they are in atmosphere, but as soon as the organism dies, the unstable isotopes start to degrade. After about 5,730 years (the **half-life**), only half the original number of unstable Carbon-14 atoms will remain. After 11,460 years, only one-fourth of the original amount will remain, and so on. When we find an organic item at a site, we can submit it to a radiocarbon dating lab, which measures the ratio of remaining Carbon-14 to the stable Carbon-12, demonstrating approximately how long ago the specimen died.

There are several limitations with radiocarbon dating. First, there have been slight fluctuations in the Carbon-14 to Carbon-12 ratios within organisms over time as a result of fluctuations in the atmosphere. These slight fluctuations can result in a significant discrepancy in dating, so radiocarbon dates need to be calibrated in order to be compared to calendar years. Second, radiocarbon dating can only be done at sites that have preserved organic materials. Third, people sometimes reuse materials, such as repurposing old ship timbers in a new ship, so if the wrong sample is chosen, resulting dates might be wrong by decades. Finally, there is an upper limit to this method: after about 45,000-50,000 years, there are no detectable Carbon-14 atoms left.

Dendrochronology, also known as tree-ring dating, has been used to provide ages for a number of shipwrecks in the Mediterranean and in Scandinavia. As the name implies, it relies on the principle that many tree species in temperate and cold environments have distinctive annual growth rings. During wet years, these rings will be wide, and during dry years, they will be thin. Dendrochronology labs create tree ring chronologies for an area, which can be used to understand past climate fluctuations and also to date wood remains at archaeological sites. These chronologies start with a living tree and they continue backward in time by adding older, dead samples (figure 3.4). By counting backward from the bark, as the ring touching the bark is the one grown during the last year of the tree's life, dendrochronologists can determine how many years are represented by the life of a tree. They can then compare the ring patterns to samples of older wood, overlapping the fresh sample with the older one, and extending the known pattern back in time. When archaeologists send in a wood sample, it is compared to the patterns of rings in the master chronology, producing a dating result that can be extremely precise. However, there are limitations with this method as well. Not all sites have well-preserved wood, not all species provide clear growth rings, and not all places have master chronologies. Wood samples have to be large enough to crosscut a substantial number of rings in order to allow for

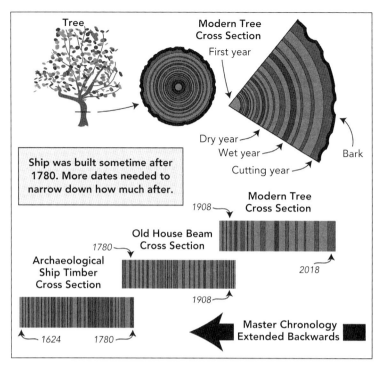

Tree

Modern Tree Cross Section

First year

Dry year
Wet year
Cutting year
Bark

Ship was built sometime after 1780. More dates needed to narrow down how much after.

1908

Modern Tree Cross Section

Old House Beam Cross Section

1780

Archaeological Ship Timber Cross Section

2018

1908

1624    1780

Master Chronology Extended Backwards

**Figure 3.4** Dendrochronology.

accurate pattern matching, and unless the sampled piece of wood still has the bark on it, it is impossible to know if the outside tree ring on the sample is the ring representing the year the tree was cut. This is a particular problem for ship timbers, which are often shaped and missing the outer rings. Finally, this method only works for as far back as the local master sequence extends. The longest is about 13,000 years in Northern Europe; most are closer to 5,000 years.

Two charged-particle dating methods are used by maritime and underwater archaeologists, though both are somewhat rare. Optically stimulated luminescence (OSL) dates when a grain of quartz sand was last exposed to light, and therefore was last at the surface of a site. There is a very low level of radiation in all sediments; when a sand grain gets buried, it slowly starts to absorb this radiation. When it is exposed to light, it releases the radiation in a burst of energy. Thermoluminescence (TL) dates when a material was last heated to the melting point. Heating releases all radiation, which slowly re-accumulates after burial. This is especially useful for cultural materials that are deliberately heated such as hearths and ceramics. TL and OSL samples are exposed to heat (TL) or light (OSL) in an analyzer that measures the burst of released radiation from this exposure. That is compared to the ambient radiation at the site, and the ratio between the two can be used to determine approximately when the sample was last heated or exposed to light. Luminescence dating has a long range, potentially up to 300,000 years ago, but it is not terribly precise. Estimated ages are approximately 10 percent of the sample age at this time, so a sample from approximately 10,000 years old would have an estimated age range of 11,000–9,000 years old. Further, because OSL samples must be collected in the dark and kept in the dark, and background radiation must be collected for either method, sampling is somewhat difficult, especially in underwater settings.

### Relative dating methods

Relative dating methods are constantly used at all archaeological sites, even when absolute dates are available. Stratigraphy, discussed above, is often a useful relative dating method, as the **law of superposition** demonstrates the relative ages of material culture at a site. This law states that cultural material buried in deeper layers is older than material in shallower layers. In other words, the first layers have to exist in order to be buried by later layers. Archeologists can understand what happened first, second, third, and so on, by examining the order in which layers were buried and which layers crosscut others. Therefore, it is very important for archaeologists to pay attention to the matrix through which we are excavating, even if it is inside a shipwreck. Differences in color, texture, compaction, or artifact content can all be clues that a new layer, including a potential feature, is being encountered. By itself, stratigraphy only allows us to know that one layer is older than others or younger than others, but stratigraphy can also be used to more precisely date items through association when there are known absolute dates. If, for instance, there is a feature at a site containing a charcoal sample that dates to 250 CE, and that feature also contained a number of stone tool fragments, we could say those tools were associated with that feature and also date to approximately 250 CE. Natural phenomena such as recorded volcanic eruptions can also produce stratigraphic layers whose date can be positively determined.

**Typologies** and seriation have been used by archaeologists to date sites for more than a century. Typologies are made by classifying artifacts using their physical characteristics or traits. Artifacts that are grouped together according to their trait similarities are known as types. The variance between types is based on differences in traits. For artifacts that seem to have served the same functions, some of these trait differences are due to changing styles over time. Thus, if the archaeologist puts artifacts into groups, and then puts those groups into order based on similarities, an evolution of the shape, style, or size of an artifact category can oftentimes be discerned, representing change over time. When this is combined with stratigraphic information archaeologists can put the artifact types in order and compare them to other sites. This is known as **seriation**. Seriation is done with frequently discovered types of artifacts that can be shaped deliberately and that have flexibility in shape or decoration, such as stone projectile points, ceramics, glass bottles, or other such items. Generally, people do not throw away everything they have when a new item becomes available. Instead, the old item is replaced as needed. Therefore, as new styles become available, they will initially be rare, then common, and then, as they are replaced, in turn, rare again. Due to this, it is possible to order artifact styles based on this overarching trend, an approach known as **frequency seriation** (figure 3.5).

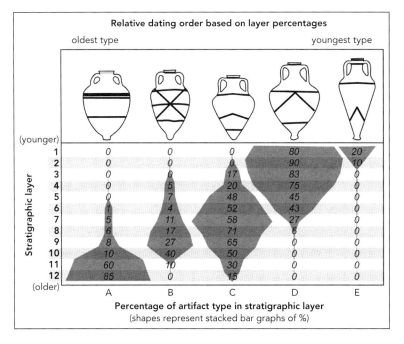

Percentage of artifact type in stratigraphic layer
(shapes represent stacked bar graphs of %)

**Figure 3.5** Seriation and frequency seriation.

*Terminus post quem* and *Terminus ante quem*, straightforward despite the Latin, are terms referring to the relative dates of artifacts and stratigraphy. *Terminus post quem* translates to approximately "date after which" and it simply means that the site, feature, or stratum was created after the youngest dated item that it contains. In other words, everything had to exist before it could enter the archaeological record. However, it is often impossible to know how much time elapsed between item creation and deposition. This is where *terminus ante quem* (date before which) is useful in combination with site stratigraphy. If the layer of interest is buried, it must be older than the oldest age in the overlaying layers. Again, it is hard to know how much older, but context clues, absolute dates, or diagnostic artifacts help narrow the age range (figure 3.6).

## Characterization, sourcing, and composition

In order to reconstruct the lifeways of past people, archaeologists aim to learn when, how and why people made their things, how they used them, and how they moved them about the landscape. Though we often use various sorts of analogies and other lines of evidence such as written records to help us understand how people in the past *might* have done things, we have also developed numerous methods to help us analyze the makeup of an artifact through **characterization**. Whether through chemical testing or naked eye observation, once we can determine the constituent materials of an artifact, we can then compare those constituent parts to known sources for each material, a technique known as **sourcing**. [11]

The types of analysis needed to characterize an artifact vary by material and type; some are destructive, others are not. For instance, pottery can often be characterized by thin-section analysis. An edge of a pottery fragment is sliced crosswise and polished until it is thin enough that a microscope can see through it. Then, the analyst, using the geological techniques of **petrography**, can classify the minerals and inclusions in the clay used to make the ceramic vessel. Further, pottery contains temper to add strength and to aid in successful firing. Tempers vary, but can include shell, sand, grog (ground up fragments of old pots), and grasses or mosses (fibers), among other things. These can also be seen and classified in the thin sections. Clays have different mineral compositions (as do the tempers) which they retain from their sources, the places from which the raw clay or raw temper material was obtained.

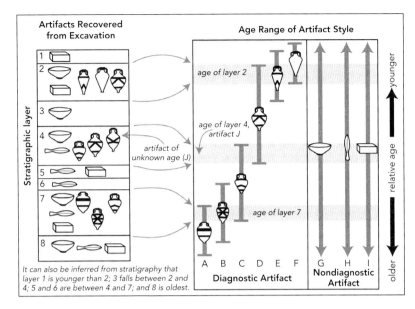

**Figure 3.6** How *terminus post quem* and *terminus ante quem* can be used to provide a relatively precise date.

Through identifying clay outcrops with similar mineral compositions to the archaeological ceramics, we can discover from approximately where the raw material was obtained in the past.

Sometimes the source may be immediately adjacent to the site, but in maritime and underwater archaeology, especially, the source may be continents away from where a ceramic entered the archaeological record. In addition to serving as trade goods themselves, ceramic vessels were frequently used as containers for other perishable trade goods such as foodstuffs, wine, or olive oil. Therefore, sourcing can help us learn a great deal about the movement of ships and their cargoes. Thin-section analysis can also be used on stone, glass, or metal artifacts, but is employed more rarely in these contexts.

Often, thin sections do not allow materials to be discriminated precisely enough. Geochemical characterization is often used instead. **Trace element analysis** refers to the categories of analysis in which an artifact sample is scanned in order to obtain its whole elemental makeup. This scanning may be done by machines emitting X-rays, lasers, or gamma rays, or by other sorts of stimuli that cause the electrons in the artifact to vibrate so that they can be read by an instrument, allowing the instrument to determine what elements are in the artifact based on these electron emissions. Some of these methods "ablate" or burn up a portion of the artifact entirely. These tend to get the most accurate reading of the elements, but, of course, they destroy the sample. Trace element analysis is focused on obtaining the percentage of each element that is in the artifact. Most of an artifact will usually be composed of a few primary elements, which are so prevalent that they are not particularly useful for determining how something was made or its origin. For instance, most samples of glass are almost entirely silica, so silica does not help discern the source of the glass. However, elements that compose only a small or barely discernable fraction of a sample may vary due to specific local geological processes or local manufacturing processes. Comparing the relative percentages of these "trace" elements can sometimes tie an artifact to its exact manufacturing facility or the source of a raw material.

**Isotopic analyses** on the other hand, focus on a single element within an artifact. Researchers compare the ratio of the various isotopes of this element to known ratios of source areas to see where an item likely came from, or sometimes, to determine the manufacturing temperature range of an artifact. Isotopic analyses are also used very commonly to analyze organic artifacts and human remains, as organic materials and people have variation in isotopic ratios due to diet, migration, and variation in drinking water. Analysis of human remains from a shipwreck, for instance, could suggest the cultural origin of the vessel's crew or passengers. Isotopic analyses can be used for sourcing, manufacturing processes, and foodways analysis, which could be used, in turn, to infer mobility patterns, possible ethnic or gender differences in a group, trading patterns, and other things.

Another sourcing and composition study that archaeologists occasionally use on human remains and organic materials is DNA sequencing. These studies are infrequent, as organic preservation is rare, and viable DNA preservation in organics is even rarer. However, the science of ancient DNA recovery and analysis is advancing by leaps and bounds. Numerous recent studies have used bioarchaeological analysis in combination with ancient DNA in order to determine how past groups were related to each other, how much past groups were likely to have interbred, whether it was the men, women, or whole groups moving across the landscape from place to place, to determine how long ago different groups were likely to have migrated to new areas based on their genetic differences from their closest relatives, and to discuss disease movements around the ancient world. DNA analyses are also conducted on organic artifacts in order to determine exactly what they are, such as the contents of a ceramic vessel, if the organism is representative of a domesticated or wild version, and to reconstruct the movement of plants and animals. These studies give us important clues about past mobility, provisioning and manufacture strategies. We can then infer larger social implications through the use of analogies and other indirect lines of evidence.

## Analogies and other indirect lines of evidence

Material culture is exceptionally useful in answering questions about *what* a culture was doing and *how*, but often gives us less direct insight into *why* a culture chose to do something a certain way. To bridge the gap between patterns of material culture and cultural meanings, archaeologists utilize as many possible lines of evidence as they can. For instance, perhaps an archaeologist discovers a mysterious stone formation offshore of the modern coast of Turkey. She knows it was made by people because of its shape and a few Bronze-age artifacts scattered around it. What was this formation? What was it used for? There could be several sources of information to help her interpret this site. If she is working in an area that is discussed by contemporary histories or literature, she will refer to the pertinent literary sources.

## Primary sources: texts and icongraphy

Textual records only apply to places that have been written about, but they can be extremely helpful for understanding what people in the past were doing and why. The written record, however, is often incomplete, inconclusive, or even inaccurate. It only occasionally contains details along the lines of "the people in this area like to make fishing platforms by dry-laying large cobbles in rows of 12 that they then cover with squared-off timbers about 2 cm thick and 10 cm wide in order to make a stable platform for launching their cast nets. The cast nets, made of intertwined cotton cables, obtained by trade with Egypt, are approximately 2 m in diameter, and are used in water depths of 5 to 15 m. All net fishing is done by teenaged boys and girls until they marry, but the fishing platforms are built by grandfathers." Usually the level of detail does not exceed "moored in small cove to fishing platform for night. Left next day . . . " because many activities of the past were so commonplace to the people writing about them that there was no need to be more specific. Further, in most times and places, relatively few people were literate and even fewer of those people were common folks writing about everyday life. Much writing, particularly the writing important enough to be curated in locations that allowed it to survive for hundreds or thousands of years, recorded financial transactions and important, life-altering events. It also must be mentioned that not all recorders of history were equally truthful or reliable for numerous reasons, so it is important to critically consider any textual source. Archaeology's ability to interpret the everyday, often capturing the life of underreported, underprivileged, or underrepresented groups, is one of its great strengths and why it complements and supplements the written record so well.

Beyond the functional and historical, most cultures developed fiction or other types of literature that may contain crucial clues to the use and meaning of material culture, the everyday treatment of ordinary things, and the interrelationships between people in a society. For instance, in our hypothetical fishing platform example, a story set in this society may be about the romance of a boy and girl who met while fishing off such a platform and could contain the influence of the gods who encouraged the platform to be built. From this, we would learn who built the platforms and why, and who was doing the fishing. In the real world, epic poems such as Homer's *Odyssey* or the *Poetic Edda* are used to provide hints into ancient seafaring, shipbuilding, sailors' lives, and navigation.

There are many times and places for which we have no relevant texts, however. After all, anatomically modern *Homo sapiens* is nearly 200,000 years old, but our oldest written records only date to approximately 3400 BCE in the Middle East and much later in most other places. Most of human history, thus, is not covered by written records, and we must look to other sources to bolster our understanding of patterns of material culture. In some places, art and iconography pre-date cohesive written records, or provide more specific details about how things actually looked or functioned. For instance, early Mesopotamian vessels are essentially known only through their representations in cylinder seals and a few sparse textual references from pre-Dynastic Egypt (ca. 3400 to 2000 BCE) (figure 3.7). Egyptian illustrations dating to ca. 3500 to 3100 BCE have also been used to discuss early boatbuilding in Egypt. Iconography, however, just like written records, is only relevant to a few cultures and is often not specific enough to offer more than impressions. As can be seen in figure 3.7, vessels are often represented schematically and not to scale, without details of rigging, construction, loading, or other particulars of interest to the archaeologist. At the same time, these images are clear enough to show differences between the vessels from Egypt and those from the Near East and to provide hints that help us interpret the archaeological record. The former seem to be long rafts with central pavilions, reeds at one end, perhaps as proto-sails, and possible banks of oars deployed on the sides. The latter seem to be made of reed bundles coming to a high peak both forward and aft, and are maneuvered by poles at both ends.

### Analogies

Where do archaeologists look when attempting to connect patterns of material culture to bigger cultural meanings if there are no texts or iconographical references to rely on? Anthropological archaeologists call the type of research used to bridge this gap **middle-range theory**. It consists of the use of information from modern contexts to interpret archaeological patterns, and it relies heavily on **analogies** of various kinds. Analogies are crucial for much of our interpretations of past people and past lifeways. They work like this: an archaeologist discovers an archaeological example of something (it could be an artifact, a feature, or a site). He wants to understand more about it, so he looks for something similar that is already known and critically examines attributes of this better-known example to see if these other aspects about the better-known may be relevant to the archaeological item; if so, they are tentatively used for interpretation of the unknown archaeological example.

This sounds complex, but often these analogies are employed almost instantaneously, based on long practice. For instance, an archaeologist finds a large triangular-shaped bronze tool with three sharp edges and a hollow end for holding something. She instantly identifies this as a spear tip because it has similar attributes such as size, shape, weight, and socket dimensions to artifacts that she has seen at other sites or to illustrations of Bronze Age spear

tips. This may seem to be premature, and occasionally studies show that our assumed classification is
incorrect, but these initial identifications also give a
starting place for understanding sites. Analogies can
come from several places. Three of the main types
that archaeologists commonly use are **ethnographic
analogy**, **ethnoarchaeology**, and **experimental archaeology**, which is also known as **replication**.

Ethnography is obtained from cultural anthropology. Ethnographers live among a culture in
which they are interested for months to years at a
time, embedding themselves fully within a society
and writing about how members of that culture live
their daily lives, including why members of the society make the choices they make. Their writings
are known as ethnographies, and details of these
ethnographies are often used to interpret archaeological data. This process of using living societies to
interpret the archaeological record is known as ethnographic analogy. Analogies are considered to be
the strongest when they are closely related to the archaeological site we are trying to interpret in terms of
culture, feature, geographic location, or other aspect.

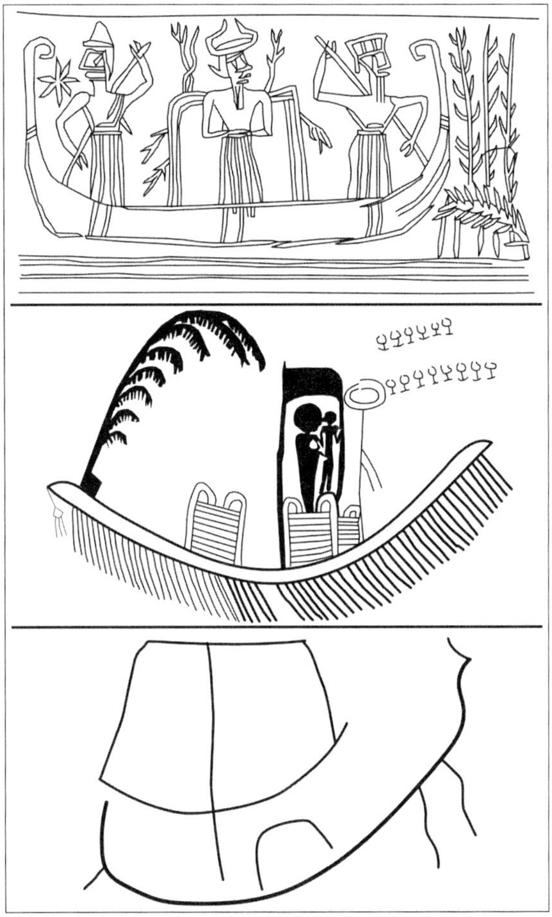

For instance, if we are trying to interpret the shipbuilding process at an archaeological site in Samoa,
it would be more insightful to look at ethnographic
data from Samoan cultures than those from Finland.
If we had no ethnographies from Samoa (which we
do), it would be better to look at shipbuilding among
other semitropical island dwellers in areas with similar natural resources. If we did not have either of
those, it would be better to look at shipbuilding
among other nonindustrial societies that were organized as complex chiefdoms. Best of all would be
if we had cross-cultural comparisons (ethnologies)
of a number of nonindustrial shipbuilding societies

**Figure 3.7** Iconography of early boats. Top, The boat
journey of the god Ea (cylinder seal impression, ca. 2300–
2150 BCE) redrawn after W. H. Ward, *The Seal Cylinders of
Western Asia*, 1910, fig. 102). Middle, Boat iconography redrawn from one panel of several containing boats from a
Naquada II pot from ancient Egypt (ca. 3500 BCE). Bottom,
redrawn Egyptian Naquada II petroglyph from Wadi Abu
Wasil (ca. 3100 BCE). Drawings not to scale.

to look at elements that are common among many or all of these societies. If a
characteristic is extremely common, it is more likely to be true of our archaeological example. The weakness of these analogies is that no modern society exists
in an isolated bubble; each has changed and modernized in its own way, so the
way people do things today may or may not be the way they were done by their
ancestors. However, ethnographic analogies have done much to enrich our understanding of past possibilities, even if they cannot and should not be used to
definitively state how people did things in the past.

# Madeline Fowler[a] and Rigney Lester-Irabinna[b],
[a]Senior Research Fellow in Archaeology, University of Southampton; [b]Professor of Education, University of South Australia, Australia

Envisage an Indigenous community connected to a shipwreck through stories of an ancestral spirit, through crew composed of members of that community, and through that community's language used in the naming of the vessel; yet, without Indigenous collaboration the interpretation of this shipwreck would likely reflect only economic value. Maritime archaeology and Indigenous collaboration can converge on many levels. Maritime archaeological research in Indigenous contexts tends to focus on material culture, landscapes, and seascapes, utilizing both Western anthropological theory and Indigenous peoples' knowledge drawn from thousands of years of custodial guardianship. Indigenous collaboration augments maritime archaeology to investigate submerged prehistoric landscapes, fish traps, stone arrangements, and traditional watercraft—eliminating an unnecessary separation of contemporary Indigenous peoples from their past. It seeks to nuance complexities of seascapes as distinctive markers of geography that have cultural significance in modern times, for example, where ancestral spirits are part of the contemporary landscape.

Or, maritime archaeological research investigating non-Indigenous landscapes and their impacts may be undertaken in a place of significance to many Indigenous peoples where the sharing of Indigenous and non-Indigenous history should occur. Indigenous peoples may connect to postcontact European sites, such as shipwrecks, through their location (many Indigenous communities have systems of past, present, and future ownership of intertidal and submerged landscapes), as well as Indigenous involvement during the life history of the ship, the wrecking and rescue event or continued visitation to the site, for example, for fishing. The material culture of maritime cultural landscapes does not reflect all elements of past lives and Indigenous collaboration can add elements otherwise missing. The material culture of a shipwreck, for example, may not reflect the cultural background of the crew or passengers onboard the vessel during its working life.

Approaches labeled as community or community-based, collaborative, consultative, decolonizing, postcolonial, and Indigenous archaeologies also embody the tenets of "Indigenous collaboration." In all these approaches, it is *process*—that is, method—that is most important. Maritime archaeologists may choose to engage with these processes at any point along a spectrum ranging from informality to elaborateness. The process should be interactive participation, not reactive. Incorporating these processes is the product of choices and actions made by the maritime archaeologist as an individual—it is the responsibility of the archaeologist to acknowledge the traditional owners of the lands and seas on which they work. In all stages of research, maritime archaeologists must adhere to ethical responsibilities and culturally appropriate behavior. This may include accepting that some information is not for public knowledge, or that some sites may be off-limits to researchers or certain members of a research team (such as gendered places).

## Research Framework
We advocate that the maritime archaeology collaboration described here enables the establishment of any project to frame research questions, aims, and objectives that build cultural and critical consciousness about landscape while involving usual scientific rigor

in developing field practices, data collection, analysis, storage, and public dissemination. The priority may even be community needs and values, over the collection of scientific data. Such an approach ensures that some level of control remains with the community and that the documentation of sites identifies different definitions of significance—to the community and for archaeology.

A research framework should also include methodologies for encompassing non-Western systems of knowledge. Intangible cultural heritage provides the principal means of accessing Indigenous knowledges by contextualizing the traditional "scientific" data collected by maritime archaeologists. Indigenous epistemologies such as knowledges, beliefs, traditions, lived experiences, worldviews, cultural practices, and lifeways can inform intangible cultural heritage. While intangible cultural heritage is accessible through several means, toponymy (the study of place names) and oral history are particularly relevant to maritime archaeology. Indigenous toponyms are not only useful as a data source; their use reveals that the privileging of certain languages is a choice. Scrutinizing discourse (appropriate word choice and terminology), and recognizing the problematic nature of some maritime archaeological terms, more generally assists in avoiding the language of colonialism. Oral histories, particularly conducted in a place-based setting, also reveal the location, as well as nuanced interpretations, of tangible archaeology while recording the past through Indigenous voices. The Indigenous spiritual world, for example, not only intersects with the natural environment, but also with aspects of the physical world introduced by Europeans, such as shipwrecks.

## Practical Outcomes

Indigenous collaboration in maritime archaeology should also have many practical outcomes for communities. This could include providing employment to Indigenous people, for example as heritage monitors during the course of the project, or enabling communities to manage their own cultural heritage in the later long-term management of sites; producing educational materials for schools; and capacity building by facilitating discipline-specific skills training—both academic, field-school and work-based learning opportunities. The restoration, reuse, and reinvigoration of sites by Indigenous communities are also under consideration as approaches for site protection and management. Maritime archaeologists must also be aware that their research is often viewed through the lens of traditional and commercial land and sea rights. Archaeological research not only informs our knowledge of the past, but also informs end-users interpretations of the past in the present.

Maritime archaeology is archaeology. Indigenous archaeology, that is, archaeology with, for, and by Indigenous people, is good archaeology. The process of Indigenous collaboration is hence applicable to non-Indigenous community-based research, reinforcing ethics in maritime archaeology more generally and providing nuanced, localized and lived histories.

Ethnoarchaeology is similar to ethnographic analogy, arising as a field of study in the mid-twentieth century due to difficulties archaeologists had with utilizing traditional ethnographies. Most ethnographic research is interesting but does not discuss the tangible material culture aspects of a society in the kind of detail that is useful to an archaeologist. Ethnoarchaeologists focus on the material culture of their study group along with the social interactions that led to those patterns of material culture. Some ethnoarchaeologists specifically study site-formation processes, or how cultural activities have left tangible traces that would be discoverable and interpretable in the future. Ethnoarchaeology also looks at how natural processes such as animal trampling, decay, scavenging, water movement, and so on can impact sites in the short term to extrapolate these processes into longer time frames. Therefore, ethnoarchaeologists may record what and where people are eating and discarding their refuse, describe how, where, and of what houses are constructed, discuss who makes what and why, and record how villages that were occupied last year or ten years ago have decomposed.

The final kind of analogy commonly utilized by archaeologists, especially common in maritime and underwater archaeology, is experimental archaeology or replication. Replication involves modern researchers attempting to recreate the material culture of the past in order to understand how it might have been constructed or used. Replication might involve everything from virtually modeling a ship as a way to test its sailing capabilities to constructing a full-scale replica of an archaeologically known vessel using traditional shipbuilding techniques, tools, and harbor installations. Replication, especially the latter case, can be a slow and expensive process, and, because the historical and/ or archaeological record is often spotty, requires a great deal of interpolation and artistry. At the same time, the process of re-creating a vessel from scratch often gives a deeper understanding of the problems people in the past had to solve when creating the original version and the reasoning behind associated decisions. These recreations often suggest explanations for previously inexplicable aspects of the archaeological record and allow archaeologists to test their hypotheses. However, it must be remembered that replications are only possible ways in which things were done, just like other sorts of analogies, and not definitive explanations.

It is important to mention one final thing about replicas. They are extremely effective methods of public outreach and do more than almost anything else to make the past accessible to the general public. People love to see history made tangible. Many of these vessels, such as the recreated Athenian trireme *Olympias* (figure 3.8), which is a commissioned vessel in the Hellenic Navy, are great sources of national pride and are used to raise historical awareness as well as draw modern visitors. Viking ship reconstructions such as the *draken Harald Hårfagre* (figure 3.9) have been sailed and rowed across the Atlantic Ocean to recreate ancient Viking voyages. These vessels are not without their troubles. The time and expense in creating and maintaining them is enormous, and they can be dangerous, just as life at sea always has been. *Olympias* has been permanently moved to an exhibition space to save on costs of upkeep and staffing. The first reconstructed Baltimore clipper, the *Pride of Baltimore*, sank in a squall off the coast of Puerto Rico in 1986, losing four members of her crew; the *Pride II* was built with modifications to make it safer as it serves as a worldwide ambassador for the port city.

### SUMMARY

All archaeologists are focused on the analysis and interpretation of material culture. Thus, our primary, but far from only, source of information is the things that people have left behind, whether by accident or on purpose. There are many types of material culture that archaeologists can recover from sites, each of which can be used to provide different types of information about the people in the past. We often compare the materials from one portion of a site to those from another portion in order to discuss whether or not there is evidence for different use of space across the site, and if there is, what those differences mean. We compare artifacts to each other to create typologies that allow us to understand when a site was used, how a site was used, and how technologies changed over time. We compare the material remains from one site to another site of a similar age to discuss variation over space, and cultural material from different ages to talk about variation over time. Some of the materials discovered at archaeological sites are not cultural in origin but can still be very informative about the site itself, sometimes

**Figure 3.8** *Olympias*, a recreated Greek trireme, under sail. (Courtesy of Hellenic Navy)

helping to interpret the site formation processes and possibly helping to date the site. We investigate the remains of plants and animals, both visible and microscopic, to understand past environments and past foodways. In order to gain the most information possible during excavation, which is a destructive process, excavators must pay very close attention to the context of all finds and document things in great detail. Archaeologists conduct a number of analyses of the material culture we recover in order to discover as much as we can about it. Finally, archaeological interpretation relies on a series of lines of evidence, both direct and indirect, in order for us to interpret past lifeways as accurately as possible.

### DISCUSSION QUESTIONS

1. This chapter discussed several categories of maritime and underwater sites. What types of material culture are likely to be recovered from each? How does this play into what we could learn about past people from each site category?

**Figure 3.9** *Harald Hårfagre*, a recreated Viking dragon (draken) ship. (Courtesy Ronnie Robertson)

2. How do site formation processes, including varying preservation rates, impact maritime and underwater archaeological sites?

3. Why does context matter so much for archaeologists? How do we keep track of context? How has technology enabled this?

4. Why are research questions so important for maritime and underwater archaeological research?

5. What do you think are the biggest challenges with utilizing indirect evidence? Why?

**FURTHER READING**

Bortolini, E. (2016). Typology and Classification. *The Oxford Handbook of Archaeological Ceramic Analysis*. A. Hunt, Ed. 651–670. Oxford University Press, Oxford.

Doran, G.H. (2002). *Windover: Multidisciplinary Investigations of an Early Archaic Florida Cemetery*. University Press of Florida, Gainesville.

Kelly, R.L. and D.H. Thomas. (2013). *Archaeology: Down to Earth*, fifth edition. Wadsworth Publishing, New York.

Swiss Coordination Group UNESCO Palafittes. (2015). Prehistoric Pile Dwellings around the Alps. Available at http://whc.unesco.org/en/list/1363.

Tycot, R.H. (2004). Scientific Methods and Applications to Archaeological Provenance Studies. *Proceedings of the International School of Physics "Enrico Fermi."* M.M.M. Martini, and M. Piacentini, Eds. 407–432. IOS Press, Amsterdam. Available at http://luna.cas.usf.edu/~rtykot/PR40%20-%20Enrico%20Fermi%20obsidian.pdf

## CHAPTER 4

# ARCHAEOLOGICAL RESEARCH IN AN UNDERWATER ENVIRONMENT

## FOCUS QUESTIONS

- How have people interacted with seas, lakes, and rivers? How was this inter-action shaped by their culture and environment? What are the similarities, differences, and outcomes of these interactions?
- What types of maritime archaeological sites are there, and how do they differ in what they can teach us about the past?
- How can the preservation of artifacts in submerged environments, which tends to be better than on land, improve our understanding of past cultures?
- How can we gather data in a precise and rigorous way while still maintaining archaeological sites and the data they contain for future societies?

## UNDERWATER RESEARCH AND THE UNDERWATER WORLD

In chapter 1, we proposed that humans are technological amphibians. Never is this more true than when conducting underwater research. Humans have invented forms of life support that allow us to work and even live under the surface of the sea for hours or days at a time. We have developed ways to communicate underwater and make precise and accurate measurements of submerged sites, but, for every hour that a maritime and underwater archaeologist spends underwater collecting data, he or she spends dozens on the surface reconstructing and interpreting a site, analyzing artifacts or samples in the lab, and writing up the results. There are many stages to conducting underwater archaeology, beginning with months of background research, and ending with (potentially) years of conservation. Part I of this book discussed what underwater archaeologists look for and why. The chapters in Part II delve into the details of how underwater archaeologists conduct their research. This chapter presents what happens before an excavation, beginning with some specifics about the underwater world, which will likely be unfamiliar to many. A brief discussion on how underwater sites form and preserve follows, as this can have much relevance to what we can hope to discover. This is followed by a description of how we look for underwater sites of various kinds. It is important to note that, while many important aspects of maritime cultural heritage are not located underwater, this chapter and chapter 5 are specifically focused on the nature of underwater research. Terrestrial research follows many of the same strategies and methodologies, but uses different equipment; for more information, consult one of the many introductory archaeology texts available.

### THE UNDERWATER WORLD

Perhaps you have seen documentaries of SCUBA divers working underwater or videos of teeming ocean life moving through a crystal-blue sea. When ocean waters are clear, it can be hard to remember that the people in the video are working in an alien environment. Obviously, humans cannot breathe water, but there are many other foreign aspects of the submerged world that are less apparent. Water affects all our senses, largely due to the fact that it is nearly 800 times denser than air; this means all divers need to have knowledge of underwater physics in order to submerge and emerge safely. These physical constraints set limits upon how deep we can work and how long we can stay submerged (see Diving Physiology box), and shape how we perceive the underwater world.

### DIVING PHYSIOLOGY

The human body, as remarkable as it is, is ill-equipped to operate underwater for an extended period. Our reliance on air, and particularly oxygen, limits the time we can naturally spend underwater without having to return to the surface to breathe. In order for archaeologists to be able to physically investigate or excavate submerged sites, they must rely on the assistance of diving equipment, whether SCUBA (Self-Contained Underwater Breathing Apparatus), surface-supplied air, or hard-hat diving. These technologies have their technical limitations, such as the capacity of individual SCUBA tanks, but the key limiting factors to dive time and depth have to do with diving physiology, or the effects of diving on the human body.

At sea level, the total force per unit area exerted against a surface by the weight of the air above that surface represents atmospheric pressure. As a diver descends deeper into a body of water, the weight of the liquid above that diver represents hydrostatic pressure. Every 10 meters of seawater imposes the same amount of pressure on a diver as the entire atmosphere does when standing on the beach at sea level. The total combined force per unit area exerted on the diver, consisting of both atmospheric and hydrostatic pressures, is referred to as ambient or absolute pressure. When diving, the ambient pressure does not only apply a compressing force on our bodies, but also on the air that we breathe from the SCUBA tanks we carry. Thus, the density of the air entering our lungs is in equilibrium with the lungs themselves as their capacity is affected by the ambient pressure. The deeper the water, the higher the ambient pressure, the more compacted a diver's lungs, and the denser the air that comes from a SCUBA tank. Though this allows a diver to be provided with sufficient oxygen in their system at any given depth, it comes with a series of potential dangers.

One of the key considerations comes from nitrogen, the primary gas that comprises atmospheric air. The air that we breathe consists of about 78 percent nitrogen and 21 percent oxygen, as well a series of trace gases. As the ambient pressure and time at depth increase, so does the amount of nitrogen inhaled by a diver and dissolved in their bloodstream. The higher concentration of nitrogen ultimately affects a diver's clarity of thought, producing the effect referred to as nitrogen narcosis. One way to think about this impairment is to correlate the effects of every 10 m of seawater with those of an alcoholic beverage. In other words, operating at 30 m of depth, an archaeologist's thinking is generally impaired to the same level as if he or she had consumed three shots of alcohol. When performing scientific tasks, taking down measurements, or recording detailed observations, this is certainly something to take into consideration.

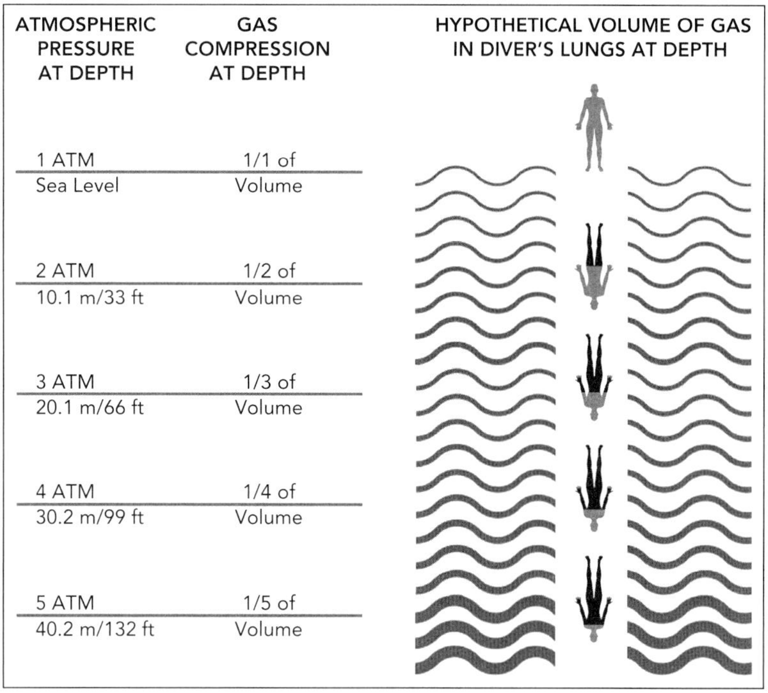

The longer a diver is at depth, and the deeper a diver ventures, the more gas saturates the bloodstream. As the diver ascends at the end of the dive, the ambient pressure decreases, and superfluous gas is exhausted with each exhalation. If, however, a diver stayed underwater for too long a period

| ATMOSPHERIC PRESSURE AT DEPTH | GAS COMPRESSION AT DEPTH | HYPOTHETICAL VOLUME OF GAS IN DIVER'S LUNGS AT DEPTH |
|---|---|---|
| 1 ATM Sea Level | 1/1 of Volume | |
| 2 ATM 10.1 m/33 ft | 1/2 of Volume | |
| 3 ATM 20.1 m/66 ft | 1/3 of Volume | |
| 4 ATM 30.2 m/99 ft | 1/4 of Volume | |
| 5 ATM 40.2 m/132 ft | 1/5 of Volume | |

Figure 4.1 Diving physiology with depth.

of time, and charged their body with too much dissolved gas, all of that gas would not be exhaled during ascent. As a result, the excess gas, which under less pressure also increases in volume, comes out of solution in the bloodstream, potentially causing several adverse health effects, such as decompression illness. As a result, a diver must pay close attention to how much nitrogen they have charged their body with and at what depth, and also take care to ascend at a controlled rate that allows exhalation to exhaust the excess nitrogen circulating in the bloodstream. There are a number of actions a diver may take to ensure this has taken place, such as conducting decompression or safety stops, where a diver pauses during the ascent for a particular length of time at a given depth. Different mixes of gases with lower percentages of nitrogen can also be used to limit the intake of the gas. Most archaeological projects, however, will endeavor to plan their diving operations without the added complexity. It should also be noted that a diver might not fully exhaust the excess gas by the time they reach the surface; residual gas can remain in the bloodstream for several hours, meaning that a diver would already be charged with excess gas if they were to return to the water during the same day. Accordingly, for planning purposes, there may need to be an extended break between dives, or divers may have to be limited to one dive a day. This all depends on the depth and duration of the first dive, which is why dive operations have to be carefully planned in advance.

There are other environmental factors that affect a diver's physiology: Cold water may affect an individual's comfort level or safety much faster than anticipated; breathing the compressed air mixture of a SCUBA tank may contribute to diver dehydration; the enhanced speed of sound through water (more than 4 times faster than air) means that divers may have a challenging time distinguishing the direction of a sound; and visibility may be impaired to the point where it makes no difference if eyes are open or closed. It is, therefore, important to be aware of the effects of the underwater environment on diving archaeologists and plan accordingly—limit time at depth, wear appropriate protective gear, plan your dive, dive your plan, and ensure there always is a safety plan. An underwater archaeologist has less time on site to do what a colleague on land must do and faces a series of environmental and logistical challenges. All this means that an underwater archaeological project requires careful consideration and planning in order to be completed successfully and safely.

The speed of sound in air at room temperature is approximately 340 m/s. In saltwater of the same temperature, sound travels at approximately 1500 m/s near the surface. As water gets warmer, saltier, or deeper, sound travels even more quickly. When working underwater, this is immediately apparent: boat motors many meters above a diver sound terrifyingly close and it is hard to discern the direction from which sounds come. Because of the penetrating nature of sound underwater, it is common for divers to be recalled to the surface by banging on a metal object or otherwise signaling just below the water. On the other hand, the human voice cannot make clearly enunciated words in water, so the noise your dive partner makes is easily heard, but the sounds are unintelligible unless he is wearing a full-face helmet or specialized mask. Some of these masks even include intercoms that allow for communication between divers and with the surface. However, most diving operations still do not have spoken-communication capabilities. Thus, archaeologists have to rely upon hand signals, written notes, and, in really dark or turbid waters, touch communication to converse with other divers. Some dedicated dive teams learn sign language to communicate more clearly, but surprisingly little conversation is actually needed for a multiple-hour dive; most researchers get by with a handful of signals and a few notes.

Sight is also impacted underwater in several ways. As implied above, underwater visibility can vary due the degree of light penetration or turbidity (dissolved matter or particulates in the water). Archaeologists have worked on sites where the visibility was so poor that they could not see their gauges even when the gauges were pressed to their masks, while other sites are privileged with clear visibility on the order of 50 m. Even in clear water, divers need to have a pocket of air around their eyes, provided by the dive mask or helmet, or they cannot resolve any details underwater due to the different light refraction properties of water. This refraction also magnifies and distorts distance. Objects viewed through a mask appear approximately 33 percent bigger and 25 percent closer than they actually are. This can be challenging when reaching for equipment, but is very helpful when trying to see tiny details on a wreck or precisely record the location of a very small artifact. Also due to the refraction and differential absorption of light, colors appear differently underwater. When light hits the surface of a body of water, it slows down and bends, much like light striking a glass prism. The different wavelengths of light have different amounts of energy, and they are absorbed as they lose energy in the water. Red light fades out by a depth of about 6 m of water. Green light is filtered out by about 15 m, while violet light can penetrate to 100 m or more. This means that colors are faded or absent in deeper waters, unless they are reintroduced through a powerful artificial light. Color discrepancies underwater can be important when recording details of a site; the human eye is well-calibrated to detect minute color differences at the surface, so we occasionally miss details underwater without color.

When archaeologists work underwater, the types of gear employed will vary with location, conditions, and the needs of the research, but all underwater work is restricted by both available technology and the limitations of the human body. There are numerous hazards to consider while working underwater. First and foremost is the inherent danger in relying upon life support in an alien environment. Many things can go wrong with air supplies or the buoyancy systems used to bring the diver back to the surface. Therefore, all archaeologists who work underwater need to be formally trained and experienced divers with well-maintained gear, and all responsible diving projects have stringent safety plans and redundant safety systems, including diving in pairs or teams. With all of these precautions, gear failure, while infrequent and frustrating, is rarely life-threatening on underwater archaeological projects.

The environment itself can cause difficulties. Currents can make it extremely challenging to stay in place during work, tiring the divers, and causing them to consume their breathing air more rapidly. Currents can also cause rapid heat loss, quickly chilling divers and hindering their motions. Tides can be dangerous by changing water depths through scouring, causing currents, and ruining visibility. Obstacles on the seafloor, boats on the surface, or objects in the water column can all serve as hazards both for the divers and for people working on the surface. Further, the fauna in the water can be dangerous. Sharks, alligators, barracuda, eels, and other animals rarely attack divers, but it can happen, and all good diving safety plans have emergency protocols for dangerous wildlife. Finally, both hypothermia and hyperthermia are very real and tangible problems for underwater archaeologists. Heat loss in water is approximately 24 times greater than in air, so even relatively warm water can be dangerous on a long dive. Therefore, in water colder than body temperature, most divers wear wetsuits. In particularly cold water, divers may wear a dry suit over an insulated thermal undersuit. Even colder conditions can be overcome with a hot water suit, which utilizes constantly circulating warm water. This thermal protection is much needed underwater, but on the surface it can be stifling. A diver in full gear on a boat deck during a hot day can become dangerously overheated, so diving operations should be planned to run as efficiently as possible to minimize the risk of hyperthermia.

As discussed in the diving physiology box, divers are subjected to increasing pressure with depth. This increasing pressure impacts both human physiology and the breathing gas mixture, placing upward limits on the amount of time a diver can safely spend underwater at a given depth due to the amount of nitrogen absorbed into the bloodstream (figure 4.2). If you pursue a diving certification, you will get in-depth training in calculating how long you can stay at a certain depth to prevent an excess intake of nitrogen. You will also discuss decompression diving, in which a diver gains more working time at the bottom through planning decompression stops at particular depths during the ascent in order to exhale excess nitrogen prior to surfacing. Decompression diving is usually restricted for recreational divers for safety reasons, but is often utilized by trained underwater researchers.

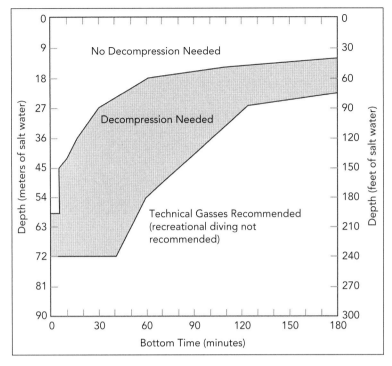

**Figure 4.2** Example recreational diving table showing time limits for diving on air (21 percent oxygen) at various depths. (Modified from DCIEM Diving Manual)

## HOW AN UNDERWATER SITE FORMS

Remember that an archaeological site is a location from which we can recover evidence of human activity. Archaeological sites form or are destroyed through a combination of cultural and natural processes. This contains an important implication—that such evidence is either preserved or accessible. Many archaeological sites are entirely destroyed after they are created. Some shipwrecks break up completely on the rocks that sank them, with all the cultural material swept away and any surviving passengers pulled ashore, leaving no trace on the sea floor. Some sites are left behind as sea level rises and are buried by sediment spewing from a river mouth while the ocean drowns them; the result is that they are invisibly interred under meters of seawater and further meters of mud. Other sites created near the coastline are compromised by the constant swash of waves breaking and moving artifacts until all primary context is gone. Although beachgoers may regularly report finding these artifacts, the story the artifacts would otherwise be able to tell is largely lost. Generally, some portions of a site are more intact, while some are heavily disturbed or completely destroyed. However, archaeologists must discover which portions are which by paying very close attention to the stratigraphy at the site and the relationship between the artifacts, ecofacts, features, and the natural stratigraphy.

Where and how it became submerged can heavily influence to what extent an underwater site is intact or disturbed. Landscapes can be submerged suddenly by catastrophic floods or closure of a dam, or gradually by sea level rise, and can be buried in mud or scoured by beaches. Shipwreck sites can be created in a myriad of ways. Ships are built, used, and discarded or lost, much like other sorts of material culture, although, of course, the loss of a ship is generally more catastrophic. Ships are created to protect humans from an alien environment and are usually very expensive to build, equip, and maintain, so the loss of one is often a great financial disaster on top of the loss of human life. Ships sink for numerous reasons, but many of them are related to human error of some kind.

Ships run aground or hit obstructions due to storm winds, poor navigation, or poor visibility. Ships spring leaks or are torn apart during storms that exceed their engineering, either because they were not built soundly enough for the extreme conditions, because they weaken with age, because they are sailed too aggressively or with poor judgment, or because ships are often at the forefront of unmastered technologies, and lack of knowledge leads to catastrophe. Ships are deliberately sunk by hostile forces. Ships catch fire or explode due to failures in the engine systems or improper storage of explosives. Throughout this text, there are examples of vessels that fall into each of these categories. As you read, note the myriad of hazards that face sailors and those who risk their lives on the seas.

Not all ships end up underwater because of catastrophe, however. Some vessels are scuttled on purpose, such as the Skuldelev ships, five Viking-era vessels deliberately filled with rocks to block a shipping channel and inhibit invasion of the town of Roskilde, Denmark, in approximately 1050 CE. Some are abandoned to slowly settle in place over time after they are no longer needed such as the USS *Jefferson*, built by the Americans to fight the War of 1812 in Lake Ontario, and left to slowly rot and sink in Sacket's Harbor, New York after the end of the war. Some are sunken deliberately to create preserves for sea life or underwater museums, such as several of the twentieth century vessels found on the Florida Panhandle Dive Trail. Therefore, while we think of shipwrecks as sudden and catastrophic, not all ships end up on the bottom by "wrecking" and the actual submersion of a ship can also be a gradual process.[1]

The method of submergence, the process of submergence, and the amount of energy involved in the submergence all have important implications for how well an underwater site will preserve and how much of the site is likely to be in primary as opposed to secondary context. Additionally, the geological setting of a site after submergence has much to do with whether or not a site will ultimately be destroyed or preserved and whether or not a site is discoverable or all but invisible. The distribution and condition of the artifacts within the site can help us determine how the site was submerged and can aid in reconstructing the site's environment before, during, and after the site was created. Obviously, the type of site also has an impact upon how likely it is to preserve, but, in general, rapid but low-energy submergence and rapid and permanent burial in anaerobic sediments lead to the best preservation of both shipwrecks and landscapes (figure 4.3). As mentioned in chapter 3, the organic preservation in submerged sites can be truly phenomenal, like the near-perfect state of the *Hamilton* and *Scourge*, both vessels that sank in one night during the War of 1812 in the cold, dark waters of Lake Ontario and were found with masts still standing more than 200 years later (chapter 12).[2]

Why did these two vessels preserve so well until their discovery? There are three main reasons: They sank almost instantly into deep water, and so were not battered by waves during or after their sinking. In fact, they were in an area of Lake Ontario where there was little to no disturbance of any kind at the bottom. The fresh water, a better preservative than salt water, was deep enough that no sunlight

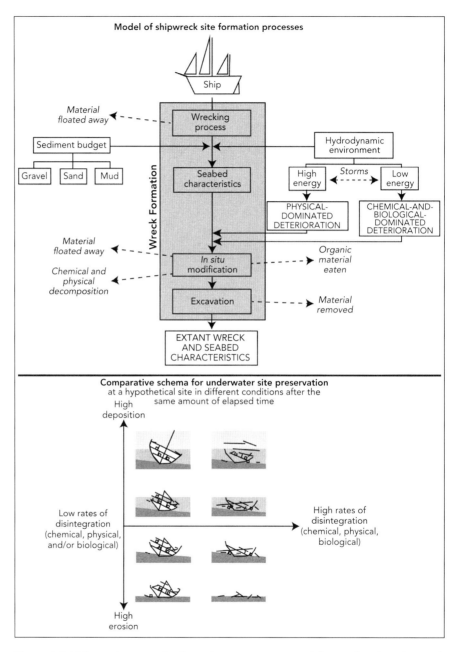

**Figure 4.3** Major underwater site formation processes, especially as related to shipwreck sites. (Modified from Ward et al. 1999, Figs. 3 and 5)

could penetrate, and cold enough to inhibit the growth of bacteria. Finally, the environment remained unchanged for hundreds of years. In general, one of the most favorable factors for site preservation is that the environment remains as stable as possible from the time a site is created until the time it is discovered. Another is that there is minimal action from the enemies of organic preservation: warmth, oxygen, and humidity. In tropical waters, "shipworms" *(Teredo navalis)*, eat any exposed wood, so rapid burial is especially important in these areas. Finally, being submerged in a low-energy environment, such as the bottom of a deep lake, is much better than being in a high-energy environment, such as a beach, as the latter will constantly expose and rebury things, and the cyclical motions of breaking waves will tear apart the wreck and destroy the context of the material culture. The Lake Ontario wrecks preserved so well because all of the most favorable factors for site preservation (table 4.1) were present. However, after hundreds of years within a stable environment, these and other deep wrecks in the Great Lakes have recently become threatened because invasive mussels of the *Dreissena* genus, brought into the lakes by transatlantic shipping vessels, have begun to infest the inland waters, attaching themselves to ship hulls and rapidly altering the formerly stable wreck environments (chapter 7). This situation illustrates that preservation is a dynamic process, even at sites that appear to be stable.

Sites in active environments present greater challenges in terms of their interpretation, as it is important to determine which portion of the archaeological record is the result of human agency and which portion is due to geological processes. For example, research at Blackbeard's ship, *Queen Anne's Revenge*, located offshore of North Carolina, (discussed more fully in chapter 12) revealed that the ship worked its way deeper and deeper into the sandy bottom of the bay by being buried and unburied repeatedly during storms.[3] This repeated exposure and reburial led to patterning between the artifacts, especially the very small artifacts, which revealed information about geological processes, as

TABLE 4.1 **FACTORS THAT FAVOR SITE PRESERVATION**

| |
| --- |
| Stability of environment |
| Little to no sunlight |
| Little to no humidity or remaining constantly wet |
| Little to no oxygen (anaerobic) |
| Submergence in a low-energy environment |
| Rapid burial |
| Submergence in cold waters |

well as storm and wave patterns, rather than human activities. Further, the stratigraphic layers at the site were scrambled because several of the storms likely scoured sediments away, winnowing out the lighter materials and depositing new sand. At the same time, the larger artifacts showed a surprising amount of correlation between their probable stowage locations within the vessel and where they were discovered in relationship to one another. Occasionally these larger artifacts also trapped the smaller ones in place. This demonstrates that even in locations where little seems to be in undisturbed context, it is possible to make reasonable assumptions about the original context, and make some inferences about human behavior.

Once an underwater site has formed and is on the continuum between preservation and destruction, artifacts themselves can either aid in or inhibit preservation. For instance, ships often used ballast weights—whether stones, pig iron blocks, or other heavy material—to stabilize and adjust how the hull floated in the water. Following a vessel's sinking, the ballast pile, located in the bottom of the hull, presses a shipwreck to the seafloor. This pile of ballast helps preserve materials trapped beneath it, including what are often the only timbers of the original hull to survive. This weight also serves to trap numerous smaller artifacts, and makes the remains of the vessel easier to detect during a survey. Some types of material culture do even more to preserve sites. For instance, shell is made of calcium carbonate, and thus has a neutral to basic pH. Most water and sediments are weakly acidic, which causes the breakdown of organic materials. Shell can help neutralize this acid; therefore, shell middens (trash heaps) tend to be filled with well-preserved food remains, protected from decomposition by the surrounding shells. In other cases, however, artifacts can actually cause the dissolution of other types of material culture through complex chemical reactions including the galvanic processes of metals in saltwater (see the Conservation box in chapter 5). It is thus important to carefully document the provenience of artifacts on a site in order to better understand what is missing and perhaps why certain artifacts fared better than others. Finally, as will be discussed in much more detail in chapter 7, both human and natural processes can impact underwater sites after they form, including trawling, introduction of new species, and changes in sea level.[4] Thus, it is increasingly important for archaeologists to fully understand the archaeological resources in their areas so that they can assess the threats to sites, and develop responsible management and mitigation responses.[5] To do this, the first step is to find and record the sites themselves.

## SURVEY: FINDING SITES

Some sites are easy to find—or do not need to be "found" because people always knew where they were, like Trajan's Harbor (chapter 7). Some sites are relatively easy to discover, once someone looks in the right place using the right technology, such as the discovery of the WWII wreck of the *Bismarck*, located by

Robert Ballard in ca. 4,800 m of water depth (chapter 12). Some others are very difficult to detect, such as inundated terrestrial sites from hunting and gathering societies (chapter 7). As with most types of archaeological research, different methods are required to locate different kinds of sites.[6]

The first method that archaeologists employ to discover sites is the simplest. We interview people who live or work in the area we are interested in researching. Almost all of the most impressive and most visible terrestrial sites, and many of the underwater sites, have been discovered this way. This works because at least a few people in most areas are interested in their local history, and people tend to notice and remember out-of-the-ordinary things like wooden ship timbers or large concentrations of artifacts that might snag fishing nets. Those who live and work on the water tend to know where the navigational hazards are that could have caused wrecks in the past, and they tend to know about historic ships that were wrecked in these areas. Shipwrecks also can act as artificial reefs, which attract fish, so even when people do not know a rough spot on the bottom is due to a shipwreck, they do know where the fish are. In other words, locals usually know more about an area than the archaeologist does, so if you can find the right person, you can save yourself days or weeks of searching for a specific site. In fact, the very first underwater excavations conducted by Bass and colleagues (chapter 2) were performed on Bronze Age wrecks that were discovered by sponge divers because saltwater sponges were attaching themselves to the rough, hard surfaces created by piles of amphorae and ballast from the wrecks.[7]

However, interviews are far from infallible. People notice the big sites, but they tend not to know about the smaller ones, or the ones that might be mostly buried, deep, or otherwise in an inaccessible location. Also, sometimes people are wrong in their memory of where a site is or what it is. Further, there are many places on the seafloor that were not especially notable to the locals. These portions *may* lack sites, but it is unscientific to merely assume that this is so.

In most cases, archaeologists need to **survey**, or conduct systematic investigations for the purpose of locating sites. Surveys are designed based on the project research objectives. These objectives can range from searching for a particular site, such as Cussler's search for the *Hunley* (chapter 2), surveying a promising area to uncover any unknown sites within a geographic area, or surveying an area that is going to be impacted by development to see if any cultural resources will be impacted.

The ultimate purpose of many surveys is to locate or relocate archaeological sites, but the first step is usually to locate **targets**. *Target* is a generic term that underwater archaeologists use to refer to any type of anomaly on or in the seafloor that warrants further investigation until it is definitely identified or discounted. Many of the anomalies turn out to be sunken logs, rock formations, abandoned boxcars, or discarded tires. Sometimes "target" is also used to refer to areas that have been reported to contain a site until the claimed site has been discovered or shown not to be there. Therefore, a target is not necessarily the result of human

## Christopher E. Horrell, Federal Preservation Officer/Senior Marine Archaeologist, Bureau of Safety and Environmental Enforcement, USA

One of the most important roles of a professional archaeologist, whether terrestrial or maritime, is working with developers. Development can mean many different things and includes a multitude of activities, ranging from small projects such as installing a dock or breakwater, to large-scale projects such as sand extraction for beach renourishment or offshore energy installations. In some cases, underwater cultural sites that were once submerged may now be located on dry land and require the expertise of a marine archaeologist to advise a developer on how to proceed. For cultural sites that are found within a body of water, in many parts of the world a developer must comply with a particular set of requirements before the commencement of any activities that could potentially damage those sites.

Professional marine archaeologists who work with developers identify and document underwater cultural heritage sites before the project begins. Most projects start with the need for information about potential archaeological sites within the project area. Marine archaeologists use a variety of field methods and tools to identify sites. The most frequently used method, and often a necessary first step, is to design and conduct a high-resolution remote sensing survey to detect any potential archaeological sites within the project area. These surveys often employ a magnetometer, side-scan sonar, and sub-bottom profiler. In addition, depending on project parameters and requirements, tools such as a multibeam bathymetric system, a sector-scanning sonar, or a Remotely Operated Vehicle (ROV) may be required. All of these tools have specific features and functions that aid in the identification of underwater cultural heritage. The marine archaeologist must understand not only how to set up and conduct a survey, but also must be able to analyze and interpret the resulting data, and ultimately produce a professional report of findings. Some projects may require the development of specialized mitigation measures to prevent or minimize impacts to underwater cultural heritage, or the implementation

of a data recovery effort to collect as much archaeological information as possible before a resource is unavoidably impacted by the project.

One of the first things that a marine archaeologist working with a developer must consider is the breadth of different types of underwater cultural heritage that may be encountered in the course of the project. These archaeological sites might include submerged prehistoric sites, shipwrecks, or other maritime features such as a lighthouse or a historic breakwater. When working with developers, marine archaeologists not only consider the types of sites that could be impacted, they must also consider preservation legislation that may protect underwater cultural heritage. In the United States, there are specific rules and laws at the local, state, and federal level, all of which may be tied to the National Historic Preservation Act of 1966. Typically, a permit must be issued before initiating a development project, and that permit will have stipulations that require an assessment of the potential for underwater cultural heritage in the developer's proposed project area. International requirements vary depending on each nation's laws and regulations. In general, marine archaeologists working with developers and their projects require a specific tool set and knowledge base that are often different than what is found in academic research.

Before selecting the appropriate methodology and high-resolution remote sensing survey equipment, the marine archaeologist must understand the parameters of the proposed project and what instrument(s) are best suited to identify potential sites. As an example, a project will require an anchored dredge to remove sand from offshore in 12 meters (40 feet) of water for a beach renourishment project. The dredge will be anchored above the sand borrow pit and carefully remove the predetermined quantity of sand required for the project. The marine archaeologist working with the developer will review the plan, the local environment, water depth, and other factors in order to consider all potential bottom-disturbing activities. These activities include the physical removal of sand from the borrow pit, associated anchor placements and anchor chain used to hold the dredge on station, and any other activities that may disturb the seafloor. At this point, the marine archaeologist will design a survey plan that covers the extent of all bottom-disturbing activities proposed by the developer. Understanding the parameters of the project and the functions of the remote sensing equipment allows the marine archaeologist to provide the maximum amount of survey coverage needed to identify submerged heritage sites that exist in the area.

Once potential underwater cultural heritage is identified, the marine archaeologist will advise the developer as to how best to proceed without impacting these potential sites. In some cases, the survey will indicate that the project area is devoid of any potential archaeological resources and the developer can proceed with the project as planned, as long as they limit bottom-disturbing activities to the surveyed project area. In other cases, the marine archaeologist will identify targets that should be avoided by the developer, if possible, or investigated if the target cannot be avoided. Avoidance is always the preferred method in order to balance the project's needs with the protection of underwater cultural heritage. Occasionally, avoidance of potential archaeological resources is not possible and further investigation is required. The marine archaeologist will advise and provide the necessary tools and techniques to investigate and document the resource. Depending on water depth and other environmental factors, this may include diver visual investigations or ROV investigations to document the site. If the developer's proposed project requires the disturbance of the site, test excavations and data recovery efforts may be necessary. When data recovery is the only option, the marine archaeologist will develop a research design and devise a data recovery plan to collect the greatest amount of data possible to thoroughly document the site under time and budgetary constraints.

Once field work is complete, conservation of recovered artifacts and analysis of the entire dataset is the next step. Using these data, the marine archaeologist will draft a report that meets the reporting standards required by the local, state, or federal government. In addition to providing an interpretation of the data, the marine archaeologist will advise the developer and the permitting entity as to how best to proceed with the project upon completion of recovery operations.

One final consideration is that archaeological data collected during a development project may also be used to aid in the interpretation of other underwater cultural heritage sites. This is accomplished in a number of different ways including the production of what is often referred to as gray literature. Gray literature consists of technical reports, working papers, white papers, and other forms of information that marine archaeologists use for research and cite as they conduct their work or future research. In addition, marine archaeologists may provide a detailed presentation to his or her colleagues at conferences. When publishing the results of their work, there are important considerations that must be made when marine archaeologists review and uses this information. These considerations may include understanding the overall distribution of sites and their relation to the amount of development in a particular area or region. In some instances, more sites might be found in areas where there is more development, potentially skewing analyses and interpretations. In some instances, new technologies are developed and introduced into the field to augment and address data needs. In other cases, new discoveries lead to further research questions and interpretations of the archaeological data. This information is vital for expanding the archaeological community's collective knowledge base as well as educating the public. While the developer will receive the benefits of completed project, the marine archaeologist has the opportunity to disseminate new and useful information providing a detailed account of how a project was conceived and completed along with a clearer understanding of past human behavior while setting up questions for further research.

activity, nor is it necessarily relevant to the project even when it represents cultural material. Targets can be obtained through active or past surveys, from maps, or from interviews. Surveys are not solely for discovering where sites are. Surveys also demonstrate where sites are not, allowing us to gain useful information about site distributions and site preservation. Therefore, even when we do not locate a specific archaeological site, a survey is useful, because it allows us to eliminate portions of the seafloor from future searches.

Surveys, however, are only effective in providing us with useful information about site distributions and site absence when they are conducted systematically. If areas are searched at random, something may be discovered, but it will be impossible to determine what this means in the broader landscape or culture. Therefore, when archaeologists plan a survey, we often begin months in advance, and many factors play into the methods and equipment to be used and how large an area we will search. As with all scientific projects, when a survey is conducted for research purposes the area to be searched will largely depend upon research questions (sidebar by Aniruddh S. Gaur). If, on the other hand, researchers are trying to determine whether there are any sites in an area before development happens, the development boundaries determine the survey area. When looking for a specific site, historic and environmental data associated with a vessel's sinking will determine the survey area. If investigating a promising area for future research, the definition of "promising" will have been determined by a number of physical characteristics of a given area. The archaeologists will then determine how much money and time is available to conduct this research and what equipment is accessible and appropriate; these constraints will be balanced with the potential types of sites we may discover and environmental conditions in the survey area in order to determine what survey strategies will have the greatest chance of success within our limitations.

## COASTAL ARCHAEOLOGY AND SHORELINE CHANGE ALONG THE INDIAN COAST

Aniruddh S. Gaur, Marine Archaeology Center, CSIR-National Institute of Oceanography, India

Coastal archaeological sites have often been used as secondary sources for determining the paleo-coastline, though they serve as a much more authentic record, since these sites can reflect the impact sea level changes have had on human society in the past. There are several literary sources that relate the submergence of ancient towns due to the wrath of divine forces; these forces represent natural phenomena such as cyclones, storms, and tsunamis. To better understand these references, maritime archaeology started in India with the objective to find the remains of the ancient town of Dwarka on the west coast of India. Subsequently, during extensive explorations around the Indian coast over the past three decades, a large number of archaeological sites dating back to the Bronze Age and the British Raj period have been brought to light. For the first time in India, we used coastal archaeological sites to determine the paleo-shoreline. I provide a brief description here.

The study of Bronze Age (Indus Civilization) sites of Gujarat suggests that over 20 percent of sites are located within 20 km (12 miles) of the coastline. The geological studies indicated that during the time of the Indus Valley Civilization, sea level was higher than today; thus these sites were much closer to the coast than they are today. The present morphology of Rann of Kachchh suggests that this was part of the Arabian Sea and must have been a shallow gulf during the Indus Valley period. The archaeological investigations at various sites in India and in the Gulf countries suggest that the Indus navigators sailed through this gulf to the hinterlands up to Harappa through the Indus River Valley and externally to Mesopotamia. Thus, the shoreline along the northwest coast of India has changed significantly during the last five millennia.

Archaeological investigations in and around the island of Bet Dwarka indicate that during the Bronze Age (2500 to 1500 BCE), surrounding sea levels were higher and the island must have been smaller than it is today; however, during the early historic period, the sea level dropped almost 2 m below the present, as three early historic settlements are found below the high water line. Based on these data, a paleo-shoreline has been drawn which suggests that Bet Dwarka was almost 40 percent larger than it is today. The remains of an 11th-century CE temple have been found in the intertidal zone of Pindara (northwest Saurashtra coast), which indicates that even during the last 1000 to 800 years before present shorelines have changed significantly.

On the east coast of India, Poompuhar, a famous site which was thought to be the capital of Early Cholas (3rd-century BCE to 6th-century CE), has been partially submerged in the sea. The early Tamil text *Manimekhalai* ascribed this inundation to punishment for failing to celebrate Indra's Festival, echoing some natural phenomena that must have led to the submergence of this ancient port town.

The coastal and underwater archaeological investigations brought to light the remains of the ancient town in the form of brick structures, terracotta ring-wells, and pottery. The underwater archaeological explorations off Mahabalipuram revealed the presence of a large number of stone structures that could have been parts of a temple, as Mahabalipuram is famous for its Pallava-period (8th- to 9th-century CE) art and architectural marvels. Based on the similarity of construction pattern, the findings from underwater may also be dated to the Pallava period.

The coastal and maritime archaeological investigations along the Indian coast provide numerous examples of the application of archaeological data in determining ancient shorelines and paleo–sea level fluctuations.

Background research can be very helpful in selecting a location for a survey. Historical records, when available, can be particularly insightful. Bottom hazards and shipwrecks tend to be mentioned on maps and in documents from an area. Therefore, these notations can precisely pinpoint where a particular ship is believed to have sunk. Of course, historic maps and records still need to be matched to locations in the real world, so, while these records help narrow search parameters, they rarely provide an exact location. Historic maps, for instance, need to be georeferenced to modern maps using known landmarks. However, coastlines change shapes, development changes stream patterns, and not all historic maps are equally accurate in terms of scale, distance, and direction, so georeferencing may or may not be a simple process.

Even when there are no specific historic records referring to a particular archaeological site, we can employ proxy data to help select areas that are more likely to contain sites of interest. For instance, researchers interested in inundated landscapes depend heavily on sea-level curves (reconstructions of prior ocean water levels based on shoreline markers now found underwater or on land) and ocean bathymetry maps, or contour maps of the seafloor showing modern water depths. If a researcher wanted to look for a coastal site that dated to approximately 9,000 BCE, she would look at her local sea-level curve and see that at that time water levels were approximately 80 m lower than they are at present. Therefore, she would look at the bathymetry maps and target portions of the seafloor that are approximately 80 m deep for her survey. If looking for shipwrecks, she may target landforms likely to cause them, like nearshore bars and reef formations, or may employ meteorological or oceanographic data to determine where prevailing winds or currents would guide vessels.

No matter which type of research archaeologists are doing, it is essential to know exactly where we are. Even in the modern day, when seemingly every cellular phone has a GPS receiver, this is extremely difficult. Most of the ocean looks like a featureless plane, and even a few miles offshore will be out of sight of land. This means that satellite navigation is what most of us rely upon today for underwater surveys. Precise location in both two dimensions (northing and easting) and three (bottom depth) are absolutely crucial to locating and relocating sites, positioning ships, and deploying and recovering divers. In the vast oceans, even a few meters of inaccuracy can lead to mission failure, especially in waters with poor visibility. For instance, converting a known wreck location from Loran-C (a radio-based navigation system used from the 1950s to the 1980s) to a modern GPS system can result in position uncertainty of up to several dozen meters. Thus, even when using recent historic records, such as maps of a shipwreck located in 1985, it might take some time to relocate known find spots. Extrapolate this into the past and even less precise means of determining locations, and you begin to get an idea of the scope of the potential complications.

## Sampling

Whether we are working on land or underwater, once archaeologists have established a desirable area to survey, we typically employ some sort of sampling strategy in order to determine where we should concentrate our efforts. It should be noted that archaeologists use the same sampling strategies to find sites and to excavate them, just at different scales, so this section is equally applicable to chapter 5. There are four main types of sampling strategies that archaeologists use whether on land or underwater, and depending upon the research questions and the natural conditions of the surrounding area, any one of them could be the best strategy for a given site. Therefore, there is no "best sampling method" for maritime and underwater archaeology. The four main sampling strategies are random, stratified random, transect, and non-random.

Random sampling is used most commonly when no previous work has been done in the survey area and nothing is known about what may be found there. To randomly sample an area, it would be divided into blocks of some size dependent upon the survey capabilities. These blocks would be arbitrarily labeled, and a given number of these blocks would then be selected using a method such as a random number generator, or some other approach that would ensure human bias was not involved in the block selection (figure 4.4a). This lack of bias is the key strength of the random sampling method—it ensures that archaeologists are not missing important sites because our preconceived notions have led us to look where we think we will find things. This randomness, however, means that we also could randomly miss all of the important sites within the promising area.

When we know a little bit about the archaeological potential of an area we tend to employ stratified random sampling (figure 4.4b). Just as previously, our potential survey area is made into a grid. Then we mark out areas that are meaningful for some reason or another. For instance, if we know that recent harbor dredging had disturbed a portion of a bay, we may choose to entirely exclude that area from our survey or make sure to investigate the disturbance. We may wish to examine or avoid a coral reef or a known recent shipwreck. The grid areas we want to examine will be placed into our random selection method, while the ones we do not want to investigate will be excluded. This narrows our search area and allows us to focus on areas believed to hold greater potential for archaeological finds. Therein lies the strength and weakness of this method. We are perhaps more likely to find things, but using this method means we only find sites where we expect to, and, therefore, we are less likely to find truly extraordinary sites that lie completely outside of our expected site parameters.

Transect sampling is used when it is important for an archaeologist to see how things are changing across a swath of space (figure 4.4c). Transects are continuous linear samples, and technically most remote sensing methods work in a transect strategy. The sonar equipment is turned on, and the boat goes in a straight line for a given distance, then returns in a straight line adjacent to the last one for a given distance. However, choosing transects as a sampling methodology usually means explicitly choosing to run along or across a geological feature or a known site of some sort because you are most interested in seeing how things are changing in space across a known parameter. The strength of this method is that it works well to show how things are varying with the geological change, such as bathymetry, or the site area, such as from bow to stern of a vessel. The weakness is its narrowness. The researcher must hope that he or she chose the most representative swaths.

Finally, nonrandom sampling is what it sounds like. Survey areas are chosen for any of a variety of reasons. For instance, in figure 4.4d, the surveyors are looking for a shipwreck that was located on a historic map and georeferenced to that area. Nonrandom surveys are also done to survey where pipelines and infrastructure are placed offshore; these surveys are limited to the area of potential impact from the project. There are many, many reasons for choosing a nonrandom sampling strategy, but because it is nonrandom, it also has the potential to be nonsystematic and provides less useful information about where sites are

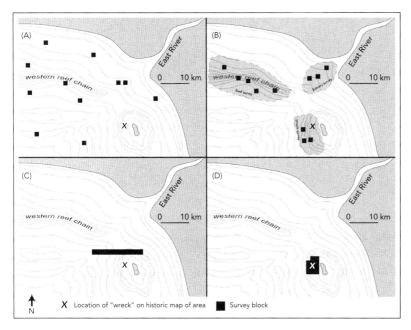

**Figure 4.4** Sampling strategies. A. Random (random number generator selecting grid locations). B. Stratified Random (random locations chosen within the major geographic features). C. Transect (linear area chosen to bisect a number of geographic features). D. Nonrandom (area chosen to pinpoint historic shipwreck).

not. No matter what sampling strategy is chosen, there are several methods that can be used to survey the chosen areas.

## Diver surveys

Many underwater archaeology projects conduct surveys using divers when the environmental conditions permit it. Diver surveys work best when the area to be investigated is relatively small, when the sites of interest are likely to be visible on the seafloor, when the water is shallow enough for divers to spend a relatively long amount of time underwater, and when water visibility is good enough for divers to see a relatively large swath of the bottom. These diver surveys can follow many different systematic patterns underwater (see Surveying with Divers box), and they have several advantages. First, trained archaeological divers are unlikely to miss any major items of interest on the surface of an area that is surveyed, as humans are remarkably good at not only finding artifacts, but also noticing irregularities in shape, color, topography, or texture, all of which may indicate the location of a site. Second, diver surveys often require less infrastructure and fewer resources than the corresponding remote sensing surveys mentioned below. Diver surveys are employed most frequently for target identification, as they tend to be more efficient at finding cultural materials when searching small areas.

However, diver surveys also have their limitations. While they are relatively cost-effective, they often only provide good pictures of small areas, and only when the conditions above are met. Diver surveys are not as helpful in covering broad regions, in deep water, in areas with poor visibility, over seafloors with heavy marine growth, or in regions with high sedimentation rates which might rapidly bury archaeological sites. Many of these conditions, however, are often what favor good site preservation, and may ironically be the sites archaeologists most want to find. In order to effectively survey such areas, researchers turn to a series of remote sensing tools.

## SURVEYING WITH DIVERS: SWIMLINE, JACKSTAY, RADIAL, AND BASELINE OFFSET METHODS

Diver-based visual surveys often prove to be the most efficient and effective method of identifying and documenting sites within smaller geographic regions. A diver can detect small differences in color, texture, sheen, shape, and other features that elude most remote sensing instruments. Even though remotely operated vehicles may be able to stay underwater longer and go deeper than divers, these vehicles often are not as efficient as a trained pair of divers in locating sites in the near-shore environment, nor are most capable of documenting sites in a similarly effectual manner. Here we will address four methods through which archaeologists can systematically survey and document sites underwater—the swimline, jackstay, radial, and baseline offset surveys.

A key premise of any successful survey is that it must follow a systematic approach. Absence of data is, at times, as important as the presence of material culture; the only way to be certain of a survey's results is to trust that the methodology gathered data in a comprehensive manner that minimized data gaps. When it comes to exploring an underwater area with the objective of locating archaeological sites or features using divers, the swimline and jackstay surveys provide two such proven methods.

The swimline survey method uses an underwater line stretched between two submerged anchors that are typically also buoyed to the surface. The line is typically deployed from the surface along a predetermined bearing, and the buoys permit the surface vessel to verify the line's correct placement, collect GPS points of the swimline extremities, and keep track of the divers below. When surveying, at least one pair of divers swims the length of the line parallel to each other, as far apart from each other as visibility permits. The two divers may hold a line perpendicular to the swimline as they swim to ensure they are maintaining position, and the diver farthest from the swimline may also carry a marker buoy so that the surface vessel can keep track of their locations. Additional divers can be positioned alongside each other to widen the swath of the area surveyed. If the line is marked, either by being intertwined with a tape measure, or through knots or other indicators (electrical tape works well), then the position of any detected target can be roughly determined by the divers themselves (e.g., 5 m south of the 25-m marker). If the line is not marked, divers can typically affix smaller buoys to a target and rely on the surface vessel to collect GPS points on the appropriate location. The length of the line is in part dependent on the desired width of a survey area, as when the divers reach the far end of the swimline, they can either turn around and swim in the opposite direction on the other side of the swimline, jump over to another established swimline, or conclude the survey. Depth, visibility, currents, whether more than one dive is planned for the day, and the physical condition of the divers all play a role in determining the appropriate extent of swimline surveys.

Jackstay surveys are more detailed and systematic than swimline surveys, but are also more time-consuming. They are sometimes used when a known site is in the area to be surveyed and archaeologists want to determine its extent, though they can also be launched in order to investigate a previously unstudied area in a more comprehensive manner. Unlike a swimline survey, which depends on a single primary line, jackstay surveys depend on two primary lines to serve as the fixed boundaries of the survey area. They are deployed in parallel to each other underwater and anchored to the seafloor or lakebed with buoys on each extremity. These lines must each be marked with distance indicators every so many meters, or be intertwined with tape measures. The space between the two lines is the desired area to be surveyed. Once the boundary lines are appropriately positioned, divers proceed to the first predetermined marker (e.g., 5 m) on the first boundary line and stretch a third, perpendicular line (the survey line) to the 5m marker on the second boundary line, affixing it in place. The divers then conduct a swimline survey along that survey line, which is usually intertwined with a tape measure, back to the first boundary line, documenting any targets along the way. Upon arriving at the first boundary line, divers move the end of the survey line to the second predetermined interval (e.g., 10 m) and affix it there. In swimming back to the second boundary line along the survey line, which now diagonally stretches from the 10-m marker on the

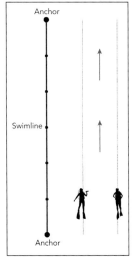

**Figure 4.5** Swimline survey.

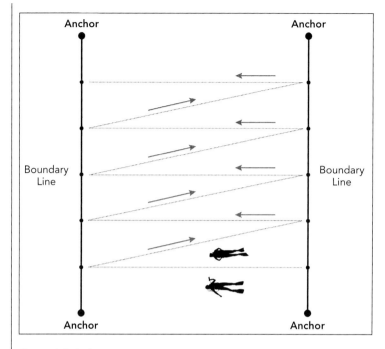

**Anchor**                    **Anchor**

**Boundary Line**                    **Boundary Line**

**Anchor**                    **Anchor**

**Figure 4.6** Jackstay survey.

first boundary line to the 5-m marker on the second boundary line, divers cover some of the same ground covered during the first swimline survey. They can either dedicate themselves to careful survey of this area, or quickly swim to the second boundary line and move the survey line to the 10-m marker on that end, thereby setting up for a second perpendicular survey between the boundary lines. This process, whether setting up diagonal or perpendicular survey lines, will repeat itself for each predetermined interval along the boundary lines. The decision as to which approach to take will vary with each project's needs, objectives, and resources; however, both ways of conducting jackstay surveys afford a much more controlled and detailed approach to surveying an area. Jackstay surveys, therefore, are common in areas with very low visibility even though they take longer to set up and perform than swimline surveys.

The radial survey, also referred to as a circular search, is a somewhat more flexible surveying approach that can be used both to investigate archaeological targets of interest and quickly map an archaeological site. In this method, a central point is selected and serves as the primary datum of the survey. This point is typically affixed firmly to the seafloor or lakebed, but extends several centimeters off the bottom to prevent snags, and may also be buoyed to the surface. Whatever the anchoring mechanism, there is usually an eyelet that allows for a carabiner attachment, or another means through which the end of a tape measure can be affixed to the central point. Two divers spread themselves out as far apart as visibility permits, one holding on to the spool of the tape measure and the other to the midpoint between the outer diver and the central point. Marking their point of origin, the divers then proceed to complete a circular course around the central point. Once that first course is completed, both divers move outward from the center, maintaining their original relationship and distance from each other. It is important to note when planning that the outer diver will exert themselves more than the inner diver. If an object of interest is discovered at any point, it can be marked with a buoy from which a surface vessel can collect a GPS point. More often, however, divers themselves mark the location of the target through collecting the distance from the central point using the tape measure, and a bearing along the outstretched tape heading back to the central point using a compass. When subsequently developing a site plan, archaeologists simply reverse the bearing and use the scaled distance to mark a location; as long as divers carefully annotate each point, a fairly complex site plan can be developed. There will, however, be a margin of error that increases as a tape measure is stretched farther away from the central point.

In the right conditions, one of the most efficient ways to create a basic archaeological site plan is referred to as a baseline offset survey. It works in much the same way as a swimline survey, although instead of attempting to locate and document objects of interest, a baseline offset survey aims to map them for the purposes of developing a more detailed site plan. A baseline, usually intertwined with a tape measure, is established, bisecting an archaeological site and extending a fair distance in each direction beyond it. A clear line-of-sight should exist from one end to the other of the line, and ideally there should be as little in its way as possible. The baseline must be affixed firmly to the seafloor or lakebed as its extremities serve as the primary datum points for the site. The "zero" end of the tape measure is affixed to one of the extremities, which then serves as the origin, or central node (0,0) on a Cartesian grid. In order to document the location of an artifact or feature, the archaeologist must mark the distance along the baseline, along with the distance perpendicularly extending toward the artifact or feature on one side of the baseline, referred to as an "offset." Beginning at the point to be measured, the archaeologist extends a second tape measure toward the baseline, attempting to meet the baseline in a perpendicular manner. The archaeologist then swings the tape measure toward and away from the origin on the baseline, until the smallest distance from the artifact is registered, representing a 90° angle. When mapping the point, one would conceptually travel the distance along the baseline to the point of intersection, and then measure out the second "offset" distance away from the baseline. This method is far swifter at providing a general impression and artifact distribution map of a site than more complex mapping methods such as trilateration. It can also be applied by using only two divers and minimal equipment. It does, however, have limitations when encountering uneven geomorphology, site features that prevent a tape measure from obtaining an accurate perpendicular reading, or an expansive site, as a tape measure stretched more than a few meters may start to bend in the current and, in doing so, provide erroneous measurements. Being aware of these limitations, baseline offsets still serve as a fundamental and common technique for preliminary documentation efforts.

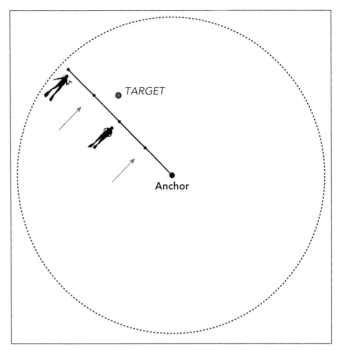

**Figure 4.7** Radial survey.

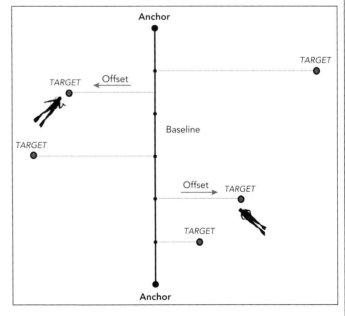

**Figure 4.8** Baseline offset survey.

## Remote sensing survey

Remote sensing is the most common survey tool for most maritime and underwater archaeologists. Remote sensing is what it sounds like—investigating an area without directly touching or seeing it. More generally, it refers to investigations that gather data without excavation. The Remote Sensing Survey box provides additional details on the various instruments commonly utilized in underwater archaeology. Most operate by attaching a sensor to a platform that travels through the water. This platform might be the hull of the survey vessel; a towfish, which is towed by cable behind the survey vessel; an autonomous underwater vehicle (**AUV**), which is programmed on deck, placed in the water, and left to run its survey route before being picked up later; or a remotely operated vehicle (**ROV**), which is placed in the water and is guided by a pilot who remains on the surface. The equipment utilized for these surveys varies greatly depending upon the research questions, water depth, types of sites that are in the area, project budget, and whether or not the sites are likely to be buried or exposed on the seafloor. For example, side-scan sonars and magnetometers are used most often for locating wrecks, while sub-bottom profilers are generally most useful for locating inundated landscapes (figure 4.9).

(A)

(B)

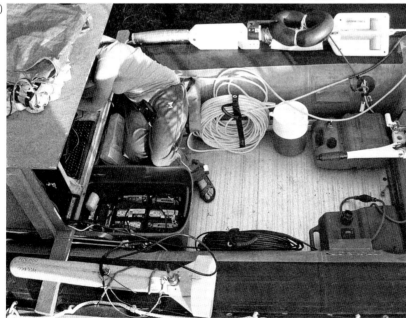

**Figure 4.9** Common sonar equipment (towfish) used in underwater research. A. Dual frequency side-scan and sub-bottom profiler. B. Side-scan sonar (bottom) and magnetometer (top) positioned for safe travel to survey area.

If you are looking for buried materials, employing a magnetometer or a sub-bottom profiler is crucial. If there may be surface exposure, acoustic sensors such as a side-scan sonar or multibeam echosounder are likely to be most effective. It is best practice to employ more than one type of remote sensing instrument at a time in order to obtain as thorough a data record for a region or site as possible. The major limitation of remote sensing surveys is that all targets need to be verified by further investigation. Sometimes targets are shipwrecks or preserved landscapes, but they are much more commonly strange geological features or twentieth century waste. This is true for diver surveys as well, but when the anomalies are visible, divers can often dismiss false targets much more quickly and efficiently than remote sensing methods can (figure 4.10).

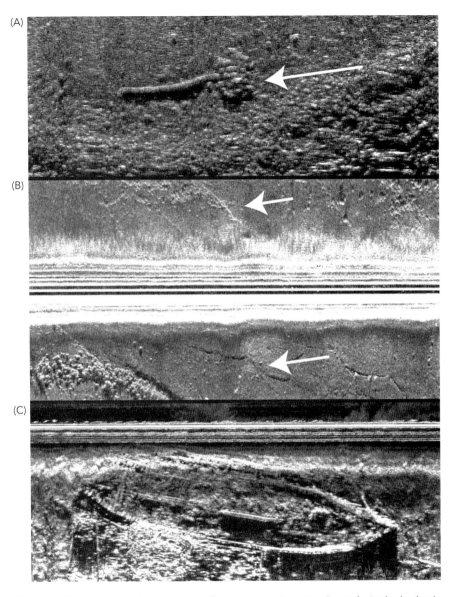

**Figure 4.10** Several targets as seen in side-scan sonar. A. a tree. B. cracks in the bedrock. C. a sunken vessel. A and B are not of archaeological interest, but C is.

Most maritime archaeologists who work in the private sector, often referred to as cultural resource managers, spend the majority of their time planning, implementing, and reporting remote sensing surveys. These sorts of surveys are most often used to discover if any cultural heritage sites are located within the area of a proposed development project. If sites are located, the planned development project is usually revised in order to avoid them, though in certain instances where avoidance is not feasible archaeological recoveries might take place. Remote sensing has several advantages that makes it the survey method of choice for industry. First, dozens of kilometers can be surveyed in the time it would take divers to survey a few hundred meters, making it much more efficient in terms of time, though potentially less precise, than human investigation. Second, much deeper depth limits apply to remote sensing equipment as opposed to human divers. While very deep water is more complicated for acoustic surveys than shallow water because of the amount of cable needed and the special housings for the towfish, useable data can still be collected. Third, remote sensing surveys can run 24 hours a day with only one or a few technicians monitoring the data feeds while the equipment is working, and usually multiple sensors are running at a time, so enormous amounts of data can be gathered with only a handful of people. Finally, it is possible to get complete coverage of the seafloor using acoustic methods, so anything visible on the seafloor should be detectable and recorded, provided the appropriate resolution is utilized to discern smaller targets. All of these advantages make remote sensing surveys incredibly powerful and incredibly useful when a large area needs to be investigated.

## REMOTE SENSING SURVEY INSTRUMENTS

Underwater archaeological surveys are typically conducted for one of three reasons: (a) to find a particular target; (b) to discover unknown targets within a promising area; and (c) to ensure no cultural heritage sites are located within an area that will be impacted by subsequent development activities. It is therefore of primary importance to be thorough and systematic in surveying, as both presence and absence of targets can be significant. Selecting the appropriate remote sensing tools for a project requires careful consideration of the nature of the survey, the marine environment, and regional site formation processes (e.g., depth, presence or absence of oxygen, sediment, wave action, and currents), as well as the types of anticipated cultural heritage sites in the given region.

Remote sensing survey instruments, which include side-scan sonars, multibeam echosounders, sub-bottom profilers, and magnetometers, are able to survey varying swaths of the seafloor and below it. Remote sensing instruments are typically able to explore and document underwater environments with greater efficiency than human divers and often collect data from areas inaccessible to humans. However, tool selection itself is an intrinsic part of developing a survey strategy, as each instrument carries with it particular strengths and drawbacks.

The side-scan sonar is one of the instruments most commonly used by archaeologists to survey the underwater environment. Typically towed behind a vessel as a towfish, the instrument carries one or more transducers mounted on each of its sides which transmit short pulses of acoustic energy in the shape of a fan traveling away from the towfish (figure 4.11). These pulses are able to reflect off the seabed or objects lying on it and are registered as returns by the transducers. As the towfish moves through the water, data from each pulse are stitched together to create a flowing, two-dimensional map of the seafloor. The strength of the returning energy will determine how a particular element is visualized—for example, a metal hull will show up as a much stronger return than soft sediment. Additionally, if a feature such as a shipwreck projects into the water-column, the acoustic pulse emanating from the towfish will be unable to penetrate it, creating an acoustic shadow behind the feature. Side-scan sonars come in a variety of frequencies, with the archaeologist typically having to balance the instrument's desired resolution with the desired range of a survey. A high frequency sonar, for instance, tends to collect data over a narrower swath, but at a higher resolution. Irrespective of frequency, the area immediately below the towfish (the nadir) is invisible to the device as no pulses are sent directly downward. Therefore, the survey must be designed so that there is the necessary swath overlap in order to avoid potentially missing important targets. Side-scan sonars are, by and large, the archaeologist's tool of choice for detecting objects on the seafloor within relatively large areas. However, these instruments do not create accurate bathymetric maps, nor are they able to penetrate into the sediment. For these benefits, one must turn to two other acoustic tools.

**Figure 4.11** Side-scan sonar in use with graphical illustration of the area covered by the instrument. (Courtesy of Kongsberg Maritime)

Unlike the side-scan sonar, which is a relatively simple tool to deploy, multibeam echosounders necessitate a more complex setup that includes being mounted to the hull of a vessel or vehicle, as well as precise positioning, movement compensation sensors, and calibration. The user is rewarded, however, with the ability to create accurate bathymetric maps of the seafloor. Multibeam echosounders use transducer arrays to emit a fixed series of acoustic beams in the shape of a fan toward the seafloor, with each beam aimed at a slightly different angle (figure 4.12). The time it takes for each beam to return from the seafloor is individually measured, as is the speed of sound through water at the given location. By factoring a beam's travel time and angle, the instrument can then calculate a respective depth corresponding to each beam within the fan, creating a swath of data. As the instrument travels through the water, successive swaths create a three-dimensional model of the seafloor and any targets upon it, composed of precise depth measurements, or points. The overall "point cloud" can be used not only to detect potential archaeological features, but also to take precise measurements from one feature to another. The raw data that are collected, however, require careful processing to produce accurate results.

Neither a side-scan sonar, nor a multibeam echosounder can effectively peer beneath the seafloor to detect buried objects. This role is fulfilled by sub-bottom profilers, which have traditionally been used to image sediment layers and geological features beneath the seafloor through the use of low frequency sound waves. They are the main tool employed by researchers searching for inundated, formerly terrestrial sites, as they are able to image features such as ancient river channels that may support the identification of submerged prehistoric landscapes (figure 4.13). However, whether towed or hull-mounted, sub-bottom profilers are not frequently used as the primary survey tool on most archaeological surveys,

**Figure 4.12** Multibeam sonar in use showing the instrument's ability to record changes in the sea bottom. (Courtesy of National Oceanic and Atmospheric Administration)

as they accumulate a single stream of data directly below the instrument rather than collecting swaths of data over an area. In the context of a survey for ship or aircraft wrecks, sub-bottom profilers are best suited for providing a nondestructive source of information about already-identified buried or partially buried sites. On occasion, they are also able to determine whether an unknown target on the seafloor continues well into the substrate, and therefore is likely a geological formation, or whether it is resting on the surface, and could represent a deposited feature such as a shipwreck.

Marine magnetometers are also able to detect buried objects. Unlike acoustic-based tools, magnetometers measure the total amplitude of the earth's magnetic field, detecting variations within it. They are passive instruments, not emitting any signals, but in an archaeological context are able to detect the presence of ferromagnetic metallic objects on or buried within the seabed. In terms of archaeological artifacts, this often corresponds to iron ballast, anchors, ordnance, machinery, and chains. Magnetometers are typically towed systems to keep away from any magnetic interference associated with the research vessel, and to allow the instrument to be closer to the seafloor. This is important, as the measured intensity of metallic artifacts depends not only on their material, size, and shape, but also on their distance to the magnetometer. More advanced systems called magnetic gradiometers are able to collect information about the location, depth, and shape of a ferrous object. The main limitation of both systems is that they are unable to detect nonmetallic artifacts or features; they also typically have more narrow ranges than acoustic-based instruments such as side-scan sonars and multibeam echosounders.

It is important to note that remote sensing instruments are not usually mutually exclusive and that a general area survey will ideally involve as many different tools as possible—a multibeam echosounder to record seafloor morphology or map specific targets, a side-scan sonar as the main survey tool to detect anomalies on the seafloor, a magnetometer to identify sites that might be buried, a sub-bottom profiler to assess the potential for buried sites, and a visual capability such as a Remotely Operated Vehicle (ROV) to inspect targets further. A target-specific survey, on the other hand, may emphasize one tool over another—if looking for a semiburied historic period wreck, focusing on

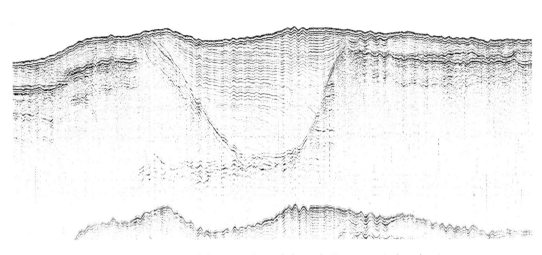

**Figure 4.13** Sub-bottom profiler record showing a buried channel. (© Wessex Archaeology)

locating its ballast pile with a magnetometer or gradiometer may be the best approach; if looking for a WWII subma-rine in flat terrain, a high-resolution sonar survey may be all that is required.

It is common practice to complete data collection through surveying parallel lines, appropriately spaced depending on the capabilities of the selected remote sensing tool(s). Potential targets should preferably be visible on multiple survey lines and, ideally, have been noted by multiple instruments in order to minimize the chances of missing or misidentifying an object of interest. The orientation of these lines may depend on the coastline, the survey area, or the selected tools themselves. Irrespective of tool selection, therefore, establishing an accurate position is critical both in ensuring proper navigation and data overlap, and also in allowing for subsequent target verification. Accordingly, all remote sensing tools have to be complemented by a capable positioning system, which in certain cases (e.g., when using a multibeam echosounder) has to be particularly accurate.

Everything in a survey should be viewed as being interrelated. One of the most important things to remember is that a survey is always constrained by its weakest link—there is little reason to opt for the highest resolution multibeam echosounder if positioning or navigational capabilities are limited. Dynamic positioning, which allows a vessel to remain stationary within a very limited footprint, is usually a prerequisite for advanced and delicate ROV operations, such as excavating a deep-water wreck. If a magnetometer is selected as the primary search tool, there is usually little reason to opt for an accompanying side-scan sonar frequency with a low resolution and wide swath, as magnetometers tend to have narrower swaths. It is therefore important when trying to match tools to resources to consider the interrelationship between all instruments and compile the toolset accordingly. Finally, remember that the human element is the measure of all things. A project may have the best platform and tools available, but may fail to accomplish its mission if it does not revolve around competent, dedicated, and knowledgeable team members.

The necessary equipment and software are expensive, and ship time on larger oceanographic research vessels can be even more prohibitively costly. To counteract the cost of buying and maintaining this equipment, many academic programs or government agencies rely upon rental or partnership arrangements when conducting research projects. These surveys need to be planned well in advance and are often paid for via grant funds. This means that large-scale surveys designed by archaeologists to determine if there are sites in a broad swath of seafloor are comparatively rare. Much more commonly, researchers will use remote sensing equipment to search a relatively small area for a specific wreck, or for areas that seem likely to be fruitful for further investigation. Researchers also employ remote sensing surveys to more fully investigate a known target of interest.

## SUMMARY

Almost all maritime and underwater archaeologists conduct surveys during their careers. These surveys can be used to locate new archaeological sites, to relocate previously recorded sites, or to determine if important cultural resources are in an area. The methods used to conduct these surveys are highly dependent upon the research questions, available time, budget, and the natural conditions of the area of interest. Sampling strategies are used to select areas to survey, with the sampling strategy chosen relative to the research questions being asked. Remote sensing surveys are generally conducted over broader areas and in deeper waters than are diver surveys, but diver surveys can seamlessly integrate target verification with target location, while remote sensing surveys locate targets that need to be verified by other methods. Whether or not an archaeological site survives underwater is highly dependent both on how the site became submerged and upon the conditions that prevailed at the site after it was inundated.

## DISCUSSION QUESTIONS

1. Numerous times in this text we have referred to humans as technological amphibians. Does this discussion of underwater research and survey convince you of this? Why or why not?
2. What are some of the reasons that archaeologists are often most interested in the sites that are hardest to find?
3. Why are research questions the primary driver of most decisions related to underwater research? Why is it important to tailor methods to research questions?
4. Why are remote sensing surveys so important to maritime and underwater archaeology?

## FURTHER READING

Blondel, P. (2009). *The Handbook of Sidescan Sonar.* Springer, Berlin.

Bowens, A. (2009). *Underwater Archaeology: The NAS Guide to Principles and Practice,* second edition. Blackwell Publishing, Portsmouth, UK.

Keith, M., Ed. (2016). *Site Formation Processes of Submerged Shipwrecks.* University Press of Florida, Gainesville.

Stewart, D.J. (1999). Formation Processes Affecting Submerged Archaeological Sites: An Overview. *Geoarchaeology* **14**(6): 565–587.

CHAPTER 5

# DOCUMENTING AND EXCAVATING UNDERWATER SITES

*Digging and Drawing without Drowning*

## FOCUS QUESTIONS

- How can the preservation of artifacts in submerged environments, which tends to be better than on land, improve our understanding of past cultures?
- What information can be gained from inundated landscapes and submerged terrestrial sites?
- What kind of information do ship and aircraft wrecks hold? What can their contents tell us about trade, colonization, warfare and the people on board?
- What do maritime technological innovations tell us about broader trends in society, history, and culture? How does naval innovation shape the rise and fall of maritime societies?
- How can we gather data in a precise and rigorous way while still maintaining archaeological sites and the data they contain for future societies?

## WHAT HAPPENS WHEN WE FIND A SITE?

In chapter 4 we discussed the various methods archaeologists use to discover underwater sites. This chapter covers what we do once we have discovered them. Despite movie portrayals of archaeologists running, swimming, or flying from site to site, breaking into long-sealed chambers to reveal gold or lost idols, most archaeological investigations are minimally invasive. In fact, comparatively few sites are excavated at all. Archaeology is a destructive science; this is a point that we keep mentioning because archaeologists are ethically bound to serve as responsible stewards for our finite maritime and underwater cultural heritage. Further, archaeological research, especially underwater, is extremely time-consuming, which means that each investigator can only properly excavate and conserve a very limited number of sites during his or her career. Finally, much research is funded by public money, so we must be careful stewards of that trust as well. Responsible archaeologists only excavate if it is necessary and if they have the ability to properly conserve the materials recovered from these excavations. What, then, makes excavation necessary? There are many answers to this question, but in essence, archaeologists excavate when excavation is the only reasonable way to answer meaningful research questions or when a site is in imminent danger of destruction.

### SURVEY FIRST, THEN EXCAVATE

After archaeologists discover a target of interest, as discussed in chapter 4, the next step is to determine what, precisely, was found. To do this, we conduct a more-intensive survey of the target area, often using the same survey method used to discover the target, but in closer intervals. If using sonar equipment, the area of interest may be covered from several different directions, for instance. This is frequently followed by a visual inspection using divers or cameras on an ROV or AUV. Many underwater sites, especially shipwrecks and aircraft, have some type of visible artifact scatter on the seafloor, so this visual inspection allows us to get a sense of the age and nature of the site.

These visual target investigations can be used for four main purposes: assessing what a target is, recording the extent and nature of a site, monitoring a previously recorded site, and conducting a topographical investigation to place a site into its broader context.[1] Several of these objectives may overlap and can be accomplished at the same time. During visual inspection, divers will use the diver survey methods discussed in the previous chapter to make an initial site map and will capture imagery of the entire site area if visibility allows. This overview, or planview, map serves three purposes: It allows archaeologists to make an initial assessment of the nature, completeness, and potential significance of the site; it gives a tangible reference point to use for planning how to organize any future work at the site, and it allows researchers to log the site with the official agency in charge of the submerged resources where they are working. Initial planview maps are drawn as though the site were on a flat surface and the viewer were floating above it like a fish. Archaeologists who are diving, unlike their terrestrial counterparts, can do just that to check the final maps for accuracy. For many sites that are never excavated, these planview maps may be all the documentation that is ever developed, so it is very important for researchers to be precise and represent as accurately as possible the exposed portions and extent of the site. If the site were to be revisited, any changes during the ensuing time would then be readily apparent.

As mentioned throughout the text, archaeologists must constantly balance answering current research questions with preserving cultural heritage for future generations to appreciate or study. They are further restricted by time and budgetary constraints. These constraints are especially relevant to underwater research, as bottom time can be very limiting for research at deeper sites, and research vessels cost the same whether a diver is actively excavating or not. Finally, recovery of any archaeological material from an underwater environment requires a long-term conservation and curation plan, necessitating additional funds, facilities, and expertise. Due to these and other constraints, archaeologists have excavated only a small percentage of the known underwater cultural heritage sites in the world. Whenever possible, archaeologists answer their research questions via non-intrusive research. For instance, the visible artifact assemblage on the seafloor is often extensive enough to determine approximately how old a shipwreck is and its probable culture of origin by comparing the observable materials to known typologies. If there are any evident ship remains, we also can assign the vessel itself to a tentative type based on the shape, framing or fastening patterns, or many other diagnostic elements (see chapter 9). In the rare cases of extremely well-preserved wrecks such as *Hamilton* and *Scourge* in Lake Ontario (chapters 4 and 12), or certain wrecks in the anoxic (less than .5 mg/liter of oxygen) and suboxic (very low oxygen and sulfur) waters of the Black Sea (see sidebar by Dan Davis), many of the questions archaeologists can think to ask can be answered without excavation at all.

## DEEPWATER ARCHAEOLOGY: A RAPIDLY EMERGING FIELD

### Dan Davis, Department of Classics, Luther College, USA

The great strides that have been made in conducting archaeological excavations underwater typically took place in diving depths of less than 50 m (164 ft). For decades the limitations of human physiology resulted in the exclusion from archaeological exploration of vast deep areas of the world's lakes, seas, and oceans. The Mediterranean, for example, known for its rich seafaring history and its deep abyssal plains, has yielded more than 2,000 shipwrecks to date, nearly all of which lie close to shore and within SCUBA depths. Until the 1980s, the technology required to provide reliable access to deeper water did not exist. In that decade, various research institutes and companies developed sophisticated remotely operated vehicles (ROVs) to enable unmanned exploration of the deep.

The field of deepwater archaeology came of age in 1989 during an expedition directed by oceanographer Dr. Robert D. Ballard and archaeologist

Dr. Anna Marguerite McCann. Hypothesizing that an ancient, open-water trade route existed between Rome's port at Ostia and the North African city of Carthage, they conducted a survey of Skerki Bank, which lies midway between those two ports in the central Mediterranean. At 800 m (2625 ft) depth they discovered the wreck of a 4th-century-CE ship, which they dubbed ISIS. The advanced ROV system *Jason/Medea* was used to map the site, and seventeen amphorae were raised for further analysis. A second expedition to Skerki in 1997 resulted in the discovery of an additional seven wrecks dating from the 1st century BCE to the 19th century CE.

Until the early 2000s, these and other deepwater archaeological expeditions consisted of wreck surveys and

*(continued)*

occasional artifact sampling. That changed in 2004–2005 when a Norwegian team conducted successful, limited ROV excavations on the early 19th-century Ormen Lange shipwreck off Norway at 170 m (558 ft) depth. In 2007, Ballard employed his advanced *Hercules/Argus* ROV system to partially excavate the fantastically preserved Sinop D wreck, which he had discovered seven years earlier at 325 m (1066 ft) depth in the Black Sea's anoxic waters. Dating to the 5th or 6th century CE, the ship lies mostly buried, its frame ends outlining a typical hull shape, but the mast remains standing and a large steering oar is visible on the main deck. At the same time, a team of archaeologists conducted limited ROV excavations of the early 19th-century Mardi Gras shipwreck (1220 m, 4003 ft) in the Gulf of Mexico. In a short time this new field has helped fill in the picture of ancient, medieval, and premodern seafaring (e.g., trade types, shipping routes, nautical technology) and now serves as a powerful complement to work in shallower waters.

Geophysical methods are essential for deepwater shipwreck searches and surveys. A typical first phase for a deepwater project consists of "mowing the lawn" with a side-scan or multibeam sonar, both of which map the seabed and permit objects to be measured accurately. Such equipment can be mounted on autonomous underwater vehicles (AUVs) that are preprogrammed for the survey, or deployed from a surface vessel. Targets are identified and assessed according to their sonar signature.

In the second phase, high-priority targets are visually identified with an AUV or ROV. AUVs can be programmed to navigate to a specific set of coordinates and initiate a local acoustic and optical survey of the seabed. Upon surfacing, their data can be downloaded and assessed. ROVs, being tethered to the research vessel, operate "live" but vary in their capability. Small, inspection-class ROVs can shoot video and still images of the wreck site with limited illumination. Larger ROVs employ powerful lights, multiple sensors, and high-resolution cameras. In general, the larger the ROV, the larger the support equipment and team required, and therefore the larger the survey vessel, and the greater the cost. Unlike excavations involving SCUBA where bottom times are limited by depth and decompression, ROV teams can operate on a 24-hour clock in rotating shifts.

Intensive investigations of shipwrecks in deep water require larger vessels outfitted with dynamic positioning (DP), a computer-controlled system that integrates thrusters, propulsion, and GPS to enable a vessel to maintain position over the wreck site in most weather conditions. In this configuration, ROVs can work on the bottom without damaging the site, or being pulled away unexpectedly. DP vessels are costly; to make such projects financially feasible, archaeologists often collaborate with oceanographers to accomplish inter- and multidisciplinary research.

If funds, expertise, equipment, and vessel allow, archaeologists can move beyond initial wreck identification and undertake site recording, artifact sampling, and excavation. The first step is to produce a predisturbance photomosaic or photogrammetric record of the site to serve as baseline for future work. A common mode of site investigation includes the recovery of a representative sample of artifact types, such as cargo, ceramics, crew possessions, and hull remains. From these artifacts researchers can glean trade practices, social history, and maritime technology.

The Ormen Lange, Sinop D, and Mardi Gras projects demonstrate that excavating a shipwreck in deep water is technologically feasible. ROVs outfitted with water jets and dredges can remove bottom sediments from around artifacts, and pilots (directed by archaeologists) can carefully excavate artifacts and move them to a basket for removal to the surface. In these cases, daily mapping runs may be made to record progress, and a digital log of all operations should be kept by the archaeologists. While methods and tools can benefit from further development, ROVs can be reliably used for archaeological excavation in deep water, even to full ocean depths.

The pace of shipwreck discoveries in deep water has increased in the past few years as archaeologists choose productive survey areas. Ballard's *Nautilus* expeditions in the Aegean and Black seas (2009–2013), for example, yielded 46 ancient, medieval, and premodern shipwrecks. The Black Sea Maritime Archaeology Project (2015–2017), discovered 60 historic shipwrecks, some of which lie extremely well preserved in the anoxic zone. While the Black Sea will continue to attract archaeological interest, other waters with similar preservation conditions (e.g., Baltic Sea, Caspian Sea, L'Atalante Basin, Orca Basin) have enormous potential to contribute to maritime history.

### EXCAVATION

In some instances, surveys do not provide enough information to answer the research questions and excavation is necessary. Many of our most interesting and complex questions can only be answered by finding portions of underwater sites that are in undisturbed context, so that we can more confidently discuss human behavior. The deeply buried sites on inundated and buried landscapes similarly require excavation to assess. Targets such as covered and preserved soil layers can be discerned through sub-bottom profiler surveys, but those subsurface layers need to be accessed directly through coring and test excavations in order to verify suspected targets and find any archaeological materials. Some sites are compromised due to environmental changes or human activities such as development, so excavation is necessary to salvage data from them before they are lost forever. Even though it would be preferable to preserve all cultural heritage sites, this is not feasible or economically viable. Thus, archaeologists excavate for two main reasons: scholarly research and data recovery to mitigate loss. These two are combined as often as possible, with excavations at a threatened site being focused on recovering information relevant to crucial research questions about the time period or culture the site represents. In fact, sites that are not considered potentially able to provide this sort of information are often not excavated at all, even if they are being destroyed, in order to reserve resources for more intact or informative sites.

Once a decision is made to excavate a site and archaeologists proceed to disturb it, we are responsible for the site and the materials we recover from it, so researchers must plan and budget for the conservation and permanent curation of the materials we remove from the seafloor. Two weeks of excavation can easily generate months of lab work and years of conservation, meaning that this responsibility cannot be undertaken lightly. As a result, archaeologists tend to sample sites, excavating only the portions necessary to answer their questions. Usually, nonrandom sampling (chapter 4) is chosen for excavation. If the site is completely buried, some sort of random grid-sampling method will be used to determine the layout and extent of the site first. If portions of the site are exposed, what is visible will guide where excavations occur to expose what is buried. Archaeologists might use probing, coring, or excavation to understand the material culture contained within a site. Excavation may occur in small test areas or in larger blocks.

## Probing and coring: exploration without digging

Probing is systematically prodding the seafloor to determine the extents of a site, often using metal rods, though water or air jets may also be used. This strategy is most often employed when the majority of a site is buried. It has the advantage of being inexpensive and time-efficient, and when employed on a grid pattern it can provide excellent information about site size, shape, depth, and even composition. Probing is best employed when working in an area with distinctly different or hard features, such as a rocky ballast pile versus a muddy seafloor as these are easy to distinguish with a probe. Probing should be used advisedly; it can be quite easy to damage site elements such as wooden timbers, especially if bottom type is not distinct from feature of interest.

Coring is next in terms of logistical complexity and amount of recoverable information. Coring involves vertically driving a metal or plastic tube through the sediments at the site, capping the tube, and pulling it out—using the suction created by the cap to keep the sediments contained inside. Coring is used by environmental scientists and geologists as well as archaeologists, so there are many types of coring devices, coring setups, and coring recommendations. Coring is occasionally employed at shipwreck sites, especially those that are buried, and it is absolutely crucial to archaeologists working on inundated terrestrial sites. Coring has several advantages: (1) It can be done from the surface using a boat as a platform (figure 5.1) or underwater with divers. (2) All it takes is a tube to collect the sediment, a means of accurately recording the coring location, a method to push the tube into the bottom, and a method to carefully extract it. (3) It is possible to gather a small cross section of all the strata (sediment layers) at the site at once; these can then be observed and sampled, allowing uncontaminated samples to be collected and the layers at the site to be described accurately.

Multiple cores can be collected in a day, so it is possible to reconstruct the geological sequence of the entire site relatively rapidly. However, coring also has several disadvantages. First, coring is usually very hard work, as some parts almost always involve brute strength maneuvering. Second, it is difficult to know what will be cored ahead of time, so it is possible to damage something important by driving a tube through it. There is also the potential to collect a core from the only anomalous portion of the site, resulting in an erroneous assessment, which is why it is important to always collect enough cores to ensure a representative sample is collected. The process of collecting cores can also deform or compress sediments within the tube by compacting them, making the strata seem thinner than they really are. Some coring methods require extracting a length of sediment and returning to the same hole to extract the next length. When doing this, it is possible to miss the original hole and collect the same sequence twice by collecting the adjacent sediments, which can make the strata seem too thick. Finally, cores are heavy and unwieldly and they must be handled carefully or the sediments within them might become mixed, making the core useless. All these caveats aside, though they require some post-field time to cut, describe, and sample, cores are many times faster than most other types of subsurface exploration.

## Excavations large and small

Both probing and coring may be done before, during, or after more extensive excavations are conducted at a site. Excavations may also proceed without probing or coring, especially when the site limits are obviously delimited on the seafloor.

**Figure 5.1** Coring a river site from a floating platform. A. Placing core tube. B. Attaching vibrocoring device. C. Driving core with coring device and manual pressure. D. Extracting core.

Most excavations begin with a small test excavation that is cleared to expose a portion of the site and provide researchers with an indication as to what is there. In shipwrecks, this test excavation, which extends either the width or length of the vessel, is often a small area around where the center of the hull seems to be, and/or a trench to expose the bow or stern of the vessel. This allows researchers to determine how big the vessel is, or, in certain instances, offers a sense of how difficult it will be to remove the ballast to look for underlying hull remains. In inundated landscape sites, a small square is excavated to expose the stratigraphy and look for artifacts within that stratigraphy. These squares are often 1 x 1 m or 1 x 2 m so that they can be excavated relatively quickly but are big enough for a diver to fit into. Several of these squares may be placed around the landscape, often near locations where coring revealed promising stratigraphy. Next, it is common to make the excavation area bigger. How much bigger is dependent upon the research questions being asked and the length of the field season, and could range from only a few more square meters to exposing the entire wreck site.

During the early days of underwater archaeology, it was very common to excavate entire shipwrecks over the course of multiple seasons, conserving all of the contents to display in museums. Some entire ships were even raised, conserved, and put on display, such as the *Vasa* (chapter 12). These full-ship excavations have many advantages: It is possible to study all of the hull remains, which allows for the most complete and accurate ship reconstruction. All of the cargo can be investigated, which sometimes causes the researchers to significantly revise their interpretations based on earlier, smaller samples from the site. People love to visit ship museums, so these sorts of excavations bring tourists, prestige, and funds that can support maintenance of the museum to an area.[2] Even so, this type of excavation tends to be less common today. Raising entire ships and conserving them is incredibly expensive and time-consuming. It is usually even prohibitively expensive to excavate entire wrecks, raise and conserve the cargo, and leave the hull underwater. Once the materials are raised, their conservation and display require both resources and appropriate facilities, but the public viewing and concordant visitor fees are not collected until months, years, or decades after the excavations have occurred, even if public interest in the site is very high.

### EXCAVATION

There is no one correct way to excavate an underwater site. In fact, the methods employed in underwater archaeology may be more variable than those for almost any other sort of science, because much of what we do and how we do it is determined by the underwater conditions at the site. These conditions can include, but are not limited to, depth, turbidity, light penetration, currents, bottom type, and marine life. At some sites, especially those in nearshore or estuary areas affected by tides, these conditions can vary greatly over the course of the day, potentially limiting when and for how long excavations can even be conducted. For all underwater excavations, diver safety must be balanced with precision in excavation and mapping. Therefore, the project director and diving safety officer (usually not the same person) will spend a great deal of pre-project planning time determining potential safety concerns. The excavations will be planned to both meet the research objectives of the project and keep the researchers safe, with safety being the first priority. If there is no safe way to collect the data with accuracy and precision, no excavations will be conducted.

## The mechanics of excavation

On terrestrial sites, archaeologists carefully use digging tools to loosen sediment that they place into buckets and transport to screens, whereupon they sift all the spoil to see if any small items were missed during digging. They generally dig in regular increments (5- or 10-cm levels are common) within each distinguishable stratum in each excavation unit, which are generally 1 x 1 m squares or multiples thereof. Larger artifacts are excavated around and mapped in place, but the smaller items are either recovered from within their corresponding trench or are found in the screen, having been removed from their context with the loose dirt. The finds for each level are recorded on a separate level form and are bagged together, so that it is very easy to see how each unit changed with depth and how each unit compared to each other at the same depth. If you are new to archaeology, we recommend consulting an introductory text for more details about how such excavations work.

Except for the difficulty of speaking with our partners, the limitations to how much time we can spend at work, the way that our tools have a tendency to float away, and the fact that our extra sediment conveniently disappears up the dredge or airlift, underwater archaeologists work in a manner very similar to our terrestrial colleagues. Very little about underwater archaeology resembles stereotypical diving. There is usually little swimming, and archaeologists spend as little time in the water column as possible. Instead, the focus is on conducting archaeological research, descending as fast as safely possible, weighing ourselves down, and, at times, even removing our fins to nullify the effects of working in an alien environment.

When excavating an underwater site, the biggest difference is that some kind of water flow is absolutely needed if the divers want to see what they are digging. Fine-grained silts easily float into the water column and can remain for hours or days in still water, obscuring any view of what is at the bottom. Occasionally, though far from typically, the currents at a site are strong enough or the sediments at the site are coarse enough (coarse sands or pebbles) that the water clears almost as fast as divers disturb the bottom. Most of the time, we need to move the sediment away from where we are digging so that small items and fine details of the area being excavated are still discernable. The two most common ways that archaeologists do this are with water dredges or with airlifts (see Excavating box). Every project has different excavation needs and constraints, so the setup of this equipment can be quite variable. Figure 5.2 shows one example of a water dredge setup. The dredge or airlift is not used as a digging tool; instead, it removes the loose sediments the diver feeds into the mouth of the suction device. Both suction devices can damage fragile items and can suck up fairly large items—including trowels, tape measures, and gloves—if the diver is not vigilant. Sediments are, instead, removed by trowel in the case of compacted sediments or hand-fanning (wafting one's hand just above the sediment to agitate the surface) in the case of sands and other loose sediments (figure 5.3).

The sediments removed by dredge or airlift are often winnowed through a series of mesh screens or bags to make sure that no small artifacts were missed during excavation. The sediment itself flows through, but items bigger than the mesh size are trapped inside the screens or bags. Mesh sizes vary greatly depending upon project parameters and available equipment; 0.635-cm (1/4") mesh hardware cloth is very commonly employed in the United States due to its regular availability.

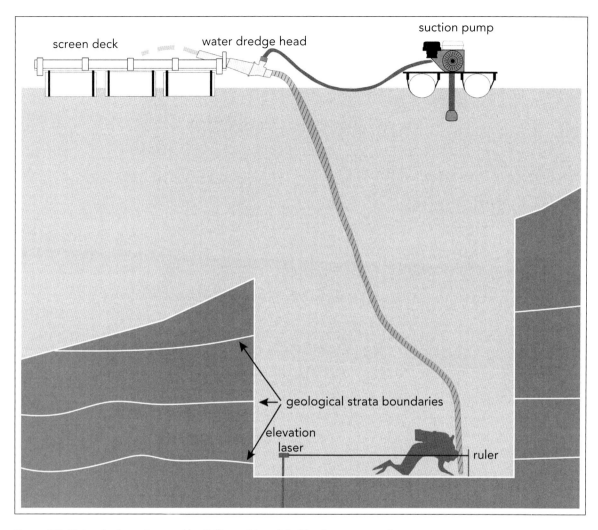

**Figure 5.2** Water dredge setup used by Halligan at inundated landscape excavations.

There are also a myriad of ways in which these screens are deployed. Sometimes the mesh bags are attached to the discharge end of the dredge or airlift and are left unmonitored. They are emptied at the end of a dive or as they fill up. Sometimes these screens are at the surface and surface support personnel monitor them regularly for cultural material that was missed by the excavation team (figure 5.2). Other methods are employed as appropriate. No matter which method is used, however, it must be noted that the materials recovered from the screen are not found in place, so they cannot provide the same sort of contextual information as those mapped in situ. Instead, these items from the screen can only be associated roughly with the other material excavated during a dive. There could still be fairly precise information about approximate artifact context if the dive team were only

**Figure 5.3** Excavating by trowel and water dredge (top), and by hand-fanning (bottom).

excavating a relatively small volume of sediment, but recovery of artifacts in the screen is much less desirable than mapping the items in place.

Just as in terrestrial archaeology, we are striving to find and excavate relatively undisturbed portions of our sites so that we can locate materials where they were left by people. Obviously, nearly all shipwrecks have been somewhat disturbed by sinking; also various portions of the wreck floated away during sinking while others eroded away prior to burial, as discussed in chapter 4. However, the relationship between the portions of the vessel and the relationship between the vessel and its cargo can still be largely undisturbed. Further, it is important to remember that ship cargos are valuable, and it may be possible that some of the patterns in the material culture are related to past salvage attempts. Finally, some of the patterns may be due to whatever caused the ship to sink in the first place, and therefore, they can tell us what ultimately happened to the vessel. Because of this, just like our dry colleagues, when we find material culture we carefully map it in place. While we dig, we pay close attention to differences in color and texture in our sediments. These differences may represent where portions of the cargo have dissolved in place, such as the slippery feel of the sands surrounding the burst flour casks in the hold of the steamship *Heroine*; or they might represent different episodes of site exposure and burial, such as the layered sands on top of and within *Queen Anne's Revenge* discussed more fully in chapters 4 and 12.

## EXCAVATING WITH WATER DREDGES AND AIRLIFTS

When diving archaeologists engage in controlled removal of sediment during the excavation process, they usually rely on one of two tools, the **water dredge** and the **airlift**. The aim of both is to remove sediment in a precise manner, affording archaeologists the ability to methodically excavate a site. The outflowing sediment of both water dredges and airlifts is usually screened, should any small artifacts accidentally be picked up in the sediment removal process.

The water dredge, also referred to as a water eductor dredge, is typically used in shallower environments, where direct access to the site from the surface can be easily established. This is because the dredge obtains its suction power directly from a pump on the surface. The head of the water dredge, which is the part manipulated by the diver underwater, receives a hose with an inflow of water pushed through by the surface pump. The shape of the head is such that the flowing water is bent and sent back out through the nozzle of a second hose attached to the head—the exhaust. The displaced water rushing out of the exhaust near the very mouth of the head creates a suction force via Venturi effect that is capable of carrying sediment, small rocks, and even larger objects, if the pump is strong enough. The mouth of the water dredge is usually 10–15 cm (4–6 in.) wide so a diver can fan sediment through it but also cover the entrance with his or her hand to prevent the inadvertent removal of artifacts in a limited-visibility environment. If any artifacts are inadvertently removed, the exhaust hose is usually either affixed to a sediment bag underwater that can be periodically recovered and screened on the surface, or is directly fed into a screen on the surface. The key challenge with a water dredge is that the surface pump needs to be powerful enough to create the necessary water flow without becoming uncontrollable. In deeper environments, the pumped water's force dissipates due to friction in the hoses and the pressure variation, and so a dredge may fail to serve its function.

In such environments, where a site's depth exceeds 10–15 m or so, an airlift is typically used. As opposed to a relying on water flow, an airlift actually uses compressed air to create suction, operating on the premise that a gas expands under less pressure. A compressor on the surface forces air down to the archaeological site through a small hose. There, an archaeologist makes use of a long, rigid tube, whose opening is about the same width as the mouth of a water dredge. In certain instances, a flexible mouthpiece is added to the tube to allow for greater maneuverability. The tube is angled with the deeper end pointed toward the area to be excavated and the shallower end aimed toward the location where the spoil is to exhaust. The tube is held in place, at the appropriate angle, using tethered weights. The compressed air hose is introduced in the opening on the deeper end of the tube; as the air rises within the tube to a shallower depth, it expands, displacing water and therefore creating suction. Airlifts are able to use this principle to remove sediments and small rocks, much like water dredges, and archaeologists can attach screening bags to the exhaust tip of airlifts to capture artifacts that are inadvertently removed. However, there needs to be enough of a depth differential between the bottom of the airlift and its top to allow for the expanding gas within to create the necessary suction. One must also be mindful of currents and wave action—not only will the airlift become difficult to handle, but if facing into a current, the exhaust may end up discharging material right back on to the site being excavated. Therefore, unlike a water dredge, which may operate freely in high-energy, shallower environments, an airlift requires a certain water depth and a greater awareness of currents and the surrounding environment. It can, however, operate at depths that are usually beyond the limits of a water dredge.

Whether a water dredge or an airlift is used, both require some practice to master. In limited-visibility environments, the archaeologist must be able to sense by hand what is being sent through either water dredge or airlift. The type of sediment being removed will usually dictate whether the archaeologist uses a brush, a trowel, hand-fanning, or hand-scooping to dislodge or release sediment into the water column and up the suction device. Rough inclusions within the sediment or cold water may mean that the archaeologist has to use gloves to protect exposed hands when excavating, limiting dexterity and tactile sensitivity. At times archaeologists cut off the tips of gloves to expose the top of their fingers as a means to maintain greater control of what is being removed. (Often excavators go through multiple pairs of gloves in a given season.) Another acquired skill is body positioning—buoyancy control is paramount as archaeologists must hover over the site when using airlifts or hold down a lively water dredge. When mastered, however, both tools can be exceptionally useful in the precise and careful excavation of an archaeological site.

There are a number of important sites discovered in waters too deep for archaeologists to visit via diving. Relatively few of these sites have been investigated to any great extent, but when they have been, it was via either small submersibles or ROVs, which are operated by pilots on board the research vessel who are running commands through an umbilical connected to the unmanned vehicle. A few of these sites have even been partially excavated by specially modified ROVs, such as the one used to carefully collect artifacts from 1,200 meters below the surface from the Mardi Gras wreck (figure 5.4).[3] At this time, most of these sites are out of the reach of ordinary academic research, but this research holds great promise for upcoming years as technology for deep exploration continues to develop and become more accessible.

## Provenience and association: mapping the site and associated finds

No matter how much of a site is eventually excavated, excavation tends to proceed in a systematic pattern in order to make sure that the data from the site are clearly and precisely uncovered and recorded. At some point, a grid, **baseline**, or control points will be placed on the site. This may be a literal grid frame that is anchored above the excavation area, allowing the divers to use it for

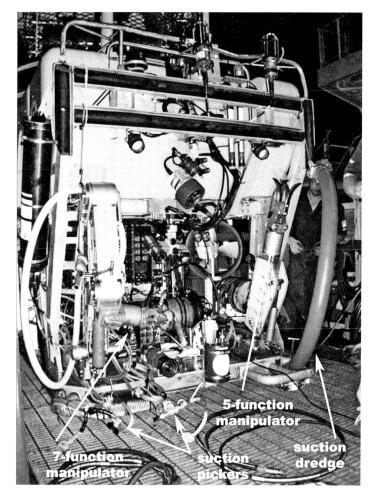

**Figure 5.4** Triton XLS-17 ROV with specialized archaeological equipment. Note the five-function manipulator on the right and the seven-function manipulator on the left, the suction dredge on the extreme right for excavation, and the suction pickers in the left foreground to lift delicate items.

measurement and stowage of equipment (figure 5.5). It may be a series of points relative to the site, such as "between frame 1 and frame 2, starboard." It may be a baseline tape measure that is affixed to the center line of the shipwreck. There may be a series of control points marked out by nails, pin flags, or other markers. In any case, these markers will be used for mapping the site and to record the **provenience,** or grid location (northing, easting, and elevation), of each find, allowing it to be tied to the master map of the site.

Remember that archaeologists are most interested in determining the context of the materials in order to recreate human activities. To do this, we have to determine how the artifacts, ecofacts, features, and sediments at the site are associated with one another. Carefully recording the provenience and finds and making maps of the natural stratigraphy at the site can help clarify these associations and also help clearly demonstrate them to other researchers.

Sometimes a site grid is placed before any excavation at all occurs. Sometimes test excavations occur first to allow the grid to be aligned to the site in a logical manner. All grids have an origin point, or **datum,** from which all other measurements are based. This point is ideally left at the site permanently, so that any future research can be oriented in the same manner and associated to the same origin point, limiting duplication of previous efforts. Accordingly, it is important to position at least this control point in a place that will not be disturbed or removed by later excavation. Ideally, it should be placed within view of the site but away from any remains. This control point should preferably be tied very precisely to a GPS location for easy relocation. All of these things can be difficult or impossible in certain underwater conditions. Accurate underwater GPS is still in the future, so marker buoys at the surface must serve to mark northing and easting (Y and X) using a shipboard GPS, while elevation (or Z) needs to be obtained by diver's depth gauges, tape measures pulled down from the surface, or other error-prone

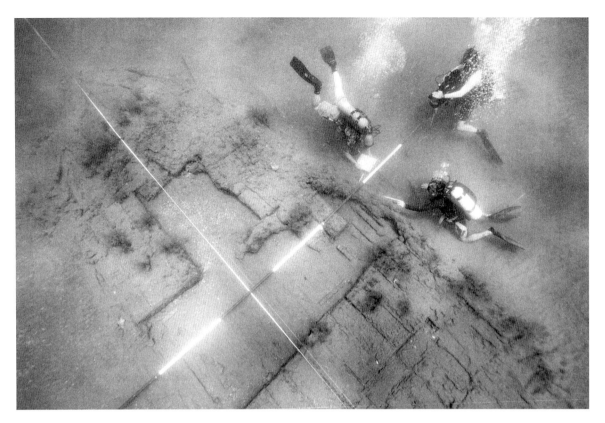

**Figure 5.5** Grid frame used on *Nuestra Señora de Encarnación* shipwreck, lost off the coast of Panama in 1688. (Courtesy of National Geographic Society. Photograph by Jonathan Kingston)

measures. Therefore, the datum at an underwater site is rarely georeferenced with the level of precision that terrestrial sites enjoy.

Even though a researcher often must accept some uncertainty in terms of the overall site location, the relative positioning of mapped elements on a site map can be extremely precise. Archaeological sites need to be mapped in three dimensions, although some maps focus more on the horizontal dimension (planview maps) while others focus on the vertical dimensions (profile or section maps). Maps can be made of the entire site, or more in-depth drawings can be created of an individual excavation area or feature (figure 5.6). Trilateration is one of the most accurate ways to make planview maps of sites with dramatic elevation changes or very irregular artifact distributions. This method is frequently employed at sites of all types with many different bottom configurations as it requires little technology, minimal setup, and only basic training. Two divers with a few control points, a clipboard, and two tape measures can quickly and rather accurately mark the locations of features on a wreck, scatters of artifacts, or the extent of a site. See the Trilateration box for more discussion of how this works.

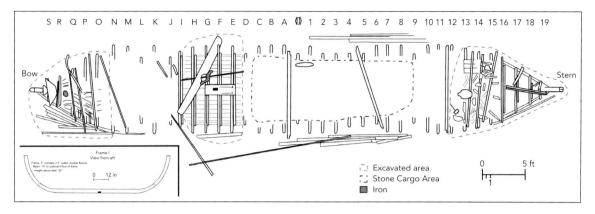

**Figure 5.6** Plan map and section recorded after minimal excavation using baseline offset and trilateration measuring techniques. Durham boat wreck located in Oneida Lake, New York.

## TRILATERATION

Several core principles and practices of archaeology—establishing provenience and the relationship between artifacts, conducting stratigraphic analyses, interpreting a site as a whole, publishing final reports so that peers can independently re-interpret collected data, and so on—rely on accurate documentation. One could argue that the very application of the scientific method to archaeology depends to a significant degree on mapping a site accurately and comprehensively, particularly when it comes to the destructive excavation process. Underwater archaeology has just as much need for precision and accuracy in mapping as terrestrial archaeology, despite the additional complexities associated with operating in a submerged environment without the surveying tools typically used on land. Several ways to map an archaeological site underwater have therefore been developed, each carrying its own mix of precision, expense, and effort. Some of the more advanced approaches map a site in three dimensions, while others represent the 3D world on a 2D site plan. Certain approaches map a site in a georeferenced manner, meaning that everything is mapped in absolute terms and can be positioned in the real world. Others rely on relative mapping, positioning each element in relation to each other, without necessarily tying everything to the real world location; in these instances, perhaps a single GPS point may be sufficient to tie the whole site to its global position. Each approach has benefits and drawbacks and selecting the appropriate one often depends on time, resourcing, and objectives.

One of the most widely accepted methods for relative mapping underwater, whether conducting a non-intrusive cursory survey or a multiseason full-scale excavation, is **trilateration**, largely because it is generally efficient, inexpensive, and accurate. The essence of trilateration mapping reflects its meaning—"of three sides." In trilateration, three specified points serve as the vertices of a conceptual triangle, where the length of each side of the triangle is related to the length of the other two sides and two vertices are control points with known locations, while the third is a measurement of interest. The recorder will set at least two datums (technically the plural of datum is data, but archaeologists ignore this grammatical convention to avoid confusion between measurements and points of reference). Datums are key positions on or around a site that will not be moved or altered for the duration of an excavation or survey; they can, for example, be iron rods staked into the ground, natural rock formations, or buckets of cured cement with a clearly demarcated central point. All other relative measurements on a site will depend on the positioning of the datums.

There can be as few as two (though more are preferable), and often times the geographical position of a single datum is used to tie the site to the real world. It is very important to collect both bearing and distance between the datums, and good practice to record in both direction— both from Datum A to Datum B, and Datum B to Datum A—as a means of verifying the accuracy of the measurement and bearing. Once the datums are established, every other desired point can be related to those datums through recording distance measurements without the need for a bearing. Though technically measurements from only two datums are necessary to position a target, three measurements are recommended as this approach provides for greater degree of certainty, as well as the ability to estimate one's range of error.

For example, let's assume four points on a site need to be mapped—the muzzle of a cannon, the eye of an anchor, the center of a piece of ballast, and an unidentified concretion. By measuring the distance of each of those points to two established datums with a tape measure, an archaeologist can reconstruct the conceptual triangle mentioned above (with the two datums and the point to be measured serving as vertices) on a 2D plan. If we want to create a 1:10 scaled plan of the archaeological site, we then draw an arc (either with a compass or digitally) 1/10 of the real measurement in the direction of the ballast from Datum A, and a second arc 1/10 of the real measurement in the direction of the ballast from Datum B. Without knowing the precise bearing of either measurements, the two arcs will intersect and pinpoint the location of the ballast in relation to the two datums. The practice can be repeated with each of the remaining three artifacts, positioning each in relation to the datums, and ultimately to each other.

If one does not know the relative location of each artifact to the datums and draws full circles around the two datums, each with its corresponding radius, a second point of intersection will occur. This is one of the primary reasons why three datums are usually considered the minimum number required to reliably map an archaeological site; the

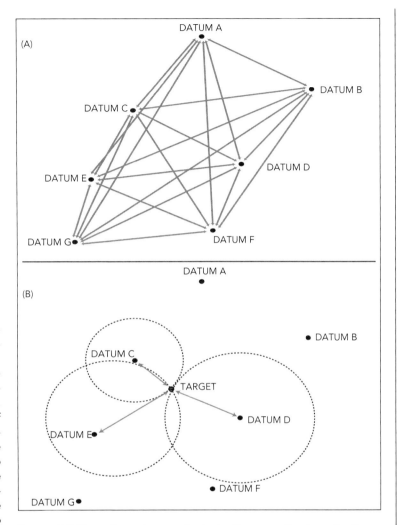

**Figure 5.7** The trilateration method. A. Datum calibration. B. Datum measurement.

addition of third measurement correctly identifies which of the two points of intersection along the circles represents the relative location of the ballast block. In fact, many archaeologists add a fourth to ensure that there is a means to correct any errors in the original measurements. Imagine if the third datum brought in above to settle the argument had a wrong measurement associated with it; instead of limiting the possibilities of accurately placing the ballast block from two to one, it would instead add to the uncertainty. In some cases, even more datums are required to account for the morphology of the site—slopes, rocky outcrops, depressions, or large artifacts often get in the way of an accurate measurement, while stretching a tape measure underwater too far will invariably bring in a degree of error. This may seem redundant, but remember, once an artifact has been removed from its context, an accurate site plan may be the only thing that accounts for its provenience.

Once the appropriate number of datum towers has been established and their positions related to each other, accurately mapping a site with just a single tape measure becomes both possible and efficient (though always bring backup tapes because many a dive has been ruined because equipment broke, was lost, or floated away!). All a diver needs to do is write down the three measurements relating the three datums to an artifact, and that artifact can be accurately positioned on a site plan. For larger artifacts, additional points might be measured so as to account for the artifact's orientation. In the case of an anchor, for example, oftentimes its eye and the tips of the two flukes are recorded. With the advent of software applications that can digitally trilaterate based on input measurements, any erroneous measurements can easily be identified and flagged; if mapping in real-time, they can be promptly retaken. Overall, with proper methodologies to ensure errors are minimized and some experienced diving archaeologists, trilateration can result in the development of site plans that are accurate to within just a few centimeters. At the same time, it is a versatile technique that can be used to quickly collect basic measurements when first encountering a site, and a tool that should be in every underwater archaeologist's tool box.

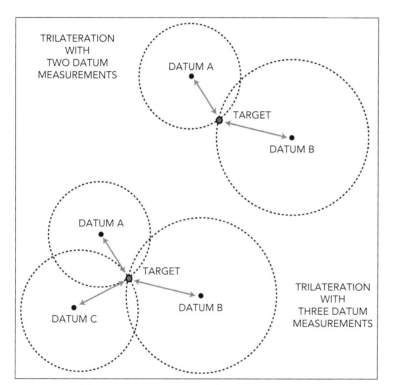

**Figure 5.8** Trilateration using two or three datums.

Often when a site is not large or we need to make a precise map of a small area, archaeologists use the baseline offset method instead (figures 5.9 and 5.10). This method was described in detail in chapter 4, and it works the same way for surveying a site and for making either a profile or a planview map. When developing planviews, the baseline is marked with a tape measure laid along the centerline of a ship's assemblage or the south wall of an excavation square; when recording a vertical section or profile view, it is often laid along a line of known elevation. A second tape measure, held perpendicular to the baseline tape, is used to measure the amount of "offset" of the point of interest. For instance, if trying to draw the curved section of a frame, a horizontally level tape line is marked above it. Measurements are taken from this tape line vertically downward to the frame at regular intervals and at every important feature (such as the ends of a timber). These distances, or offsets, can be recorded on a chart, which can be used to later draw the outline of the frame, or they can be directly drawn on gridded drafting film underwater.

Ships are full of curved parts fitted together in a myriad of complicated ways, so shipwrecks can be especially challenging to record. If any portion of the hull remains, accurately recording the curves of this hull can be critical for reconstructing the size, shape, and type of the vessel. Even the small amount of potential error that is introduced by using an offset measurement can be too much. For curved ship timbers, we can improve measurement precision through the use of a goniometer, or digital angle measuring tool, placed in a waterproof housing. The goniometer is positioned at one end of the timber and the angle of the curve is recorded on a chart. It is then moved so that the right end starts exactly where the left end stopped for the first measurement, the next angle is taken, and so on, until the entire length of the timber is recorded. The length of the goniometer housing is then recorded, so that we know how far apart our angle measurements were. We can then transfer this information to graph paper with a ruler and compass, and accurately draw the shape of the timber to scale.[4]

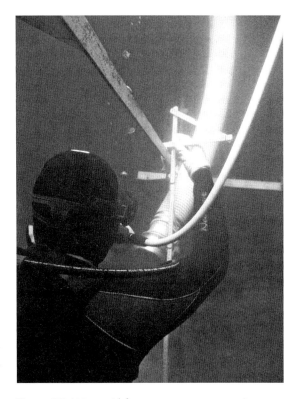

**Figure 5.9** Using grid frame to map an excavation area. North and east measurements are collected directly from the frame. Elevation is measured below the frame, which is at a known depth. Diver is recording soil layers at an inundated terrestrial site.

**Figure 5.10** Using a control point and baseline to map a site. The laser (the instrument at right center) is at a known elevation, northing and easting. North and east are collected by stretching a tape from this point to another control point on the grid 1 m away to use as the baseline, as seen in image, while the second tape is used to measure the offset of the point of interest. Elevation measurements from this point are taken by tape measure below the laser line that shines across to the location of interest.

Whenever possible, archaeologists will also photograph the site during every stage of excavation. Sometimes the underwater visibility is too poor for video or photography, but having a visual record can serve as a valuable backup to field notes and can help to resolve fine details during project writeup. When these photos are planned properly, and appropriate grid markers are made visible, they can be used to make photographic site plans, or photomosaics, by fitting them together (figure 5.11). Recent software innovations have also made photogrammetry increasingly useful to archaeological applications (see Photomosaics and Photogrammetry box).

Between diver mapping and photographic recording, sites can be recorded in two and three dimensions with ever-increasing precision. This is very important.

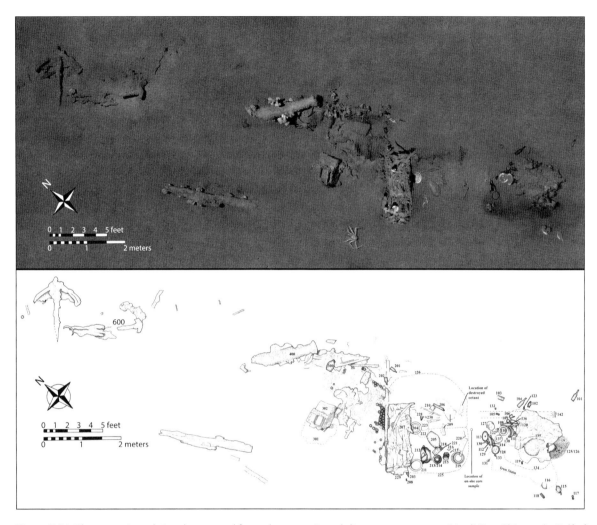

**Figure 5.11** Photomosaic and site plan created from photomosaic and direct measurements. Mardi Gras Shipwreck, Gulf of Mexico. (Ford et al. 2008)

Divers can get cold and tired or suffer from nitrogen narcosis, and fingers get numb on long dives, and occasionally some measurements are missed, recorded incorrectly, or measured incorrectly. Therefore, it is important to also begin drawing the desired map, plan, profile, or section as soon as possible after the dive, so that inconsistencies can be noted immediately and corrected during the subsequent day's diving. A video is an excellent backup, but it is no replacement for close human scrutiny, and should not be used as such unless the site is inaccessible to divers.

## PHOTOMOSAICS AND PHOTOGRAMMETRY

The limited visibility often encountered in underwater environments, combined with the scale of some underwater archaeological sites, means that it is frequently not possible to photograph them in a single frame. Since the 1950s, therefore, photomosaics have been used to document underwater sites by creating composite 2D images composed of multiple photographs, with each depicting a section of the whole. Photographs leading to a photomosaic can be taken by divers, ROVs, or AUVs. Irrespective of the method, however, there are several elements that go into producing an accurate photomosaic of a site in order to mitigate or minimize distortions resulting from parallax, lenses, camera angles, and height of exposure.

Among the key areas that need to be considered when planning for a photomosaic are the height of the camera over the site to be documented, the degree of overlap between sequential images, and the systematic pathway of the camera. In order for images in a photomosaic to share the same magnification, they must be taken at approximately the same height from the seafloor or feature to be documented. Height selection is dependent upon the illumination and clarity of the water. It is important to determine at what elevation the desired level of detail fades away and if a strobe light can be used, or if the flash will merely illuminate particulates in the water column. Finally, the time available for documentation of the site can be paramount. The closer to the seabed one is, the more photographs will be required to record the whole site. Height, therefore, cannot be considered independently, for it is intrinsically tied not only to the time available, but also to the degree of overlap between sequential images. Due to a series of distortions and errors associated with underwater photography, which are accentuated the farther away one gets from the center of an image, a significant degree of overlap is required between images to create an accurate photomosaic. Typically, the extreme edges of a photograph are simply cropped to limit distortion, meaning that each sequential image should

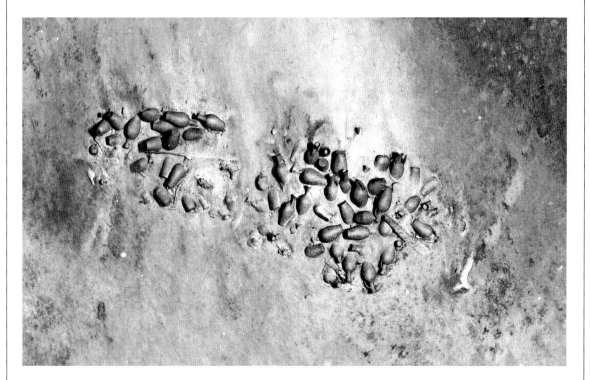

**Figure 5.12** Photomosaic of Chersonessos A. (Courtesy of Ocean Exploration Trust / C. Roman (URI))

overlap in content with the one that preceded it by as much as 50 percent. Finally, the path—whether a grid, track, or otherwise—which the camera will follow must be planned in advance, and the prescribed methodology must also take into account how fast the diver or vehicle holding the camera will be moving, and how frequently a photograph will be taken. Ultimately, once all the images are collected and digitally processed with today's digital darkrooms, the results can be visually flawless.

It is important to remember that, although accuracy is consistently on the rise, photomosaics are still usually relied upon as complements to other survey methods. This is not always the case, though, particularly in deepwater

**Figure 5.13** Photogrammetry model of Alexandria, VA shipwreck 44AX229 (right) and photogrammetric recording (left). The image at right is not a single photograph but a 3D model of the shipwreck created from many photographs. (Courtesy of George Schwarz and Tiago Fraga)

environments where photomosaics collected through the use of advanced ROVs and AUVs may now serve as the primary means of documenting a site. In such instances, bathymetric data collected at the same time can serve as a framework upon which a digital photomosaic can be draped, combining the two datasets to develop a photorealistic virtual model of a site.

Photogrammetry attempts to create three-dimensional models through the collection and processing of photographs without the need for additional data sets. First introduced in the context of underwater archaeology in the 1960s on the Yassıada Byzantine wreck, stereophotogrammetry permitted 3D measurements to be obtained from overlapping pairs of stereometric photographs. Requiring precise camera positioning, both in terms of distance from the subject and between parallel lenses typically mounted on identical cameras, stereophotogrammetry also usually necessitated a professional photogrammetrist to postprocess the collected images. More recently, the advent of digital image-capturing and purpose-developed software led to a new technique called convergent photogrammetry. In this type of photogrammetry, software utilizes the position of a camera when a photograph is taken, including distance from the subject and angle of the lens, to project lines from the camera into space. When three or more photographs capture the same feature identified by the user from different angles, a 3D point in space can be interpolated through the use of software calculations that correlate the intersection of the associated line projections. This process is aided by the inclusion of reference points within photographs that can be recognized by the software or identified by the user in the postprocessing phase. A plethora of images from a variety of angles is required to create accurate photogrammetry models, and significant time and computing power is spent post-processing the visual data.

The benefits of convergent photogrammetry over stereophotogrammetry are numerous and substantive, including the fact that photographs can be taken with handheld cameras, positioning does not have to be prescribed, and photographs at different magnification levels can be interrelated. Provided that a sufficient number of photographs from a sufficient number of angles are taken, and points are carefully interrelated to the greatest resolution possible (sometimes down to the pixel level), a 3D photorealistic model of the archaeological site can be created. Convergent photogrammetry models are based on an underlying point-cloud, much like those resulting from laser scans, and though not yet quite as accurate as the latter, permit the derivation of measurements from an archaeological site that can meet or exceed hand measurements in accuracy and consistency. In addition, such models can be easily scaled to document entire sites, or individual artifacts, and the same process can be undertaken in the field or in a laboratory, with little in terms of equipment costs. Photogrammetry, therefore, is expected to become increasingly common as a documentation method, adding another level of information to the otherwise 2D photomosaics.

## Recovering material culture: from ships to soils to sherds

After we have mapped our material culture in place, we have to decide what to do with it. This may seem obvious; after all, we are excavating to find things. Should we not then be bringing our finds to the surface to study them more completely or to display in a museum? We do need to recover some artifacts in order to study them, but not all material culture is recovered from every excavation, depending upon the research questions. For instance, if a ship is covered in several hundred tons of ballast stone, is it really necessary to collect every stone? If the cargo was a load of coal or bricks, how much could we learn from seven tons that we could not learn from seventy pieces? How much of a ship do we raise? The entire thing? Only a fragment? None at all? If we do the former, we need to have an enormous amount of infrastructure in place in order to responsibly conserve the recovered materials. If the latter, will we be able to effectively address our research questions? Permanent storage space is limited, as is the resourcing necessary for conservation. Material left on the bottom is oftentimes in a relatively stable state and in a relatively stable environment, so leaving it in place at the wreck site can be a viable and cost-effective solution for site preservation. In short, maritime and underwater archaeologists commonly collect relatively small samples of the materials from underwater sites.

For instance, if there are thousands of sherds of amphorae, we may institute a random sampling strategy in order to collect a representative sample for sourcing studies, typological studies, residue analyses, or other sorts of studies as discussed in chapter 3. If there are intact barrels of goods, only a few may be raised, or all of them may be recovered for more in-depth analyses. At a shipwreck site, we may only raise loose timbers, or we may selectively collect timbers representing key portions of the site, such as the keel, hull planking, and frames. In fact, we may collect wood samples for several purposes. Species identification and DNA studies may help determine where the ship was built and the strategies employed to build it. Wood samples are also used for dendrochronology and/or radiocarbon dating, though it is important to be selective when choosing a wood sample and to date several samples if possible because ships can be used for years before sinking. Larger cores of wood—at least 5 cm—are best for dendrochronology, as the lab needs to assess a large number of rings for comparison purposes. For radiocarbon dating, it is best to select samples representing the shortest-lived species possible, as such samples are more likely to reflect the actual age of the site. For both of these analyses, it is important to keep recovered samples wet until sending them to the lab. Drying wood cracks and deforms, and rapidly becomes useless. For radiocarbon samples, keeping them in the dark prevents UV damage—it is also important to refrain from adding any chemicals if possible. The laboratory conducting the desired analysis typically provides sample collection and handling guidelines in line with the latest methodologies, and, at times, might also be directly involved in the field collection process itself.

We can learn important things from ecofacts as well, and they are nearly always sampled rather than collected in their entirety. Divers will collect sediments from around and within the site to analyze for site-formation processes, and to sample them for microfossils and/or residues of various kinds. Such sediments may be collected from cores, from grab samples while excavating, from within artifacts, or from excavation walls. Ballast stone is sampled for sourcing studies and to help understand how the vessel was moving about the oceans. It is common to collect portions of the barnacles attached to the wreck or of the shell scattered within the site's sediments for similar reasons and to help understand site-formation processes. We may sample some or all of the bone at the site depending upon whether we think it was introduced to the site via human agency or due to natural processes.

How, then, do we recover these materials? Some are small, and they are simply put into plastic bags filled with water and brought to the surface. Many others require creativity. A trip to the surface with large, awkwardly shaped, or fragile artifacts can be quite difficult for both artifacts and divers, who need to carefully ascend at a set rate and monitor gauges with one hand, leaving only one for managing samples or artifacts. Fragile artifacts need to be stabilized before they can be brought to the surface, so we frequently place them in some sort of supporting framework or bin. We also may have lift mechanisms in place to allow items to be raised by team members on the surface or have dive teams swim items to the surface in tandem. For large and bulky items, we often utilize lift bags, which are bladders that are brought to the seafloor, attached via ropes to the item, and filled with air just until the item starts to float very slightly. These can be tricky because as the item is swum to the surface, the diver must monitor the bag and let air out to keep it from ascending uncontrollably and endangering the artifact as the air expands due to decreasing pressure. Lift bags come in various sizes, with corresponding variance in lift capability, ranging from a few kilograms to a few metric tons, allowing archaeologists to raise a small timber or an entire marble column drum (figure 5.14).

Archaeologists and marine salvors have also invented numerous ways to raise very large pieces of vessels or entire vessels. If a vessel is intact enough, this might include filling the hull with air, or if the vessel is more fragile, it will require a supporting frame or series of straps, a crane, and some sort of platform, such as was used for the Medieval cog raised from the Ijssel River in the Netherlands in 2016, or the *Mary Rose*, flagship of Henry VIII, which was raised in 1982 and underwent decades of conservation (see chapter 12)[5]. In both of these cases, an active conservation plan was in place prior to recovery.

Less well-thought-out was the raising of *Alvin Clark*, a lumber schooner built in 1847 and sunk 1864 in Green Bay, Wisconsin. It was raised in 1969 by sport diver Frank Hoffman who ran steel cables under the ship, attached them to a barge, and winched it to the surface. At the time of its raising, it was so intact that the ship still floated and could be re-rigged (figure 5.15). Hoffman, who had no conservation plan for the vessel, displayed it as a tourist attraction, but the vessel started

**Figure 5.14** Using lift bags to lift a column capital from the Kızılburun shipwreck, Turkey. (Courtesy of Institute of Nautical Archaeology. Photograph by Don Frey)

to deteriorate soon after being removed from its stable environment at the bottom of the lake, and the museum did not generate enough money to offset the costs of raising the vessel, much less pay for conservation. This led to decades of the vessel slowly degrading while Hoffman tried to find a buyer. In 1994, after almost entirely rotting away and being partially burnt, the remnants of the vessel were bulldozed and demolished completely.

## Some practical considerations

Because of the tension between economics—budgets and time—and data, archaeologists need to be very practical about how we excavate. Underwater archaeology is almost always much more expensive than its terrestrial counterpart for several reasons. First, and most obviously, in most cases, it requires people to work underwater, which requires diving gear, motors to provide air supply or compressors to refill air tanks, and redundant safety systems for life support. This includes surface support staff, usually almost equal in number to the divers, and pairs of divers to work together to complete the same task. Second is the mechanics of excavation: while it is possible, depending on project budget, to have a large number of excavators at terrestrial sites, there can only be a few people excavating an underwater site at a time due to logistical and safety considerations. Further, during an ordinary day at a terrestrial site, an excavator may dig for eight or more hours. A three-hour dive is extremely long when working at most underwater sites, and two dives over the course

**Figure 5.15** The *Alvin Clark* soon after raising. (Courtesy of Great Lakes Historical Society Collection—Historical Collection of the Great Lakes at Bowling Green State University)

of the day is the most that is usually possible. Each underwater team typically needs its own dredge, airlift, or other form of sediment remover and usually its own power source to run it. Safety personnel need to monitor this system. If sediments are being screened, each screen also needs to be monitored periodically. There also needs to be a person logging finds and beginning initial conservation.

Excavation notes need to be completed at the end of each dive, before a diver can return to the water. If record-keeping is not emphasized, much of the excavation data will be lost and the time underwater wasted. Excavators and surface staff need to be hydrated and divers usually need to warm up and decompress after their dives. Pumps, generators, and breathing air systems need to be cleaned, maintained, and fueled. During the working day, anywhere between two and ten small engines will be running, creating a cacophony on the surface. This is when everything is working properly. On an average day, a small amount of time is lost to malfunctioning equipment or weather delays; on unfortunate days, hours are spent repairing critical support paraphernalia or storms delay the project for the day.

Why, then, is the expense of underwater excavation worth it? This textbook provides numerous examples of the wealth of information about past people that can only be found underwater. The excellent organic preservation that can be found in underwater sites is one of the main reasons to conduct maritime and underwater excavations. Many of the things that can be found underwater cannot be discovered anywhere else in the world. Ships were rarely stored on land for posterity, so the *only* place shipping technology and elements of seafaring culture are systematically preserved is underwater. Other types of sites may have originally underwater versions have better organic preservation, such as the Page-Ladson site discussed in chapter 7. The excellent preservation of inorganic artifacts such as ceramics or glass bottles recovered from underwater sites may provide a context through which universally applicable artifact typologies or dating sequences are developed. Some exceptional artifacts, such as ancient Greek or Roman bronze statues, have almost exclusively been found underwater; on land, the valuable raw material prompted reuse and recasting. While these well-preserved artifacts can provide a wealth of information about past lifeways, excavation and recovery require conservation and special care immediately after they are discovered. After all, as soon as they are exposed to light, oxygen, and warmth, they begin to decompose and degrade, potentially leading to their complete loss if they are not cared for.

### CONSERVATION AND CURATION OF ARCHAEOLOGICAL MATERIAL

Maritime and underwater archaeology is dependent upon conservation. It may take years or even decades before the excavated materials are properly conserved and stable. Therefore, it is especially important to budget for these potential expenses during initial project planning. Preservation and stabilization of these materials is often the realm of specialists in maritime conservation, who ideally are involved with the project from the outset. In general, archaeologists try to keep an artifact as stable as possible from the time of its excavation until it begins conservation. Therefore, after initial recovery, we try to keep all artifacts wet in the same water as they came from, in rigid bins with lids to avoid evaporation. We try to keep them as cool and dark as possible to avoid the growth of fungi or bacteria. Finally, we label everything with clearly marked tags associated with provenience information in order to be able to tie the items back to their proper location on the site map.

In the conservation lab, the materials will begin the slow process of final conservation. Artifact conservation methodologies vary greatly according to, among other things, material type, size, and the environment from which an artifact was recovered (see the Donny L. Hamilton sidebar; see also the Conservation: What Can Be Found? sidebar in chapter 13), making conservation a very complex science involving equal parts chemistry, physics, and artistry. Organic materials must be treated differently than inorganics. Metals must be treated differently than stone. Different metals must be conserved differently than one another, and composite artifacts—those that contain multiple materials, such as an axe with a steel head and a wooden handle—must often be conserved differently than either component alone would require. Further, materials recovered from saltwater are typically processed differently than those recovered from fresh water, as any salts that have permeated into an artifact must be slowly and carefully removed prior to further treatment.

During this process, new discoveries are often made as fine details become apparent through the painstaking process of removing decades of encrustations and marine growth. Drawings, photographs, and videos are used to record all of the recovered material from the site as it undergoes various stages of analysis and conservation in order to track its progress and condition throughout the entire process. Artifacts may also be imaged in other ways, especially if they were recovered from saltwater contexts. For instance, it is often impossible to tell what might be located within a single concretion, a corroded mass that forms in marine environments in the presence of and around iron. Concretions are therefore regularly x-rayed, permitting researchers to non-invasively gain an impression of what lies within. X-rays can be very useful for determining what might be within a concretion, or even if any of the original materials remain extant. If the original artifact within a concretion dissolved away leaving behind a void, conservators can still create a cast of the artifacts, gaining a replica that is useful for study.

## BASIC CHEMISTRY AND TECHNIQUES OF ARCHAEOLOGICAL CONSERVATION

Donny L. Hamilton, Director, Center for Maritime Archaeology and Conservation, Texas A&M University, USA

Conservation of excavated artifacts from archaeological sites should be a given for all areas of archaeology; however, as I tell my students, "Maritime archaeology is the only field of archaeology that is totally tied to the conservation laboratory," for without proper conservation most of the excavated artifacts will degrade and be lost for a myriad of reasons. The major problems created for conservators when treating artifacts from maritime sites are:

1. high levels of soluble salts in seawater and brackish water,
2. disfiguring maritime encrustation encapsulating metal objects, and
3. corroding metal artifacts.

Any porous archaeological material such as ceramic, bone, wood, or leather (most organic material for that matter), and even sedimentary stone will absorb soluble matter in seawater or brackish water. This includes high levels of sodium chloride (common table salt), which have to be removed. Otherwise, once the salts in the porous artifacts dry, they expand and create enough pressure to cause the material to split, crack, and exfoliate the outer surfaces; pottery and bone artifacts can

*(continued)*

be severely damaged. The soluble salts are removed by taking an artifact though a series of baths of fresh water, or by placing it in a vat with fresh water continually running through it until the removal process is complete. After desalination, the surface of porous and fragile ceramic and siliceous artifacts usually needs to be consolidated with a synthetic resin such as polyvinyl acetate or Paraloid B-72.

On the majority of maritime archaeological projects, and especially those that pertain to shipwreck sites, wood is the most commonly found organic material. When wood is submerged in water its soluble elements—starches, sugars, mineral salts, and tannins—start leaching out, making it more porous and consequently more waterlogged. The water then starts to break down the cellulose in the wood and eventually even the lignin in the cell walls. Ultimately, the water itself may be the only thing maintaining the overall shape and physical integrity of the wood. Following desalination, if a wooden artifact is not further stabilized, the surface tension of the evaporating water may cause its cells to collapse, which results in an artifact shrinking severely, warping, and splitting. The most common stabilization treatments in such cases involve either (1) replacing the water within an artifact with polyethylene glycol (PEG), a water-soluble wax; (2) freeze-drying; or (3) a combination of both.

Other organic material such as leather, cork, and a lot of plant material will be completely saturated with water. If the water is not replaced with something to support the underlying cellular structure, severe shrinkage will occur. Leather reacts in water much the same as wood does, with the tanning material and soluble substances being leached out. If not conserved, the leather typically shrinks into an inflexible, stiff, brittle, dark-colored version of its former self. Leather can be treated by the same PEG treatments and freeze drying techniques used for waterlogged wood. The molecular weight of the PEG used determines the degree of flexibility.

Even glass, which is usually the most stable material in a historic site, will break down in water. The sodium or potassium in the glass surfaces can leach out, leaving a layer of dull-colored devitrified "dead glass" on top of a well-defined layer of preserved glass below. If the "dead glass" flakes off, the original surface of the glass is removed, leaving an uneven layer of unaltered glass. In some instances, the glass can be completely devitrified. The devitrified surface can harbor soluble salts, which, once crystalized by drying out, will flake the dead glass off the surface. Thus, any soluble salts have to

be removed with water baths and then consolidated with polyvinyl acetate, Paraloid B-72, or silicone oil to secure the corroded glass surfaces in place.

The conservation of metal artifacts is a major component of maritime archaeology. For the most part, such conservation deals primarily with the metals of antiquity—gold, silver, cupreous metals (copper, bronze, and brass), lead, tin, iron, and zinc—with iron, cupreous metals, and silver presenting the biggest challenges. More recently, however, modern materials such as aluminum alloys have been added to the mix, challenging previous conservation approaches.

A primary problem in the conservation of metal artifacts from a marine environment, especially in subtropical and tropical areas, is the formation of marine concretion around their outer surfaces. This is particularly true for objects made of iron and, to a lesser degree, those made of other metals. The concretion layer can form around a small, single artifact, such as a nail, or around massive or complex pieces such as anchors, cannons, and machinery parts. Encrustations can weigh several thousand pounds and often encapsulate a large number of different artifacts. Every encrustation needs to be stored wet, in an alkaline solution that both retards metal corrosion and keeps the concretions from drying out, which will make them considerably harder and more difficult to remove.

A variety of tools, such as hammers and chisels, pneumatic chisels, and even dental picks are used to remove concretion layers. In order to alleviate the risk of any damage to the encapsulated artifacts, radiographic x-rays are required to identify the location of different materials and the condition of the artifacts themselves. The encrustation may also contain natural molds of small artifacts that have completely corroded away, leaving hollow forms that can be cast with epoxy to create a perfect replica of the original artifact. In order to support the archaeological interpretation of artifacts and maintain the association between them, or between natural molds, the conservator is required to document all the artifact associations in each encrustation.

Once an encrustation is carefully removed, the conservation of the extracted metal artifacts can then proceed. When present, wrought iron and cast iron have traditionally presented the biggest challenges. One has to be aware of the fact that alone of all the metals of antiquity, iron does not appear anywhere on Earth in a metallic state other than in iron meteorites. Basically, iron does not like to be in a metallic state, and in the presence of moisture and oxygen it oxidizes to a rusty ferric state. The problem is that when the iron converts to a ferric state, it expands to more than twice the volume of the original iron. In the process of transforming into expanded, exfoliated layers of rusty iron, the original surface of an iron artifact may be destroyed. An additional compounding problem is the presence of any iron chloride corrosion products; these convert to hydrochloric acid, which then attacks any remaining metallic iron, creating more iron chlorides. The corrosion process continues until there is no metallic iron remaining.

Electrolytic reduction is the main conservation technique used to remove any residual concretion and iron chlorides. In the process, the ferrous corrosion products are reduced to magnetite, which preserves the corrosion layers and thus the original surface of iron artifacts. Wrought iron and mild steel are by far easier to conserve than cast iron, which I refer to as the "metal from hell," because of the enormous size and weight of some cast iron artifacts, and problems such as brittleness and graphitization that corrodes the iron, leaving a fragile graphite framework in its stead.

Following electrolytic reduction, the iron artifacts are rinsed thoroughly to remove any residual chemicals and are then coated with a tannic acid solution to convert the surfaces to corrosion-resistant ferric tannate, which also turns the surface of the iron black. The artifact is then sealed with microcrystalline wax or marine paint in order to create an environmental barrier. However, a conserved iron artifact is still made of iron that will corrode once more if exposed to moisture and oxygen. Thus, all conserved iron artifacts have to be properly curated or displayed, and periodically evaluated and retreated if necessary.

Cupreous metals preserve much better in marine environments, second only to gold, but they are all subject to copper chloride corrosion products. In such instances, cuprous chloride converts to hydrochloric acid, which attacks any remaining metal in a manner similar to that described for iron above. Therefore, it is important to remove the chlorides from the metal.

Again, electrolytic reduction is commonly used to solve this problem and is generally effective in converting the copper corrosion products back to a metallic state.

It might be assumed that, being composed of a noble metal, silver artifacts excavated from an archaeological environment would be found in good condition. In a marine context, however, if silver artifacts are buried in sediment and covered with marine encrustation, an anaerobic environment is created where anaerobic sulfate-reducing bacteria produce hydrogen sulfide, which in turn attacks the metal, creating silver sulfide. In some cases, a coin can be completely converted to silver sulfide, which is very brittle and crumbles easily. In fact, sulfide corrosion products are some of the most common corrosion products found on metals of antiquity recovered from a marine environment. By electrolytic reduction or by a chemical reduction process using sodium hydrosulfite and sodium hydroxide, the silver corrosion products can be converted back to a metallic state, preserving the details present in the corroded sulfide layers. Silver corrosion products do not present any detrimental problem for long-term preservation as most are reduced to a metallic state during the treatment of the silver. The conservation is oriented toward preserving the details on the silver surfaces.

Similarly, artifacts of lead, tin, and pewter (an alloy composed of varying percentages of tin, copper, and lead) do not need to be conserved in order to ensure their long-term preservation, but are treated to reveal additional details otherwise obscured, and to make them look more like the metals they represent. Electrolytic reduction and a variety of chemical treatments are used as deemed appropriate.

In conclusion, conservation is a critical part of any maritime archaeology project. It cleans the artifacts so the diagnostic attributes can be seen, it stabilizes the objects for long-term preservation and museum display, and it contributes as much data as the actual excavation, guaranteeing the overall success of the archaeological project.

Sometimes, especially with extremely fragile items, CT (computed tomography) scans are used to generate three-dimensional (3D) representations of the interior of artifacts, ecofacts, or human remains. A CT scanner works by taking a series of sequential X-rays, known as "slices," which are then combined by computer. It is also increasingly common to gather and generate 3D models of the exterior of objects using laser scanners or photogrammetry. These techniques allow us to create virtual models that can be shared with researchers, be used as documentary records, fulfill outreach functions, or even be printed to create 3D copies of artifacts. These new technologies have allowed us to share underwater and maritime archaeology with the general public in new and exciting ways, and helped collaborative research by making it possible to share data to a degree that was difficult in the predigital world. When conservation is complete, the materials may be put on display, such as *La Belle* and its contents at the Bullock Texas State History Museum (chapter 6), or they may be returned to the excavators for final analysis, publication, and stable storage.

As we will discuss in more detail in chapter 6, the final, and most important, step in all excavations is publication and outreach. If the data from an excavation are not made available to other researchers and the general public, no matter how painstaking the excavation, the effort did not represent professional archaeology; instead, it was slow and inefficient looting. Unpublished excavation is, in many ways, worse than no excavation, because the site has been destabilized and materials were removed from their original context with no concurrent gains in knowledge. Because of the time it takes to conserve the material from underwater sites, publication of these sites can take longer than many terrestrial sites, but publication remains crucial.

## SUMMARY

In this chapter we have discussed the methods used to excavate underwater sites, justifying the effort and the expense because of the unique nature of underwater material culture. It is comparatively rare to excavate entire shipwrecks or other underwater sites due to cost and the logistical complications of raising and conserving the materials. In fact, archaeologists today usually only excavate when it is the sole way to answer their research questions, or to recover information from a threatened site before it is destroyed. Archaeologists have developed numerous techniques to recover precise information from these underwater sites. We can make very accurate maps through various drawing and documentation techniques. We can excavate very precisely with water dredges and airlifts. We can recover even very small materials, including microfossils, by collecting bulk samples and cores and by screening the materials we have excavated. There are many ways to excavate underwater sites, and the most appropriate method for a given site will be one that correctly balances the research questions and budget with the environmental constraints of the site, such as depth, visibility, and water temperature. All underwater materials need to be conserved if they are raised, which needs to be considered in the project budget from the very beginning. This process can take years, delaying the final, most important stage of the research: publication.

**DISCUSSION QUESTIONS**

1. What are the main considerations that constrain underwater excavations? How might these differ from the concerns of terrestrial archaeologists or underwater researchers in other fields?
2. Chapters 4 and 5 have presented a brief overview of underwater fieldwork. What aspect of underwater research seems most appealing to you? Why?
3. Why is it often more important to not excavate a site?
4. Why is maritime and underwater archaeology "the only field of archaeology that is totally tied to the conservation laboratory?" What benefits do you see potentially arising from this relationship? What challenges?

**FURTHER READING**

Bowens, A. (2009). *Underwater Archaeology: The NAS Guide to Principles and Practice,* 2nd edition. Blackwell Publishing, Portsmouth, UK.

Green, J. (2016). *Maritime Archaeology: A Technical Handbook,* 2nd edition. Routledge, New York.

Hamilton, D. L. (1999). Methods of Conserving Archaeological Material from Underwater Sites, Revision 1. *Conservation Files: ANTH 605, Conservation of Cultural Resources I.* Texas A&M University, College Station. Accessible at http://nautarch.tamu.edu/CRL/conservationmanual/ConservationManual.pdf.

Kelly, R. L. and D. H. Thomas (2013). *Archaeology: Down to Earth,* 5th edition. Wadsworth Publishing, New York.

Mary Rose Museum (2017). The Mary Rose Museum. Mary Rose Trust, Portsmouth, UK. Accessible at http://www.maryrose.org/.

Underwood, C. (2013). Excavation Planning and Logistics; The HMS *Swift* Project." *Oxford Handbook of Maritime Archaeology.* A. Catsambis, B. Ford and D. L. Hamilton, eds. 133–160. Oxford University Press, New York.

## CHAPTER 6

# PUTTING IT ALL TOGETHER

## *How to Get from Site to People*

### FOCUS QUESTIONS

- How have people interacted with seas, lakes, and rivers? How was this interaction shaped by their culture and environment? What are the similarities, differences, and outcomes of these interactions?
- What information can be gained from inundated landscapes and submerged terrestrial sites?
- What kind of information do ship and aircraft wrecks hold? What can their contents tell us about trade, colonization, warfare, and the people on board?
- What do maritime technological innovations tell us about broader trends in society, history, and culture? How does naval innovation shape the rise and fall of maritime societies?
- How did maritime people shape world history?

### ARCHAEOLOGICAL SITES ARE EVIDENCE OF HUMAN BEHAVIOR

The previous chapters describe how we do underwater and maritime archaeology, but the work of an archaeologist does not stop with excavation or even artifact conservation. The last step is always the interpretation and dissemination of the new information that was uncovered, answering the questions "What does the site tell us about the human condition?" and "How can we share that information with others?" The sites and artifacts that we find are mute. They cannot speak for themselves, so it is up to the archaeologist to interpret them. We do this by working backward from the recovered object to its conceptualization, and along the way we learn a lot more about the people who had the idea and made the object. As the archaeologist David Hurst-Thomas once said, "Archaeology is not what you find, it's what you find out."[1]

TABLE 6.1 **SCALES OF INTERPRETATION**

| Scale | Social Unit | Data |
|---|---|---|
| Locale | Individuals | Artifacts and Features |
| Site and Environs | Group | Sites and Isolated Finds |
| Domain | Culture | Sites and Landscapes |

The task of making sense of the finds is best completed by the archaeologists that recorded the site. They have the most intimate knowledge of the site, saw it in person, and have the firsthand memories to fill any gaps in what was recorded, making them the best suited to form the necessary connections and breathe life into the people that created and inhabited the site. More than just a practical issue of knowing the site better than anyone else, publication is an ethical mandate. If an archaeologist excavates a site but does not interpret and publish the results, she or he is no better than a looter who pillages a historic shipwreck for personal gain. An important part of archaeology is sharing what we find with other archaeologists and the general public.

When interpreting an archaeological site it is useful to think about it at three scales: (1) the artifacts and features that make up the site, (2) the site and its immediate environs, and (3) the larger, even global, framework of the site's inhabitants (table 6.1).

## Artifacts and features

Artifacts and features are the most direct evidence of past cultures because they are the residue of earlier human activities. The meals that people ate, the tasks they completed, the ways they passed their leisure time all tend to leave behind some mark in the archaeological record. By carefully analyzing the context of individual artifacts and features and by determining associations between artifacts and features based on that context, archaeologists can reconstruct what happened in a particular part of a site. This is usually recorded as a series of measurements, drawings, and, increasingly, digital data describing the horizontal and vertical position of everything found at the site. With that information, it is possible to determine what features and artifacts are close to each other, which were used earlier or later in the life of the site, what artifacts were found within a particular feature, and other important observations. The interpretation of what happened in that specific part of the site at a specific moment is based on the associations between finds, and the associations are based on context.

For example, a hypothetical early boatbuilding location might appear as a scattering of stone tools and a bit of burned earth (figure 6.1). Through context we would know that these artifacts and features are associated because they all occur on the same former ground surface and are in close proximity. While studying the

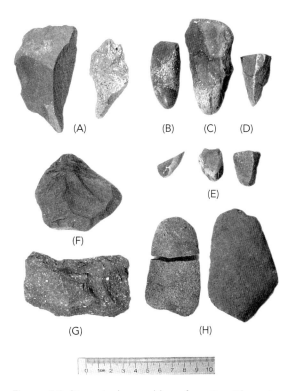

**Figure 6.1** Stone tool assemblage from San Clemente California that is associated with early Holocene boat-building. (Courtesy of Jim Cassidy)

context of the finds we might also note that they are near a shoreline and that there is a vacant place in the spread of tools where something is missing (maybe the boat). Analysis of the tools would reveal that they were used for woodworking and a reading of ethno-historic accounts would reveal that fire was often used to char the inside of boats to make the wood easier to scrape and shape (figure 6.2). The relationships between the finds led to the conclusion that they are related, which led to an interpretation of how they came to be associated; in this case through the process of building a boat. If a later group of people came to the same place and built a ship, the artifacts and features from that activity would be near the boatbuilding finds but in a stratum closer to the modern surface. We would not say that this material culture was associated with the older material because it was found in a different layer, making it clear that it was deposited at a different time. Because these materials were not associated, we would not interpret them as being part of the same activity, although we would certainly take note of the continued use of the same location for similar activities through time.

As in the case of the boatbuilding location, there is always a deductive leap from what is found to how those items were used. This act of interpretation is what makes archaeology, archaeology. It is also what introduces the subjective, the art, to what would otherwise be a technical endeavor of collecting field data. Diving can be learned in a weekend and a competent excavator trained in a matter of weeks, but the knowledge and skill to properly interpret an archaeological site takes years of study. For that reason, interpretation is not something to take lightly. Proper interpretation must take into account all of the available data and must weigh that data against all other possible interpretations. Each interpretation is the product of applying everything that the archaeologist has experienced, learned, and read to the relationships between the features, artifacts, and surrounding environment. Even then, there is no guarantee that the interpretation is correct, so the archaeologist also tests and retests earlier interpretations as new finds become available. The pattern of artifacts and features described above could have been created through other activities, but the archaeologist may deem that none of the known potential activities fit the available data as well as the process of building a boat, so for the time being the boatbuilding interpretation stands. Through the publication process, however, other archaeologists are able to reassess the same basic set of data

**Figure 6.2** Native Americans of the eastern United States using fire to remove the interior of a log boat. Also note the use of fire to fell the tree in the background.

reported by the original excavator, and in doing so revise or refine the original interpretation until a general consensus arises.

## The site and its environs

Once an archaeologist has interpreted one set of associated artifacts and features, she or he moves to the next scale of interpretation by analyzing the site and its environs as a whole. This is done by combining all of the associations from across the site to form an interpretation of what happened in all excavated areas of the site. The same rules of context apply at this scale, and the archaeologists construct their interpretation based on the parts of the site that are contemporaneous. For instance, the boatbuilding location may have only been one part of a larger site. The site may have included a place for repairing nets, an area where fish were smoked, a shrine to ask for safe and prosperous journeys, houses, and an array of other activity areas that made up daily life for the folks that lived there. There may have also been nearby places outside of the site such as fields where crops, including gourds to be used as floats, were grown, outcrops where stones to be used as net sinkers were gathered, and special houses where sailors purified themselves before a long voyage. In order to understand life at the site, the archaeologist needs to interpret all of these pieces and bring the elements together in much the same way that one of the site's inhabitants could have moved from activity to activity and from role to role during the course of a day.

## The larger framework

Just like your normal life plays out in a relatively limited number of places, moving from home, to school, to work, people in the past had a relatively circumscribed lifestyle. For the most part, the unscripted drama of their lives played out on the stage of an individual site. However, just like you are affected by overseas wars, the global economy, or an international trip, people in the past formed part of larger cultures and a wide network of social relationships that stretched far beyond the confines of a single site. This became increasingly true as humans traveled farther and farther across the water. For this reason, it is valuable to look well beyond a single site when forming an archaeological interpretation.

The maritime people of a culture almost certainly interacted with family, friends, partners, rivals, and leaders who never left the shore. Part of understanding maritime archaeological sites is understanding the associated nonmaritime sites. Both the maritime and nonmaritime people of a society are represented by sites spread across the domain of that society. This domain might be very large. At the height of its empire, Spain claimed much of North and South America, as well as lands along the coasts of Africa, in the Middle East, India, Southeast Asia, and islands in the Pacific. This global empire was serviced by Spanish ships crewed by sailors from disparate portions of this empire. Thus, any single Spanish shipwreck from the Imperial Period should be viewed as part of this larger network. Maritime peoples also often found themselves affected by outside events. Many of the peoples that the Spanish invaded as they spread their empire had coastal and maritime adaptations of their own. The coming of the Spanish caused them to adapt their culture to best survive, avoid, or take advantage of the situation as they perceived it at the time. Thus, these indigenous maritime peoples were impacted by the developments in Europe that led to Spanish expansion even though many of them were not previously aware of Europe. If we, as archaeologists, have the goal of understanding past cultures, we need to draw on a wide range of archaeological sites and, when available, written, iconographic, and oral histories to contextualize our finds within the tangled web of past human existence.

Looking beyond an individual site and its environs also allows us to compare sites through time. Cultures spread and interacted through time similarly to how they spread and interacted through space. One of the strengths of archaeology is its ability to look at how cultures change over long periods of time, and to compare cultures across time and space to elucidate what makes them similar or unique. We are not limited by human memory or the antiquity of writing; we can investigate and compare human behaviors from hundreds of thousands of years ago through yesterday. Pulling together comparative information from across the spectrum of human existence allows archaeologists to make important and well-supported arguments about what it is to be human. It also requires archaeologists to keep up to date with new developments and finds in the archaeological and anthropological literature, as well as to conduct a thorough literature search whenever interpreting a site.

To return one last time to the boatbuilding location described above, an archaeologist could use that site as an entry point to explore how boatbuilding developed in that area through time and as a way to investigate how cultures with a similar technology solved the problem of building boats in a variety of different regions. These investigations would then lead to interesting interpretations of how human cultures develop, how they adapt to seafaring, and what other factors affect a group's ability to thrive in a maritime environment.

### THE INTERPRETATION OF MARITIME AND UNDERWATER SITES

Much of the preceding discussion applies as well to terrestrial archaeology as it does to underwater archaeology. Interpreting maritime and underwater sites, however, does vary in subtle ways from what is practiced on land. In particular, maritime and underwater archaeology requires the ability to reconstruct human habitation of now submerged landscapes, to view the maritime environment from a range of perspectives, and to be able to reconstruct a ship from a few timbers.

## Draining away the water

In order to study submerged settlements and determine how past peoples used a landscape, we need to virtually drain away the water and reconstruct what the landscape looked like before it was inundated. This is both one of the most technologically and most anthropologically demanding tasks in underwater archaeology.

Archaeologists often become aware of submerged sites through serendipity: artifacts found in dredge spoils, tools and bones recovered from fishing nets, underwater finds reported by recreational divers, or items washed ashore. This mode of identifying sites supports the truism that archaeologists rarely discover anything. More often than not, someone already knows about the sites we are seeking. It is up to the archaeologist to build the relationships and ask the questions that allow community members to lead them to the site, and then, most importantly, it is up to the archaeologist to properly study and interpret the site so that its lessons can be broadly understood and disseminated. For these reasons, it is very important for archaeologists to build relationships and trust within local communities through good communication and an understanding that goodwill and information must flow in both directions.[2]

## Marc-André Bernier, Manager, Underwater Archaeology, Archaeology and History, Parks Canada, Canada

When asked about the most important thing one has done in a career in underwater archaeology spanning almost three decades, the question that comes to mind is: "Did I even do something important?" But while struggling with the original question, the answer to the second one quickly became quite clear to me. And the moment when it occurred is still as vivid in my mind as if it happened yesterday. The date was 10 November 1990. The place was the North Shore of the Gulf of St. Lawrence, in Quebec.

I was one of three members of Parks Canada's Underwater Archaeology Team who had just been sent there to take possession for the Receiver of Wreck of two cannon that had been recovered by sport divers presumably from the 1693 *Corossol*. As our flight from Ottawa stopped in Quebec City, a Royal Canadian Mounted Police (RCMP) officer boarded the plane with the Receiver of Wreck himself to deliver us a mandate letter to recover the cannon. Freshly hired by Parks Canada (I had started in June of that year), I was quite impressed with the flamboyance of this man, barging into a plane with a Mountie to save historic goods from the villains. But this, I also thought, may turn out to be a more dangerous venture than I expected if they were acting with such "conviction."

Once arrived in Sept-Îles, Pete Waddell, Jim Ringer, and I took our rental van to the house of one of the so-called culprits. Winter was already there, and winter on the North Shore is brutal. I was glad that Pete, an ex-linebacker from some midwestern university, was one of us, and that Jim (slightly smaller but with a biker's mustache) was as well. When the door opened, I was stunned to see our "bad guy": Jeannot Michaud, a short, rounded man with a gentle voice. A high school teacher, as it turned out. He showed us one of the two cannon, lying in his backyard under a foot of snow. The other cannon was in the basement of his friend, Richard Tachereau, who had decided that a couple of coats of shellac was better for heritage than 30 cm (12 inches) of snow.

We had a good chat with these guys. They had all been afraid of us, federal government officials sent by the RCMP. We quickly informed them that we were as surprised as they were to see how this had escalated so quickly. And we took the time to listen to their story. It turned out that they had recovered the two cannons and brought them to the local museum to prove that the long-sought-after *Corossol* had finally been found. All with good intentions. The next day, we all worked together to put the cannon back in the water, facing -20°C (-4°F) temperatures and uncooperative winds (I have to admit, if I had brought a good pair of mitts for the two-hour open-boat ride, that alone may have qualified as the most important thing I did . . .). We ended up working on the *Corossol* with the Sept-Îles group in 1991 and again in 1994, side by side on a wreck that, in the end, had very little aside from 8 cannon scattered between huge boulders. But it is one of my favorite wrecks.

Then it happened again. In 1994, seeing the project and partnership going so smoothly, I was approached by another diver from the area, intrigued by the unexpected collaboration between government and sport divers. He wanted to show me something but was testing me beforehand. I listened to him, he listened to me. I explained what we were doing. It took a while, a few other encounters, before he trusted me enough. And then Marc Tremblay finally took me to his cottage where he handed over some of the artefacts he had recovered from the *Corossol* shortly after its discovery. He had spent years looking for it, and couldn't help but go out to it when he heard the news that it had been found.

The day after Christmas of 1994, I came back to my apartment after spending the holidays at my inlaws'. Among the endless messages from relatives and friends captured by the answering machine wishing us a Merry Christmas was one from an excited Marc Tremblay. While snorkeling out to recover his boat mooring before the bay in front of his cottage froze over, he saw a wreck in 3 m (10 ft) of water. Filled with hundreds of objects.

Muskets, pistols, shoes, pipes, bones. A week later, I was on a snowmobile with Tremblay and his buddy Patrice Deschênes en route to his Baie-Trinité cottage, dive gear in tow. We dove together on what we later found out was the *Elizabeth and Mary*, a 45-ton New England barque carrying militiamen from Dorchester, Massachusetts, lost on its return trip to Boston after the unsuccessful 1690 siege of Quebec City. For the next three summers, the *Elizabeth and Mary* blessed us with an incredible collection of more than 6,000 unbelievably well-preserved artifacts and an unforgettable experience. Divers from an avocational organization born out of the project—the Groupe de Préservation des Vestiges Subaquatiques de Manicouagan or GPVSM—spent half of the 2,100 hours underwater excavating alongside archaeologists. Twenty years later, the GPVSM still exits. They have been, and still are, an active voice in the preservation of the rich maritime heritage of the North Shore.

I've had the chance to be part of wonderful projects, discoveries, and publications, and have had the privilege to represent my peers and field at UNESCO. But in retrospect, I could probably not have been as successful with these if on 10 November 1990, I had not learned the value of listening to members of the community to hear their perspective on underwater heritage. And this is likely the most important thing I did as an underwater archaeologist: learn to listen.

In areas where archaeologists suspect there might be submerged settlements but none are reported, it becomes necessary to apply the remote sensing tools described in chapter 4 to peer through hundreds of meters of water and also through the seafloor or lakebed. In order to narrow the search area, archaeologists use predictive modeling. Predictive modeling is a GIS technique that uses a series of georeferenced superimposed maps (e.g., terrain, proximity to water, etc.) backed with databases to determine the most likely locations for settlements based on what we know about how people used similar landscapes. This is a highly anthropological technique that requires the archaeologist to consider why people used a landscape and what sorts of factors figured into those uses. Archaeologists often answer these questions through the analogies discussed in chapter 3. Based on these analogies, it is possible to input specific variables into the model and predict the likelihood of human settlement on previously unstudied areas. By combining the map of what was destroyed by rising seas and the areas with the highest probability of containing archaeological sites, it is possible to create a new map showing the highest probability areas that are still intact—the areas indicated on this final map become the first place to look for submerged settlements.[3] Whether anything is found or not, the resulting information is entered into the predictive model to help refine its parameters, increasing the chances of success on the next expedition.

Recent work by archaeologists from the University of Michigan along the Alpena-Amberley Ridge in Lake Huron (figure 6.3) nicely illustrates the process of reconstructing a submerged human landscape. They realized that during times of lower water (approximately 10,000 to 8000 years ago), the Alpena-Amberley Ridge would have been an exposed landform connecting modern Michigan and Ontario. Using existing data about the ridge, they were able to model when it would have been exposed and begin to reconstruct its environment. Taking this one step further, the archaeologists enlisted the help of computer scientists to create a learning

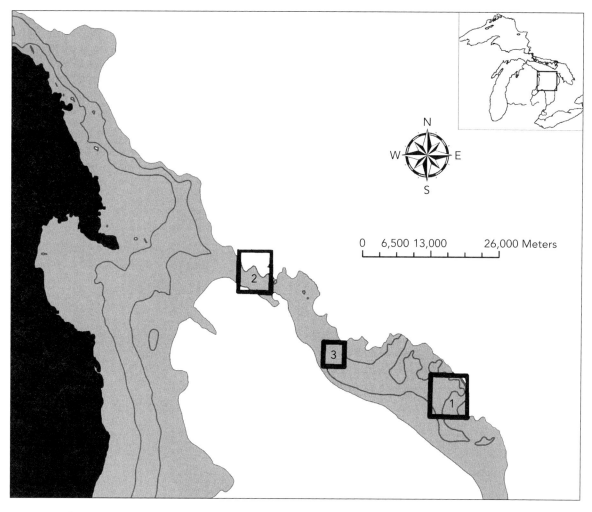

**Figure 6.3** Alpena-Amberley Ridge survey areas (black squares). The modern land is shown in black, the area exposed at low water in grey, and the surrounding water in white. (Reprinted with permission from Sonnenburg, Lemke, and O'Shea, *Caribou Hunting in the Upper Great Lakes* (University of Michigan Museum of Anthropology 2015), page 109)

virtual reality model to predict how generations of caribou may have migrated across the ridgeline. This model and other data helped identify survey areas where sonar was used to map the lakefloor. In some of these locations, the Michigan archaeologists identified stone hunting blinds and drive lanes that were likely used by some of the earliest residents of North America to hunt caribou (figure 6.4). The drive lanes were structures used to direct the movement of caribou toward the hunting blinds where the hunters hid waiting for them. That these are human-made features is attested by the presence of stone tools and debris around them. These findings indicate that the hunters were shifting from following herds to building permanent facilities to take advantage of migrating herds and have implications for how early communities adapted to shifting environments and

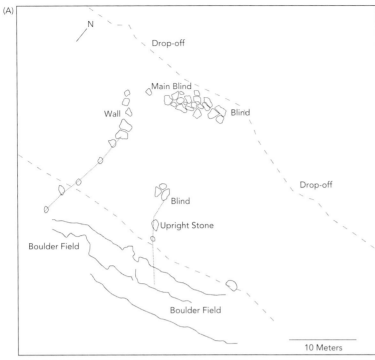

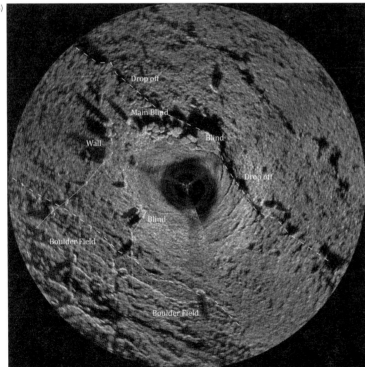

**Figure 6.4** Example of submerged hunting structures on Alpena-Amberley Ridge. Bottom image is a scanning sonar image, top is an archaeological interpretation. (Reprinted with permission from Sonnenburg, Lemke and O'Shea, *Caribou Hunting in the Upper Great Lakes* (University of Michigan Museum of Anthropology 2015), page 128)

resources. Future work will continue to explore how indigenous Americans used the ridge and how they adapted as it sunk beneath Lake Huron.[4]

## Seeing water through another's eyes

A fundamental aspect of maritime archaeology is to understand how maritime people perceived and interact with the water. Yet, we all see water in our own way— a way influenced by our personal interactions with water, and, more powerfully, through how our culture and subculture interacts with water. Think about all of the stories you have read about water and seafaring, all of the warnings you received about water ("don't swim for at least 30 minutes after you eat, or . . ."), and all of the other subtle and not-so-subtle ways that the people around you have influenced your perception of different types of water bodies. The same thing happens in practically every culture, especially those that are adapted to seas, lakes, or rivers.

The way that a society perceives the water is translated into its interactions with water, which, in turn, leave a material record that archaeologists can find and interpret. Cultures build docks, fish weirs, dams, ports, and other structures to facilitate their use of water and its resources. They fill some areas, dredge others, and reserve specific locations for specific activities, both sacred and profane. They pollute some areas and keep others remarkably clean. The decisions behind these and other practices are based in the economic, social, religious, and other structures that undergird that particular culture. In this way, the landscape is a form of material culture just like an artifact: It starts as an idea in someone's mind, an idea that is formed by their experiences and culture, and is then made physical and is recoverable through archaeological methods. However, while most artifacts and features have a short life, lasting for a generation or less, landscapes are formed over multiple generations, and the changes of one generation affect the next generation, so that each generation works with not only the natural environment but the environment as modified by those who came before.

The coasts of Ireland provide a good example of these processes. Different cultures have settled and resettled the same locations along the Irish shore. In some instances, earlier uses influenced later uses, such as the consistent use of certain places to trap fish. In other cases, new technologies caused inhabitants to re-envision their relationship with the sea, such as the use of tides to power mills as well as trap fish. Some aspects of being adapted to a maritime world were consistent across millennia of Irish coastal residents, including aligning their lives to the rhythms of the tides or appreciating both the horror and potential windfall of a shipwreck through the bodies and goods that wash ashore. Other aspects changed through time as different groups brought their own worldviews to the shorelines. In recent times there has been a shift from coasts as difficult places of work to places of recreation and beauty, which has drawn new populations who use and treat the coasts differently. A similar pattern is also evident in the Pacific Northwest of North America where urban dwellers are increasingly moving to the coast for its recreational value and in the process destroying culturally important indigenous archaeological sites.[5]

The landscape is also literally and metaphorically a living thing that prompts and reacts to human activities. It includes plants and animals that move, return, and regrow in response to human activities, but which also strongly influence where and how humans do things through their presence, absence, and ability to flourish in a given environment. The landscape also includes sediments that accumulate or erode like the calluses on a hand, tides that rise and fall like breathing, weather that seems to attack, and many other nonorganic processes that through their own complexity and the complexity of their interactions with each other give the impression of a living thing, or at least a thing controlled by more-than-human powers. Thus, the landscape is not simply the receiver of human changes or the stage setting of human actions, it is an active player in cultural adaptation and human-nature interactions. Humans and the environment have a recursive relationship in which changes to either has the potential to affect the other. This back and forth between humans and nature, with subsequent cultures building on and adapting to the landscapes of their predecessors, causes many maritime archaeological landscapes to become **palimpsests**, with material culture from multiple periods layered on top of each other.

Since interaction with a landscape varies with culture, two or more groups living in the same area can easily have multiple perceptions of, and interactions with, the same physical space. Especially during the colonial periods, very different views of the same landscape could come into contact. Another example from the North American Great Lakes illustrates this point. Both indigenous and European groups recognized the Great Lakes as important places that facilitated travel and contained valuable resources, but which were also dangerous to the unprepared or the unlucky. They disagreed, however, on the source of the danger. Europeans tended to focus on storms as the major source of danger, seeing the lakes themselves as relatively benign. For many native peoples, the threat came from within the lake in the form of an other-than-human entity named Mishebeshu who variously took the form of a horned serpent or panther, lived beneath the lakes, and was responsible for many of the accidents on them (figure 6.5). While associated with waves, Mishebeshu was distinct from storms and was, in fact, the enemy of the Thunderers.

Native and European residents of the Great Lakes during the 17th to 19th centuries saw the same water but saw it in fundamentally different ways. In part, this may have had to do with differences in their watercraft. Native American bark canoes were susceptible to swamping and puncture but were generally safe from storms because they tended to be worked near the shore. If a storm arose, the canoe could be easily pulled ashore until the weather passed. It is worth noting that Mishebeshu often lived where a sheer rock face met the water, and was considered most dangerous when crossing open water, the two instances when a canoe was most at risk. European ships, on the other hand, were relatively safe from normal waves or submerged branches, but were at risk during storms that could drive the vessel uncontrollably ashore—the very place where canoes are the safest. The types of watercraft and perceptions of danger are only two of the many religious, economic, and seafaring traditions that formed a self-reinforcing feedback loop between how each group saw, used, and interacted with the Great Lakes landscape.[6]

Agawa rock painting, Ontario

Parkers Landing petroglyph, Pennsylvania

Darky Lake rock painting, Ontario

Ojibwe Mide chart

**Figure 6.5** Representations of Mishebeshu.

## Reconstructing ships from shipwrecks

The last major interpretive skill that sets maritime and underwater archaeology apart from its terrestrial sibling is the ability to reconstruct an entire ship from the few surviving pieces that often remain on an archaeological site. The site formation processes discussed in chapter 4 are important in determining what portions of the ship survive and how the remaining timbers relate to each other. Since ships were among the most complicated machines that any culture made, it stands to reason that their interpretation is a bit more complicated than the average archaeological site. Much of this complication is because of the related facts that a working ship is a volume, not a surface, and that ships were designed to survive various and fluctuating pressures as they moved through the water. In order to interpret a shipwreck, we need to reconstruct it in three dimensions from the flattened and incomplete remains, understand how it functioned as a vehicle, and interpret the nature and roles of people and cargo that were carried on board. The artifacts found within a shipwreck site help archaeologists orient themselves within the ship since specific activities were often confined to specific places on the ship. The artifacts also allow the archaeologists to reconstruct life aboard the ship. Many artifacts were specific to seafaring life, but many more were also used on land so their analysis follows many of the processes used by terrestrial archaeologists and it is important for a maritime archaeologist to be cross-trained in the material culture contemporaneous with the shipwrecks that they investigate.

Archaeologists have traditionally reconstructed watercraft through a series of drawings, called **lines** and **construction drawings**, which are roughly equivalent to the architectural rendering and blueprints for a building. The lines show the three-dimensional shape of the hull in a two-dimensional form (figure 6.6), while the construction drawing shows the major timbers and pieces that formed the vessel, and how they were positioned together to shape the whole (figure 6.7). In recent years, lines and construction drawings have been replaced with digital reconstructions. The computer-aided reconstructions have the advantages of allowing multiple iterations to test hypotheses and the ability to make rapid edits, as well as being readily input into other programs to test the seafaring capabilities of a hull. Whether the reconstruction is completed on paper or on a computer, the process is largely the same.

**CONNECTING THE DOTS OF MARITIME ARCHAEOLOGY AND HISTORY**

Kevin Crisman, Professor, Nautical Archaeology Graduate Program, Institute of Nautical Archaeology, Texas A&M University, USA

If there is one lesson I've learned over nearly four decades of directing maritime archaeological projects under the water and in archives, it is that you need to do your own primary historical research. When seeking the truth about the past it pays to be a skeptic and to verify what you read in the history books. Also, good historical research before going into the field allows you to identify your discoveries and determine their importance with a high degree of confidence. My most memorable experiences over nearly forty years as a maritime archaeologist are those occasional "aha" moments when you get to attach a name, a story, and significance to a previously unknown shipwreck or un-identified artifact. There is the thrill of detective work successfully accomplished, certainly, but also the sat-isfaction of knowing your research ultimately helps connect the people of today (and tomorrow) with the generations of people who preceded us. In this regard maritime archaeologists are especially fortu-nate: the roving, transient, perilous careers of ships and mariners—and their vital role in linking cultures—tend to make their stories compelling.

One such "aha" moment I like to recall occurred in 1981 while diving with several colleagues on a graveyard of abandoned War of 1812 warships at the southern end of Lake Champlain. Diving conditions were not good, with less than 1 ft (30 cm) of visibility, so we were pretty much working by feel. We located a wooden wreck that had fallen over when sinking; most of its port side was intact up to the level of the main deck. Several gunports were preserved, so we knew it was a warship, but the question remained: which one? Five large 1812-era ships were said to have been abandoned at this location. Measuring the overall length of the wreck was one way to find out. Using an extra-long tape measure, I started at the sternpost and followed the keelson forward until the curved timbers of the lower stem appeared. At the point where the wreck ended, the tape read 115 ft (35 m). At that moment I knew that a hull of this length, at this location, could only be the U.S. Navy's *Eagle*, a 20-gun brig that had a brief but illus-trious career on the lake in 1814. Finding and identifying the wreck was a thrill, but it was just the first step. It took two more years of diving and research in before we could prepare a re-construction of the brig's "as built" appearance and a book telling the story of *Eagle*'s design, assembly, and history.

In most cases determining the name of the vessel takes a lot longer than with *Eagle*. In 1983 Arthur Cohn and I directed a survey that found a mostly buried mid-18th century wreck. The location of the hull and its length suggested it *might* be the 1759 British sloop *Boscawen*, but there was no proof of this. It ultimately took two years of excavation and recording, an exten-sive look at the history of the ship, a comparison of French and British construction techniques, and the dis-covery of the sloop's single mast step to confirm our hypothesis. This kind of complex, multisource puzzle solving is truly one of the best parts of being a maritime archaeologist.

More recently, in 2014–2016, Carolyn Kennedy and I led a three-season project to record the wrecks of four 19th-century steamboats scuttled adjacent to one an-other in a "boneyard" in central Lake Champlain. We were initially guided by an old map purporting to show the location and name of each wreck, but two of the four steamboats were clearly misidentified. Our archival re-search showed that the wrecks we found were too small to match those shown on the map. One of the mystery wrecks was identified during the first year, but the other required three years of underwater and archival sleuthing before the correct identification—the 1820-built *Phoenix II*—was deduced from its construction techniques and dimensions. Right after we concluded that this wreck had to be *Phoenix II*, a team member working around the en-gine support timbers found an iron chisel with the stamp "SB Phoenix" on the shank. That was what you might call a confirmational "aha!" moment.

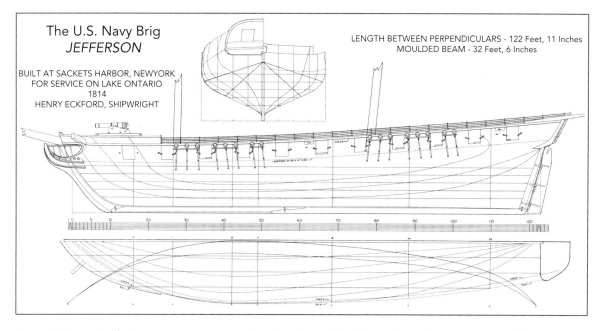

The U.S. Navy Brig
*JEFFERSON*

BUILT AT SACKETS HARBOR, NEW YORK
FOR SERVICE ON LAKE ONTARIO
1814
HENRY ECKFORD, SHIPWRIGHT

LENGTH BETWEEN PERPENDICULARS - 122 Feet, 11 Inches
MOULDED BEAM - 32 Feet, 6 Inches

**Figure 6.6** Example of a lines drawing based on archaeological data. The US Navy Brig *Jefferson*. (Courtesy of Kevin Crisman)

The use of lines to design a ship dates back to the 18th century and was an important part of the development of naval architecture. Lines gave the ship designer a way to envision a ship and its characteristics before it was built; for the archaeologist, they provide a way to extrapolate the original design from the physical remains. Lines can be thought of as a topographical map where each line shows the shape of the hull along a vertical, horizontal, or transverse plane (figure 6.8). The straight lines on the lines drawing are these planes and the curved lines are where the sides of the vessel intersect those planes. Since the vessel curves in all three dimensions, three views of the hull are necessary to capture all of the aspects of its shape. The three views are: the sheer plan that shows the vessel from the side, the half-breadth plan that is the view looking straight down onto the vessel, and the body plan that is actually split in half with one half showing the view looking at the bow and the other the stern. Since all of these plans are interrelated and depict a single unified whole, all of the intersections between the lines have to correspond. If you look at a lines drawing closely, you will note that the intersections of any two lines on one plan are matched exactly by the intersection of the same two lines on the other plans. When all of the lines intersect properly on all three plans and the resulting curves form appropriate arcs, the lines are said to be "fair."[7]

The relationships between the various line plans makes them a powerful means for the archaeologist to reconstruct a ship from its shipwrecked remains. More often than not the shipwreck will be fragmentary. If we are lucky,

**Figure 6.7** Example of construction drawing based on archaeological data. The US Navy Brig *Jefferson*, showing both construction features and crew activities. (Courtesy of Kevin Crisman)

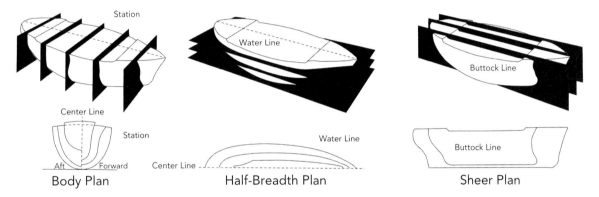

**Figure 6.8** The hull of a ship divided with planes to demonstrate the relationships between the lines on a lines plan.

we find the bottom of the hull, one side that collapsed as the ship deteriorated, and a few disarticulated timbers. In many cases, however, all that is found are a few pieces of the hull with large gaps in between. Nevertheless, even with only a small amount of surviving hull, it is possible to begin to position the pieces relative to each other and transfer their curves to a lines drawing. The fact that the lines must intersect and form fair curves helps to guide the reconstruction and acts as a check to the final product. Reconstruction is also aided by the fact that most vessels tend to be symmetrical, so once we get one side we can mirror it to the other side. The more complete the shipwreck, the easier it is to reconstruct the builder's original design, but in most archaeological cases it is necessary to apply some extrapolation to complete the lines plans. This extrapolation might be simply completing a curve in a manner consistent with the rest of the hull, or it might require referencing other shipwrecks and artistic representations to determine the shapes of vessels from that period.

The lines only define the outer surface of the frames and hull timbers—the surfaces to which the hull planking was affixed. This is the important surface in terms of designing a vessel for understanding how it would handle and how much it could carry, but it is a long way from depicting how the watercraft was actually built. To illustrate and analyze how it was built, archaeologists create construction drawings. These often mirror the lines plans with multiple views, but instead of showing the shape of the hull, they focus on the size and shape of the timbers that were used to build the vessel. The construction drawings also show the positions and attachment of the decks, as well as all of the other pieces that made the ship work, such as the attachments for the mast, the steering gear, the pumps, and in some cases the engines. Much of this information comes from the wreck itself, such as the size of the frames and planking, the way the pieces were assembled, and how everything was fastened together. Other details have to be inferred from other similar archaeological examples, artistic depictions, and documentary descriptions. Like the lines, the construction drawing is a mixture of hard archaeological evidence and scholarly interpretation based on the best available evidence.[8]

Armed with the lines and construction drawings, or a computer model, of the hull, the archaeologist can calculate how much cargo the vessel held, how it sailed, if it was fast, if it was safe or prone to tipping over, and several other aspects of how the vessel functioned as a vehicle. It is also possible to interpret the vessel as material culture; it provides a window on that culture. For example, how a culture counted is evident in the basic units used to design the ship, and its appetite for risk or available resources is evident in how a vessel balanced speed and safety or how lightly or heavily built the hull was. By comparing ships across the wide range of recorded shipwrecks, it is also possible to study technology and culture change.

The French ship *La Belle* illustrates the process of reconstructing a ship from its shipwreck. *La Belle* was one of four ships that sailed from La Rochelle in 1684 with the goal of establishing a French colony on the Mississippi River under the direction of Robert Cavelier, Sieur de La Salle. La Salle had already established strongholds on the Great Lakes and traveled down the Mississippi. Based on these previous expeditions, he understood that controlling the Great Lakes and the Mississippi would give France access to much of the interior of North America and a major advantage over the other European colonizers. Unfortunately for La Salle, the 1684 expedition suffered several misfortunes, including the loss of a ship to pirates and missing the mouth of the Mississippi by more than 480 km (300 miles). All hope of a successful endeavor ended when *La Belle* sank in Matagorda Bay, Texas, in 1686. More than three centuries later, in 1995, it was discovered by archaeologists from the Texas Historical Commission (THC).[9]

The THC built a cofferdam around the wreck and pumped the interior dry so that *La Belle* could be excavated like a terrestrial archaeological site (figure 6.9). The remains of the cargo and supplies were excavated first and then the hull itself was documented and removed, deconstructing the ship in its entirety. At every step of the process, detailed records were collected so that the entire shipwreck could be virtually reconstructed and refilled with its contents. Because all of the artifacts and ship structure were waterlogged and saturated with salts, everything also needed to be conserved. This was a lengthy process, stretching over more than a decade, but it allowed for every item and the ship itself to be carefully studied. The artifacts represent what La Salle felt would be necessary to found and sustain a colony on the frontier. They

**Figure 6.9** *La Belle* shipwreck during excavation. The metal wall in the background is the interior of the cofferdam. (Courtesy of Texas Historical Commission)

tell us much about La Salle's logistical abilities as well as about how the French viewed the New World. The hull itself is a trove of information about the state of French nautical technology. This is particularly true because *La Belle* was originally designed as a kit to be carried in the hold of another ship and assembled upon arrival. Many of the timbers are marked to aid in assembly and there is a French ledger that records the principal measurements of the ship. With this information, it has been possible to understand the mathematics behind the original design of the vessel, as well as the thought process of the designer, making the hull a 3D treatise on contemporary French scientific knowledge. Following the conceptual reconstruction of the vessel from the data recovered during the archaeological excavation, and the completion of the conservation treatment in 2016, the hull was physically reconstructed within the main hall of the Bullock Texas State History Museum. It serves as the museum's permanent centerpiece, surrounded by interpretive displays dedicated to the people and the artifacts located within it.

### DISSEMINATION, PUBLICATION, AND OUTREACH

*La Belle* is also an excellent example of the final, and very important, step of archaeological investigation: the dissemination of results. Like most archaeological investigations, the *La Belle* project was funded in large part with public monies, and the researchers were conscientious to ensure the people of Texas a good return on their investment. In addition to the museum exhibit, several books and articles for both the general and scientific communities have been published on the shipwreck, along with a detailed website containing images of many of the artifacts, and a K-12 curriculum.[10]

An archaeological project is never finished until there is an easily accessible publication that summarizes its results and interpretations. It is important to remember, however, that a publication does not necessarily mean that a project is over, as interpretation and reinterpretation can go on for decades. The nature and medium of publications will depend on the project, but it is good practice to produce at least one publication for the general public and another that contains the details that are of interest to archaeological specialists (table 6.2). These could take the form of a website with general summaries backed by digital data, a scholarly journal article combined with a newspaper writeup, or a wide array of other forms of dissemination. The savvy archaeologist will continue to use the latest technologies and platforms to reach the widest possible audience in order to meet this fundamental responsibility of our field—to share the knowledge we gained through the study of the past.

## SUMMARY

Interpretation and dissemination are two of the most important, and most fulfilling, parts of an archaeological study. Archaeologists have an ethical duty to interpret what they find and to share that interpretation with the public. Archaeological finds are generally interpreted at three scales: the individual features and artifacts of the site, the site and its immediate environs, and the site in a larger, sometimes global, framework. Each of these scales of interpretation allow a different, but interrelated understanding of what life was like for the people who inhabited the site or sailed on a foundered ship. This is analogous to studying a leaf, the tree, and the forest—each scale is important to our understanding of biology. Maritime and underwater archaeology also has particular interpretative challenges, such as reconstructing now submerged landscapes, interpreting the different ways that different groups interacted with water in general as well as specific bodies of water, and rebuilding a ship from sometimes scant shipwreck remains. All of these interpretations need to be published so that the general public, who directly and indirectly fund nearly all archaeology, and archaeological specialists can learn from what was discovered.

## DISCUSSION QUESTIONS

1. The artifacts from archaeological sites eroded by changing sea levels are often considered to have little interpretive value. Why is this the case, and what interpretive value might these artifacts have?

TABLE 6.2 **MAJOR DISSEMINATORS OF MARITIME AND UNDERWATER ARCHAEOLOGY**

| |
|---|
| **Websites** |
| The Museum of Underwater Archaeology |
| MaritimeArchaeology.com |
| Advisory Council on Underwater Archaeology |
| Sub-Arch Listserv |
| **Journals** |
| *International Journal of Nautical Archaeology* |
| *Journal of Maritime Archaeology* |
| *Mariner's Mirror* |
| *Historical Archaeology* |
| *INA Quarterly* |
| *Journal of Archaeological Science* |
| **Magazines** |
| *Archaeology* |
| *National Geographic* |
| *Sea History* |
| **Conferences** |
| International Congress on Underwater Archaeology (IKUWA) |
| International Symposium on Boat and Ship Archaeology (ISBSA) |
| International Symposium on Ship Construction in Antiquity (Tropis) |
| Society for Historical Archaeology (SHA) |

2. How do you view the water? Do you see different bodies of water differently (e.g., an ocean versus a river)? How might these perceptions influence how you interact with the water? What would be the archaeological remains of your interactions with water?

3. Do you find one of the scales of interpretation more interesting than the other two? Why?

4. What can be learned through the process of reconstructing a ship from shipwreck remains?

5. Do you believe that archaeologists have an ethical mandate to publish their results for both the general public and other archaeologists? Why or why not?

**FURTHER READING**

Benjamin, J., C. Bonsall, C. Pickard, and A. Fischer, Eds. (2011). *Submerged Prehistory*. Oxbow Press, Oxford.

Bruseth, J., A. Borgens, B. Jones, and E. Ray, Eds. (2017). La Belle: *The Archaeology of a Seventeenth-Century Vessel of New World Colonization*. Texas A&M University Press, College Station.

Ford, B., Ed. (2011). *The Archaeology of Maritime Landscapes*. Springer, New York.

Lipke, P., P. Spectre, and B.A.G. Fuller, Eds. (1993). *Boats: A Manual for Their Documentation*. American Association for State and Local History, Nashville, TN.

Roberts, A., J. McKinnon, C. O'Loughlin, K. Wanganeen, L.-I. Rigney, and M. Fowler. (2013). Combining Indigenous and Maritime Archaeological Approaches: Experiences and insights from the "(Re)locating *Narrunga* Project," Yorke Peninsula, South Australia. *Journal of Maritime Archaeology* 8(1):77–99.

Sonnenburg, E., A. Lemke, and J. O'Shea, Eds. (2015). *Caribou Hunting in the Upper Great Lakes*. Memoirs of the Museum of Anthropology, Number 57. University of Michigan, Ann Arbor.

Steffy, J.R. (1994). *Wooden Ship Building and the Interpretation of Shipwrecks*. Texas A&M University Press, College Station.

# HUMAN ADAPTATIONS TO WATERY WORLDS

## CHAPTER 7

# INTERACTING
# WITH THE ENVIRONMENT

## FOCUS QUESTIONS

- When and how did maritime societies emerge?
- How have people interacted with seas, lakes, and rivers? How was this interaction shaped by their culture and environment? What are the similarities, differences, and outcomes of these interactions?
- What types of maritime archaeological sites are there, and how do they differ in what they can teach us about the past?
- What information can be gained from inundated landscapes and submerged terrestrial sites?

## RELATIONSHIPS BETWEEN PEOPLE AND THE WORLD'S WATERWAYS

So far this text has discussed the nuts and bolts of how to do maritime and underwater archaeology and how to interpret the data thus collected. In this chapter, we change tack and discuss what has been learned from maritime and underwater sites. Whereas earlier chapters were focused on methods, using case studies to illustrate those methods, now we will be discussing larger themes, with case studies to exemplify those themes, touching briefly on some of the major highlights of the past century of maritime and underwater archaeological research. Any one of these case studies could be the focus of an entire career, and there are many specialized books and articles available on these topics. The references in the text and the "Further Reading" sections at the end of each chapter suggest avenues for further investigation, and some case studies will appear in multiple chapters to demonstrate how maritime and underwater archaeology can help elucidate the past through numerous lenses.

This chapter will focus on the broad theme of human-environment interactions. In the context of this chapter, the term "environment" refers to the natural world, including climate, topography, flora, fauna, river courses, sea levels, and salinity. For the moment, we will exclude the environmental factor of proximity to, and contact with, other human groups. This latter factor is so relevant to maritime societies that these interactions will be discussed at length in ensuing chapters.

Unlike most creatures, humans adapt to their environments mainly through cultural innovations, so this chapter will discuss the large-scale environmental changes most relevant to maritime and underwater archaeologists that human societies have had to address over the millennia. While natural environments do not determine human cultures, environmental parameters often provide significant constraints. There are some general patterns to the strategies people choose in given environmental conditions, but also many unique aspects to every culture. For instance, given access to open water, people almost universally figure out ways to use it and the plants and animals that live in and on it, but cultures differ greatly in how they engineer ways to make things float to better access those aquatic resources.

While it can be tempting to classify human interactions with the watery world as either functional or symbolic, in practice, there is seldom a clear threshold between these categories. It is more useful to consider these interactions as on a spectrum, spanning from direct material and physiological utilization and extraction to spiritual and cognitive motivations. For the purposes of this discussion, material interactions are those focused on directly utilizing the watery resources, such as fishing, shipping goods or people, hunting whales, harvesting reeds, and so on. Cognitive interactions with the aquatic include the religious teachings, symbolism, and mythologies surrounding watery places and the folklore guiding how, why, and when a given resource should be used. To archaeologists, the material activities more often leave tangible and interpretable traces, while the cognitive might primarily be accessed through inference and from additional contextual knowledge. This chapter will interweave cultural and archaeological aspects of human-environment interactions, discussing how human activities and the environment shape each other. This chapter will also discuss how the archaeological record is created, maintained, and destroyed by both environment and human activities.

Human interactions with the environment are often recursive, with the natural world influencing human cultures, and human cultures shaping the natural world. This creates a dynamic relationship between human and environmental responses, with human cultures and multiple natural systems feeding back on each other. Because these interactions occur at multiple scales, many small adjustments are needed to maintain equilibrium, and a large change on either side must elicit response from the other. Archaeologists have long been interested in trying to understand these larger changes, especially those in human societies. The archaeological record provides detailed evidence for the long-term consequences of these interactions for humans and the larger ecosystem which may be of use to modern people striving to make sustainable decisions, such as the 17 sustainable development goals adopted by the UN in 2015.[1] Maritime and underwater cultural heritage especially provide information related to the environment (goals 11–13) and life on land and under water (goals 14 and 15), but maritime and underwater sites also provide key evidence about how the world became the way it is today, which can be applied to the origins of inequality, and discussions about development and infrastructure.

Early researchers often thought either that major environmental changes forced people to change, or that suddenly people became more capable or learned new technology from their neighbors. We now know that things are not that simple. People constantly weigh potential costs and potential benefits, and often major changes only occur when the perceived benefits seem overwhelming or the risks seem small—at least for the people who get to make the decisions. As this chapter will demonstrate, there are often unforeseen consequences to these changes that require further adjustments in the future; this is especially true for the large-scale specialized endeavors of politically complex societies, such as the industrialized economies of the late Modern era.

## THE ENVIRONMENT HAS ITS EFFECTS: SUBMERGED TERRESTRIAL SITES AND LANDSCAPES

As we have mentioned, the world in which the genus *Homo* evolved was a dynamic one. The Pleistocene (ca. 2.6 million–11,500 years ago) was marked by repeated cycles of glacial (cold) and interglacial (warm) periods. This warming and cooling led to major fluctuations in sea levels, river channels, lake size and shape, plant and animal communities, rainfall, ocean currents, and other natural systems. This was a world in which adaptability and flexibility would have been extremely useful. Recent evidence places the oldest stone tools in East Africa at 3.3 million years ago, while the oldest skeletal remains of the genus *Homo* date to 2.8 million years ago, nearly coincident with the onset of the Pleistocene. Multiple species of hominins evolved and developed culture, spreading out of Africa and throughout Eurasia against the backdrop of growing and shrinking glaciers, falling and rising seas, and speciation and extinction. By approximately 14,000 BCE, *Homo sapiens* had spread throughout all continents except Antarctica, colonizing the Americas and reaching the modern extent of our species. Well before the beginning of the Holocene (ca. 11,500 years ago, 9450 BCE), *Homo sapiens* was the only hominin species left.[2]

This brief foray into human evolution is relevant to our current discussion because these environmental changes between glacial and interglacial may well have triggered or enabled the appearance and disappearance of certain species and major cultural changes, including the global diaspora of modern humans. No matter what relevance they had to hominin lifeways, these large-scale climatic fluctuations definitely had an enormous impact upon the archaeological record of these early humans by determining which sites have been preserved and which were destroyed.

## Climate change in brief

Climate change has become a tremendous concern to current human societies for a number of reasons, including the significant impact it may have on the billions of people settled near the world's present coastlines. Climate is defined as the long-term weather conditions in an area, but "long-term" is a relative term, often an average over approximately thirty years. Archaeology, however, is designed to look beyond the generational time scale. Through the long archaeological perspective, it is clear that climate has been quite variable, and adapting to climate change has often been a factor in human history. With good historical weather data existing in most places for only the past few decades or centuries, archaeological sites are an extremely important source of past climate and paleoenvironmental data.

Most of what we know about past climates is interpreted indirectly through various sorts of **proxy records**; for instance, we commonly determine sea levels by dating shoreline or nearshore features found in deep water or far up on dry land. We know how deep or high these coastal features are found today, and the date we get from them tells us approximately when the coast was in that location. We determine how relatively cold or warm it was in the past by looking at the isotope records from deep-ocean and ice cores. The relative percentages of oxygen, nitrogen, and carbon isotopes vary as it gets colder and warmer. Paleoenvironmental scientists date samples from the cores and examine the isotope ratios within the samples to see if they are indicative of colder, warmer, or similar-to-modern temperatures. Microfossils and sediments at sites can be used to interpret local conditions. For instance, the presence of wind-blown sediments and pollen associated with scrub-tundra within a core collected from the now-submerged Bering Land Bridge could be used to infer an open, wind-blown tundra environment at a given point in time before inundation. See sidebar by Mark Dunkley for more discussion of this.

Archaeological sites can be very useful for understanding past climates and environments because archaeologists regularly collect and analyze a wide range of ecofacts, aim for excellent temporal control of samples, and can provide a context of human behavior for this environmental information. First, as discussed in chapter 3, archaeologists analyze many types of ecofacts because it is not known in advance which will be most helpful to understanding past human behavior. For instance, pollen, phytoliths, diatoms, and some types of wood can inform us about the places and environments a ship has passed through. Second, a site with good preservation of ecofacts is also likely to be comparatively well-dated, so rich environmental records can be easily tied to a specific time. Third, these archaeological datasets can speak to how humans were using (and sometimes

## MARITIME ARCHAEOLOGY AND ENVIRONMENTAL CHANGE

# Mark Dunkley, Maritime Archaeologist, Historic England, UK

The warming of global climate is now unequivocal. Since about 1950 there have been many recorded observations of environmental change comprising increasing air and ocean temperatures and the widespread melting of snow and ice. While some of these changes have been linked to human influences, there is abundant evidence that the rises and falls of eustatic sea level are indicative of long-term processes that originated in the late glacial period around 12,000 years ago.

The identification of major environmental threats to cultural heritage and the built environment has therefore been one of the core strands of Historic England's strategy. Here, work has already begun to assess the potential effects of climate change by identifying natural and environmental threats to the historic environment in order to devise adaptive responses to those threats.

The oceans play an important role in mitigating climate change. Using data collated by the Intergovernmental Panel on Climate Change (IPCC), research has evolved around four broad effects of changes on oceanic processes which individually have the potential to affect the future management of underwater cultural heritage: (i) sea temperature, (ii) sea level, (iii) carbon dioxide and ocean acidification, and (iv) circulation, suspended particulate matter, turbidity, salinity, and waves.

### Sea temperature

The globally averaged combined land and ocean surface temperature data shows a warming of 0.85°C (1.5°F) between 1880 and 2012. On a global scale, the ocean warming is largest near the surface, and the upper 75 m (246 ft) warmed by 0.11°C (0.2°F) per decade over the period 1971 to 2010. Warmer oceans are indicative of more energetic oceans, so erosion in shallow contexts may be enhanced, controlled by local seabed topography.

One noticeable effect of ocean warming is the northward migration of invasive species; of particular relevance is the blacktip shipworm (*Lyrodus pedicellatus*)—a species of shipworm that consumes the wooden hulls of sunken ships, is active all year, and appears to have migrated from more southerly latitudes, possibly as a result of sea temperature increase. In 1980, *L. pedicellatus* was recorded at 40° N but by 2007 it had migrated to 50° N. Current research places it around 51° N.

### Sea level

Over the period 1901 to 2010, global mean sea level rose by 0.19 m (7.5 in.), principally through thermal expansion (water expands as it warms) and the melting of the cryosphere. While the effects of thermal expansion might be tempered by a more vigorous hydrological cycle with increased evaporation, the effect of sea-level rise on archaeological diving projects will be to incrementally reduce the amount of time (and therefore productivity) an air-breathing diver can safely spend underwater. For example, a 20-percent increase in diving depth between 25 ft (7.62 m) and 30 ft (9.144 m) can result in a 32-percent decrease in dive time.

In addition, sea-level rise increases the risk of accelerated coastal erosion or increased flooding, while the infusion of land with salt may create difficulties related to in situ management methodologies at the coast edge. It also allows larger waves to approach the shore leading to damage and risk to coastal structures and monuments

### Carbon dioxide and ocean acidification

Carbon dioxide is present naturally and released from anthropogenic sources. The oceans take up and store about a quarter of anthropogenic $CO_2$ emissions through a combination of biological processes, solubility, and circulation patterns. Since preindustrial times, the ocean has naturally absorbed about 30 percent of the emitted anthropogenic $CO_2$, causing ocean acidification—between 1751 and 1994, average ocean surface pH is estimated to have decreased from approximately 8.25 to 8.14.

A more acidic ocean will have a detrimental effect on metal structures and shipwreck sites, and the wider consequences for all underwater cultural heritage, including the corrosion potential of metal-hulled shipwreck sites, needs to be explored. The rates of potential

*(continued)*

decay are not well understood, and so work is needed to further our understanding of the potential effects and impact of changes in ocean chemistry.

Increased acidification will also have an effect on biogeochemistry by harming native marine fauna that build shells of calcium carbonate, such as the shipworm *Teredo navalis*. The indirect effects of this harm upon wooden archaeological remains and coastal structures are not yet known.

### Circulation, suspended particulate matter, turbidity, salinity, and waves

The general circulation of the oceans defines the average movement of seawater and follows a specific pattern. This pattern exchanges seawater with varying characteristics, such as temperature and salinity, within the interconnected network of oceans and is an important part of the heat and freshwater fluxes of the global climate. It is thought that changes in ocean temperatures and wind patterns, resulting from the combined effects of overall environmental change, will affect and alter oceanic currents and will include changes in rainfall affecting the runoff from rivers.

For underwater cultural heritage, the immediate impact is likely to be twofold: First, the effect of increased turbidity will be to decrease underwater visibility for diving archaeologists and second, changes to the nature of particles entering the marine environment may enable better in situ preservation by reducing biological decay (though this may be offset by shallow-water erosion). However, as yet there are no detailed projections of change for suspended particles and turbidity, let alone sufficient understanding to scale down national and/or regional predictions to a particular locality.

Oceanic environmental change presents both opportunities and challenges for how maritime archaeology is managed. Without checks and intervention, the negative effects of change are likely to cause increased attrition of archaeological sites and objects underwater. However, the adoption of a thematic approach, aligned to the potential impacts of the four broad effects of oceanic climate change, highlights where initial research should be prioritized.

The *Sixth Assessment Report* of global environmental change from the IPCC is expected in 2022. This report will be of interest to policymakers and researchers as it will facilitate an increased understanding of the rates of oceanic change and will review of progress toward the universal goal of keeping global warming to well below 2°C (3.5°F).

affecting and being affected by) local environments. Contrasted with many other types of paleoenvironmental studies that only examine one or two proxies, archaeology can be among the best sources of accurate broad-ranging paleoenvironmental reconstruction.

Many environmental changes are relevant to human cultures, so nearly all archaeological publications contain a section discussing what is known about the environmental setting, along with explicit discussion of how the environments have changed over time. In general, global climatic conditions were far less relevant to a given human culture than their very local conditions, and these conditions vary greatly from place to place. In most places, the natural climate, flora, and fauna became somewhat similar to modern conditions around approximately 3000 BCE, but this does not mean things remained unchanging for the past 5000 years. Instead, our proxy records indicate that there were similar plants and animals, and average annual temperatures were comparable to now, but there were many spans of locally colder-than-average or warmer-than-average temperatures during the past five millennia.

## Sea level changes and the impacts on human societies

Of most relevance for maritime and underwater archaeology, global sea level also reached approximately modern levels at around 6500 years ago (or ca. 4550 BCE), rising more than 130 m from the last major glacial period that ended approximately 20,000 years ago. Figure 7.1 shows these sea level fluctuations throughout the Pleistocene.[3] During cold periods, sea levels were as much as 140 m lower than present, and during warm periods they were as much as 10 m higher than present. During glacial periods, much of the world's water was tied up in enormous glaciers, some of which were more than a mile thick. As a result, huge swaths of the continental shelves were exposed—making them dry landscapes with lakes, rivers, forests, prairies, and full complements of wildlife. As the world warmed, these shelves were drowned and plants, animals, and people needed to move farther inland. The warmer saline ocean waters were rapidly diluted by a massive influx of cold, fresh water from melting glaciers, which affected ocean currents and circulation patterns and marine life as well. Sometimes this sea-level rise was happening so quickly that people would have been able to see the shorelines change on an annual or decadal basis.

During these times, it is likely that nearshore habitats would have been very unstable, and the marshes, lagoons, shellfish beds, and fish that are often attractive to human groups would have either been missing or unpredictable. We know, from a site in South Africa, that people were using shellfish by approximately 165,000 years ago (chapter 2), but shell middens (piles of shell debris, often the waste from food consumption) become common worldwide during the early Holocene—sometime after

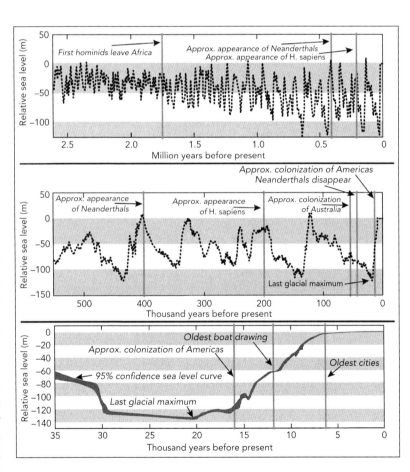

**Figure 7.1** Generalized sea level chart for entire Pleistocene (top) and last 500,000 years (middle), with more precise curve for past 35,000 years (bottom), showing selected major events in hominid history in italics. Sea-level curve redrawn from Hansen et al. 2013 and Lambeck et al. 2014.

9000 BCE and before 5000 BCE in most places—as Mesolithic foraging societies begin to use broad-based and more sedentary subsistence strategies. Some of these Mesolithic cultures can even be considered true maritime communities. For instance, settlement patterns, shell middens, and isotopic evidence from human burials indicate that some Jomon foragers in Japan were living semiper-manently in coastal villages focusing upon maritime resources by 5000 BCE.[4] Our oldest direct evidence of boats also dates to the Mesolithic, or, as it is known in the Americas, the Archaic period, with dugout canoes more than 7000 years old having been recovered from wetland sites in the Americas and Europe (chapter 8).

## Rising seas and sinking lands: formation and preservation of underwater sites

We know very little about how people were using coastal resources during the Pleistocene because most of the Pleistocene coasts are far underwater and many kilometers offshore. Many of the early Holocene coasts are also submerged, al-though not quite as deeply. This has had an enormous impact on what we can hope to know about early people, as natural processes and the logistics of under-water research constrain our knowledge for several reasons. Relatively few sites are likely to have endured the submergence process, as the churning action of nearshore waves tends to destroy primary context. Therefore, the more time a site spends in the surf zone, the less likely that any of its features or the contextual relationship between artifacts, ecofacts, and features will survive. Thus, when sea level rises rapidly, it is more likely that sites or portions of sites will survive in-tact, as they spend relatively little time in the breaker zone. On the other hand, when sea level is rising rapidly, people are not likely to create much infrastruc-ture on their coasts, so any coastal sites created are likely to be temporary and small, which means there is less to preserve and the sites are inherently harder to discover. It is also difficult to determine where the coastline would have been at a moment in time when it is changing on a yearly or semiannual basis, so it is hard to find a coast, much less a coastal site, from these periods of rapid rise.

As discussed in chapters 3 and 5, sites survive best in stable, low-energy environments, preferably after being buried quickly (figure 7.2). It is likely that a large number of sites—although a small percentage of the original total—in what are now offshore areas were preserved in this way. The late Pleistocene to mid-Holocene sea-level rise occurred as massive amounts of glacial water entered the oceans. This water got into the oceans via furiously flowing flooded rivers, many of which were also carrying enormous amounts of mud into the ocean basins. This mud settled to the seafloor and likely buried a large number of sites under meters of sediment. However, these deeply buried sites are much more difficult to find and excavate than their terrestrial counterparts. As discussed in chapter 4, we can only discover them by finding evidence of buried land surfaces via sub-bottom profiler surveys and collecting sediment cores. At this time, no

deeply buried offshore archaeological site has been excavated,
although a few have potentially
been discovered.[5]

There are other areas where
not very much sediment was
deposited on the continental
shelves and the submergence process was relatively gentle. Sites
have been discovered on the
seafloor in these settings buried
by only a small amount of sand.
In some cases, subsurface features
have even preserved, such as the
Neolithic wells discovered off
the coast of Israel (sidebar by
Ehud Galili). More often, artifacts
are scattered on the surface but
show evidence of having been
moved around by wave action
and small animals. For instance,
archaeologists caught a sea urchin using a ca. 5000-year-old spearpoint in its defense on a middle Holocene site in the Florida Gulf of Mexico (figure 7.3). These
discoveries, however, demonstrate that inundation is not always completely catastrophic (sidebar by Michael K. Faught).

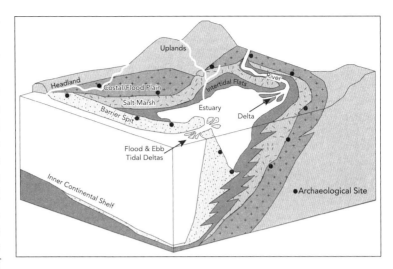

**Figure 7.2** Preservation potential for inundated coastal/flood plain sites. Three-dimensional schema shows coastal settings and common archaeological site locations. Top is current environment and site locations; the depth represents the extent of those environments at lower sea levels and the location of sites that may have preserved if they were distributed the same as currently. (Redrawn from original courtesy of William Chadwick)

---

## FROM THE NEOLITHIC TO THE 20TH CENTURY: UNDERWATER ARCHAEOLOGY IN ISRAEL REVEALS 10,000 YEARS OF MARITIME HISTORY

### Ehud Galili, Senior Researcher, Zinman Institute of Archaeology, University of Haifa, Israel

Ancient civilizations left behind numerous remains on the sea bottom and the coasts of Israel. Among these are settlements inundated by the sea, ancient coastal cities, shipwrecks, harbors, and anchorages spanning the last 10,000 years. These cultural assets represent important historical milestones in the man–sea relationship. They reflect important chapters and events in the history of humanity, including the Neolithic revolution, the appearance of the first empires and the foundation of the major mono-theistic religions. The two underwater projects briefly described below repre-sent the extremes of the timespan cited above, from

*(continued)*

the Neolithic Period to the Second World War. Both examples, however, highlight the importance of inter-disciplinary and international collaboration and innovative thinking, which are two key concepts I have tried to advance in my career in maritime archaeology. The first case study pertains to coastal prehistoric villages inundated by the last postglacial sea-level rise along the Carmel coast. The second addresses the wreck of the Italian submarine *Scirè*, sunk in 1942 off Haifa.

## Lost prehistoric civilizations: submerged villages off the Carmel coast

The existence of a complex of inundated, formerly coastal, Neolithic villages off the Carmel coast was first acknowledged in 1965, when the Neolithic/Chalcolithic site of Tel Hreiz was described. I started investigating the inundated sites in 1981 and have been studying them continuously ever since. Archaeologists, anthropologists, zoologists, botanists, geologists, and other researchers joined me in a collaborative, international research project spanning decades. We have developed and used innovative methods, such as allowing sea storms to remove the overlaying sand. The newly exposed sites were explored, documented, and mapped. Special features were excavated manually by applying similar methods used in terrestrial prehistoric archaeology. These methods were converted and developed so they could be used underwater.

The people residing in these sites simultaneously experienced two major global revolutions. One was the last global sea rise after the last glacial melting. The second was the Neolithic transition to farming. The archaeological evidence suggests that the Neolithic inhabitants struggled against sea-level rise, trying to rescue their villages and water sources. But eventually the rising sea won and the sites were evacuated. These now-submerged prehistoric villages are among the best preserved in the world and provide important information about the material culture, economy, social behavior of the coastal Neolithic population. The submerged sites include a Pre-Pottery Neolithic C settlement named Atlit-Yam, and five late Neolithic/early Chalcolithic settlements belonging to the later Wadi Rabah culture. The sites are exposed by sea currents removing the overlaying sand; they are well-preserved and reveal the secrets and way of life of these vanished civilizations through the multidisciplinary research approach and methods we developed.

The Atlit-Yam site is some 200–400 m (656–1312 ft) offshore, at 8–12 m (26–39 ft) depth, and covers ca. 40,000 m² (9.9 acres). It is dated to 9180–8550 years BP (calibrated). Stone-built water wells, the earliest known, indicate the typical South Levantine need for a permanent water source in the rainless summer. Foundations of rectangular dwellings, ritual megaliths and storage and production installations were recovered, as well as eighty-five human skeletons. Remains of cultivated cereals, domesticated sheep/goats, pigs, dogs, cattle, and fish remains suggest that the settlement was one of the earliest known Mediterranean fishing villages subsisting on agro-pastoral-marine resources.

The later Pottery Neolithic (PN) sites, Kfar-Samir, Kfar-Galim, Tel-Hreiz, Megadim, and Neve-Yam, are submerged at 0–5 m (0–16 ft) depth, and were dated to 8100–7300 years BP (calibrated). Finds from these sites include water wells built of tree branches and stones, paved surfaces, and wall foundations, as well as stone, bone, pottery, and flint artifacts. Installations for olive oil extraction, the typical secondary product of the Mediterranean, provide the earliest evidence for such industry. One of the earliest known organized cemeteries, containing stone-built cist graves separated from the living quarters was discovered at Neve-Yam. The PN settlements' economy was fully agricultural, based mainly on terrestrial resources, cultivation, and herding.

## The tragic end of the Italian submarine *Scirè*

The submarine *Scirè* carried divers aiming to attack the then-British port of Haifa. It was tracked by the Royal Navy through communication intercepts and was sunk on 10 August 1942 in Haifa Bay, with no survivors. The location of the wreck, which lies at 30 meters (98 feet) depth, was known and reported by the Israeli Navy to the Italian Navy in 1950. During the sixties, an Italian delegation repatriated to Italy some parts of the wreck and two warriors who had drifted ashore soon after the battle and were buried in Haifa. In 1982, we dove on the wreck and documented human bones. The Italian authorities were notified, and, in the following years, the submariners were repatriated. As a local underwater archaeologist, I cooperated with the Italian divers using my knowledge of the underwater terrain and the wreck. In 2014, a ceremony was held in Italy where the role of all involved was acknowledged and the wreck was declared a war grave and a protected heritage site. During that period, the underwater antisubmarine system of the British port of Haifa was discovered. An indicator loop system and the associated coastal watchtowers, very advanced for their time, played a major role in the sinking of the *Scirè* and its crew. It was abandoned and forgotten when the British left the area. To study that underwater system, we collaborated with an Australian expert of such systems, Italian historians, and divers. The ongoing project has involved archival studies, underwater and coastal archaeological research, and interviews of veteran navy divers, all aiming to reveal the details of the *Scirè*'s last battle. In retrospect, a dive to a forgotten wreck by an underwater archaeologist created a cultural heritage site and an international project of collaboration on submarine warfare during WWII. Although applied to an entirely different context, the same innovative, inquisitive, and inter-disciplinary approach to studying underwater cultural heritage allowed for a much fuller understanding of both sites. It is pursuing and fostering such a research environment that I view as my most meaningful contribution to our field.

## Preserving the cultural heritage for future generations

Underwater archaeological relics are threatened by nature (sea level rise, waves and currents) and man (looting, quarrying and construction of marine structures), resulting in rapid erosion and destruction of coastal and underwater sites. If this process continues, a significant portion of the coastal and marine cultural heritage of Israel will disappear and archaeological, touristic, and economic assets of great value will be lost. It is necessary to preserve them and reveal the archaeological and historical information carried in such sites. Accordingly, Israel conducts ongoing underwater rescue surveys and mapping of the sites, formulates regulations, risk assessment surveys, and preservation and protection masterplans, and applies law enforcement and monitoring to protect this cultural heritage for future generations.

**Figure 7.3** Projectile point being used as camouflage by an urchin at a submerged offshore site in the Florida Gulf of Mexico. White arrow points to projectile point. (Courtesy of Michael K. Faught)

## Michael K. Faught, Vice President and Treasurer, Archaeological Research Cooperative; Maritime Archaeologist, SEARCH, Inc., USA

I started out as a graduate student at the University of Arizona proposing that Paleoindian and early Archaic sites (dating from ca. 13,000–9,000 years ago) could be found offshore in northwest Florida, in Apalachee Bay, as a lot of terrestrial sites from these periods had been found onshore. It worked, and I spent the next 30 years working on such sites as a student, professor, and professional archaeologist.

As sea levels used to be much lower, I figured that early archaeological sites would continue offshore, as people would have experienced and exploited a much larger landscape—probably near drowned river channels. Because there was little posttransgression sedimentation in this Big Bend region of Florida, much of the paleolandscape is exposed, or shallowly buried. Therefore, one can sample by several methods from small or larger boats, depending on the available budget. Another benefit was that sites we were finding (I had help from a lot of volunteers and colleagues) were located in shallow water, mostly between 6 and 18 ft (1.8–5.5 m) deep. This aspect of the Big Bend sites meant that students and researchers could stay underwater for long periods of time doing visual or mapping surveys, transect collections by hand fanning round pits like shovel test pits, or induction dredge excavations of single- and multiple-meter-square test units. More than 40 locations of artifact finds (sites) were recorded by my research in the Big Bend; about five of these were substantial in terms of size and numbers of artifacts, the remainder were probably small scatters.

I was fortunate to have been able to write some successful grant proposals and obtain funding to organize eleven forays with both small and large vessels. We carried all the usual heavy dive gear, but also gloves, tape measures, trowels, ropes and string, rebar coordinate markers, and small-engine-powered hydraulic dredges for transect collections and dredge excavations, as well as diesel-powered surface-supplied breathing air. All this research was accomplished with the help of enthusiastic volunteers (including EarthWatch volunteers), graduate students who served as staff for field schools, and field school participants. With remote sensing equipment loaned and operated by partners, and then later paid for by startup and grant monies, we methodically investigated many nautical square miles of seabed using side-scan sonar and sub-bottom profiler technologies. There is much boat time needed for this kind of research, something compounded by the distance from shore and weather conditions. It is my experience that staying for multiple days out at sea on a bigger, more comfortable boat is the most effective—and costly—approach.

I then had the opportunity to teach students some of my ideas and opinions about the processes and protocols of finding and working on submerged prehistoric sites, and the substantial differences between prehistoric and shipwreck archaeology. In the course of presenting classes, I taught that shipwreck archaeologists, particularly western hemisphere shipwreck archaeologists, generally work on "nation-state" shipwrecks (Spanish, French, English, Dutch, Union or Confederate, etc.) and these kind of wrecks can be found in a number of geographic locations around the globe. Therefore, the historic underwater archaeologist can conduct research virtually anywhere. This contrasts with the geoarchaeologist's threefold task of needing to know local and regional prehistoric sequences (i.e., artifacts and site types expected at different depth zones offshore), the local and eustatic sea level curves, and, finally, the geology and antecedent topography or landscape morphology pertinent to identifying where sites might occur offshore. There is also a difference in the application of remote sensing tools once an appropriate region has been identified. The shipwreck archaeologist needs the side scan and magnetometer to find "sites"; the marine geoarchaeologist only needs the side-scan sonar or the multibeam echosounder if the paleolandscape is exposed or shallowly buried; however, the sub-bottom profiler is almost always required to identify river pathways.

I have tried to organize and publish on principles, methods, and protocols for finding and conducting research on continental shelf prehistoric sites—especially with regard to procedures that can be applied to cultural resource management-driven projects. It is my opinion that profit-driven marine development projects (wind farms, beach renourishment projects, pipeline laying, and others) have the vessels and the remote sensing gear needed for work farther offshore in deeper water (i.e., earlier in human history). The data gained from these and other mapping projects are useful tools to identify site locations and explore new areas that carry exciting potential to teach us about the extent of human activity in now-submerged places. I think the most important thing I have done in underwater archaeology is to bring the prehistoric potential of the offshore to both academics and industry.

Similar research in the North Sea has discovered that much of the landscape that existed while the British Isles were connected to mainland Europe has preserved. Sediment cores and sonar data collected from this landscape, known as Doggerland, show that it contained lakes, rivers, and a lush coastal environment for the Paleolithic and Mesolithic foraging societies who lived upon it. Bone and stone artifacts and hundreds of bones from terrestrial animals have also been discovered on this landscape, mostly by being caught in fishing nets, but systematic investigation has increased during the past twenty years as more hydrocarbon development has occurred offshore in this area.[6]

Another consequence of this major sea-level rise is that inland areas became coastal areas and freshwater lakes and rivers filled up. River channels often changed abruptly, and old riverbeds and floodplains were buried, drowned, or abandoned. Often, these fluvial processes destroyed sites as massive amounts of sediment were relocated during this process, but some sites were deeply buried and protected. Sites that were buried before becoming part of the fluvial system, such as the Page-Ladson site in Florida, can be fantastically well-preserved. This site is found 10 m down in the bottom of a sinkhole in the riverbed of the Aucilla River. Within this sinkhole is a 5-m deep sediment deposit that contains an extensive archaeological, paleontological, and paleoenvironmental record. The deepest cultural component at the site dates to ca. 12,600 BCE and is one of the oldest archaeological sites in North America. This component consists of a few stone tools and a mastodon tusk that had been cut with stone tools, all left on the edge of a small spring-fed pond after butchering a mastodon. As sea levels rose and the modern river system formed, the remains were buried in a perfectly preserved layer of sand and mastodon dung that was radiocarbon dated to unambiguously establish the age of the site (figure 7.4). The site is only about 9 km from the ocean today, but when it was occupied, it was nearly 100 km inland, as more than half of Florida's late Pleistocene landmass has been lost to sea-level rise (figure 7.5).[7]

Many new lakes were created as more water became available from the melting glaciers. These bodies of water formed over inland areas that were formerly dry land and drowned many of the sites on these landscapes. This process of drowning

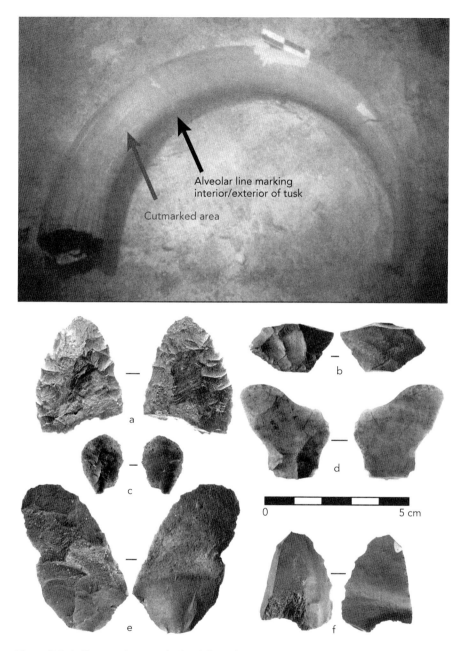

**Figure 7.4** Artifacts and cut-marked tusk from the ca. 12,600 BCE cultural component at Page-Ladson. Top is mastodon tusk with cut marks highlighted. Artifact a is a stone knife fragment, b-f are flakes from stone tool manufacture.

is often slower, with much lower energy than coastal submergence, so many sites inundated by these lakes may have survived. The Alpena-Amberly Ridge caribou hunting structures discussed in chapter 6 and the lake villages (palafittes) discussed in chapter 3 are both excellent examples of these sorts of sites.

Some formerly freshwater lakes and rivers became connected to the oceans as bays, inlets, and lagoons. A famous theory has suggested that Noah's flood of biblical fame recorded an instance of this happening in the past. During the Pleistocene, the Black Sea was a freshwater lake, but, as sea levels rose, the saltwater eventually breached the landmass on the Bosphorus, separating it from the Mediterranean Sea. Some researchers suggested that this breach

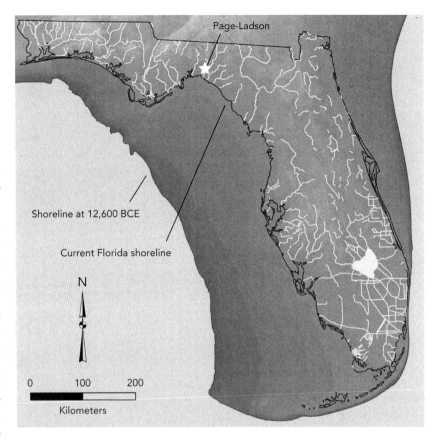

Figure 7.5 Late Pleistocene Florida landmass and current Florida shorelines, showing loss since Page-Ladson, the oldest dated Florida archaeological site, was occupied. Contour intervals are 10 m. The differences in exposed landmass between the western and eastern coasts also demonstrates the relationship between shelf slope and horizontal distance inundated by each meter of vertical sea-level rise.

would have been catastrophic, causing an almost-instantaneous flood as lake levels rose at least 50 m in only a few years' time, which would have wiped out settlements. Newer research indicates that the breaching may not have been abrupt, so there may not have been a flood at all. If there was a flood, it would have only been a few meters of abrupt rise at the most, although it would have flooded prime agricultural land with saltwater—which would have killed the crops and disrupted the local economies, so it may still have had an important impact on people.[8]

Sometimes the archaeological record actually is formed by catastrophic natural events, and sudden submergence can lead to relatively excellent preservation. The city of Port Royal, Jamaica was known as the "wickedest city on Earth" in the mid-17th century. After taking Jamaica from the Spanish in 1655, the British built six well-armed forts around Port Royal. Because of these forts, Port Royal was one of the best-protected settlements in the New World, and the town rapidly expanded. Its deepwater harbor allowed large ships to easily access the area for loading and unloading, attracting merchants and vessels involved in the sugar and slave trades. By 1692, the city boasted as many as 10,000 inhabitants, of whom possibly a third were slaves, and about 2000 buildings, many of which were relatively elaborate brick structures, indicative of the city's wealth. The city was also a hub for officially sanctioned privateers and less-official pirates. Some estimate that in its heyday nearly half the population of Port Royal was involved in piracy and privateering, bringing enormous amounts of wealth to the island of Jamaica.

At approximately noon on 7 June 1692, an earthquake shook the city, followed by a tidal wave that liquefied the sand upon which the city was built. Two-thirds of the city and all of its six forts sank beneath the waves within a matter of minutes, being drowned by 3–12 m of water. Approximately 5,000 of the city's 10,000 inhabitants died from the disaster and ensuing disease. While the remaining portion of Port Royal is occupied to this day, the city never regained its prominence. Underwater archaeologists began investigating the site in the 1950s, with a large-scale excavation conducted from 1981–1990 by Texas A&M University and the Jamaica National Heritage Trust. This investigation discovered many well-preserved buildings with in situ artifacts and human remains from the disaster, having sunk almost directly downward into the harbor to be buried in anoxic sediments. One building was partially covered by a ship that crashed into it during the disaster (figure 7.6). Within the bounds of these structures, archaeologists were able to investigate the material goods and structures of a city involved in both illicit and legal trades. The excavated portions of the site have revealed a warehouse, several taverns, at least two residences, fish and meat markets, a cobbler shop, a possible bakery, and the yards separating these structures. Some buildings were similar in layout to those that would have been found in England at the time; some were quite different. There were a great number of luxury goods discovered at the site, including ceramics from many nations, and, unsurprisingly, many artifacts associated with alcohol and tobacco sales.[9]

Likewise, the Greek city of Pavlopetri, occupied from ca. 3500 BCE through the Mycenaean period until ca. 1100 BCE, known as the world's oldest underwater city, was submerged under approximately 3 m of water by a series of at least three earthquakes that caused the city to settle deeper and deeper into the Mediterranean. The Roman city of Neapolis in modern-day Tunisia was washed away by a tsunami in 365 CE and rediscovered in 2017. Other cities were and are slowly slipping beneath the waves as the land upon which they are built subsides. Portions of Alexandria, Egypt sank between approximately 200 and 600 CE have been rediscovered and explored by divers since the mid-2000s, and the modern cities of New Orleans and Venice are famous for their continued subsidence.[10] Some of this subsidence is due to natural processes, but some of it is caused by the weight of human construction on sediments inadequate to hold it. Subsidence is also caused by people extracting hydrocarbons from the land and seafloor, literally making the earth sink by sucking oils out from within it.

Often slow subsidence leads to slow abandonment of the now-submerged land or to people building upward to keep the shoreline where it was (see next section) with the possibility of cultural material being deeply buried under later cultural material, while rapid subsidence requires abandonment without planning, so artifacts are less likely to be buried under later cultural material, but are often buried in geological deposit; if they are buried shallowly or not at all, people tend to salvage their belongings after the disaster, so the archaeological signature is relatively small.

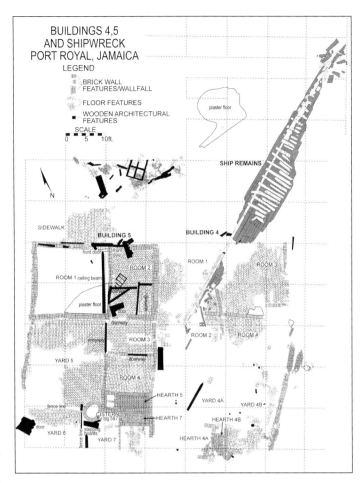

**Figure 7.6** Partial plan of the submerged portions of Port Royal, including the remains of a ship that wrecked through a building wall during the submergence. (Courtesy of Institute of Nautical Archaeology/Texas A&M University)

## HUMANS HAVE THEIR EFFECTS: ANTHROPOGENIC IMPACTS ON MARITIME ENVIRONMENTS AND SITES

Humans have shaped and tried to control our environments for nearly as long as our environments have shaped us. There is evidence that *Homo erectus* may have deliberately used fire as long as 1.5 million years ago, though most researchers do not think they could create it. Both Neanderthals and early modern humans definitely used fires for cooking plant and animal remains, creating materials, and for symbolic purposes.[11] By the end of the Pleistocene, human foraging societies everywhere on the planet were using a wide range of strategies to exploit a broad variety of the resources in their local environments. Recent studies are showing that people were selectively modifying floral and faunal communities and relying on coastal resources for much longer than we previously thought, so human impacts on the natural world have been ongoing for tens of thousands of years.

### Humans as earth movers: Landmaking and its impacts

The first section of this chapter discussed how sea level rise drowned landscapes, pushing people—and entire ecosystems—landward. In many places, people have also pushed the land seaward through deliberate landmaking and accidental siltation of river mouths and harbors. The shell middens mentioned above have created patches of higher, well-drained ground in marshy areas for millennia. Inland activities can have dramatic impacts upon the coastlines; for instance, clearing land for agriculture or creating urban areas increases runoff and sediment input to rivers, causing siltation and infilling at the coasts. Conversely, damming rivers starves them of sediments, causing them to downcut within their channels, drying formerly marshy areas. .

Expanding port cities all over the world need more space for docks and warehouses, more places for people, and more deep water for larger vessels. Deeper water and safer ports are often obtained by dredging harbors, and natural river mouths and deltas are reshaped to be more useful. Sometimes the dredge spoil is used to fill in marshy areas and create more waterfront property. Sometimes structures or old ships are sunk and filled to provide the base for more land, or sea walls are created and used to support more infill. Sometimes more "waterfront" is gained by permanently anchoring vessels in the harbors that are no longer sound enough for sailing; these can be used as warehouses, hotels, and bars, among other things.

The city of Boston, Massachusetts, has expanded its total territory by some 12,000 hectares via aggressive landfill projects from 1630 through the modern day. The city cut down some hills to create fill, dredged the harbors and dumped harbor mud onto the land, sunk cribs to provide support for land, and dumped refuse behind sea walls all to turn a small, but attractive, harbor into one of the biggest port cities in the world. The Netherlands used a sophisticated complex of technologies to reclaim, create, and maintain habitable and arable land. They began to create *polders*, which are areas of drained land surrounded by dikes, as early as the 11th century CE, and intensified efforts in the 16th century. Approximately 17 percent of the country's modern territory is kept dry through human agency. New York City followed suit. The Ronson ship, known as the "ship who held up Wall Street" was an early 18th century merchant vessel, probably the *Princess Carolina*, built in Charleston in 1717. It was discovered in a remarkable state of preservation during a development project on Water Street in Manhattan in the 1980s, and provided important information about merchant shipping at the time and the process of making new land in New York. New Yorkers of the 18th century were granted water lots by the city, extending approximately 200 ft (61 m) into the water from their current properties. In a specified number of years, the grantees were required to fill those 200 ft and provide a municipal road. They used a variety of means to fill these lands, including old ships.[12]

Deliberate landmaking through human agency is not new, nor is accidental reworking of the coast through unforeseen consequences of inland actions. Portus, probably the largest and most intricate port of Imperial Rome, is an excellent example of both. Located at the mouth of the Tiber River, approximately 30 km from Rome, Portus was created almost from nothing by order of Claudius starting in 42 CE, and greatly enlarged by Trajan in 113 CE. Although located in an exposed portion of the Tiber mouth and needing regular dredging because of the increasing agricultural runoff, a deepwater port was needed for the grain ships that fed Rome. The elaborate harbor was created, starting with sinking ships filled with *pozzonlana*, the hydraulic concrete so important to Rome's major construction projects, and eventually including an impressive lighthouse. Temples, warehouses, canals, roads, and aqueducts joined the port, which was used and improved in the ensuing centuries until at least 879 CE. We know much of this from the historical record; a major construction project such as this required a bureaucratic body to track resources, and the primary supply line for one of the principal cities in the world is mentioned in many types of writings. Through these writings, we know that the harbor was no longer navigable by the 12th century and today it lies nearly 2 km inland. Although Leonardo da Vinci Airport lays adjacent to the harbor of Trajan, covering portions of Claudius's port, and the Tiber River has long since changed course, much of Portus's Roman infrastructure is visible today (figure 7.7).[13]

Many archaeologically studied ports show evidence of accumulating enough silt to make them useless for shipping, which makes them equally valuable for maritime and underwater archaeologists. One of the largest excavations in modern Europe took place in such a harbor at the site of Yenikapı in Istanbul, Turkey. Yenikapı is the remains of the silt-filled Harbor of Theodosius, and has yielded the remains of at least 37 ships dating from the 5th–11th centuries CE.[14] Excavation and analyses of these vessels has greatly enhanced our understanding of medieval seafaring and shipbuilding technologies by providing several examples of vessels otherwise completely unknown, or only known through writing or iconography.

**Figure 7.7** Portus, more specifically the remains of Trajan's harbor (outlined in white), outside of modern Rome. Note distance inland due to siltation and landmaking. (Base imagery courtesy of Google Earth)

## Humans as keystone predators and meddlers: Altering the food web and its impacts

Human subsistence strategies regularly and permanently alter the floral and faunal biomes surrounding human communities, and evidence suggests that this trend has been occurring for many thousands of years, even by hunting and gathering societies. Neanderthals were selectively hunting immature marine mammals and gathering mollusks in Gibraltar more than 40,000 years ago. Modern *Homo sapiens* were even more likely to use coastal resources, and, by 21,000 BCE, there is some evidence that shellfish populations were experiencing size reduction from human predation. Fully maritime societies that were regularly utilizing boats to catch fish only obtainable in deep waters were occupying the shores of the Mediterranean by 9000 BCE. Hunting sea otters off the coast of California after 7000 BCE led to an explosion in sea urchin populations and local disappearance of kelp forests, which was, in turn, alleviated by human use of the urchins. Indigenous peoples on the west coast of the Americas regularly built "clam gardens," rocky intertidal terraces for growing large and sustainable shellfish populations; the time depth of these gardens is unknown, but they were in regular use long before Europeans arrived in the New World. Thus, well before the industrialized world, there is ample evidence that humans were shaping the maritime food webs around them.[15]

As human societies became larger and more complex, permanent coastal settlements became established throughout the world. These coastal villages, towns, and cities fed themselves through a combination of terrestrial and marine resources, and over time people became extremely clever at capturing fish and large mammals from the sea, developing specialized boats, nets, and weaponry. Eventually, this led to industrialized exploitation of marine resources on the global market, often causing international regulation of these fisheries as, one after another, the various targeted resource populations crashed to near-unsustainable levels.

One of the earliest examples of this is the development of the whaling industry. Peoples in Japan, North America, and Northern Europe began hunting whales as much as 4,000 years ago, using whale oil for fuel, whale meat and blubber for food, and whale bones and skins as construction materials and tools. Whale oil and baleen became increasingly popular in Europe throughout the Middle Ages, and by the 16th century, there was enough demand for whale resources that enterprising whalers were making specialized trips to the New World to hunt them. The Basque had developed an especially effective strategy, returning annually to Red Bay, on the coast of Labrador, from 1543 into the 18th century. During their peak use of the area, a fleet of 15–30 ships would hunt, butcher, and render bowhead whales on site, packing approximately 1000 casks of whale oil per vessel—the remains of about 20 whales—for the return trip to Spain. Archaeologists have been investigating the remains of this industry since 1978. The remoteness of the area helped preserve the terrestrial processing areas extremely well, while the cold water of Red Bay contains many of the whale bones and the wrecks of three ships and several of the smaller vessels in near-pristine condition. This excellent preservation allowed the entire whaling process to be more completely understood.[16]

By the mid-19th century, the United States' whaling fleet included more than 2700 ships, barks, brigs, and schooners, with many other nations, including Japan, Norway, Britain, and France also hosting substantial fleets. By 1846, the United States had cornered the market on the whaling industry, owning more than three times the amount of registered whaling vessels as the rest of the world combined (735 out of 900 total worldwide vessels), and whaling was the fifth-largest sector of the American economy. Specialized whaling vessels and whale-processing stations allowed industrial whale harvesting to continue apace. From the 16th century until chemists learned to refine petroleum-based oils during the mid-19th century, whale oil and spermaceti were important lubricants, lighting fuels, and ingredient in paints and soaps. The baleen of whales was also harvested to produce items that required flexibility, such as corsets and umbrellas. In the record year, 1853, American whaling vessels dispatched 8,000 whales and had vessels in every part of the world's oceans from Australia to the Arctic. Whales, which originally were reliably to be found in the Arctic oceans at specific times of the year, had become increasingly unpredictable as their populations were hunted to near-extinction. This industry began to decline soon afterward, partially due to the increasing rarity of whales, but also due to changes in the American labor market and the increasing reliance on petroleum. Whale populations still remain low throughout the world and many countries have instated laws forbidding or strictly restricting hunting.[17]

One of the most dramatic ways in which humans impact maritime ecosystems is through introducing exotic species, whether intentionally or not. Many of the world's seas and lakes are fighting a losing battle against infestations of invasive weeds, fish, and shellfish that were transported within the bilges and on the hulls and props of ships and boats. These exotics often thrive in the new environments, colonizing empty niches in the ecosystem or outcompeting the plants and animals that already live there, transforming the entire biome within a few years. This can cause economic as well as ecological impacts, as these changing ecosystems often have unintended impacts upon species of financial importance. This invasion can also threaten the archaeological record. Stable conditions after a site is created is one of the most important factors for continued preservation of an intact archaeological site. Introduction of an invader, almost by definition, impacts this stability.

For instance, zebra mussels (*Dreissena polymorpha*) and quagga mussels (*Dreissena bugensis*) left Russia and entered the Great Lakes of North America via ballast water in a transatlantic vessel sometime in the late 1980s. The lakes were the ideal environment for them and less than a decade later, they had rapidly colonized all available hard surfaces on the lake beds, including the previously well-preserved wooden and steel shipwrecks found in the deep waters of the lakes. Quagga mussels are now outcompeting zebra mussels in the lakes. They have spread to a majority of freshwater bodies in the United States and Canada and to many other portions of the world. In addition to upsetting the lake ecosystems, this colonization of the wrecks is leading to rapid deterioration of the sites, possibly due to carbonic acid released by the mussels during respiration. Figure 7.8 displays an excellent example of this at the popular dive site of the railroad car ferry *Milwaukee*, built in 1903 to carry 28 freight cars at a time across Lake Michigan from Wisconsin to Michigan, avoiding the extra miles needed to go around the lake. It sank with all hands in 1929 during a tremendous storm. It was rediscovered in 1972 in 38 meters of water and has featured in several documentaries since. Currently, members of the Wisconsin Historical Society are monitoring the wreck's condition while the quagga mussel colonization threatens site stability.[18]

Human disruption of the food web also can have severe impacts on the archaeological record. Bottom trawl fishing, the practice of dragging enormous nets along the seafloor, not only captures a wide variety of fish, many of which

**Figure 7.8** Quagga mussel colonization of the railroad car ferry *Milwaukee* (1903), sunk on 22 October 1929 in 38 m (125 ft) of water in Lake Michigan. Top, pilothouse in 2004 and 2014, Bottom left, pilothouse door in 2004; Bottom right, degradation of pilothouse door after only 10 years of mussel activity in 2014. (Courtesy of Tamara Thomsen, Wisconsin Historical Society)

are not consumed by humans, but also removes sediment and smooths out the seafloor. This smoothing tends to have severe impacts on shipwrecks and other sites near the surface of the seafloor. Michael Brennan and colleagues documented destruction and damage to 45 wrecks in the Black and Aegean seas using high-resolution sonar data. These images showed that wrecks were turned over, exposing timbers and dumping contents, and some wrecks were dissipated over larger areas. Occasionally, the nets become entangled on more intact wrecks, tearing apart both nets and wrecks, and providing additional entanglement hazards for archaeologists working on the site in the future.[19]

## Humans as waste makers: disposal of trash underwater and its impacts

Since ancient times, the underwater world has been seen as a place of no return. What goes beneath the surface no longer needs to be considered. Whether it is the glass beer bottle one has just finished drinking, an unwanted witness, or barges filled with a city's waste, people regularly dispose of their extra encumbrances under the waves. We saw hints of this earlier, when discussing how cities make land, but many cultures—perhaps even most—have considered it not only acceptable, but prudent, to use the oceans, rivers, and lakes to manage garbage of various kinds whenever possible. After all, if organic remains, including human waste, are dumped underwater, dangerous predators and scavengers and noxious smells are minimized. The modern sewage systems of most countries are an extension of this idea; it was only in the mid-19th century, after Dr. John Snow's study of a cholera epidemic in London demonstrated that a contaminated pump was providing the water that was killing people, that doctors realized that polluted water could make people ill.[20]

Greeks of the 6th century BCE considered the sea to be an "away place" that could be used to dispose of things forever, including people. Choosing to dispose of valuable things permanently by flinging them into the sea, could, thus, be a way to court the favor of or avoid the disfavor of the gods, while dangerous items or people could also be committed to the deep to get rid of them. This latter is an attitude that has proven persistent. Although many countries have strict regulations about what may or may not be dumped into the oceans, most of these regulations were only passed in the latter part of the 20th century.

Many of the world's governments and industries dumped millions of gallons of low-level radioactive nuclear waste into the oceans in sealed containers in at least 50 different deepwater sites between 1946 and 1982. Most countries ceased this activity after a 1982 London Convention. However, dumping the waste into deep water was seen as one of the safest means of disposal of the radioactive materials because of the low level of radioactivity and the distance the materials would be removed from humans, and some countries have continued the process. More concerning to most researchers is the amount of garbage, especially chemicals, nitrates, sewage, and nonbiodegradable plastics reaching the world's rivers, lakes, and oceans through illegal dumping, runoff, and poor waste-management practices; many suggest the solution to this problem is through better management of terrestrial disposal, especially in poorer nations.[21]

The archaeological impact of these activities is twofold: (1) creating sites and (2) impacting older sites and the archaeologists who try to excavate them. The trash itself is an archaeological deposit that provides evidence of human activities. This occasionally provides valuable clues about past cultures; much more often, however, it tells us about the poor waste-management practices of the recent past. As noted in the remote sensing survey section of chapter 4, an inordinate number of "targets" we observe turn out to be modern trash that was dumped in the water either intentionally or unintentionally. In many northern communities, for instance, it is common annual winter practice to place a disposable car, drained of all fluids, on the ice of a lake or pond, with a communal betting pool based on the day the ice will thin enough for the car to fall through. Less officially, there has long been a habit of pushing items out on the ice so that they would "disappear" when it melted. These items, ranging from shipping containers to washing machines to couches to plastic bags of trash, have been observed in numerous sonar images.[22]

Modern debris also impacts older archaeological sites. For instance, a red plastic drinking cup was found wedged onto the deepwater Mardi Gras site, more than 50 km from land and 1220 m below the surface. This is interesting because it displays the ubiquity of plastics, but did not strongly affect site integrity. More damaging are the trawling activities and nets mentioned above. Even when investigating targets in rivers and streams, archaeologists need to come armed with knives to cut the numerous fishing lines that are often attached to any preserved wreck, impacting the site and providing an entanglement and drowning hazard to the excavator. We need to wear gloves to protect ourselves from the ubiquitous fishhooks, as well. Many underwater sites also are found within now-polluted waters, damaging the delicate balance that allowed the wreck to preserve initially and providing a threat to any researcher who attempts to investigate the site. Many of these sites are so significant that archaeologists accept the health risks to research these sites, such as the intrepid team of Frank Goddio, who discovered the sunken portions of Alexandria within one of the world's most polluted harbors or the members of Luc Long's team who dove into the sewage- and refuse-filled Rhône River in France to map a Roman dump and a number of Roman river vessels.[23]

Not all dumping is equally harmful, however. In many portions of the world, we are now purposefully sinking stable items like former subway trains and derelict vessels to provide hard, rough bottom surfaces for corals to grow on. These artificial reefs provide homes to a wide variety of marine life and are areas with comparatively high degrees of biodiversity, which also leads them to become popular recreational dive locations.[24] Usually, the "reefs" are chosen to be nonreactive, and all dangerous chemicals are removed from them prior to sinking. Ecological studies of these artificial reefs are ongoing, but they generally seem to be providing a benefit to many marine animals. Obviously, these reefs are also deliberately created archaeological sites, so these studies are also helping us to understand the rate and timing of marine colonization of wreck sites and how colonization impacts sites.

## WATER ON THE MIND: THE COGNITIVE ASPECTS
## OF HUMAN-WATER INTERACTIONS

The first two-thirds of this chapter have focused on the directly observable material aspects of human/environmental interactions. This final section will discuss how archaeologists study the more cognitive and spiritual aspects of these interactions, much of which is only accessible to us through analogy, iconography, and the written word. While it is more difficult to define a culture's spiritual beliefs than it is to determine what a group was eating, it is very important for archaeologists to try to discover these beliefs if the goal of archaeology is to understand people in the past. It can be hard to separate spiritual activities from material ones; how a society views the water strongly shapes how it uses (or does not use) its access to maritime resources, while the nature of the seas surrounding a culture can shape its view of the water. **Cognitive archaeologists** focus on understanding the belief systems of past cultures and how these systems influenced daily life. This subfield of archaeology came into its own in the early 1980s in Europe and has been gaining ground ever since. It has greatly influenced the maritime and underwater archaeology of northern Europe especially, and has provided us new and fruitful ways to think about people in the past.

As we have noted throughout this text, the watery world is not naturally part of the human purview, but most human societies have gained facility with traversing and using this foreign environment and mitigating, to some extent, the dangers, in order to reap its rewards. Perhaps because of this juxtaposition of danger and opportunity, it is extremely common for water to feature prominently in the art, poetry, literature, myths, legends, histories, ceremonies, and ideologies of maritime nations. Waterways are represented as an agent of change, source of devastation, and birthplace of wealth. These representations are based in fact; loss of a vessel at the wrong time could lead to the destruction of a formerly affluent merchant family, while a fleet coming ashore a day before a rival's could make the fortunes of another. Maritime trade was the original high-risk portfolio.

Long, unintentional sea voyages are extremely important in literature ranging from Homer's *Odyssey* to Viking sagas to modern novels such as *The Life of Pi*. The voyages are full of death-defying danger and allow the characters who survive to be tempered by the journey. Shakespeare used shipwrecks as a plot device, usually as a means of catalyzing events, in at least seven of his plays. The idea of discovery and opportunity on long voyages is also extremely important. This is especially true regarding voyages to (and shipwrecks on) islands.

As literal lands apart, islands represent the exotic, rare, and primitive, mixed with opportunity and danger. They have been understood as such in popular culture since the *Odyssey's* land of the lotus eaters. The legend of Sinbad, immortalized in the *Thousand and One Nights*, a series of Middle Eastern tales recorded sometime between 800 CE and 1400 CE, tells of Sinbad's five voyages to island after island, each of which was not what it seemed, and each of which contained its own dangers, from cannibals to giant birds. Somehow Sinbad survived all of his mishaps, acquiring diamonds and princesses on the way. This view of islands as exotic and primitive in European popular culture has also led to an implicit bias in much European scholarship toward considering island inhabitants themselves to be insular, isolated, and simpler than their mainland brethren. While some island cultures did consider their islands to encompass the entirety of the world, there is ample evidence that most islands in the past were rarely disconnected from the worlds around them, and many island and coastal dwellers saw their coastlines as bridges, rather than walls.[25]

Many people today consider water to be a barrier and shorelines to be a hard edge, but in numerous past and present cultures, people perceived and perceive the waterline differently. Waterways present varying opportunities because waterways are changeable. For instance, people in northern climes anxiously await the freezing of lakes in order to set up elaborate ice fishing villages, where the social opportunities are more important than the actual fishing for many occupants. These icy lakescapes were also regularly used to connect the United States and Canada via carefully planned ice roads on the Great Lakes throughout the 19th and 20th centuries; one could argue that this is a functional use of the landscape, but it was enabled by the way in which folks around the lakes viewed themselves as interconnected, international borders notwithstanding.[26]

Fragments of stories of how people viewed their watery worlds have survived in almost every known maritime culture, and they have some common attributes. The sea is often considered to be a capricious being that has both positive and negative attributes and demands careful and respectful treatment. As pointed out by Robert Van de Noort, the waters of the oceans are often considered to have agency, or the ability for deliberate action. Therefore, there are many rituals and taboos surrounding the proper way to approach and appease these fickle beings (chapter 10). At the same time, as the oceans and their coasts are not homogenous, neither are the cultures reliant upon them. Not only do maritime cultures transform over time, these cultures vary greatly from place to place. For instance, in the early 20th century, it was rare for North Sea sailors to know how to swim; this was a deliberate choice, because being able to swim was likely only to prolong death in the frigid waters. Now it is an entrance requirement in many navies to pass a swim test.[27]

In many maritime societies, the sea, while dangerous, was and is seen as the source of opportunity and prosperity. Therefore, a busy harbor town with forests of masts was considered to be a positive symbol, projecting images of success and safety. These images have permeated artistic representations, from the extremely popular paintings of seascapes that dominated the late 19th and early 20th century art of Europe and the Americas to medieval illuminated manuscripts. These artistic representations at the same time outline a contradiction in the general English lexicon. *Landscapes*, in the general use of the word, are tangible portions of the terrestrial world shaped and understood by people.

*Seascapes*, on the other hand, are artistic representations of coastlines, usually with some human elements included. These renditions always seem to include land, and usually include some water as well.

This difference in definition between landscape and seascape may well reflect the larger cognitive disconnect between the dry and wet for landlubbers. Sailors had a different vocabulary, rarely referring to the "shore" as a singular feature seen from land, but, instead referring to portions of it as important features as seen from the water. The vocabulary of coasts and the oceans, in fact, differ in many ways from that of the inland. Partly this is because the refractive properties of wave, shoreline, humidity, and deep water lead to space and distance being perceived through markedly different lenses. Partly this is because the "coast" and the oceans are not the uniform thing casual beachgoers would take them for, and different portions provide different opportunities and hazards, and there-fore, need to be approached with different technologies. All of this has its own vocabulary in English and in many other languages as well, demonstrating that, for many coastal people, the seascape, just like the landscape, actually was a tan-gible and bounded portion of the maritime world shaped and understood by people.[28]

Many maritime researchers have realized this, referring to this "seascape" as a "maritime cultural landscape," a term coined by Christer Westerdahl to clarify that both sides of the waterline are important in how people conceive of and therefore utilize their maritime worlds.[29] In fact, many coastal societies perceive themselves as more similar to other coastal societies, even those separated by great distance, than they do to neighboring land-oriented groups. For instance, recent research has demonstrated that the flooding of the North Sea at the end of the Pleistocene initially fractured groups into numerous smaller cultures, but as seafaring technology became more and more reliable, the North Sea was reg-ularly used to create contacts between coastal groups as demonstrated by similar material culture pan-Scandinavia and Scotland by ca. 2800 BCE.[30]

The cultural traditions on these maritime landscapes can be enduring, lasting over centuries and, possibly, millennia. For instance, wetlands are lit-erally marginal environments, occupying the margin between land and water. In many societies in Northern Europe, these marginal environments served as liminal zones in which specific rites and rituals were enacted, such as the sacrifices of people that became today's famous bog bodies. In the Medieval period, these wetlands became the domain of liminal women, such as nuns. Islands and remote coastal domains were the realm of monastic communities of the Medieval British Isles, whose battles for survival in harsh maritime environments represented their battles against evil and temptation. The writings of the time indicate that these liminal zones were chosen on purpose for spiritual motives. Pre-Christian pagan imagery and writing provide pos-itive representations of the maritime, while Christian imagery sends a mes-sage of the oceanic world as a tricky, devious enemy that needs controlling, in contrast to freshwater, which is a source of life, hope, and succor. By the 13th century, these views had expanded as monks became increasingly interested in mapping and exploring the physical world, including participating in actual explorations and pilgrimages.[31]

## SUMMARY

People affect their environments; environments and environmental changes influence human cultures in turn. Many of these impacts leave tangible traces that may preserve in the archaeological record. Further, both anthropogenic and environmental activities can impact the archaeological record itself, including determining if and to what extent the archaeological record will even preserve. Less tangible in the archaeological record, but very important for our understanding of past peoples, the maritime and underwater environment has also shaped the way people perceive the world in significant and dramatic ways. These spiritual perceptions, in turn, shaped the functional aspects of how people approached and utilized the maritime world. Archaeologists look to indirect evidence and proxy records to interpret the broad environmental trends and the very specific spiritual aspects of human/maritime interactions; the archaeological record tends to speak most clearly about the more material aspects of these interactions. Maritime and underwater archaeology can provide direct information about past human/environmental interactions that can offer useful lessons for modern cultures.

## DISCUSSION QUESTIONS

1. If you were living during the late Pleistocene environmental change, what would have been the most troubling aspect to you? Why do we say that creativity and flexibility would have been important for people living in the late glacial world?
2. Why is it important for maritime and underwater archaeologists to have some basic understanding of geology, hydrology, and physical oceanography?
3. Why is it so challenging to differentiate causation and correlation between cultural and environmental changes? What are some approaches that can help to clarify the relationship between people and environment at a given site?
4. Which of the modern human activities we mentioned do you think are most likely to adversely impact maritime and underwater archaeology? Why and how?
5. Given that spiritual aspects of maritime cultures are so variable in time and space, why is it important for archaeologists to try to access these aspects?

**FURTHER READING**

Dolin, E. (2007). *Leviathan: The History of Whaling in America.* W.W. Norton, New York.

Evans, A.M., J. Flatman, and N. C. Flemming, Eds. (2014). *Prehistoric Archaeology on the Continental Shelf: a Global Review.* Springer, New York.

Flatman, J. (2010). Wetting the Fringe of Your Habit: Medieval Monasticism and Coastal Landscapes. *Perspectives in Landscape Archaeology.* H. Lewis and S. Semple, Eds. 66–77. Archaeopress, Oxford.

Halligan, J. (2016). Inundated Freshwater Settings. *Encyclopedia of Geoarchaeology.* A.S. Gilbert, Ed. Springer, Dordrecht.

Hamilton, D.L. (2000). The Port Royal Project: Archaeological Excavations. Nautical Archaeology Program, Texas A&M University, College Station. Available at http://nautarch.tamu.edu/portroyal/archhist.htm.

Lawler, A. (2007). Raising Alexandria. *Smithsonian Magazine.* https://www.smithsonianmag.com/science-nature/raising-alexandria-151005550/.

Lindenlauf, A. (2003). The Sea as a Place of No Return in Ancient Greece. *World Archaeology* **35**(3): 416–433.

Rainbird, P. (2016). Islands Out of Time: Towards a Critique of Island Archaeology. *Journal of Mediterranean Archaeology* **12**(2): 216–234.

Rick, T.C. and J.M. Erlandson. (2009). Coastal Exploitation. *Science* **325**: 952–953.

University of Nottingham. (2017). The Pavlopetri Underwater Archaeology Project. Available at http://www.nottingham.ac.uk/pavlopetri/index.aspx.

Van de Noort, R. (2011). *North Sea Archaeologies: A Maritime Biography, 10,000 BC to AD 1500.* Oxford University Press, Oxford.

## CHAPTER 8

# INHABITING THE COAST

## FOCUS QUESTIONS

- When and how did maritime societies emerge?
- How have people interacted with seas, lakes, and rivers? How was this inter-action shaped by their culture and environment? What are the similarities, differences, and outcomes of these interactions?
- What types of maritime archaeological sites are there, and how do they differ in what they can teach us about the past?
- What information can be gained from inundated landscapes and submerged terrestrial sites?
- How did maritime people shape world history?

## MARITIME ARCHAEOLOGY DOESN'T HAVE TO BE WET

Maritime archaeology does not necessarily have to take place underwater. There are many examples of terrestrial archaeological sites that reflect a culture's mar-itime lifestyle. While these sites are occasionally located a surprising distance inland, the majority are clustered along shores and coasts where people have their most direct contact with the wet environment. As the seer Tiresias implied when he told Odysseus to walk inland until the inhabitants mistook his oar for a winnowing fan, the farther you get from the shore, the less likely you are to encounter maritime peoples. In this chapter, we will explore the archaeology of coasts, ports, shipyards, and artificial islands to better understand the relationship between sailors and landlubbers, between maritime and terrestrial adaptations, and between maritime and terrestrial archaeologies. Many of these topics are combined in what archaeologists refer to as **maritime cultural landscapes**.[1]

## DEVELOPMENT OF MARITIME ADAPTATION

Humans have no inherent affinity for the water. We lose our webbed fingers during the first trimester in the womb, about the same time our tails fade away. Our ability to enter a wet environment after birth is almost entirely dependent on cultural adaptations—everything from the ability to swim, to predicting the weather, to building boats—are learned behaviors. Not only does it take time for us to learn these skills, it took our ancestors time to develop them. Human evolution could be summarized as hominids moving from the forests to the plains to the oceans, with the last step indicating the development of fully *Homo sapiens sapiens* cognition and allowing for our worldwide distribution.[2] The spread of humans to the shore, along the shore, and onto the water was a cultural adaptation likely springing from the movement of hunter-gatherers in search of food and resources. As *Homo sapiens sapiens* developed in Africa, some groups used coastal resources as part of their regular resource procurement strategy. Over time, some of these groups began to focus more and more on maritime resources and developed technologies to take fuller advantage of those resources. Once adapted to the coast, these groups likely spread along the shoreline, moving into unsettled areas with less competition for resources, following the migrations of animals, and shifting as plants and animals migrated in response to climate change. In this way, humans moved out of Africa then throughout southern Asia, eventually reaching Australia. Similarly adapted groups also spread into the islands of the Mediterranean, while other groups were likely involved in the settlement of the Americas. All the while, other humans with different cultural and technological adaptations moved (though usually more slowly) into the inland portions of Asia, Europe, and the Americas.

In time, some of the coastally adapted groups became fully maritime or seafaring cultures. In more recent times, these seafaring cultures are better described as subcultures within larger ethnic or national cultures. In either case, the shore remains the juncture between human maritime systems and terrestrial systems. Most of our major cities are ports (figure 8.1), because ports are the nodes where the goods, resources, and people collected from, and transported across, the seas intersect with the inland transportation routes that allow those people and items to be distributed across the various continents. This is true today despite air transportation, and was even more of an imperative in earlier times. Sailors do not spend all their time at sea, and many have families who never leave dry land. It is also true that both ships and sailors are most often conceived on land. Both ships and sailors are terrestrial products that must cross the waterline to fulfill their purpose. This relationship continues throughout their lives. Ships return to ports to load and unload cargoes, take on new crews, undergo repairs, and often end their careers wrecked or abandoned on or near the shore. Shore communities exist around ports and landing places to support the ships and sailors. The most important aspects of these communities were the relationships

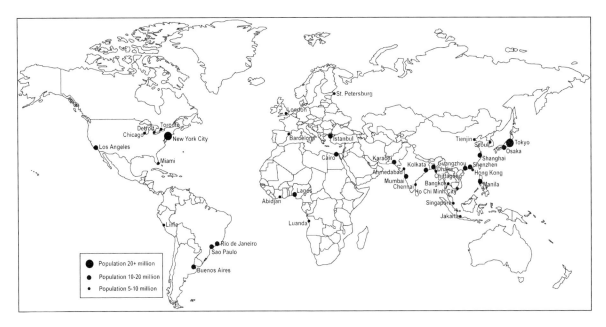

**Figure 8.1** Major coastal cities.

between people—their shared experiences that gave a community its character and provided the mutual support that humans needed to thrive. Archaeologically, we can recognize these roles of shore communities in the homes, places of worship, stores, entertainment establishments, and other institutions that catered to sailors and their families, as well as the docks, warehouses, shipyards, and other infrastructure that provided for the ships.[3] Since sailors spent portions of their lives both afloat and ashore, and because their families derived much of their sustenance from the sea while living on land, maritime archaeologists need to study the lives of these people on both sides of the waterline. That means investigating not only shipwrecks, but also the coastal sites that relate to maritime peoples. These coastal sites form an important link between the domains of terrestrial and underwater archaeology since much of what we find on shipwrecks was intended for use on land and many of the people and goods studied by terrestrial archaeologists were transported over water.[4]

An example of the interrelationship between terrestrial and maritime archaeology at the coast comes from the south shore of the North Sea, in what is now Belgium, during the Late Medieval period. People in these coastal communities were involved in both fishing and farming. Fishing was the primary task of men but was not sufficient to support most families, so many supplemented their income with terrestrial pursuits. With the men away fishing, women became involved in what are cross-culturally male-dominated occupations such as animal husbandry, hunting, net mending, agriculture, and trading. In some communities, families of these farmer-fishers maintained two residences: a farmstead and a separate small building that occasionally housed the fisherman, but was primarily for the storage of nets, lines, barrels, and boats. From the perspective of archaeology, these separate structures could appear to belong to two different groups, despite being maintained by the same individuals. As the hinterland population grew and the demand for fish increased, many of the families could make a living entirely by fishing and added a permanent residence to their fishing building. During this transition, it was not uncommon for fathers to pass the farm to one son and the fishing equipment to the other, allowing both to establish families, leading to population increase and culture change. As clearly demonstrated in this example, an understanding of maritime archaeology and the roles of maritime peoples within the larger study of archaeology requires an appreciation of coastal archaeology.[5]

## THE ARCHAEOLOGY OF LANDING PLACES, PORTS, SHIPYARDS, AND ARTIFICIAL ISLANDS
### Landing places

The earliest and most common juncture between land and sea occurred at landing places. "Landing place" is a generic term for an unmodified or lightly modified location where a boat can be pulled ashore. For most of human seafaring history, boats were shallow-drafted and nearly flat-bottomed. These vessels included the earliest reed and log rafts as well as the log, plank, and skin boats made by later preliterate peoples. All these vessels have the advantage of being easily beached on any gently sloping shore, and wear on the bottoms of known examples confirms that this was common practice. These boats could, and no doubt were, pulled ashore anywhere it was convenient, but they were also regularly and repeatedly beached at specific locations. These locations could be close to a settlement or resource and may have been a ferry landing or any other place that figured into regular human interaction with the wet environment. Most of these locations took advantage of the natural landscape, but, at places of regular beaching, we can find archaeological evidence of humans modifying the environment to make landing more convenient. This may take the form of **jetties** (small **piers**), **hards** (prepared, firm surfaces that make it easier to beach a boat), **causeways** (log- or stone-raised roads that span the muddy stretches between land and water), **slipways** (changes to the slope of the shore such as a cut in the bank or cleared stones), concentrations of artifacts lost during loading and unloading, or other lines of evidence.

Many landing places took advantage of rivers and river mouths where the landing was protected from waves by the natural setting and discharged sediments offered a gradual slope on which to beach the boat. In areas where there was sufficient tidal range, it was common to moor a boat, allow it to settle on the bottom with the outgoing tide, load or unload, and then refloat it with the incoming tide.[6] This practice allowed substantial boats carrying heavy cargos to be loaded and unloaded with very little infrastructure. Landing places could also serve as portage locations. **Portage**, the process of moving a boat overland from one body of water to another, could be done between rivers or to cross an isthmus. Smaller, lighter boats, such as skin boats, were easily carried from one water body to the other. In some locations, a prepared way allowed much larger vessels to be portaged, such as at the Diolkos, which allowed ships to be pulled over the Isthmus of Corinth in Greece, thereby avoiding the need to circumnavigate the Peloponnese.[7]

The use of landing places continued even after the development of larger ships that required formal ports and harbors. Anywhere that people continued to use boats that could be run ashore, landing places persisted. In many countries, the most prevalent modern example is canoe landings. A canoe can be put in the water anywhere, but specific access points are more commonly used than others. To understand the archaeological signature of a landing place, think about the infrastructure of canoe access points (e.g., parking areas, small boat ramps or muddy slopes) and all the artifacts (e.g., glass bottles, sunglasses, and cell phones) that litter the bottom around them.

A much older example comes from North Ferriby, England, where the remains of four sewn-plank boats were discovered on the banks of the Humber River between 1937 and 1996. The Ferriby boats, dating to 2030–1680 BCE, are important in their own right as early examples of large (approximately 15.2 m [50 ft] long) plank boat construction in northern Europe (figure 8.2). The associations between the boat remains and other recovered artifacts are also important as an example of a landing place and boatyard. While one of the boats was likely abandoned largely intact, another two, which were found lying atop a prepared hard surface of wood poles, appear to have been in the process of repair. Combined with a piece of a repair patch, chips from shaping planks, and the remains of yew withies for stitching the planks together, is these provide strong evidence

**Figure 8.2** Reconstruction of a Ferriby boat approaching a landing place. (Courtesy of Ferriby Heritage Trust Ltd.)

**Figure 8.3** Tulum, Mexico. El Castillo is the large building closest to the cliff and the landing place is visible immediately adjacent. (Base imagery courtesy of Google Earth)

that boats were repaired, if not built, at North Ferriby. The site also contains the remains of what may be a windlass for hauling boats out of the water, two paddles, a net weight, a bronze knife, and several pieces of pottery. The excavators interpreted these artifacts as evidence that the site was a landing place, and the location is a natural point for a ferry across the Humber. The landing place and boatyard at North Ferriby, therefore, provided the means and location for travel across (and likely along) the Humber estuary, moving people, livestock, flint, pottery, and other goods.[8]

Similar landing places elsewhere in Britain also facilitated the diffusion of goods and ideas between the island and mainland Europe.

The Mayan site of Tulum in Mexico, which flourished during the 13th to 15th centuries CE, also provides a good example of a landing place (figure 8.3). El Castillo, one of the largest buildings at the site, presents a nearly blank stone face toward the sea, except for two small windows in the upper story. When illuminated, these windows likely guided oceangoing Mayan canoes through a narrow passage in the surrounding coral reef and toward one of the few beaches that break the sea cliffs of the region. This natural setting may have been why Tulum was founded, and likely led to its development as a prominent port. Artifacts from throughout Mexico and Central America have been found at the site, accentuating how an established site can develop alongside an expanding network of intercultural exchange.[9]

## Ports

Many landing places occur along portions of the coast that are naturally protected from wind and waves. They also tend to be easily identified from the water, facilitating a boatman's ability to reliably find them. These protected and identifiable areas that are large enough to shelter a ship are referred to as **harbors**. Many harbors occur naturally, but are often augmented with piers, breakwaters, lighthouses, or other artificial structures. The natural setting and artificial improvements of harbors allow larger ships, those that cannot be pulled ashore at a landing place, to shelter while taking on or discharging cargo. This includes piers that stretch out to deeper water so that a ship can remain afloat while easily transferring cargo. The earliest evidence of a pier comes from Lothal, India, where archaeologists have found evidence of a ca. 3700 BCE wharf. In ports with no piers or where the ships were too deep to approach the available piers, ports often offered lighters—boats that shuttled between the shore and the ship to transfer cargo and people. As locations where ships regularly loaded and unloaded cargo, as well as places where ships and sailors frequented, many harbors developed ports. **Ports** are settlements associated with harbors that grew up around the commerce of the harbor, storing and selling cargos, collecting custom dues and taxes, repairing ships, housing and entertaining sailors, and all the other cultural activities linked to a harbor. The relationship between the harbor for the ship and the associated port settlement is so strong that "harbor" and "port" have become synonymous.[10]

Ports were the first coastal sites investigated by archaeologists and they remain a significant research focus with major projects stretching from the Mediterranean to Australia. Archaeologists were first drawn to Mediterranean ports with substantial architectural remains at sites such as Portus, Piraeus, and Caesarea Maritima. Piraeus was the military and commercial port of ancient Athens, while Portus served Rome and Caesarea Maritima was built by Herod to benefit Roman Judea. All three were impressive engineering feats that illustrate the political and economic organization of classical Greece and Rome.

Piraeus, which actually consisted of three harbors located approximately 12 km (7 mi) from the landlocked city of Athens, was developed and fortified during the 5th century BCE. The harbor itself was protected by walls, and a walled roadway connected the port and Athens so that materials and goods could continue to flow back and forth even during a siege. Piraeus is Greece's largest harbor and now part of modern Athens, so the archaeological site of Piraeus has been heavily disturbed by later construction. Nonetheless, through analysis of the archaeological remains, some of which are still visible along the waterline, archaeologists have been able to reconstruct large portions of the ancient port. Much of this work has focused on the trireme shipsheds in the harbor of Zea (figure 8.4). Triremes, the principal warship of the Athenian navy, relied on their speed and maneuverability to ram or board enemy ships. Consequently, waterlogging, infestation by marine growth or marine borers, and the general wear and tear of storms and weather while moored in the harbor were significant threats to their wartime effectiveness. To protect their valuable warships and keep them in top fighting maintenance, the Athenians built enough shipsheds to house more than 300 triremes by the 330s BCE. The shipsheds consisted of stone and timber ramps covered by tile roofs supported by stone columns so that the triremes could be hauled completely out of the water and protected from the elements. Inscriptions from the shipsheds, as well as the size and features of the sheds themselves, are an important line of evidence about triremes, helping

**Figure 8.4** Shipsheds at Zea Harbor, 4th Century BCE (From Lords of the Sea: The Epic Story of the Athenian Navy and the Birth of Democracy by John R. Hale, © 2009 by John R. Hale. Used by permission of Viking Books, an imprint of Penguin Publishing Group, a division of Penguin Random House LLC. All rights reserved)

us extrapolate characteristics such as the vessel dimensions. Because of their light construction, triremes do not survive well as shipwrecks, so the shipsheds are one of the few physical links to these important ships. They also illustrate how important the triremes were to ancient Athens. The shipsheds were a major building project, with the sheds at Zea alone covering more than 55,000 m$^2$ (13.6 acres), and were among the largest roofed structures in antiquity. Beyond their practical purpose, the size and visibility of the sheds broadcasted the might of the Athenian navy to anyone who visited the port.[11]

As impressive as Piraeus was, the Romans invested even more effort into building numerous artificial harbors, in some instances completely reworking the landscape to place a large harbor where nature had provided almost nothing of the sort. These harbors illustrate just how far the Romans and their allies were willing to go to facilitate maritime trade. They are also monuments to Roman engineering and the importance of maritime trade in the Roman world. Two of the best-known Roman harbors are Portus (discussed in chapter 7) and Caesarea Maritima.

Caesarea Maritima, the harbor and city built by Herod on the coast of modern Israel in the last decades BCE is among the best-studied examples of Roman hydraulic concrete engineering (figure 8.5). Hydraulic concrete is a form of concrete that sets underwater. When built, Caesarea Maritima was the largest artificial harbor of its time, requiring 100 to 150 shiploads of volcanic ash to be imported from Italy to concoct the concrete. Archaeological investigations of the breakwaters suggest that the engineers were experimenting with different construction techniques, trying to find an effective and efficient method to position the hydraulic concrete and hold it in place while it set. The technology, volcanic ash, and name of Caesarea Maritima, all imported from Italy, as well as the flow of Roman goods and soldiers, served to physically and culturally project Rome onto Judaea. Caesarea Maritima also illustrates the active role of nature in human-water landscapes. No matter how well-built a harbor is, dramatic and subtle environmental processes are constantly at work. Geoarchaeological analyses at Caesarea Maritima indicate that seismic action caused the breakwaters to tilt downward during the late 1st or early 2nd century CE so that they no longer protected the harbor. The inner harbor continued to be used until the early 6th century CE when the accumulation of silt limited its ability to shelter ships.[12] Today, Caesarea Maritima is part of a national park and divers can follow underwater trails to explore the harbor.

While the ports of Caesarea Maritima and Piraeus were planned, other ports developed organically. Bryggen, London, and San Francisco evolved without a unified vision and continue as major port cities today. As such, most of the port archaeology in these cities is a result of modern development, providing small windows on the past through the excavated foundations of new buildings.

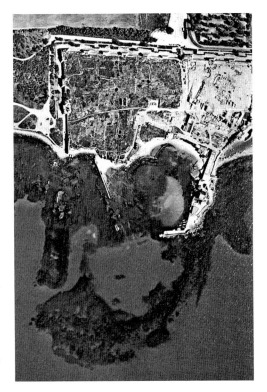

**Figure 8.5** Caesarea Maritima viewed from above. The dark, submerged shapes are the breakwaters of the outer harbor, while the remains of the inner harbor are still visible above the water. (Courtesy of the Caesarea Ancient Harbor Project)

At Bryggen, the historic port of Bergen, Norway, the archaeological research opportunity came as a result of a major fire that destroyed several buildings in 1955. Bryggen was founded some time before 1070 CE, but its historical significance is tied to the 14th to 16th centuries, when it was a major trading port of the Hanseatic League. During that period, Bryggen was the economic center of Norway. Today, the district is a UNESCO World Heritage Site with many buildings dating to the early 1700s, but the character and layout of the town extends back into the Medieval Period (figure 8.6). The 1955 fire, while disastrous for the standing structures, allowed archaeologists to explore how far back the city patterns extended. They found evidence of at least eight historically recorded fires that formed recognizable stratigraphic layers, making dating much easier. With each rebuilding, the houses, warehouses (often the houses and

**Figure 8.6** Workers posed on the docks of Bryggen with the historic warehouses and homes in the background.

warehouses were in one structure), and piers crept farther out into the harbor, so that the current settlement is more than 91 m (300 ft) in front of the original shoreline. Despite creeping forward, the layout of the town and style of buildings remained largely the same. In some cases, families dragged the crib-work foundation of their burned building farther into the harbor and rebuilt on top of it. Moving farther and farther into the harbor was done, in part, to access deeper and deeper water to facilitate loading and unloading larger and larger ships, but it was also a result of uncontrolled rubbish removal. The archaeologists found thick layers of trash that were swept off the piers and dumped from ships. This constant dumping filled the harbor and required rebuilding to allow ships to approach the piers. The trash, however, is an important record of the town's economic development. Much of the debris is ceramics, some of which appear to have been broken in transit and been deposited directly from the ships. Circa 1200 CE, there is a notable transition from continental wares to those made in England, reflecting a change in the merchants' trading patterns.[13]

London, one of the oldest ports in northern Europe, aptly exemplifies the transformation from landing place to major port. The transition from beaching and floating vessels as the tides fell and rose to major harbor infrastructure allowing ships to be unloaded, no matter the tide, happened multiple times as various groups inhabited and re-inhabited different sections of the Thames within the bounds of the modern city. Similar to Bryggen, the quays and harbor walls of London pushed farther and farther into the river over time to accommodate larger and larger ships and to create more room for warehouses (figure 8.7). The progression of these waterfronts and the changing methods of building them are evident in the archaeology, datable with dendrochronology samples drawn from the timbers preserved through constant saturation.

Founded by the Romans ca. 50 CE, the port became the capital and largest town in the province of Britannia, but is only mentioned ten times in the surviving classical references, so archaeology is the major source of information about this important period in the city's history. Subsequent periods of development generally included many of the same features, though of varying quality. During the 1200s, for example, individual landowners were responsible for shoring up their own waterfronts, leading to a hodgepodge of materials and techniques.

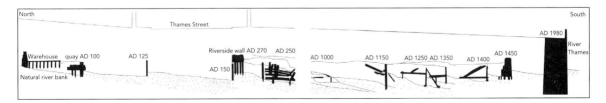

**Figure 8.7** London's advancing waterfront, 1st Century CE to modern times. (Redrawn from Gustav Milne, *The Roman Port of London*)

Changes in the depth of the harbor, construction of quays, and artifacts found along the waterfront all relate to changes in the political and economic power of London, the urban development of the city, and changes in ship design and technology more broadly. As with many waterlogged environments, the London waterfront has produced some impressive archaeological evidence of trade, including an intact Roman amphora containing 6000 olives (figure 8.8). The tidal range and dark water of the Thames means that it is still yielding archaeological finds. Today, there are active avocational groups that constantly scan the shores at low water for new finds.[14]

Like Bryggen and London, San Francisco developed organically, but much, much faster. Prior to 1849, San Francisco was a sleepy little harbor dominated by mudflats at low tide, but the discovery of gold nearby drew hundreds of ships and thousands of people to the harbor in a matter of months. In 1848, approximately a dozen ships arrived in San Francisco; the next year more than 500 ships anchored in the harbor. Most of these ships came carrying "forty-niners" hoping to make a fortune in the gold fields, but when the sailors also decided to join the Gold Rush, ship owners were unable to find enough crew to sail their vessels, and the harbor was littered with abandoned ships. The influx of miners also quickly overtaxed the town's existing infrastructure so that there were not enough buildings to fulfill the normal port functions. Taking advantage of the glut of ships to fill this need, entrepreneurs began to buy abandoned ships and repurpose them as restaurants, hotels, stores, churches, offices, and even a prison, but most were used as warehouses. Between 1849 and 1851, approximately 200 ships were converted into buildings (figure 8.9). Many of these vessels remained afloat, while other were dragged ashore, but as the waterfront quickly expanded into the harbor, most found themselves incorporated into the city grid. *Niantic*, which arrived at San Francisco in July 1849, was three blocks inland by 1851. On 4 May 1851, *Niantic* was among the nearly 2000 structures destroyed by fire. Rather than clear the debris, the town covered the area with sand and began to rebuild, encapsulating *Niantic* and the rest of the early port beneath the modern city. In 1978, archaeologists excavated part of *Niantic* ahead of a new building on the site. Today, it is not uncommon for new construction to uncover a ship several blocks from the modern waterline.[15]

**Figure 8.8** Amphora found in the Thames estuary and the pits of the 6000 olives that it contained. (© National Maritime Museum, Greenwich, London)

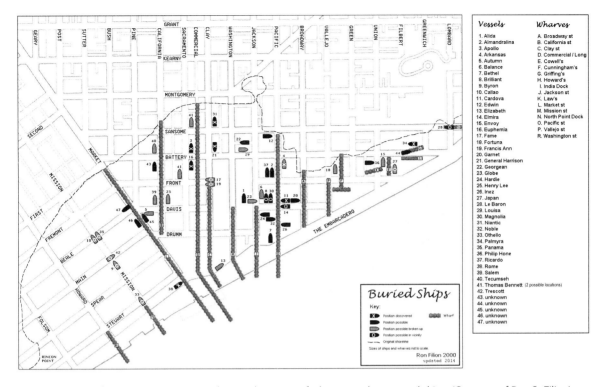

**Figure 8.9** Map of modern San Francisco showing locations of wharves and converted ships. (Courtesy of Ron S. Filion)

## MARITIME ARCHAEOLOGY OF BURIED SHIPS AND HARBORS

### James P. Delgado, Senior Vice President, SEARCH, Inc., USA

On 30 April 1913, the *New York Times* announced that "workmen excavating a site for the new building of the National Biscuit Company at Tenth Avenue and Fifteenth Street unearthed the curved skeleton timbers of an old sailing vessel buried some ten feet beneath the surface of the street." Twelve years later, in July 1925, the *New York Times* reported that "the excavation for the foundations of the new Seamen's Church Institute at 25 South Street took the aspect of an archaeological expedition yesterday morning, when the employees of the Foundation Company, 120 Broadway, announced the discovery of a buried ship, the second to be dug up in two days." The find was two "ancient Dutch ships" with rum bottles, coins, and cannon.

The discoveries were not unique in New York, nor confined to New York. They were part of a global phenomenon in which natural and human modification of harbors and coastlines buried that which was once beneath the sea or inland waters, resulting in latter-day discoveries of maritime sites on ostensibly "dry" land. In

*(continued)*

other instances, ships were being found in burial sites on land as part of funerary rituals. These discoveries had a profound impact on the nascent discipline of nautical archaeology. The first detailed examination of ancient and medieval shipwrecks, as well as more "modern" craft, came from sites like these on European, Mediterranean, and American shores and harbors in the 19th and early 20th centuries. These included sites like the County Hall ship in London, buried vessels from the California Gold Rush rediscovered beneath landfill as San Francisco rebuilt after the earthquake and fire of 1906, and ancient Greek wrecks unearthed during waterfront construction in Marseilles. As the mid-20th century and the early 21st centuries brought increasingly deeper and greater areas of excavation, hundreds of ships and large portions of ancient and forgotten harbors have been uncovered and excavated.

In the 21st century, archaeologists recognize that "buried ships" continue to provide unique opportunities in nautical archaeology. At the same time, modern maritime archaeologists are also realizing that a more holistic view of maritime sites on land provides opportunities to assess the growth and decline of ports, port-related infrastructure and technology, and activities such as fishing, as well as broader perspectives on maritime activity and maritime cultural landscapes in now land-filled port sites.

This has particularly been the case in Istanbul, Turkey with the Yenikapı site (3rd–10th century CE), in London (2nd–16th centuries CE), in Pisa (1st century BCE to 4th century CE), in New York (17th–19th centuries CE) and in San Francisco (1849–1907 CE). The largest quantity of sites exist in areas where marshes, sea-level change, river channel shifts, siltation, or deliberate land-filling or drainage (notably, in the case of the polders in the Netherlands, where substantially well-preserved ships, most from post-medieval contexts, have been discovered and excavated) have buried ships.

There is a significant body of work that has been accomplished at "dry-land" sites such as buried ships, ports, harbor facilities, and cargoes from all periods of history, but the future potential of nautical and maritime archaeology encompasses sites where sea-level changes have covered former bays, river courses, ports, and harbors. This includes anchorages and ports of ancient cities, such as Troy, where the Bronze Age port now lies beneath modern fields, and Greek and Roman port cities such as Miletus and Ephesus. While still unexcavated, the former port areas of sites such as these will likely yield significant evidence of maritime activity, including the remains of vessels.

The seemingly dry but frequently "wet" sites, often encapsulated by water-saturated mud, have yielded incredibly well-preserved discoveries. Examples include a number of stunning sites, and among them vessels of considerable antiquity where the only contemporary detailed evidence for vessel construction comes from ships recovered from land. This includes every known example of logboats and early watercraft as far back as 6000 bc. The finds at Yenikapı have provided a new understanding of Byzantine shipbuilding that cannot be overemphasized. Future excavations on land will recover additional and significant vessels and greatly add to our knowledge of shipbuilding as well as of the history and development of ports. From port infrastructure to derelict vessels, and lost and discarded cargoes in port contexts, land excavations on reclaimed land also offer a unique opportunity to archaeologically assess ports from antiquity up to the modern era. While excavation underwater will continue to provide access to shipwrecked cargoes within the context of the vessel itself, excavations on land offer the same potential, as a number of the polders wrecks contained cargoes. It has been observed by some prescient nautical archaeologists that the new frontiers of nautical archaeology lie both at great depth and beneath parking lots and fields that cover former waterfronts.

Mid-19th century San Francisco is notable for the number of ships that were repurposed, but reusing ships to build port infrastructure was common in many ports, including London, Bryggen, and Portus. Probably the best-known example of this practice is the Ronson Ship that archaeologists discovered beneath New York's Water Street in 1982 (chapter 7).[16] Ships were part of the ecosystem of a port. Ports grew, shrank, and changed in response to technology, economics, and environment. As trade increased, ships grew in size, and as sediment filled a port, local entrepreneurs and governments were forced to adapt, taking advantage of whatever means they had at hand and often in competition with other ports on the same water body. How individuals and the port as whole adapted to these pressures provide archaeologists with insights into what was important to residents of the port and how they viewed the world around them.

## Shipyards

Many ports included the facilities to build and repair ships. Shipyards, as the terrestrial birthplaces of ships, provide one of the strongest links between life afloat and life ashore, and were nearly always situated directly on the littoral. These were sites where cultures brought together cutting-edge technology with massive amounts of raw materials to build some of the largest and most complex machines of their time. The ability of a society to effectively amass technologies, techniques, and materials at shipyards gave it distinct commercial and military advantages over its regional, and, in some cases, global, competitors.[17] Shipyards were major factors in the trajectory of world history. They are also one of the locations within a port where the exchange of ideas between maritime cultures is most evident. Ship and boat builders were constantly watching the harbor for different types of vessels, construction techniques, and means of propulsion that they could incorporate into their own designs. These patterns played out at a wide variety of shipyards, ranging from a pleasant and convenient stretch of shore such as the Ferriby boatyard described above, to massive industrial complexes with steam engines and dry-docks, as we will discuss below.

An example of an ancient shipyard comes from the port city of Dor located on Israel's northern coast. The Canaanites settled Dor during the second millennium BCE, but the port saw a wide range of masters as different groups controlled the area over the ensuing four millennia. It is the best-recorded harbor definitively identified with the elusive Sea Peoples, it was a remote port of the Athenian navy, it is mentioned several times in the Bible, and it supported a Knights Templar fort during the Crusades. In many respects, Dor parallels Caesarea Maritima just to its south, but while Caesarea Maritima was planned, Dor grew organically. Like Caesarea Maritima, the excavations at Dor have taken place both on land and underwater, so that the gates, houses, and temples of the city are matched with its quays, shipyards, fish storage tanks, and the dyeing facilities that specialized in making the valuable Tyrian purple from sea snails. The complexity of these maritime facilities was compounded by sea levels that fell away from the original waterline and then rose well above it during the occupation of the port. These natural changes not only caused the waterline to move, but also affected the entire shape of the harbor and the accumulation of sediments. The site records a series of adaptations by the residents: moving seaward as the water receded, cutting a channel so that tidal flow could flush sediments from the harbor, and eventually abandoning part of the harbor.

The remains of a Hellenistic period (323–31 BCE) shipyard are intermingled among the complex remains that not only built up over time but also shifted horizontally with changing sea levels. The shipyard included three slipways cut into the bedrock that allowed finished hulls to be lowered into the central harbor. The shipyard area was large enough to accommodate several ships and, once the hulls were afloat, the small, protected central harbor was likely used to complete and outfit them.[18]

The same basic features, although on a more massive scale, are on display at the later large shipyards of northern Europe. Archaeological investigations of the British Royal Navy Dockyard at Woolwich and the Dutch East India Company (abbreviated VOC for Verenigde Oostindische Compagnie) shipyard at Oostenburg illustrate the scale and sophistication of these preindustrial ship factories that produced some of the largest vessels of their time. Both Oostenburg and Woolwich operated during the same period and at approximately the same scale. Oostenburg produced approximately 500 ships between the 1660s and 1799, and employed 1200 people in 1750, while Woolwich operated from 1512 to 1869 and had 1111 employees in 1774. Both drew materials from throughout Europe to build and outfit their ships. In the case of Oostenburg, the shipyard also pulled in goods from Asia on returning VOC ships, while Woolwich likely used timber imported from North America. In both instances, they demonstrate the centralizing power of shipyards, bringing together materials from throughout a culture's domain to build and repair ships that were then used to expand and exploit that domain. Both also tell us about the social and technological organization of shipyards with the processes of building a ship spread between groups of artisans. At Woolwich, these tasks were divided among very specific structures, such as covered saw pits for cutting timbers, a pitch house for heating pitch, and a separate building for bending the heavy planks that covered the outside of British warships. Both also included major infrastructure for building ships. At Woolwich there were two **dry-docks**, one of which was capable of holding two ships (figure 8.10). A dry-dock is an excavated area that can be pumped dry once a ship is safely secured inside of it. With the water removed, the entire hull is easily inspected and repaired. Dry docks were also used for building ships—once the hull was completed or repaired, water was let in and the ship floated, avoiding the potentially dangerous event of sliding the ship into the water. This more traditional means of launching a ship was used at Oostenburg (figure 8.11), but the launching ways there were designed so that the angle of the ways could be changed by adding or removing soil within a heavy foundation.[19]

Both Woolwich and Oostenburg also demonstrate the value of archaeology even at well-chronicled historical sites. The British Crown and the VOC invested large sums in these shipyards, and so they were heavily documented with maps, models, and drawings. So much so, that it is reasonable to ask if archaeology can tell us anything new about these sites. In both cases, archaeological research demonstrated that the historical documents were largely accurate, something that

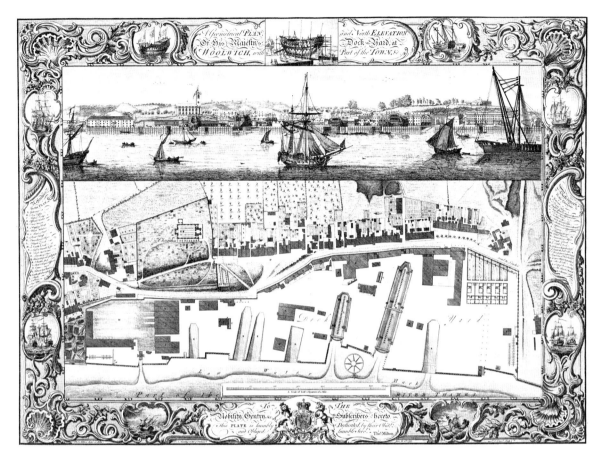

**Figure 8.10** Woolwich Shipyard, 1753. Note the two dry-docks near the center of the shipyard, as well as the launching ways on either side.

should never be taken for granted, but that they also missed many important details. The ingenious launching ways of Oostenburg were glossed in historical documents, while Woolwich tended to be depicted as being more orderly than it truly was. The excavators of Woolwich discovered that many of the shipyard's structures were built using timbers reused from other structures, dismantled ships, or shipyard waste. In an instance of particular parsimony, one timber was reused twice.

Slightly earlier but as large, if not larger, than Woolwich and Oostenburg was the Nanjing Treasure Shipyard on the Yangzi River in China (figure 8.12). The shipyard takes its name from the so-called Treasure Ships of Zheng He that traveled on diplomatic and commercial voyages as far away as East Africa during the first three decades of the 15th century (more on Zheng He and his massive fleets in chapter 11). In the early 2000s, Chinese archaeologists excavated one of the basins associated with the shipyard. This is a small fraction of the massive

'T OOST INDISCHE MAGAZYN. EN SCHEEPS-TIMMER-WERF .

**Figure 8.11** Oostenburg Shipyard, 1726, with a ship on the launching ways and ship timbers arranged around the yard.

shipyard; as late as 1944 there were 13 visible basins. Gates on the river ends of the elongated basins once connected them to the Yangzi River. Whether they functioned as dry-docks is unknown. Within the 421 m x 41 m (1381 ft x 134 ft) basin, archaeologists identified 34 structures made of pilings driven into the bottom and topped with beams that are interpreted as platforms to support the ships during construction. Based on the size of the basin and the position of the structures, it is likely that more than one ship was built in each basin. Workshops and fields filled the spaces between the basins. The fields probably grew hemp for ropes and other products used in ship construction, as well as food for the workers. This arrangement suggests a more integrated shipyard than Woolwich or Oostenburg, with much of what was needed for fabrication produced on site, and the workers, in some cases, living within the shipyard. Marks on the timbers found within the Nanjing basin suggest that the wood for construction was a tightly controlled resource. Archaeologists found similar marks on timbers at Woolwich, and in both cases they are interpreted as inventory marks to track this valuable commodity. The basin also produced two rulers and two rudder posts. The "foot" rulers both measure 31.3 cm (12.3 in.) and suggest the measurement standard used in building the Treasure Ships. This is valuable information, since the Chinese foot, like most early measurements, varied with time and space. The teak rudder posts both measured over 10 m (33 fet) long. The rudder posts, basin structures, and rulers are some of the only hard evidence regarding the size of Zheng He's ships, which have been argued to be as large as 137 m x 56 m

彩版二 (II)

**Figure 8.12** Nanjing Treasure Shipyard during excavation. One shipbuilding basin with exposed wooden structures is in the foreground. Two additional, flooded basins are in the background. (Courtesy of Nanjing City Museum)

(449 ft x 184 ft). What remains of the shipyard is now a commemorative park, memorializing China's early maritime expansion.[20]

As with most archaeological sites, it is also helpful to consider shipyards and other coastal sites from a landscape perspective, stepping back to look at how these sites are arranged in their settings to answer different questions. A specific shipyard site is good for addressing how shipbuilders answered specific problems of supply, logistics, and layout; how they adapted to new ideas of ship design and technologies; the relationships between workers, ship designers, and managers; the transition from craft production to industry; and many other interesting questions. Analyzing multiple shipyards in a region makes it possible to address more general trends of how shipbuilders adapted their environments, what they thought a shipyard should look like, and how they interacted with the communities around them. As is true of most archaeological data, shipyards can be analyzed both qualitatively and quantitatively. GIS is a powerful tool in quantitative landscape studies. For example, it was possible to compile the archaeological, geographical, and historical data for wooden shipbuilding sites in the state of Maryland into a GIS and then analyze the data to statistically determine what factors the shipbuilders considered when picking the location of their shipyards. The data showed that shipbuilders preferred protected areas with a slope between 3 percent and 11 percent, but were generally unconcerned about the stability of the soils because they were able to reinforce the launching ways with stone or wood foundations. They also preferred areas within 8 km (5 miles) of urban centers, if not actually within a town, so as to be close to workers and clients. Maryland shipbuilders also seem to have wanted oak nearby, but did not necessarily require it to be within the immediate property. Finally, and maybe most interestingly, the shipbuilders avoided any soil that might support tobacco. During much of the historic period, tobacco was king in the Chesapeake region, and it was apparently seen as foolish to waste such valuable land with something like ship construction.[21]

Qualitatively, we can compare shipyards across large distances to identify similar patterns that different cultures settled upon, as we did with Treasure Shipyard, Woolwich, and Oostenburg. It is also possible to compare shipyards through time. One trend that was regularly repeated at shipyards was consolidation due to industrialization. As ships transitioned from being made of wood and powered by wind to iron hulls and steam propulsion, the amount of capital, the size of the workforces, and the variety of skills needed to build them put many smaller shipyards out of business. The larger shipyards that remained also tended to be in urban areas where they could access other industries and transportation networks. These changes in ship construction led to changes in the organization of the shipyards and shipbuilding labor as shipbuilding transitioned from craft to science.[22]

## Artificial islands

Humans regularly alter their physical environment to better suit their perceived needs, and the coast is no exception. As already discussed in chapter 7, most major ports have a history of filling to create more and better land along the waterline. Rather than expand the entire shoreline, other cultures opted to take a different approach and build their homes or communities on artificial islands. Good historical examples of this come from Ireland, Scotland, Guatemala, and Mexico, while in places like Dubai we continue to claim the sea, building land outward into what was formerly water.

**Crannogs** are possibly the best-known archaeological examples of artificial islands. Located predominantly in Ireland and Scotland, with at least one example in Wales, crannogs are most often found in lakes and marshes. Crannogs were often a wooden structure built on top of a mound of peat or brushwood supported by a retaining wall of logs and linked to shore by a causeway or bridge, but there are also examples with retaining walls, causeways, and superstructures made of stone (figure 8.13). This type of house was popular for a long time. While often associated with the Iron Age (800 BCE–100 CE), there were precedents

**Figure 8.13** Artist's reconstruction of Buiston Crannog, Ayshire, Scotland. (© Historic Environment Scotland. Illustration by Alan Braby).

in the Neolithic era and some were occupied into the 18th century. Over this period, the popularity of crannogs waned and resurged, with sites often being reinhabited after long periods of abandonment. The form, function, and symbolism of the sites also shifted throughout their history.

Most crannogs appear to have been homesteads associated with farms and livestock situated on the adjacent lands. All recently excavated crannogs have evidence of cereal crops and many have contained animal dung that suggests livestock were stabled on the crannog and only grazed onshore. There is also evidence of some crafts, such as bronze and iron working, taking place on crannogs. In later periods, some crannogs seem to have been inhabited by upper-class citizens, but nearly all walks of land-owning society likely lived on them during all periods. The widespread use of crannogs begs the question of why people went to the considerable effort of building artificial islands when there was perfectly good land available. The most common explanation is defense; however, recent studies have argued that crannog gates provided more the appearance of defensibility than actual defensibility. Another explanation is that the artificial islands made the settlements more conspicuous, while also giving the appearance of exclusivity. Their setting would have helped the residents to claim the adjacent farmland, which was often of above average quality. Combined with the appearance of defensibility, visibility and exclusivity may have functioned similarly to a modern gated community. There was also likely a spiritual reason for inhabiting crannogs. Local Bronze Age and later peoples viewed lakes as a gateway between this and other worlds, between life and death. There is archaeological evidence of many bodies and weapons being deposited in watery places during this period; this has come down to us today through the myth of Excalibur and the Lady of the Lake. More than likely, the choice to invest in home sites requiring so much work was a result of multiple causes that shifted somewhat with time and place as cultural decisions are almost always multifaceted.[23]

Other European cultures, such as the Neolithic and Bronze Age peoples of the Alpine lakes, built their homes along lakes, but in Central America, we see islands sculpted into urban and ceremonial centers. At the site of San Lorenzo, the Olmec (ca. 1500–400 BCE) reworked a natural island into a regional capital. The residents augmented the island, a plateau overlooking the wetlands of the Coatzacoalcos River, with bushels of earth and terraced fields into its sides. San Lorenzo was an integral part of its surrounding fluvial landscape, but its height and architecture would have also made it stand out strikingly from the surrounding environment. Stone-lined drains carried water away from the center of the site, while causeways or dikes within the floodplain supported houses, served as quays for canoes, and may have provided some flood control. The sculpted plateau, rising above the surrounding wetlands, was dotted with the colossal heads that the Olmec are famous for, as well as other monuments, not the least of which were the drains that demonstrated Olmec power over the important resource of water. The surrounding floodplain provided waterfowl and fish, as well as wild plants to eat and reeds for roofs and baskets. Floods irrigated and fertilized fields where crops could be grown. Today, the area around San Lorenzo is dotted with small artificial islands where farmers smoke fish caught in the surrounding rivers, and it is likely that Olmec had a similar practice. The river also provided convenient transportation of both mundane and exotic goods that helped the city flourish and added tax revenues to the wealth of the elites. When San Lorenzo collapsed around 900 BCE, the Olmec center shifted to another modified island at La Venta.[24]

## THE COAST AS A BRIDGE BETWEEN THE HINTERLAND AND THE HINTERSEA

The hinterland is literally the "land behind" a port or city. It is the inland country that is economically tied to the urban center. The hinterland produces the goods, raw materials, and foodstuff that flow into the port for export to other areas. The hinterland also absorbs much of what is imported into ports. Since goods and materials are never traded without the ideas that underlie their production, use, and value, there is also an active exchange of culture between a port and its hinterland. We can also think of ports as having a "hintersea," the maritime parallel to the hinterland that also produces and absorbs goods, materials, and culture. In this model, the port and its surrounding coast act as a bridge between the wet and dry domains of a culture. Landing places, ports, shipyards, and artificial islands are all examples of these bridges, allowing people, ideas, and things to flow freely from land to sea and back again. The aggregation of terrestrial products at a shipyard to build a vehicle to carry other terrestrial items across the water is possibly the clearest example of this practice.

Archaeologists trace the relationships between hinterland and hintersea through evidence of food, industry, commodities, and trade. All of these things leave a physical residue that archaeologists can find and analyze. By tracing overseas artifacts or commodities that moved inland from the coast, we can begin to define the catchment area around a port. For example, in England nearly all of the 7th- to 9th-century coins recovered through metal detecting and excavation have been found within 15 km (9 mi) of the coast, suggesting that international trade extended at least that far inland. Importantly, these coins were found all along the coast, implying that landing places, and not just ports, were heavily used for exchange.[25] The distribution of imported goods such as ceramics or exotic materials, as well as landscape features like rivers and roads, can be traced to understand the network of routes that connected the coast and the hinterland. Similarly, the distribution of shipwrecks and their cargos provide archaeological evidence for the network of fishing and trading routes that laced the hintersea, ultimately leading to other shores. By connecting the dots of trade goods, shipwrecks, and other finds, archaeologists expose the entire network that carried items from place to place. This network always narrows to cross the shore at specific places in much the same way that a street network tends to narrow to cross a river at bridges.

## SUMMARY

There is a terrestrial component to all maritime cultures. Human adaptation to the sea developed slowly and eventually facilitated the expansion of people across the globe. Even in cultures that were fully adapted to seafaring, some members lived on land and there was always a need to move goods, people, and watercraft across the waterline. The primary examples of maritime archaeology of the coasts are landing places, ports, shipyards, and artificial islands. These types of sites demonstrate the flow of goods, materials, and ideas across the coasts, connecting inland and overseas settlements.

### DISCUSSION QUESTIONS

1. How many of the items on your person right now were imported from overseas? Was the pattern the same in the past? How far into the past?
2. What advantages might there have been to reusing ships as structures, wharves, and landfill within expanding ports?
3. What are the practical and symbolic aspects of the sites discussed in this chapter?
4. Ferriby and Dor were in use at roughly the same time. Can the evidence from one inform our interpretations of the other? Why or why not?
5. Why is it likely that human migration happened faster along the coasts than on inland routes?

### FURTHER READING

Aberg, A. and C. Lewis, Eds. (2000). *The Rising Tide, Archaeology and Coastal Landscapes*. Oxbow, Oxford.

Danish Institue at Athens. (2017). Piraeus, the Zea Harbor Project. Danish Institute at Athens, Athens. Available at http://www.diathens.gr/en.

Delgado, J.P. (2009). *Gold Rush Port, The Maritime Archaeology of San Francisco's Waterfront*. University of California Press, Berkeley.

Ford, B. (2018). *The Shore Is a Bridge: The Maritime Cultural Landscape of Lake Ontario*. Texas A&M University Press, College Station.

Henderson, J. and R. Sands. (2013). Irish and Scottish Crannogs. *The Oxford Handbook of Wetland Archaeology*. F. Menotti and A. O'Sullivan, Eds. 269–282. Oxford University Press, New York.

Milne, G. (1985). *The Roman Port of London*. B.T. Batsford, London.

Moser, J.D. (2011). Shipyard Archaeology. *The Oxford Handbook of Maritime Archaeology*. A. Catsambis, B. Ford, and D. Hamilton, Eds. 834–855. Oxford University Press, New York.

Raban, A., M. Atzy, B. Goodman, and Z. Gail. (2009). *The Harbour of Sebastos (Caesarea Maritima) in Its Roman Mediterranean Context*. BAR International Series 1930. Archaeopress, Oxford.

Wright, E. (1990). *The Ferriby Boats, Seacraft of the Bronze Age*. Routledge, New York.

CHAPTER 9

# SHIPS

## FOCUS QUESTIONS

- When and how did maritime societies emerge?
- How have people interacted with seas, lakes, and rivers? How was this interaction shaped by their culture and environment? What are the similarities, differences, and outcomes of these interactions?
- What types of maritime archaeological sites are there, and how do they differ in what they can teach us about the past?
- What kind of information do ship and aircraft wrecks hold? What can their contents tell us about trade, colonization, warfare and the people on board?
- What do maritime technological innovations tell us about broader trends in society, history, and culture? How does naval innovation shape the rise and fall of maritime societies?
- How did maritime people shape world history?

## SHIPWRECK ARCHAEOLOGY

Archaeology, specifically the subfield known as nautical archaeology, is our primary tool for understanding how our forebearers tackled the problem of moving themselves and their possessions across large bodies of water. The earliest known drawing of a boat comes from Gobustan National Park in Azerbaijan and dates to approximately 10,000 BCE, relatively late in human development, while the first documentary mention of shipping does not appear until a late third-millennium BCE Mesopotamian inscription. Among the subsequent written accounts, there are a few exemplary documents that include details about how boats were built, such as an 1800 BCE Mesopotamian tablet that describes building a huge vessel to transport pairs of animals. Most of these descriptions, however, are fairly vague. Writers and artists recognized the importance of ships and included them in art and records, but generally represented them as complete objects with little concern for how they were built or the root of the technology. They were so ubiquitous that they often escaped close inspection.

It was not until the 15th century CE that shipbuilders began to describe their process in any detail, and, in many places, ship construction remained an art passed, without records, from master to apprentice well into the modern period. Shipbuilders of some periods also tended to be secretive about their designs and technology in an attempt to retain an advantage over competitors. As a result, much of human–sea interaction escaped documentation, leaving us with only the archaeological record. Archaeologists certainly use historic and artistic descriptions, including ship plans, iconography, and text descriptions, but much of what we know about how ships appeared, were built, and functioned comes from the process of excavating, recording, and interpreting their physical remains.[1]

This chapter provides a summary of the development of ships. As with all the chapters in this book, this is an entry point. There is much more known, and to be known, about ship construction. Ships are one of the true outlets for human ingenuity, and people have devised many, many ways to employ them and to cross bodies of water.

### SHIPS AS MATERIAL CULTURE

Archaeologists can interpret ships from both functional and symbolic perspectives. Functional interpretations often focus on the relationships among the environment, available resources, function, technology, and form. Functional questions, thus, run along the following lines: how far is the voyage, what is being transported, what weather is expected, will the ship be used for warfare, is the primary concern speed or capacity? The environment provides the resources that are the basic building blocks of seafaring technology. As cultures expanded geographically through sea travel, different resources became available, but the basic technology of shipbuilding often remained rooted in the materials that were originally available, and the mental templates passed from generation to generation that defined the essence of a ship. The available resources and technology, combined with the needs of the boatbuilders or their clients, drives the form and construction of the final vessel. By disentangling these various factors, archaeologists can learn a lot about a culture's priorities, wants, and abilities. Modern automobiles are a useful analogy here. The investment in, and uses of, a pickup truck are very different from those of a subcompact car. Large portions of their form are a result of their function.

Ships also served a symbolic function. To different peoples they represented power, freedom, wealth, danger, or other forces. These symbolic roles also manifest themselves in the physical remains of ships, including construction, decoration, modification, and maintenance. Again, think about automobiles and what traits you associate with a hybrid car versus a pickup; a rusty Hyundai versus a pristine Porsche. Together, the symbolic and functional interpretations of shipwrecks allow archaeologists to form conclusions about how people perceived and interacted with the world around them.

These interpretations, however, are based on wrecks. This is the equivalent of basing interpretations of automobiles on the archaeology of automotive salvage yards. Shipwreck archaeology is the archaeology of failure and disaster. At best, a shipwreck is a vessel that was abandoned at the end of its useful life, but most of the shipwrecks that have been scientifically investigated were lost because of a catastrophic event. This in no way invalidates the conclusions based on shipwrecks—it is possible to learn a lot about a culture based on its failures. But it is important to remember this fundamental nature of shipwrecks when interpreting them. In nearly every case, the captain and crew misjudged themselves, their vessel, their location, or their situation, or were caught in circumstances that were beyond their control, such as a storm that could not be avoided. These disasters are part of the life of the vessel and often influence what archaeologists find. It is worth considering the skewed nature of the shipwreck record and the specifics surrounding the loss of a vessel when interpreting a shipwreck.

## EARLY VESSELS AND THEIR MORE RECENT DESCENDANTS

As mentioned in the previous chapter, early boatbuilding is evidence of the expanding cognitive abilities of our hominin ancestors. The ability to assess and use the attributes of multiple materials and tools to build a boat is evidence of a creative and flexible mind. Unfortunately, much of the evidence for the earliest boats has been lost due to both rising sea levels and the perishable materials used to build these vessels, as discussed in chapters 3 and 7. Instead, archaeologists rely on the few preserved vessels and vessel fragments that have been recorded, along with rock art and other early depictions, and ethnographic examples to hypothesize what the earliest vessels looked like. The use of ethnographic examples to understand early boats makes the important point that many of these technologies are still in use today. In many cases, the earliest technology is still the best for building a functional craft with local and inexpensive materials. The continued use of these technologies demonstrates their usefulness as well as the long-term and continuous adaptation of many cultures to maritime lifestyles.

Among the earliest and simplest boats were floats and rafts (figure 9.1). A **float** is anything that a person can cling to while crossing a waterbody. Floats could be a buoyant log, a bundle of reeds, or an inflated animal skin. **Rafts** tend to be built from the same materials as floats, but have the advantage of keeping the occupant out of the water. Rafts consist of any material that floats lashed together to form a platform. These can be large or small, and were a convenient

(A)

(B)

(C)

(D)

**Figure 9.1** Raft (A), reed boat (B), logboat (C), and skin boat (D).

and expedient way to move people and things across calm waters using readily available materials and simple tools. Rafts are still widely used today as ferries or for fishing, especially in rivers. For navigating larger or more treacherous bodies of water, people developed more complicated **boats** made of skin, wood, and reeds—the same materials as rafts, just organized in a more masterful way. A boat is any small open vessel and can be defined in opposition to a ship, which tends to be larger and decked. There is some ambiguity between these two categories but, in general, a ship might carry boats onboard but never the reverse.

Hollowing out a log to form a boat allowed early mariners to protect themselves and their cargos from waves in a stout watercraft. The oldest surviving example of a boat is a log boat from the Netherlands dating between 8040 and 7510 BCE. This boat was relatively small, only 3 m (10 ft) long, but others, such as the circa 400 BCE Hasholme boat from England, were much larger (12.8 m; 42 ft long). Log boats required considerable work to make, with many hours spent hollowing the interior and shaping the exterior, but the resulting boat could be as large as the builder could handle, would last for years, and was capable of going to sea. Builders also began to modify the single log craft to form more complicated log boats. The sides of the log could be expanded, or the log might be split with a plank added to the centerline, to create both a more stable and more capacious boat. In other cases, planks were added to the sides of the log to create more **freeboard**, making the boat drier and more seaworthy.[2]

In areas where there were no trees suitable for log boats, or where the trees were covered with bark that could be peeled in large strips, hide and bark boats developed. These boats were generally a waterproof skin stretched over a frame of wood, bone, or other material. Even at their simplest, these boats required more technological knowhow than a log boat, but they could also be a relatively expedient affair. The least complicated skin boat type is a **coracle**; found world-wide, they are formed by a hide covering a bowl-shaped framework of small branches. Other hide and bark boats were much more sophisticated, such as the **kayaks** and **canoes** of northern North America. Examples of these boats recorded by early European explorers and surviving in museum collections are evidence of generations of refinement and the erudite use of available materials to create sleek, stable, and useful watercraft. The bark canoe was an open craft made of thin wood frames covered most often with birch bark that had been sewn to-gether and waterproofed with pitch. Kayaks were built where there were typically no trees and so had frames of drift wood or bone covered with animal hide. Both kayaks and canoes were paddled well out to sea to hunt and fish. Hide kayaks existed in North America into the modern period, as did skin boats in other parts of the world. For example, 17th-century Irish **curachs** were 8-m (26-ft) long, hide-covered, wicker structures with an external keel, **rudder**, and sail.[3]

Hide and bark boats were less durable than log boats, so we have fewer ar-chaeological examples, but they were also easy to repair and incredibly port-able. Log boats tended to be left in a body of water, often intentionally filled with stones and sunk to preserve them, also increasing the likelihood that they entered the archaeological record. For example, more than 100 canoes, dating be-tween 7000 and 4300 BCE, were recovered from a single lake in Florida. Hide and bark boats, on the other hand, were light enough to be **portaged**, so that only one boat was required for a trip that might take a paddler from a lake to a river to the sea. There is linguistic evidence that log boats were seen by some Native Americans as things, while bark and hide boats were described as animate with personal pronouns, like a traveling partner.[4]

Reed boats were among the earliest vessels developed in Egypt, the Indian Ocean, Australia, South America, and elsewhere. These boats were made by bundling reeds together and then assembling the bundles into a wide variety of vessel shapes. In Peru, for example, bundles of reeds were built into large cargo vessels and smaller fishing boats used far from shore. In this tradition, the bundles were compressed so that the boats were rigid and less likely to become waterlogged. Perhaps the most famous reed boats, however, were the papyrus boats used by ancient Egyptians on the Nile. Artists often depicted these vessels in tomb paintings and models, and like the Peruvian reed vessels, they had upturned ends to help them cut through the water and remain afloat. Papyrus boats became such a part of the Egyptian idea of what a boat should look like that they continued to build vessels in a similar form long after they had transitioned to wooden shipbuilding and the wider range of shapes wood allowed.[5]

Some reed vessels could be quite large. A Mesopotamian account of a great flood and a hero who survived it in a large ship filled with pairs of animals specifically describes the ship as being made of plant fiber. The story, written in cuneiform sometime between 1900 and 1700 BCE, describes this ark as a circular vessel covering an area of 2600 m$^2$ (27,986 ft$^2$). It was built in much the same way as similar early 20th century Iraqi boats, just much, much larger.[6]

## The transition from boats to ships

As the Mesopotamian ark story implies, sometimes you just need a larger vessel. As the early boatbuilders refined their craft, they created vessels with ever-increasing capacities; however, the construction material eventually limited the builders' ability to build bigger. This limitation was reached first by the builders of skin, bark, and reed craft, and, much later, by shipbuilders using wood. In the case of wood, builders began to conceive of the tree as planks rather than logs and devised ingenious ways to attach the planks to one another to build massive wooden ships. Eventually, even the largest wooden ships would be dwarfed by those made of metal.

While metal dominates the ships of today, the earliest ships included no metal at all. Instead the planks were lashed or sewn together, or joined with **mortise-and-tenon join**ts like fine cabinetry. For example, the planks of the Ferriby boats (2030–1680 BCE) discussed in chapter 8 were positioned using wooden dowels driven through cleats carved into the surface of the planks and then the planks were lashed to each other with strands of yew and hazel rope (figure 9.2). The lashings passed through paired holes in the planks that were drilled so that the plank protected the exterior face of the rope, and moss was used to waterproof the joints.[7] Only later were metal fasteners used to hold ships together, and, as we will see below, the use of metal is still not universal. Lashed boats could be quite large. The approximately 4000-year-old Ferriby boats were 15.2 m (50 ft) long, while the Abydos boats, buried circa 3100 BCE in Egypt, were 23 m (75 ft) long and could have carried 30 paddlers. As the size of the vessels increased, the planks of the hull alone were not sufficient to counterbalance the pressure of the water displaced by the hull. To keep the surrounding water from crushing the vessel, **frames**, **beams**, and other internal structures were added to strengthen the external shell. Similarly, as ships grew longer, the tendency to **hog** or **sag** increased, so shipbuilders increased the dimensions of the center planks of the vessel, leading to **keels** and **keelsons**. Changes in how ships were designed and built happened slowly and developed differently in different parts of the world as shipbuilders responded to varying local environments, needs, and resources, leading to the development of divergent shipbuilding traditions.

### DEVELOPMENT OF REGIONAL SHIPBUILDING TRADITIONS

Archaeologists use the term **tradition** to group cultures or industries that are similar to each other because they developed together or from one another. These relationships often stretch over long periods of time and tend to be regional as generation after generation learned a set of habits from their ancestors and refined them through interactions with their neighbors. A shipbuilding tradition is an approach to building and conceptualizing ships that is shared through time by the shipbuilders of a region. These traditions have definable characteristics

**Figure 9.2** Ferriby Boat reconstruction demonstrating the use of cleats and lashing to join the planks. (Courtesy of National Maritime Museum Cornwall)

that are distinct enough that even a casual observer can distinguish ships from different ones, but traditions do change over time and space and tend to blur together at the borders where they overlap. In some instances, shipbuilding traditions change due to internal forces as innovators within a culture find new ways to solve seafaring problems. In other cases, the change comes from outside as shipbuilders borrow ideas from foreign vessels. The challenges of seafaring and the wide-ranging nature of ships provided plenty of fodder for both innovation and the diffusion of ideas.

## Mediterranean

Like the smaller Ferriby and Abydos boats, the oldest known ship was also held together with lashing. The Khufu vessel was one of five buried adjacent to Khufu's pyramid, among the Great Pyramids at Giza, in approximately 2566 BCE (figure 9.3). These vessels were for the pharaoh's use in the afterlife and may have also been used to carry the pharaoh's mummified body along the Nile before he was interred—thus serving both a functional and a symbolic role. Three

**Figure 9.3** Kuhfu ship. (Courtesy of Berthold Wener)

similar vessels were looted in antiquity and one remains entombed. The Khufu vessel was excavated in 1954 and, following 14 years of reassembly, was reconstructed in its entirety. The frames of the ship, which was 43-m (140-ft) long, were each lashed to their neighbors and the hull was sewn together with continuous bands running from side to side to further secure the pieces together. Frames and beams were also lashed to the planking, providing transverse strength. The wood for the hull was imported from Syria, Lebanon, or southern Turkey, suggesting the lengths to which Egyptian shipbuilders had to go in order to procure appropriate timbers. The difficulty of procuring wood is also likely why many of the timbers are relatively small for a vessel of this size. While the hull was built of wood, the shape still looked as if it was made of papyrus with graceful curves, upturned ends, and no keel. The papyrus heritage may have been exaggerated in the Khufu vessel because of its ritualistic use, but other Egyptian ships tended to retain many of these aspects.[8]

In addition to lashing, the Khufu vessel was held together with wooden tenons. The tenons prevented the planks from sliding past each other and the lashing prevented them from separating. This use of tenons presaged what became the dominant form of shipbuilding in the Mediterranean for much of antiquity, but the transition from lashed to mortise and tenon occurred in fits and starts. To join two planks with a mortise-and-tenon joint, corresponding recesses were cut into the edges of adjoining planks to form mortises. A piece of wood the same size as the mortises, called a tenon, was inserted into one and then the other of the plank edges, joining the planks. The Uluburun shipwreck, lost off the coast of Turkey circa 1320 BCE, was built using large mortise-and-tenon joints, with pegs holding the tenons in place (figure 9.4). In this instance, the mortise and tenons were so large and so numerous that they essentially formed internal frames. No true frames were recorded at the site. The ship also had a proto-keel that was larger than the neighboring planks but extended into, rather than out of, the hull.

Five hundred years later Greek shipbuilders were still using lacing to assemble their ships. Several shipwrecks from before the 5th century BCE demonstrate remarkable consistency in how ships were built throughout the Greek world. The builders used small cylindrical tenons to align the planks and stop them from slipping laterally, but held the planks together with a sophisticated lacing system. Widely spaced frames were shaped to fit over the lacing and were lashed and treenailed in place. **Treenails** are wooden dowels used to join two pieces of timber; this is a technology that continued to be used until the end of the wooden shipbuilding period.

A major shift occurred in Greek shipbuilding between the last quarter of the 6th century and the first decade of the 5th century BCE when shipbuilders gave up lacing and adopted mortise-and-tenon construction. In terms of naval architecture evolutions, this change was rapid and sweeping, affecting almost every ship type. We are able to date the

**Figure 9.4** Reconstruction based on Uluburun shipwreck.

transition so precisely because of several well-preserved shipwrecks from this period. Early in the transition, some ships retained lacing at the bow and stern, the most complex parts of a hull, and frames shaped to pass over lacing were retained, even though they no longer served a functional purpose. The Ma'agan Mikhael shipwreck, the remains of a 14.4-m (47-ft) long merchant vessel lost off the coast of Israel circa 400 BCE, is an example of one of these transitional hulls. By the time of the Kyrenia shipwreck (ca. 300 BCE), the entire hull, which included timbers reused from an older laced vessel, was assembled with pegged mortise-and-tenon joints. The Kyrenia ship also had larger and more closely spaced frames than earlier laced vessels, and the frames were fastened to the planks with copper nails. It is unclear why the Greeks altered their longstanding building tradition so profoundly, but it may have had to do with increased transportation of bulk cargo in **amphorae**, the development of the Greek **trireme**, the adoption of foreign technologies, and rapidly expanding state-sponsored naval fleets. The mortise-and-tenon ships would have been less flexible and more durable than the laced ships. Yet, laced vessels persisted in the Adriatic Sea as late as the early 2nd century CE, perhaps because they remained well suited for their environment and purpose. So, while mortise-and-tenon construction was present in the Mediterranean as early as 1320 BCE, 1500 years later ships were still being laced together. The slow and regionally specific transition from laced to mortise-and-tenon construction is evidence of how shipbuilding technology often develops in relation to the environment where the ship will be used, and how the technology tends to change only when an economic or other need arises. Archaeologists' ability to link a given vessel to the homeland of its builder, even when the ship wrecked a thousand or more kilometers (620 miles) from home, speaks to the cultural connection between maritime peoples and their ships. Ships are profoundly culturally specific.[9]

Even as Mediterranean shipbuilders changed how they fastened their planks, they retained the underlying belief that the planks defined the shape and strength of a vessel. This belief was apparent in the lack of frames in the Uluburun ship and the widely spaced frames of the Greek laced vessels, but was belied in the later, more heavily framed Kyrenia ship and Adriatic laced vessels. The second major shift in Mediterranean shipbuilding was the transition from **shell-first** to **frame-first** construction. Shell-first construction was manifested in the laced and mortise-and-tenon ships. This shipbuilding technique saw the hull planking as the basis for the shape and strength of the vessel, and the ship was designed longitudinally, along the length of the planks. When building a shell-first vessel, the planks were built up row by row and joined along their edges, first with lacing and, later, with mortise and tenons or other fasteners (figure 9.5). Only at the end were frames added to reinforce the hull, if they were added at all. This approach required the individual crafting, often carving, of planks, but allowed the shape of the hull to be changed as construction progressed.

Frame-first construction rotated the focus 90 degrees and concentrated on the frames that ran transversely across the ship. In this method, the frames define the shape of the hull and provide much of the vessel's structural strength. The shipbuilder erected some or all of the frames and attached them to the keel, before shaping the planking around them (figure 9.6). The approach required the frames and the hull to be preplanned, since it was difficult to alter the shape of the hull once the frames were formed, and eventually led to the modern science of ship design. This was a fundamental shift in how ships were built, requiring a complete reorientation of how shipbuilders thought about, designed, and assembled their ships.[10]

As might be expected, the transition from shell-first to frame-first did not happen overnight and there were regional variations that persisted. The process of moving toward frame-first construction began as early as the 2nd century CE and is visible in the declining size and frequency of mortise-and-tenon joints found in dated shipwrecks (figure 9.7). By the 6th and 7th centuries CE, frame-first construction was present throughout the Mediterranean. During the transition period, there were vessels constructed using mixed approaches, where both shell-first and frame-first ways of building and thinking about a ship's design and strength were employed, and the pace of transition varied from region to region and from vessel type to vessel type. In later centuries, these various frame-first building styles intermingled as the cultures and shipbuilding traditions of the Mediterranean and beyond moved and mixed. In this way, tracing the roots and branches of frame-first construction has more to do with cultural interaction than the technical decisions of ancient shipbuilders.

It is also worth noting that Mediterranean shipbuilders often preserved the basic shapes of their vessels even while the philosophy and techniques of shipbuilding transitioned from shell-first to frame-first. This implies that shipbuilders and their clients were content with how these ships moved through the water, but were trying to fix a different problem. Frame-first ships were possibly more durable and were likely more efficient to construct because they could be preplanned and overseen by a single lead shipbuilder, while shell-first vessels required every builder to be a craftsperson. It may have also been a response to the increasing availability of metal fasteners, which were required for frame-first, but not for shell-first, construction. There may have been other social, economic, geographic, and environmental drivers for the change. For example, with the ability to preplan a hull comes the ability to standardize vessel forms: Naval fleets can come to rely on proven hull shapes that are quicker and less costly to reproduce. Merchants can order hulls whose volumes will be known, addressing cargo and taxation considerations. Authorities can tax more effectively, knowing the standardized volume of cargo for a class of vessels. Now that archaeologists have clearly identified the nature of the change, with more than 25 shipwrecks defining the temporal and regional variation within the Mediterranean, they can begin the important job of explaining the change. [11]

The third major development in Mediterranean shipbuilding during antiquity had to do with how sailors harnessed the wind and propelled their vessels. Beginning with the Egyptian vessels that traveled along the Nile, **square sails** dominated the region. A square sail is a roughly rectangular sail that is oriented perpendicular to, or square to, the long axis of the ship. Sometime before the 300 BCE Kyrenia ship,

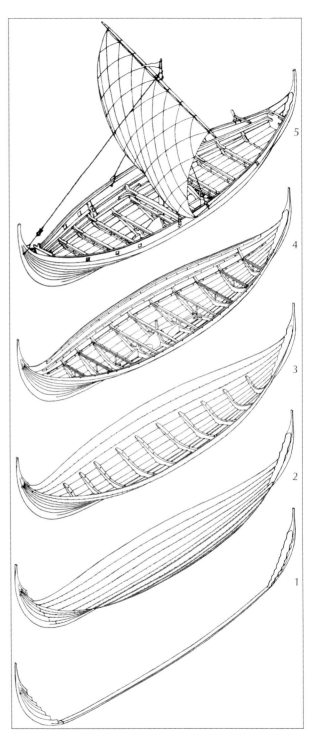

**Figure 9.5** Shell-first building sequence as demonstrated by Skuldelev 3. (Courtesy of The Viking Ship Museum)

**Figure 9.6** Frame-first building sequence. In this image, looking from the starboard side of the bow, the keel and frames have been assembled and the builders are beginning to attach the hull planking. ("Fitting Garboards," page 129. *The Evolution of the Wooden Ship* by Basil Greenhill, Illustrations and Commentary by Sam Manning, 1988, The Blackburn Press)

and becoming more common in the CE period, a new type of sail called a **fore-and-aft** sail began to appear in the Mediterranean. Fore-and-aft sails were often, but not exclusively, triangular and oriented parallel to the longitudinal axis of the vessel, so that the sail runs from fore to aft. Fore-and-aft sails are somewhat easier to work near shore and were likely used on coastal vessels. Because sails do not often survive in the archaeological record, archaeologists have drawn much of their evidence for changes in propulsion from artistic representations. The deep-relief carvings practiced by the Romans have proven particularly useful for the interpretation of sail features. Indirect evidence of the sails can also be used to build this argument. The Kyrenia ship had a single mast step, where the foot of the mast was secured, and it was far forward in the hull (figure 9.8 as compared with figure 9.4). This location would be appropriate for a fore-and-aft sail, but not a square sail.[12]

More efficient and versatile sailing rigs and different ways to design and build hulls were closely linked to how ancient Mediterranean peoples made their livings. The great merchant cultures of the Minoans and Phoenicians depended on their ships to move cargoes, and, along with those cargoes, ideas, throughout the region. The classical Greeks relied on ships to connect their homelands with the colonies they built around the rim of the Mediterranean (see chapter 11). The Romans used ships, some of them truly massive, to bring Rome to their far-flung empire while also reaping the benefits of that empire in the form of raw materials and exotic goods. For example, the Madrague de Giens shipwreck, discovered off the French coast near Marseille, was a 1st century BCE merchantman that measured 40 m (131 ft) long and was capable of carrying nearly 8000 amphorae. The needs of these cultures drove changes in ship design and construction, and changes in ship design and construction allowed new enterprises to flourish.

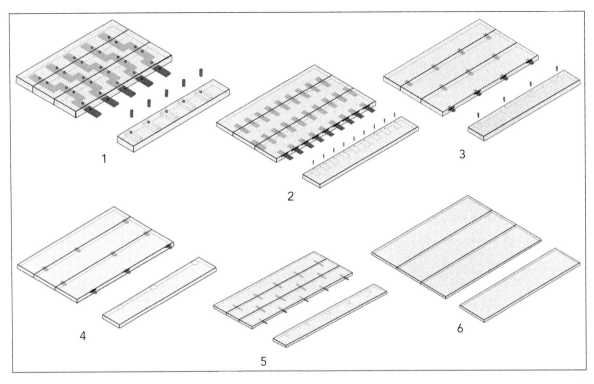

**Figure 9.7** Diminishing use of mortise-and-tenon joints. 1. ca. 1325 BCE (Uluburun); 2. Late 4th century BCE (Kyrenia); 3. 4th century CE (Yassıada 2); 4. 7th century CE (Yassıada 1); 5. ca. 900 CE (Yenikapı 14); 6. ca. 1025 CE (Serçe Limanı). (Redrawn from figure courtesy of Cemal Pulak, Institute of Nautical Archaeology)

## Indian Ocean

Mediterranean sailors were not the only ones using ships to expand their reach and their markets. Shipbuilders in the Indian Ocean were simultaneously honing their craft and making decisions that distinguished their ships from those built in the Mediterranean. There is a long tradition of maritime connections between the Indian Ocean and Mediterranean Sea. Egyptian ships were carried across the desert from the Nile and reassembled to ply the Red Sea, while later Greek and Roman merchants traded in the Indian Ocean. Arabian captains sailed on the Mediterranean Sea, Red Sea, and Indian Ocean. These seafarers linked the Indian subcontinent and Southeast Asia to eastern Africa, Arabia, and the portions of Asia, Africa, and Europe that border the Mediterranean. Most of these linkages were in the name of trade, but along with the goods came ideas about writing, religion, technology, and many other forms of culture, including shipbuilding. Because of these longstanding linkages, it is often difficult to determine where specific technologies, such as the fore-and-aft sail, developed.

**Figure 9.8** Kyrenia II under sail, 1987. (Courtesy of Harry Tzalas)

Based on ship timbers found in Oman, Indian Ocean shipbuilders were constructing sewn-plank, shell-first vessels by 2500 BCE. However, while their neighbors to the west began to build mortise-and-tenon, and then frame-first, ships, Indian Ocean builders continued to sew their vessels. Even when they adopted nails for some types of ships, shell-first remained the dominant approach into the modern period. The Indian Ocean shipbuilders were certainly aware of changes in Mediterranean shipbuilding, but made the conscious decision to retain sewn-plank vessels.

The **dhow**, the quintessential Indian Ocean vessel, helps explain this apparent conservatism (figure 9.9). With its high ends, flat bottom, and sewn planks, the dhow is designed to be beached. The flat bottom allows the vessel to come into shallow water and rest upright on the beach, while the high ends prevent waves from coming into the ship. The sewn planks are better at riding the surf and withstanding the shock of beaching (figure 9.10). The sewn seams also have the benefit of breaking before a plank, so that repairs are relatively easy to make. This, combined with a fore-and-aft sail and a rudder mounted on the centerline of the hull (likely introduced from China), make the dhow uniquely suited for coastal trade. It can be agilely steered near the shore and beached at a convenient location; it can then use the rising tides to float away and travel to another location. This type of ship construction allowed dhows and other Indian Ocean craft to be employed where there are limited port facilities, greatly expanding the opportunities for trade throughout the region.[13]

Comparatively little is known about ancient Indian Ocean shipbuilding. While nearly 1000 Mediterranean shipwrecks have been investigated, almost no premedieval shipwrecks have been found in the Indian Ocean. One of the few exceptions is the Belitung shipwreck, which dates to circa 830 CE. It was found in between Borneo and Sumatra filled with a cargo of Chinese ceramics but was likely built

**Figure 9.9** Dhow illustrated in the 13th century CE manuscript al-Hariri's Māqāmat. (Courtesy of Bibliothèque nationale de France)

in Arabia or India. Despite its uniqueness, the cargo of the Belitung shipwreck was sold and the ship received less attention than it deserved—clear evidence of the damage that commercial exploitation can do to submerged cultural heritage. This paucity of wrecks has in part to do with the types of cargos that Indian Ocean vessels carried, as well as with the warm waters of the area. Many Indian Ocean goods were perishable and carried loose in the hull. Without durable goods or containers to hold the shipwreck to the bottom and protect it from deterioration, the hull tends to disappear. In the Mediterranean, many shipwrecks have been found pinned beneath piles of amphorae or durable cargoes. Similarly, the warm waters of the Indian Ocean support many animals and microbes that consume the wood and organic cargoes of shipwrecks, essentially eating the shipwreck out

**Figure 9.10** Sewn planking on interior of a dhow.

of the archaeological record.[14] It remains possible that ship remains are preserved in deep water. As the technology to access these sites expands, the Indian Ocean is one of the growth fields of nautical archaeology where new investigations can make major contributions.

## East Asia

The Belitung ship was carrying Chinese ceramics when it wrecked, but evidence of direct trade between Arabia and China goes back even earlier, to at least the 6th century CE. Despite this regular exposure to other ways of building watercraft, the shipbuilders of East Asia, like their Indian Ocean counterparts, developed and retained their own unique shipbuilding characteristics. In East Asia, these characteristics included the use of **bulkheads** to reinforce edge-fastened, shell-first hulls that relied heavily on the use of iron (figure 9.11). Just as in the Mediterranean, there was significant regional variation throughout East Asia as shipbuilders with similar ideas about what a ship should look like modified their construction techniques over multiple generations.

Most East Asian vessels were built with a shell-first mindset. Many of the hull planks were grooved to receive the next plank above them and then edge nailed together. If a repair or additional

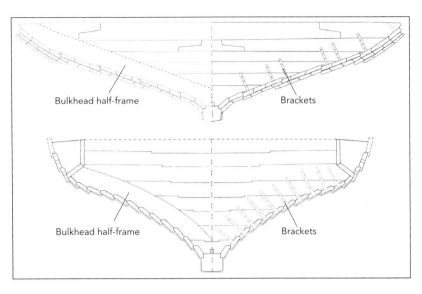

**Figure 9.11** Cross-sections of the Quanzhou ship (top) and the Shinan shipwreck (bottom). Note the multiple layers of hull planking and presence of bulkheads. (Courtesy of Jun Kimura)

strength was necessary, additional layers of hull planking, five or more layers in some cases, were laid on top of the existing planking, clearly indicating that the planking was seen as the main structural element of the ship. Rather than mortise and tenon or sewing, East Asian shipbuilders began to use substantial amounts of iron in their vessels sometime before 1000 CE. In addition to long nails to hold the planks together, they employed iron brackets to attach internal bulkheads to the side of the hull. These bulkheads were essentially wooden walls that ran across the inside of the ship, dividing the hold into several compartments. Bulkheads began to appear during the Han Dynasty and became nearly ubiquitous by circa 600 CE. They served the same purpose as frames in Mediterranean ships: they reinforced the hull and helped prevent the external water pressure from crushing the vessel. Bulkheads were also used to support masts. With masts mounted to bulkheads and supported by deck beams, Chinese shipbuilders did not have to rely on the spine of the vessel to bear the force of the wind and could place masts off-center. Larger Chinese ships carried several masts and sails staggered across the deck, so that each sail was better able to catch the wind without another sail blocking it.[15]

During the 1st century CE, Chinese shipbuilders began to add a centerline rudder to some of their vessels. This was a major innovation in ship design. Previous vessels in China, as well as in the Mediterranean, Europe, and elsewhere, used steering oars or rudders hung from the sides of the vessel to guide it through the water. Whereas vessels in other parts of the world continued to be built with both a pointed bow and pointed stern, Chinese shipbuilders early on developed a **transom**, or flat, stern. The transom stern likely made other forms of steering cumbersome and led to the development, or coevolution, of the centerline rudder. By placing the rudder along the centerline of the vessel, the Chinese increased the efficiency of steering, eventually allowing for larger ships (such as the Nanjing Treasure Ships mentioned in chapter 8) and longer voyages. This is, of course, the way that most modern ships, as well as airplanes, are steered. Based on archaeological data, it appears that the Chinese were the first to develop this important technology. It is less certain whether the centerline rudder diffused through the Indian Ocean into the Mediterranean, or if Mediterranean shipwrights independently invented the same technology.[16]

Chinese shipbuilders retained many of these innovations and they came to typify what is often referred to as the Chinese **junk**. "Junk" entered the Western lexicon as a result of Portuguese colonialism and is a generic European term for a wide variety of East Asian ships. It is a widely used, but not very specific term. Many of the characteristics associated with the junk type are present in the earliest Chinese shipwrecks and, while they changed with time and varied with location, were still common in the 19th century CE. Unfortunately, during the 20th century, traditional Chinese shipbuilding fell out of practice. As a traditional, nonliterate form of knowledge, practiced by builders who held the plans in their heads rather than on paper in their hands, lack of practice means that this form of shipbuilding is in danger of being lost after nearly a thousand years. At the same time, the wisdom of the early Chinese shipbuilders is borne out as their innovations appeared in later Western ships. For example, bulkheads became ubiquitous in iron ships constructed in the 19th century and later. Chinese junks also tended to have hulls that were widest aft of the **midship**. This is the opposite of most European ships built during the last several hundred years, which were wider near the bow and narrower at the stern. Modern racing yachts, however, when viewed from above, are often wider aft of midships.[17]

## Pacific Islands

While the major shipbuilding peoples of Egypt, Greece, Rome, China, and elsewhere were developing ships to, both intentionally and inadvertently, increase contact with one another, the navigators of Micronesia, Melanesia, and Polynesia used watercraft to push into the unpopulated expanses of the Pacific Ocean. Departing the islands of Southeast Asia around 4000 BCE, and making a major push beginning circa 1500 BCE, these seafarers populated many of the Pacific Islands by 1250 CE, when they settled New Zealand, settling Hawaii (ca. 600 CE) and Rapa Nui (Easter Island, ca. 700 CE) along the way.[18] Geographically, this was one of the largest migrations in human history, and it was perpetrated entirely by water.

Despite the number of vessels used in this movement and the fact that many were no doubt lost looking for new islands or traveling between known islands, the archaeological evidence for these watercraft is thin.[19] Pacific Island craft were lightweight and carried little or no durable cargo or ballast. When wrecked, there was very little to pin them to the seafloor and most of these vessels likely broke up and floated away. Even if one of these craft did sink intact, finding such a

**Figure 9.12** Polynesian double canoe, *Hōkūle'a*. (Courtesy of The Polynesian Voyaging Society and 'Ōiwi TV)

small site remains a challenge. The same vast expanses of ocean that made the feats of Polynesian navigation so impressive also daunt any archaeologists interested in surveying for a Polynesian shipwreck. Despite the paucity of archaeological data, however, ethnographic data and traditional knowledge extending into the 21st century, as well as European accounts from the 18th and 19th centuries, provide abundant information about these watercraft.

Polynesian boatbuilders built canoes with and without **outriggers**. An outrigger is a framework supporting a float beside the main hull. It increases stability and allows the canoe to be sailed with less risk of capsizing. Outrigger canoes were the everyday craft of the Polynesians, used for moving around a single island, fishing, and trade and transportation between the islands in an archipelago.

For longer-distance travel or for displays of power, they built ships referred to as double canoes, similar to a large modern catamaran (figure 9.12). These consisted of two long, narrow hulls, usually 15–27.5 m (49–90 ft) in length, joined by a platform. The two hulls meant that they were very stable and the platform provided ample space for shelters, supplies, crops, animals, passengers, and to work the sails. Double canoes could carry upward of 140 people, making them ideal for exploration and colonization of new islands. The hulls of these ships were sewn together

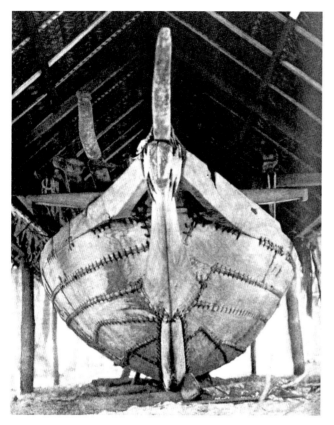

**Figure 9.13** Sewn Polynesian voyaging canoe.

in much the same way we have seen elsewhere (figure 9.13). On islands with abundant trees, the lower portion of the hull was a hollowed-out log, or several logs joined together lengthwise, with additional planks built up to form the necessary height and displacement. Where wood was rare, considerably smaller planks were used and much more sewing was necessary. The lengths that shipbuilders went to build their vessels is understandable in the context of the importance of these vessels. Not only did the double canoes connect islands, they were often equated with islands, such that one lived both on islands and on canoes and both islands and canoes plied the sea.[20]

These canoes were steered with large paddles, often one on both sides and a third near the middle. Propulsion for double canoes, and many smaller canoes, came from sails made of palm leaf mats. There was a wide variety of these sails, representing various regional preferences, but, in general, they were in the form of an apex-down triangle. This type of sail, unknown to Europeans, allowed Polynesian navigators to sail across the wind and more than likely sail into winds coming from approximately 75° off the bow.[21] Sailing off the wind was important because Pacific Island migration was generally from west to east—into the wind. Since sailing ships derive their motive force from the wind, it is impossible for them to sail directly into the wind. To move against the prevailing wind, sailors often sail at an angle to the wind and then shift their direction to cut across the direction of the wind. This practice, called tacking, leads to a zig-zag pattern. The outbound portion of Pacific Islander voyages, therefore, was slower and more difficult because it was generally into the wind, but that also increased the chances of a safe return home; if vessels turned around when half of their supplies were exhausted, they should have been able to make the journey with food and water to spare. This is similar to the "rule of thirds" used by experienced divers when exploring inside a shipwreck. If a dive team only penetrates the wreck as far as one-third of their breathing gas will allow, they should be able to exit with a full third remaining to accommodate any unforeseen incidents.

Much of our understanding of the capabilities of double canoes comes from the work of the Polynesian Voyaging Society and their 19-m (62-ft) voyaging canoe *Hōkūle'a*. *Hōkūle'a*, like other modern versions of ancient ships, is a floating hypothesis: It allows us to test ideas about the capabilities of past seafarers and ships. While we cannot argue that the capabilities of present-day reconstructions directly reflect those of the original vessels, building and sailing ships such as *Hōkūle'a* helps in our understanding of the past and expands the questions we can put to the archaeological record. *Hōkūle'a* was launched in 1975 and has since been used for several long-distance voyages, including a three-year circumnavigation of the globe, demonstrating the seaworthiness of double canoes and the sophistication of traditional Polynesian navigation without modern instruments.[22]

## Northern Europe

While Southern Europe, North Africa, South Asia, and Southeast Asia were all connected by nearly uninterrupted water, accessing Northern Europe was more difficult because it involved sailing out into the Atlantic Ocean. There are accounts of ancient Mediterranean explorers venturing beyond the so-called Pillars of Hercules at the Straits of Gibraltar that mark the western end of the Mediterranean Sea (see chapter 11) and by circa 50 CE the Romans had established a significant port at modern-day London.[23] Clearly, Northern Europe was not cut off from the rest of the world, but with more than a thousand kilometers (600 mi) of land and the often-tumultuous Atlantic separating Northern European shipbuilders from those to the south, they developed a unique shipbuilding approach.

Boatbuilding in Northern Europe began with skin and log boats, but, as builders in Polynesia and elsewhere had discovered, it was possible to build larger vessels by splitting a log into planks and attaching the planks to each other. Rather than attach the planks side by side with **caulking** between the short dimensions of each plank, however, Northern European shipbuilders overlapped them so that there was a seam between the top of one plank and the bottom of the next. This overlapping, called **lapstrake** construction, required more wood, a resource abundant in Northern Europe, but provided an excellent surface for caulking and fastening (figure 9.14). The Hjortspring boat, which was built circa 350 BCE and later ritually deposited in a shallow Danish lake with a

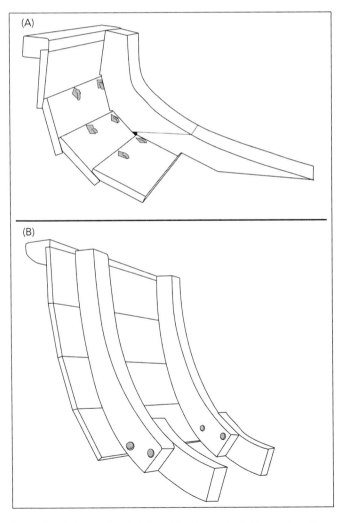

**Figure 9.14** Examples of clinker (A) and carvel (B) ship construction.

variety of weapons, is a good example of this boatbuilding technique. Its planks were sewn to each other, but within a few hundred years, local builders had begun to use iron nails to fasten the planks. The Nydam boat, dated to 200 CE and found just six miles from Hjortspring, was built by nailing through the overlapping plank edges and then bending the nail over a metal washer called a **rove** to secure it in a technique called **clinker** construction.[24]

Clinker ship construction is one of the distinguishing features of the Nordic ship-building tradition, often referred to as "Viking shipbuilding" after its most famous practitioners. These ships were built in a shell-first manner with the primary shape and strength of the vessel coming from the hull planks. The planks were split radially out of logs, which made them stronger than if they had been sawn across the grain. Only after the hull was at least partially complete were frames inserted to provide additional strength. Since the planks were not flush, the frames had to be carved into a stepped, or **joggled**, shape to fit snugly against the inside of the hull (see figure 9.5). This type of construction was firmly in place by the beginning of the 7th century CE when the Sutton Hoo ship was dragged ashore and repurposed as a royal burial chamber (figure 9.15). In addition to being an important step in the evolution of Northern European ship construction, Sutton Hoo is evidence of the importance of careful excavation. The 27-m (89-ft) long vessel survived only as stains in the surrounding soil, punctuated by badly corroded nails that once held the planks together. The stains were all that remained of the wooden components that had rotted away long ago, but by carefully removing the unstained soils the excavators were left with a nearly perfect impression of the original vessel.

Throughout the next 500 years, Nordic shipbuilders continued to advance their craft by increasing the height of the vessel sides and refining their methods for reinforcing the hull with cross-beams and **knees**. There was also a diversification of ships from general purpose forms to ships built specifically for war, trade, or other tasks. A variety of these vessels were sunk deliberately in the 11th century to obstruct a channel in the Roskilde fjord in Denmark. These five vessels referred to as the Skuldelev ships were excavated between 1957 and 1962. This pioneering excavation led to the recovery, conservation, documentation, and reconstruction of all five vessels, now on display at the Viking Ship Museum, alongside nine others—the Roskilde vessels—discovered during the construction of the museum. The Skuldelev and Roskilde ships date to the middle fifty years of the 11th century and offer a snapshot of fully formed Viking shipbuilding (figure 9.16). They were built across much

**Figure 9.15** Sutton Hoo ship during excavation.

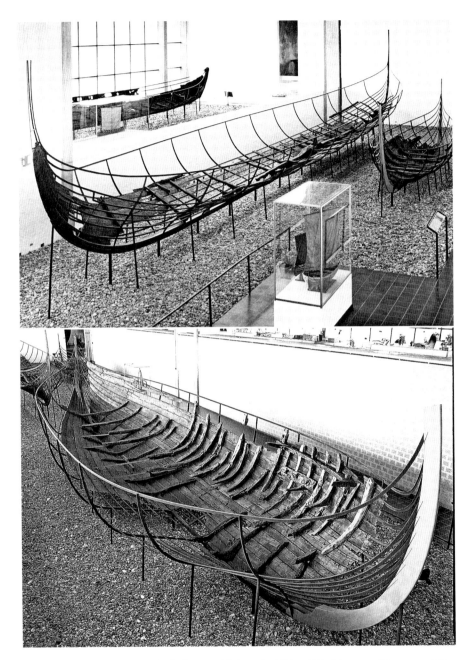

**Figure 9.16** Skuldelev 1 and 2 hulls on exhibit at the Viking Ship Museum. (Courtesy of The Viking Ship Museum)

of the European Viking realm, but all ended their days as part of a defensive blockade. The ships were staked to the seafloor and filled with stones to block a channel and defend settlements deeper in the fjord. Skuldelev 1 was an ocean-going cargo ship, while the slightly smaller Skuldelev 3 was likely used for coastal trade. Skuldelev 2 was a 30-m (98-ft) longship, the quintessential Viking warship. Skuldelev 5 was also a longship, but approximately half the size of Skuldelev 2. Skuldelev 6 was originally built as a fishing boat, but may have been converted to coastal trade later in its career. Ranging in length from 11.2 to 30 m (37–98 ft) and built of a variety of woods, all five Skuldelev ships shared clinker construction, joggled frames, and transverse reinforcing timbers called *biti*; were single-masted; had sweeping double-ended shapes; and had carved end **posts** that typify Nordic shipbuilding.

Despite more than a millennium of development, there were clear connections between the Hjortspring boat and the later Viking ships at Skuldelev. All were built using lapstrake construction and had carved end posts. Some Viking shipbuilders went as far as to carve the end posts to continue the shape of the overlapping strakes onto the post. These vessels also had a focus on rowing. The Hjortspring boat was propelled entirely by human muscle. The later Viking ships were built with a single mast that supported a square sail, but all were also capable of being rowed. Rowing allowed them to maneuver the ship in calm weather, and, in the case of longships, to sweep into an unsuspecting port no matter the weather. The use of a paddle or oar to steer the Hjortspring boat also lived on in the quarter rudder mounted on the side of Viking ships.[25]

Meanwhile, a little farther south, shipbuilders developed an approach in which the shape of the vessel was defined by the bottom. This **bottom-based** construction approach appears in several late 1st- and 2nd-century CE shipwrecks such as the Blackfriars Wreck 1, the Bevaix Boat, and the Zwammerdam barges. All of these vessels date to a period when the Roman Empire extended throughout Europe, but the fundamental idea of bottom-based construction seems to have been indigenous. In bottom-based construction, the bottom planks are often temporarily attached to each other, then framing timbers are placed and the bottom trimmed to shape, before the temporary fasteners are removed (figure 9.17). The sides of the vessel are then built up from the bottom, using the shape of the bottom to define the overall shape of the vessel. The resulting hull tends to be flat-bottomed and to have a hard turn of the **bilge**, where the bottom and sides meet. Because the resulting vessel can be built long and narrow, with a shallow **draft**, and because flat-bottomed hulls tend to perform poorly in open water, many of these vessels were intended for use on rivers and inland waterways. Bottom-based construction can be seen as a shipbuilding philosophy parallel to shell-first and frame-first construction described above. It was most famously practiced in Europe, but appears worldwide.[26]

Bottom-based and clinker construction came together sometime around 1100 CE to form a vessel type called a cog (figure 9.18). The cog type likely originated around the Baltic Sea and was typified by a primarily flush-planked, keel-less bottom that defined the shape of the ship, and high, straight, lapstrake sides. Cogs also tended to have straight stems and stern posts. Importantly, even revolutionarily for the region, a centerline rudder was hung on the sternpost. Centerline rudders had appeared previously in Southeast Asia, but the stern rudder, hung from the straight stern post on hinges like a contemporaneous European door, became the standard form of rudder throughout Europe and elsewhere during the second millennium CE. A single sail provided propulsion. More than 20 cog shipwrecks have been found, but the Bremen cog is among the most complete, and, in many ways serves as the archetype. The Bremen cog was likely washed away while under construction in 1380 CE. It was nearly finished but the rudder was yet to be hung, the upper works were not complete, and the wreck was full of shipbuilding tools. Its excellent state of preservation allowed archaeologists to match its shape to the many illustrations of cogs found in historical depictions.[27]

### CONVERGENCE OF SHIPBUILDING TRADITIONS

All boatbuilding traditions started essentially the same way with reed boats, log boats, and skin or bark boats. From these basic technologies, shipbuilders adapted to local conditions and created larger vessels in divergent ways, leading to the variety of shipbuilding traditions discussed above, as well as throughout this book, and many others that space does not permit us to highlight. Eventually, however, shipbuilding technologies and designs traveled along with cargoes, weapons, and people to trade with and conquer other areas, in a process that resulted in a con-vergence of shipbuilding methods. The mixing of ships and shipbuilders between regions led

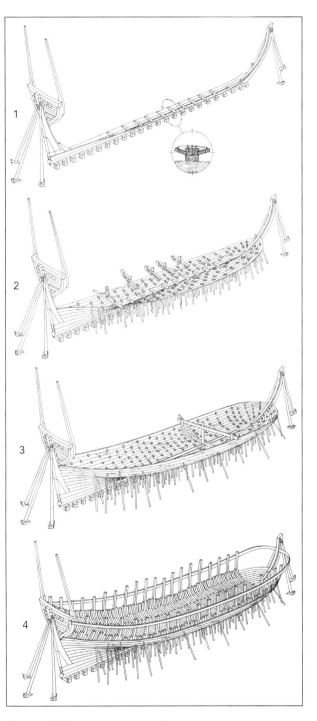

**Figure 9.17** Bottom-based ship construction sequence. (Drawing by A.J. van den Heuvel)

**Figure 9.18** Bremen Cog reconstruction, *Roland von Bremen*. (Courtesy of Heiner Trappmann)

to hybrid vessels that borrowed from more than one ship-building tradition to create a new type of ship that performed better or more efficiently. The hybridization of ship construction was part of larger processes of **ethnogenesis** as cultures came into contact. Ethnogenesis is visible in artifacts, foods, and languages, but is particularly poignant in watercraft because ships were often the vectors of culture contact. Watercraft evolved from common roots into myriad designs that were constantly influenced by other designs from regions near and far.

The convergence of shipbuilding traditions was evident in antiquity across many regions, but accelerated, particularly between the Mediterranean and Northern Europe, beginning in the 12th century CE. There were Mediterranean-style ships in Northern Europe before this period, such as the County Hall ship, excavated in London but built in a markedly Roman manner around 295 CE. Northern European ships had also entered the Mediterranean, a result of Viking raids during the 9th through 11th centuries. During the 12th century CE, however, the Crusades brought large numbers of European ships into the Mediterranean and, by the 14th century, Mediterranean merchant ships were common in Northern Europe. As a result, the hybridization of ship designs quickened.

Some cogs reflected the influence of Mediterranean shipbuilding techniques likely picked up during the Crusades. For example, the builders of the Bremen cog incorporated **through beams**—large beams that spanned the hull and protruded through the sides—and were in the process of building a **sterncastle**—a high superstructure above the transom—when the ship was lost. Both through beams and sterncastles had been present in the Mediterranean since antiquity but were relatively recent additions in Northern Europe. Still, cogs remained decidedly Northern European in design and construction.

The advent of a new ship type, the **carrack**, in the 14th century CE represented a fuller hybridization of shipbuilding in which Northern European shipbuilders adopted several key aspects of Mediterranean shipbuilding, eventually leading to the dissemination of these building techniques across the globe. Carracks had flush hull planking, multiple masts, wooden castles at bow and stern, and a stern rudder (figure 9.19). Flush planking, called **carvel planking** (see figure 9.14),

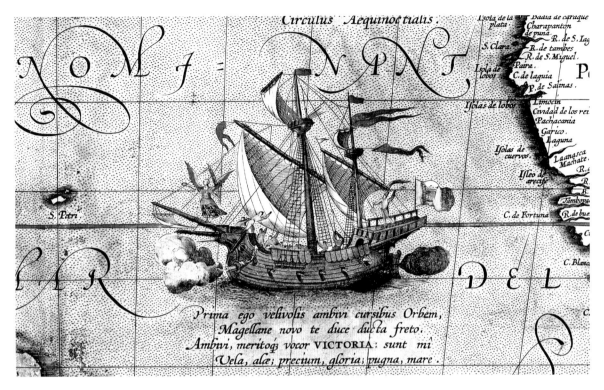

**Figure 9.19** Carrack (Magellan's *Victoria*). Detail of *Maris Pacifici* by Abraham Ortelius (1589).

entered Northern Europe from the Mediterranean via southwestern European trading vessels called *caravelas*. This form of planking was based on a frame-first way of viewing ship construction and so eventually required northern shipbuilders to transition away from shell-first and bottom-based approaches. Giving up these long-held traditions must have had perceived benefits, which likely included savings in iron and labor that made it more economical to build more and larger ships. Carvel-built ships were also easier to repair, allowed for more flexibility in hull shape, and made gunports easier to construct and seal. Whether the latter two benefits were apparent to late 14th- and early 15th-century shipbuilders is unknown, but they became important in world history. Carracks also took advantage of the Mediterranean fore-and-aft sail and combined it with the traditional Northern European square sail. These sails were deployed on two different masts, itself a novelty in Northern Europe. The square sail allowed the ship to be efficiently driven by following winds, while the fore-and-aft sail made the vessel more maneuverable, especially when winds were not optimal. This began a period of sail innovation. By 1409, a third mast was added and by the late 15th century CE, a sail under the bowsprit and a topsail were added. Together, these sails allowed the ship to catch winds that would otherwise not be used. Dividing the sails between multiple masts and placing more than one sail on a mast meant that each individual sail could be smaller. Smaller sails were easier to handle, so that the crew sizes could be smaller, reducing one of the major costs of operating a sailing ship.[28]

Carracks also carried forward the previously-adopted habit of including sterncastles and forecastles and stern rudders. Sterncastles and forecastles, basically wooden fortifications rising above both ends of a ship, were particularly helpful in the pre-cannon age of naval warfare as they gave soldiers a high place to rain projectiles down on an adversary's ship. They were also present on merchant ships, in part because the distinction between naval and merchant ships was vague at this time, with ships being used for both purposes during their lives. The stern rudder was at this point a well-known component of Northern European shipbuilding and was adopted by Mediterranean shipbuilders at about the same time that the carrack became the prevalent large vessel in Northern Europe.

The carrack marked a significant change and deserves a moment of focus. Cultures in general tend to change slowly. Culture is how humans define ourselves and cultural adaptations are our primary means of survival. These adaptations make up for our profound deficits—the lack of claws, shells, fleetness, mass, and other physical attributes that many animals use to make their way in the world. Because it is linked to our identity and our survival, most groups are slow to make fundamental changes to their culture. This is particularly true when it comes to ships and seafaring. Ships were expensive to build, carried valuable cargos, and were crewed by large numbers of people sailing into a dangerous environment. The weight of this responsibility encouraged shipbuilders to change their designs and techniques even more slowly than other craftspeople and to cling to what had traditionally worked until an improvement was demonstrably proven. The change that we see as relatively quick from an historical and archaeological perspective—something that happened over a century or two, rather than millennia—still spanned several generations and was probably accompanied by a lot of arguments between established builders and the brashest of their apprentices.

The shipwrecks that illustrate this transition should be seen as the product of these arguments, as well as evidence of other less-durable phenomena such as the practices of maneuvering sails or determining course. Archaeologists should imagine the worry and debates that likely accompanied all the changes in shipbuilding discussed in this chapter: the adoption of a sail or rudder, changes in navigation techniques, alterations in shipbuilding methods, the decision to go to sea in a type of vessel no one had seen before, or to be the first to sail for the horizon. These were all life-and-death decisions. The technological changes that archaeologists record in shipwrecks are our window on the personal worlds of shipbuilders and sailors. In the case of the adoption of carvel planking, this was not a smooth transition. Clinker vessels continued to be built until modern engines made them unpractical and some shipbuilders continued to build bottom-based ships into the 17th century CE, but adapted their methods so that the result looked like a frame-first carvel ship. Other ships were substantially reworked to take advantage of the new techniques.

The Woolwich Ship, which is likely the remains of the English warship *Sovereign*, was converted from clinker to carvel during its lifetime. If it is the remains of *Sovereign*, it was built in 1488 and rebuilt in 1508, demonstrating that in some instances the change came within a generation.[29]

The hybridized carrack and the ships that followed it were better suited for long-distance ocean voyages than nearly any vessels except contemporaneous Chinese vessels and the Polynesian double canoes. Unlike the double canoes, the hybridized ships could carry large numbers of people and supplies as well as cannon. The fact that the Chinese decided to end their overseas expansion at just the moment that Europeans began theirs demonstrates the fragility of historical developments. Columbus' *Santa Maria* and Magellan's *Victoria* were both carracks. Carracks had global reach and were steered by cultures with global ambitions. In this way, these ships, which represent the convergence of Northern European and Mediterranean technologies, served as the first vectors for the global convergence of cultures beginning with European expansion in the 15th century CE (see chapter 11).

### TRANSITION FROM ART TO SCIENCE, FROM WOOD TO IRON, AND FROM SAIL TO STEAM

The previous discussion has been almost entirely about wooden ships, but any trip to a modern port clearly shows that that is not where the story ends. The convergence between the Mediterranean and wider worlds discussed above extended far beyond shipbuilding. This trend included developments in science, technology, and mathematics that eventually also had repercussions for shipbuilding over the next 500 years.

The earliest shipbuilding instructions were similar to the first recorded recipes: they assumed a huge amount of prior knowledge on the part of the reader and served more to remind an expert of a few key points rather than act as a step-by-step cookbook for the novice. By the 15th century CE, however, the more universal language of mathematics was being used to communicate basic hull forms. These instructions still required a good deal of practical knowledge to complete, but the shape of a vessel was now more a product of science than art. Previously, shipbuilders had built primarily by eye, aided by years of experience and simple tools such as flexible pieces of wood bent across principal frames to determine the curve of the hull. Mathematically determined vessel forms allowed good designs to be saved and reproduced. Mathematics additionally allowed a successful design to be rendered on a few pieces of parchment and communicated to a shipbuilder who had never seen the ship in question. Planned ship construction fit well with the Renaissance mindset. This was a time when mathematics and ratios were popular, so the rationalization of shipbuilding through mathematics made sense to many contemporary shipbuilders.

## THE SCIENCE OF SHIP DESIGN

Eric Reith, Director of Research Emeritus, CNRS, LAMOP, Musée national de la Marine, France

Any boat or ship can be delineated schematically on a technical plan as an abstract piece of architecture, and at the same time as a machine equipped with mechanical systems of propulsion, direction, and even warfare. In the historical period, a vessel's intended purpose, the marine environment, architectural theories, and a number of other factors informed the scale and nature of these architectural and mechanical representations. Though any boat or ship is subjected to the universal constraints of stability (static and dynamic), friction, maneuverability, and performance, these constraints may vary in complexity depending on the type of vessel considered. It is thus obvious that between a ship-of-the-line and an inshore fishing boat the manners in which these constraints are addressed vary greatly in technical terms.

It is during the general design phase that the most innovative technical approaches to naval architecture are formulated. Up until the end of 16th and the beginning of the 18th centuries, depending on the country concerned, ship design generally rested on a set of unwritten rules, which, for the definition of the shape of the hull in particular, called upon the application of "practical geometry" by shipyards. This method of proportions utilized a master-mold frame (and the rising square) as an intermediary between a ship's architectural concept and its physical manifestation. The method of "whole molding," in its various configurations, relied on the progressive rising and narrowing of each frame as the shipwright moved away from the master-mold toward the extremities of the vessel. In this manner the proportional rising and narrowing of each frame determined the shape of a vessel's hull, always operating at a 1:1 scale.

It was in the years 1570–1580 CE that a clear intellectual break with these traditional design practices appeared in England, through the famous figure of the royal master shipbuilder Mathew Baker. Baker made several innovations into the process of ship design that influenced the field as a whole, including the conceptualization of ship architecture, the manner of training future shipbuilders, and the elevation in social stature of shipbuilders. Using a constant reduced scale and a standardized template—including the plan view, the longitudinal side view, and the cross-section—Baker drew on paper the hull lines of a ship. Within this framework, the drawing of the master-frame, for example, whose role is central in the design of the shape of a hull, rests on a geometrical construction containing several tangent arcs of a circle. Starting from such a geometrical representation on reduced scale, a shipyard could then utilize the master-mold method at the appropriate scale to construct vessels. From this point on, the design of a ship was separated from the time of its construction, and the social status of the shipbuilder parted from that of the carpenter.

Another notable innovation was the recourse to what Baker referred to as "two supporting sciences," and geometry, when defining the architecture of a vessel. One of the first applications of this mediation of mathematics is related to the calculation of a vessel's tonnage prior to its construction. The capacity to intellectually envisage characteristics of a vessel—such as tonnage—in advance, as opposed to evaluating such characteristics postconstruction, represents a remarkable advancement in the science of ship design. It should be underlined that the ability to make such preconstruction calculations was only made possible by the visual aid of hull lines, as it was the measurement of the various curved layouts of a hull that allowed the mathematical calculation of surfaces and volumes.

Baker and his *Fragments of Ancient English Shipwrightry* marked the first step in a long and gradual evolution that followed variable regional chronologies and saw ship design transition from a method based on vernacular rules of architectural practice to one based on scientific and mathematical principles. Alongside, though perhaps below the surface, was the evolution of a profession gradually changing the status of a marine carpenter, formed on a shipyard by means of practical training, to that of a naval engineer trained in the scientific disciplines and the theory of naval architecture within the framework of a school.

In France, for example, this progression toward a scientific design of ships was punctuated by a series of thinkers and publications which resonated across Europe. In 1697, Paul Hoste, a Jesuit professor of mathematics, published *Théorie de la construction des vaisseaux*, in which, among other matters, he precisely defined the concept of a transverse projection plan in three views: the plan view, the longitudinal side view, and the cross-section. In 1746, the famous physicist Pierre Bouguer published his *Traité du navire, de sa construction et de ses mouvemens* in which he defined for the first time a series of hydrostatic and hydrodynamic concepts, including that of metacenter, which constitutes a fundamental reference for the measurement of a ship's stability. It is interesting to note that these two authors do not belong to the professional and social environment of shipbuilders, but to that of science, thus affirming the increasingly important role granted to science and theory compared to that afforded to technique and practice. A further illustration of the developing relation between science, technology, and naval architecture was provided by the famous Swedish naval engineer Fredrik H. af Chapman through his collection of plans, *Architectura Navalis Mercatoria*, published in 1765, and his 1775 treatise *Tractat om skepps-byggeriet*. These publications instantly became authoritative references illustrating the application of scientific thinking to the design of merchantmen and warships.

What intellectual connections exist between the methods of a naval engineer and those of a nautical archaeologist? Their respective reasoning presents a certain number of analogies. Starting with the excavation or investigation of a shipwreck, an archaeologist aims to restore the vessel in all its aspects, both as an architectural concept, and as a machine. The archaeologist desires to draw the plan of the hull, and to define its architectural characteristics (dimensions, proportions, hydrostatic and hydrodynamic capacities, stability, light displacement, fully loaded displacement, and tonnage). It is a question for the archaeologist of reconstructing, to some extent, the original architectural concept and, in the final analysis, of being in the same place as that of the naval engineer of the past vis-a-vis the earlier architectural projection. The analogy is also found on the level of the work methods. Like the naval engineer, the nautical archaeologist begins by drawing the plan of the hull; for a long time, work was carried out manually, on the drawing table. Today, the computer and design software are the usual instruments of work. The subsequent phase—that of analyzing the reconstructed ship plan—is facilitated by the use of naval architecture software and 3D simulations that make it possible to give "life" to the recreated vessel.

In short, there exists, in addition to a frequent passion shared for the universe of the naval architecture, an authentic intellectual relationship between the "scientific spirit" of the nautical archaeologist and that of the naval engineer. Perhaps it is not by chance that two of the most famous nautical archaeologists, the Danish Ole Crumlin-Pedersen (1935–2011) and the American J. Richard Steffy (1924–2007), stemmed from a scientific formation: Ole that of a naval architect and Dick that of an engineer.

Some of the first evidence for planned ship construction comes from archaeology, rather than documentary sources. The Serçe Limanı shipwreck (1025 CE), which was lost off the coast of Turkey carrying three tons of glass, is among the earliest shipwrecks showing evidence of mathematically planned construction. Its frames show evidence of the repeated use of a "foot" measurement, predetermined frame locations to control the hull shape, and proportional rising and narrowing of the frames. A refinement of these techniques is evident in the remains of an early 14th century CE coastal trading vessel known as the Culip VI ship that wrecked off the northern coast of Spain. The surviving frame timbers were marked with scratches at the edges of the keel and the turn of the bilge, as well as with Roman numerals that increased sequentially from the midship frames toward the ends. Based on these marks and the proportions of the frames,

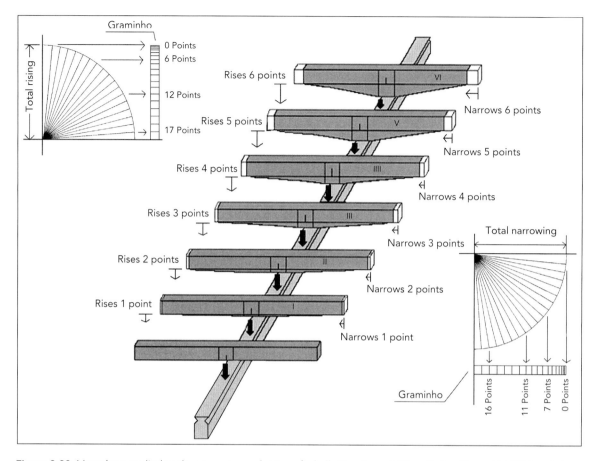

Graminho

0 Points
6 Points
12 Points
17 Points

Total rising

Rises 6 points
Rises 5 points
Rises 4 points
Rises 3 points
Rises 2 points
Rises 1 point

VI
V
IIII
III
II
I

Narrows 6 points
Narrows 5 points
Narrows 4 points
Narrows 3 points
Narrows 2 points
Narrows 1 point

Total narrowing

Graminho

16 Points    11 Points    7 Points    0 Points

**Figure 9.20** Mezzaluna applied to the narrowing and rising of a hull. (Courtesy of Filipe Castro, Texas A&M University)

the excavators determined that the hull was designed using the *mezzaluna*—a technique not recorded in written form until more than a century later. The *mezzaluna* takes its name from the half-circle (or moon) that governed its application. Half of the *mezzaluna* was used to determine how the frames narrowed and the other half dictated the rise of the frames above the keel as the vessel rose and narrowed toward each end (figure 9.20). Each half of the *mezzaluna* was divided into a set number of angles and the angles were then transferred to a gauge that was used in the actual building process. With a few short notes about the radius of the circle and the number of divisions, the *mezzaluna* allowed the shape of a hull to be communicated. The resulting gauges were then used to shape the frames, the frames were numbered as seen on the Culip VI shipwreck, and then assembled. The Culip VI wreck also showed how the shape could be further modified. The narrowing of Culip VI began on either side of the midship frames, but the rising did not commence until four frames later. The sophisticated application of this technique to a mundane vessel in a region not generally considered a center of shipbuilding innovation suggests that planned shipbuilding was well established considerably earlier than the documentary record would suggest.[30]

The mathematics used to design ships became more intricate in subsequent centuries, allowing for increasingly complex ships. During this time, ship design transitioned from the practical knowledge of the shipyard to the theoretical knowledge of the drafting table, so that by the 18th century one of the great books on ship design, Pierre Bouguer's 1746 *Traité du navire*, was written by a mathematician and astronomer with no shipbuilding experience. The development of naval architecture meant that ships could be visualized and their characteristics, such as capacity and stability, could be predicted before a single piece of timber was cut. The lines drawings that naval architects and nautical archaeologists use to represent the 3D shape of a hull on a 2D piece of paper grew out of these developments (figure 9.21). Traditional ship designing techniques, including building by eye, using flexible strips of wood to determine the curve of the sides, or sculpting small models of the hull to visualize the relationship between frames and the finished vessel began to be replaced, but were common into the 19th century CE and are still practiced today.[31]

Naval architecture was in full force by the time that wooden shipbuilding reached its height during the 19th century CE. Among the most sophisticated and iconic vessels of this period were the **clipper ships** (figure 9.22) These ships were to ship design what *art moderne* was to architecture: they were so simplified and so clearly represented their essential nature that they approached the realm of art. For clipper ships this essential nature was speed. These vessels had nearly flat keels, paralleling their equally flat decks that were devoid of any obstruction that would prevent the crew from working the truly huge amounts of canvas stretched across three or more masts. Clipper ship hulls tended to be long and narrow with a sharp bow. This hull shape and the frightening amount of sail meant that clipper ships could cruise through the water at more than twice the speed of the average ship. This speed came at the cost of safety and cargo space. Clippers were only economically viable in specialized trades, such as transporting tea to Britain or miners to the Australian and American gold rushes, where people were willing to pay substantial sums to arrive first. These ships also required daring captains and crews that were willing to push the ship to, and sometimes beyond, the bounds of safety in any weather.

One of the few archaeological examples of a clipper ship, the *Snow Squall*, ran aground on the Falkland Islands while sailing from New York to San Francisco in 1864. More than a century later, *Snow Squall*'s bow was raised and put on display at the Maine Maritime Museum, not far from where the ship was built (figure 9.23). Even more famous, the *Cutty Sark* (1869) is intact and on display in Greenwich, England. *Cutty Sark* was one of the last and fastest clipper ships built, famously traveling 672 km (418 mi) in one day (an average sailing day in this period was less than 300 km, 186 miles). It took advantage of the lessons learned, and preserved as ship plans, by previous generations of ship designers.

**Figure 9.21** Shipwrights using plans at a shipyard from *Élémens de l'architecture navale* by Henri-Louis Duhamel du Monceau, 1752.

**Figure 9.22** Clipper ship *Sovereign of the Seas*. (Henry Hall, 1884, *Report on the Ship-Building Industry of the United States*, fig. 33, page 76)

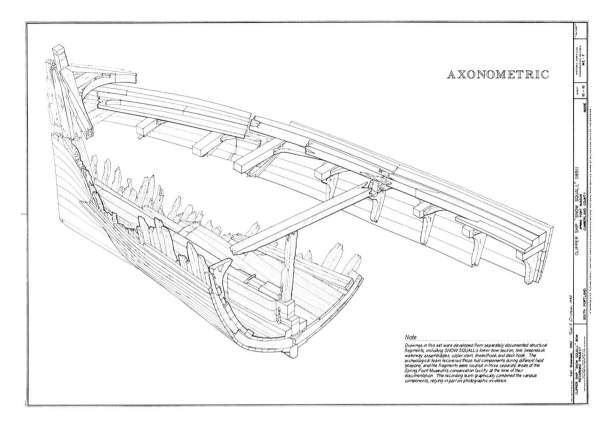

**Figure 9.23** The bow of *Snow Squall* based on archaeological remains. (Courtesy of Historic American Buildings Survey)

*Cutty Sark*, and clipper ships in general, were also a harbinger of the next major change in shipbuilding. *Cutty Sark* was built using **composite construction**: iron frames covered with wood hull planking. This was a bridge to completely iron construction, which was more expensive and not fully trusted at the time. The iron frames could offer the same strength as wood, with smaller dimensions, leaving more space for cargo. Between 1853 and 1870, 27 clipper ships were built using composite construction, while 33 were entirely made of wood and 5 were framed and sheathed in iron.[32]

The growing use of iron, and later steel, in ship construction increased the importance of naval architecture. It also increased the size of ships that could be built. By the close of the 19th century CE, the design of oceangoing ships was largely separate from their construction, mirroring much of the white-collar/blue-collar divide that also became apparent in manufacturing more broadly. Ship design was the domain of engineers who planned increasingly massive ships to fulfill specific roles. Materials for these ships were imported from greater and greater distances and were often the result of other industrial processes, such as iron making. At the shipyard, the jobs of forming and assembling the frames and hull were increasingly delegated to laborers who had no input on the design or construction. Shipbuilding had become fully industrialized.

Initially independent from the development of metal shipbuilding, but eventually intersecting it, the transition to steam power also occurred during the 19th century CE. Steam-powered vessels had their roots in the 18th century, but the early 19th century saw the first economically viable applications of the technology. Steam technology spread most quickly on the rivers of North America and Europe. Archaeological examples of these early steamboats include the *Eric Nordevall*, launched in 1837 and lost in Sweden's Lake Vättern, and the *Heroine*, which was launched in 1832 and sank six years later in the Red River between Oklahoma and Texas. While separated by an ocean, these two ships share several similarities such as their wooden hulls, relatively flat bottoms, and the use of side-mounted paddlewheels for propulsion. Steamships also began to be used on the oceans, and in 1819 the SS *Savanah* became the first steamship to cross the Atlantic. *Savanah*, like many early steamships, carried a good deal of sail as an insurance policy for finicky and underpowered engines, and much of its famous voyage was in fact made under sail.[33]

The transition to steam was as, if not more, momentous than the transition to iron shipbuilding. Steam-powered vessels were able to follow a strict schedule, regardless of the winds and tides, they were able to work against the currents of rivers, and they could be more easily maneuvered within ports. Steam power essentially removed shipping from the control of nature and handed much of that control to the captain. Steam ships also required a smaller crew to operate since they did not have large sails that required many hands to haul.

When steam power and iron hulls came together the result was as fundamental a shift in shipbuilding as any that had been seen previously. Just as the Industrial Revolution completely changed production on land, these revolutions utterly altered shipbuilding. Captains and crews had to master the new technology, and countless burned and exploded steamship wrecks attest that they struggled. Shipbuilders also struggled to incorporate the new materials and propulsion systems into their repertoire of skills. Entirely new crafts had to be learned and incorporated into the shipbuilding process. New craftsmen such as boilermakers and punch and shear operators for cutting out the iron and steel elements of the ship and engines had to be hired. Builders and designers also had to account for how the new materials and engines affected each other. Engines required space within the hull and put new and different stresses on the hull that were not present with wind power. Steam also benefitted from hull shapes that differed from sail, and iron shipbuilding made some of these shapes possible. Ultimately steam allowed for increasingly larger ships and cargos to be propelled through the water, as metal ship construction greatly increased the upper limit of ship size. Shipyards themselves had to be expanded to include engineering works for the construction of boilers and additional equipment to facilitate working large pieces of iron. Beginning in the early 1800s, there was a consolidation of shipbuilding into a few yards in centralized locations. Gone were the days when the bulk of the materials needed were available from the local environment and a handful of individuals could master all the skills needed to build a vessel. Instead, this new mode of ship construction depended on materials that were not locally available, so shipbuilders positioned themselves near importation centers; located not only in major ports, but near railheads. These shipyards were now corporations, often with "iron works" in the company title. Within these companies, naval architecture and engineering allowed ship designers to determine in advance how to fit all of the new machinery into the hull, how to maximize cargo or passenger space, how the shape the hull for best performance and efficiency, how to limit the amount of materials required for construction, and, importantly, to rationally balance these different demands to form a commercially successful ship.

The first of these modern ships, the SS *Great Britain*, was launched in 1843 (figure 9.24). *Great Britain* was iron-hulled and powered by a propeller. It was the first such ship to cross the Atlantic Ocean. The designer of the *Great Britain*, Isambard Kingdom Brunel, was one of the great minds of the 19th century and

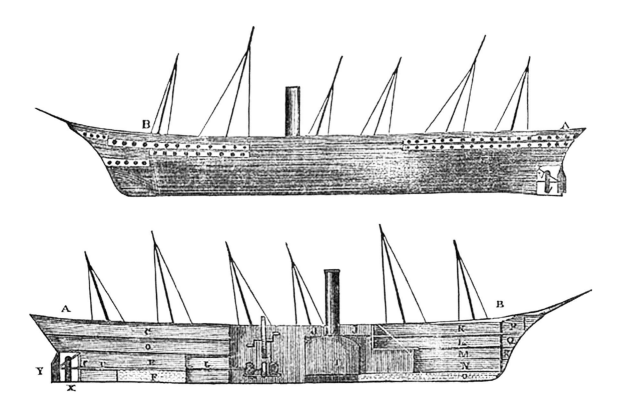

**Figure 9.24** Diagram of SS *Great Britain* showing hull shape, decks, and propeller.

also designed bridges and railways. Like *Snow Squall, Great Britain* ended its career in the Falkland Islands, but in 1970 it was brought back to England as a museum ship. *Great Britain* is also the immediate ancestor of possibly the most famous shipwreck, the *Titanic*. While half the size of *Titanic, Great Britain* shared similar construction and power. Brunel was the first to incorporate water-tight bulkheads in modern European shipbuilding and the first to build a large ocean-going ship with a predominately flat bottom, both attributes of *Titanic*. If the designers of *Titanic* had incorporated another Brunel innovation, a double hull with space between the inner and outer skins, *Titanic* might have fared better in its collision with the iceberg.[34]

### LOSS AND CONTINUATION OF LOCAL SHIPBUILDING

The industrialization of shipbuilding and the spread of industrialized ships throughout the world as a result of trade and colonialism had a deleterious effect on global ship variety. Nearly everywhere that iron, engine-driven ships took hold, the more diverse local shipbuilding industries suffered, and sometimes collapsed. In some instances, this was because the new ships offered real advantages, in others, it was because those in power wished to appear modern and expressed a preference for the new ships, even when the traditional vessels were a better fit for the environment. In many locations, however, traditional shipbuilding continued long after the arrival of iron and steam. Local vessels did particularly well in regional trades where larger, more expensive vessels had a hard time achieving an economy of scale. In many of these areas, dedicated local builders continue to build craft in much the same way their ancestors did. In others, much of the traditional shipbuilding knowledge has been lost, and archaeology offers one way to retrieve it. Shipwrecks offer modern builders the clearest picture of how earlier shipbuilders shaped and assembled their vessels.

Archaeologists can also learn a great deal from interacting with traditional craftspeople. As mentioned above, shipbuilding is often a conservative occupation where change happens slowly. At times, archaeologists assume that local shipbuilders reached equilibrium with their environment early on and have had little cause to change how they build watercraft for hundreds of years, or possibly even longer. This is a dangerous assumption, since culture is always in flux, and, just as our technology changes, we would expect the technologies of other cultures to change. Despite that caveat, shipbuilders working in the same region as their ancestors and deriving their skills from the same traditions are often our best starting place for understanding the vessels built by earlier generations. Studies among living builders become a hypothesis that can be tested against what is found in the archaeological record.

Ethnography among traditional builders is also valuable because it can teach us how people think about their vessels. There are many shipbuilding practices that do not manifest themselves in the wrecks that archaeologists record.

Similarly, there are many aspects that archeologists find in ships that are not the product of purely rational decisions (at least not from a post-Enlightenment, Western perspective). Discussing the how and why of shipbuilding with a local master-builder helps repopulate the ancient shipyard with people engaging in shipbuilding practices and beliefs.[35]

### SHIPS ARE MORE THAN TOOLS AND TECHNOLOGY

Understanding the beliefs of those who built and used ships is as important as understanding how the resulting vessel was put together. This chapter has largely focused on how ships were built, propelled, and steered because it is useful to understand how something functioned before attempting to understand what it meant to the users. Frankly, it is also easier for archaeologists to describe the physical things they observe than to intuit the far less tangible beliefs that formed those things. The following chapters will attempt to put some flesh and muscle on the technological skeleton described in this chapter. The truth, however, is that archaeology still has a long way to go before we truly understand what ships meant to their builders and sailors, and what the remains of those ships mean to us today.

### SUMMARY

The earliest watercraft were largely similar worldwide and consisted of floats, rafts, log boats, reed boats, and skin or bark boats. While these technologies are still employed today, the need for larger and more seaworthy vessels led to a proliferation of shipbuilding techniques. The three major philosophies of shipbuilding included shell-first, frame-first, and bottom-based approaches. Within these approaches shipbuilders used sewing, mortise-and-tenon joints, nails, and other means to fasten the parts of vessels together. Different regions also developed different types of sails to propel and rudders to steer their ships. Trade and communication by sea resulted in the transfer of ideas between regions, but shipbuilding remained largely regional until the 12th century CE when Mediterraneans and Northern Europeans began to build hybridized ships. The global diversity of ship types began to decline and naval architecture increased as the hybridized ships spread and evolved. During the 19th century another revolution in shipbuilding occurred with the widespread adoption of iron ship construction and steam propulsion. Most modern ships are the direct result of this latest transition.

### DISCUSSION QUESTIONS

1. Why did ships develop so differently across the world given their relatively similar beginnings?

2. Why is the continuation of traditional boat and shipbuilding important?
3. How is shipbuilding technology linked to the spread and expansion of a culture?
4. If you could build any type of ship, what type would you build and why?
5. Why do we have many examples of certain ship types and none of others?

### FURTHER READING

Adams, J. (2013). *A Maritime Archaeology of Ships*. Oxbow Books, Oxford.

Delgado, J. (2019). *War at Sea: A Shipwrecked History from Antiquity to the Twentieth Century*. Oxford University Press, New York.

Ferreiro, L. (2007). *Ships and Science: The Birth of Naval Architecture in the Scientific Revolution, 1600–1800*. The MIT Press, Cambridge.

Greenhill, B. (1988). *The Evolution of the Wooden Ship*. Facts on File, New York.

Hocker, F.M. and C.A. Ward, Eds. (2004). *The Philosophy of Shipbuilding*. Texas A&M University Press, College Station.

McGrail, S. (2014). *Early Ships and Seafaring: European Water Transport*. Pen and Sword Archaeology, Barnsley, UK.

Steffy, J.R. (1994). *Wooden Shipbuilding and the Interpretation of Shipwrecks*. Texas A&M University Press, College Station.

## CHAPTER 10

# LIFE AFLOAT

## *Sailors and Seafaring*

### FOCUS QUESTIONS

- How have people interacted with seas, lakes, and rivers? How was this inter-action shaped by their culture and environment? What are the similarities, differences, and outcomes of these interactions?
- How can the preservation of artifacts in submerged environments, which tends to be better than on land, improve our understanding of past cultures?
- What kind of information do ship and aircraft wrecks hold? What can their contents tell us about trade, colonization, warfare, and the people on board?
- What do maritime technological innovations tell us about broader trends in society, history, and culture? How does naval innovation shape the rise and fall of maritime societies?
- How did maritime people shape world history?

### SEAFARING SUBCULTURE

Ships are complex machines. They need to withstand the dynamic pressure of water attempting to crush the hull as well as the motive force of engines, wind, or oars, while protecting cargoes or passengers from the elements. And do this all economically. Many of the complex machines that we know from our modern, technological age are black boxes in which ever-smaller processors and circuitry made of exotic materials function in a way that few of us comprehend. We use them but we do not necessarily understand them. Ships, especially sailing ships, are the opposite. The majority of ships that archaeologists study were made of simple, organic components—wood, rope, canvas. Their complexity came from human imagination and the ways that we arranged and combined these materials. The strength and size of the hull were determined before the ship was launched and tended to be static throughout the vessel's career. Propulsion, especially by wind, was dynamic. The sails had to be constantly manipulated to capture the right amount of wind and propel the vessel in the desired direction. Officers and sailors had to constantly adapt and make decisions to keep the ship functioning. Humans were part of the machine; they were the processors and circuitry that made decisions and carried them out to navigate the ship across expanses of water, responding to the weather and conditions as they shifted.

Many seafaring communities were constituted of maritime peoples who learned the sea from a young age in the same way that they learned to speak the local language. The ocean was the constant background noise of their lives, stories of family members that had gone to sea populated their childhoods, and the arrival of tides and ships structured their daily schedules. The skills and knowledge necessary to work offshore were enculturated almost from birth. These abilities to command or work a ship were transferrable from vessel to vessel, even across nationalities, so that ships became cultural melting pots. Diverse populations of varying nationalities and ethnicities congregated on ships. Overlaying these differences was the unifying aspect of seafaring, with its similar practices and beliefs. The result was disparate groups of men living in small spaces and forced to interact in often-stressful situations so that cultural traditions were readily transferred between individuals. They also learned and shared practices dictated by the environments where they worked and the physical structures of the ships they sailed. Superstitions and attitudes promulgated from ship to ship as seafarers spread word of what had helped them survive a challenging situation. In this way, seafarers became not only a subculture of their own societies, with their own foods, ceremonies, language, rules, and punishments, but also a subculture that cut across multiple contemporary societies creating traditions that have extended over centuries. This chapter explores some of the practices and beliefs of seafaring peoples.

Some of what follows is drawn from the wealth of historic accounts about seafaring. However, these accounts are limited to literate societies, and the literate members of those societies, leaving most seafarers out of the narrative. The archaeological record provides clarity where information was misrecorded or misconstrued by an uninformed or unsympathetic observer, or simply not recorded because no one was able to, or considered it necessary to, write it down. The written record provides wonderful depth and detail about life at sea, but the archaeological record provides a more democratic and unvarnished view that reflects how things really were, not how someone wanted them to be recorded.

## NAVIGATION

One of the primary challenges of seafaring is knowing where you are and, more importantly, how to get from where you are to where you want to be. For many early navigators, this problem was solved by staying within sight of shore and using known landmarks to gauge their location. However, since the shore is one of the most dangerous places for a vessel and because some destinations can only be reached by sailing over the horizon, sailors eventually learned to navigate in the wilderness of the sea.

## Maps and sailing directions

One way to know your place in the world is by description. If you have ever stopped for directions or called a friend when you were lost, you know the power of good oral directions. This was the form of the earliest "maps." Ship captains collected knowledge about the winds, tides, animals, coastal features, bathymetry, and other details that they encountered on their routes and built this knowledge into a mental map of the waters they sailed. Eventually this knowledge was written down, and only much later was it turned into the visual representation that we call maps and charts.

The earliest sailing directions were held only in the mind of the captain who learned them—having made the trip many times, he or she knew the route well. But in order to share a lifetime of learning, the captains, and likely generations of captains, had to encapsulate their knowledge in a form that would stick to the mind of a hearer, even if that person had never sailed the route before. One way to do this, used by many oral cultures, is to embed the information in a story. By learning the story, a neophyte navigator learned what to look for while making a passage and the details that made the story memorable helped to fix the mundane aspects of sailing in the mind of the hearer. Polynesian seafarers told stories that included not only how to locate distant islands but the best times of year to sail. The *Odyssey*, one of the oldest works in Western literature, similarly preserves aspects of an earlier oral tradition, among which are the details of Odysseus' voyage in the western Mediterranean. For example, modern scholars have placed the paired dangers of Scylla and Charybdis in the treacherous straits between Sicily and mainland Italy.[1]

The transition from a completely oral tradition to the written word of the *Odyssey* is a good reminder that archaeologists rarely find the first of anything. Much of culture is intangible, and it is only on special occasions that culture is made material. Even if the archaeological example is also the first example that was ever created, the item was probably discussed and thought about for some time beforehand. Some of the earliest examples of **sailing directions**, such as the 1st century CE *Periplus of the Erythean Sea* (figure 10.1) and the 9th- or 10th-century *Landnámabók*, describing sailing routes in the Indian Ocean and around Iceland, respectively, were almost certainly derived from the combined knowledge of several individuals.[2] These descriptions, observations, and lists of bearings and distances (usually measured in sailing days) were only translated into a graphical form resembling a modern nautical chart beginning in the 13th century CE Mediterranean.[3] Six hundred years later there were still large bodies of water that had not been charted. In the modern age, where GPS is ubiquitous, it is hard to

**Figure 10.1** 1658 map showing locations in the *Periplus of the Erythean Sea*. Jan Jansson's *Erythraei sive Rubri Maris Periplus*.

imagine the sheer guts involved in crossing open water with no land in sight, some-times for days or weeks. Yet for much of human history, sailors had the courage and faith in their abilities to leave land behind without a graphical representa-tion of their location. Instead, they carried a chart in their mind and used various techniques to estimate their position and speed within that mental map.

## Position and speed

For millennia, the primary navigation technique was dead reckoning. **Dead reckoning** is the approximation of direction and distance based on constantly updated estimates of speed, sea conditions, winds, and currents (figure 10.2). If the sailors know the direction of their destination, the combined force of winds and currents pushing them off of that heading, and their speed, they can adjust their heading to compensate for the drift and estimate how far they have come and how far they still have to go. With experience, this is a reliable way to cross hundreds of miles, but it could also result in missing the destination by a substantial distance if they misjudged any of the variables.

The monsoon winds that drove much of the expansion discussed in chapter 11 are an example of the effective use of environmentally aware dead reckoning. The word "monsoon" comes from the Arabic "*mausim,*" meaning the season of the wind, and describes the strong seasonal winds that sweep the Indian Ocean. Between June and September, these winds blow from the southwest and then reverse from November through April. Sometime before 600 BCE seafarers realized that these winds facilitated sailing between East Africa, India, and Southeast Asia on a yearly cycle propelled outbound by the winds in one season and home when the winds shifted in the next season. The force of these winds necessitated a stout vessel and, because the desired routes seldom ran parallel to the wind direction, an understanding of the effect that the wind had on the direction of travel.

In order to effectively use dead reckoning, the navigator needed a means to reckon speed and heading. Speed is impossible to measure without a point of reference. In the open ocean, reference was gained by throwing something overboard and noting how quickly the mostly stationary floating object receded from the moving vessel. By 1600 CE, this practice had

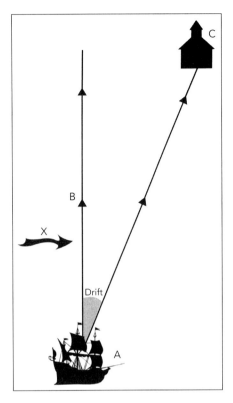

**Figure 10.2** Dead reckoning. A is the position of the vessel, C is the destination and B is the heading that the vessel must sail to reach C while being pushed by tides and winds in direction X. A-C is the actual route sailed.

been formalized into a wedge-shaped piece of wood, known as a log, which was attached to a line with knots tied in it. The log, shaped so as to resist the water, was tossed over the side and the number of knots, spaced 14.6 m (48 ft) apart, were counted as they passed through a sailor's hand during a 28-second period. The number of knots equaled the rate in nautical miles (1.85 km) per hour and eventually gave its name to the measure of speed over water. The 28-second interval was measured using a small "hourglass" called a **sand-clock** (figure 10.3). Sand clocks were being produced in various sizes in Venice by the late 13th century and provided a way to measure time on ships and elsewhere. By the 19th century, an instrument that calculated speed based on the rotations of a propeller replaced the wooden log. Sailors still had to throw the instrument over the side of the vessel. Until the invention of these more precise ways to measure speed, navigators measured the average speed of the vessel as "days" in early sailing directions. A "day" was an estimate of the distance a fast ship would cover

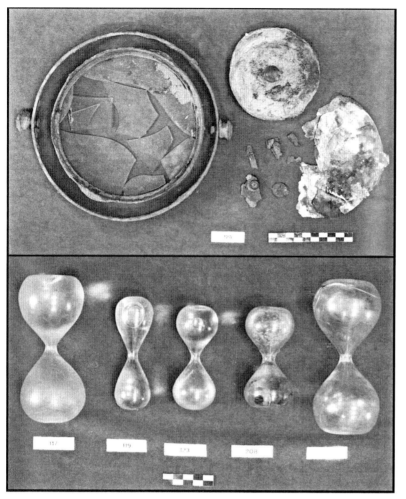

**Figure 10.3** Sand clocks of various sizes and a compass recovered from the early 19th century Mardi Gras shipwreck. (Courtesy of Conservation Research Laboratory, Texas A&M University)

in good conditions and provided an approximation of the time and distance between two points. Based on their sense of their own vessels' speed, captains had to adjust their locational estimate accordingly.[4]

With a means to estimate speed, a sailor only needed to determine the vessel's heading to sail with dead reckoning. Today we would use a compass to maintain a heading, but that was not possible for much of seafaring history. The Chinese likely used a magnetized stone, called a lodestone, to find directions during the 1st century CE, but it was not until the end of the 11th century that Persian and Arab sailors employed a magnetized needle on passages in the Indian Ocean. A similar compass, initially constructed with a needle floating in water and later with the needle suspended from a brass pin and pointing to directions on a card, appeared in Italy in the late 12th century and was widespread in Europe by the 15th century. Even then, these compasses were often a luxury and could be lead astray by the large amounts of iron contained on many vessels. The advent of iron ships in the 19th century exacerbated this problem and led to the addition of iron spheres, magnets, or screws on either side of the compass to correct the bearing.

In the absence of a compass, the simplest way to maintain a steady heading was to keep the wind or ocean swells at a consistent angle to the hull. Combined with a sounding lead, this was often all that early mariners needed to cross large bodies of water. A **sounding lead** is a heavy object, often made of lead, which can be thrown over the side of the vessel to test water depth. Many of these leads contained a pocket of a sticky substance that collected a sample of the bottom material. Sounding leads were important for safety so that the vessel did not run aground, but were also useful to determine position as the vessel approached shore, even if the shore was still out of sight. In many locations the shape and composition of the bottom were known and a sounding lead allowed the sailor to deduce what part of the coast they were approaching. Other evidence of an approaching shore might include clouds massing over the land, changes in the water color, variation in the swells as they deflected off the coast, and the presence of animals such as birds and sea snakes.

At some point, now lost in time, mariners realized that stars rose and fell in a consistent manner and that those patterns changed with location. Armed with this knowledge, Polynesian seafarers were able to sail constellation routes following a sequence of stars to travel from one island to another. In other places, such as Greece and Persia, the celestial pole, the point around which the stars appear to rotate, was identified with a specific star and that location was used as a reference point to determine bearings. By aligning the pole star with any of the many ropes or upright timbers that populate a ship, the navigator had a constant nightly point of reference. The height of known stars above the horizon could also be used to determine **latitude**, or the vessel's north-south position. Initially this measurement was likely made using hand-widths. By the end of the 9th century CE, Arab navigators were using a device called a *kamal* to make similar measurements (figure 10.4). A *kamal* consists of a tablet attached to a knotted string. The tablet is moved away from the eye until it fills the space between the horizon and the star and the number of knots were counted and converted into degrees latitude. Later navigational instruments such as the astrolabe, quadrant, and sextant operate on a similar principle, but with increasing degrees

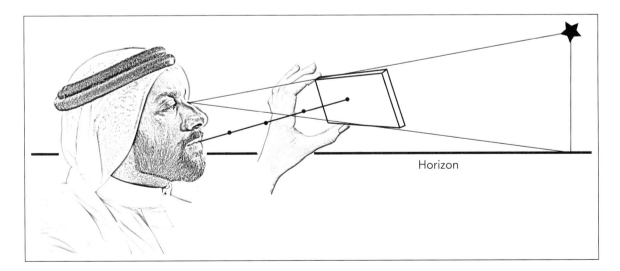

Horizon

**Figure 10.4** *Kamal* navigation tool in use.

of precision and accuracy. All also suffered from the same limitations—they required a cloudless sky and calm water so that the celestial body could be accurately sighted. While many of these instruments are only rarely preserved on shipwrecks, astrolabes are occasionally found because they consisted of a metal disk (figure 10.5). Even still, the oldest known archaeological example of an astrolabe dates to circa 1500 CE, but similar instruments had existed since at least 771 CE.[5]

It is no coincidence that these technologies bloomed first while Arabian merchants were expanding their overseas interactions and again when western European nations began their colonial expansion. Improved navigation instruments aided in these maritime exploits, while measurements taken along the routes and in far-flung ports also provided the raw data that astronomers needed to refine the instruments and make them more useful. There was a scientific feedback loop between the development of these instruments and their use in overseas expansion.

All of these instruments only measured latitude. As a result, mariners through the 18th century CE did not regularly sail the most direct route between two points. Instead they sailed north or south until they reached the latitude of their destination and then turned toward the destination using dead reckoning and regular maintenance of their latitude based on the sun and stars to reach the desired port. This was a safe method with a high rate of success, but required the vessel to sail two legs of a triangle rather than the much shorter hypotenuse. This method also meant that navigators could easily miss an end point along an east-west oriented coast. The *La Belle* shipwreck discussed in chapter 6 illustrates

**Figure 10.5** Astrolabes from the 1606 *Nossa Senhora dos Mártires* shipwreck. (Courtesy of Filipe Castro, Texas A&M University)

the dangers of not being able to calculate **longitude**. *La Belle* was lost on the coast of Texas, more than 480 km (300 mi) west of its intended destination at the Mississippi River because of bad maps and no means to check them with longitude. This mistake ultimately cost one of the great explorers of the 17th century, Robert La Salle, his life. *La Belle* was just one of many naval disasters, which included the loss of four British warships and 1550 seamen off the Isles of Scilly in 1707 when longitude was again misjudged. The problem of calculating longitude at sea was not solved until John Harrison devised his chronometer in the 1760s.

In theory, longitude is easy to calculate. Every 15 degrees east or west is equivalent to one hour earlier or later than a base location. By knowing the time at the base location and comparing it to the local time it is possible to calculate the change in longitude. By the end of the 15th century astronomers had developed full sets of tables based on the sun at noon, but while noon at your current location is obvious based on the height of the sun, it is much more difficult to know when noon occurs at the base location. One way to know the base time is a clock set to that time, but the humidity and rocking of ships wreaked havoc on most clocks prior to Harrison's chronometer. The chronometer included several novel solutions that allowed it to maintain accurate time. Set at the base location, the chronometer allowed the navigator to compare noon at the base location to noon at the ship's location and thereby calculate longitude. Solving the longitude problem was the last of the major navigational developments, but not the end of improvements to navigation. Every year, the sea becomes safer with new means to measure speed, position, and water depth; improved charts to illustrate the surrounding waters and lands; and advances in navigational aids to make reefs, shores, and channels more visible.[6]

### SOCIETY AFLOAT

Those responsible for navigation were only a small portion of a much larger crew that populated a vessel. Many other hands were necessary to work sails, maintain the vessel, feed engines, handle cargo, nourish and care for crew, and, occasionally, defend the ship. In some societies, such as those in the Pacific Islands or maritime Arctic, nearly everyone spent time on the sea. In other instances, such as late medieval Mediterranean **galleys**, serving on a ship was not a choice but a condition of slavery. Much of the rest of the history of seafaring lies between these poles, with sailors choosing their occupation (although often from a limited selection of options) and forming a distinctive and recognizable subculture of a society. Much of what defined these subcultures was intangible and so documentary, ethnographic, and artistic representations are useful in interpreting shipboard life. These representations become more plentiful as we approach the modern period and tend to bias our discussion toward the last several hundred years of Western society.

## Archaeological evidence

Shipwrecks also provide evidence to expand and refute the conclusions drawn from documentary sources. Archaeologists regularly discover intact artifacts and organic items on shipwrecks allowing the artifacts to be readily identified and the entire toolkit of the ancient sailor to be reconstructed. Even more important, the relationships between the artifacts can be preserved, allowing archaeologists to understand how they were used together—to understand how sailors organized their floating world, and to reconstruct the activities that were taking place just before the ship sank.[7]

*Mary Rose*, Henry VIII's warship, discussed at length in chapter 12, provides an excellent example of how much we learn about shipboard life from archaeology. Because the starboard side of the vessel and its contents were embedded in the dense sediments of the Solent, this shipwreck yielded a wide variety of material culture, providing an unparalleled glimpse of life afloat in 1545 (figure 10.6). Nearly intact hats, clothes, and shoes were found throughout the ship, illustrating the fit, function, and fashion of clothing worn by various classes in Tudor England, as well as insight into how these garments were constructed. Entertainments such as books, dice, dominoes, and board games were found, alongside complete sets of tools and a wide variety of personal knives representing the work and leisure activities that took place on the ship. Many of the tools would be expected, such as mallets and measuring sticks, but others might be surprising, including tools for weaving and sewing. There were also combs for removing lice, the remains of fleas, flies, and larvae recovered from sediments within the wreck, and a chest containing the instruments and medicine jars of the ship's surgeon, all of which suggest that the "good old days" could have been better.

Further evidence of this came from the skeletons recovered from the wreck. When *Mary Rose* sank, over 500 men drowned, so that skeletons were found throughout the site. Some of the skeletons had particular wear on their clavicles and spines that suggested they were professional archers, while others showed signs in their pelvis, leg, and foot bones of long periods of work in an unstable environment, and may have been professional mariners attuned to walking on a shifting deck. Analyses of these skeletons also showed that many of them suffered from childhood diseases and malnutrition. The availability of regular meals may have attracted some to service in the King's Ships. *Mary Rose* also contained substantial evidence of what was eaten and how it was eaten. The variety of animals bones, from both fresh and preserved meats, and the range of ceramic, pewter, and wood, plates and tankards left no doubt that social class was reinforced through food. *Mary Rose* is only one of many examples of the variety and types of archaeological evidence that comes from shipwrecks. Because of the preservation offered by submerged environments, these finds are often more complete than on land and allow archaeologists to not only interpret life at sea but to also come to conclusions about contemporary life ashore. Many terrestrial archaeologists have referenced shipwreck assemblages to better understand their subjects.[8]

**Figure 10.6** Personal artifacts recovered from *Mary Rose*. Top: jerkin with a comb in the pocket; Middle: early backgammon board; Bottom: wooden dishes and spoons. (© Mary Rose Trust)

## Johan Johan Rönnby, Professor, MARIS, Södertörn University, Sweden

It is possible to regard maritime archaeology most of all as an exciting adventure. There is nothing necessarily wrong with such an attitude. Exploring, regardless if it is about space, the distant past, or the bottom of the ocean, is perhaps something which is embedded in the human mind. We are curious and want to know more just for the sake of it. Exploration, not least underwater, is therefore a fun and engaging activity. Maritime archaeological projects also bring different kinds of people together and stimulate creativity and cooperation.

But most archaeologists would probably agree that we should also try to make knowledge and the results of archaeological research relevant to our contemporary society. One could go so far as to state that good research in a social discipline such as archaeology should in the end always aim to critically consider, question, and examine structures, conditions, and ideas in our modern world

The skill of a maritime archaeologist in diagnosing, for example, the technicalities of frames, joints and lashings, and so on, must therefore also be integrated with theoretical creativity and interpretation. Comparative material and contexts that provide relevant explanations for a site are neither predetermined nor inherent in the object which is studied. Rather, such interpretation depends on the archaeologist's ability to conceive possibilities and parallels. The real challenge is to construct explanations and narratives that are not only scientifically credible but also have general relevance for modern society, other humans, and ourselves.

Let me give two short examples. The brackish, cold, dark water of the Baltic Sea and the absence of *Teredo navalis* often preserves shipwrecks in a remarkable way in this northern European region. Shipwrecks several hundred years old can stand fully intact on the sea bed. This means it is actually possible to "go on board" either by diving down to them or via remotely controlled cameras. To do this is almost to visit the past, to travel to an unknown long-forgotten place. It is a kind of "knowledge diving" that results in a personal experience that changes one's perspective. Based on personal insights

and reflection, it may then be possible to come closer to aspects of past people's lives that are normally beyond our reach.

The so-called Ghost ship is an exceptionally well-preserved Dutch small-sized fluyt from the mid-17th century. The wreck lies at a depth of 130 m (426 ft) in the middle of the Baltic Sea and is almost completely intact with its masts still standing. To look inside the small cabin in the stern where a crew of six or seven spent much of their time around a simple wooden table offers a unique insight into days long gone. In this very limited space, which often necessitated a crouching position, the crew attended to personal hygiene, drying of clothes and the preparation and consumption of meals. To accommodate everyone, they must have rested and slept in turns. This view is quite different to the impression of hierarchical arrangements offered by, for instance, larger naval vessels. On board a fluyt, not only discipline but also consideration and cooperation must have been prerequisites for an endurable life. To "go on board" the Ghost ship deepens our understanding of the people behind the internationally successful Dutch seaborne trade and the rising global economy of the time. A patriarchal structure, a very strict reformist morality, and constant piety would have characterized personal relations in the single, small, crowded, dark and damp cabin. The shipwreck is, in this way, a materialization of a 17th-century mentality and ideology, which, with its strict work ethic and sense of duty, was a prerequisite for the later development and spread of modern capitalist thinking!

Some warship wrecks on the Baltic seabed can be characterized as being archaeological "smoking guns." One such example is *Mars* (1564). The newly built ship, known as "*Mars* the Miraculous" because of its great size (60 m [197 ft] long, around 1800 tons), took part in a May 1564 battle against a joint fleet from Denmark and the town of Lübeck. After being boarded by the enemy, the vessel exploded while the fighting on board was still going on. Blinded by smoke and deafened by the noise from the guns, seamen and soldiers on *Mars'* decks were shot, impaled by debris, burned to death, or drowned. More than 800 people followed the ship down to a depth of 75 m (246 ft).

The archaeological documentation of the wreck site, with its heavily burned timber, damaged hull, and disfigured osteological remains, emphasizes the violent course and the chaotic, deadly, and dangerous environment on board during the battles. *Mars* in this way offers a unique snapshot of the grueling nature of the fight. The wreck provides a frozen moment of the battle, not least due to the several very large bronze guns that are still in place in the ports of the lower gun deck, giving the impression that they have just been in use (see figure 1.4).

The wreck of *Mars* therefore represents not just the remains of a great new Renaissance ship, but the site of a well-preserved "maritime battlefield." Associated marine archaeological investigations have provided new insights into unknown solutions related to practical issues in naval battles during early modern times. But the scope of the research has gone further than that. The opportunity to study the "battlefield space" has invited discussion and reflection on the mental and psychological aspects associated with warfare in general, and human behavior in such situations and environments. An archaeological documentation of an early modern battleship can in such a way also serve as a more general anthropological study of war and violence.

I have been diving and working on different archaeological sites for many years and have also been involved in and responsible for several high-tech underwater expeditions. But I would like to believe that my most important research contribution has been to infuse cultural interpretations and the concept of societal relevance in maritime archaeological research. In fact, interpretation and relevance are both very important parts of being a maritime archaeological explorer, and make the work even more fun!

## Gender, ethnicity, and hierarchy

Shipboard life tended to be male dominated. There were notable exceptions, but for much of history they were notable because they were exceptions. During the 18th century, and likely earlier, women such as Anne Bonny and Mary Read (figure 10.7) joined sailing crews dressed as men. By the next century, it was increasingly common for women to accompany their husbands aboard British naval vessels. While officially prohibited, these women shared their husbands' bunk and rations, aided in shipboard duties, and birthed children aboard warships. There were also thousands of women who accompanied their husbands, often the captain, aboard merchant and whaling vessels. Some of these women, such as Mary Patten, who took command of the clipper ship *Neptune's Car* when her husband became ill—putting down a mutiny and commanding the last two months of the voyage while pregnant—became famous for their skills and daring, but most quietly survived at sea like the majority of male sailors. Millions of other women remained at home and raised seafaring families and worked in port businesses.[9]

For the men that formed the majority of the sailing community, there was a wide variety of reasons for going to sea. For many, it was an honorable profession spanning several generations. For others it was a way to escape poverty and social limitations. For Africans, Native Americans, and other indigenous peoples affected by European colonialism, as well as Europeans from the lowest echelons of their societies, seafaring offered one of the few chances for advancement and consistent pay. The clearly defined hierarchies of shipboard life also offered some shelter from the more random injustices they often faced on land.[10]

**Figure 10.7** Contemporary engraving of Anne Bonny and Mary Read. Bonny and Read were famous pirates in the 18th-century Caribbean.

Different types of ships attracted different types of sailors because merchant, fishing, and naval vessels offered different work schedules, dangers, amounts of pay, and degrees of flexibility. Military vessels tended to be the most regimented, but offered regular pay and required less labor because they had large crews, while merchant vessels carried fewer guarantees of pay and food in exchange for often better pay and opportunities for advancement.

Upward mobility for ambitious and intelligent sailors hinged on the economic value of ships and the rigid hierarchy common in many sailing societies. Ships are expensive and complicated machines that often operated in dangerous conditions where an instantaneous and absolute decision is better than reaching consensus. In a storm, where the handling of sails needs to be coordinated, the benefits of a single, unquestioned captain becomes apparent. This absolute power often spread to all operations of a ship outside of port and was supplemented by additional layers of hierarchy to buttress and communicate the captain's power. Hierarchy also served as a filter for talent. Through hard work and "learning the ropes" it was often possible to advance through the ranks, although the upper ranks in some services were limited to those from specific social classes. The experiences of Charles Tyng in early 19th-century Boston illustrates the possibility for advancement. The son of a not-particularly affluent lawyer, Tyng had a middle-class upbringing but no wealth and no interest in school, so he decided to join a voyage to China as a **ship's boy**, the lowest rung in the hierarchy. Despite being abused during this first, 18-month-long voyage and walking away from other undesirable ships, Tyng regularly took on extra duties and responsibilities and rose to the position of **first mate** by the time he was 19. In his early 20s he was the captain of his own ship and eventually owned multiple vessels.[11]

Hierarchy was reflected in the clothes, food, and spaces of ships. While small merchant and fishing vessels might be operated by literal or fictive family so that everyone ate, slept, and relaxed together, most larger vessels maintained order through clear indications of status embedded in social and physical barriers. Sleeping space was among the clearest and most consistent signals of rank among many seafaring cultures. Generally, the closer to the stern and the more space, the higher the rank, with the captain in a private cabin at the stern and the common sailors crowded together forward of the mast. This arrangement had some practicality—the steering apparatus is at the stern—but also provided the captain with the most spacious and comfortable quarters. Most ships are wider at the stern than bow and, because the stern is not driving through the waves, it is a dryer and less-tossed place. Since ships often also had their toilet, the **head**, at the bow where waves were more likely to wash away waste, the bow was more convenient for the numbers of men sleeping there, though also likely more malodourous. The only consolation a seaman attempting to sleep in the damp, crowded, smelly, rocking **forecastle** of a ship might take was that he was under cover during storms, but even that was a relatively recent innovation. Prior to the 17th century and the adoption of hammocks from the New World, most crews slept on deck.[12]

## Diet and disease

Food also served to distinguish the upper echelons of shipboard society. Sailors often took their meals communally with groups eating from a single dish, but those in charge regularly ate different foods separately from the crew. While common, especially from the medieval period on, this distinction was not as universal as reserving the stern for the captain, and small crews often ate together. The types of foods eaten on vessels also varied through time and from culture to culture. For much of seafaring history, during which voyages were relatively short, food could be purchased in port and prepared using a simple hearth onboard or prepared ashore, as coastal traders pulled into coves for the night. What was available might vary in each port but the food preparation techniques tended to resemble those of the cook's homeland. As voyages became longer during the post-medieval period, food preservation on ships became an increasing concern. Away from shore for months, mariners turned to drying, salting, and pickling to preserve foods, as well as selecting foods, such as root crops, that were naturally slow to rot. Foods such as salted beef and ships' biscuits, or **hardtack**, became common during this period. While many nations settled on similar sailors' diets, there was still regional variation. For example, oatmeal, dried peas, suet, vinegar, and rum were more common among British mariners, while Spanish and Portuguese seamen ate more beans and rice, and flavored their meals with garlic, olives, raisins, and oils. Some vessels carried live animals for the officers' table where wine was also on offer. While still being identifiable with their home foods, shipboard diets diverged not only in terms of ingredients but also preparation. Most vessels did not include an oven, so meals were usually boiled or stewed in large pots attached to a central stove, when the weather permitted. These food preparation techniques led to some interesting cuisines with even more interesting names, such as boiled baby and spotted dick, when the weather was calm, and cold meals when it was not.[13]

Such diets, with limited fresh foods, limited nutrients, and salt levels that far exceed modern recommended limits tended to exacerbate the already unhealthy conditions of many sailing vessels. With a dense population living in a confined, damp, space, many diseases did quite well on ships. History is full of literal plague ships that imported illness as well as their cargoes. In 430 BCE, during the Peloponnesian War, a sickness from Persia or Egypt arrived at the Athenian port of Piraeus and quickly spread to Athens where it resulted in a massive loss of life. This plague killed so many people that it seems to have curtailed the Athenians' ability to maintain their labor-intensive trireme navy, and eventually led Athens to surrender to Sparta in 404 BCE. Roughly 940 years later, the bubonic plague began spreading in waves across the Old World, carried by the extensive and expanding maritime trade networks of the period.[14]

Expanding trade networks eventually led to the best-known seafaring ailment: **scurvy**, which results from a lack of vitamin C. It begins with weakness, and progresses to gum disease and bleeding from the skin, before resulting in changes in personality, wounds that will not heal and eventually death (figure 10.8). As long as sailors landed often, they obtained enough vitamin C through their regular diet, but as voyages began to stretch over a month, the vitamin C-poor diets of sailors made scurvy an increasing problem. Among the crews of early European explorers such as Magellan and Vasco da Gama, scurvy wreaked havoc and the causes were not well understood. Even as late as the 19th century, scientists debated the sources of scurvy. This persisted despite James Lind demonstrating in 1747 the healing effectiveness of citrus juice in one of the first controlled clinical trials in the history of medicine. Eventually lime juice was adopted by the British Merchant and Royal navies as preventative, giving rise to the slang term "limey" for a British person and the cocktail mixer Rose's lime juice.[15]

Scurvy is only the best-known of a host of ailments that troubled sailors. Scurvy, typhus, tuberculosis, venereal diseases, alcoholism, and other ailments killed nearly 40 times more men than combat on ships in the 18th century. Lice, fleas, and other vermin were common, and the damp and dirt of ships led

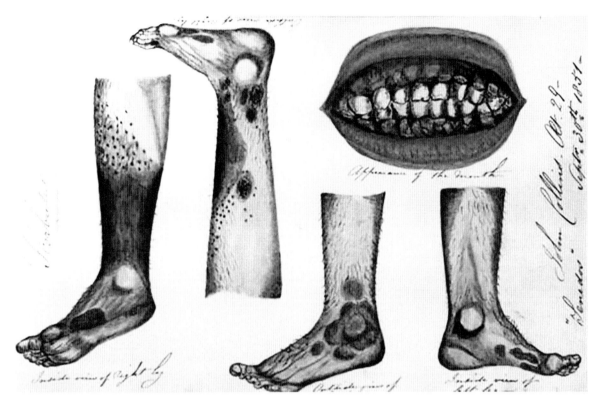

**Figure 10.8** 19th century medical drawing of the effects of scurvy.

even small wounds to fester much worse than on land, adding to the discomfort and dangers of seafaring. Climbing ladders, stairs, and rigging, and, sometimes, just walking aboard a constantly pitching vessel also led to many sprained joints, broken bones, and amputations. A lack of sleep and regularly interrupted sleep also had long-term effects on the health of mariners. Once injured or sick, sailors did not have ready access to medical treatment. Naval and large merchant crews commonly included a surgeon by the 18th century, but earlier and smaller vessels had to get by with a lay practitioner, sometimes assisted by a box of medicines and a manual of diseases. Medieval vessels through the 16th century were serviced by a barber-surgeon who pulled teeth, set bones, and performed bloodletting and minor surgeries, when not cutting hair. The disease, dangers, hard work, and poor food of a seafaring life is what Samuel Johnson had in mind when he quipped, "being in a ship is being in a jail, with the chance of being drowned."[16]

Sailors did take steps to keep their vessels and themselves clean despite the conditions around them. For example, clothes washed in saltwater take longer to dry and when dry are stiff and uncomfortable, so sailors collected rainwater for this purpose. They used fine-toothed combs to remove lice from their hair.

There are also accounts of enemas believed at the time to help counteract the effects of diet and the injection of mercury into the urethra to fight syphilis. They attempted to keep the ship clean by scrubbing the decks with sand or a piece of sandstone called a **holystone**. Understanding that the dampness inside of the hull caused health maladies, as well as leading to rot, post-medieval seafarers attempted to circulate air within the vessel, used stoves to dry the lower decks, and fumigated the depths of the hull with a mixture of vinegar and sulfur sprinkled over hot coals to create poisonous fumes. Most of these cures created more work for the crew and in some cases put them at increased risk, while doing little to improve the healthfulness of shipboard life.[17]

## Recreation

Life afloat was not all drudgery. There were extended periods with no necessary tasks to be completed. The boredom coming with this leisure time could be as damaging to morale as bad food and flea infestations. To pass this time sailors played games, created artworks, and made music. Evidence of various portable games such as dice, dominoes, and board games like backgammon have been found on shipwrecks since antiquity, as well as artifacts interpreted as gaming pieces for games to which the rules have long been forgotten. Sailors also used their time to perfect various arts and handicrafts. Taking advantage of the small pieces of rope that were common on most sailing vessels, many sailors became adept at **knot-work**. They created coverings and lanyards for various tools and useful items such as mats, bowls, and monkey's fists that made it easier to throw a line (figure 10.9). This was one of the least expensive ways to pass the time, but also represented the sailor's pride in their craft. Knot tying and rope work was central to the role of seamen in the age of sail. The sailor had to be able to fasten, repair, or make almost anything out of rope in order to keep his vessel functioning until it reached a port. Knotwork developed and showcased those fundamental skills. Other sailors created art. There are sketches and paintings created by sailors, but many sailors opted for carving or **scrimshaw**. Using the point of the ubiquitous sailor's knife or a sailmaker's needle, mariners carved images into tools, pieces of wood, or, on whaling vessels, bone or tooth. Rubbing soot into the lines made the image stand-out and allowed sailors to personalize items, remember loved ones on the shore, or simply create art for the sake of art. Other unknown sailors whittled, leading to surprising and endearing finds such as the palm-sized representation of a Spanish galleon recovered from the wreck of an actual galleon off of Florida's Emanuel Point. Some also brought instruments to sea with them, while others passed the time by creating lyrics to accompany the music. Finally, a few sailors were literate. These individuals spent their off hours reading and writing correspondence for their less-educated crewmates. They also, thankfully, kept journals, which provide some of our best evidence for seafaring life, especially during the last 500 years.[18]

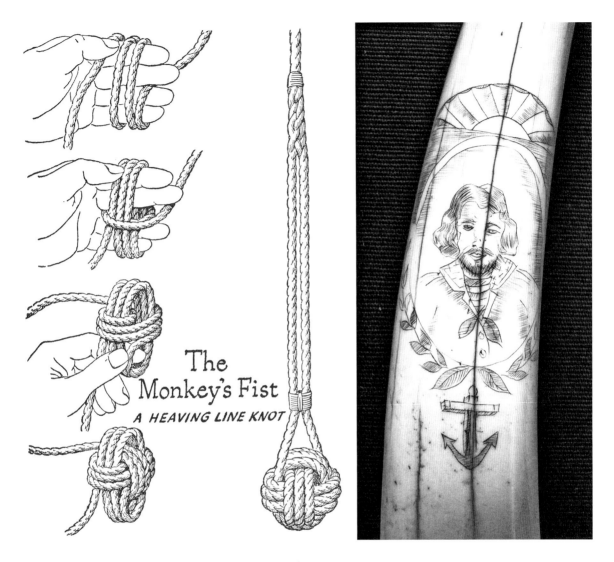

**Figure 10.9** Example of rope-work (left) and scrimshaw (right).

## Beliefs and ceremonies

Ships and the sea hold a special place in the beliefs and rituals of seafaring peoples. The amount of time spent at sea, the investment of resources in ships and cargoes, and the dangers of sailing away from land all contribute weight to the actions and precautions taken by seafarers. The importance of maritime occupations also led maritime aspects of culture to seep into daily terrestrial lives and appear in rituals on land. In some cases, these beliefs are only reproducible with ethnographic information, such as the linguistic overlap between ships and islands among Polynesian seafarers. In other instances, such as the spectacular

Anglo-Saxon ship burials found at sites like Sutton Hoo, the archaeological evidence is unequivocal.

In his famous, early anthropological study of the Trobriand Islanders, Bronislaw Malinowski noted that the islanders had specialized rites when fishing in the open sea, but not for fishing within the island lagoon. Malinowski interpreted this as a response to anxiety and risk with the rituals preceding open water fishing as a way to mitigate the increased risk and uncertainty that came with fishing outside of the lagoon. The rituals may have also served to bond the sailors together, increase cooperation, and acclimate them to the absolute authority of the captain; in other words, mentally conditioning the crew for survival at sea.[19]

In many cases, maritime beliefs and their associated rituals overlapped those on land, with similar gods and ways of accessing those divinities. For example, in Christian iconography the anchor has come to symbolize "hope." The fact that the anchor may be the last and only thing holding a vessel away from shore and preventing it from wrecking instilled these items with symbolic power. Stone anchors used by Lebanese sponge divers during the 19th century were inscribed with crosses, crescents, and prayers to increase their chances of holding. One read "I place myself in God's keeping," reiterating the message of hope associated with Northern European anchors. Earlier, in the ancient Mediterranean, stone anchors appear in seaside temples. These were likely votives left by sailors asking for a safe passage. As powerful as the symbolism of anchors is through the ages, it was only one part of the larger suite of maritime beliefs. The same sailors that deposited anchors at the temples of Byblos, Ugarit, and Kition also likely carried small idols to perform rituals at sea during times of danger and made sacrifices when entering port to offer thanks for a safe journey. As on land, religion took many forms and varied with culture and time. Archaeologists are only recently beginning to explore the physical remains of these beliefs and rituals.[20]

The archaeological interpretation of maritime rituals is complicated by the fact that, in addition to the rituals with parallels on land, many more were unique to the sea. For example, many seafaring peoples practiced initiation rites the first time a new sailor passed a specific landmark. This could be the first time the sailor left the safety of a port or lagoon or the first time that he passed a specific seamark associated with a long journey. The most famous example of this is was when a sailor or officer became a Son of Neptune the first time he crossed the equator. The "crossing the line" ceremony goes back to at least the early 17th century and certainly grew out of earlier ceremonies. In most accounts of the crossing the line ceremony, the hazing of uninitiated sailors begins days before the ship reaches the equator, and a crew member crudely dressed as Neptune appears the day before to announce his intention to initiate the "pollywogs." All of this serves to build the suspense and apprehension of the uninitiated. At the appointed time, each initiate is blindfolded and taken individually before Neptune, where he is roughly handled, repeatedly dunked, doused, or forced to swallow sea water; smeared with tar and grease before being literally or figuratively shaved; and compelled to take an oath to Neptune (figure 10.10). At the end of the ceremony the "pollywog" is a "shellback," or a Son of Neptune, and a full member of the crew.[21]

This rite of passage illustrates several aspects of ceremonies at sea that are important to archaeologists and that apply to many other sailors' rites through time. First, this ceremony can be analyzed using well-established anthropological approaches to studying rites. The crossing the line ceremony allowed an inversion of power, such that usually subservient sailors had momentary control over their own movements and could impose their will on any officer or seaman who had not previously passed the equator. This freedom acted as a safe way to relieve tensions that often built during long voyages. The ceremony was also

**Figure 10.10** Crossing the Line ceremony during the 19th century.

a rite of passage that forced neophytes through a traumatic experience so as to bind them together and connect them to the identity of a long tradition. In this way, the ceremony increased cohesion among the specific crew and sailors in general. Second, the ritual was completed using mundane objects in a special way. Neptune's wig, beard, and robe were often made from rope and sail; his trident, a fish spear. The other implements often included buckets and barrels, as well as a razor, all of which had other uses aboard the vessel. Without a historical record, the presence and significance of this ritual would require keen observation and a significant dose of archaeological luck.

## HISTORICAL MARITIME ETHNOGRAPHY

Despite the wealth of material culture excavated from shipwrecks there are still important aspects of sailors' lives that we are not likely to ever recover archaeologically. That does not mean, however, that these aspects are unknowable. By using the techniques of our colleagues in cultural anthropology and history, many of these aspects can be reconstructed for the periods with written records and pushed through analogy into periods and places with no records. Two immaterial, but important, components of shipboard life that can be recovered in this way are shanties and tattoos.

Shanties are maritime work songs in which the emphasis of the syllables are used to coordinate multiple hands working together to pull a line, work a pump, or push a capstan. Usually these songs were sung in a call-and-response manner with the leader singing a verse and the crew responding with the chorus. For example:

> Were you ever in Quebec,
> *Bonnie laddie, Highland laddie,*
> Stowing timber on the deck,
> *My bonnie Highland laddie-O.*

This arrangement allowed the leader to insert specific instructions when needed to direct the task. Various types of work required different rhythms and were accompanied by different songs. For example, a shanty sung while quickly tightening a sail by hauling on a halyard would quickly exhaust a crew working the pumps or raising an anchor. While shanties were limited to work and were often short and repetitive, sailors also composed uniquely maritime folk songs during their leisure times.

Many of these songs are no longer sung, or exist in a popularized form that only vaguely resembles their original form, though during the early 20th century a substantial number were collected from elderly European seamen, as well as active sailors in places where shanties were still sung, such as the West Indies.[22] The written and audio recordings of these intact work songs allow for linguistic anthropological analysis. The work environment and mindset of the sailors figure prominently in these songs, describing their tasks and concerns, including the mundane such as loading timber in the example above; the romantic including references to leaving loved ones; the less-than-romantic with an entire vocabulary for prostitutes; and the job specific, so that whaling shanties often differed from those in the merchant service or navies. Other songs dealt with the hierarchies of sailing life and the injustices, perceived and real, that accompanied them. Shanties were often translated into various languages reflecting the international nature of seafaring, but the rhythms remained consistent linking each song with a specific type of work. Many of these characteristics are represented by the song *Reuben Ranzo:*

> Oh, poor old Reuben Ranzo,
> *Ranzo, me boys, Ranzo*
> Oh, poor old Reuben Ranzo,
> *Ranzo, me boys, Ranzo*
>
> Oh, Ranzo was no sailor
> *Ranzo, me boys, Ranzo*
> So he shipped aboard a whaler
> *Ranzo, me boys, Ranzo*
>
> Oh, Ranzo was no beauty
> *Ranzo, me boys, Ranzo*
> So he couldn't do his duty
> *Ranzo, me boys, Ranzo*
>
> Oh, because he was so dirty
> *Ranzo, me boys, Ranzo*
> He give him five and thirty
> *Ranzo, me boys, Ranzo*
>
> Oh, the skipper's daughter Suzy
> *Ranzo, me boys, Ranzo*
> Well, she begged her dad for mercy
> *Ranzo, me boys, Ranzo*
>
> Oh, she give him wine and water
> *Ranzo, me boys, Ranzo*
> And a bit more than she ought to
> *Ranzo, me boys, Ranzo*
>
> Well, he got his first mate papers
> *Ranzo, me boys, Ranzo*
> He's a terror to the whalers
> *Ranzo, me boys, Ranzo*
>
> Now he's known wherever them whale-fish blow
> *Ranzo, me boys, Ranzo*
> As the hardest master on the go
> *Ranzo, me boys, Ranzo*[23]

This song is paced for hauling on halyards and originated in the whaling fleets but spread throughout American and British ships. "Ranzo" may be a corruption of "Lorenzo" indicating one of the many Portuguese sailors who were recruited onto whaling vessels in the Azores.

Tattoos also formed an important but fleeting aspect of seafaring culture, especially beginning in the 19th century. Anthropologists have done substantial work on the importance of tattooing as a means to mark meaning on our skin. Tattoos are a very personal way to remember an event or experience, and often the act of being tattooed is part of a larger life transition so that the tattoo serves to indicate group membership. Despite this significance, with very rare exceptions, the tattoo only lasts for the life of the person. Because human skin does not often preserve in the archaeological record, tattoos are considered ephemeral at archaeological time scales.

Tattooing did not start with sailors, but they did popularize it. There is possible evidence of tattoos in cave art as far back as 30,000 years ago and strong evidence from Egypt circa 4000 BCE. So, while tattooing is a longstanding tradition in the Old World, it was the exposure of whalers to tattooing in Polynesia that began the trends in tattooing that extend into the modern period. In Polynesia, tattooing was part of a rite of passage often associated with reaching maturity. Polynesian tattoos include geometric shapes representing locally significant items, such as palm fronds and canoe paddles. Among sailors, tattooing was associated with the adoption of a seafaring life, and the images were no less esoteric or culture-specific, including anchors, crosses, and women (figure 10.11). First whalers and then sailors more generally brought the art to widespread attention in Europe and the Americas, but it remained associated with the lower echelons of society, which included sailors, until the late 20th century when tattoos rapidly gained acceptance.

One of the main sources of data on early maritime tattooing is protection certificates. These certificates verified a sailor's citizenship and protected them from being forced into service on another nation's warship. Many of these certificates include identifying information such as descriptions of tattoos. These sources indicate that approximately 10 percent of the circa 1800 British sailing population was tattooed with names, dates, anchors, mermaids, hearts, crucifixes, and initials. Accounts written by sailors offer additional context for the descriptions recorded in the certificates. Charles Tyng, introduced earlier in this chapter, was tattooed on a voyage to China in 1817 by a sailor who learned the craft while imprisoned in Dartmoor, England, during the War of 1812. Tyng received intertwined hearts with red roses and cupid arrows on his left arm, Christ on the cross with blood dripping from his wounds on his right arm, an anchor and the letter T on the back of his left hand, and a heart on his left middle finger. While most of his shipmates were similarly decorated, Tyng grew to regret his tattoos as he transitioned from being an ordinary seaman to serving as a captain and owning his own vessels. Later in life he attempted

**Figure 10.11** World War II-era sailors displaying their tattoos.

to remove them with chemicals and cut the anchor off his hand leaving a bad scar.[24]

Tyng felt that his tattoos marked him as a sailor and were inappropriate as he moved up the social hierarchy. Tattoos indicated membership in the maritime subculture to both sailors and non-sailors, but they also carried meanings that were only likely to be understood by another sailor. For example, members of Neptune's Court who had crossed the equator were entitled to images of turtles and Neptune. Other tattoos might represent a long voyage traveled; for example, swallows were popular because they fly long distances but always return home. Crossed cannon or harpoons indicated service in a particular fleet, navy or whaling, respectively. Tattoos were also used to ward off disaster, so that pigs and roosters on the feet or lower legs were believed to prevent drowning because these animals often survived shipwrecks, and crosses on the soles of the feet were intended to prevent a shark attack. Thus, while a landlubber might be able to identify a sailor as a sailor by their tattoos (as well as clothes and hair), a fellow sailor could read the career of his mate on his skin.

Like the crossing the line ceremonies, shanties and tattoos allowed sailors to express their individuality and gave them some control over their bodies in what was an otherwise often domineering environment. That sailors repeatedly gravitated to specific songs, tattoo motifs, and ceremonies, and that these characteristics were different from what was practiced on land is clear evidence that sailors represent a distinct population and that these characteristics, even if ephemeral, are important to an archaeological understanding of maritime culture.

## SUMMARY

Ships are complicated machines that require constant human attention to operate. The offshore lives and activities of sailors form an important component of maritime archaeology. Finding their way at sea was a major concern for sailors of all nationalities and time periods. As voyages became longer, the difficulties of navigation, as well as health and recreation increased. Seafarers contended with many diseases, most notably scurvy, and found numerous ways to pass periods of inactivity. Eating, music, tattooing, art, games, and reading helped to entertain sailors. While not all of these activities are apparent in the archaeological record, a combination of archaeology, ethnography, and history allows much of sailing life to be reconstructed. Sailors also developed beliefs and ceremonies that are apart from those practiced on land. Many of these were rites of passage that were attempts to offset the otherwise uncontrollable dangers of seafaring. With its strict hierarchies, and particular foods, clothes, language, and beliefs, seafaring formed a distinct subculture within and across many national and ethnic identities.

## DISCUSSION QUESTIONS

1. Seafaring is often depicted as a romantic and free existence. Does the archaeological and historical evidence support or refute this perception?
2. What nautical words or phrases exists in your vocabulary?
3. How much can archaeologists understand about seafaring life, given that not all aspects of culture are preserved in the archaeological record?
4. How do science, technology, and maritime commerce converge in navigation?
5. How might archaeologists go about identifying the presence of women, indigenous peoples, and ethnic minorities within shipwreck sites?

## FURTHER READING

Beck, H. (1973). *Folklore and the Sea*. Mystic Seaport, Mystic, CT.

Druett, J. (2001). *She Captains: Heroines and Hellions of the Sea*. Simon and Schuster, New York.

Gardiner, J., Ed. (2005). *Before the Mast: Life and Death aboard the* Mary Rose, *The Archaeology of the* Mary Rose, volume 4. Mary Rose Trust, Portsmouth, UK.

Harland, J. (2016). *Seamanship in the Age of Sail*. Naval Institute Press, Annapolis, MD.

Redknap, M., Ed. (1997). *Artefacts from Wrecks: Dated Assemblages from the Late Middle Ages to the Industrial Revolution*. Oxbow Books, Oxford.

Spalding, S. (2014). *Food at Sea: Shipboard Cuisine from Ancient to Modern Times*. Rowman and Littlefield, New York.

Tyng, C. (1999). *Before the Wind, The Memoir of an American Sea Captain, 1808–1833*. Viking, New York.

Van Tilburg, H.K. (2007). *Chinese Junks on the Pacific, Views from a Different Deck*. University Press of Florida, Gainesville.

## CHAPTER 11

# EXPLORATION, COLONIZATION, TRADE, AND EXTRACTION

## FOCUS QUESTIONS

- How have people interacted with seas, lakes, and rivers? How was this interaction shaped by their culture and environment? What are the similarities, differences, and outcomes of these interactions?
- How can the preservation of artifacts in submerged environments, which tends to be better than on land, improve our understanding of past cultures?
- What kind of information do ship and aircraft wrecks hold? What can their contents tell us about trade, colonization, warfare and the people on board?
- What do maritime technological innovations tell us about broader trends in society, history, and culture? How does naval innovation shape the rise and fall of maritime societies?
- How did maritime people shape world history?
- How do we balance the needs of modern societies with the preservation of cultural heritage sites?

## FROM FROGS TO 9/11

Plato described the ancient Greeks, their colonies, and Mediterranean neighbors as frogs around a pond. The sea connected them and any city-state that jumped into the "pond" caused ripples that affected the others. They were linked, both through intentional trade and conflict and through unintended consequences, by the waters they sailed. The same was also true of other seafaring peoples in other parts of the world. As the centers of maritime activity, including the Mediterranean, began to expand beyond their home waters in pursuit of new resources, their "ponds" grew and overlapped, and cultures increasingly found themselves in contact with one another.

This process began more than 4000 years ago and has been picking up speed ever since. Expansion was relatively slow and fitful at first, but, by the 15th century CE, European and Asian powers were systematically and deliberately spreading across the oceans in search of new resources to trade and extract. These movements created and reworked the global economy, so that, for example, gold from the Americas expanded European coffers and destabilized West African economies. These movements led to the spread of religions and diseases that tested faiths while giving rise to much of the modern religio-political map. These movements also reworked entire ecosystems. Humans expanded some plant and animal ranges both intentionally and inadvertently through trade and colonization, while other species were outcompeted or hunted to extinction.

Throughout the process of maritime expansion, the world became both larger and smaller. The average person was increasingly aware of others beyond his or her town, region, or country as increasingly exotic goods, materials, and ideas flowed through maritime trade, so people were more engaged with a widening world. At the same time, the world became smaller and more interconnected in the sense that events in Southeast Asia or South America might have a profound effect in Europe or Africa. This interconnectedness grew into a hallmark of **modernity**, evident today in international communication, business, and travel. Much of the strife in the modern world also has its roots in this interconnectedness. The convergence of people of different economic, social, political, and religious worldviews has led to both incredible innovations and significant friction between groups. Many people experience these frictions every day, but the average American became most acutely aware beginning on 11 September 2001 when planes designed for international travel were repurposed as weapons in a dispute over political, social, and religious ideologies. The attack on the World Trade Center and our global future have their roots in a history of maritime expansion and trade.

Since for much of this history people were too busy trying to survive or profit to leave many records, and the records that they did leave often intentionally misrepresent the individuals on the other side of the exchange, archaeology plays an important role in understanding how the modern world was formed by maritime expansion, extraction, colonization, and trade. Archaeology acts as a vital check on these accounts. Whether it was the headless peoples that Herodotus reported in his *Histories* or the giant birds and snakes of Sinbad's journeys, accounts of distant lands tended to accentuate the fantastical. While it is tempting to ignore these as fiction, headless people were still being ascribed to northeastern South America in the 1600s (figure 11.1) along with many subtler misrepresentations. The grounded perspective of archaeology is necessary to combat these biases and give all sides a voice in describing what happened when cultures came into contact.

**Figure 11.1** Engraving in a 1603 German edition of Sir Walter Raleigh's 1595 *Discovery of Guiana*.

### ANCIENT TRADE

Some of the earliest archaeological evidence of international maritime trade comes from the site of Mersa Gawasis on Egypt's Red Sea coast (figure 11.2). The Egyptians traded with Punt from circa 2500 to 1000 BCE and royal fleets utilized the natural harbor at Mersa Gawasis from at least 2055–1650 BCE. The exact location of Punt is still debated, but it was likely located at the southern end of the Red Sea, nearly 2000 km (1243 mi) from Mersa Gawasis. Ships built on the Nile were transported overland to Mersa Gawasis where they were outfitted and launched. Upon their return, the ships were broken down, with the timbers scraped clean of marine growth and either recycled onsite or transported back to the Nile shipyards. The cargos were removed from sealed shipping boxes and transferred to sacks to be carried overland to the Egyptian heartland along the Nile. The sealed boxes indicate the value of the cargoes from Punt, which included incense, gold, ivory, and ebony wood. Despite the

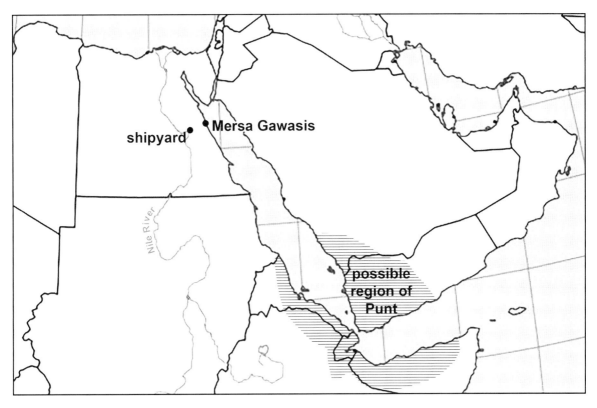

**Figure 11.2** Map showing Mersa Gawasis, Nile shipyard, and possible locations of Punt.

importance of these voyages, Mersa Gawasis was a temporary harbor, only inhabited during the time around an expedition. No permanent houses were found at the site, but there were rock-cut chambers to store supplies between trips, ceremonial monuments to ensure or commemorate successful voyages, and a slipway for launching and retrieving ships. The monuments include stela dedicated to maritime gods and indicate that there was a degree of risk and pride in executing one of these voyages. As with many ancient harbors, Mersa Gawasis eventually became filled with sediment so that the modern coastline offers only the slightest hints to the prosperous ancient landscape that once functioned there.[1]

Actual shipwreck evidence of international trade comes from the Uluburun site off the coast of Turkey, which is among the earliest known shipwrecks (figure 11.3). This vessel was lost carrying a variety of raw materials and high-status Late Bronze Age trade goods dating to the end of the 14th century BCE. While the vessel likely originated from a port on Cyprus or the Syria-Palestine coast, it contained goods from no less than nine cultures ranging from Mesopotamia to northern Europe. The bulk of the cargo was 10 tons of copper ingots and 1 ton of tin ingots that were destined to be combined into bronze. The ship was also

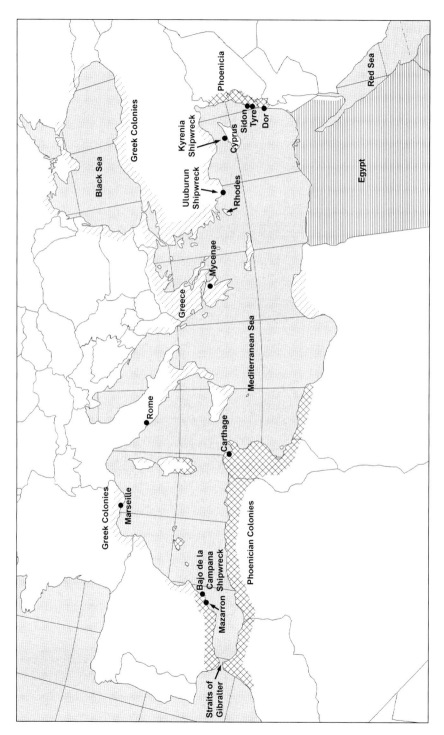

**Figure 11.3** Ancient locations described in chapter 11.

carrying glass ingots and more than 100 jars of a turpentine resin. In addition to these valuable raw materials, the cargo included ebony logs, hippopotamus and elephant ivory, ostrich shells, usable and scrap gold and silver, precious stones, and a swan-shaped ivory cosmetic box. The variety and value of the entire cargo, which includes many goods that the Egyptians sought in Punt, indicate that international trade was well-established at this early date. The excavators believe that at least part of the cargo may have been royal gifts, and that the ship was carrying Mycenaean envoys in addition to the crew and merchants from the southeastern Mediterranean. Such exchange between elites likely facilitated the movement of goods between widely distributed kingdoms, and allowed exotic items to enter local markets and then further circulate.[2]

Mycenaean and Egyptian power declined circa 1200 BCE as the Sea People swept through the Mediterranean (see chapter 12). The Sea People are still poorly understood, and may have been displaced maritime peoples from elsewhere in the region, but made at least part of their living through piracy and coastal raiding. The Phoenicians, who were already established along the coast of the eastern Mediterranean, stepped into the economic vacuum created by the Sea People and became one of the first major trade-based economies. Rather than focusing primarily on production at home, the Phoenicians developed their sailing, navigation, and mercantile skills to draw the Mediterranean and Red seas into a single trade network that also extended well into the adjoining hinterlands and acted as middlemen for their neighbors, the Egyptians and Assyrians. Archaeologists have excavated the Phoenician harbor at Dor (already described in chapter 8) and their port cities of Tyre and Sidon, but only a half-dozen Phoenician shipwrecks are known (figure 11.4). Two of these wrecks, dubbed Tanit and Elissa, consisted of amphorae piles discovered in deep water, indicating that the Phoenicians plied direct, open-water routes between their destinations, rather than hugging the coasts. Both ships, likely swamped in a storm between 700 and 750 BCE, had cargoes consisting of wine transported in remarkably standardized amphorae, Lebanese cedar, wool, and potter's clay. A third vessel, the Bajo de la Campana shipwreck, dating to circa 600 BCE, sank when it struck a shallowly submerged rock pinnacle off the coast of Spain. It was carrying a mixed cargo that included elephant tusks, many of which were votive offerings inscribed with Phoenician letters, copper and tin ingots, galena used in the extraction of silver, pottery including amphorae, plates, bowls, and lamps, ostrich eggshells, and furniture. The location of the Bajo de la Campana shipwreck in Spain, on the opposite end of the Mediterranean Sea from the Phoenician homeland, is indicative of the reach of the Phoenicians. They established colonies along the coasts of North Africa, Spain, and Sardinia, were importing tin from as far away as Cornwall, and ventured down the coasts of Africa through both the Straits of Gibraltar and the Red Sea possibly as far as the equator.[3]

**Figure 11.4** Excavation of Phoenician hull remains at Mazarron 1 site, Spain. (Courtesy of Spanish National Museum of Underwater Archaeology Archive/ J. A. Moya)

## COLONIES AND EMPIRES IN THE MEDITERRANEAN

The Bajo de la Campana shipwreck included many of the same goods that were carried by the Uluburun shipwreck and imported to Egypt from Punt. The continued trade in hard-to-acquire raw materials and expensive finished goods relates to the general self-sufficiency of preindustrial peoples. For much of human history, most of what was needed was produced locally; only special items required long-distance transport. Unlike these earlier examples, the Bajo de la Campana ship was likely not traveling internationally but shuttling between Phoenician colonies. The development of Phoenician colonies, including Rome's adversary Carthage, indicates that maritime expansion was becoming more permanent.

**Colonies**, which develop from settling peoples of one nationality or ethnicity in a distant land to control that land, were often established so the parent nation could benefit economically from the colonized region. The benefits took many forms, including access to raw materials, intercepting existing trade routes, increasing lands for cultivation, and allowing the expansion of the citizenry, their wealth, and, thereby, the tax base. In many instances, these colonies were dependent on water transport for their existence. Ships carried settlers to the colonies, transported goods between the colonies and the homeland, and protected the sea routes that allowed the colonial system to function. As colonial systems became more developed, it was also necessary to move materials between colonies to combine the various colonies into a network of economic production. For example, the galena carried on the Bajo de la Campana ship was loaded in one colony and was destined for another, where it would be used to extract silver from ore, while the luxury items were probably intended for high-ranking local officials to help maintain relations between the municipalities. Ultimately, and probably indirectly, the silver and other wealth fed the coffers of Phoenicia.[4] The Greeks and, later, the Romans, expanded on this model with colonies feeding wealth back to the mother city, or *metropolis* in Greek.

Greek colonies were situated in the eastern and northern Mediterranean Sea, as well as along the shores of the Black Sea. Each colony was linked to a specific city-state, though city-states often had many colonies and colonies could create their own subsequent colonies. Through the symbolism of transporting a fire from the metropolis to the colony and through very real political and economic bonds, the colonies were an extension of their homelands. Greek explorations took them along the western coasts of Africa and Europe, although these voyages largely repeated Phoenician trips. An exception that also demonstrates the economic drivers of Greek expansion is the voyage of Pytheas of Massalia (modern Marseille). Pytheas traveled north from Marseille around 325 BCE, eventually exploring much of Britain and the Baltic, as well as crossing into the Arctic and becoming the first person known to write about (though, obviously, not to see) the midnight sun. Much of his journey was by ship, and he was ultimately forced to turn south by drift ice north of a land he called Thule. Along with describing the people and places he saw, Pytheas noted the sources of valuable commodities such as tin in Cornwall and amber in the Baltic.[5]

Connecting their established colonies, the Greeks developed an expansive trade network based on merchant ships called *holkades* (figure 11.5). These were deep, broad sailing vessels built to safely carry substantial cargos. There was regional and temporal variation in these ships, but an example from approximately the time of Pytheas' voyage was found off the north coast of Cyprus near the town of Kyrenia. Built circa 325 BCE and lost perhaps 30 years later, the Kyrenia ship was 14 m (46 ft) long and 4.2 m (14 ft) wide. Not particularly large and with only one square sail, the ship was likely worked by four sailors, as indicated by several sets of four eating utensils and dishes. In addition to the small crew, the owners of the vessel attempted to squeeze as much use as possible out of the ship, making several repairs over its lifetime. A crack in the keel had been mended and the outside of the ship was covered with pitch and lead to make it more watertight and protect it from marine borers. The mast step was also moved, possibly to make room for a larger pump, necessitated by an increasingly leaky hull. On its last voyage, the Kyrenia ship likely sailed south off the coast of Turkey taking on and offloading cargo at various island ports, before loading wine at Rhodes, identifiable by the predominance of amphorae from that island. The ship then turned east and nearly made it to safety before sinking only a mile from the port at Kyrenia. Given its age and worn condition, it is possible that the ship simply gave out in a storm. Similar scenarios are common in the archaeological record—a parsimonious owner attempting to get one more voyage at the end of one more sailing season pushed his vessel too far only to lose the cargo and, often, his life (the ship being doomed to demolition in a breaking yard if not a shipwreck).

However, there is growing consensus that Kyrenia may have instead been taken by pirates. Eight javelin heads were found among the ship's hull remains, with indications suggesting that they had been in contact with the exterior lead

**Figure 11.5** Cross-Section of the Kyrenia ship, an archaeologically recovered *holkades*, on display at the Kyrenia Castle on Cyprus.

sheathing of the vessel. The absence of certain finds was also curious—there were no balance scales or sets of weights common among coastal trading vessels of the time, and only a few bronze coins of small denominations remained, most of which may have originally been polished to attract fish as part of a net (they were found among clusters of cast-net weights). Based on the size of the vessel, more than a ton of cargo appears unaccounted for, though it could have also been composed of perishable items that left no trace. Inside the hull, excavators found a lead curse tablet, folded in an envelope of lead and pierced through by a clenched copper spike. Such tablets from Greek and Roman sites have been found planted in graves or thrown in wells and are often inscribed with text associated with binding victims down to the netherworld. Could this have been an attempt by pirates who overpowered an old, overloaded merchant vessel, to call on dark magic and the sea to hide their evil deeds?[6]

As the Romans came to dominate the Mediterranean Sea, what they called *Mare Nostrum*, "Our Sea," they worked to eliminate piracy and turn the sea into a highway connecting their far-flung empire. The Romans seldom ventured into areas that the Phoenicians or Greeks had not already explored, but they solidified economic and social control over many of those areas. They exported bureaucrats and soldiers, along with foodstuffs such as olive oil and wine, to their colonies and trading partners in exchange for metals, wheat, fish, spices, and exotic materials. By inserting Roman officials, backed by soldiers, into local governments, the Romans were able to extract trade and taxes from a wide range of colonies. The movement of commodities from these colonies and the movement of Roman foods and goods to those stationed in the colonies required a highly developed maritime trade network that was integral to Roman civilization. For example, much of the grain to feed Rome came from North Africa and Egypt, and the western Mediterranean was the source of much of the fermented fish sauce known as *garum* that was the mustard or ketchup of its day. The scale of olive oil transportation is attested by Monte Testaccio along the Tiber River in Rome. The artificial hill is 35 m (115 ft) high, a kilometer in circumference, and contains the remains of an estimated 53 million olive oil amphorae mostly imported from Spain. This massive pile of trash is a monument to the trade of a single commodity within a trade network that included dozens of commodities. Rome was also indirectly connected to China through middlemen as Roman craft and the Qin, Han, and other dynasties expanded trade in the Indian Ocean. Rome exported glass and luxury items to China in exchange for silk and spices. However, the indirect nature of this trade is evident when the well-defined routes of the Periplus of the Erythraean Sea (discussed in chapter 10) are compared to Roman descriptions of locations farther east (figure 11.6).[7]

A wide variety of ships was necessary to move the plethora of commodities between ports large and small, far and near. The Godavaya shipwreck off the coast of Sri Lanka provides direct evidence for Roman trade in the Indian Ocean. This ship was lost during the 1st or 2nd century BCE while carrying a cargo of iron and glass ingots, ceramics, and carved stone. At the other end of the empire, the County Hall ship was found more than 6 m (20 ft) below the modern streets of London. Sunk in 295 CE, the County Hall ship was built locally using Roman shell-first construction techniques including mortise and tenon. Within the Mediterranean, there are several well-preserved examples of Roman merchant ships, including those found at l'Anse des Laurons, France and Marausa, Sicily. Combined with graphical representations such as the Torlonia relief that shows the harbor of Portus, archaeologists have a good idea what Roman merchant ships looked like and how they were built (figure 11.7). They tended to have flat bottoms with curved **bilges**, a curved vertical stem, and a high stern, with an upper deck. The hull was reinforced with **through beams** and heavy **wales**. Most tended to have a single, square sail, with a smaller foresail that aided in steering the vessel. Otherwise, steering was provided by side rudders.[8] The Romans also built specialty ships for specific commodities. These ranged from the mundane, such as a vessel designed with an internal tank to keep fish alive during transport, to the monumental, including a vessel to transport a 500-ton obelisk from Egypt to Rome.[9]

**Figure 11.6** A Renaissance reconstruction of Ptolemy's 1st projection, indicating the Land of Silk (*Serica*) in northeast Asia at the end of the overland Silk Road and Qin (*Sinae*) in the southeast at the end of the maritime routes. (© The British Library Board, Harley 7182 f60v-f61)

## NORTHERN EUROPEAN EXPANSION

In the early 6th century CE, Saint Brendan purportedly sailed west and north from Ireland in a curach and discovered a series of legendary islands. While much of his story is too fantastic to be believed, Brendan was a real person and the tale does include references to what were likely bizarre but real phenomena such as icebergs and volcanoes. Brendan's journey also symbolizes the very real movement of Irish monastic hermits through the northern islands as far west as Iceland. About a century behind these monks, the Vikings reached the Faroes in 650 CE, Iceland in 860, Greenland circa 980, and Newfoundland circa 1000 (figure 11.8). The Viking advance led to larger settlements and active trade, but they tended to kill or enslave the monks who were already living on many of these islands.[10]

The movement of the Vikings through the northern islands is indicative of two facets of their expansion: sea raiding and settlement. The beginning of the

Viking age is often set in the late 8th century when they began prowling the British Isles; raiding the coasts and rivers of much of Europe and Asia was certainly a source of wealth and prestige for Vikings. Less dramatic, but supporting at least as large a portion of the Viking population, settlement of new lands was also a major economic and social driver for Viking expansion. In some instances, they seized existing settlements, such as Dublin, but in many others they founded their own low-density agricultural hamlets. In spreading more than 3200 km (2000 mi) from their homeland to Newfoundland, the Vikings were likely looking for resources to extract and trade in Europe, but their legacy was the settlements they founded.

**Figure 11.7** Torlonia Relief from Portus showing a Roman merchant ship coming into port.

The ships of the Vikings are discussed in chapters 9 and 12, but the variety of ships found at Skuldelev reveal the various forms of Viking expansion. We know that the longship Skuldelev 2 was built near Dublin, based on the woods used to build it, and it may have been used to expand the Viking domain through raiding. Meanwhile, Skuldelev 1 was a substantial cargo vessel capable of sailing the North Sea and would have been useful for carrying settlers to, and goods from, Viking colonies. It is still debated just how far west similar ships carried the Vikings, but archaeology tells us that they certainly made it to Newfoundland. On the northernmost tip of the island is a site called L'Anse aux Meadows where a small group of Vikings settled briefly circa 1000 CE. The hamlet consisted of eight buildings, including an iron smithy and carpentry workshop, and was likely used, in part, to repair ships used to further explore the region. From sites such as L'Anse aux Meadows, the Vikings interacted with the indigenous peoples of North America. In some instances, there was peaceful trade; in others, one side or the other attacked. One of the factors that may have prevented the Vikings from pressing farther into North America was the presence of densely settled, organized groups of Native peoples. The inability to establish friendly relations with Native peoples, as well as the logistical difficulty of connecting a far-flung and diffuse population across the difficult waters of the North Atlantic, eventually caused the Vikings to withdraw. They likely left North America not long after the settlement of L'Anse aux Meadows and withdrew from Greenland circa 1450 CE.[11]

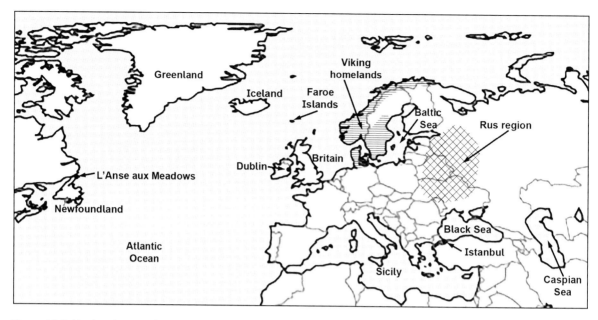

**Figure 11.8** North Atlantic and European locations described in chapter 11.

The Vikings did not only expand west, they also traveled south along coasts and rivers. They raided down the west coast of Europe, entered the Mediterranean, and eventually conquered Sicily in 1040 CE. They traveled the rivers between the Baltic, Black, and Caspian seas, settling and trading with people in the borderlands between Europe and Asia. The new culture that grew out of this contact was called the Rus' and provided a direct link between Vikings and the Islamic world. This connection led to significant cultural contact that we know about from the historical writings of Ahmad ibn Fadlan who traveled among the Rus', as well as archaeological finds such as rings and pieces of cloth at northern Viking sites that are inscribed to Allah. Other evidence of this contact appears in the Viking runes marked in Istanbul's Hagia Sophia by members of an elite Viking unit of the Byzantine army called the Varangian Guard.[12]

As with many Europeans, the Vikings were interested in the goods coming out of southwest Asia, many of which were imported from much farther east. Westerners had been expanding east to more directly access these goods since the Phoenicians and Romans. Arabian merchants established themselves in Sri Lanka by 414 CE and were regularly sailing to China by the mid-8th century.[13] This expansion took advantage of the monsoon winds and navigation techniques described in chapter 10 and was carried out in the laced ships described in chapter 9. Arabian trading in the Indian Ocean gave rise to the fictional stories of Sinbad the Sailor, set during the reign of Harun al-Rashid (786–809 CE), and paved the way for the much better–substantiated voyages of Muhammad Ibn Battuta (1325–1354) and Marco Polo (1271–1295). Neither Polo nor Ibn Battuta was the first to travel to East Asia, but they were among the first to record their voyages. Their tales not only tell us about the different cultures of the region but also about the power of writing. The fact that their journeys were written down and widely circulated is what makes them famous today. It is also noteworthy that many of Polo's credible observations were not believed in his time but some of his fabrications were accepted as fact. Early exploration literature should serve as a check of our own modern prejudices. While it is easy to see misconceptions in the past, the tendency to misunderstand other cultures is very much a concern of the present—we tend to believe what we want to believe, especially when it is about someone else.[14]

Journeying east from Venice, Polo traveled mostly by land, but on his return he sailed from Quanzhou, China. It is a happy coincidence that the shipwreck of a junk dating to the time of Polo (circa 1270 CE) was discovered in Quanzhou Bay in 1973. This substantial oceangoing ship measured more than 34 m (112 ft) long and demonstrated many of the characteristics of East Asian shipbuilding, including many bulkheads dividing the inside of a hull that was composed of several layers of overlapping planks (figure 11.9). For his part, Ibn Battuta traveled across the entire Islamic world from his home of Tangier in Morocco to China and Vietnam, and then home again over a nearly 30-year span. He traversed

**Figure 11.9** Quanzhou Bay shipwreck during excavation, note the bulkheads running across the hull. (Courtesy of Municipality of Quanzhou)

120,000 km (75,000 mi) over land and water and likely sailed on nearly every type of vessel available at that time.

### THE MARITIME SILK ROAD

Both Polo and Ibn Battuta traveled at least in part on the Silk Road, a network of trade routes that spanned Asia. This network moved finished goods and exotic materials in all directions, including bringing many of them to Arabia where they were traded to Europe (figure 11.10). Paralleling the overland route was a Maritime Silk Road that has drawn recent attention due to shipwreck finds such as the 9th-century Belitung and 13th-century Nanhai No. 1 shipwrecks. The Belitung ship was originally from Arabia and was lost in the Java Sea on a return journey carrying ceramics, worked silver and gold boxes, and other goods. Nanhai No. 1 originated in China and sank in the South China Sea carrying a primary cargo of porcelain. These shipwrecks are just beginning to teach archaeologists about the materials that traveled the Maritime Silk Road and the types of ships that carried them. Just as on land, the Maritime Silk Road did not simply run east to west, but was a network that connected many ports in Japan, Korea, China, Indonesia, India, Arabia, and elsewhere, allowing ideas and technologies, as well as goods, to move and mingle throughout the region.[15]

The products traded along the terrestrial and maritime Silk Roads are readily apparent in the archaeological record. Through stylistic and chemical analyses, it is possible to identify where an artifact or raw material originated. The picture that is beginning to appear as we discover new sites and reanalyze old finds is of a highly interconnected Asia and Europe. It is no accident that many of the advances in navigation discussed in chapter 10 occurred during the 13th century when long-distance trade was also increasing. Technology and commerce fed one another. Similarly, European expansion along the west coast of Africa and east through the Indian Ocean was driven by a desire to directly access the goods of East Asia, and cut out the middlemen that inflated the prices of these goods.

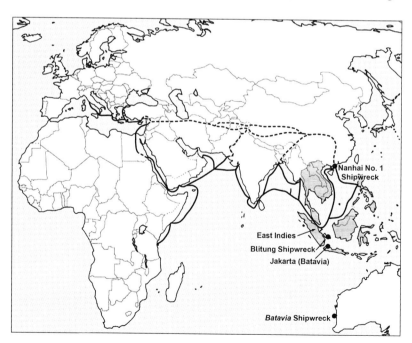

**Figure 11.10** Maritime Silk Road (solid line) and Silk Road (dashed line).

The expansion was not exclusively west to east. Between 1405 and 1433 CE, Zheng He commanded seven voyages on behalf of the Ming Dynasty, eventually reaching the east coast of Africa. His massive fleets included hundreds of vessels, some of which may have been 137 m (449 ft) long, although estimates of 67 m (220 ft) might be more realistic. For comparison, Columbus' *Santa Maria*, built half a century later, measured only 18 m (60 ft) long. Ships the size of Zheng He's often suffer from hogging, but the use of bulkheads may have alleviated this problem. Similarly, propulsion can be difficult because large ships require more or larger sails. Zheng He's largest ships may have had nine masts that were staggered across the main deck so that they did not steal wind from each other. This would be impossible on a European ship where the masts are mounted to the keelson, but was possible with the masts attached to the bulkheads (chapter 9) (figure 11.11). Traveling with the monsoon winds, the fleet visited many of the ports of the Indian Ocean to improve trade relations and extract tribute. This was a largely nonviolent voyage, although Zheng He did crush a large force of pirates near Sumatra and the sheer scale of the fleet and ships likely cowed most of the governments it visited.[16] There are many parallels between Zheng He's fleet and the Great White Fleet that circumnavigated the world under Theodore Roosevelt demonstrating the power of the United States Navy's new steel battleships. We will revisit the political ramifications of Zheng He's voyage in the conclusion of this chapter.

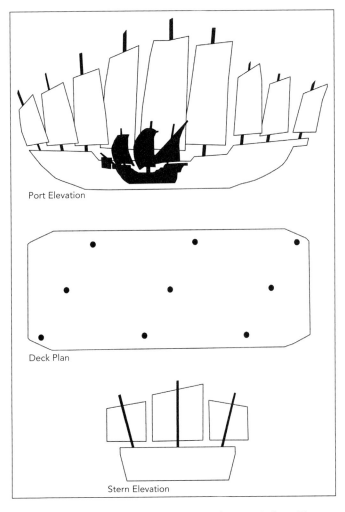

Port Elevation

Deck Plan

Stern Elevation

**Figure 11.11** Schematic of a large ship in Zheng He's fleet. The various views show the likely sail plan. The outline of Columbus' *Santa Maria* is superimposed on the upper image for scale.

## THE (SO-CALLED) AGE OF DISCOVERY

One of the greatest maritime expansions occurred beginning in the 15th century CE as Europeans steadily spread along the coasts of Africa, into the Indian Ocean, and ultimately to South and North America. Other expansions, such as the movement of Polynesian peoples through the Pacific, rival the European expansion for geographic scale, but few can match the speed of this expansion or its effects on the modern world. These, however, were not voyages of discovery except from a shortsighted, contemporary European perspective. Archaeology has shown repeatedly that not only had these lands been discovered by indigenous peoples millennia earlier, but, in many cases, Europeans had previously visited them. The previous example of Vikings in North America and their interactions with Native peoples is a classic example of how little new discovery actually happened during the Age of Discovery.

The early 15th century rapid and large-scale expansion of European peoples is often associated with the Portuguese prince Dom Henrique, better known as Henry the Navigator. Henry certainly used his position to drive this expansion, but he was also a product of his time. The voyages of Marco Polo were well known, as were the riches of northern and western Africa that included local gold and goods traded via Saharan routes. In fact, Portuguese African expansion began with the capture of Ceuta in 1415 (figure 11.12). Located in Northern Africa on the south side of the Straits of Gibraltar, Ceuta provided the Portuguese with a foothold in Africa. In subsequent years, Henry, who rarely left Portugal, instigated voyages that claimed the Azores and Madeira, and explored the West African coast. By mid-century, Henry's ships had reached modern Senegal, circumventing the Muslim-controlled overland trade routes and giving the Portuguese direct access to African gold. By the time Henry the Navigator died in 1462, Portuguese navigators had ventured as far south as modern Sierra Leone. Twenty-eight years later, in 1498, Vasco da Gama rounded the Cape of Good Hope and became the first European to reach India completely by sea. The likely wreck site of a ship from da Gama's second voyage to India (1502–1503 CE) has recently been discovered off the coast of Oman. While little of the ship's hull remains, the archaeological assemblage from this site is a window on how the Portuguese proposed to access and control trade in the Indian Ocean.[17]

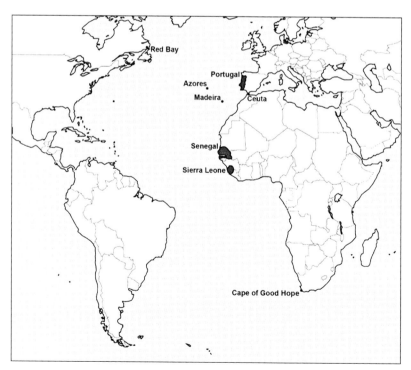

**Figure 11.12** European expansion beginning in the 15th century.

Much of the early Portuguese expansion took advantage of the **Volta do Mar** ("turn of the sea") sailing techniques. Near the equator, the "trade winds" tend to come from the northeast, but in the mid-Atlantic they are southwesterly. To take advantage of these winds, sailors had to sail far to the west before turning north and east and following the winds back to Europe. This counterintuitive discovery paved the way for Columbus to sail to the Americas . . . and return. Later, Ferdinand Magellan took advantage of the outbound Volta do Mar winds to begin his 1519–1522 circumnavigation of the globe. While Magellan himself did not survive the voyage, the return of his decimated crew to Spain further fueled this era of maritime expansion. It is worth noting that neither Columbus nor Magellan set out to discover new lands; instead they were attempting to open new routes to already known places.

As mentioned in chapter 10, navigational techniques and technologies were significantly refined during this period of European expansion. Advances in measuring position and finding the way between locations allowed increased certainty in sailing across the seas and establishing colonies on distant shores. The observations recorded in these distant places also provided a breadth of measurements that permitted astronomers and navigators to further develop existing technologies. Shipbuilding similarly benefited from the recursive relationship between the desire to press farther afield and the lessons learned from earlier voyages. It was during this time that Henry the Navigator's shipwrights developed the **caravel** (figure 11.13). The caravel was a small (13–18 m [42–60 ft] long), sturdy, maneuverable vessel with one or more lateen sails. Caravels were small enough to explore up rivers, maneuverable enough to return home despite difficult winds, and durable enough to survive long voyages along the African coast or into the Atlantic. While caravels appear in historical images, much of what made them such successful exploration vessels was not widely recorded (as you would expect for a trade secret) and can only be inferred from archaeologically recorded examples of Spanish and Portuguese vessels.

Approximately 20 Portuguese and Spanish, collectively referred to as Iberian, shipwrecks from the 15th and 16th centuries have been archaeologically recorded. The low number is the result of deterioration in warm waters and destruction by salvors seeking treasures, real and imagined, in these wrecks. Many Iberian ships did in fact carry treasure as part of the Spanish *flota*. These were convoys of ships that carried goods, including timber, silver, gold, sugar, tobacco, and pearls from the Americas to Spain. From the recorded shipwrecks,

**Figure 11.13** A caravel from Vasco da Gama's 1502 Portuguese India Armada (*Livro des Armadas*).

archaeologists have learned that the frames of Iberian ships were connected with dovetail joints, treenails, and spikes. The hull planking was similarly attached with both treenails and iron nails. The use of multiple means of attachment made construction more complicated and expensive but also stronger—the equivalent of wearing both a belt and suspenders. The Iberian shipbuilders also used naturally curved pieces of wood to frame the sterns of their vessels, making this crucial, and often weak, transition between the bottom and sides of the vessel particularly strong. Finally, the mast step was an expanded portion of the keelson and buttressed by extra timbers, reinforcing the main point of stress between the mast and the hull, and making it an integral part of the hull. Taken together, these construction techniques are largely unique to Iberian vessels of this period and argue for a sophisticated shipbuilding tradition focused on building rugged vessels.[18]

Parks Canada archaeologists found one of the earliest and most intact examples of an Iberian ship in Red Bay, Labrador (see also chapter 7). Discovered in 1978, in the northern latitudes rather than the Caribbean, and representing a Basque whaling galleon, rather than a Portuguese exploratory caravel, the 1565 shipwreck believed to be *San Juan* demonstrates how quickly and fully the Iberians came to exploit the New World. The village of Red Bay was a whaling station during the 16th century when whalers from the Basque region of southern France and northern Spain traveled to the area to hunt right and bowhead whales from small boats called *chalupa*. The whale blubber was then rendered into oil on shore and loaded into galleons to be transported to Europe. *San Juan* was one of these galleons and was loaded with whale oil when it was blown ashore by a storm and sank. Archaeologists found much of the hull of *San Juan* on the bottom of Red Bay, its sides splayed open and a *chalupa* pinned beneath its rudder and starboard stern (figure 11.14). In addition to these finds, Red Bay contains the wrecks of at least two additional galleons and three other *chalupas*, as well as the remains of shore facilities and a whaler graveyard. This largely intact maritime landscape is one of the premier underwater archaeological sites in the Americas and was designated a UNESCO World Heritage Site in 2013.[19]

## TRADE AND COLONIZATION SINCE 1500 CE

The Iberians were not alone in probing beyond their national boundaries. The French, English, Dutch, Swedish, and others established colonies in the Americas, Africa, and Asia. The remains of these overseas colonies dot many of the world's coasts and the wrecks of the ships that connected them have been variously searched for and recorded.[20] As these nations became increasingly comfortable with the rough outlines of Earth's coasts, they turned their attention from geographic exploration to scientific exploration. These later waves of exploration were aimed at mapping and collecting to better understand the shapes and

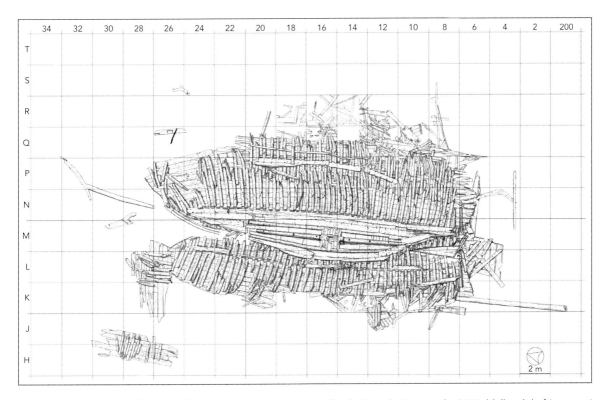

**Figure 11.14** Site plan of *San Juan*, Red Bay, Labrador. (Courtesy of Parks Canada. Drawing by P. Waddell and drafting team)

economic potentials of these lands. The earlier waves of exploration were aimed at claiming lands by drawing colonial lines on a map, while the later waves of exploration were intended to fill in the details within those lines. Charles Darwin's famous voyage on the converted 10-gun British naval brig *Beagle*, for example, mapped the coasts of South America and located islands in the Pacific, while also collecting geologic and biological specimens. That Darwin's observations during this voyage led to his revelations about evolution was, at the time, secondary to a fuller understanding of British colonial holdings. In this and many other ways, the Age of Exploration quickly became the Age of Exploitation.

## Colonialism

The goal of most of the European countries that engaged in expansion beginning in the 15th century was to occupy other lands with settlers and exploit those lands economically. By expanding their control across the seas, the European powers expanded their home economies and exported their excess, and frequently problematic, populations, often to the detriment of the residents of the colonized countries. The archaeology of colonialism is an important topic that extends well beyond the scope of this book, but the maritime component of colonialism must be acknowledged.[21] The example of one Dutch East India Company shipwreck illustrates the maritime nature of colonialism from the 16th century onward.

Founded in 1602, the Dutch East India Company, or Verenigde Oostindische Compagnie (VOC), was history's first multinational corporation, as well as the first to sell shares of stock to the public. Much of the VOC's early success was based on a government-backed monopoly over the Dutch spice trade with Southeast Asia, and it eventually came to have near-governmental powers of its own, including the ability to wage war, imprison people, and establish colonies. Within two decades of its founding, the VOC had established Batavia, now Jakarta, as its center in Asia, from which it would grow a network of hundreds of bases across India, China, Japan and the East Indies. Two, and later three, fleets would sail each year from the Netherlands, around the Cape of Good Hope at the southern tip of Africa, and across thousands of miles of open ocean before turning north toward the East Indies on a transit that lasted eight months and brought spices and fabrics back to Europe. Dutch **East Indiamen** were ships purposefully constructed for the lengthy voyage. Early 17th-century Dutch East Indiamen were much smaller than contemporary Spanish and Portuguese **galleons** due to the shallow waterways, tidal currents and sandbanks they needed to navigate in the Netherlands. They were, however, sturdy, with a large enough hold to accommodate cargo and multiple months of supplies. They were also heavily armed, prepared to take on pirates and enemy vessels, blurring the line between cargo carriers and ships of war.

## MY MOST IMPORTANT CONTRIBUTION TO MARITIME AND UNDERWATER ARCHAEOLOGY

Bruno E.J.S. Werz, CEO, African Institute for Marine & Underwater Research, Exploration & Education (AIMURE), South Africa

My career in underwater archaeology started in 1980, when I became the youngest diver on the now world-famous *Mary Rose* (1545) Project. During the second dive on this shipwreck, I knew that there was nothing more I wanted than to become a maritime archaeologist. Many other projects followed. These included not only Dutch East India Company (VOC) shipwreck excavations, such as *Vliegent Hert* (1735) and *Amsterdam* (1749), but also the recording of submerged prehistoric landscapes off the Isle of Wight. During the mid-1980s I was selected to join the Royal Dutch Army Underwater Reconnaissance and Diving Unit, where I was trained as a military and professional diver. Then in 1988, an appointment as Senior Lecturer

in maritime archaeology at the University of Cape Town followed. At present, I am CEO of the African Institute for Marine & Underwater Research, Exploration & Education (AIMURE).

In South Africa, I have undertaken various archaeological projects, including the first scientific underwater excavation in this part of the world. This was executed during the 1990s and concerned the VOC ships *Oosterland* and *Waddinxveen* that both sank during a storm in Table Bay on 24 May 1697. Both were on the return voyage and laden with Oriental products such as spices, tin and copper, as well as diverse collections of Chinese and Japanese porcelain. Careful study of the archaeological information in combination with detailed archival research contributed to more knowledge of late 17th-century Asian economy and provided the first practical evidence of private trade among VOC personnel. In 2008, I was appointed the Principal Investigator by the Namibian government for the excavation of a shipwreck discovered in a diamond mine in Namibia. This project became known as the Oranjemund shipwreck excavation. Research has since confirmed that the vessel is the oldest wreck ever excavated in sub-Saharan Africa: the Portuguese merchantman *Bom Jesus* that foundered in 1533 during an outward-bound voyage from Lisbon to India. This project instantly became international front-page news and was featured in, among others *National Geographic*, and on CNN and BBC News. The reason for this was not only the age of the wreck, but also the fact that it contained more than 2000 very rare coins, making it the biggest gold "treasure" ever found in Africa outside Egypt.

But what project is the most important one for me? Although thousands of valuable coins were recovered from the wrecks of the *Vliegent Hert* and the *Bom Jesus*, as well as hundreds of exquisite porcelain vases and figurines from the *Oosterland* and *Waddinxveen*, the lure of treasure has never been a driving factor. After all, treasure hunting is diametrically opposed to the code of ethics true archaeologists abide by. For me, the overall importance of maritime archaeology is the uncovering of new information on the human past. This past belongs to us all and it, the material witnesses, and the intangible information it has created must be kept for the benefit of society. To this day, I feel very privileged to

have been able to contribute to this by discovering the oldest-known submerged evidence for hominin activity.

When excavating the *Oosterland* and the *Waddinxveen*, I decided to study the stratigraphy underlying both shipwrecks, so test holes were excavated down to bedrock. At the bottom of the first hole and immediately overlaying the bedrock was a compact layer of red-brown sand. This distinct layer was some distance below and isolated from the shipwreck material. Upon excavating this layer that was later identified as an old land surface or palaeosol, I discovered an Acheulean hand axe in situ. The hand axe shows no signs of wind or water abrasion and has extremely sharp edges, indicating that it was deposited soon after use at the location where it was found. Other finds include a second hand axe found 750 m from the first, a bifacial tool that is probably an unfinished hand axe, and some smaller lithic fragments.

Dating of the implements was based on typology, indicating their approximate age as between 300 thousand years ago and 1.4–1.6 million years ago. The implements were produced from locally occurring quartzite, confirming their regional origin. Local circumstances that explain why these finds were preserved in such a pristine condition include a combination of their rapid burial by beach and aeolian sediments, the low seabed gradient, constructive wave action and additional burial in sediment deposited by adjacent rivers. This contributed in a positive way to their preservation when the hand axes were most likely to be exposed at the waterline during changing sea levels.

One of the most important aspects of this discovery is that it proves that even prehistoric material from the Early Stone Age can be found and survive in situ under the sea. The finds from Table Bay must have witnessed several marine trans- and regressions over many millennia. These Acheulean tools represent the oldest artifacts ever found under the sea and have thus opened the way for future explorations into humanity's "deepest past."

In October 1628, a fleet of six ships, under the direction of the newly constructed flagship *Batavia*, left Texel in the Netherlands headed for its namesake. Bypassing the Portuguese territories along the coast of Africa and into the Indian Ocean, the fleet rounded the Cape of Good Hope and set sail east for the East Indies. *Batavia*, however, missed the critical turn to north into the East Indies and ended up on the treacherous western coast of Australia, becoming the first Dutch ship to sink in Australian waters. About 300 of the 341 crew and passengers on board survived and found shelter on the uninhabited Abrolhos Islands. A party of some 48 people led by the captain and senior officers left the wreck site in one of *Batavia*'s boats to seek help in Batavia, returning three months later to find that as many as 125 of the survivors had been massacred by a group of men instigated by Jeronimus Cornelisz. The Dutch authorities ultimately prosecuted, convicted, and executed many of those responsible. *Batavia* had completely broken up within days of the vessel's wrecking and was not rediscovered until 1963.

*Batavia* was excavated by the Western Australian Museum between 1973 and 1976, and the site was subsequently revisited in 1980. As of this writing, *Batavia* is the only early 17th-century Dutch East Indiaman whose hull remains have been scientifically excavated and conserved (figure 11.15). The 20 tons of recovered timbers represent approximately 3.5 percent of the original vessel and yet were sufficient to ascertain that the vessel's construction was largely consistent with 17th-century VOC shipbuilding records and what is known of contemporary shipbuilding practices. These vessels had a gun deck, a full three-masted rig, fore- and sterncastles, and heavy wales girdling the ship to provide strength. They were built according to a bottom-based construction method typical for northwestern continental Europe, rather than using the frame-based construction methods seen elsewhere. The hull itself consisted of five layers of planking, including two layers of oak, with offset seams and layers of goat hair applied with a resinous substance on all outboard surfaces of hull planking. This made for

**Figure 11.15** Reconstructed Dutch East Indiaman *Batavia*. (Courtesy of Malis)

a remarkably thick and waterproof hull, and one uniquely suited for the exceptional stresses of long transoceanic journeys. The hull was further protected by an exterior layer of pine sheathing, often referred to as sacrificial planking, together with closely spaced iron nails affixing it to the hull that would rust and provide a layer of iron corrosion. This exterior of rust layer was meant to inhibit damage caused by the teredo worms found in the warm waters Indiamen would spend months transiting.[22]

Excavations relating to the *Batavia* survivors' camp contributed to an often overlooked aspect of shipwreck archaeology: what happens to those who survive a shipwreck. By comparing the archaeological remains of shipwreck survivor camps across Australia, archaeologist Martin Gibbs has begun to identify similarities in how the survivors organize themselves, subsist, prepare for rescue, and interact with indigenous peoples. This archaeology of crisis has much to teach us about what it is to be human. In the case of *Batavia*, the survivors turned on each other and nearly half of those who escaped the wreck were murdered.[23] This grisly behavior illustrates one of the many negative aspects of colonialism. Removed from the normal social structures and repercussions of their home countries, some colonists allowed their less-humane urges to manifest. Combined with disease, greed, and a sense of ethnic superiority, this lack of social restraints led to a prodigious amount of death, rape, and torture during the Colonial period.

The VOC continued to experiment and evolve its shipbuilding techniques, adjusting to resources and enhancing efficiencies. Unfortunately, however, the scarcity of archaeological data means that very little is empirically known about Dutch ships of the later 17th century. By this time, the Dutch had grown into a major maritime power, wresting control of the East Indies trade routes from the Portuguese, who were facing additional competition from emerging rival England. The global scale of these maritime powers cannot be overstated. Extending from the Portuguese probing along the coast of Africa and into the Atlantic during the 1400s, the European empires expanded rapidly. When Francis Drake sailed around South America and began attacking Spanish treasure ships in the Pacific in 1578, European expansion entered a new phase in which distance was a progressively shrinking barrier. Ships became ever more seaworthy as they were increasingly called upon to sail long distances and stay at sea for long periods. By the time Charles Darwin departed on his famous journey in 1831, even a ship as mundane as a small naval brig could be trusted to circumnavigate the globe in a voyage lasting almost five years.

## Transporting commodities

One of the purposes of colonialism is to send valuable commodities to the home country. As European colonialism advanced, the movement of commodities became more complicated, with some commodities moving between various colonies before the finished product or accumulated wealth was shipped back to

Europe. The various triangular trades that existed in the Atlantic from the late 16th to early 19th centuries illustrate this practice (figure 11.16). Humans from West Africa were brought to the Caribbean where they were forced to work on plantations producing sugar and in factories that transformed that sugar into molasses. The molasses was then shipped to New England where it was distilled into rum. The profits from the sugar and rum were used to purchase finished goods, which were shipped to Africa to purchase more people. Alternatively, enslaved Africans sent to the Americas more broadly were forced to produce cotton, tobacco, indigo, and other commodities that were then sent to Europe where they were processed into manufactured goods and then returned to Africa and used to acquire more humans. In both instances, the wealth of the investors tended to ratchet up with each transaction. While it is shocking to consider enslaved Africans as a commodity, these people were commodified from the moment of their enslavement in Africa, during the Middle Passage from Africa to the Americas, and after. This is another example how maritime archaeologists have begun to investigate the benefits and horrors that colonialism spread across the globe.

Few shipwrecks definitively associated with the Middle Passage have been found, let alone systematically investigated and reported, although not for a lack of effort.[24] Among the most fully reported is the Danish frigate *Fredensborg* that sank near Arendal, Norway in 1768. On its final voyage, *Fredensborg* sailed from Copenhagen, Denmark to Accra, Ghana carrying a mixed cargo of finished goods dominated by alcohol, gunpowder, flints, and muskets. These goods were exchanged for enslaved Africans and a small amount of other goods such as ivory before the ship next sailed to the Danish West Indies. Thirty Africans died in the passage across the Atlantic. *Fredensborg* left St. Croix with a cargo of primarily sugar and tobacco, but also cotton, cinnamon bark, mahogany, and dyewood, much of which was lost when the vessel ran aground in a storm. Much of what is known of *Fredensborg* is recorded in primary documents, but the shipwreck provided a good deal of detail not found

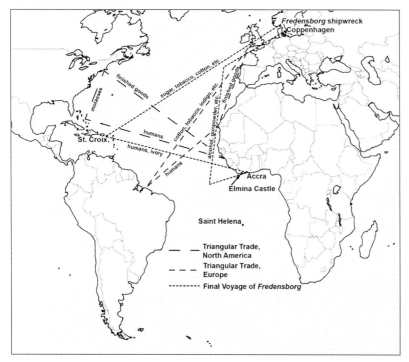

**Figure 11.16** Triangular trades.

in the papers. These details included much about the mundane lives of both the sailors and the enslaved peoples, including foods, the means to conduct trade, and the fancy shoe buckles worn by some of the crew (figure 11.17). As important, the shipwreck serves as a touchstone, a tangible link to the horrors that can be glossed as "thirty Africans died in the passage across the Atlantic." In this way, *Fredensborg* is one part of the physical heritage of slavery that stretches across four continents and includes not only sites directly related to slavery but those built with the profits of slavery (which include many universities and institutions).[25]

Among this broad heritage landscape of the slave trade are a wide range of maritime-oriented terrestrial sites. The Portuguese shipped nearly all the materials necessary to build Elmina Castle to what is now Elmina, Ghana, in 1482, making the castle the oldest European building in sub-Saharan Africa. Elmina gave the Portuguese access to African trade and served as an important waystation for both inbound and outbound East Indiamen. The castle, town, and surrounding region transferred from the Portuguese to the Dutch to the British as the strengths and shapes of the European colonial empires shifted during the 15th through 20th centuries, before becoming the independent country of Gold Coast in 1957. Elmina castle was one corner of the triangular trade: European goods were exchanged for enslaved peoples who had been captured in the interior and brought to the castle to be held before being exported to Brazil and other parts of the Portuguese colonial world. From the late 15th century until the Dutch abolished their portion of the slave trade in 1814, tens of thousands of people passed through Elmina Castle. The castle illustrates the two poles of colonialism. The dungeons beneath the castle held nearly 1500 people at a time in dark, cramped conditions where it was impossible to lie down and diseases and rape were rampant. Those who survived confinement left through the aptly named "Door of No Return" for a Middle Passage voyage that was often worse. Immediately above the dungeon, however, were government quarters where European officials lived lives of relative ease and comfort. Despite the dominating presence of the castle, archaeology at the site has also shown a remarkable continuity of West African beliefs and culture within the town of Elmina.[26]

**Figure 11.17** Artifacts recovered from the *Fredensborg* slave ship wreck, including cargo and personal effects.

Evidence of those who left through the "Door of No Return" has come to light on the island of Saint Helena. From 1840 until the 1860s, Saint Helena, the isolated island in the middle of the South Atlantic that famously housed the exiled Napoleon Bonaparte, supported a British Naval station engaged in the eradication of illegal slave trading. Britain outlawed the slave trade in 1807. The Navy sent 439 slave vessels to Saint Helena, of which 87 were carrying slaves. Many of the enslaved people were dead upon arrival at the island and many others soon succumbed to the injuries and illnesses they had suffered during their captivity. The graves of some of these people were discovered in 2006 as the result of a road and airport construction project. The burials are unique because they represent a very short window of time and comprise entirely people born in Africa. **DNA**, chemical, and morphological analyses of the bones and teeth of the exhumed skeletons have begun to shed light on the origins of the enslaved peoples, as well as how they began to adapt to slavery from the very beginnings of their captivity. The results indicate that people from a large swath of West Africa and the interior were brought together on the slave ships and that, despite language and cultural difference, the enslaved peoples were possibly forming new communities that helped them persist in the face of oppression.[27]

The transition from legal to illegal slave trading led to smaller and faster slaving vessels with a better chance of evading Navy patrols. Other vessels also began to emphasize speed as the market demands of the 19th century increasingly rewarded the first to reach port. This phenomenon was particularly noticeable in the shipping of tea from China to Britain and the transportation of miners to goldfields in the United States and Australia aboard the clipper ships mentioned in chapter 9. In the case of tea, the first cargoes to arrive each season relieved a scarcity that had developed since the last vessel of the previous season, making early tea considerably more valuable than if it arrived a week later. Clipper ships were also used to move opium from India to China in order to increase the buying power of British merchants in China, eventually precipitating the First Opium War, during which Britain employed gunboat diplomacy to enforce its ability to import narcotics to China. Clipper ships also saw heavy use during the Australian and American gold rushes, when the first miners to arrive had the right to stake the most promising claims. In all these cases, a high price was paid for space in the clipper's hull in exchange for reaching the destination as quickly as possible. However, the clipper ships were inefficient and expensive to operate with holds of limited size and large crews, so they depended on low-bulk, high-value cargoes for their existence. These ships drew on designs from earlier fast ships including Baltimore clippers and French frigates, but added new innovations that made them radical for the time. With their fine lines, flaring bow, sleek appearance, reaching masts, and ability to hold speeds previously unobtainable, clipper ships not only served this purpose but also caught the public's attention (figure 11.18). Aided by evocative names, such as *Flying Cloud*, *Lightning*, and *Storm King*, and flamboyant

**Figure 11.18** Advertisement for the clipper ship *Ocean Express* emphasizing the speed of the vessel and its captain, even surpassing the steamship in the background.

captains who drove their vessels and crews through horrific weather, often resulting in exciting exploits recounted in newspapers, these ships captured thrilled the public during the mid-19th century. Like most fads, however, their time was fleeting. With the United States Panic of 1857 and the decline in world markets, combined with the rise of steam-powered ships and the opening of the Suez Canal, clippers disappeared almost as quickly as they appeared. Many of these ships were scrapped, removing them from the archaeological record, while others were simply abandoned in out-of-the-way places and have yet to be studied.[28]

## Extracting commodities

The extraction of marine commodities was not only a result of colonial expansion but also a driver of expansion and contact. Whaling ships from the northeastern United States discovered more than 400 islands in the Pacific as whalers hunted farther and farther afield. The demands of home markets drove the expansion of marine extraction, just as they drove the development of terrestrial extractive industries such as timbering, mining, and trapping, leading to the commoditization of much of the natural world. Extraction from the seas tended to be less bounded than on land because the seas were treated as more of a commons, with nations largely free to pursue resources where they could find them. As a result, fishing and whaling industries often reached areas soon after or before more official exploratory missions. In many instances these fishers, whalers, and sailors became the unintentional emissaries of the expanding Euro-American world. The commoditization of terrestrial resources led to profound landscape alterations with significant changes to the plants and animals as native species were removed and replaced with species intentionally and unintentionally imported from throughout the colonial world. Marine extraction similarly led to profound changes in the distribution, size, and diversity of many marine species. It destabilized the marine food web in some cases, while also leading to a redistribution of foods such that preserved fish like mackerel, cod, and shad have been recovered from archaeological sites more than 1600 km (1000 mi) inland.[29]

As discussed in chapter 7, whaling was among the most geographically expansive and historically important marine extractive industries. Whaling can be undertaken from either the shore or from ships, but became increasingly ship-based as whale populations shrank and the whales changed their behaviors to avoid hunters. In either case, whalers often spent long periods away from home, often interacting with local populations, to procure and process a commodity that was shipped home to feed other industries. The resulting social and economic networks laced across much of the globe, transcending colonial boundaries.[30]

The Basque whaling station at Red Bay we discussed above is an example of shore-based whaling where the crews lived on land, went to sea in small boats to hunt whales, and dragged the whales back to the station for processing. The *San Juan* and other ships were only used to transport the crews and oil back and forth across the Atlantic Ocean. Other significant work on the archaeology of shore-based whaling has been done in Australia on primarily 19th-centruy whaling stations. Confined by the requirements of the environment, whaling practice and their cultures, Australian whalers were remarkably consistent in the locations they chose for their stations. They favored places with a protected harbor, a gently sloping beach for hauling out whales and boats, high ground or trees nearby to give them a good vantage to look for whales, and flat ground to build their **try works** and quarters. The areas around these sites also tend to be littered with the bones of whales, representing the remains of carcasses that were deposited in the waters around the station. While most whaling stations were outposts of European nations and relied heavily on imported foods to sustain them, some whalers did form relationships with local populations and lived with indigenous communities in places such as New Zealand and Canada.[31]

Pelagic, or offshore, whaling moved the shore station aboard a capacious, durable vessel and allowed the whaling enterprise to roam the seas, taking and processing whales where they found them (figure 11.19). This is the form of whaling that tends to dominate the popular imagination due to stories such as *Moby-Dick* and real events like the sinking of the whale ship *Essex*. The *Essex* was sunk by a whale, leaving its crew adrift in the middle of the Pacific Ocean, resulting in cannibalism, and inspiring Herman Melville to write *Moby-Dick*. Adventure aside, whaling ships were a major part of 19th-century commercial fishing fleets. The operation of whaling ships and sailors' lives on whaling voyages, which often stretched for years, are well recorded in the administrative documents of the captains and companies, as well as in less-formal documents and art created by sailors during the long periods when no whales were within sight. Among the best physical evidence of whaling ships comes from the *Charles W. Morgan* now docked at Mystic Seaport in Connecticut. The *Morgan*, built in 1841 and measuring 32 m (106 ft) long, was an average whaling ship of its time, albeit a particularly lucky ship. After eight decades of service and 37 whaling voyages, the *Morgan* was retired and preserved while other similar vessels were lost or scrapped, making it the last wooden whaling vessel. Archaeological evidence also comes from the considerably less lucky *Two Brothers* that struck a shoal within what is now the Papahānaumokuākea Marine National Monument. *Two Brothers* was captained by George Pollard, Jr., who had previously lost the ship *Essex* to a whale. The shipwreck was identified based on its location and the presence of whaling equipment, such as harpoons and try pots, which date to the 1820s. Additional investigations of *Two Brothers* will hopefully yield information about how the ship was organized and used.[32]

CUTTING IN & TRYING OUT.

**Figure 11.19** Whalers processing a whale at sea. Strips of blubber are removed alongside the vessel and boiled in the try pot on deck. (Image from *Etchings of a Whaling Cruise: With Notes of a Sojourn on the Island of Zanzibar: And a Brief History of the Whale Fishery, in Its Past and Present Condition.* J. Ross Browne, 1846)

The pursuit of whales took whaling ships throughout much of the Pacific, Atlantic, Indian, and Southern oceans, with stops to provision along the coasts of nearly all the continents and innumerable islands. Seldom able to be selective of the crews that would sign on for a long and dangerous voyage and offering substantial payouts for a successful voyage, whale ships attracted many men who had not previously been to sea. As a result, many farm boys found themselves on South Pacific islands interacting with, in all conceivable ways, the local populations. Whaling ships also became floating microcosms of 19th-century globalization with heterogeneous crews of people broadly describable as Pacific Islanders, Europeans, Euro Americans, Africans, African Americans, Native Americans, and Asians, but with many important ethnicities glossed in these broad categories, living and working aboard individual vessels. The whale ships brought new technologies, religions, alcohols, and languages to the places they visited, but the visits also had a profound effect on the whalers, not too dissimilar to what some students experience during a semester abroad (only longer and less chaperoned). The example of tattooing from chapter 10 is but one aspect of Pacific Island culture that returned with the whale ships.

### INLAND WATERWAYS

The movement of ideas and cultures was not limited to sea crossings. As discussed previously in this chapter, the Vikings very successfully moved along the rivers of Europe and Asia, forming a new ethnicity that spanned the two continents. Earlier, the Romans used boats to move commodities and troops throughout much of Europe. Even earlier than that, going back to the earliest boats, watercraft regularly provided the easiest and most efficient ways to move people and things long distances and to interact with neighbors many miles away.[33]

Within the Americas, inland communication and expansion took many forms. Prior to the arrival of Europeans, much inland movement was by canoes made of bark or log (see chapter 9), some of which were quite large. Columbus' son, Ferdinand, described one canoe as being as long as a galley and 2.5 m (8 ft) wide.[34] Similar canoes continued to be used by Europeans and Native peoples, especially when traveling on the unimproved rivers of the interior. Fur traders in North America, for example, used bark canoes well into the 19th century because the canoes could carry a substantial cargo over very shallow water and were light enough to carry between rivers, allowing traders to nearly span the continent from east to west. While these craft themselves are not preserved in the archaeological record, they have left archaeological and ethnographic records. Archaeologists have excavated sites created when fur trade canoes capsized in rapids. This "whitewater archaeology" has produced nested pots, beads, trade axes, musket balls, and a wide variety of tools that give a sense of the goods that traders carried inland to exchange for pelts.[35] The passages of these boats are also recorded in the Métis people of Canada who trace their origins to the union of Native peoples and European traders and settlers.

As the economy of North America expanded and people of European descent spread farther and farther west, it became necessary to send larger and larger vessels along the rivers. These social and economic pressures were initially fulfilled by a variety of boats designed to work on the shallow and often treacherous rivers between the Appalachian and Rocky Mountains. During the 19th century, shipbuilders began to experiment with **steamboats** on these western rivers (figure 11.20). Initially the steamboats resembled those being built for coastal and ocean voyages, but builders rapidly adapted their techniques to the challenge of floating a powerful, oscillating engine—which Charles Dickens described as sleeping next to a gunpowder mill—in a few feet of water.[36]

Given that these vessels were built only 200 years ago, it would be reasonable to expect copious records detailing their construction, operation, and maintenance. That is not the case. The shipbuilders did not leave plans and did not

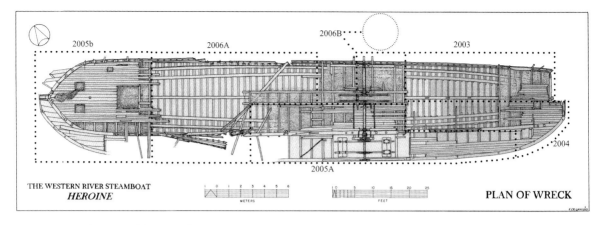

**Figure 11.20** Plan map of the steamboat *Heroine* shipwreck, Red River, Oklahoma. The wider deck preserved on the port side of the hull extended above the water providing some protection for the paddle wheels and more space on deck. (Courtesy of Kevin Crisman)

write much about their process. While there are many paintings and drawings of steamboats, it was largely left to archaeologists to determine the details of their internal workings. What *has* become apparent from archaeological investigations is that steamboat builders employed a wide variety of means to reinforce their vessels: notching timbers and using iron chains to keep the ends from sagging, strengthening the nearly right-angle turn between the bottom and sides, adding forward bulkheads to prevent the hull from flooding if the steamboat ran into a submerged log, and employing large amounts of timber and cross-bracing to absorb the erratic motions of early steam engines. Some even added poles to help leverage the entire ship over sandbars. The ingenuity of steamboat operators also becomes apparent in the frontier fixes that they employed to keep their ships running when they were damaged in regions where the only industrial support was the local blacksmith. Operating these vessels was similar to the grueling Baja 1000 race, but in the name of commerce, rather than sport. And the commerce was impressive. As with the fur trade canoes, the excavated cargoes of steamboat shipwrecks give a unique glimpse of what was needed on the frontier. The cargo of the steamboat *Bertrand*, now on display at the DeSoto National Wildlife Refuge, included meats, oysters, pepper sauce, mustard, alcohol, alcohol-soaked cherries, fruit, clothing, clocks, housewares, building supplies, and medicine. These vessels were essentially a Walmart motoring up shallow and shifting rivers to bring necessities and comforts to the edges of the Anglo American world.[37]

### PROBLEMATIZING THE ROLE OF SHIPS IN EXPLORATION, COLONIZATION, AND EXTRACTION

There are various sides to the role of ships in human expansion and contact. Some of these ships carried tremendous wealth—wealth that changed the course of nations and global history. When these treasure-bearing ships sank they became the treasure wrecks that many members of the public expect of every shipwreck and which fuel the global industry specializing in the plunder of historic shipwrecks. Other ships carried peoples' ancestors and provide their roots in the countries that they now call home. These vessels are part of a people's heritage. These vessels also represent past glories. They are touchstones for major industries, fortunes made and lost, and exciting stories. Whale ships and steamboats combine these threads in single ships, in part explaining the popularity of whaling and steamboats in popular history and fiction. Yet, we must also contend with the other realities of human expansion over the past half-millennium. Ships also brought cruelty, disease, and violence to new shores in quantities that indigenous peoples had not previously witnessed. These same voyages also began a process of decreasing cultural diversity that continues today with more languages and traditions lost each year. In addition to humans, ships brought invasive species, new farming techniques, and perceptions of the landscape that led to often-destructive effects on the environment. Whether these effects were intended or unintended matters much less than the repercussions that continue to ripple across the globe. Said simply, the ships discussed in this chapter were harbingers of the modern age, but that is an unequal age where some have benefited at the expense of others.

The political ramifications of these ships did not end when they sank. Modern governments occasionally look to shipwrecks and past maritime expansion as precedent for modern expansion. For example, many recent Chinese scholars and politicians represent the voyages of Zheng He as peaceful voyages of diplomatic and economic capacity building for the region. Some draw parallels between the goals of the Ming Dynasty in Zheng He's voyages and modern Chinese political expansion in the region. Others argue that a focus on the generally peaceful nature of Zheng He's interactions with other nations is an attempt to revise history and obfuscate the goals and repercussions of modern China's increasing regional influence.

In the Arctic, similar questions of previous expansion are intersecting with the warming climate and shipwrecks. The wrecks of HMS *Erebus* and HMS *Terror* were found by Canadian archaeologists in 2014 and 2016, respectively. Both were lost during John Franklin's failed 1845 attempt to find the Northwest Passage and have been remarkably well preserved by the cold Arctic waters. These shipwrecks will resolve historical mysteries about the fate of the Franklin expedition, provide additional information about how Arctic expeditions were outfitted and how the ships were modified, and may contain scientific samples that bear on modern ecological questions. They are also part of Canada's assertions of sovereignty in the Arctic—sovereignty that will likely allow access to the region's oil and gas reserves. As the planet warms and ice recedes, these important economic resources will become easier to access. Canada's claims became slightly stronger in 2017 when the United Kingdom gave the ships to Canada, recognizing the sites, and, thereby, their locations, as Canadian.[38] As with all political issues, there is more than one way to view Zheng He and the Franklin shipwrecks, and it is not the place of a textbook to tell you what to think about these issues. It is, however, the goal of this text to get you to think about the role of ancient ships in the modern world.

## SUMMARY

With their ability to float heavy cargos across the largely frictionless surface of the oceans, ships have long played a role in human expansion, trade, and extraction. Colonialism, commerce, and the extraction of natural resources during the last five centuries led directly to the modern world. The movement of Europeans beginning in the 15th century CE led to widespread colonialism, the Atlantic slave trade, and an irreversible reworking of global environments and cultures. These themes, however, also existed in the ancient world. Greeks, Phoenicians, and Romans founded colonies and moved significant commodities huge distances. This ancient trade made Europeans aware of the goods available in East Asia, eventually leading to the more aggressive European expansion of the Age of Exploration. These maritime movements and actions reverberate today and it is incumbent on maritime archaeologists to situate the study of the past within the context of the modern world.

## DISCUSSION QUESTIONS

1. What does the study of past interactions between cultures tell us about our own perceptions of different nationalities and cultures?
2. Why did early trade focus on rare or luxurious items?
3. What drivers beyond the purely economic led people from the ancient world onward to make connections with new cultures?
4. Why is it that so much poor behavior accompanied culture contact during the past 500 years? Was this a new phenomenon or always part of culture contact?
5. Do you think the increasing globalization of human societies has, on the whole, led to most people leading better or worse lives? Why?

## FURTHER READING

Bass, G. (1996). *Ships and Shipwrecks of the Americas*. Thames and Hudson, New York.

Crothers, W. (2000). *The American-Built Clipper Ship, 1850–1856*. International Marine, Camden, ME.

Dreyer, E. (2007). *Zheng He, China and the Oceans in the Early Ming Dynasty, 1405–1433*. Pearson, New York.

van Duivendvoorde, W. (2015). *Dutch East India Company Shipbuilding: The Archaeological Study of Batavia and Other Seventeenth-Century VOC Ships*. Texas A&M University Press, College Station.

Fernández-Armesto, F. (2006). *Pathfinders: A Global History of Exploration*. W.W. Norton, New York.

Grenier, R., M.-A. Bernier, and W. Stevens, Eds. (2007). *The Underwater Archaeology of Red Bay: Basque Shipbuilding and Whaling in the 16th Century*, 5 vols. Parks Canada, Ottawa.

Kahn, A. and J. Bouie. (2015). The Atlantic Slave Trade in Two Minutes. Available at http://www.slate.com/articles/life/the_history_of_american_slavery/2015/06/animated_interactive_of_the_history_of_the_atlantic_slave_trade.html.

Kane, A. (2004). *The Western River Steamboat*. Texas A&M University Press, College Station.

Lawrence, S. and P. Davies. (2011). *An Archaeology of Australia Since 1788*. Springer, New York.

Svalesen, L. (2000). *The Slave Ship* Fredensborg. Indiana University Press, Bloomington.

## CHAPTER 12

# WARFARE AT SEA

- How have people interacted with seas, lakes, and rivers? How was this interaction shaped by their culture and environment? What are the similarities, differences, and outcomes of these interactions?
- What types of maritime archaeological sites are there, and how do they differ in what they can teach us about the past?
- What kind of information do ship and aircraft wrecks hold? What can their contents tell us about trade, colonization, warfare, and the people on board?
- What do maritime technological innovations tell us about broader trends in society, history, and culture? How does naval innovation shape the rise and fall of maritime societies?
- How did maritime people shape world history?
- How do we balance the needs of modern societies with the preservation of cultural heritage sites?

## VESSELS OF WAR

As we have seen, a ship is primarily a functional item aimed at transporting goods and people for transit, trade, and exploration. To these, one must add one more purpose—warfare. In fact, in the realm of ship design and construction, naval warfare has served as a key catalyst for development. As early boats evolved into larger, more specialized, and more complex structures, warships and naval tactics advanced along with them. Seeking every advantage over an adversary, warships borrowed heavily from technological innovations and new materials used elsewhere on land and sea, and in turn many developments associated with naval warfare eventually came to be incorporated into vessels serving other purposes. Despite these exchanges, warships were a distinct category of watercraft from very early on—a category of ships that came to project power and control of the seas, and epitomize a society's technological achievements, and, in some instances, even a society itself. The archaeology of naval warfare is a broad topic involving the study of not only ships but also shore infrastructure; shipsheds, supply depots, coastal fortifications, and a series of other structures. This chapter will concentrate on the ships that engaged in war at sea over the course of the last few millennia, relying largely on knowledge gained from archaeological investigations.

Beginning in antiquity, a merchant vessel's main objective was to transfer goods from one location to another. Its wide hold was therefore designed to swallow cargo at the expense of maneuverability. Speed was secondary when compared to tonnage, and, through large swaths of history, the sail was the preferred means of propulsion. Though wind was not always dependable, and sails did not always allow for navigating in the desired direction, as a means of propulsion sailing was relatively inexpensive and required correspondingly little in terms of manning. By contrast, in the heat of battle, speed and maneuverability could spell the difference between life and death. The ability for a warship to navigate irrespective of the direction of the wind was therefore pivotal. Accordingly, one of the first key points of divergence between merchantmen and warships was the development of the galley: slender, shallow-draft vessels propelled at least in part by oarsmen. These finer hulls enabled vessels to cut through the water by minimizing the drag associated with the wider, rounder hulls of merchant vessels.

### OARS, RAMS, AND MEN

On the outer wall of Pharaoh Ramses III's mortuary temple at Medinet Habu, near Luxor, Egypt, is one of the earliest depictions preserved in the archaeological record of a naval battle involving galleys (figure 12.1). The scene represents an event that took place in 1176 BCE, when Ramses III defeated a coalition of the mysterious Sea Peoples who had emerged during the Late Bronze Age from what appear to have been cataclysmic upheavals associated with mass migrations in the eastern Mediterranean.[1] The Egyptian victory spared the kingdom from the fate that had beset regional powers (such as the Hittite empire) at the hands of this enigmatic but formidable enemy. The depiction at Medinet Habu conveyed the pharaoh's triumph to the world and serves as the starting point in our discussion of the galley, though we can be certain that naval engagements on the water went back centuries earlier.

## The Mediterranean

During the period of laced Greek ship construction (chapter 9), the *penteconter* was the dominant galley. In contrast to merchant vessels, the penteconter was slender in shape and propelled by 50 oarsmen. A square sail offered additional propulsion, though records indicate that the sail was removed when battle was

RAMSES III AND HIS FLEET IN BATTLE WITH THE FLEET OF THE SEA PEOPLES
COMPARE PLATES 38-41

**Figure 12.1** Drawing of limestone relief at Medinet Habu depicting Ramses III and his fleet in battle with the fleet of the Sea Peoples. (Courtesy of the Oriental Institute, University of Chicago)

imminent. Despite its prevalence, no archaeological remains of a penteconter have been yet located. As these light wooden warships carried no weighty cargo or ballast, some suggest that these vessels may have largely broken apart on the surface instead of sinking intact to the sea floor. What is known of penteconters is based on historical and iconographical records, which indicate that they primarily served as platforms for archers and heavily armed foot soldiers, or hoplites.

Between the 6th and 4th centuries BCE, a sweeping technological shift occurred that transformed this early ship construction tradition into one based on pegged mortise-and-tenon joinery and the use of double-clenched copper nails.[2] This new tradition dominated ship construction in the Mediterranean for centuries, and yet it was not entirely new; its underlying features had been largely used in the Levant since at least the middle of the 14th century BCE (consider the Uluburun wreck, mentioned in chapter 9). Though it is not entirely clear what prompted the dramatic change to occur when it did, the mortise-and-tenon construction method permitted the construction of stronger and more durable hulls, and was a critical element in the development of a new kind of warship—the Greek trireme. In fact, it has been suggested that advancements pertaining to the trireme were among the key reasons why mortise-and-tenon joinery was widely adopted across the spectrum of naval shipbuilding.

Triremes were named after the three series of oarsmen that were positioned along each side of the vessel granting this form of galley unprecedented propulsive power when thrusting its main offensive weapon, a bronze ram mounted on the bow, against the enemy. Hundreds of such triremes descended into the straits of Salamis, near Athens, in 480 BCE in what would be the decisive naval battle of the Persian Wars. On the fateful day the Persian ships were defeated in

**Figure 12.2** Hypothetical drawing of an Athenian trireme in the process of ramming a Persian trireme during the Battle of Salamis in 480 BCE. (Courtesy of Y. Nakas © Zea Harbour Project)

a single naval engagement that altered the course of the war, allowing Athens to flourish into its Golden Age (figure 12.2). It is therefore understandable why one of the earliest underwater archaeological surveys anywhere took place near Salamis in 1884. The Greek state-sponsored expedition was unable to locate evidence of the Battle of Salamis, but set the stage for professional archaeological standards being applied in the underwater environment. Lacking an archaeological example of a wrecked trireme, what we do know about these formidable galleys comes from other sources. The closest we can get to sizing up these vessels at the moment is through the famous shipsheds in the Athenian port of Piraeus that housed them, excavated in recent years under the auspices of the Danish Institute at Athens and the Greek Ephorate of Underwater Antiquities. Elsewhere, 4th-century BCE inscriptions found on marble blocks in Piraeus indicate that contemporary triremes were equipped with 170 oarsmen classified into three categories. The precise arrangement of these three teams of oarsmen is still a matter of debate. What we do know is that naval tactics employed by oarsmen took advantage of the maneuverability of the triremes, ramming the side of an enemy vessel, as well as attacking between two forward-facing enemy galleys, aiming to break off all the oars along one side of an adversary, thereby incapacitating the vessel and devastating the oarsmen within.[3]

The formula of oar-powered galleys stacked with oarsmen proved successful and soon the trireme was followed by the *quadrireme* (the "four") and the *quinquireme* (the "five"). As the Mediterranean world entered the Hellenistic Age following the death of Alexander the Great, the fierce competition between Hellenistic monarchs led to the development of even larger polyremes, spanning from sixes to reportedly even thirties, which may have only served a symbolic purpose to project power and wealth. The most direct archaeological evidence for the various polyremes of the Hellenistic Age at present is a monument built following the Battle of Actium in Nikopolis, Greece in 31 BCE. There, Octavian, having defeated the fleet of Mark Antony and Cleopatra, incorporated into the stone monument 36 bronze rams from captured ships. Only the sockets that originally held the rams remain today, but their sizes correspond to the ten types of vessels that participated in the battle.[4] We do, however, have an example of a Hellenistic ram discovered in 1980 near the village of Athlit in Israel (figure 12.3). The isolated find was the first ram ever discovered and provided the first tangible evidence of the construction of Hellenistic warships. Within the bronze ram lay a heavy central timber and side timbers that distributed ramming stresses born by the half-ton bronze ram along the entire hull. The beautifully decorated three-finned Athlit ram was designed to splinter timbers and split the seams of an adversary without bending, breaking, or becoming entangled.[5] Other rams

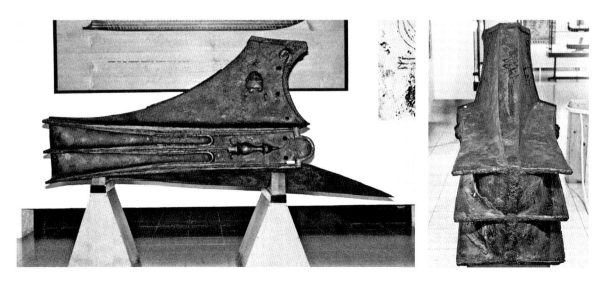

**Figure 12.3** The Athlit ram on display at the National Maritime Museum, Haifa, Israel. (Courtesy of Asaf Oron)

have been found since that time, including most impressively from a site near the Egadi Islands, Italy, dating to the First Punic War in 241 BCE. Recent investigations in the area have located more than 10 bronze rams, along with helmets and amphorae, allowing for the first in situ ancient naval battlefield assessment, and a whole new dataset through which to study ancient warships.[6]

The galley continued to serve as the primary vessel of war for centuries. The Roman bireme galleys of the later period had a fully enclosed deck placed over the oarsmen for protection, where previously a narrow walkway separated the banks on either side. These galleys evolved in a number of directions, including the larger Byzantine *dromons* appearing in late antiquity and early medieval times. Rather than the earlier square sails, galleys came to be propelled by lateen sails, making them more maneuverable. The ram, originally aimed at inflicting damage below the waterline to incapacitate a ship, evolved to a spur-like projection above the water, serving as a means for boarders to pour across onto the decks of an enemy vessel and engage in combat. In the 7th century CE, the introduction of Greek fire, a flammable liquid launched from tubes mounted on the bows of Byzantine ships, signaled a major shift in weaponry. No longer did a vessel have to get directly entangled with the enemy; inextinguishable with water, Greek fire could engulf an adversary from a distance (figure 12.4). Though its precise composition remains unknown, it served as a cornerstone of the Byzantine Empire's naval arsenal.[7] Vessel construction methods themselves were also evolving. Recent excavations at the silted-in ancient Port of

**Figure 12.4** Greek fire engulfing a galley. Miniature from the Madrid Skylitzes, 11th–12th century. (Courtesy of the Biblioteca Nacional, Madrid)

Theodosius in Istanbul, Turkey, have yielded remains of 37 shipwrecks dating from the 5th to 11th centuries CE, including among them the first archaeological evidence of Byzantine galleys. Distinguished from contemporary merchantmen by their long, slender hulls, thwarts for oarsmen, and oar-ports, they also provide substantiating evidence for the primary development of the age—the transition from shell-first construction to frame-first construction.[8] With the advent of frame-first construction came an increased ability to use proportions to plan the design of a ship in advance. In the commercial realm, this meant a greater flexibility in designing larger, more boxlike holds and the ability to standardize hold sizes for such things as tax purposes. In the military sphere, construction using proportions meant the ability to effectively replicate successful designs, standardize fleet vessel types, and more cost-efficiently expand state navies.

## Northern Europe

While these developments were taking place in the Mediterranean, in northern Europe clinker construction had continued to evolve (chapter 9). By 600 CE, the simpler overlapping planks of the 4th-century BCE Hjortspring boat had been superseded by large, open-decked galleys such as the Sutton Hoo vessel. During the excavation of a burial mound on the Gokstad farms in Norway in 1880, excavators discovered the extensively preserved Gokstad ship dating to around 890 CE (figure 12.5). At over 23 m (75 ft) long and 5 m (16 ft) wide, the seaworthy and graceful vessel was propelled by sixteen pairs of oars and a single sail. The multipurpose Gokstad ship dates to the period in Scandinavia referred to as the Viking Age, spanning the 9th to the turn of the 12th centuries CE. As discussed in chapter 11, new trading nodes and seafaring routes were opening, bringing with them the aggressive expansion of the Vikings to places such as England and Ireland. This expansion could scarcely have been possible without the development of the iconic Viking warship, the **longboat**. These vessels permitted small raiding parties the mobility to attack and withdraw with speed and efficacy that proved lethal.

Clues as to what Viking longboats looked like emerged in 1934 in Funen, when the impression of a ship in yet another burial mound was excavated. It was not, however, until the middle of the 20th century that preserved examples of a Viking longboat were identified among the Skuldelev vessels. Among them are two warships—Skuldelev 2 and Skuldelev 5. Skuldelev 2 has a reconstructed length of almost 30 m (98 ft) and could accommodate up to 60 oarsmen. Interestingly, dendrochronological analysis has shown that the keel and planks, felled in May or June 1042 CE, had grown in southeastern Ireland, near Dublin and Waterford, both towns founded and inhabited by Vikings. Though there are modest differences with contemporary examples built in Scandinavia—the broad and shallow lower frame timbers could be an adaptation to use in the open Irish Sea—Skuldelev 2 is remarkably consistent in its design with Scandinavian

**Figure 12.5** The Gokstad ship built toward the end of the 9th century CE. (Courtesy of the Museum of Cultural History, University of Oslo)

construction methods. Skuldelev 5, meanwhile, probably represented an example of the smallest category of warship, a *snekkja*, which also served commerce and exploration purposes. Among its most interesting features is a wooden structure running along the gunwale, behind which shields could be placed for protecting the crew. These wrecks were later complemented by others such as Roskilde 6, dating to approximately 1025 CE. Roskilde 6 is estimated to have been 36 m (118 ft) in length and to have accommodated 78 oarsmen, making it the longest Viking ship yet discovered and highlighting the continuing prowess of longboats in the Late Viking Age.[9]

## SAILS AND GUNS

### East Asia

Across the globe, the Mongols, under the leadership of Khubilai Khan, would soon become the dominant force in East Asia. Following the subjugation of

Korea, the emperor turned his sights toward Japan, sending naval forces across the Tsushima Strait in 1274 CE, and again in 1281 CE, having conquered the Southern Song dynasty in the interim. The second time around Khubilai Khan would dispatch a fleet of more than 400 and perhaps as many as 4,400 vessels from China and Korea that massed near the island of Takashima. As the fleet assembled, a powerful typhoon struck, bestowing on the Japanese what they considered a divine wind, or *Kamikaze*, and crushing the vast majority of the Mongol vessels. In the early 1980s, archaeologists began uncovering artifacts and remains of hulls associated with the failed invasion (see sidebar by Randall Sasaki). Three decades later, in the fall of 2011, an intact vessel from the second invasion was discovered by Ryuūkū University, prompting the first designation of an underwater site as a National Historic Site by the Japanese Agency for Cultural Affairs. Though the particular vessel was not recovered, nor was a second one discovered in 2015, the study of the more than 500 timber fragments that have been recovered over the course of investigations affords archaeologists insights into Khubilai Khan's well-organized fleets. The ships were not poorly built watercraft that were easily overcome by the typhoon as some suspected. Instead, several were well-constructed, while some even showed repairs prior to being launched. Vessels were divided according to their function, with flat-bottom ships serving as landing craft to establish a beachhead, V-shaped hulls serving as cargo ships for carrying provisions, and round-hulled riverine craft repurposed for reconnaissance and other tasks. The diversity of the remains also reflected a

---

**MY MOST IMPORTANT CONTRIBUTION TO MARITIME AND UNDERWATER ARCHAEOLOGY**

## Randall Sasaki, Researcher, Kyushu National Museum, Japan

In 1281, while attempting to attack the island of Takashima, the ill-fated fleet of the Mongol Empire was destroyed by the so-called divine wind. Historical sources tell us that the Emperor Khublai Khan amassed more than 4,000 ships to invade Japan. Memorialized in contemporary documents, the site of the invasion has never been forgotten.

The first underwater archaeological project on the island took place more than 30 years ago, and several research institutions led initiatives in hopes of locating the site of a shipwreck associated with Khublai Khan's fleet. However, all that was found were scattered artifacts related to the battle, including a collection of anchors, various weapons and armor, storage jars, bundles of coins, and fragmented pieces of hull remains. I joined a project

led by the Asian Research Institute for Underwater Archaeology in 2003. Wherever we searched, we found evidence of the battle, but we never came across a complete hull. Some isolated hull remains were located, but the majority of wooden remains we discovered appeared to be driftwood.

Beginning in 2005, a new project was organized by the University of the Ryukyus. By using the most up-to-date remote-sensing technology, the new effort began to detect a few targets that were thought to correspond to possible shipwrecks. Despite having a limited budget, in 2011 the decision was made to excavate

*(continued)*

one of the more promising targets. Some of us believed that this would have been the last chance to run such an operation; it was difficult to find support for an ambitious excavation as all the projects of the past twenty-five years had been successful only in finding bits and pieces and artifacts. However, we persisted, and there it was—a more-or-less compete hull from the Mongol invasion buried beneath the seafloor. The vessel was named Takashima No.1 Ship. In 2015, to our surprise, another vessel was discovered. I had a chance to see this second, Takashima No. 2 Ship. Because of its narrow hull and the sharp bow, it was obvious this was a vessel made for speed. The shape of the hull, the use of bulkheads, and the use of iron nails prevalent in Southern China, but not found elsewhere, all suggested that the vessel was indeed made in Southern China. The hull was so complete that it was not difficult to identify such characteristics in just one dive.

A few years have passed since the two discoveries which, at the time, I thought were what we had been waiting to uncover for thirty years. I now hold a different opinion. The greatest discoveries, I now believe, had already been made in the preceding decades. It was the bits and pieces of the remains that were important; it was the collection of small things that made up the entire site itself that was the greatest treasure trove of information. What I originally thought were insignificant finds turned out to be truly insightful, together forming the Takashima Underwater Site. The seascape as a whole holds various mysteries that must be answered, and sometimes a small clue can lead to answering a big question.

I will mention one such example here, a single bundle of copper coins, composed of 88 individual pieces. All the coins were of the same kind, inscribed with the phrase *Tai-Ping*, meaning "great peace." The number 88 is considered a lucky number, and the word *Tai-Ping* also refers to a calm ocean, as in the Pacific Ocean (Tai-Ping Ocean). The coins were a good luck charm, representing the wish of the people who came to invade Japan. They wished for tranquil ocean and a safe voyage, but instead they vanished. It took me a few years to realize that the coins had such a meaning behind them. When I did realize their significance, I felt a stronger connection with the people of the past. There are many such stories that I did not recognize at first, including one particular mystery I helped to solve.

At the time, I was conducting a research project on recording and categorizing timber remains that had been recovered from across the site. I was looking through the results of the wood species analyses and I stumbled upon a peculiar set of data. I had counted close to one hundred possible pieces of firewood (or driftwood), and it turned out that over 80 percent of these pieces of wood were identified as pine. It became obvious that someone had intentionally selected pine. There should be a reason, I surmised, why the invading fleet brought pine with them, instead of oak or another wood species. I studied the characteristics of pine to find the answer. Pine, it turns out, is a fast-burning wood, does not have to be seasoned, and burns even when damp. In addition, pine, which is a softwood, makes a large amount of smoke compared to hardwood. Therefore, pine is not only a perfect candidate to be used as firewood on a long sea voyage, but it is also an excellent type of wood for burning as a beacon, as the ensuing smoke can be spotted for miles at sea. Suddenly, I realized that the firewood may hold a key to solving a puzzle. It was a mystery how the invading ships were able to reach Japan without being lost, given relatively simple navigation tools and only a handful of experienced captains. There is no need for sophisticated navigation tools, nor a large number of experienced navigators, however, if a few navigators can guide a large number of ships through the use of smoke signals by burning pine wood throughout the voyage. The archaeological evidence seems to suggest this was the case.

It may not sound exciting, but great discoveries are often made not in the field, but in the laboratory, in a library, or at home. I was fortunate to have come across a site that can continue to provide insights and discoveries when I least expect them. Even a small discovery holds the power to instantly change an ordinary day into an exciting one. And that small discovery may also lead to answering a greater mystery unsolved for centuries. Investigating the Takashima Underwater Site through this newly found perspective represents my most important contribution to our field.

number of contemporary East Asian shipbuilding traditions, revealing how geography shaped each one. Prevalent common features such as the importance of bulkheads, the use of consistent wood species, and the ubiquity of nail joinery, however, also suggests a common origin for the ships of the Mongol fleet.

Swords, helmets, and iron-tipped arrows were among the weapons found during the excavations, though among the more interesting finds were fragments of at least 21 *tetsuhau*, or ceramic bombs (figure 12.6). These serve as the earliest archaeological evidence of shipboard explosive ordnance on any battle site. The ceramic bombs were packed with scrap iron and had flat-bottomed, thicker bases to ensure that they did not accidentally roll. As a fuse was lit, the weapons were catapulted, spreading shrapnel, fire, and a thunderous sound. The age of naval guns would soon be upon us, and the world was shrinking—in fact, the Venetian

**Figure 12.6** *Tetsuhau* ceramic bombs recovered from the site where Khubilai Khan's 1281 CE invasion fleet was struck by a typhoon near the island of Takashima, Japan. (Courtesy of Matsuura City Board of Education, Nagasaki. Provided by the Kyushu Maritime Museum. Photograph by Ochiai Haruhiko)

traveler Marco Polo would bring word of the might of Khubilai Khan to the West in his book *The Description of the World,* composed in 1298 CE.[10]

## The Mediterranean

Back in the Mediterranean, Venice and other nations were dependent on maritime trade for their survival and strategically extended their influence eastward, facilitating exchange with central Europe. Between the mid-13th century and the end of the 14th century, the Italian maritime cities sent their fleets of galleys into battle, repeatedly inflicting wounds on one another's merchantmen to control the main maritime trade routes. Around that time, authorities began regulating state-sponsored shipbuilding by means of decrees, the later iterations of which serve as some of the oldest surviving shipbuilding manuscripts. Venice even used a system of conscription to provide rowers for the fleet, while around the turn of the 14th century, Genoa put to sea the largest fleet ever launched by an Italian city, consisting of 165 galleys and 35,000 men. It was not until the advancement of the Ottoman Empire in the 15th century that the balance of power in the eastern Mediterranean shifted.

Galleys themselves were also evolving, and in dramatic fashion—by the 1530s, bronze guns firing cast-iron shot introduced at the end of the 15th century were taking hold. These guns replaced the earlier and smaller stone-slinging counterparts that had come into use in the preceding decades. The prow was beginning to function as a platform supporting three to five heavy guns, with several lighter, short-range guns flanking the sides of the oared vessels and positioned on maneuverable swivels to serve primarily as antipersonnel arms. By the 1540s even larger vessels, propelled by sails as well as oars, began carrying eight or more heavy guns. Larger galleys necessitated more men, and more resources, while at the same time depending on a smaller number of harbors that could accommodate them. Soon, the cost of maintaining a fleet of full-sized oared vessels capable of achieving major strategic goals became prohibitive. The galley would surrender its crown as the preeminent naval warship, though not before serving in the largest European engagement of the 16th century, the last fought almost entirely by rowed warships, and the first to be decided by firepower—the Battle of Lepanto (figure 12.7). Off the coast of western Greece, on 7 October 1571, the Ottoman fleet was decisively defeated by the Holy League, which consisted primarily of the Venetian and Spanish fleets. This served as the first significant victory of a European naval force over the Ottoman Turkish fleet, which lost or relinquished some 170 galleys and 30,000 men. Six **galleasses**, a new type of vessel consisting of a three-masted converted merchant galley with high bulwarks, heavy cannon and protected fore and aft castles, had played a determinative role.[11]

## Western and Northern Europe

As the concentration of power in Europe was shifting westward and northward toward the Atlantic, vessels capable of open sea warfare were taking center stage.

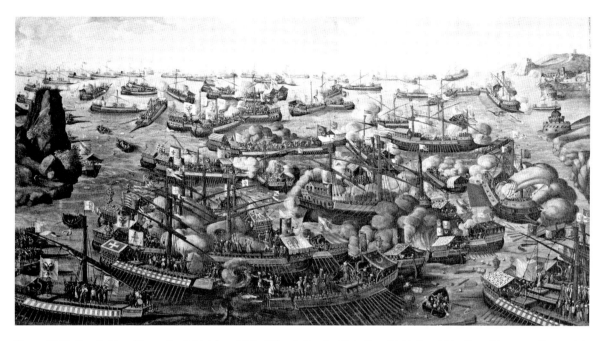

**Figure 12.7** The Battle of Lepanto, 7 October 1571. Oil painting by H. Letter. (© National Maritime Museum, Greenwich, London)

By the turn of the 15th century, Iberian shipwrights had adopted the carvel construction method. The flush planking, affixed to a full skeleton of frames, provided added strength, greater complexity in rigging, and an increase in the size of vessels. Three- or even four-masted sailing vessels were being constructed, facilitating the dawning age of discovery and colonization, as well as the growing use of guns. When King Phillip II of Spain, having just annexed Portugal, attempted to invade England with the famed Spanish Armada of 1588, there were but a few galleys in the fleet of 130 vessels. Instead, the Spanish king rested his unsuccessful attempt on large galleons, armed merchant men, invasion transports, and a small number of galleasses. The remains of eight such armada wrecks have been discovered thus far along the coastlines of Scotland and Ireland, reflecting the variety of vessels involved and providing us with insights about this transitional period.[12]

The English force that defeated the Spanish Armada had been developing for most of the 16th century. The earlier clinker construction tradition, epitomized by the overlapping triple-thickness planking of King Henry V's *Grace Dieu* launched in 1418, was coming to an end. The same could be said for boarding tactics and naval battles that largely resembled land engagements at sea. The prominence of guns, on the other hand, was on the ascent. *Grace Dieu* carried three or so small guns. By 1511, *Great Michael*, the flagship of the Scottish navy, was making use of **gunports**, and was capable of firing broadsides with 12 cannon per side. In the same year and in the midst of a major naval expansion by Henry VIII of England, *Mary Rose* was finished and had its first voyage.[13]

*Mary Rose* was a carvel-built carrack, with a deep and broad hull, four masts, a high clinker-built sterncastle, and a large overhanging forecastle. One of the first English warships with multiple levels of guns, *Mary Rose* supplemented its two gun decks with additional arms projecting from the forecastle and sterncastle. The formidable vessel was manned by 185 soldiers, 200 mariners, and 20–30 gunners and fought over the course of more than 30 years in three wars with France. Refitted in 1535–1536, the vessel's structure was reinforced, and additional gunports were likely cut, accounting for as many as 76 wrought- and cast-iron and 15 cast-bronze guns of different types. On 18 July 1545, the French fleet of galleys engaged the English in the Battle of the Solent at long range. The following morning, calm weather allowed the French an opportunity to outmaneuver the English; suddenly, *Mary Rose* heeled over. Contemporary accounts suggest the sinking was due to an abrupt turn and a gust of wind that allowed water to enter the open lower gunports. Other theories, however, have suggested that the vessel was overloaded with guns and soldiers, or that the French struck the hull with a cannonball low enough to cause water to flood in.

Salvage attempts on the *Mary Rose* began in 1545 but failed to recover much other than some sails and yards. In 1836, the wreck was rediscovered by a diver employed by fishermen to disentangle their nets. Salvage attempts once more ensued, this time using underwater explosives and resulting in the recovery of four bronze guns and parts of wrought-iron guns, along with wooden elements and other small finds. Once those salvage attempts ceased in 1843, *Mary Rose* once more lay in rest until its rediscovery by divers in 1971. The ship was placed under the Protection of Wrecks Act and excavation by The Mary Rose Trust followed between 1979 and 1982, when, using an immense crane and a purpose-built lifting cradle, a large portion of the surviving hull was recovered in front of a worldwide television audience of 60 million. For the next ten years, *Mary Rose*'s hull was continually sprayed with chilled water as sediment was carefully removed, and the structure was stabilized. Over the next twenty years, the hull was sprayed with polyethylene glycol (PEG), until 2013, when the timbers entered the final phase of conservation and were allowed to dry in environmentally controlled conditions within a purpose-built museum in Portsmouth (figure 12.8). *Mary Rose* now represents the only 16th-century warship on display and is still answering questions about naval developments in northern Europe. The discovery in 2011 of the near-contemporary *Mars*, one of the largest and most heavily armed ships of its time, will help fill in gaps in our knowledge. Lost during the Nordic Seven Years' War in 1564, the Swedish warship became one of the first ships to sink a principal enemy vessel with its guns, of which it had more than 100. The wreck's remains now lie in the cold waters of the Baltic and are being investigated in detail.[14]

**Figure 12.8** The *Mary Rose* at the Mary Rose Museum in Portsmouth Historic Dockyard. (© Mary Rose Trust).

By the second quarter of the 17th century, Sweden was on the ascent, having brought lands in modern-day Russia, Estonia, Latvia, and Lithuania under its control. Russia and Poland had given way, leaving Denmark to serve as the main regional rival and the Netherlands and Spain as contenders farther afield. Sensing an opportunity to consolidate his power, King Gustav II Adolf initiated the construction of two ships belonging to a new class of warship. The Swedish navy at this point was composed of about 30 warships, with the typical large warship carrying a single deck of 12-pound guns. The new warships, *Vasa* and *Äpplet*, would have two full gundecks and would be armed with 72 bronze cannon, each weighing 1200 kg and firing 24-pound solid iron balls. It would be a few decades more before cast-iron guns would come to replace their heavier, more expensive bronze counterparts. As a consequence, manufacturing such a large number of guns required tons of molten bronze that had to be heated and poured in one continuous operation. It was, in fact, so resource-intensive that few ships could be so equipped and the two new vessels, though not the largest in the world, would be the most powerful. Although two-decked vessels with 60–80 guns would eventually become the norm, only a few two-gundeck warships had been built in Europe by this time. Shipwrights were challenged by the much higher load carried on the upper gundeck, inherently lessening stability, and the fact that the lower gundeck had to be closer to the water line.

*Vasa* was ultimately launched on 10 August 1628, armed with 64 bronze guns and more than 700 brightly colored carvings projecting the nation's power. Having traveled less than a nautical mile on its maiden voyage, a gust of wind filled the warship's sails and the hull suddenly heeled to port; a second, stronger gust came as the vessel was righting itself, submerging the open lower gunports. In front of hundreds, if not thousands, of people who had gathered to witness the launch, *Vasa* sank. Salvage attempts started just three days after the sinking and during the course of the 17th century all but three of the vessel's guns were recovered. It was not, however, until 1956, when the ship was rediscovered, that a salvage operation intent on recovering the vessel as a whole was put in motion. Within five years, *Vasa* was lifted free of the seafloor using pontoons, raised to the surface, and transported to a dry dock where the excavation of the vessel's interior began. More than 30,000 objects were recovered during 5 months, and a 17-year PEG-based conservation process was initiated in 1962. The purpose-built Vasa Museum welcomed the impressive ship in 1988, where it is on display receiving more than one million visitors a year, and continuing conservation and preservation measures aim to stabilize the unique structure (figure 12.9).[15]

**Figure 12.9** The *Vasa* as viewed from the stern quarter in the Vasa Museum, Stockholm.

*Vasa* proved too small below the waterline to carry so much firepower, and was too heavily built above it. Naval engineers soon recognized the importance of placing heavier guns in the lower gun deck, and smaller, lighter guns on the deck above. Aiming to inflict the greatest damage on an adversary through firing broadsides, fleets would come to engage in a naval tactic that would have opposing vessels position themselves in two columns, forming the line of battle. These larger, "ship-of-the-line" warships grew in size, primarily in width, and settled deeper and lower in the water to allow for enhanced stability. Naval power, however, was not merely concentrated in these ships-of-the-line, which would represent the peak of naval technology for nearly two centuries; the world was changing, getting smaller, and capitalism was beginning to blur the line between state and commercial interests.

## Colonialism and the East Indies

As noted in chapter 11, the formation of the VOC in 1602 CE marked a new period in global history characterized by the heightened competition between established European powers for access to, and control of, new colonies and markets. The case of *Batavia*, discussed in the same chapter, illustrated that the boundaries between what constituted a naval vessel and what constituted a merchant vessel were being crossed. By the end of the 17th century, the Dutch had used this new strategy and their naval prowess to grow into a major maritime power, wresting control of the East Indies trade routes from the Portuguese, who were facing additional competition from emerging rival England. Evidence of

Portugal's waning influence is perhaps exemplified by what was the first, and still represents a rare, archaeological investigation of a Portuguese shipwreck of this era.

Between 1696 and 1698, Fort São Jesus, which served as a Portuguese trading station guarding the harbor of Mombasa, Kenya, found itself under siege by Omani Arabs. Over the previous two centuries, Portuguese voyages of discovery had opened a direct sea- route to the East that needed to be protected. Portuguese forts and colonies dotted the route around Africa and across the Indian Ocean, controlling the route. After nearly a century of exploitation, the Omani Arabs re-belled against Portuguese taxes levied on their vessels trading in East Africa, while the English and Dutch competition were constraining what was left of the former Portuguese trade monopoly. Portugal's declining sea power was being tested in the Persian Gulf at precisely the time when the siege of Fort São Jesus was put in place. In response, the 42-gun Portuguese frigate *Santo Antonio de Tanná*, origi-nally built in Bassein, India, led a squadron from Goa, Portugal's major colony on India's west coast, to break the siege. Delivering supplies and men in the winter of 1696, *Santo Antonio de Tanná* headed for Mozambique, reluctantly re-turning to Mombasa the following year to aid the beleaguered fort once more. By this time, Portugal's India fleet consisted of only five **frigates**, warships built for speed and maneuverability, but not quite as large ships-of-the line, and 17 smaller vessels. Endangering *Santo Antonio de Tanná*, therefore, was a risk not taken lightly. Finding itself under enemy fire upon arrival, the frigate eventu-ally lost all of its mooring lines and ran aground on a reef adjacent to the fort. In the course of salvage operations the ship sank below the reef as the stranded Portuguese forces were preparing to scuttle it in order to prevent enemy capture. A little more than a year later, in December 1698, Fort São Jesus surrendered.

In 1976, the Institute of Nautical Archaeology and the National Museums of Kenya's Fort Jesus Museum partnered to investigate the site. The National Museum of Kenya funded the first conservation laboratory specializing in wa-terlogged materials in Africa to treat the artifacts recovered from *Santo Antonio de Tanná*, many of which are now on display at Fort Jesus. Among the 15,000 artifacts recovered between 1977 and 1980 were iron shot, musket shot, a sword hilt, wooden powder flasks, ceramic incendiary devices, grenades, cannon quoins used to adjust the angle of gun carriages, and two bronze swivel guns. Examination of the ordnance revealed that *Santo Antonio de Tanná* was carrying a very small arms complement for the vessel's size and mission when it sank; this, together with the lack of standardization in the ordnance assemblage, and the fact that guns had to be taken from Murmugao Fortress in India to aug-ment Santo *Antonio de Tanná*'s own before the relief mission, reflected the chal-lenging economic conditions facing the Portuguese by this time. The hull of the vessel, which was reburied after the excavation, revealed a lightly built *fragata*, an agile Portuguese seagoing warship with two decks. The study of the hull also demonstrated that cargo capacity was afforded greater importance than either speed or maneuverability, indicating the importance of the vessel's trading role.

With the close of the 17th century, Portugal's hegemony of the East India trade network was behind it; as rivals were developing new and specialized ship designs, the Portuguese appear to have held fast to a tradition that would cost-effectively enable them to rely on less-specialized designs capable of serving in multiple capacities. Unfortunately, as much has been lost by the looting and commercial salvaging of Iberian vessels over the last several decades, only additional archaeological research will help provide a fuller picture of this tumultuous time in history.[16]

## Piracy

Just as the lines between merchant vessels and warships often blurred, the same can be said for those vessels engaged in the act of piracy. Evidence of piracy in the archaeological record is millennia-old, with the Kyrenia shipwreck of the 4th century BCE potentially having fallen victim (chapter 11). Piracy has plagued merchant vessels across the globe with evidence and reports of piracy evident in nearly every period. No age, however, has come to be associated more with piracy than the often-romanticized New World of the 17th and 18th centuries.

In November 1996, researchers in North Carolina discovered a tangible link to the infamous pirate Edward Teach, more commonly known as Blackbeard. Nearly 300 years earlier, in June 1718, Blackbeard purposefully grounded his 40-gun ship *Queen Anne's Revenge* alongside the sloop *Adventure* in an attempt to rid himself of the vessel. Captured less than a year earlier as the French vessel *La Concorde*, which had served as a privateer and then a slave trader, the ship was taken by Blackbeard and his company as it approached Martinique in the West Indies. Blackbeard also took with him 14 French crewmen and as many as 100 enslaved Africans, capturing several other vessels on his way to the Bay of Honduras. His fleet, eventually consisting of the renamed *Queen Anne's Revenge* and three sloops, sailed up the Atlantic seaboard sealing the port of Charleston, preventing shipping traffic and seizing additional vessels. Extracting ransom from the city, the flotilla continued up the coast to where *Queen Anne's Revenge* was abandoned. Within a few months, Blackbeard, who had continued to raid along the Atlantic coast from Pennsylvania to Bermuda, was killed by a contingent sent by Virginia's Governor to end his reign of terror.

It was only after eight years of surveying under a North Carolina state permit that Intersal, Inc. located the remains of an early 18th century shipwreck by employing archival research, a magnetometer, and divers. Nine cannon and two large anchors were originally observed on the site, which included cannonballs and a bronze bell stamped with the date 1705 that was recovered early on in an attempt to identify the wreck. A four-week expedition launched in 1997 documented the wreck further using nondestructive archaeological techniques and sampling. The investigation found 6 additional cannon, a grappling hook, rigging elements, and a large number of ballast stones and concretions. It became clear that the site would yield thousands of artifacts, and that it carried a large assortment of arms. Archaeological fieldwork in 1998 continued to provide intriguing evidence linking the discovered shipwreck to *Queen Anne's Revenge*. The bow pointed to shore according to the position of its anchors and had not suffered from a catastrophic wrecking event, which would have spread its contents across a far larger area. The artifact assemblage, which by that time included a total of 18 cannon and a small amount of gold dust, continued to resemble the wreck of *Whydah*, a near contemporary pirate vessel located in 1984. Meanwhile, geophysical studies revealed that over the course of the last three centuries in at least five instances the adjacent inlet passage had migrated over the wreck, scouring the site and settling artifacts, subsequently reburying it with sand as the entrance moved farther on. During the fall of 1999, archaeologists observed considerable damage to the site caused by a series of hurricanes that had impacted the area that year, prompting an emergency recovery that ultimately evolved into a longterm excavation of the site. More than 300,000 artifacts had been recovered through 2017, including elements of the hull and 24 of the approximately 30 cannon located on the site.

Among the first finds to be recovered were a blunderbuss and a brass musketoon barrel, representing short-range, close-combat firearms often favored by pirates. These were followed by thousands of small-caliber lead shot, grenades, and a diverse and wide assortment of arms. A concreted conglomerate of small lead shot, nails, and glass shards surrounded by fabric may have represented the remains of cannon bag shot, intended to inflict significant damage to personnel at close range. One cannon was found loaded, containing wads of cordage and three worn wrought-iron drift pin fragments, along with a round iron shot and powder residue; known as langrage, this crude kind of projectile was used by privateers, pirates, and merchantmen to inflict damage on personnel, masts, and the sails of an adversary. Langrage carried a significant risk to the gunners themselves and was likely avoided in standard military practice. This was not the only gun found loaded for combat, and the collection of recovered guns represents an array of sizes and sources of origin, including England, France, and Sweden. The assortment lacks the typical regimented order one would expect to find in a naval warship. As this intriguing site continues to be studied, and recovered artifacts complete conservation in the purpose-built *Queen Anne's Revenge* Laboratory, archaeologists will continue to learn more about artifact patterns and assemblages that can be associated with pirate vessels.[17]

## Pressed Into Service

Much as the pirate vessel *Queen Anne's Revenge* represents a captured privateer and slave trader, many naval vessels themselves originated as merchant vessels converted into service. In the year 1813, the armed schooners *Hamilton* and *Scourge* formed part of the American Squadron facing the British in a bid to control Lake Ontario. The previous year, the United States had declared war on Britain over maritime rights, including the impressment of American sailors by the British Royal Navy. The conflict came to be known as the War of 1812 and neither side was prepared for conflict. On the naval front, following a series of single-ship engagements, the adversaries turned to shipwrightry for control of the Great Lakes. *Hamilton*, the former merchant schooner *Diana*, and *Scourge*, the former merchant schooner *Lord Nelson*, were purchased and seized, respectively, by the US Navy. The vessels were refitted, armed, and pressed into service. The weight of the added guns, however, compromised their seaworthiness, making the schooners unstable by upsetting their center of balance. In a sudden early morning squall, *Hamilton* and *Scourge*, at the time preparing to confront the British fleet off Niagara, listed and foundered. Fifty-three men were lost, making this the single greatest loss-of-life incident in the Great Lakes during the war.

More than 150 years later, in 1971, the Royal Ontario Museum set out to find the two wrecked schooners using a magnetometer and a side-scan sonar. In 1973, a promising target was identified. Two years later the location of both wrecks was confirmed, and a remotely operated vehicle relayed images of *Hamilton* to the surface that conveyed an exceptional state of preservation. The near-freezing, deep, dark, and virtually currentless freshwater of Lake Ontario had permitted the vessels to resist deterioration, remaining upright with intact bowsprits, figureheads, and masts still standing in about 90 m (300 ft) of water. The vessels were designated a National Historic Site of Canada in 1976, and in 1982 a full-scale photographic survey resulted in their first archaeological documentation (figure 12.10). A series of nonintrusive investigations followed over the next two decades. These led, between 2005 and 2009, to the most thorough survey to date, which permitted for 3D mapping and high-definition recording of the wrecks. Unfortunately, the latest survey also confirmed reports of technical divers who had observed invasive quagga mussels colonizing the wrecks as early as 2000. The degree to which these mussels have and continue to cause physical or chemical deterioration of the preserved schooners is yet to be fully determined; however, this new threat is not limited to *Hamilton* and *Scourge*. In recent years additional impressively preserved wreck sites have been located in the Great Lakes, including the American Revolution–era gunboat *Spitfire* discovered in 1997 in Lake Champlain, and the contemporary 22-gun HMS *Ontario* located in 2008 in Lake Ontario. Evaluating the effect of and response to invasive quagga and zebra mussels on the preservation of these fragile archaeological sites in the Great Lakes are among the most complex challenges faced by the heritage managers responsible for these resources (see chapter 7).[18]

### STEAM AND SHELLS

The 19th century began with Britain confirming its naval supremacy through victory at the Battle of Trafalgar in 1805, when 60 ships-of-the-line belonging to the

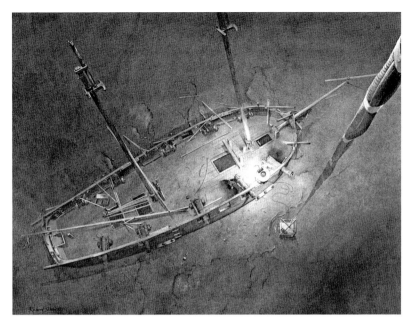

**Figure 12.10** Reconstructed view of the 1982 archaeological investigation of *Scourge* illustrating the exceptional state of preservation of the vessel. (Courtesy of Richard Schlecht/National Geographic Creative)

British, French, and Spanish fleets engaged in a pivotal contest that would end Napoleon's aspirations of invading the island nation. The War of 1812 that followed did not have such lasting geopolitical effects, but it did signal a new era of rapid and pivotal advancements in naval warfare; advancements that would soon leave navies unrecognizable to the sailors who fought at Trafalgar. In October 1814, the newly developed steam engine first appeared in warships. *Demologos*, designed for the US Navy by engineer Robert Fulton, was a wooden catamaran armed with 32-pounder guns and propelled by a single, centrally positioned and protected paddle wheel. Though it never saw action, as it was built toward the end of the war, it was a harbinger of things to come.

By 1827, the War of Greek Independence had raged on for several years as a newly forming Greek state was attempting to wrestle itself free from the Ottoman Empire. The Battle of Navarino, fought in October of that year, would alter the balance of power and ultimately lead to the creation of an independent Kingdom of Greece. In the southwest corner of the Peloponnese peninsula, the allied squadrons of Britain, France, and Russia, which had arrived to negotiate an armistice, came face to face with a far larger contingent of Ottoman Turkish and Egyptian vessels. In a decisive victory marking the final major engagement between sailing warships, the superior ships, guns, and crews of the allies effectively sunk the Ottoman fleet. The millennia-old means of propulsion would soon give way to the power of steam.

The naval powers met again within a few decades during the Crimean War, fought between 1854 and 1856. This time, Britain, France, and Ottoman Turkey faced Russia. Naval vessels were now for the first time powered by steam, firing explosive shells as opposed to solid iron shot, and protected by armor. Around this time, breech-loading guns were introduced, drastically decreasing the time it took to reload weapons, and limiting the exposure of personnel. Rifling of gun barrels added spin to projectiles, lending them greater force and accuracy. The Civil War in the United States, fought between 1861 and 1865, produced two more revolutionary advancements in naval warfare: The first cemented the shift from the wooden-hulled sailing warship to iron-hulled, steam-propelled vessels; the second applied improvements in boiler technology and surface ship design to the underwater realm.

During the Civil War, the Union Navy blockaded all Southern ports, severely inhibiting their commercial viability. The Confederacy needed relief, which in part came from the famed blockade runners; however, they did not suffice. Necessity spurred on risk, innovation, and the application of new naval technologies to help break the Union blockade. On 8 March 1862, a steam-powered ironclad vessel, CSS *Virginia*, armed with a ram and a small number of guns, set out to wreak havoc among the wooden-hulled Union ships patrolling Hampton Roads, Virginia. The armored vessel caused considerable damage to USS *Congress* on the way to sinking USS *Cumberland*, before returning to USS *Congress* and setting it ablaze. With its two large guns out of order, armor loosened, and ram lost during the engagement, CSS *Virginia* went on to attack USS *Minnesota*, damaging the enemy vessel before retiring from the engagement. The following day, 9 March 1862, marked a new era. The Union ironclad USS *Monitor* had transited from New York, arriving in Hampton Roads to meet CSS *Virginia* at daybreak, intercepting the oncoming renewed attack on USS *Minnesota*. Armed with two 11-inch guns encased within a rotating turret, the steam-propelled USS *Monitor* could angle its guns irrespective of its own heading, marking the end of the line of battle. Fighting the Confederate ironclad to a standstill after a four-hour engagement, with both warships damaged and running low on shot, USS *Monitor* kept the Union blockade intact as CSS *Virginia* retired. The world had just witnessed the first naval engagement between iron-armored warships (figure 12.11).

In December of the same year, USS *Monitor* departed Virginia under tow for Beaufort, North Carolina. On New Year's Eve, 1862, the ironclad foundered in a storm off Cape Hatteras, killing four officers and 12 sailors. More than a century later, in 1973, a team of scientists from Duke University, the North Carolina Department of Cultural Resources, the Massachusetts Institute of Technology, and National Geographic Society discovered its inverted hull resting on the seafloor. In 1975 the site was designated the first National Marine Sanctuary in the United States, under the management of the National Oceanic and Atmospheric Administration (NOAA). Following several site investigations and a careful consideration of options, NOAA issued a long-term management plan for the site in 1998, determining that the collapse of *Monitor*'s hull was imminent. A difficult decision was made to recover certain key artifacts and components of the vessel, in the process assisting with the stabilization of the remaining site in situ. Within a month, *Monitor*'s propeller and sections of the propeller shaft were recovered, followed by multiple expeditions culminating in the 2002 recovery of *Monitor*'s 30-ton steam engine, revolving gun turret, and guns. These iconic elements of the ironclad, along with thousands of additional artifacts, are currently undergoing

PUBLISHED BY CURRIER & IVES.
MINNESOTA.
Entered according to act of Congress, in the year 1862, by Currier & Ives, in the Clerks Office of the District Court of the United States, for the Southern District of New York
152 NASSAU ST NEW YORK.
REBEL STEAMERS.

THE FIRST FIGHT BETWEEN IRON CLAD SHIPS OF WAR.

TERRIFIC COMBAT BETWEEN THE "MONITOR" 2 GUNS & "MERRIMAC" 10 GUNS.

IN HAMPTON ROADS, MARCH 9TH 1862.

In which the little "Monitor" whipped the "Merrimac" and the whole "School" of Rebel Steamers.

**Figure 12.11**  1862 Currier & Ives lithograph based on a sketch by F. Newman memorializing the first battle between ironclad vessels USS *Monitor* and CSS *Virginia* (formerly *Merrimack*). (Courtesy of the Chrysler Museum of Art. Museum Collection # 74.0.31)

conservation and study at a purpose-built facility associated with the Mariner's Museum in Newport News, Virginia.[19]

A few years after the Battle of Hampton Roads, in February 1864, the sinking of USS *Housatonic* by a submarine warship demonstrated to the world that the best-prepared surface ship was entirely vulnerable to underwater attack. *H. L. Hunley* was not the first submarine to have been developed; however, it was the first to sink an enemy vessel in combat, altering the perception of submarine warfare's potential. Building on a series of prototypes, *H. L. Hunley*, which itself sank and was recovered twice in the course of preparing for deployment, was to serve as the weapon that would loosen the Union's blockade around the port of Charleston. As the sun set on 17 February 1864, the hand-crank-propelled submarine made of repurposed boiler material set out to accomplish its objective. Watchmen aboard the barely two-year-old USS *Housatonic*, which was enforcing the blockade, observed what seemed at first to be a porpoise. Within moments, as *H. L. Hunley* was receiving fire from small arms, the submarine's torpedo, tethered to a rigid spar fixed to the bow of the submersible, exploded, tearing a hole in the side of *Housatonic* large enough to drive a horse and cart through. Nearly every man aboard the ship was thrown to the deck by the force of the explosion; one minute later, *Housatonic*'s stern touched bottom. Though successful in accomplishing its mission, *H. L. Hunley* never returned to shore. The Confederacy was never able to challenge the blockade in the same way again, and the siege of Charleston was never lifted. One year to the day after *H. L. Hunley*'s attack, the city fell to the Union Army.[21]

In May 1995, more than 130 years after the submarine was last seen and following a 14-year search, a partnership between the nonprofit National Underwater and Marine Agency and the South Carolina Institute of Anthropology and Archaeology (SCIAA) discovered *H. L. Hunley*'s resting place. The submarine was buried in sediment about 300 m (ca. 1000 ft) east of the wreck of USS *Housatonic*. Following a site assessment in 1996 by the United States National Park Service, Naval Historical Center (now Naval History and Heritage Command), and SCIAA, confirming the identity of the find and determining its state of preservation, an ambitious project was launched to recover the submarine. In August of 2000, *H. L. Hunley* broke the surface of the water and was placed in a custom-designed facility, the Warren Lasch Conservation Center, now part of Clemson University. What followed were six months of meticulous excavation of the interior of the submarine, which was entirely filled with sediment. The remains of all eight of the vessel's crew were preserved inside, along with personal effects such as jewelry and a gold pocket watch, as well as utilitarian items such as a canteen, binoculars, and an oil can. Forensic analysis, combined with genealogical study, has revealed much about the men, whose remains were reinterred in the historic Magnolia Cemetery in Charleston in 2004. The submarine itself is still under conservation, with removal of an accrued concretion layer beginning in 2014 and desalination still underway (figure 12.12). The mystery of what sunk *H. L. Hunley* remains to be solved.[21]

Within 50 years of the US Civil War, naval warfare would be fundamentally transformed again. In 1906, the launching of HMS *Dreadnought* made all other warships obsolete. Powered by steam turbines, the steel-armored battleship could make 21 knots and carried ten 12-inch guns in twin turrets. The vessel sparked an arms race and the modern era of naval warships. Ten years later, in 1916, the two greatest naval powers of the time—Britain and Germany—met off the coast of Denmark for what would be the largest naval battle of World War I. By the time it was over, the Battle of Jutland claimed 25 ships and more than 8,500 men. Yet it also served as the last full-scale engagement between battleships, for Germany was unable to contest British control of the seas for the remainder of the war, and developments in naval warfare altered the balance of naval power in World War II.

Advancements over and below water would take center stage by the second quarter of the 20th century. In January 1911, the light cruiser USS *Birmingham* served as the cradle of naval aviation, launching the first naval aircraft into flight. Soon, the aircraft carrier would become the iconic form of naval power projection, playing a pivotal role in the outcome of World War II's Pacific Theater. Meanwhile, below water, the German U-boat threat matured to pose a significant hazard for merchantmen and warships alike.

### OIL AND STEEL

Maritime archaeology of 20th-century naval warfare is somewhat different than the study of the centuries and millennia that preceded it. The rate of change aside, nuclear submarines, jet-powered aircraft, and engagements of a scale unimaginable prior to the course of two world wars have left behind physical and emotional scars that transcend cultural heritage sensitivities. Many of the lost vessels serve as war graves, the final resting places of those sailors who sacrificed for their cause and country. Oil, which replaced coal as the dominant fuel by the end of World War I, now poses a potential environmental hazard as it sits trapped in the hulls of hundreds of ships across the globe. Public safety concerns are also raised by the unexploded ordnance

**Figure 12.12** The *H. L. Hunley* submarine immersed in its purpose-built conservation vat at the Warren Lasch Conservation Center. (Courtesy of Friends of the Hunley)

associated with these wreck sites. At the same time, oral histories, firsthand accounts, and mass-production of vessels and aircraft all put into question the value of marine archaeology in this context. To these questions, archaeologists have responded with respect and perseverance, filling in or correcting the historical record, while at the same time recognizing the broader importance of these sites. After all, simply because these traces of naval warfare are more recent and made of more durable materials does not mean that they do not have much to teach us; nor will they be preserved for future generations without a determined effort. The plethora of archaeological investigations directed at more recent heritage sites is a testament to what can be learned and the multi-stakeholder interest that surrounds these resources.[22]

The larger, metal hulls of modern warfare have also enabled the archaeological study of submerged battlefields or collections of craft to a degree that was previously harder to attain. Recent archaeological investigations of the Battle of Jutland have identified 22 of those vessels, and have aimed to complement what is known to have transpired through the often-times-conflicting historical and eyewitness accounts.[23] As part of the armistice agreement that concluded World War I, the ships of the German High Seas Fleet were interned in the waters of Scapa Flow, a large natural harbor in the north of Scotland which served as Britain's main naval base during both World Wars. In June 1919, under the impression that the armistice talks were about to falter, 52 of the 74 interned German naval vessels were sunk at the hands of their own crews to prevent the ships from being used against Germany in future conflicts. Only seven wrecks, those of three battleships and four cruisers, have survived subsequent salvage and scrapping efforts (figure 12.13). Many of the ships sunk during the D-Day

**Figure 12.13** Rendering of the wreck of light cruiser SMS *Cöln*, scuttled in Scapa Flow on 21 June 1919. (Courtesy of 3deep Media/Mike Postons).

landings on Normandy in World War II suffered a similar fate, as steel became a valuable and scarce commodity in the interwar and postwar periods. Historic Scotland, and the US Naval History and Heritage Command, respectively, have both launched surveys to better understand the sites that remain. In the case of the latter, the host nation France is also in the process of nominating the D-Day beaches as a UNESCO World Heritage site. Illegal scrapping remains to this day a serious threat to 20th-century naval warship wrecks, as evidenced by the recent destruction of British, Dutch, Australian, and American vessels in the Java Sea and beyond. Fortunately, however, some of the most pivotal engagements ever fought at sea are still reflected on the seafloor. Among the most striking examples are the dozens of Allied and Imperial Japanese Navy warships in Ironbottom Sound, in the Solomon Islands. These wrecks, associated with key naval battles of World War II, were first explored and documented in 1992 by oceanographer Dr. Robert Ballard, who had alongside him veterans of the Naval Battle of Guadalcanal. Around the same time, the US National Park Service was concluding its own assessment of the vessels sunk by the 1946 atomic bomb tests of Operation Crossroads in Bikini Atoll, one of the first assemblages of mid-20th century naval ships to be studied from a submerged cultural resources management perspective. More recently, archaeologists have been able to undertake even broader theatre-of-operation studies, such as assessing over 60 World War I and World War II U-boat wrecks in the English Channel, employing archaeological data to correct the imperfect historical record of where each vessel reportedly sank, and the relationship between them.[24]

Beyond naval battlefields, the public's captivation with World War II, which has in part driven research and exploration priorities, encompasses iconic wreck sites, whether close to shore, such as the USS *Arizona* memorial and National Historic Landmark in Hawaii, or in deep water. The sinking of USS *Indianapolis* at the conclusion of the war has been regarded as one of the most dramatic losses of life at sea. Having just completed a secret mission of delivering components of the atomic bomb later used on Hiroshima, USS *Indianapolis* had left Guam heading west when it was torpedoed by the Japanese submarine I-58 in July 1945. Roughly 400 of the nearly 1,200 sailors on board died in the initial attack; however, only 300 or so survived the subsequent four to five days of drifting at sea, succumbing to hypothermia, dehydration, exposure, and shark attacks. The story inspired research teams including Vulcan, supported by philanthropist and Microsoft co-founder Paul Allen, to search for the wreck in time for the commemoration of the 75th anniversary of its loss, and while a few of the survivors were still with us. Combining the latest in remote sensing technologies, archival research, and funding, Vulcan located the wreck at a depth of about 5,500 m (ca. 18,000 ft) in the Pacific Ocean during the summer of 2017, bringing closure to the families of the lost, and documenting the wreck's impressive state of preservation.[25]

The technologies and techniques applied in the 2017 discovery of USS *Indianapolis* have come a long way since they were first employed in the latter part of the 20th century. The interest in the wrecks of iconic ships of war, however, has spanned this period of development. One of the first deepwater archaeological surveys was tied to one of most powerful battleships ever built, *Bismarck*. The battleship served as the symbol of German naval power as it embarked on its first and only mission in May 1941, aiming to definitively alter the balance of power in the Atlantic. *Bismarck* was spotted by a British reconnaissance aircraft as it was leaving the Norwegian coast, leading the Royal Navy to concentrate its naval forces on the vessel's possible routes into the Atlantic Ocean. In one of the most symbolic naval engagements of the war, *Bismarck* and heavy cruiser *Prinz Eugen* were first met by battle cruiser HMS *Hood* and HMS *Prince of Wales*; the early round went to the *Bismarck*, which sank HMS *Hood* sending shockwaves through London. The chase only intensified; a torpedo biplane attack from the British aircraft carrier *Victorious* was followed by a second biplane attack from carrier HMS *Ark Royal* a day later, as *Bismarck* steamed toward the air cover provided by German airplanes in France. The second attack proved fateful, hitting the giant's stern and disabling its rudder. What followed was an all-out assault that found *Bismarck* engaging with British battleships *King George* and *Rodney*, until heavy cruiser *Dorsetshire* ultimately sank the German battleship with torpedoes. Two found their mark, though by that time the order to scuttle and abandon the ship had already been given. This was confirmed by Dr. Ballard when in 1989 he located the wreck of *Bismarck*, nearly 4,800 m (ca. 15,750 ft) below the surface sitting upright on the seafloor. There was no sign of implosion damage, caused by air trapped within the hull of a vessel succumbing to the enormous pressures of the deep; the ship had been full of water before it sank, as would be the case if it had indeed been scuttled before the torpedoes struck.[26]

### FLIGHT

It is telling that what incapacitated the German battleship *Bismarck* was not the mighty force of a comparable vessel, but an obsolete biplane. By the end of the war, the modern symbol of naval power shifted to the aircraft carrier, representing the combined might of scores of naval fighter planes and bombers (figure 12.14). Though long recognized for their value as reconstituted museum pieces, and at times salvaged unceremoniously from the seafloor for parts or reconstructions, beginning in the 1990s sunken naval aircraft have been viewed across the world as submerged cultural resources meriting preservation. A recent example of such consideration comes from aircraft sunk during the Japanese air raid of Darwin, Australia, on 19 February 1942, which constituted the single largest attack on Australia by a foreign power, and the first of scores of Japanese air raids against the country during World War II.

**Figure 12.14** USS *Lexington* (CV-2) aircraft carrier underway. (Courtesy of the Naval History and Heritage Command, NH 63549)

In 2008, a gas pipeline development project led by INPEX Operations Australia necessitated dredging along the route of the pipeline near shore installations in Darwin Harbour. Six Consolidated PBY Catalina amphibious aircraft were known to be located in the harbor's East Arm, three belonging to the Royal Australian Air Force and three, associated with the Japanese air raid, to the United States Navy. Archaeological investigations in 1999–2000 had documented and positively identified five of these aircraft. Predisturbance surveys conducted in preparation for the development project identified the position of the sixth aircraft and nearshore infrastructure and associated dredging was subsequently designed to avoid disturbance of all six aircraft wrecks. Additional marine geophysical surveys using side-scan sonar, multibeam echosounder, and gradiometer sensors continued to be conducted along the prescribed pipeline route and, in 2011, previously unidentified aircraft components associated with a US Navy PBY Catalina were located. By this time the development project was in a rather advanced stage, meaning that rerouting the pipeline was no longer possible. In coordination with appropriate authorities in both Australia and the United States, an archaeological consultant documented the wreckage components in situ and developed detailed recovery methodologies for each. Once recovered, the components were documented once more using a 3D scanner, and were then redeposited in proximity to the aircraft they were associated with. The three PBY Catalina aircraft involved in the Japanese air raid were all declared heritage places by the Northern Territory Government. The tide has turned for naval aviation archaeology and hopefully these heritage sites will soon be universally regarded as being equally as important as contemporary naval shipwreck sites.[27]

### THE NUCLEAR AGE

No discussion of naval warfare toward the end of the 20th century could be complete without reference to the silent service. *H. L. Hunley* opened the prospect of undersea naval warfare. By the 1880s, the internal combustion engine, lead-acid storage battery, and self-propelled torpedoes, had developed to a point where naval designers began proposing submarine prototypes to navies in Europe and the United States. Submarines, and in particular German U-boats, struck fear among merchant and naval vessels during both World Wars, leading to the trans-Atlantic convoy system in an effort to protect commerce, as well as antisubmarine warfare tactics and weapons, such as depth charges. It was not, however, until 1954, when USS *Nautilus* (SSN 571) was launched that the submarine adopted its most lethal form (figure 12.15). *Nautilus* was the first nuclear-powered submarine in the world, meaning that it could remain submerged for far greater periods of time, travel faster underwater than any previous vessel, and do so nearly silently. *Nautilus* was designated as a National Historic Landmark in the United States in 1982 for its pioneering role, prior to being put on display at the Submarine Force Museum in Groton, Connecticut. Shortly after the launch of *Nautilus*, submarines came to be armed with ballistic missiles, putting in place a key element of the nuclear deterrence strategy that played such a pivotal role during the Cold War. A number of these nuclear-powered submarines now rest on the seafloor, poised to become cultural heritage sites of the future.[28]

### SUMMARY

The last few millennia, and in particular the last two hundred years, have seen a tremendous advance in the way our species has pursued the conquest and control of the seas. Developments in shipbuilding, sailing rigs, and related technologies spurred on the human-propelled oared galleys that would dominate for centuries. Oars gave way to sails, then to coal-powered steam, oil, and finally nuclear fuel. Ramming gave way to boarding, which gave way to guns, torpedoes,

**Figure 12.15** USS *Nautilus* (SSN-571) underway in June 1965. (Courtesy of the National Archives and Records Administration, K-30256)

and air-dropped bombs. The ships themselves grew in size and capabilities, culminating in the naval aircraft carriers of the 20th century, when combatants no longer needed to see the enemy or engage with them directly. These dramatic developments all accentuate the role of naval warfare in human societies, as dominion of the seas has, until recently, been the only means through which to conquer, vanquish, or control an enemy whose land borders you do not share. Throughout recorded history, advanced and iconic naval vessels have been the means through which to project power to distant foes and control over restless allies. Marine archaeology has been able to tell the story of much of this development, and is continually refining and complementing what is known about some of the most dramatic moments in human history.

### DISCUSSION QUESTIONS

1. What do you regard as the most pivotal developments in naval ship construction over the last few millennia?

2. How have naval shipbuilders adapted their vessels to different climates and geographical contexts over time?
3. Identify historical examples of naval vessels being used to project power. Is this practice still in place, and has it been effective?
4. What impact have changes in the means of propulsion of naval vessels had on their development?
5. Have naval ships spurred on technological developments, or merely benefited from them?

## FURTHER READING

Broadwater, J.D. (2012). *USS* Monitor: *A Historic Ship Completes Its Final Voyage.* Texas A&M University Press, College Station.

Delgado, J. (2019). *War at Sea.* Oxford University Press, New York.

Gardiner, R. (1995). *The Age of the Galley: Mediterranean Oared Vessels since Pre-Classical Times.* Conway Maritime Press, London.

Hocker, F. (2011). *Vasa.* Oxbow Books, Oxford.

Marsden, P. (2003). *Sealed by Time: The Loss and Recovery of the* Mary Rose. *The Archaeology of the* Mary Rose *Volume I.* Oxbow Books, Oxford.

Neyland, R. and H.G. Brown, Eds. (2016). H.L. Hunley *Recovery Operations.* Naval History and Heritage Command, Washington, DC.

Sasaki R.J. (2015). *The Origins of the Lost Fleet of the Mongol Empire.* Texas A&M University Press, College Station.

Skowronek, R. and C. Ewen, Eds. (2006). *X Marks the Spot: The Archaeology of Piracy.* University Press of Florida, Gainesville.

PRESERVING OUR MARITIME HERITAGE

## CHAPTER 13

# MANAGING AND VALUING UNDERWATER CULTURAL HERITAGE

## FOCUS QUESTIONS

- What types of maritime archaeological sites are there, and how do they differ in what they can teach us about the past?
- How can the preservation of artifacts in submerged environments, which tends to be better than on land, improve our understanding of past cultures?
- How can we gather data in a precise and rigorous way while still maintaining archaeological sites and the data they contain for future societies?
- How do we balance the needs of modern societies with the preservation of cultural heritage sites?

## HERITAGE MANAGEMENT

This chapter begins the final section of the book, in which we discuss how both national governments and individuals can be involved in protecting maritime and underwater archaeological sites. The management of underwater cultural heritage is just as important to the field of maritime and underwater archaeology as conducting research on archaeological sites. Yet, even though the scientific and technical standards that apply to archaeological research are coalescing around a fairly universal set of approaches that are evolving in tandem across geographic regions, underwater cultural heritage management practices vary greatly across the globe. Underpinning this diversity are historical trends, cultural norms, available resources, and legislative frameworks. In some societies, underwater cultural heritage is managed as is any other cultural property on land. In many others, underwater cultural heritage is viewed as something different, requiring its own legislation and management approaches. Elsewhere still, it has yet to be recognized as a contributing element to a society's cultural narrative. This chapter will concentrate on the particularities of managing underwater cultural heritage, though the reader may note several areas of overlap with the management of cultural heritage on land, particularly when concerning maritime resources in the foreshore environment.

The primary resolution that a society must come to—the one that underpins all others—is that underwater cultural heritage retains value, and therefore merits treatment as a public asset to be preserved and understood. This value may be attributed to the diverse knowledge about our past contained within heritage sites as discussed in previous chapters, or to the broader relationship between underwater cultural heritage and the environment or the economy. Once a decision has been made to consider underwater cultural heritage sites as valuable, the key questions that follow are which classes of archaeological sites benefit from protected status, and what types of protective measures apply to such archaeological sites. Fundamentally, these questions involve addressing the balance between the rights of an individual or a small group to attain some form of private gain from exploiting or ignoring heritage sites, and the benefits to a society as a whole that are gained from preserving, learning, and developing communal economic gain from them. Addressing this balance, and answering these questions, typically leads to the establishment of a legislative framework, which in turn leads to the employment of cultural heritage managers, the increased cultivation of a public awareness of the importance of underwater cultural heritage, and ultimately—hopefully—a cycle of public engagement that continually refines this process. It is therefore the responsibility of any archaeologist to help foster a better public understanding and appreciation of cultural heritage sites.

### THE VALUE OF UNDERWATER CULTURAL HERITAGE

The value of cultural heritage is ubiquitously recognized, questioned, and reassessed. The overall trend in the latter part of the 20th century, however, was to intensify efforts to preserve cultural heritage sites because of the greater understanding they foster regarding our identities, cultures, and past. United National Educational Scientific and Cultural Organization (UNESCO) international agreements instituted World Heritage Sites, prohibited the illegal trade of antiquities, emphasized multinational cooperation in the protection of underwater cultural heritage, and promoted care for cultural property even in times of war.[1] On a national level, countries have been implementing antiquities laws recognizing the value of their cultural heritage since the 19th century, beginning with Greece in 1834. Yet the discussion remains open, and questions of value persist. Why should maritime cultural heritage sites be viewed as a public good to be preserved? And how can the worth of something whose utility is recognized (though not always fully supported) on such a widespread level and across societies be so challenging to convey?

# The continuing case for preserving (underwater) cultural heritage

A country's laws are often seen as a reflection of that society's ethics and norms. Given the plethora of laws, international agreements, court cases, and treaties in existence, it would seem the main philosophical divide between whether cultural heritage is communal and worth preserving or whether it may be exploited for private purposes has been settled. This, however, is not entirely the case. Ethics do not carry universal validity, and neither do laws. It is important to remember that something of "heritage value" to one group or nation may carry no such value to another. Concepts of historic preservation have not developed in corresponding manners among nations with disparate economic, social, cultural, and political priorities. Furthermore, as nations have established heritage preservation frameworks independently of each other, areas between them, such as the high seas, are marred by competing notions of ownership, rights, and responsibilities. Sunken vessels present a unique set of challenges as they were originally constructed to transcend cultural and political boundaries. In this opaque arena, private economic interests have at times managed to supersede the interests of preserving cultural heritage, whether through legal or illicit activities. Along with such material culture, knowledge about the human experience is irretrievably lost.

## DETERMINING WHAT SHOULD BE PRESERVED

There is no universally applicable set of standards establishing what material traces of the past located underwater are worthy of consideration and preservation as underwater cultural heritage. Disparate approaches to underwater cultural heritage reflect broader societal discussions of what heritage sites are worthy of preserving. Certain societies have attempted to establish wide-ranging criteria that guide the determination of a site's heritage value (e.g., association with an important person, event, technological achievement). Others set specific definitions for what constitutes underwater cultural heritage; for example, historic shipwrecks (variously defined) and their cargo, but not historic aircraft wrecks. It seems most have opted to establish a generic cultural heritage definition and to rely on temporal horizons, which, once crossed, bestow various degrees of protections upon a site. In many cases, a series of chronological dates can be found in the same heritage law that serve as guides dictating when a site merits increasing levels of protection. These dates usually correspond to historical events (e.g., a national independence day) or eras important to a given society, with the older material typically viewed as deserving greater reverence.

Setting a particular date before which cultural material deserves protection serves as a clear marker when it comes to uniformly enforcing violations. However, it also potentially raises questions as to whether the practice relies on an arbitrary means of attributing heritage value. A further approach, which attempts to recognize the shifting perceptions of heritage value through time, while preserving a clear line for enforcement purposes, is one based on the establishment of what can be called a buffer period. This approach stipulates that if a site meets the generic definition of cultural heritage and is a certain number of years old, then it falls under the material to be considered for preservation. Establishing the extent of the buffer period often depends on the individual history of the society involved, but it permits for cultural material originally not covered by preservation laws to be gradually placed under the umbrella of protection as time goes on. In the international arena, discussed below, the UNESCO Convention follows just such a buffer period approach, placing the marker of 100 years as the delineating temporal horizon in the definition of underwater cultural heritage.

Ultimately, how heritage resources are delineated depend on societal concerns, norms, beliefs, and precedent. Even within the same nation, different jurisdictions may approach the matter in a disparate and sometimes inconsistent manner, such as the case of individual states within the United States of America. To some degree, these discrepancies challenge the ability of heritage professionals to develop a clear public message when promoting heritage preservation. On the other hand, such individualized approaches permit each society to attain a tailored balance of competing interests and priorities.

### BALANCING PRESERVATION MEASURES AND STAKEHOLDER EQUITIES

The sea affords human societies many benefits—it is a source of nourishment, energy, and natural resources, a means of efficiently transporting goods across large distances, a medium upon, over, and within which to wage war, and an environment of recreation. As a consequence, there are many different **stakeholders**—people or entities who have an interest or equity in a matter— whose concerns and priorities must be considered when assessing the types of protective measures that can be implemented in an attempt to preserve underwater cultural heritage sites.

Harbors with millennia-old histories and centuries-old infrastructure may remain in use today, necessitating that any attempt to preserve their historic fabric, both above and below water, be done in a manner that takes into account the economic impact of restricting current commerce. The energy industry's impressive technological advancements in obtaining hydrocarbons from ever-increasing depths—resulting in an extensive network of undersea pipelines, platforms, and structures—must cohabit the same marine space as underwater cultural heritage. The fishing industry's need to harvest marine fauna—at times using trawling methods that greatly impact the seafloor—has to coincide with a desire to protect historic resources located among the most fruitful fishing grounds.

In fact, underwater cultural heritage sites themselves can serve multiple functions: engines of economic growth through tourism, artificial reefs promoting healthy marine ecosystems, and, of course, repositories of knowledge about the past. This multifaceted nature of underwater cultural heritage is perhaps best exemplified in the relationship between heritage preservation professionals and the diving community. Sites themselves can serve as sustainers of a vibrant diving industry in the vicinity, but can also be a victim of the increased attention. An avocational diver may see little harm in picking up a small artifact as a memento—however, how many artifacts can be removed from a site before its value is significantly diminished, both as a repository of cultural knowledge, but also as a diving site? At times, the removal of simply one artifact may suffice in foiling any attempt by archaeologists to identify the craft and provide it with its historic context. Meanwhile, the anchoring of tens of vessels over a site will invariably lead to the destruction or displacement of artifacts below. Inexperienced divers may involuntarily cause harm when facing buoyancy issues. What could be seen as a set of adversarial interests—those of divers and archaeologists—can, however, also be viewed as potentially allied. It may be responsible divers who inform authorities of any clandestine efforts that impact a site. It may be divers who are able to help raise awareness among the public of the importance of underwater cultural heritage. And it may be the very interest expressed by responsible divers that serves as the economic impetus to place protective measures over a site in the first place. The extent of those measures may vary from complete prohibition of diving and anchoring—an approach that entirely favors preservation over diving equities—to restricting or controlling diving by providing mooring sites, limiting the numbers of visitors, or having authorities lead guided tours. Except in instances of particular concern over a site's preservation, the more common approaches attempt to harness the positive contributions of the responsible diving community and limit the potential harm through education and public outreach initiatives. Oftentimes, these approaches are accompanied by the deterrence provided through legal protection mechanisms and associated fines for willful disturbance of heritage sites.

Identifying and promoting an alliance of communities and interests is not always feasible. At times, interests are so diametrically opposed that both sets of equities cannot coexist in the same space. Bottom-trawling is so impactful to the seafloor that the benthic animal community and underwater cultural heritage sites are devastated by its impact. The two set of interests—trawling and heritage preservation—cannot be reconciled in the same physical region. Here, the balancing act of equities is much more challenging to address and often results in one party being significantly disadvantaged over another. For example, certain regions or marine preserves may prohibit bottom-trawling, but for any cultural heritage sites located in areas that are not protected, there is little that can typically be done to avoid impacts. Unfortunately, underwater cultural heritage is oftentimes a lower priority when evaluated against certain more powerful economic interests. However, here too opportunities for alliances exist, in this instance primarily with the environmental movement that shares common concerns about the impacts of bottom-trawling. In fact, as the world community begins to pay greater attention to the importance of our oceans, seas, and coastal areas in terms of their environmental, economic, and sustenance contributions, the premise of conservation and responsible use of marine resources, including underwater cultural heritage sites, will only gain in importance. It is incumbent upon archaeologists to recognize such heritage sites as more than repositories of knowledge, and view them as part of this greater, holistic approach to maritime resources, contributing to the conversation surrounding the sustainable use of our oceans.[2]

In most cases, clear preferences among different uses of marine resources must be established, though the impact of those preferences may be mitigated without one set of equities being greatly disadvantaged. In the case of undersea hydrocarbon exploitation, for example, energy companies often see it as in their best interests to thoroughly map the route of an intended pipeline with the highest resolution remote sensing equipment available. This allows engineers to appropriately plan and design the pipeline, minimizing uncertainties that could lead to delays and unexpected costs down the road. The same dataset that is collected for engineering purposes can serve as both an environmental and a cultural heritage planning resource, often leading to a better inventory of submerged heritage sites. Should a site be observed along the proposed pipeline track, it is relatively inexpensive in terms of the overall project budget for the pipeline to be slightly redesigned to avoid impacting it. At the same time, the company limits any uncertainties caused by a physical obstacle along the route and potentially benefits from a positive public reception of its discovery and its responsible actions in avoiding unnecessary impacts to underwater cultural heritage.

Although this account of possible stakeholders is not intended to be exhaustive, a final prominent group that must be discussed is the archaeological community itself, as, at times, archaeologists carry the potential to cause the greatest disturbance of all parties through activities such as full-scale excavations. As mentioned earlier, archaeology is a destructive science and excavations often necessitate the systematic disarticulation of cultural heritage sites. It is often incumbent upon government authorities to establish the standards and procedures through which a public asset, the underwater cultural heritage site, is to be scientifically excavated to preserve the greatest degree of knowledge and material. A balance must be struck between making such standards and professional qualifications so rigorous as to discourage research altogether, and so lacking or open-ended as to allow for the destruction of a site without the necessary documentation, conservation, analyses, and reporting.

Underwater cultural heritage management, therefore, often involves balancing disparate interests and equities. This is naturally reflected in the types of preservation measures that are adopted with the aim of maintaining the integrity and developing a better understanding of underwater cultural heritage. Such measures span from establishing maritime zones within which certain activities are banned or restricted, to requiring that heritage sites be taken into account during infrastructure projects, to controlling or limiting visitation or impactful activities, to establishing appropriate scientific protocols and standards for research-driven disturbance, and, importantly, to raising public awareness and appreciation of submerged cultural resources. Having accepted the value of underwater cultural heritage and determined what it consists of, a society is called upon to negotiate reaching this delicate balance of preservation measures through which to empower the heritage management professional.

## ESTABLISHING INTERNATIONAL NORMS: THE UNESCO CONVENTION ON THE PROTECTION OF THE UNDERWATER CULTURAL HERITAGE

Thus far the discussion has accentuated the variation that exists between individual societies when it comes to determining what constitutes underwater cultural heritage, as well as the degree and manner through which it should be preserved and researched. There is, however, a set of international ethical norms, principles and practices emerging that represent a consensus of appropriate standards intended to transcend individual societies. The sea is not limited to territorial waters within which an individual nation has full sovereignty, nor are the remnants of past human activity. These universal sets of norms aim, therefore, not only to guide the management of underwater cultural heritage within the territories of sovereign nations, but also in the international waters between them. They are most prominently codified in the UNESCO Convention on the Protection of the Underwater Cultural Heritage which was adopted in 2001 (figure 13.1).

The UNESCO Convention followed on the heels of another landmark agreement, the 1982 United Nations Convention on the Law of the Sea, which broached the concept of an international responsibility to protect underwater cultural heritage, as well as the precedent set by the International Council of Monuments and Sites in its 1996 International Charter on the Protection and Management of the Underwater Cultural Heritage. One of the basic aims of the 2001 UNESCO Convention was to extend to underwater cultural heritage the same protections offered to archaeological heritage sites on land.[3] At the same time, the United Nations General Assembly also noted a growing awareness that underwater cultural heritage was threatened by unauthorized activities, increasing commercial exploitation, and incidental negative impacts of other legitimate activities. The Convention, therefore, proceeded to outline basic principles for the protection of underwater cultural heritage, set out provisions for an international framework of cooperation and coordination between nations, and aimed at enhancing capacity building in the field of underwater archaeology and cultural heritage management. The Convention entered into force on 2 January 2009 when the twentieth state acceded the agreement. As of 2019, more than sixty nations, referred to as States Parties, have joined the Convention,

**Figure 13.1** Representatives from dozens of nations attend a plenary session of the United Nations Educational, Scientific and Cultural Organization General Conference. (Courtesy of UNESCO)

establishing what is, by far, the most influential international set of norms in the field of underwater cultural heritage management and research.[4]

There are four main principles that are expanded upon within the main text of the agreement and its accompanying annex:

1. States Parties to the UNESCO Convention have a responsibility to preserve underwater cultural heritage.
2. In situ preservation—preserving sites undisturbed in their original location—is to be considered the primary management approach for underwater cultural heritage.
3. Underwater cultural heritage should not be commercially exploited for trade or speculation, and should not be irretrievably dispersed.
4. States Parties are to cooperate, exchange information, promote training, and support public awareness of the importance of underwater cultural heritage.

Importantly, it also presents an agreed-upon definition for "underwater cultural heritage," which means:

All traces of human existence having a cultural, historical or archaeological character which have been partially or totally under water, periodically or continuously, for at least 100 years such as:

  (i) sites, structures, buildings, artefacts and human remains, together with their archaeological and natural context;

 (ii) vessels, aircraft, other vehicles or any part thereof, their cargo or other contents, together with their archaeological and natural context; and

(iii) objects of prehistoric character.[5]

The annex, entitled "Rules concerning activities directed at underwater cultural heritage" (hereafter Annex Rules), consists of a series of 36 recognized principles and guidelines that pertain to the responsible treatment and research of underwater cultural heritage. Given their detailed nature, the Annex Rules have gained prominence equal to, if not greater than, the main text when considering their effect on underwater cultural heritage management practices.

Foremost among the Annex Rules is the protection of underwater cultural heritage through the adoption of in situ preservation as the preferred management option. Scientific research should be minimally intrusive and use nondestructive techniques and survey methods wherever possible, in preference to artifact recovery. The latter should only be authorized when it can lead to a significant contribution to the protection, knowledge, or enhancement of the heritage site.[6] The Annex Rules are also clear in stipulating that underwater cultural heritage may not be traded, sold, bought, or bartered as commercial goods, and that activities directed at heritage sites must be strictly regulated to ensure proper recording of cultural, historical, and archaeological information.[7] Beyond stating principles, the Annex Rules establish what are considered professional best practices. A project design with prescribed components is mandated, preliminary research must be undertaken in advance of intrusive work, funding must be secured to finance a project through completion, a project timetable has to be established, and contingency plans formulated.[8] Scientific research may only be undertaken under the direction, control, and regular presence of a qualified underwater archaeologist with the scientific competence appropriate to the project. Further requirements pertain to documentation, conservation, and site management programs, as well as safety and environmental parameters.[9] Finally, the Annex Rules discuss the need and contents of interim and final reports, which are to be deposited as public records, and the curation of project archives.[10] It is important to note that public education, popular dissemination of information, and public access to underwater cultural heritage are all encouraged, with or without conditions, throughout the Annex Rules.

These internationally agreed upon sets of norms are increasingly being viewed as guidelines within national, local, and regional underwater cultural heritage management programs, even by nations that have not signed on to the UNESCO Convention. Nevertheless, variations remain within the archaeological community itself, let alone across authorities at the national, regional, and local levels.

## WHAT MATTERS IN UNDERWATER ARCHAEOLOGY IS THE THINKING, NOT THE SINKING

### Thijs J. Maarleveld, Professor of Maritime Archaeology, Department of History, University of Southern Denmark, Denmark

When I submitted my doctoral thesis, I gave it the blatantly presumptuous motto *"what matters in underwater archaeology is the thinking, not the sinking."* I felt slightly apprehensive about it at the time. I still had to defend my thesis, after all. But by now, and perhaps this is even more presumptuous, I stand by it firmly, and think that it captures my contribution to the discipline quite well. The pun, of course, is that as a Dutchman, I have problems pronouncing "th"; not in my own name, but in English. From my mouth, sinking and thinking sound the same. But clearly, they mean quite different things. And where maritime archaeologists engage with the results of sinking, it is the thinking that counts.

Most of my career was fundamentally affected by my role in policy development. Integrating maritime aspects in thinking about archaeology and heritage, and the promotion of archaeological thinking where it doesn't prevail, have therefore been the mainstays of my profession. Research that I promoted or undertook supported the arguments. It served to give pride of place to maritime aspects and maritime areas in strategies for the promotion of heritage protection, enjoyment and use on the one hand, and planning and development on the other. As a result, it has been very diverse. Some had a direct bearing on research questions to do with ships, notably early modern merchant ships. Much of it benefited maritime archaeology only indirectly, as it served to inform my understanding of the sedimentary geology of coastal and offshore areas, of processes positively affecting preservation, or of opinions, habits and practices that affect discovery and appreciation of certain categories of finds, but not of others; in short, of all those circumstances that create the opportunities for the "record" and the discipline to develop.

Field research, however, and developing methods for direct observation under adverse circumstances, or finding patterns and archaeological proxies for historical inferences have steered my thinking just as much; far more, in fact, than the acceptance of existing narratives or received knowledge. It is in the detailed nitty-gritty of archaeological craftsmanship that thinking really matters and that archaeology can make a difference.

In 1980, after five years of work as an excavation technician, I was employed by the Dutch Ministry of Culture. Subsequently, I worked as a civil servant for 25 years, representing the government in different capacities, but always with the problems and challenges relating to underwater archaeology at the core of my portfolio. Problems that occurred once divers found "old" things needed to be solved. Many significant finds had been made, and many a contentious issue had arisen. Most related to systematic discovery in the dynamic, awkwardly accessible, but archaeologically rich tidal basins and estuaries that constitute the Dutch coastal environment, but at least as contentious were searches around the world for wrecks documented in Dutch archives.

In both instances, the motto that "thinking matters" is not a tautology at all. Thinking is easily put on hold where the discovery or valuation of "old" shipwrecks are concerned. Excitement tends to prevail. Not that excitement would be bad, of course. Quite to the contrary. Enthusiasm is what should steer all endeavors. But if excitement is met by unthinking indifference, it can easily lead to unacceptable practices. Without a theoretical and normative framework, greed tends to become the leading principle. This happens at a small scale, but also in extensive business plans for deliberate search parties.

An overall framework was—and is—of the essence. It should be applicable irrespective of location or type of archaeological site. While dealing with sunken landscapes and buried settlements, as well as sunken or abandoned ships, it should be based in thinking, and can hardly put the sinking first. Continuing rights and interests can and should be respected, but they cannot be the basis for the framework as such. It is heritage values after all, and thus the overriding public interest that should guide decisions, and not the private interest that—quite rightly—prevails in salvage regulations resolving the issues related to current sinking events.

Devoting time and thinking to the processes by which such an overall framework could be consolidated in law, regulations and guidelines, or recommendations on planning and management, is probably the most important thing I have done in the field of maritime archaeology. Although I was one of many, I was to play a rather consistent role in these issues, at the national, at the regional and local, but also at the international level. Partly, this was a function of my regular work, partly it came through my commitment to professional organizations. Internationally, the triad of the ICOMOS Charter of 1996, the UNESCO Convention of 2001 and the Manual for Activities directed at Underwater Cultural Heritage of 2013 are tangible results to which I substantially contributed, as negotiator and as individual professional. I am glad I did, much as it distracted from other interesting things that ultimately define why maritime archaeology is important.

But while charters, conventions and manuals can give guidance and inspiration, they cannot—and should not—replace creative thinking. It is thinking that matters. Without creative thinking, essential competences such as diving, or even observation and recording, become of very limited value. Although the discipline is in dear need of craftspeople who combine all these skills and practical competences, and who can work in a stressful environment in order to transform destructive developments into creative research, they can only do so if they can think innovatively and archaeologically. Forgetting this will only lead to the dull application of procedure and the uncritical acceptance of received truths. What matters in underwater archaeology is the thinking . . . far more so than the accidental sinking of even the most significant ship.

## COMPONENTS OF AN UNDERWATER CULTURAL HERITAGE MANAGEMENT PROGRAM

Once underwater cultural heritage has come to be valued as a public asset and a society has determined what sites should be preserved and what mechanisms are permissible to use in doing so, the management of underwater cultural heritage is typically undertaken by a local, regional, or national government authority. Though this is not always the case, effective stewardship of underwater cultural heritage often benefits from a legislative framework empowering the appropriate level of government agency with certain responsibilities and rights. Such legislation typically conveys either management authority over certain categories of heritage sites (e.g., Naval warships), a responsibility to manage cultural (and other) resources within a particular geographic jurisdiction (e.g., marine preserves, national boundaries), or identifies a role in a consultative process that results from the potential disturbance of heritage sites. With a legal mandate promoting their mission, government authorities are typically in a better position to execute overall heritage management responsibilities than nongovernmental partners, though the latter can and often do play a vital role that at times exceeds the capabilities or resourcing of public authorities. At times such government authorities specialize in the management of underwater cultural heritage, given the particular nature of submerged sites; elsewhere underwater cultural heritage is addressed by a government entity responsible for stewardship of cultural heritage at large, or by offices responsible for the human environment.

## George Koutsouflakis, Director, Department of Underwater Archaeological Sites, Hellenic Ministry of Culture and Sports, Greece

Though antiquarians had developed an interest in ancient art retrieved from the sea by the 19th century, the importance of underwater cultural heritage was persistently understated in early legislation. While recognized in several countries as a fraction of the broader corpus of terrestrial cultural heritage, governments did not feel the need for specific protective regulations directed at submerged heritage sites.

The invention of SCUBA in 1943, and the widespread adoption of recreational diving that followed, forever changed the relation between man and the underwater world. Overnight, formerly inapproachable fields of cultural heritage became accessible to a continuously growing number of divers. While underwater archaeology, at the time in its first formative stages, was struggling to adjust scientific practices to the new physical realm, national governments proved unable and unprepared to meet the requirements of time. Archaeologists constantly found themselves intervening in the wake of looters. Amphora cargoes were dismantled during the 1960s and the 1970s throughout the Mediterranean as a result: a huge loss to humanity and science.

Modern nation-states are much more eager to define and protect their underwater cultural heritage whether within territorial waters or beyond them, such as in other maritime zones over which a certain country exercises relevant jurisdiction.

Governments are first of all responsible for defining the nature of what should be included under the term "underwater cultural heritage." Different schools of thought engender disparate approaches, and experience has shown that items recovered from underwater might not share the same universal value. Most national legislations set stable or movable chronological limits that define the boundaries between what should be protected as heritage and what is susceptible to exploitation and salvage. While the 2001 UNESCO Convention on the Protection of the Underwater Cultural Heritage places a general chronological boundary at 100 years, the Greek State, for example, extends the chronological range of underwater cultural heritage protections

to any relic of a shipwreck or aircraft that has remained underwater for more than 50 years.

Governments are also responsible for setting terms and conditions under which underwater sites of cultural interest should be physically approached, surveyed, documented, excavated, and studied. In most advanced countries underwater archaeology is organized, qualified, or licensed by state authorities, according to the widely accepted principle that underwater heritage, as with cultural heritage in general, is fundamentally a public matter, and as such should be supervised and protected by a legitimate authority. Once again the treatment and accessibility of underwater sites can vary significantly between nations. While several countries follow very restrictive policies allowing access only to officials, others adopted approaches that promote generalized access, putting in place only a minimum of restrictions. The same applies to the scientific study of these sites. In several countries underwater archaeology is practiced only by a limited number of state-sanctioned professionals (who are not always in a position to meet the demands of the scientific research potential), while others are more open to cooperate with long-established universities, institutions, and foundations. In some cases, even self-proclaimed underwater researchers that hold no academic background obtain the right to conduct research in the underwater environment and even, at times, receive "in kind" compensation.

Governments above all, have the obligation to provide a protective legal shield against any acts that would possibly endanger underwater archaeological sites. Yet, despite the growing public interest in underwater cultural heritage, several nations offer such sites no legal protection, or provide only a rudimentary framework of protective laws. Effectively safeguarding underwater cultural heritage also demands adequate means to apply and enforce the law, a challenge that even advanced national governments do not entirely suffice to answer.

The lack of legal protection and the absence of enforcement leave space for the exploitation and appropriation of objects from underwater sites by private salvors, companies, or associations who often operate in the interstices of the archaeological legislation and claim rights of ownership according to the parallel applicable maritime laws.

Furthermore, only a small part of the world's oceans fall within the exclusive territorial jurisdiction of any one nation. There developed, therefore, an urgent need for an international legal instrument to encourage cooperation between countries. A first step toward a common understanding among governments was the 1982 United Nations Convention of the Law of the Sea (UNCLOS). Although dominated to a great extent, as maritime law does, by the doctrine of the "freedom of the high seas," the UNCLOS treaty articulated for the first time the obligation between States Parties to protect underwater cultural heritage. The 2001 UNESCO Convention on the Protection of the Underwater Cultural Heritage that followed almost two decades later elaborated further through codifying commonly held basic principles and minimum professional requirements within an international agreement specifically dedicated to the protection of underwater cultural heritage.

The 2001 UNESCO Convention recognizes this heritage as part of the cultural inheritance of humanity and provides for a detailed cooperation system for States Parties through which to facilitate the application of protective measures. For its purposes, the term "underwater cultural heritage" is used to mean "all traces of human existence having a cultural, historical or archaeological character which have been partially or totally under water, periodically or continuously, for at least 100 years . . . " (Art. 1 para. 1(a)). The 2001 UNESCO convention forms a firm basis of practical rules for the treatment of underwater cultural heritage.

The number of states ratifying the 2001 UNESCO convention, 62 in 2019, might still seem low in contrast to the 168 parties of the earlier UNCLOS convention. While the basic articles of the 2001 UNESCO Convention are supported by most of the negotiating members, several states—some with a major influence in the scene of international politics—backpedaled from ratifying the entire text as they felt that certain issues remained unresolved. National agendas, geopolitics, and strong economic interests prevented others from ratifying. The reasons often have little to do with the protection of underwater cultural heritage itself.

The tendency, however, among academic institutions in countries that influence the evolution of best practices and the management of cultural heritage, is to press forward with the international dialogue and assuage governmental reservations. It is expected that if some of the leading maritime powers ratify the agreement in the years to come, the 2001 UNESCO Convention will attain a much greater degree of global acceptance.

Irrespective of host agency, cultural heritage management involves the development and implementation of appropriate policies, tools, and resources that allow for the identification, administration, preservation, and interpretation of designated cultural sites. Broadly speaking, agencies charged with administering underwater cultural heritage execute their mission through the fulfillment of four primary functions. The first, heritage management, involves elements such as inventorying sites and developing appropriate policies to foster research, preservation, and public awareness of underwater cultural heritage. The second, archaeological research, fulfills the need for sound and reliable data upon which to make prudent decisions and permits for underwater cultural heritage sites to contribute to our knowledge about the past human condition. The third, artifact conservation and collections management, ensures that the investment made in the responsible recovery of artifacts from an underwater cultural heritage site is preserved and maximized through additional research and educational opportunities. And finally, the fourth, public outreach, is in the eyes of many the most important, as it engenders public support of measures aimed at preserving cultural heritage, and fulfills an underlying purpose of archaeology, which is the pursuit and dissemination of knowledge.

## Cultural heritage management

A fundamental component of cultural heritage management is the need to identify resources under a program's management, something that carries its own particularities when addressing heritage sites located in an underwater environment. Accordingly, a management program is grounded upon its ability to develop an inventory or database of resources under its purview. This database is oftentimes derived from a combination of sources—archival documents, scientific surveys, public reporting, contributions from other management agencies, and, unfortunately, the looting of sites. The fields in such a database provide resource managers with information that could help identify, interpret, evaluate, and develop an appropriate management plan for a particular entry. In some instances, the inventory may also contain information about important aspects of sites that are not associated directly with their cultural value, such as whether a wreck site contains environmental or public safety hazards.

Some of the most important fields within the database are associated with the coordinates of a site, its boundaries, and the degree to which the location of a site is positively known. A location derived solely from historical sources may not be as dependable as one derived from a report received from a member of the public who has visited a site in person; in turn, locations derived from a scientific research project are generally considered even more dependable. It is important for a heritage manager to be able to differentiate between empirically verified sites and locations, those that have been reported but not verified, and those that are expected to exist but have not been reported at all. Locational data remain fundamental in terms of cultural heritage management because the data serve as the center of one of the most powerful tools at the hand of a heritage manager—a Geographic Information System (**GIS**) (figure 13.2).

A GIS permits a heritage manager to visually overlay a series of georeferenced datasets to effectively interpret and analyze facets of a site under management. Let us assume that one dataset represents the locational data originating from the management program's database, along with the designated degree of confidence in that locational data—a trait that can be visualized through the use of different icons. Using a GIS, the user can import cartographic data, nautical charts, geopolitical boundaries, bathymetric data, satellite imagery, marine protected area boundaries, and so on, all tied into their position in the physical world. The heritage manager can now, knowing little more than the location of a site, potentially determine the approximate depth of the wreck, the prevalent currents in the area, the political region it falls within (and hence the appropriate authorities with whom to coordinate), whether it is located within a

**Figure 13.2** A Geographic Information System (GIS) illustrating the superimposition of georeferenced data layers—in this case maritime zone jurisdictions and the boundaries of national marine sanctuaries off the coast of California—that can be used when developing management approaches for underwater cultural heritage sites in the region. (Courtesy of MarineCadaste.Gov)

marine preserve, the nearest port from which to launch operations, and so forth. Critically, a heritage manager can utilize a GIS to determine whether they have any management authority over the site to begin with, as different provisions apply to sites depending on locational jurisdiction or ownership. Whether a site falls within a marine preserve, a nation's territorial sea, a nation's contiguous zone, or a nation's exclusive economic zone may directly determine what legal protections apply (figure 13.3). A sovereign nation has diminishing levels of control and enforcement authority in each of these maritime zones as one gets farther and farther from shore.

Another critical element to consider is whether there is a discernible owner of a particular cultural heritage site—in many nations, underwater cultural heritage, by definition, represents a formerly abandoned property and comes under the management of the state as a public asset. In other jurisdictions, ownership is not universally declared; a consultation process takes into account the public value of underwater cultural heritage and ensures the public's interest is considered when it comes to site management. There are also special categories of heritage sites, such as sunken military vessels, which generally remain the property of the sovereign state they served at the time of their sinking. Accordingly, the consolidated dataset present within a GIS and its associated database assists the heritage manager in balancing these various considerations when determining

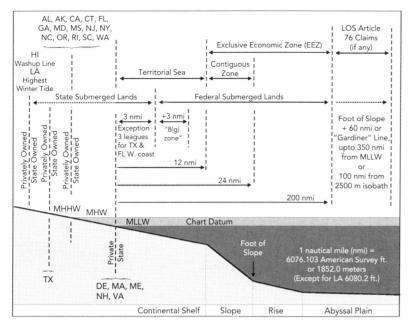

**Figure 13.3** Summary graphic produced by the Bureau of Ocean Energy Management to explain the extent of maritime boundaries to stakeholders in the United States offshore oil and gas industry. It illustrates the potential complexities associated with delineating maritime zones within which different legal protections for underwater cultural heritage may apply. (Courtesy of the Bureau of Ocean Energy Management)

what actions may be appropriate in any given scenario. It may only be a starting point—with further archival research, empirical studies, legal reviews, or stakeholder consultations being necessary to arrive at any conclusions—but a GIS serves as an invaluable reference that often take years to fully develop.

As the use of geographic application tools is becoming more commonplace in our everyday lives, it important not to underestimate the underlying knowledge required to maintain a heritage management GIS. For example, locations may originate in multiple different coordinate systems, collected through a variety of equipment and methods (before and after the advent of the Global Positioning System), and may be represented in a series of cartographic projections, all of which can introduce error or uncertainty in terms of a site's actual location. Knowing whether a site falls within or outside a marine preserve may be crucial for its management and preservation potential. Being a few tens of meters one direction or another (a margin of error very easily accrued) may mean the difference between the site enjoying protected status or not. It is therefore crucial that the responsible cultural heritage manager is appropriately trained and that selected data sets originate from reliable and credentialed sources.

Once resources under management have been identified, located, and captured in a management program's database and GIS, high on the list of priorities for a cultural heritage manager is assessing the condition of cultural heritage sites under the program's purview. Condition assessments sometimes take the form of desktop studies but are generally far more effective and accurate if they involve onsite archeological research (figure 13.4). Assessments may examine, for example, the current state of preservation of a site. To what degree has the site been impacted by human activity (e.g., fishing, trawling, diving, or looting)? To what degree has the site been impacted by the surrounding environment? To what degree is the site impacting its surrounding environment? Is it under threat? Is it

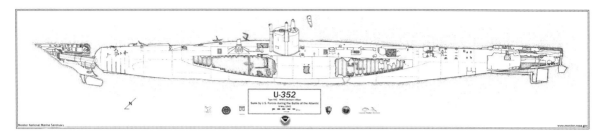

**Figure 13.4** Archaeological site plan of U-352, a World War II–era German submarine sunk off the coast of North Carolina, developed by the Monitor National Marine Sanctuary as part of a site condition assessment. (Courtesy of the National Oceanic and Atmospheric Administration)

a threat? What is its preservation potential and do management actions need to be taken to strengthen it? What is the site's research potential and should it be prioritized for future research activities?

The surrounding environment and human activity, whether directly or indirectly, play a determining role when it comes to how a site's condition evolves. Sedimentation over centuries or millennia has buried underwater cultural heritage sites, leaving no trace behind. Shallow-water high-energy reef environments have battered them to the point that little remains. Powerful storms have been known to alter the seafloor and archaeological sites located along their paths. Oftentimes the heritage manager has to be aware of such impacts to better understand site formation processes, but remains a mere observer documenting what is occurring or has transpired in an attempt to mitigate potential future threats.

In certain instances, though, those threats are the result of expected human activity. For example, the natural progression of a river may be impacted by an infrastructure project, such as a dam, resulting in a dramatic effect on underwater cultural heritage sites located downstream. The dam may alter water levels, current or erosion patterns, sedimentation rates, and even salinity or oxygen levels. Expected human activities may also include sanctioned archeological excavations that, in the process of recovering data in order to mitigate impacts from dredging or infrastructure development, profoundly alter the character of the site that remains (figure 13.5). Unknown or unplanned types of human activities may be even more disruptive over time, as they often impact sites without either forethought or concern for site preservation. Many such activities are legal and are deemed necessary—drag net fishing, for example, or, in many areas, bottom trawling. Some are legal, but questionable—in some jurisdictions authorities may grant salvage awards to private entities who undertake artifact recovery from heritage sites for private monetary gain. In other instances, the activities are illicit—the unauthorized recovery and scrapping of metal from the hull of World War II warships for private profit, or the looting of cultural sites for the black-market value of their historic artifacts (figure 13.6). With advances in technology, making navigation, remote sensing tools, and information accessible to

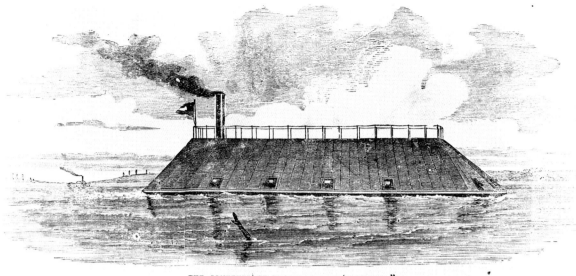

THE CONFEDERATE IRONCLAD RAM "GEORGIA."

**Figure 13.5** Line engraving depicting CSS *Georgia*, an ironclad floating battery that served in the defense of Savannah, Georgia, during the American Civil War. Between 2015 and 2017 an archaeological excavation under the US Army Corps of Engineers took place outside the port of Savannah to recover the remains of CSS *Georgia* that had come to rest in the middle of what is now a major shipping channel. (Courtesy of the Naval History and Heritage Command, NH 58722)

**Figure 13.6** A salvage barge crowded with the remains of O 16, a World War II–era Royal Netherlands Navy submarine sunk in the Gulf of Siam. The submarine, considered a war grave, was unceremoniously recovered for the scrap metal value of its hull in 2012. (Courtesy of ABC News)

an ever-widening swath of the population, the risk of unauthorized disturbance is a growing concern. Heritage managers may no longer be able to rely on a site's inaccessibility or obscurity as its primary means of protection. This is one more reason why condition assessments are so important, as they document a baseline from which any deviation can be measured. It is far more effective for a cultural heritage manager to enforce violations for unauthorized site disturbance if the site postdisturbance can be compared directly with what it looked like before looting took place.

It is important to pause here and recognize certain particularities surrounding underwater cultural heritage sites. They are often associated with marine tragedies. Most ship and aircraft wrecks tell of abrupt and catastrophic moments in time associated with weather, accidents, or enemy actions. A ship may go down with many of its sailors and, in more recent eras, laden with oil; a warship may founder while still carrying ordnance aboard. These elements require heritage managers to contend with sensitivies that extend beyond the normal historic preservation priorities; for example, the sanctity of maritime graves, or the mitigation of risks to public safety and the environment. Consider also that underwater cultural heritage sites often provide a substrate for entire colonies of benthic communities by serving as artificial reefs.

An assessment of the potential environmental and human impacts, direct and indirect, that may affect the preservation potential of a site, as well as the potential impacts a site may have on its surrounding environment, often results in the development of site-specific management plans or broader-reaching heritage management policies. In developing these precedents and policies, an underwater cultural heritage management program can greatly influence research of underwater cultural heritage, site preservation, and public opinion. In tandem with mandates such as pertinent laws or regulations, a management program often has the ability to establish permitting programs controlling access to heritage sites, outlining the manner through which they may be scientifically studied, and setting the standards and professional credentials and qualifications necessary for practitioners to lead such research endeavors. When a site is to be disturbed for archaeological research purposes, it is therefore incumbent upon heritage managers to, for example, assess and refine research design proposals, ensure that any material to be recovered is appropriately conserved, verify that long-term curation of recovered artifacts is secured prior to recovery, and ensure that a suitable publication of the results of the research follows within a prescribed timeframe—these are just some of the parameters typically addressed in research permitting programs.

In this section, we have reviewed the importance of heritage management tools and practices such as an archaeological site inventory and GIS, condition assessments, management plans, and research permitting programs. The role of a cultural heritage manager, however, is directly related to the earlier discussion on laws, regulations, and policies. For instance, does building the hypothetical dam in the earlier example require consideration of the project's effects on underwater cultural heritage? If so, heritage managers typically serve as stewards and representatives of underwater cultural heritage within multistakeholder discussions aimed at reaching an appropriate balance of economic and historic preservation interests. In the case of illicit site disturbance, the heritage manager is called upon to represent the public good, coordinate with appropriate authorities, and, to varying degrees, pursue legal and enforcement means to curb such activity. On the whole, therefore, a heritage management program places significant emphasis on developing and fostering consistency in applicable laws, regulations, and policies, aiming to influence the preservation and research of underwater cultural heritage sites well into the future.

## Archaeological research

The importance and contributions of archaeological research at large is discussed throughout this text; from the standpoint of a cultural heritage management program, such research serves a series of distinct purposes: Archaeological research assists with both inventorying efforts and site condition assessments. It provides the empirical data upon which sound heritage management decision-making is based and is the most reliable and often most current source of information about the characteristics of a cultural heritage site. The archaeological research itself complements, supplements, and, at times, corrects the historical record. Given its potential for public benefit, archaeological research is also seen as a mechanism through which to mitigate potential disturbance of a site. Construction of a new marina may impact a historic pier and a shipwreck located alongside; full architectural documentation of the pier and excavation of the shipwreck may serve as the compromise through which the new development addresses the harm it would otherwise cause to the material record. Archaeological research is also a key way to raise public awareness of the past and the value of underwater cultural heritage. At the same time, in executing archaeological research, staff of a heritage management program remain current in their awareness of the latest methods, techniques, and accepted practices of the field, support future advances, and enhance their standing as an authority responsible for managing sites and setting standards. For these and other reasons, conducting and overseeing archaeological research is a fundamental component of any comprehensive and effective underwater cultural heritage management program.

## Conservation and collections management

The responsibility for managing underwater cultural heritage is typically not limited to archaeological sites; any artifacts that are recovered from a site also tend to be the heritage management agency's responsibility. Though some management programs refrain from collecting artifacts, or infrequently engage in recoveries, for many other programs it is a desirable or unavoidable part of their purview. There are usually three avenues through which material is recovered and retained, each of which typically requires some combination of documentation, conservation, and curation.

The first avenue, underwater archaeological excavations—whether the product of internal research, a consequence of permitted activities, or a part of mitigation efforts—result in the recovery of artifacts that need immediate stabilization and analysis. It should be noted here that while internal research is planned for and controlled, mitigation excavations and permit-controlled excavations are often externally driven and therefore not always predictable. As a result, an artifact collection under management may increase unexpectedly, which means a heritage management program must be able to address such an unanticipated growth in its collection.

The second avenue comes in the form of what are referred to as orphaned collections: artifacts recovered in the past, often prior to the passage of protective legislation, that are now in need of an institutional home and usually treatment. Here too, accessioning of such artifacts is an unplanned but often necessary occurrence if the management program holds responsibility for the site of origin or the associated collection.

The third avenue through which material is recovered, which is the most detrimental, is through illicit site disturbance. Here, persons have either knowingly or unknowingly violated prohibitions on disturbance of archaeological sites and have proceeded to bring artifacts to the surface. More often than not, the consequences of such actions are significant, and not only to the site that has been impacted underwater. Proper and immediate conservation treatment has usually been withheld from illicitly recovered artifacts through lack of knowledge of its necessity or lack of inclination or resources to perform the necessary treatment. As a result, when a management agency becomes aware and eventually recoups the material that has been recovered without authorization, it is often in a fragile or compromised state. Vital information may have been lost in the process of artifact degradation beyond that lost in terms of provenience and context (see "Archaeological Conservation: What Can Be Lost" box). At times, crude or uninformed "treatments" applied by those engaged in the unsanctioned recovery actually further hamper professional conservation efforts.

Irrespective of the route an artifact takes to arrive to the appropriate cultural heritage management program, there is a core need for most programs to have a specialized conservation capability and facility, staffed with conservators who are intimately familiar with the treatment of artifacts recovered from a waterlogged or underwater environment. This need to stabilize the material record is supplemented by the invaluable contribution that the conservation process makes toward the understanding and analysis of the artifacts recovered. In essence, laboratory-based conservation treatments often serve as the continuation of the archaeological excavation within a controlled environment (see "Archaeological Conservation: What Can Be Gained" box).

## ARCHAEOLOGICAL CONSERVATION: WHAT CAN BE GAINED

(A)

(B)

**Figure 13.7** Cannon from CSS *Alabama*. A. Cannon being recovered. B. View of jaw in concretion. (Courtesy of the Naval History and Heritage Command)

On 19 June 1864, the American Confederate raider CSS *Alabama* was sunk by USS *Kearsarge* off Cherbourg, France. *Alabama* had been tremendously successful at its mission, capturing or burning ships throughout the North Atlantic, West Indies, and Southeast Asia, intercepting cargo, interrupting Union commerce, and even sinking the Union side-wheeler USS *Hatteras*. On this day, however, *Kearsarge* was to prove the better vessel, and, within an hour of the first shot, struck *Alabama* a fatal blow.

One-hundred and twenty years later, the French Navy minesweeper *La Circe* discovered the remains of the wreck in approximately 60 m (200 ft) of water, spurring years of research and an international agreement between the United States and France regarding the management of the site. A series of excavation seasons ensued. A large cast-iron 32-lb cannon, one of three raised from the site, was among the artifacts recovered (figure 13.7a). The cannon was immediately placed in professional care and shipped to the Warren Lasch Conservation Laboratory in Charleston,

South Carolina for desalination. The conservators initiated the careful process of removing a layer of concretion that had accumulated around the original surface of the cannon. In 2002, several months after the cannon had been placed in treatment, conservators came across the unexpected. A heavily encrusted and stained jawbone fragment associated with a series of teeth was found enveloped in the concretion layer (figure 13.7b). The fragment had not been noticed during the excavation, the recovery, the packing, the shipping, or the desalination process; it could not have been, as it was concealed in concretion. It was a key reminder as to why conservation is a methodical, time-consuming process, and of the premise that excavation of recovered artifacts continues in the laboratory. Had the concretion layer simply been removed, the jaw fragment would have gone unnoticed, and, by 2002, the untreated cannon would have already shown signs of degradation. Instead, by 2003, the jaw fragment arrived at the Naval History and Heritage Command's Underwater Archaeology Branch.

What followed was a thorough osteological and DNA analysis of the fragment. Despite the fact that the mandible was covered in thick, heavy, reddish-brown concretion and had remained underwater for the better part of a century and half, diagnostic information could still be derived from the study. The mandible belonged to a young- to middle-aged adult, likely Caucasoid, whose teeth indicated a European or American ancestry. Isotopic analysis demonstrated that the person's diet was made up primarily of cereal grains including wheat, rye and barley, as well as animal protein from animals subsisting on the same grains. It also showed a heavy reliance on terrestrial, domesticated animal protein, characteristic of European-derived diets of that era. This indicated to researchers that the individual was likely of European origin, as the jaw fragment nearly excluded maize and cane sugars consistent with a North American diet, or sorghum and millet representative of the contemporary African diet. The individual also likely smoked a pipe, as his teeth showed a distinct mark consistent with the habitual clamping of a pipe stem.

*Alabama* carried eight cannon aboard, each necessitating a dedicated gun crew. It seems when the ship finally succumbed to the sea in its last engagement with *Kearsarge*, the fateful cannon crushed one of its gun crew members. Thanks to the meticulous work of archaeologists, conservators, and forensic archaeologists, we now know something about the unfortunate sailor, who saw the world aboard the infamous commerce raider. Perhaps future research will permit an even more precise identification of the sailor, using archaeological and historical information to complement what has been learned in the laboratory. This tantalizing prospect is only possible because conservators were brought into the project at an early stage, initiated treatment non-intrusively, methodically engaged in the cannon's de-concretion, and were prepared to address the unexpected. A lot more than what is anticipated may be learned in the laboratory, including about artifacts that were not even identified in the field. A successful archaeological project, therefore, takes advantage of this potential avenue of data by fully incorporating the conservation process into the project's research design, and, ideally, in the excavation phase itself.

## ARCHAEOLOGICAL CONSERVATION: WHAT CAN BE LOST

In the summer of 2010, the Underwater Archaeology Branch (UAB) of the Naval History and Heritage Command received an unexpected call. A leather wallet had been recovered from a German U-boat located off the New England coast by a recreational diver, and its deteriorating state had prompted action. The remains of U-853 serve as a testament to the horrors of World War II; entombed within it were its sailors, who lost their lives when depth charges dropped by the US Navy hit their intended mark. The war grave is now visited by divers, not all of whom respect its sacrosanct nature. In a thoughtless moment on one such dive, the wallet was brought to the surface; with it was a photograph of a sailor, a prayer card with handwriting on it, and two coins. The wallet and its associated artifacts were kept in private hands, until its rapid rate of degradation became cause for alarm. The divers who recovered it ultimately did the responsible thing by seeking assistance from authorities.

Following coordination with the German Embassy in Washington DC, the US Navy agreed to stabilize the artifacts. When it reached UAB, the wallet, having been recovered from a marine environment with no conservation plan, was in need of significant care. Chlorides from the marine environment had permeated the leather, as is typical for organic materials such as rope, textiles, or wood. When the wallet was removed from the sea near Rhode Island, it was allowed to dry. On a cellular level, this proved devastating; with the seawater evaporating, the salts captured within crystallized, expanded, and wreaked havoc on the material's structural integrity. The once-intact wallet arrived in a fragmentary and exceptionally friable state (figure 13.8a). It was immediately resubmerged in de-ionized water and stored in that manner prior to treatment in attempt to halt the degradation and begin a controlled desalination process. Following ethanol and acetone baths, the wallet fragments were treated with British Museum leather dressing (figure 13.8b). The damage that had been done, however, could not be undone—the fragments could only be stabilized. Upon completion of the treatment, the delicate fragments are now in a position to be placed on

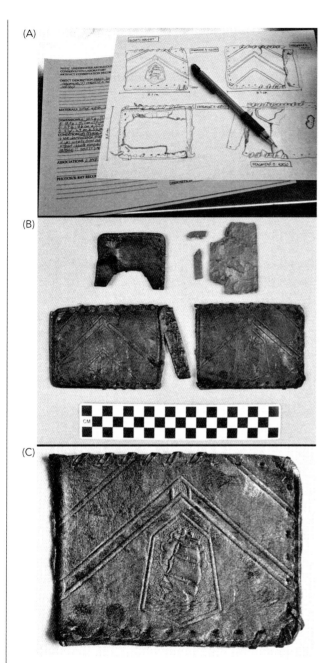

(A)

(B)

(C)

**Figure 13.8** Personal wallet from U-853. A. Drawing and notes upon arrival at conservation lab. B. Materials post conservation. C. Wallet detail showing sailing vessel. (Courtesy of the Naval History and Heritage Command)

exhibit at the request of the German government. The fragments, however, are too delicate to be reconstructed into an intact wallet, nor can they provide us with the trove of data that would have been associated with the wallet's original context.

A beautiful sailing vessel is stamped into the leather amid chevrons on one of the fragments, tantalizing researchers with one of the most personal of personal artifacts (figure 13.8c). The crew list of U-853 is known, as is the likely location of individuals during battle. Knowing where on the submarine the wallet was recovered could provide insights as to whom it may have belonged; the same can be said for the photograph and the annotated prayer card. When the former reached UAB alongside the wallet, the emulsion had peeled off, leaving behind only the backing paper as a reminder of what was lost. The prayer card never made it to the laboratory; it disintegrated somewhere between recovery and the Washington Navy Yard, along with any information it had to share with us.

There are many stories captured within this one artifact—it represents one of the final engagements of World War II, a personal story of a sailor who was tragically lost alongside his peers in the dwindling moments of the war, a war grave, an artifact of an enemy now being cared for by a friend, the importance of a responsible diving community, the opportunities that lie in better relations between the diving community and authorities, and the repercussions of irresponsible actions and unsanctioned recoveries. Without a professional conservation plan ready to be applied at the moment of recovery, and in many instances before the recovery itself, we risk losing not only artifacts, but all of the stories they could tell us. Who was represented in the lost photograph? Who gave the perished sailor the prayer card? What was the handwritten message? Who was this sailor whose final resting place was disturbed? Archaeological conservation is not only about stabilizing artifacts, but also about continuing the archaeological and analytical process in a controlled environment in order to more fully tell the story of people in the past. It is about making new observations, collecting new data, and informing the interpretation of a site. Without its proper application, we lose much more than just material culture.

Once artifacts in a collection are stabilized, that collection must continue to be managed following professional curatorial standards and under controlled environmental conditions if the original investment in the conservation of the collection is to be preserved. Accordingly, conservation laboratories are often associated with curatorial facilities that serve as the long-term repository for the artifacts under their management. From there, artifacts can be loaned to suitable museums and educational or other cultural organizations in furtherance of the management program's objectives, such as public education or facilitating external research into the collections. Therefore, in addition to artifact stabilization and treatment, conservators and collection managers working within underwater cultural heritage management programs are also often responsible for continuing inventories, artifact assessments, loans, and exhibits.

## Public outreach

As noted in this chapter's introduction, making the case that cultural heritage is something to be valued, invested in, managed, researched, and learned from is a responsibility for all archaeologists. An underwater cultural heritage management program is at the forefront of this effort when it comes to underwater cultural resources—whether in fulfillment of the program's role as a public steward of cultural heritage, furthering the purposes of archaeology, or promoting the strategic management objective of raising appreciation and therefore respect for underwater cultural heritage. Public outreach has been, and continues to be, vital to the cultural heritage preservation movement, both in the passage of stronger preservation mandates and in the execution of those already in place. Though penalties in laws and regulations may serve as a deterrent against disturbance of cultural heritage sites, it is hard to ignore the effectiveness of public engagement when it comes to changing attitudes toward underwater cultural heritage. Whether in the form of educating the diving community on the importance of not impacting sites during visits, policy-makers on the multifaceted nature of underwater cultural heritage, student groups on the fascinating lessons to be learned about the past, or sailors about the struggles and achievements of those who came before them, enhancing public awareness of cultural heritage and its management is, in the eyes of many practitioners, their primary, most fulfilling, and most effective contribution to the field .

Demonstrating value through educational initiatives is a key means through which public programs dedicated to heritage management, archaeological research, conservation, and collections management earn their keep. Outreach efforts can take many forms, but often include lectures and presentations, popular, and scholarly publications, a digital presence, media and documentary coverage, internship programs, stewardship programs, avocational archaeologist training sessions, site visits, facility tours, or museum loans and exhibits. Initiatives are tailored to the capabilities, strengths, and desired outcomes of individual heritage management programs. Ignoring this vital component of heritage stewardship risks undermining the very mission of management programs through compromising the preservation and knowledge potential of sites and impacting dedicated public funding streams.

There is significant variation across management programs regarding the emphasis placed on each of the four aforementioned functions, and an equal degree of variation when it comes to the authorities each program relies on and the resources each program can draw from. It is, however, the intertwined and mutually supportive nature of cultural heritage management, archaeological research, artifact conservation and collections management, and public outreach that makes these four elements the conceptual pillars of underwater cultural heritage management.

## MY MOST IMPORTANT CONTRIBUTION TO MARITIME AND UNDERWATER ARCHAEOLOGY

### Kim Faulk, Chief Operating Officer, PAST Foundation, USA

Underwater archaeology lends itself to daydreams of diving into undiscovered shipwrecks in exotic locales, living on boats, being the first to make a discovery, and commuting to work via SCUBA. These are all possible but not without understanding the fundamental responsibilities of being a good archaeologist. Of these many responsibilities, it is paramount to continually advocate for the protection of our cultural heritage. If we want to protect underwater cultural heritage and gain the trust of the public, we must act with integrity in all aspects of our lives. Saying what we mean and standing behind our beliefs often means having uncomfortable conversations with the public, politicians, colleagues, and others. But this steadfast adherence to principles gains respect from our adversaries and trust from others. I cannot claim to have made discoveries that will rewrite our understanding of humanity's existence, or to have been a groundbreaking leader within our field. I can, however, say without pause that I have served my community with integrity and advocated for our field and for the protection of our underwater cultural heritage fearlessly. That is the most important thing that I have done.

When elected to the Advisory Council on Underwater Archaeology (ACUA) I was honored to have an opportunity to make a difference in our field. In my eight elected years on the board, we addressed difficult issues that impact archaeologists globally: sexual harassment and discrimination, the gap between what students are being taught and what employers need, the ratification and adoption of the 2001 UNESCO Convention on the Protection of the Underwater Cultural Heritage, the exploitation and sale of underwater cultural heritage (UCH), and the perception that underwater cultural heritage is different than terrestrial cultural heritage and therefore less in need of rigorous scientific investigation.

Advocating for protecting underwater cultural heritage is not limited to my role on the ACUA; it is a critical component of my daily professional life as well. After working for both museums and state archaeological groups, I moved to cultural resource management (CRM) work in the offshore energy industry in 2005. Unlike state government or museum work, the energy sector is filled with people who have a variety of scientific backgrounds, and who have demanding budgetary timelines that must be adhered to. Since entering the industry in 2005, I have advocated for UCH with my clients, my colleagues, and other industry groups. As a result, I have seen attitudes about underwater archaeology and underwater cultural heritage change dramatically. Archaeology has now shifted from being a fringe science in the industry to a respected and valued discipline.

This has not been easy. There have been uncomfortable meetings when, as the only archaeologist in the room, I have had to fight for UCH. Nonetheless, by honestly and fearlessly defending the data, the regulations, and best practices with my clients, regulators, and colleagues, I have created a foundation of trust that allows honest dialogue about what needs to be done. We must build bridges between our discipline and others to illustrate the full value of archaeology. Acting with integrity takes daily effort and it requires that we act in accordance with what we believe is right. Watching a paradigm shift within the energy sector, and the archaeological community, about what we can accomplish together has been truly rewarding. As an example, in 2011 when the NOAA *Okeanos Explorer* undertook its first deepwater archaeological surveys in the Gulf of Mexico my colleagues and clients watched the dives spellbound. For the first time deepwater archaeological sites known only by the CRM archaeologists and individual clients were available to everyone. Clients and companies clamored to know if their site was the one we looked at that day. The amount of pride in being able to "own the discovery" of each visited shipwreck shown by my clients was truly inspiring. By comparison, my archaeological colleagues outside of the energy sector suddenly understood the value of the contributions of my peers within the industry. We were no longer just "working with industry," we were doing legitimate deepwater archaeology as a collaborative effort.

In the end, the most important thing I have done has very little to do with me. Rather, my service, my advocacy for UCH and against UCH's exploitation, and for the right of archaeologists to pursue their research free from harassment is about making our discipline a better place. The incredible members of the ACUA and Society for Historical Archaeology Boards I have worked with and learned from and my colleagues in the energy industry have all strengthened my willingness to serve. We can all make a contribution to the discipline we love, and to society as a whole, if we commit to work, live with integrity, and serve when asked.

## SUMMARY

One cannot discuss the management of underwater cultural heritage without addressing the fundamental questions: Which heritage sites retain value and are worth preserving, to what degree, and in what manner? The specific answers to such questions do indeed vary across and within regions of the globe, driven by societal factors. The fundamental determination, however, remains that underwater cultural heritage must be viewed as contributing to the public good and therefore deserves a leading seat at the table when balanced against other private interests and communal equities. As the field of underwater archaeology is maturing and coalescing around a common series of ethical standards and professional practices, it is incumbent upon field practitioners to advocate for these common norms and continue to raise the level of public awareness of the value of underwater cultural heritage across boundaries.

## DISCUSSION QUESTIONS

1. How would you define underwater cultural heritage? Would you apply a temporal horizon or a buffer period to that definition?
2. What do you see as the greatest contribution of maritime and underwater archaeology?
3. In what instances would in situ preservation not be the most desirable management approach?

4. In addition to archaeologists, conservators, and curators, what other kinds of professionals would you see as an important part of an effective underwater cultural heritage management program?

5. What groups or communities do you believe would have common interests with archaeologists and cultural heritage managers when it comes to the preservation of underwater cultural heritage sites?

6. Who owns cultural heritage? If an early 19th century British ship that was headed to the British Museum carrying an ancient Egyptian sarcophagus sank off the coast of modern-day Portugal, who is responsible for the managing the site, and who has a vested interest in it?

### FURTHER READING

Dromgoole, S. (2014). *Underwater Cultural Heritage and International Law.* Cambridge University Press, Cambridge.

Hall, J. (2007). The Black Rhino. *Journal of Maritime Archaeology* **2**(2): 93–97.

Maarleveld, T.J. (2013). Ethics, Underwater Cultural Heritage, and International Law. *The Oxford Handbook of Maritime Archaeology.* A. Catsambis, B. Ford, D. Hamilton, Eds. 917–941. Oxford University Press, New York.

UNESCO. (2001). Convention on the Protection of the Underwater Cultural Heritage. Records of the General Conference: 31st Session Paris, 15 October to 3 November 2001. Available at http://unesdoc.unesco.org/images/0012/001246/124687e.pdf.

## CHAPTER 14

# THE FUTURE OF MARITIME AND UNDERWATER ARCHAEOLOGY

### FOCUS QUESTIONS

- How have people interacted with seas, lakes, and rivers? How was this interaction shaped by their culture and environment? What are the similarities, differences, and outcomes of these interactions?
- How can we gather data in a precise and rigorous way while still maintaining archaeological sites and the data they contain for future societies?
- How do we balance the needs of modern societies with the preservation of cultural heritage sites?

### WHERE TO GO FROM HERE?

The ultimate aim of archaeology—to illuminate the past human condition and experience—is also shared by many of archaeology's related fields, including history, ethnography, and cultural and physical anthropology. Archaeology is uniquely positioned within these fields to contribute to our understanding of the past. As discussed throughout this volume, the material record often reflects many details of past existence that escape historical mention; it can offer a more concrete chronology and represent more strata of society, more parts of everyday life, more disparate sources of data, and more views of the same story, even during well-documented periods. Archaeology has the ability to extend continuously through periods of time where gaps may exist in the written record. Its very reliance on scientific methods and theory set it apart from many of its sister fields in the humanities. Furthermore, the fact that the archaeological record of the past is constantly expanding through the discovery of new sites is in contrast to what, in many cases, is a relatively static primary written record. Hence, archaeology fills the gaps, provides new insights, and reaches people, interactions, cultural exchanges, environmental impacts, economic and social trends, and a whole host of other past activities that would otherwise remain unknown or more poorly understood. In its ability to study and learn from a great number of sources in a growing number of ways, archaeology is peerless within the range of scholarly fields that study past human cultures and behaviors.

Maritime and underwater archaeology, in turn, should be viewed in the context of archaeology as a whole. Having benefited from many of the methods, theories, and lessons learned through the growth of terrestrial archaeology, maritime and underwater archaeology was able to make notable contributions from early in its development. Underwater sites, which form only a part of the maritime archaeological spectrum, represent an entirely new concentration of information that was previously inaccessible. These include material evidence for, among other things, shipboard life, trade, environmental adaptation, intercultural contact, naval architecture, port construction, and technological advancements. Sea travel, which has been fundamental to the development of the human species and instrumental in exploration, trade, cultural exchange, and war, can now be understood in a way that was previously not possible.

Underwater sites often produce a whole spectrum of artifacts that are rarely, if ever, found (or found intact) on terrestrial sites due to different site formation processes and preservation/degradation rates. The until-recent inaccessibility of most of these sites means that there has been no reusing or resmelting of artifacts and no razing or reconstructing of the sites themselves—all practices that frequently limit our understanding of material culture and sites located on land. Intact artifacts that are usually found degraded and fragmented on terrestrial sites are commonly associated with submerged cultural sites. Not only do such artifacts strike the imagination and push forward public education initiatives, but for researchers these artifacts often provide stylistic and dating comparanda that are otherwise nonexistent. The artifacts of a wreck site, provided the site remains undisturbed, are de facto contemporary, at least as far as time of loss is concerned. In terms of dating sequences for land and underwater archaeologists alike, this information is invaluable when reconstructing chronologies and patterns of development. Through placing inundated or submerged sites in context within larger maritime cultural landscapes, the ability to undertake a systemic analysis emerges, allowing for a greater understanding of a society as a whole. Maritime and underwater archaeology, therefore, when placed in the context of archaeology at large, is of ample use for studying the past and human identity, culture, development and decision-making.

While the past does not repeat itself in a literal way as conditions, civilizations, and specific circumstances change, humankind in its development tends to encounter the same types of problems, trends, processes, and situations. War, economic cycles, intercultural relations, and environmental challenges have and will continue to be with us. The usefulness of the past, therefore, comes in part from learning how people reacted to similar conditions and the outcomes and consequences of those actions. Through focusing on, for example, archaeological sites that contain information on how humans interacted with their local and regional environment, or with environmental and climatic change itself, we can be more informed about similar decisions we face today. In an age of heightened environmental sensitivities, such insights can be of broad interest to a general audience. The same can hold true for subjects such as the nature of public versus private good, cultural changes, human diversity and evolution, religion, and war—all processes and key trends that are important to people of today.

We have organized this text around answering ten Big Questions, or over-arching themes, aimed at demonstrating the uniqueness and importance of our maritime and underwater cultural heritage. We began by illustrating what maritime and underwater cultural heritage is. This included a detailed discussion of how underwater sites are created and how their continued preservation depends on numerous factors remaining in balance. We discussed how we find and excavate our submerged cultural heritage, and provided exacting detail into the types of information we can learn from the materials we discover at these sites. This was followed by the third portion of this text, in which we provided a discussion of what maritime and underwater archaeology has taught us over the past century of research. Through this synopsis, we attempted to provide a sense of the breadth of the field and give an overview of two main concepts: first, how underwater research has enhanced our understanding of human history and, second, how human ingenuity has allowed many different cultures to become technological amphibians, utilizing rivers, lakes, and oceans to gain access to new opportunities and resources, while overcoming novel challenges. Finally, especially in the previous chapter, we discussed some of the ethical and legal considerations surrounding our maritime and underwater cultural heritage.

This final chapter focuses on the present and future of maritime and underwater archaeology, and addresses how you personally can become more involved with maritime and underwater archaeology. Maritime and underwater archaeology is a diverse, multidisciplinary, and ever-changing field that combines the art of humanities with the analysis of the hard sciences. As should be evident by now, the scope of the field is broad and so are the opportunities to get involved, whether to fulfill a personal interest or to help shape the discipline through a career of contributions. Whether you choose to pursue a degree or a career in maritime and underwater archaeology or a related field such as history, anthropology, or oceanography, or whether this is the only archaeology text you ever read, there is much that you can do to help protect and promote our maritime cultural heritage (table 14.1).

TABLE 14.1 **GET INVOLVED IN MARITIME AND UNDERWATER ARCHAEOLOGY!**

| How? | Where? | What will you do? |
|---|---|---|
| Volunteer! | regional avocational groups | archival research, field research, conservation work, or public outreach initiatives |
| Learn more! | universities and academic institutions (archaeology, anthropology, history, or marine studies departments) | certificate, diploma, and degree programs |
| Become a maritime or underwater archaeologist! | the private sector, in the nonprofit sphere, government agencies, or academia | fieldwork, teaching, conservation, or public outreach |
| Become an advocate! | in your local community and with your family and friends | share what you have learned in this course with those around you |

## CAREERS IN MARITIME AND UNDERWATER ARCHAEOLOGY

If you want to become a maritime and underwater archaeologist, an increasing number of universities and academic institutions across the world are now offering not only individual courses, but certificate, diploma, and degree programs. These programs may reside in archaeology, anthropology, history, or marine studies departments and often specialize in different areas of research. As campuses regularly edit their curriculum, the most current information about these programs will be obtained by internet searches for maritime or underwater archaeology degree programs and courses.

Regardless of where you are studying, your undergraduate training should focus on gaining a wide variety of skills and experiences in fields such as history, anthropology, archaeology, or coastal and marine sciences. You should concentrate your coursework on one of the fields in which maritime and underwater archaeologists work; focus on the one that interests you most, but take courses in the others. During your undergraduate career, get involved in as much research and fieldwork as you can.

Get to know your professors; this will help you learn more about what they are doing and it will allow them to know you and your interests, which will aid them in advising you. They frequently offer field schools or accept students on field projects as volunteers (figure 14.1). Gaining such practical experience is an excellent avenue into the field and may help you determine whether to pursue further academic training. Prior to participating in these field projects, you should take additional courses in subjects related to maritime and underwater archaeology to help you become better prepared for the types of research you may encounter. These could be geology or oceanography courses, or they

**Figure 14.1** Students at Florida State University's underwater archaeology field school learning how to map a site on land before moving underwater.

could be history, archaeology, or anthropology courses. Look especially for ones focused on the time period and area relevant to your interests and, if you can, take a course with the professor running the project prior to working with him or her in the field.

Participate in field schools investigating terrestrial as well as underwater sites. The more types of experience you have, the better an archaeologist you will be. Once you have completed your undergraduate degree, you are qualified in most countries to work on excavation projects as a field technician. You can assist in excavations and fieldwork and can get a job as an archaeologist working under other archaeologists with advanced degrees. However, most maritime and underwater projects and almost all full-time maritime and underwater archaeology jobs will require a minimum of a master's degree, so you should plan to continue your studies, either immediately after graduation or after working as an archaeologist for a few years.

## Stella Demesticha, Associate Professor of Maritime Archaeology, University of Cyprus, Cyprus

My interest in shipwreck archaeology began before I graduated from the University of Athens. It was in 1989, during the excavation of the Early Helladic Shipwreck at Dokos, an important project of the Hellenic Institute of Marine Archaeology that became a spawning ground for enthusiastic maritime archaeologists in Greece at the time. But it was eighteen years later that I embraced maritime archaeology, not by taking part in another project but by directing one. In 2007, I undertook the investigation of a 4th-century BCE shipwreck, off the south coast of Cyprus, as a visiting lecturer in the Department of History and Archaeology at the University of Cyprus. The excavation of the Mazotos shipwreck, named after the village on the nearest coast, became the first Cypriot underwater archaeological excavation, carried out more than 40 years after the Kyrenia excavation, which was conducted in Cypriot waters by nonlocal institutions.

I only later realized the commitment that such a project entailed. The archaeological significance of the shipwreck alone was intimidating enough, but being the only maritime archaeologist on the island was eye-opening. No infrastructure related to systematic underwater archaeological fieldwork existed on Cyprus at the time: This included everything, from easy-to-acquire items, like excavation equipment and conservation tools, to human expertise, which proved to be the most difficult asset to get. Thus, what seemed like an interesting venture in the beginning gradually turned into a painstaking and time-consuming management and logistical effort that sadly (as I then felt) had a disproportionally limited beneficial impact on my career.

No shipwreck excavation is a simple or a low-cost project. And, the better preserved a shipwreck is, the more elaborate the project becomes—with the degree of difficulty increasing exponentially when the waters are deep, the site is far from the coast, and, of course, when funding is not secure. These are widely appreciated constraints in the realm of maritime archaeology nowadays, especially after the Annex of the UNESCO 2001 Convention became a common reference for good fieldwork practices. All the above notwithstanding, underwater archaeologists find their fieldwork so rewarding that little can stop them from pursuing it.

In this respect, I cannot see anything exceptional at all in the fact that I initiated and am still conducting the Mazotos shipwreck excavation, despite its high degree of difficulty. What I distinguish, however, is that I had the foresight to pace myself from the beginning. I took the necessary time to prepare the ground, by building capacity

and infrastructure, establishing and testing collaborations, and training team members. After ten years of effort, in and out of the water, there is now a team of enthusiastic young archaeologists and divers on the island, fully qualified to meet the endless challenge of a deepwater project in the open sea. Moreover, the excavation and documentation methodology has been tested and optimized, mistakes have been corrected, and tools have been properly modified. Procedures like meticulous sieving, precise recording, and professional diving standards are now considered common practices. And last, but far from least, successful collaboration with the Department of Antiquities of Cyprus led to the establishment of a conservation laboratory for the treatment of waterlogged finds. By necessity, we have also developed an efficient system of in situ preservation, with a lot of precious (and costly) fieldwork time on the Mazotos shipwreck being spent placing sandbags on exposed portions of the site to protect them from environmental impacts. At a depth of 45 m, this was quite the feat . . . but it was unavoidable: Due to the limited conservation infrastructure on land, it was certain that it would be years before any substantial part of the hull could be brought to the surface.

All this has been a long process of trial and error that I trust many excavators are familiar with (but seldom share with the community). It goes without saying that I was never alone in any of the above, because underwater archaeology is not a one-person job. Many institutions and individuals have supported the project and have done a great deal for maritime archaeology, beyond the Mazotos excavation per se. A good project can have a very significant impact on cultural heritage management policies and legislation changes, research trends or, equally important, on career decisions—as my experience at Dokos taught me years ago. So what I can allow myself to be proud of is exactly that: With the challenging freedom that only starting from scratch allows, I treated the Mazotos shipwreck excavation as a platform for inspiration, collaboration, and sustainable development of maritime archaeology in Cyprus. And, it seems to have worked; I am not the only qualified underwater archaeologist working on the island anymore. . . .

If you wish to work underwater, you will need to obtain diving certifications, and in many countries, you will also need to obtain scientific or commercial diving licensing prior to participating in field schools or on field projects (figure 14.2). The initial open water certifications can be completed in a matter of days, but scientific and commercial diving training courses are often intensive, several-week or semester-long classes that require many hours of classroom time along with dozens of dives in various environments and using various types of equipment. Therefore, they can be quite expensive, depending upon whether they are offered through your university, a state agency, or through a private entity, and you should plan far ahead to schedule these courses, as they tend to be offered infrequently. However, if you are not certain that you wish to commit to this time and expense prior to being sure about pursuing a degree in maritime and underwater archaeology, there are often numerous crucial surface support positions for non-divers.

The specialized nature of the field and the select number of positions within it sits in stark contrast to its breadth in terms of the diversity of professional opportunities. Though there are regional differences in terms of the number and

**Figure 14.2** Students at Florida State University's underwater archaeology field school mapping artifacts underwater.

types of professional pathways, generally speaking, professional opportunities may lie in the private sector, in the nonprofit sphere, in various levels of government agencies, or in academia.

Not all national legislations foresee a role for private sector archaeology, viewing cultural heritage, its management, and its interpretation as the sole responsibility of the state. Those that do, foster maritime archaeologists in areas including the offshore energy industry, engineering and infrastructure development, and heritage management consultancies. These positions tend to be the most active in terms of field work, and, in certain parts of the world, constitute the majority of practicing professionals. They are complemented by those maritime archaeologists who serve government agencies, and whose focus tends to be directed more toward management of cultural heritage, setting policies and regulations, and establishment of appropriate standards. Specific responsibilities differ depending on the nature of the government agency, as maritime archaeologists can be found at the city or municipal government level, the regional level, the national level, and even at the United Nations helping to foster international collaboration.

Museums may also employ archaeologists as curators or researchers in the private, public, and nonprofit sectors. Research institutions or educational organizations may hire maritime and underwater archaeologists to find, excavate, curate, or interpret sites. Research organizations are more likely to be focused on the first three functions, while educational organizations are generally responsible for interpreting sites. Many nonprofit positions work to raise awareness of maritime cultural heritage; archaeologists employed by these organizations may often find themselves not doing very much field archaeology, but will instead be interpreting finds for the public or will be tasked with presenting cultural resources as something worth preserving.

**MY MOST IMPORTANT CONTRIBUTION TO MARITIME AND UNDERWATER ARCHAEOLOGY**

Jennifer McKinnon, Associate Professor, Maritime Studies Program, Maritime History and Archaeology, East Carolina University, USA

The most important thing I have done in maritime and underwater archaeology is moving overseas and working for an extended period of time. I cannot overstate the value of doing this. Living and working in a country different to my own, as cliché as it sounds, really did expand my understanding of the field of maritime archaeology and the value of underwater cultural heritage. Throughout my early career, I developed an understanding of the cultural constructs that influence a particular system, including the laws that protect sites, the way that sites are managed, the value the public gives to heritage sites, how sites are researched, what methods are used, and even how those sites are defined. To begin to understand how cultures can value heritage differently, however, a person must step outside of their own culture and immerse themselves in other systems. This understanding of other cultures is the foundation of anthropology as a discipline and can be significant in the way one conducts themselves as a maritime archaeologist.

Living, teaching, and researching in Australia allowed me to reset my assumptions of historical and maritime archaeology. I gained significant knowledge from working with Australian academics and heritage professionals, and also Indigenous Australians. Educated in the postcolonial context of the United States, I had a sense of how archaeology was a colonial endeavor there, but to see that pattern repeated in a different land with a different set of people allowed me, first, to accept and confront that past, and second, to understand that the United States is not the only country with a difficult colonial past. Although I understood that the British colonized other places in much the same way, the experience allowed me to see colonialism in a different context, and that helped me to develop a better understanding of how it is that archaeologists operate on a professional level.

In many ways, I was in awe of the methods by which terrestrial archaeologists in Australia were forwarding a better way of doing archaeology, specifically through approaches to Indigenous Archaeology which were de-centering the archaeologist as the expert and re-centering the Indigenous perspective, and also privileging Indigenous oral histories over written colonial histories. But at the same time, I was disappointed that the strides terrestrial colleagues were making were not being translated into maritime archaeology. Less than a decade ago, there was little concern for the Indigenous voice in maritime themes and, save a few nods to the need to be more inclusive, maritime archaeologists generally didn't work with Indigenous communities and peoples to explore their own past or revisit the colonial past. In fact, I had one prominent maritime archaeologist tell me he'd never consider working with Indigenous communities because it was "just too difficult."

Fortunately, at that time there were some young students coming up through the ranks who were interested in maritime archaeology and had studied with some of the most insightful terrestrial archaeologists. They started to challenge the discipline of maritime archaeology in Australia to not only "incorporate" Indigenous perspectives, but to focus squarely on the Indigenous past and work with Indigenous communities. I also began collaborating with some of those terrestrial archaeologists to develop new research and reconsider my own approach to archaeology as a community effort. This was the point at which I understood that, as in the United States, an old guard held sway but that the future was very bright because a new generation was shifting the dialogue. This shift had a profound effect on me as an archaeologist, and I'm forever thankful for having experienced working with my Australian colleagues and teaching enlightened students. Ten years later, and I'm now teaching in the United States again, and I am still filled with awe at this new generation of maritime archaeologists and hope that the next will be exploring and challenging the discipline to push it forward in ways my own generation and those before could never conceive.

Finally, an expanding number of academic institutions are teaching courses or programs associated with maritime and underwater archaeology, which necessitate a corresponding increase in faculty members and instructors. Though some universities or academic institutions focus entirely on teaching, others place an emphasis on research, so faculty members may find that they become heavily involved in field investigations and publications, in addition to teaching. Faculty positions in maritime and underwater archaeology tend to be rarer than the other types of job opportunities, and almost all faculty positions require the applicant to have a doctoral degree, while many of the other job categories only require a master's degree in most cases.

Maritime and underwater archaeology is likely to remain a rarer subset of archaeological research for the same reasons that underwater research is difficult in the first place. It is time-consuming and expensive, both to gain the training to participate in these excavations and to conduct the excavations. It takes years and additional training to conserve the materials recovered from the excavations. However, it is also enormously rewarding, and, according to some recent research, there is likely a great deal of our underwater cultural heritage left to discover with new technologies and new methods. This research indicates that even though we may have already peaked in our rate of discovering new shipwrecks in the more obvious places, there are likely many left to discover in the places we have not yet investigated, and deepwater archaeology and inundated landscape archaeology have barely begun.[1] Remember, as we stated in Chapter 1, less than 0.05 percent of the world's oceans have been mapped at a resolution to allow us to see shipwrecks. There is much left to discover in our underwater world.

## ADVOCATING FOR MARITIME AND UNDERWATER ARCHAEOLOGY

Even if you decide that a career in maritime and underwater archaeology is not for you, it can easily remain a lifelong interest. Several regional avocational (nonprofessional) groups dedicated to supporting scientific research afford opportunities to engage in archival research, field research, conservation work, or public outreach initiatives. Oftentimes, avocational groups partner with national or regional government agencies or universities in pursuing their activities. For instance, if you are a SCUBA diver, the Advisory Council on Underwater Archaeology (ACUA) maintains a list of maritime and underwater archaeology organizations that collaborate with recreational divers.[2] Elsewhere, avocational groups represent the grassroots, community-driven desire of local societies to preserve their maritime heritage that ultimately spur on government efforts. For instance, the SCAPE Trust in Scotland founded the Scotland's Coastal Heritage at Risk (SCHARP) program that has made information about at-risk coastal sites available through a smartphone app, asking citizen volunteers to help monitor and record the condition of these threatened sites. Similar programs are found in many countries, including in the United States, such as the Florida Public Archaeology Network's Heritage Monitoring Scouts (figure 14.3). These organizations are relatively new, and more and more of them are likely to be organized in the near future, as sea-level rise continues to threaten coastal heritage sites. Responsible involvement of citizen-scientists and the general public has been one of the recent trends in maritime and underwater archaeology, partially in response to archaeologists' ethical duty to make our research public, but also in response to the overwhelming need for assistance with managing threatened coastal sites.[3]

Certain volunteer and non-government organizations have expanded beyond a regional influence to become international agents of change. Among these groups is the Nautical Archaeology Society (NAS). Based in the United Kingdom,

**Figure 14.3** Florida Public Archeology Network (FPAN) avocational archaeological diver training. (Courtesy of Florida Public Archaeology Network)

NAS has regional partners across the globe, offers specialized training programs, and publishes both a newsletter and the peer-reviewed *International Journal of Nautical Archaeology*. The society offers courses to people of all ages and all skill levels, and provides ways for professionals to work with nonprofessionals. The organization also published one of the most commonly used handbooks covering basic training in nautical archaeology.[4]

Even if you are not seeking to pursue a career in maritime and underwater archaeology and are not able or compelled to support volunteer organizations, consider sharing what you have learned in this course with those around you. Maritime cultural heritage is fragile and irreplaceable, yet fascinating and of intrinsic value. The more of us that recognize its importance and care for its protection and interpretation, the more likely that some of the threats to this heritage can be mitigated, and the lessons we can learn will be preserved for future generations. Throughout this textbook, the case studies have demonstrated how much more we have been able to learn from our maritime and underwater heritage with each succeeding generation of technology. We have become exponentially better at finding, excavating, conserving, and interpreting these sites; in a few decades, if our cultural heritage is still preserved, the amount we will be able to learn is unimaginable now.

### STAYING INFORMED

No matter how you choose to involve yourself with maritime and underwater archaeology in the future, the training you have received in this class and through this text means that you are already better-informed about maritime and underwater archaeology than the average person. You probably have started to see that stories about maritime and underwater archaeology are very popular in the media. It seems like almost every time a notable shipwreck is discovered, it makes a brief worldwide splash. Your family and friends will probably start forwarding these stories to you and they will be excited to hear your opinions on the finds.

As you encounter these stories, use the tools you gained in this course to consider them critically. Remember that many of these stories are published immediately after a discovery is made, and so very little analysis has been completed. Therefore, the initial conclusions may or may not be borne out by further research. Others are based on press releases with a particular objective in mind, or on assumptions that would not withstand scrutiny. The initial furor of many stories often leads reporters to exaggerate the importance of the finds or the controversies surrounding them. When reading them, consider the source and the media outlet. Are they published by a respected news agency, or, better yet, in a science magazine? If so, the stories are much more likely to be well-vetted and the claims much more likely to be consistent with what the scientists investigating a site reported. Examine where the articles came from, but also examine who is supposed to have done the research. Is this even a real university? Is the site plausible? A few seconds of internet searching in another window should help to answer this. Further, real stories tend to be covered by multiple media platforms. These stories are most likely to help keep you up to date on the major new discoveries.

Public news articles are less likely to provide you detailed information about advancements in maritime and underwater archaeological research. This course provided you with an introduction into the breadth and depth of this field. There is more than a century's worth of published articles, books, and news stories related to maritime and underwater archaeology. We reference many of them in this text, but consider exploring further. If you want to learn the newest details about what people in the field are discovering, you should contemplate attending a conference, such as the Society for Historical Archaeology annual conference on historical and underwater archaeology or the Archaeological

Institute of Americas conference, both held every January, or one of the Nautical Archaeology Society meetings.

The most current state of knowledge is usually presented through conference papers, which are then developed into research articles that are published in journals or conference proceedings. To get the detailed discussions of maritime and underwater research, access journals in which scholarly research is published. *The International Journal of Nautical Archaeology,* the *Journal of Maritime Archaeology,* and *Mariner's Mirror* are some of the preeminent English-language journals in which maritime and underwater archaeologists publish, but there are a number of sources that present shorter, less-technical summaries for scholars and lay-people alike such as the *INA Quarterly,* produced by the Institute for Nautical Archaeology, or the *AIMA Newsletter,* published by the Australian Institute for Maritime Archaeology. There are also a number of influential monographs and edited volumes that can provide you with specific details about a single site or topic.[5]

## USING MARITIME ARCHAEOLOGY TO TEACH THE WORLD

### Annalies Corbin, President and CEO, PAST Foundation, USA

One of the beautiful things about maritime archaeology is its inherent complexity. Actually, that is the beauty of archaeology in general—on land, underwater, and from deep space. Great archaeological outcomes are based on a robust understanding of the complexity of the questions in play and the singular opportunity to bring all our thinking to bear.

As archaeologists we are the scientists of humanity. Simply put, we study and strive to understand complex human interactions and outputs based on the web of debris left behind. We open a sealed "container" every time we investigate a site, we destroy evidence as we excavate, and, although we are master documenters, we can never really re-create all of the variables that make up an archaeological site once we begin excavation. As a discipline we owe it to humanity to be meticulous, to be flawless, to be thorough and inclusive in our pursuit of answering the questions, "What is this place/thing? Who left it behind and what does it mean?" This is why archaeology as a process and a methodology make the perfect tool for teaching. When applying the principles of sound research and field methods to any discipline of study, traditional teaching and learning are instantly transformed.

As archaeologists, we can use this very philosophy—we can train teachers, students, and communities in the art of asking probing questions, in applying the scientific method and in designing thinking to solve complex problems, therefore linking learning to real life. Time and again, archaeologists around the world have demonstrated the power of utilizing the archaeological method and design thinking as a mechanism for teaching. For example, we can use basic excavation techniques with first-grade students to explore career pathways through "Digging Jobs in a Box."

The Lincoln Zoo School partnered with archaeologists to conduct research at the site of the Marshall Hotel in Yellowstone National Park. Although students and teachers participated in the onsite excavations, the real teaching and learning took place back at school where the students conducted intense investigations of artifact concretions from the Firehole River. Students identified a

*(continued)*

rare sulfate-reducing bacteria present only in the thermal river environments of the Yellowstone geyser basins.

*Telltales to Learning* is an educational and field training project in maritime heritage along the North Shore of Massachusetts which leverages Maritime Heritage to provide teachers professional development through transdisciplinary problem-based learning. By design, the program offers immersive educational field programs to middle and high school students. Students gain experience tackling complex problems in the form of a beached shipwreck. They learn to evaluate, brainstorm, design, build, and share potential interpretations of their findings all while becoming all-important stewards of maritime cultural heritage along the way. Participating teachers have the opportunity to experience the power of applied learning firsthand and, through a comprehensive teacher professional-development component of the project, teachers have the opportunity to translate that experience into lessons to take back and apply in their own classrooms.

Many cultural heritage advocacy groups are using public archaeology projects as a direct application to the transformation of teaching and learning. PAST Foundation has formalized and amplified the approach of scientific field investigations (archaeology) and applied it to the theory of full educational transformation via an anthropologically based School Design process we call P3—Problems, Projects, and Products—which is quite simply the same design thinking process every great archaeologist applies to excavating sites. How will you apply your work to make a broader impact?

### SUMMARY

Maritime and underwater archaeology has a bright future, even though much of our shared maritime cultural heritage is threatened. If you are interested in pursuing a career in the field, there are many possible professions available to you. If you are not, there are multiple ways in which to become involved as a citizen-scientist or even as a critical audience of news articles found in the social media and online news realms. This book gave you the beginnings of what there is to be learned from maritime and underwater archaeology. Please keep reading; there is so much more information out there. Talk to a local archaeologist or your professor about ways you can become involved in archaeology in your area!

### DISCUSSION QUESTIONS

1. What do you think you could do to protect and promote maritime and underwater cultural heritage after taking this course?
2. What do you think you would find to be the most satisfying career path in maritime and underwater archaeology? Why?
3. Why is it so important to critically analyze online media and news stories about archaeology? What possible harm could be caused by incorrect stories?

### FURTHER READING

Advisory Council on Underwater Archaeology (ACUA). (2017). Organizations Providing Maritime Heritage Training to Recreational Divers. Advisory

Council on Underwater Archaeology. Available at https://acuaonline.org/. Accessed 12/24/2017.

Catsambis, A., B. Ford, and J. Halligan. (2017). Maritime Archaeology. *Oxford Bibliography in Anthropology*. J. John Jackson, Ed. Oxford University Press, Oxford. Available at DOI: 10.1093/OBO/9780199766567-0176

Florida Public Archaeology Network. (2017). Heritage Monitoring Scouts. Available at https://fpan.us/projects/HMSflorida.php.

Nautical Archaeology Society (NAS). (2017). Nautical Archaeology Society. Available at https://www.nauticalarchaeologysociety.org/.

Society for Historical Archaeology. (2017). Guide to Graduate Programs in Historical and Underwater Archaeology. Available at https://sha.org/students-and-teachers/guide-to-higher-education/.

# GLOSSARY

**ABSOLUTE DATING** dating method that gives an actual age in calendar years (11,000 BP; 800 BCE; or, even, 780-820 BCE). Common absolute dating methods include historical chronology, radiocarbon, optically stimulated luminescence, and dendrochronology.

**ABSOLUTE PRESSURE** total amount of pressure, including hydrostatic and atmospheric pressure, on a diver at a given depth. Also known as ambient pressure.

**AIRLIFT** a pressure-based device used to remove sediments from an underwater site. More useful in deeper water than a water dredge. A long, vertical pipe has compressed air injected into the lower end of the pipe, creating suction in its wake as the air bubbles rise and expand.

**AMPHORA** large ceramic container used to transport many different commodities in the ancient world.

**ANALOGY** in archaeology, comparing two things (cultures, artifacts, etc.), one well-understood and the other less-understood (and usually from an archaeological context), upon multiple dimensions under the premise that if they are alike in some ways, they likely are in others as well, so the known can be used to further understand aspects of the unknown.

**ANTIQUARIAN** person who collects objects of ancient societies for display and historical study; antiquarianism was a form of protoarchaeology common in the 18th and 19th centuries.

**ARCHAEOBOTANY** also known as paleoethnobotany, the analysis of floral remains discovered in archaeological contexts.

**ARCHAEOLOGY** the study of past human societies through the analysis of their material remains.

**ARTIFACT** portable object made or modified by humans.

**ASSEMBLAGE** the entire group of artifacts from an archaeological component or a site (or the group of artifacts that occurs together in a given culture).

**ASSOCIATION** demonstrable relationship between two items of material culture, such as an artifact being found within a feature.

**ATMOSPHERIC PRESSURE** amount of pressure applied by the atmosphere above a person.

**AUV** (Autonomous Underwater Vehicle) robot that can travel underwater and collect data without direct input from an operator. Operating parameters are generally input before the AUV is deployed and the AUV is recovered after its mission so that the data can be downloaded.

**BASELINE** straight line laid on a site from which to take measurements, using right-angle offsets

**BEAM** a timber, perpendicular to the long axis of a vessel that provides lateral strength and can support decks.

**BILGE** the curve or juncture between the bottom and side of a ship hull.

**BIOARCHAEOLOGY** the analysis of human remains discovered in archaeological contexts.

**BIOME** naturally cooccurring community of plants and animals.

**BOAT** small open vessel.

**BOTTOM-BASED** a shipbuilding philosophy in which the bottom of a vessel defines the hull form.

**BOW** forward part of a hull.

**BULKHEAD** vertical partition within a hull.

**CALIBRATION** the process of making one measurement system correlate with another. Must be done to convert radiocarbon ages to calendar years.

**CANOE** small, narrow boat with an open hull.

**CARAVEL** small, maneuverable vessel with one or more lateen sails.

**CARRACK** ship type demonstrating both Mediterranean and Northern European characteristics, including a carvel planking, multiple masts, castles, and a stern rudder.

**CARVEL PLANKING** flush planked so that plank seams were aligned.

**CAULKING** fibrous material driven into a plank seam or placed between two planks to form a watertight seam.

**CAUSEWAY** raised surface that extends between land and water.

**CHARACTERIZATION** determining the makeup of an artifact, often through geochemical analyses.

**CLINKER** form of lapstrake hull construction where overlapping planks are fastened with clenched nails.

**CLIPPER SHIP** type of ship with a nearly flat deck and keel, and a sharp bow.

**COGNITIVE ARCHAEOLOGY** branch of archaeology that attempts to understand the belief systems of past cultures.

**COLONY** area under the control of, and inhabited by settlers from, a distant country. The colony is often exploited for the economic benefit of the colonizing country.

**COMPONENT** all the evidence that can be grouped into a single time period at an archaeological site. Sites may be single-component (only containing evidence of a single period of occupation/use) or multiple-component (containing evidence of multiple periods of occupation/use).

**COMPOSITE CONSTRUCTION** the use of iron frames and wood planking in a single vessel.

**CONSTRUCTION DRAWING** drawing of the major components of a hull showing the size, shape, and position of the components within the vessel.

**CONTEXT** the relationship between artifacts, ecofacts, and features within a site and the relationship of sites to one another.

**CONTROL SAMPLE** 1. samples collected from a nonarchaeological context in order to determine how natural deposition differs from the cultural material recovered from the site. 2. cultural material from a context withheld from a scientific analysis to determine how the analysis alters the material or to save some material for future analyses.

**CORACLE** small round boat, often constructed of a waterproof covering over a wickerwork frame.

**CRANNOG** dwelling constructed on an artificial island in a lake or marsh.

**CRIB** framework of heavy timbers used as the foundation for a structure.

**CURACH** a medium to large boat, built similarly to a coracle, but designed for use in open water.

**DATUM** as used in archaeology, the origin point for a site grid, or the origin point from which measurements are taken.

**DEAD RECKONING** the approximation of direction and distance based on constantly updated estimates of speed, sea conditions, winds, and currents.

**DECOMPRESSION ILLNESS** illnesses that can happen to divers if they ascend too quickly without following proper procedures; includes arterial gas embolism and decompression sickness (also known as "the bends").

**DHOW** ship with high ends and a flat bottom often associated with the Indian Ocean.

**DIAGNOSTIC ARTIFACT** artifact that is only made during a known limited range of time, by a known culture, or both.

**DNA ANALYSIS** characterization technique that analyzes the genetic makeup of organic material culture or human remains.

**DRAFT** depth of a hull at the water surface.

**DROMON** Byzantine war galley prevalent in late antiquity and early medieval times across the eastern Mediterranean Sea.

**DRY-DOCK** basin that can be flooded to allow a ship to enter and then drained to allow the ship to come to rest on a dry surface.

**EAST INDIAMAN** general term for a ship operated by any of the European East India companies.

**ECOFACT** natural materials used by humans but not directly modified, such as stones used in buildings or the bones of an animal used for food.

**ETHNOARCHAEOLOGY** study of a living culture focusing upon the patterns of creation, use, discard, and decay of its material culture in order to use this information to further understand archaeological sites.

**ETHNOGENESIS** formation and development of an ethnic group.

**ETHNOGRAPHIC ANALOGY** the methods of inferring the use or meaning of an artifact, feature, or site from observations of living peoples. Applying ethnographic data to the archaeological record.

**ETHNOGRAPHY** the intensive anthropological study of a single culture, or the published research of this study.

**EXPERIMENTAL ARCHAEOLOGY** also known as replication, when researchers attempt to recreate materials found in the archaeological record, often using tools or materials that would have been in use in the past.

**FEATURE** nonportable object made by people, such as houses and other structures.

**FIRST MATE** officer immediately below captain.

**FLOAT** aid to flotation that requires the user to be partially immersed.

**FOODWAYS** food and all of the activities and social norms that surround obtaining, processing, and consuming foods.

**FORE-AND-AFT SAIL** sail oriented parallel to the long axis of a ship. Often, but not exclusively, triangular.

**FORECASTLE** also spelled fo'c'sle. Sailors' living quarters on an upper deck forward of the foremast.

**FRAME** timber, or assembly of timbers, that extends perpendicular to the long axis of a vessel. Planking is fastened to frames.

**FRAME-FIRST** shipbuilding philosophy focused on the frames. Frames define the shape of the hull, provide much of the vessel's structural strength, and were erected before planking was added.

**FREEBOARD** distance between the water surface and the upper side of a vessel.

**FREQUENCY SERIATION** using relative abundances (in percentages) of artifact styles to arrange artifact assemblages in relative time.

**FRIGATE** term used to describe a number of fast, relatively small warship types evolving from the 17th century onward. In addition to engaging with the enemy, frigates often served as scouts or escorts to merchant vessels, or engaged in commerce raiding.

**GALLEASS** type of vessel that developed from large merchant galleys converted for military use. Galleasses often carried more sails than galleys and were larger, slower and more heavily armed.

**GALLEON** large sailing vessel with a high stern, usually with three or four masts, carrying square sails on the forward masts and a lateen sail on the aft mast.

**GALLEY** long, slender ship propelled primarily by rowing.

**GEOARCHAEOLOGIST** specialist focused on reconstructing site context, stratigraphy, and dating using geological methods to answer archaeological questions.

**GIS** (Geographic Information System) computer program that allows multiple maps and spatial data sets to be combined and analyzed. Sometimes also referred to as geographic information science to denote the practices and theories of analyzing spatial data.

**GUNPORT** opening, typically on the side of a ship above the waterline, through which a gun may be fired.

**HALF-LIFE** number of years after which only half the original amount of a radioactive isotope will be left (for Carbon-14, this is 5730 years).

**HARBOR** a natural or humanmade coastal location where a ship may find shelter.

**HARD** a prepared surface for beaching boats.

**HARDTACK** also called ship's biscuit or sea biscuit. Simple, inexpensive, long-lasting cracker common on long sailing voyages.

**HEAD** ship's toilet, often located at bow of a sailing ship.

**HISTORIC** from a culture or time period for which there are written records.

**HOG** condition when the ends of a vessel droop.

**HOLYSTONE** book-sized piece of soft sandstone used to scrub ship decks.

**HULL** main body of a vessel.

**HYDROSTATIC PRESSURE** amount of pressure exerted by a fluid at a given depth; in diving, the amount of pressure applied by the water column above the diver.

**IN SITU** (in place) term used by archaeologists to mean that the artifacts were found in their original context of deposition.

**ISOTOPIC ANALYSIS** characterization technique that captures the relative percentages of the isotopes of a single element.

**JETTY** small pier.

**JOGGLE** notches cut into the face or edge of frames so that they better fit the hull planking.

**JUNK** traditional Chinese sailing vessel.

**KAMAL** navigation instrument to measure latitude developed in Arabia, consisting of a tablet attached to a knotted string. The tablet is moved away from the eye until it fills the space between the horizon and the star and the number of knots are counted and converted into degrees latitude.

**KAYAK** small, narrow boat with an enclosed hull.

**KEEL** the main longitudinal timber, or assembly of timbers, in most vessels. In frame-first construction most other structural components are attached to the keel.

**KEELSON** internal longitudinal timber, or assembly of timbers, that parallels the keel.

**KNEE** piece of timber used to reinforce the junction of two timbers in different planes, such as frames and beams.

**KNOT-WORK** rope tied into a series of knots to create artistic and/or functional pieces.

**LAPSTRAKE** form of vessel construction where hull planks are overlapped.

**LATITUDE** geographic coordinate specifying a north-south position.

**LATEEN SAIL** triangular sail set on a yard set at a 45° angle to the mast. A form of fore-and-aft sail.

**LAW OF SUPERPOSITION** in undisturbed stratigraphy, deeper layers are older than shallower layers.

**LINES DRAWING** set of three, interrelated drawings that render the three-dimensional shape of a hull on a two-dimensional page.

**LONGBOAT** long, slender, clinker-built vessels of the Viking Age, propelled by oars and a single square sail. Also called a longship.

**LONGITUDE** geographic coordinate specifying a east-west position.

**MARINE TRANSGRESSION** geologic processes of sea level rising relative to land and the shore line advancing toward higher ground.

**MARITIME ARCHAEOLOGY** study of human societies dependent upon waterways for their livelihoods.

**MARITIME CULTURAL LANDSCAPE** collections of submerged archaeological sites, or combinations of terrestrial and submerged sites that reflect the relationship between humans and the water.

**MAST STEP** timber that supported the bottom of the mast; the step often helped transfer the force of the sails to the hull.

**MATERIAL CULTURE** physical, tangible remains of human activities, including objects that were used, displayed, lived in, built, and discarded.

**MATRIX** the material surrounding an artifact, often noncultural (such as the sand filling the hull of a shipwreck), but occasionally the result of human activity (such as the sediment in a pit feature).

**MIDDEN** trash dump.

**MIDDLE RANGE THEORY** archaeological research that uses various types of analogies to bridge the gap between patterns of material culture and overarching questions about human behavior.

**MIDSHIP** middle of a ship; can refer to a general area on a vessel or one or more frames at the center of a ship.

**MODERNITY** quality of being modern, generally made up of ideas and attitudes that developed in Europe and its colonies since the end of the medieval period.

**MORTISE AND TENON** form of joinery where a piece of wood (tenon) is fitted into corresponding sockets (mortises) in adjoining pieces of wood.

**NAUTICAL ARCHAEOLOGY** study of shipwrecks and their contents and the study of past shipbuilding technology.

**NITROGEN NARCOSIS** drowsy and or intoxicated feeling induced by breathing nitrogen in air at higher than atmospheric pressure.

**ORGANIC** item that contains carbon and once was alive. Item is able to be radiocarbon dated, but preservation of organic materials is rare.

**OUTRIGGER** framework supporting a float that extends next to the main hull.

**PALEOETHNOBOTANY** also known as archaeobotany, the analysis of floral remains discovered in archaeological contexts.

**PALIMPSEST** surface that has been reused or altered, but which still retrains traces of its original form or uses.

**PALYNOLOGY** study of pollen grains.

**PENTECONTER** ancient Greek war galley with a removable sail propelled primarily by fifty oarsmen.

**PETROGRAPHY** geological technique of analyzing and classifying rocks and minerals, especially through thin sections. Used to characterize artifacts in archaeology, especially for sourcing.

**PIER** structure that extends from land into the water; traditionally used to land ships, but also used for fishing and recreation.

**PLANKING** outer surface or shell of a hull.

**PORT** settlement associated with a harbor. Often used as a synonym for a developed harbor.

**PORTAGE** to transport a vessel between waterbodies.

**POST** vertical timber, or assembly of timbers, that forms the ends of a vessel. May be specified as the stem (bow) or sternpost (stern).

**PREHISTORIC ARCHAEOLOGY** archaeology of societies without written records. The cultures grouped under this category recorded their history orally or through other nonwritten means.

**PRIMARY CONTEXT** material culture that was not disturbed after its initial deposition, so it is most informative about past human activities.

**PROVENIENCE** horizontal and vertical position of a find within the site's grid. Northing refers to the distance north from the arbitrary origin of the grid; easting is how far east the item is from the origin of the grid, and elevation is the distance above or below the origin point.

**PROXY RECORD** especially in reference to paleoenvironmental studies, when the presence or absence of a given type of data at a site is used to infer the presence or absence of a specific environmental condition at the site.

**RADIOCARBON DATING** absolute dating method that uses the radioactive decay of Carbon-14 to determine the time since death of once-living materials.

**RAFT** simple type of boat that derives its buoyancy from the buoyancy of its individual components.

**RELATIVE DATING** dating method that only provides a relative age (older than x or younger than x). Common relative dating methods include *terminus post quem, terminus ante quem*, stratigraphy, seriation, and association.

**REPLICATION** also known as experimental archaeology, when researchers attempt to recreate materials found in the archaeological record, often using tools or materials that would have been in use in the past.

**ROV** (Remotely Operated Vehicle) tethered robot that is often used where it is unsafe or impractical to send human divers. Commonly used in deep-water environments.

**ROVE** small square iron plate used as part of the fastening method in clinker ship construction.

**RUDDER** timber, or assembly of timbers, that could be rotated or moved to control the direction of a ship.

**SAG** the condition when the center of a vessel droops.

**SAILING DIRECTIONS** written descriptions of maritime routes that connect ports.

**SAND CLOCK** two connected glass globes containing a granulated substance such as sand or lead. The flow of grains from one globe to the other is calibrated to measure a set amount of time. Commonly called an hourglass, although many measured shorter periods.

**SCRIMSHAW** images engraved into bone, ivory, wood, or other materials and highlighted with soot or other pigment.

**SCUBA** (Self Contained Underwater Breathing Apparatus) acronym referring to one of the most common forms of diving, in which divers carry their air with them in compressed air tanks.

**SCURVY** potentially fatal disease resulting from a lack of vitamin C. Causes weakness, sores, gum disease, and hair loss.

**SECONDARY CONTEXT** when material culture was disturbed after its initial deposition, so that original context between items has been altered or destroyed, making items less informative about past activities.

**SERIATION** placing an artifact type in relative age order by changing stylistic attributes.

**SHANTY** maritime work song or chant.

**SHELL-FIRST** shipbuilding philosophy that saw the hull planking as the basis for the shape and strength of the vessel, so that the ship was designed longitudinally, along the length of the planks.

**SHIP** oceangoing vessel.

**SHIP'S BOY** also called a cabin boy. A young boy who carried messages and did odd jobs on a ship.

**SITE** location from which tangible evidence of human activity (material culture), including artifacts, ecofacts, and features, can be recovered.

**SITE FORMATION PROCESSES** how an archaeological site is created; this includes the cultural activities that left tangible traces behind (cultural formation processes) and the natural processes of destruction and decay that impact the site after people have abandoned it (natural formation processes).

**SLIPWAY** portion of shore where the slope has been altered to make hauling out and launching ships and boats easier.

**SOUNDING LEAD** weight, often made of lead, attached to a line, used to measure the depth of water beneath a vessel. Often included a pocket of soft material, such as tallow, to collect a sample of the bottom material.

**SOURCING** determining where the constituent parts of an artifact came from by comparing them to known raw material sources.

**SQUARE SAIL** often trapezoidal sail oriented perpendicular to the long axis of a ship.

**STAKEHOLDER** people or entities who have an interest or equity in a matter.

**STEAMBOAT** steam-propelled vessel. "Steamboat" generally refers to vessels used on inland waterways, even if large, while "steamship" refers to oceangoing vessels.

**STERN** rear part of a hull.

**STERNCASTLE** high superstructure above the transom.

**STRUCTURE** composite features that were probably used for containing things and are large enough for humans to enter. The term "structure" implies that the function is unknown.

**SURVEY** systematic investigation for the purpose of locating archaeological sites.

**SYSTEMIC CONTEXT** social system that surrounded and informed the creation, use, and loss of an artifact, feature, or ecofact.

**TAPHONOMY** study of how natural processes introduce (false and noncultural) patterning in the remains at a site through burial, decomposition, and so on.

**TARGET** in survey, an item of interest that needs further verification, which could be a site, artifact, or feature, but also could merely be an anomaly in the geology of the area.

**TERMINUS ANTE QUEM** ("date before which") relative dating method that determines the latest date something could have happened based on the oldest possible date of the layer above the context of interest.

**TERMINUS POST QUEM** ("date after which") relative dating method that determines the earliest date something could have happened based on the youngest material culture in a given context.

**THROUGH BEAM** large beam that spanned the hull and protruded through the sides.

**TRACE ELEMENT ANALYSIS** characterization technique that captures the entire elemental signature of an item, with a focus on accurately capturing the relative percentages of the rare (trace) elements.

**TRADITION** group of cultures or industries that developed together or from one another, usually over an extended period of time.

**TRANSOM** portion of hull perpendicular to the keel and affixed to the stern post; it generally gives a vessel a squared-off or rounded, rather than a pointed, stern.

**TREENAIL** wooden dowels used to fasten two pieces of timber, most often planking to frames. Pronounced and also occasionally spelled "trunnel."

**TRILATERATION** using three (or more) points whose relationship to one another is known as datums to accurately map a site in three dimensions by measuring the distance from each known datum to each point of interest.

**TRIREME** ancient Mediterranean warship known for being fast, maneuverable, and armed with a bronze ram to smash the hull of opposing vessels.

**TRY WORKS** a heating apparatus used to render whale blubber into oil. Usually consisting of one or more pots atop a masonry furnace.

**TYPOLOGY** categorization of artifacts into different and exclusive groups based upon their attributes (such as function, shape, decoration, size) for the purpose of comparing different types and different sites.

**UNDERWATER ARCHAEOLOGY** study of material culture found underwater.

**VOLTA DO MAR** sailing technique used during European expansion that allowed both an outbound and return voyage with following winds. Near the equator, the "trade winds" come from the northeast while the winds are southwesterly in the mid-Atlantic. Ships would sail out into the Atlantic and then turn north in order to return home.

**WALE** particularly thick exterior hull plank that strengthens and protects the side of the vessel.

**WATER DREDGE** also known in as a water eductor, a pump-based device used to remove sediments from a shallow underwater site. An angled tube injects a high-speed water jet into the dredge head, creating a Venturi suction effect pulling material through the attached dredge hose.

**ZOOARCHAEOLOGY** analysis of faunal remains discovered in archaeological contexts.

# REFERENCES

**CHAPTER 1**

1. Museo Nacional de Arqueología Subacuática. (2018). Nuestra Señora de las Mercedes. Available at http://www.mecd.gob.es/mnarqua/en/colecciones/yacimientos/ns-mercedes.html.

   Anonymous. (9 November 1805). Notices. *London Gazette*, p. 1402. Available at https://www.thegazette.co.uk/London/issue/15861/page/1402.

2. Alderman, K. (1 June 2010). High Seas Shipwreck Pits Treasure Hunters Against a Sovereign Nation: The Black Swan Case. *American Society of International Law Cultural Heritage and Arts Review, Spring 2010*; Univ. of Wisconsin Legal Studies Research Paper No. 1135. Available at https://ssrn.com/abstract=1619330.

   Museo Nacional de Arqueología Subacuática. (2018). Nuestra Señora de las Mercedes: Third Campaign: August 2017. Available at http://www.mecd.gob.es/mnarqua/investigacion/proyectos/nsm.html.

3. Yerkes, R.W., E. Galili and R. Barkai. (2014). Activities at Final Pre-Pottery Neolithic (PPNC) Fishing Village Revealed through Microwear Analysis of Bifacial Flint Tools from the Submerged Atlit-Yam Site, Israel. *Journal of Archaeological Science* **48**: 120–128.

4. Stringer, C. (2000). Palaeoanthropology: Coasting out of Africa. *Nature* **405**(6782): 24–27.

   Laskaris, N., A. Sampson, F. Mavridis, and I. Liritzis (2011). Late Pleistocene/Early Holocene Seafaring in the Aegean: New Obsidian Hydration Dates with the SIMS-SS Method. *Journal of Archaeological Science* **38**(9): 2475–2479.

   Reeder-Myers, L., J.M. Erlandson, D.R. Muhs, and T.C. Rick. (2015). Sea Level, Paleogeography, and Archeology on California's Northern Channel Islands. *Quaternary Research* **83**(2): 263–272.

   NASA. (2012). Oceans: The Great Unknown. Available at https://www.nasa.gov/audience/forstudents/5-8/features/oceans-the-great-unknown-58.html.

5. Sandwell, D.T., R.D. Müller, W.H.F. Smith, E. Garcia, and R. Francis. (2014). New Global Marine Gravity Model from CryoSat-2 and Jason-1 Reveals Buried Tectonic Structure. *Science* **346**(6205): 65–67.

   Copley, J. (2014). Just How Little Do We Know About the Ocean Floor? *Scientific American*. Available at https://www.scientificamerican.com/article/just-how-little-do-we-know-about-the-ocean-floor/.

6. Anderson, A., J. Barrett, and K. Boyle, Eds. (2010). *The Global Origins and Development of Seafaring*. Oxbow Books, Oxford.

Bednarik, Robert G. (2014). The Beginnings of Maritime Travel. *Advances in Anthropology* 4: 209–221.

Strasser, T.F., E. Panagopoulou, C.N. Runnels, P.M. Murray, N. Thompson, P. Karkanas, F.W. McCoy, and K.W. Wegmann. (2010). Stone Age Seafaring in the Mediterranean: Evidence from the Plakias Region of Lower Paleolithic and Mesolithic Habitation of Crete. *Hesperia: The Journal of the American School of Classical Studies at Athens* 79(2): 145–190.

7. Grant, R.G. (2011). *Battle at Sea: 3,000 Years of Naval Warfare*. DK Publishing, New York.

8. Benjamin, J., C. Bonsall, C. Pickard, and A. Fischer, Eds. (2011). *Submerged Prehistory*. Oxbow Press, Oxford.

9. Empereur, J.-Y. (1998). *Alexandria Rediscovered*. George Braziller Publisher, New York.

Goddio, F., and D. Fabre, Eds. (2008). *Egypt's Sunken Treasures*. Prestel, Munich.

La Riche, W. (1996) *Alexandria, The Sunken City*. Weidenfeld and Nicolson, London.

10. Muckelroy, K. (1978). *Maritime Archaeology*. Cambridge University Press, New York.

11. von Arbin, S., and A. Daly (2012). The Mollö Cog Re-Examined and Re-Evaluated. *International Journal of Nautical Archaeology* 41(2): 372–389.

Crumlin-Pedersen, O., and O. Olsen, Eds. (2002). *The Skuldelev Ships I: Topography, Archaeology, History, Conservation and Display*. Viking Ship Museum, Roskilde, Denmark.

Gardiner, Robert, Ed. (1994). *Cogs, Caravels and Galleons*. Conway Maritime Press, London.

Hoffmann, G., and P. Hoffmann. (2009). Sailing the Bremen Cog. *International Journal of Nautical Archaeology* 38(2): 281–296.

Vermeersch, J., and K. Haneca. (2015). Construction Features of Doel 1, a 14th-Century Cog Found in Flanders. *International Journal of Nautical Archaeology* 44(1): 111–131.

Williams, G. (2014). *The Viking Ship*. British Museum Press, London.

12. Pomey, P., Y. Kahanov, and E. Rieth. (2012). Transition from Shell to Skeleton in Ancient Mediterranean Ship-Construction: Analysis, Problems And Future Research. *International Journal of Nautical Archaeology* 41(2): 235–314.

13. Fernández-Armesto, F. (2007). *Pathfinders: A Global History of Exploration*. W.W. Norton, New York.

14. Foucault, M. (1984). Of Other Spaces: Utopias and Heterotopias. *Architecture, Movement, Continuité* 5: 46–49.

## CHAPTER 2

1. Friends of the Hunley. (2018). Hunley. Available at https://hunley.org/.

2. Bass, G. (2011). The Development of Maritime Archaeology. *Oxford Handbook of Maritime Archaeology*. A. Catsambis, B. Ford, and D. L. Hamilton, Eds. 3–22. Oxford University Press, New York.

Ucelli, G. (1950). *Le Navi di Nemi*. Libreria dello Stato, Rome.

3. Bass, G. (2011). The Development of Maritime Archaeology. *Oxford Handbook of Maritime Archaeology*. A. Catsambis, B. Ford, and D. L. Hamilton, Eds. 3–22. Oxford University Press, New York.

Catsambis, A. (2006). Before Antikythera: the First Underwater Archaeological Survey in Greece. *International Journal of Nautical Archaeology* 35(1): 104–107.

Weinberg, G.D., V.R. Grace, G.R. Edwards, H.S. Robinson, P. Throckmorton, and E.K. Ralph. (1965). The Antikythera Shipwreck Reconsidered. *Transactions of the American Philosophical Society* 55(3): 3–48.

4. Bass, G. (2011). The Development of Maritime Archaeology. *Oxford Handbook of Maritime Archaeology*. A. Catsambis, B. Ford, and D. L. Hamilton, Eds. 3–22. Oxford University Press, New York.

Carlson, D. (2011). The Seafarers and Shipwrecks of Ancient Greece and Rome. *Oxford Handbook of Maritime Archaeology*. A. Catsambis, B. Ford, and D. L. Hamilton, Eds. 379–405. Oxford University Press, New York.

5. Adams, J. (2013). Pathways and Ideas. *A Maritime Archaeology of Ships*. 1–14. Oxbow Books, Oxford.

Bass, G. (2011). The Development of Maritime Archaeology. *Oxford Handbook of Maritime Archaeology*. A. Catsambis, B. Ford, and D. L. Hamilton, Eds. 3–22. Oxford University Press, New York.

6. Adams, J. (2013). Pathways and Ideas. *A Maritime Archaeology of Ships*. 1–14. Oxbow Books, Oxford.

Andersen, S.H. (1987). Tybrind Vig: A Submerged Ertebolle Settlement in Denmark. *European Wetlands in Prehistory*. J.M. Coles and A.J. Lawson, Eds. 253–280. Oxford, Clarendon Press.

Clausen, C.J., H.K. Brooks, and A. B. Wesolowsky (1975). The Early Man Site at Warm Mineral Springs, Florida. *Journal of Field Archaeology* 2(3): 191–213.

7. Ballard, R.D. (2008). *Archaeological Oceanography*. Princeton University Press, Princeton, NJ.

8. Søreide, F. (2011). Maritime Archaeology and Industry. *Oxford Handbook of Maritime Archaeology*. A. Catsambis, B. Ford, and D. L. Hamilton, Eds. 1010–1031. Oxford University Press, New York.

9. Flatman, J. (2003). Cultural Biographies, Cognitive Landscapes and Dirty Old Bits of Boat: "Theory" In Maritime Archaeology. *International Journal of Nautical Archaeology* 32(2): 143–157.

10. Barker, P. (2005). *Techniques of Archaeological Excavation*. Third Edition. Taylor and Francis, New York.

11. Bass, G. (2011). The Development of Maritime Archaeology. *Oxford Handbook of Maritime Archaeology*. A. Catsambis, B. Ford, and D. L. Hamilton, Eds. 3–22. Oxford University Press, New York.

Kleeburg, J.M. (2013). A Critique of the Fundamentals of the "Commercial Salvage" Model of the Excavation of Historic Shipwrecks: An Examination of the Profitability of Six Commercial Salvage Ventures. *Technical Briefs in Historical Archaeology*. **7**: 19–30. Available at https://sha.org/assets/documents/Technical_briefs_articles/TechBreifs.pdf.

12. Flemming, N.C., J. Harff, and D. Moura. (2017). Non-Cultural Process of Site Formation, Preservation and Destruction. *Submerged Landscapes of the European Continental Shelf: Quaternary Paleoenvironments*. J.H. Nicholas, C. Flemming, Delminda Moura, Anthony Burgess, and Geoffrey N. Bailey, Eds. 51–82. John Wiley and Sons, Inc. Hoboken, NJ.

**CHAPTER 3**

1. Swiss Coordination Group UNESCO Palafittes. (2015). Prehistoric Pile Dwellings around the Alps. Available at https://www.palafittes.org/homepage.html.

2. Delgado, J.P. (2009). *Gold Rush Port: the Maritime Archaeology of San Francisco's Waterfront*. Berkeley, University of California Press.

3. Hooge, J. (2013). *Underwater Geoarchaeology at Spring Lake, San Marcos, Texas*. Unpublished Master's Thesis, Texas State University, San Marcos.

4. Muckelroy, K. (1978). *Maritime Archaeology*. Cambridge University Press, Cambridge.

5. Flemming, N.C., J. Harff, and D. Moura. (2017). Non-Cultural Process of Site Formation, Preservation and Destruction. *Submerged Landscapes of the European Continental Shelf: Quaternary Paleoenvironments*. J.H. Nicholas, C. Flemming, D. Moura, A. Burgess, and G. N. Bailey, Eds. 51–82. John Wiley and Sons, Inc. Hoboken, NJ.

6. Fatovich, R., and K.A. Bard. (2015). Mersa/Wadi Gawasis and Ancient Egyptian Maritime

Trade in the Red Sea. *Near Eastern Archaeology* **78**(1): 3–11.

Greene, D. (2001). Ozette Village. *Encyclopedia of Archaeology: History and Discoveries*. T. Murray Ed. 505–506. ABC-CLIO, Santa Barbara, CA.

Ingstad, A.S., E. Seeberg, and H. Ingstad (1977). *The Discovery of a Norse settlement in America*, Universitetsforlaget, Oslo.

7. Doran, G.H. (2002). *Windover: Multidisciplinary Investigations of an Early Archaic Florida Cemetery.* University Press of Florida, Gainesville.

8. Metcalfe, T. (10 November 2016). Oldest Beer Brewed from Shipwreck's 220-Year-Old Yeast Microbes *LiveScience*. Available at https://www.livescience.com/56814-oldest-beer-recreated-from-shipwreck-yeast.html.

9. Rickman, G.E. (1980). The Grain Trade Under the Roman Empire. *The Seaborne Commerce of Ancient Rome: Studies in Archaeology and History.* J. H. D'Arms and E. C. Kopff, Eds. American Academy in Rome Memoirs **36**: 261–275. Rome.

Brophy, J.K., and K. Crisman, (2013). A Taphonomic Evaluation of Three Intact Pork Barrels from the Steamboat Heroine (1838). *Historical Archaeology* **47**(4): 71–85.

10. Schmandt-Besserat, D., J.L. Swauger, M.A. Powell, J.P. Allen, M. O'Connor, W.D. Whitt, and W.D. Whitt. (1996). Writing. *Oxford Companion to Archaeology*. B.M. Fagan Ed. 761–769. Oxford University Press, Oxford.

11. Tycot, R.H. (2004). Scientific Methods and Applications to Archaeological Provenance Studies. *Proceedings of the International School of Physics "Enrico Fermi"*. M.M.M. Martini, and M. Piacentini, Eds. 407–432. IOS Press, Amsterdam. Available at http://luna.cas.usf.edu/~rtykot/PR40%20-%20Enrico%20Fermi%20obsidian.pdf.

**CHAPTER 4**

1. Crisman, K.J. (2014). *Coffins of the Brave: Lake Shipwrecks of the War of 1812.* Texas A&M University Press, College Station.

Crumlin-Pedersen, O., and E. Bondesen, Eds. (2002). *The Skuldelev Ships I: Topography, Archaeology, History, Conservation and Display.* Viking Ship Museum, Roskilde, Denmark.

Underwater Archaeology Division, Division of Historical Resources, Bureau of Archaeological Research, Florida Department of State. (2014). Florida Panhandle Shipwreck Trail. Available at http://www.floridapanhandledivetrail.com/.

2. Keith, Matthew, Ed. (2016). *Site Formation Processes of Submerged Shipwrecks.* University Press of Florida, Gainesville.

Crisman, K. J. (2014). *Coffins of the Brave: Lake Shipwrecks of the War of 1812.* Texas A&M University Press, College Station.

3. Price, F.H. (2016). More than Meets the Eye: A Preliminary Report on Artifacts from the Sediment of Site 31CR314, *Queen Anne's Revenge*, an Eighteenth-century Shipwreck off Beaufort Inlet, North Carolina. *Southeastern Archaeology* **35**(2): 155–169.

4. Stewart, D.J. (1999). Formation Processes Affecting Submerged Archaeological Sites: An Overview. *Geoarchaeology* **14**(6): 565–587.

Ward, I.A.K., P. Larcombe, and P. Veth. (1999). A New Process-based Model for Wreck Site Formation. *Journal of Archaeological Science* **26**(5): 561–570.

5. Anderson, D.G., T.G. Bissett, S.J. Yerka, J.J. Wells, E.C. Kansa, S.W. Kansa, K.N. Myers, R.C. DeMuth, and D.A. White. (2017). Sea-Level Rise and Archaeological Site Destruction: An Example from the Southeastern United States Using DINAA (Digital Index of North American Archaeology). *PLOS ONE* **12**(11): e0188142.

Hambrecht, G., and M. Rockman (2017). International Approaches to Climate Change and Cultural Heritage. *American Antiquity* **82**(4): 627–641.

6. Ballard, R. D., and R. Archbold. (2005). *The Lost Ships of Robert Ballard.* Thunder Bay Press, San Diego.

Keay, S., M. Millett, and K. Strutt. (2008). Recent Archaeological Survey at Portus. *The Maritime World of Ancient Rome*. R. L. Hohlfelder, Ed. 97–104. University of Michigan Press for the American Academy in Rome, Ann Arbor.

Sonnenburg, E., A. Lemke, and J. O'Shea, Eds. (2015). *Caribou Hunting in the Upper Great Lakes*. Memoirs of the Museum of Anthropology, Number 57. University of Michigan, Ann Arbor.

7. Bass, G. (2011). The Development of Maritime Archaeology. *Oxford Handbook of Maritime Archaeology*. A. Catsambis, B. Ford, and D.L. Hamilton, Eds. 3–22. Oxford University Press, New York.

**CHAPTER 5**

1. Bowens, A. (2009). *Underwater Archaeology: The NAS Guide to Principles and Practice,* second edition. Blackwell Publishing, Portsmouth, UK.

2. Bass, G. (2011). The Development of Maritime Archaeology. *Oxford Handbook of Maritime Archaeology*. A. Catsambis, B. Ford, and D.L. Hamilton, Eds. 3–22. Oxford University Press, New York.

3. Ford, B., A. Borgens, and P. Hitchcock. (2010). The "Mardi Gras" Shipwreck: Results of a Deep-Water Excavation, Gulf of Mexico, USA. *International Journal of Nautical Archaeology* **39**(1): 76–98.

Horrell, C. and Borgens, A, Eds. (2017). The Mardi Gras Shipwreck: The Archaeology of an Early Nineteenth-Century Wooden-Hulled Sailing Ship. *Historical Archaeology* **51**(3): 323–461.

4. Cozzi, J. (1998). The Goniometer: An Improved Device for Recording Submerged Shipwreck Timbers. *International Journal of Nautical Archaeology* **27**(1): 64–80.

5. Ghose, T. (17 February 2016). Medieval Shipwreck Hauled from the Deep. *LiveScience*. New York, Live Science. Available at https://www.livescience.com/53734-dutch-shipwreck-hauled-from-water.html.

Mary Rose Trust. (2017). The Mary Rose Museum. Mary Rose Trust, Portsmouth, UK. Available at http://www.maryrose.org/.

**CHAPTER 6**

1. Hurst-Thomas, D. (1989). *Archaeology* Holt, Rinehart and Winston, New York.

2. Roberts, A., J. McKinnon, C. O'Loughlin, K. Wanganeen, L.-I. Rigney, and M. Fowler. (2013). Combining Indigenous and Maritime Archaeological Approaches: Experiences and insights from the "(Re)locating *Narrunga* Project," Yorke Peninsula, South Australia. *Journal of Maritime Archaeology* **8**(1): 77–99.

3. Enright, J.M.R. Gearhart II, D. Jones, and J. Enright. (2006). *Study to Conduct National Register of Historic Places Evaluations of Submerged Sites on the Gulf of Mexico Outer Continental Shelf*. U.S. Department of the Interior, Minerals Management Service, Gulf of Mexico OCS Region, New Orleans, OCS Study MMS 2006-063.

Evans, A.M., M.E. Keith, E.E. Voisin, P. Hesp, G. Cook, M. Allison, G. da Silva, and E. Swanson. (2012). *Archaeological Analysis of Submerged Sites on the Gulf of Mexico Outer Continental Shelf*. U.S. Department of the Interior, Bureau of Ocean Energy Management, Gulf of Mexico OCS Region, New Orleans, OCS Study BOEM 2013-011110.

4. Sonnenburg, E., A. Lemke, and J. O'Shea, Eds. (2015). *Caribou Hunting in the Upper Great Lakes*. Memoirs of the Museum of Anthropology, Number 57. University of Michigan Museum of Anthropological Archaeology, Ann Arbor.

5. Hutchings, R.M. (2017). *Maritime Heritage in Crisis: Indigenous Landscapes and Global Ecological Breakdown*. Routledge, New York.

O'Sullivan, A., and C. Breen. (2007). *Maritime Ireland: An Archaeology of Coastal Communities*. Tempus, Stroud, UK.

6. Ford, B., Ed. (2011). *The Archaeology of Maritime Landscapes*. Springer, New York.

Ford, B. (2017). *The Shore Is a Bridge: The Maritime Cultural Landscape of Lake Ontario.* Texas A&M University Press, College Station.

7. Lipke, P., P. Spectre, and B.A.G. Fuller, Eds. (1993). *Boats: A Manual for Their Documentation.* American Association for State and Local History, Nashville, TN.

8. Hocker, F.M., and C.A. Ward, Eds. (2004). *The Philosophy of Shipbuilding.* Texas A&M University Press, College Station.

Steffy, J.R. (1994). *Wooden Ship Building and the Interpretation of Shipwrecks.* Texas A&M University Press, College Station.

9. Bruseth, J., Ed. (2014). *La Belle, The Ship that Changed History.* Bullock Texas State History Museum, Austin.

Bruseth, J., A. Borgens, B. Jones, and E. Ray, Eds. (2017). La Belle: *The Archaeology of a Seventeenth-Century Vessel of New World Colonization.* Texas A&M University Press, College Station.

10. Texas Beyond History. (2008). *La Belle* Shipwreck—Teaching Resources. Texas Archaeological Research Laboratory, University of Texas, Austin. Available at https://www.texasbeyondhistory.net/belle/teachers.html.

**CHAPTER 7**

1. United Nations. (2018). The Sustainable Development Goals. Available at https://www.un.org/sustainabledevelopment/sustainable-development-goals/.

2. Halligan, J.J., M.R. Waters, A. Perrotti, I.J. Owens, J.M. Feinberg, M.D. Bourne, B. Fenerty, B. Winsborough, D. Carlson, D.C. Fisher, T.W. Stafford, and J.S. Dunbar. (2016). Pre-Clovis Occupation 14,550 Years Ago at the Page-Ladson Site, Florida, and the Peopling of the Americas. *Science Advances* **2**(5).

Harmand, S., J.E. Lewis, C.S. Feibel, C.J. Lepre, S. Prat, A. Lenoble, X. Boës, R.L. Quinn, M. Brenet, A. Arroyo, N. Taylor, S. Clément, G. Daver, J.-P. Brugal, L. Leakey, R.A. Mortlock, J.D. Wright, S. Lokorodi, C. Kirwa, D.V. Kent, and H. Roche. (2015). 3.3-Million-Year-Old Stone Tools from Lomekwi 3, West Turkana, Kenya. *Nature* **521**: 310.

Villmoare, B., W.H. Kimbel, C. Seyoum, C.J. Campisano, E.N. DiMaggio, J. Rowan, D.R. Braun, J.R. Arrowsmith, and K.E. Reed. (2015). Early *Homo* at 2.8 Ma from Ledi-Geraru, Afar, Ethiopia. *Science* **347**(6228): 1352–1355.

3. Hansen, J., M. Sato, G. Russell, and P. Kharecha. (2013). Climate Sensitivity, Sea Level and Atmospheric Carbon Dioxide. *Philosophical Transactions of the Royal Society A: Mathematical, Physical, and Engineering Sciences* **371**(2001).

Lambeck, K., H. Rouby, A. Purcell, Y. Sun and M. Sambridge (2014). Sea level and Global Ice Volumes from the Last Glacial Maximum to the Holocene. *Proceedings of the National Academy of Sciences* **111**(43): 15296–15303.

4. Habu, J. (2014). Post-Pleistocene Transformations of Hunter-Gatherers in East Asia. *The Oxford Handbook of the Archaeology and Anthropology of Hunter-Gatherers*. V. Cummings, P. Jordan, and M. Zvelebil, Eds. 507–520. Oxford University Press, Oxford.

5. Evans, A.M., J. Flatman, and N.C. Flemming, Eds. (2014). *Prehistoric Archaeology on the Continental Shelf: A Global Review.* Springer, New York.

6. Flemming, N. C., J. Harff, and D. Moura. (2017). Non-Cultural Process of Site Formation, Preservation and Destruction. *Submerged Landscapes of the European Continental Shelf: Quaternary Paleoenvironments.* J. Harff, N.C. Flemming, D. Moura, A. Burgess, G, N. Bailey, Eds. 51–82. John Wiley and Sons, Inc., Hoboken, NJ.

7. Halligan, J.J., M.R. Waters, A. Perrotti, I.J. Owens, J.M. Feinberg, M.D. Bourne, B. Fenerty, B. Winsborough, D. Carlson, D.C. Fisher, T.W. Stafford and J.S. Dunbar. (2016). Pre-Clovis Occupation 14,550 Years Ago at the Page-Ladson Site, Florida, and the Peopling of the Americas. *Science Advances* **2**(5).

8. Giosan, L., F. Filip, and S. Constatinescu. (2009). Was the Black Sea Catastrophically Flooded in the Early Holocene? *Quaternary Science Reviews* **28**(1): 1–6.

9. Hamilton, D.L. (2000). The Port Royal Project: Archaeological Excavations. Nautical Archaeology Program, Texas A&M University, College Station, Texas. Available at http://nautarch.tamu.edu/portroyal/archhist.htm.

   JNHT (Jamaica National Heritage Trust). (2009). The Underwater City of Port Royal. UNESCO World Heritage Nomination. Available at http://whc.unesco.org/en/tentativelists/5430/.

10. Empereur, J.-Y. (1998) *Alexandria Rediscovered*. George Braziller Publisher, New York.

    Nield, D. (5 September 2017). A Lost City Has Been Found 1700 Years After a Tsunami Sank It. *Science Alert*. Available at https://sciencealert.com/this-lost-underwater-city-has-been-found-1-700-years-after-a-tsunami-sank-it.

    University of Nottingham. (2017). The Pavlopetri Underwater Archaeology Project. Available at http://www.nottingham.ac.uk/pavlopetri/index.aspx.

11. Berna, F., Goldberg, P., Horwitz, L.K., Brink, J., Holt, S., Bamford, M., and Chazan, M. (2012). Microstratigraphic Evidence of in situ Fire in the Acheulean Strata of Wonderwerk Cave, Northern Cape Province, South Africa. *Proceedings of the National Academy of Science* **9**(20): E1215–E1220.

    Henry, A.G. (2017). Neanderthal Cooking and the Costs of Fire. *Current Anthropology* **58**(S16): S329–S336.

12. Hoeksema, R. J. (2007). Three Stages in the History of Land Reclamation in the Netherlands. *Irrigation and Drainage* **56**(S1): S113–S126.

    Riess, W. (2014). *The Ship that Held Up Wall Street*. Texas A&M University Press, College Station.

    Seasholes, N.S. (2003). *Gaining Ground: A History of Landmaking in Boston*, MIT Press, Cambridge.

13. Keay, S., M. Millett, and K. Strutt. (2008). Recent Archaeological Survey at Portus. *The Maritime World of Ancient Rome*. R.L. Hohlfelder, Eds. 97–104. University of Michigan Press for the American Academy in Rome, Ann Arbor.

14. Kocabaş, U. (2015). The Yenikapı Byzantine-Era Shipwrecks, Istanbul, Turkey: A Preliminary Report and Inventory of the 27 Wrecks Studied by Istanbul University. *International Journal of Nautical Archaeology* **44**(1): 5–38.

    Pulak, C., R. Ingram, and M. Jones. (2015). Eight Byzantine Shipwrecks from the Theodosian Harbour Excavations at Yenikapı in Istanbul, Turkey: An Introduction. *International Journal of Nautical Archaeology* **44**(1): 39–73.

15. Rick, T.C., and J.M. Erlandson, Eds. (2008). *Human Impacts on Ancient Marine Ecosystems: A Global Perspective*. University of California Press, Berkeley.

    Starkovich, B.M., N.D. Munro, and M.C. Stiner (2017). Terminal Pleistocene Subsistence Strategies and Aquatic Resource Use in Southern Greece. *Quaternary International* **465**: 162–176.

    Stringer, C.B., J.C. Finlayson, R.N.E. Barton, Y. Fernández-Jalvo, I. Cáceres, R.C. Sabin, E.J. Rhodes, A.P. Currant, J. Rodríguez-Vidal, F. Giles-Pacheco, and J.A. Riquelme-Cantal. (2008). Neanderthal Exploitation of Marine Mammals in Gibraltar. *Proceedings of the National Academy of Sciences* **105**(38): 14319–14324.

16. Grenier, R., M-A. Bernier, and W. Stevens, Eds. (2007). *The Underwater Archaeology of Red Bay: Basque Shipbuilding and Whaling in the 16th Century*, Parks Canada.

17. Dolin, E. (2007). *Leviathan: The History of Whaling in America*. W.W. Norton, New York.

18. Cohn, A. (1996). *Zebra Mussels and Their Impact on Historic Shipwrecks*. Lake Champlain Maritime Museum, Burlington, VT. Available at http://www.lcbp.org/wp-content/uploads/2013/03/15_ZebraMusselsImpact_HistoricShipwrecks.pdf.

Personal communication with Tamara Thomsen, Maritime Archaeologist with the Wisconsin Historical Society, Wisconsin State Historic Preservation Office, on 12/21/2017.

United States Department of Agriculture (2017). Quagga Mussel. Available at https://www.invasivespeciesinfo.gov/aquatics/quagga.shtml.

19. Brennan, M.L., D. Davis, R.D. Ballard, A.C. Trembanis, J.I. Vaughn, J.S. Krumholz, J.P. Delgado, C.N. Roman, C. Smart, K.L.C. Bell, M. Duman, and C. DuVal. (2016). Quantification of Bottom Trawl Fishing Damage to Ancient Shipwreck Sites. *Marine Geology* **371**: 82–88.

20. Johnson, S. (2007). *The Ghost Map: The Story of London's Most Terrifying Epidemic—and How It Changed Science, Cities, and the Modern World.* Riverhead Books, New York.

21. Calmet, D. (1989). Ocean Disposal of Radioactive Wasted: Status Report *International Atomic Energy Bulletin* 4/**1989**: 47–50. Available at https://www.iaea.org/sites/default/files/31404684750.pdf.

Lindenlauf, A. (2003). The Sea as a Place of No Return in Ancient Greece. *World Archaeology* **35**(3): 416–433.

Raubenheimer, K., and A. McIlgorm. (2017). Is the Montreal Protocol a Model that Can Help Solve the Global Marine Plastic Debris Problem? *Marine Policy* **81**: 322–329.

Yamaguchi, M. (27 November 2017). Fukushima Meltdown: Japan Urged to Dump Radioactive Waste in Pacific Ocean by Nuclear Experts. *Independent* Asia Section. Available at http://www.independent.co.uk/news/world/asia/fukushima-meltdown-japan-dumping-radioactive-nuclear-waste-pacific-ocean-a8077481.html.

22. Enger, J. (31 March 2017). How Long Will It Take for Car to Fall through Ice? Make a Bet for This Minn. Tradition *MPR News.* Available at https://www.mprnews.org/story/2017/03/31/cass-lake-lions-club-fundraiser-ford-escort-car-ice.

23. Ford, B., A. Borgens, W. Bryant, D. Marshall, P. Hitchcock, C. Arias, and D. Hamilton. (2008). *Archaeological Excavation of the Mardi Gras Shipwreck (16GM01), Gulf of Mexico Continental Slope, OCS Report MMS 2009-037.* U.S. Department of Interior, Minerals Management Service, Gulf of Mexico OCS Region, Bureau of Ocean Energy Management, New Orleans, LA. Available at http://www.boem.gov/BOEM-Newsroom/Library/Publications/2008/2008-037.aspx.

Kunzig, R. (2014). Romans in France: An Ancient Wreck Tells of Romans in France. *National Geographic.* Available at http://ngm.nationalgeographic.com/2014/04/roman-boat/kunzig-text.

Lawler, A. (2007). Raising Alexandria. *Smithsonian Magazine.* Available at https://www.smithsonianmag.com/science-nature/raising-alexandria-151005550/.

24. Parke, P. (27 February 2015). Dumping Subway Trains into the Ocean . . . in a Good Way. *CNN* World Section. Available at http://www.cnn.com/2015/02/26/world/subway-cars-coral-reef/index.html.

25. Fitzpatrick, S.M., and A. Anderson. (2008). Islands of Isolation: Archaeology and the Power of Aquatic Perimeters. *The Journal of Island and Coastal Archaeology* **3**(1): 4–16.

Rainbird, P. (2016). Islands Out of Time: Towards a Critique of Island Archaeology. *Journal of Mediterranean Archaeology* **12**(2): 216–234.

26. Ford, B. (2018). *The Shore Is a Bridge: The Maritime Cultural Landscape of Lake Ontario.* Texas A&M University Press, College Station.

27. Van de Noort, R. (2011). *North Sea Archaeologies: A Maritime Biography, 10,000 bc to ad 1500.* Oxford University Press, Oxford.

28. Stilgoe, J.R. (1994). *Alongshore.* Yale University Press, New Haven, CT.

29. Westerdahl, C. (1992). The Maritime Cultural Landscape. *International Journal of Nautical Archaeology* **21**(1): 5–14.

30. Ballin, T.B. (2017). Rising Waters and Processes of Diversification and Unification in Material Culture: The Flooding of Doggerland and Its Effect on North-West European Prehistoric Populations between ca. 13 000 and 1500 cal BC. *Journal of Quaternary Science* **32**(2): 329–339.

   Van de Noort, R. (2011). *North Sea Archaeologies: A Maritime Biography, 10,000 bc to ad 1500*. Oxford University Press, Oxford.

31. Flatman, J. (2010). Wetting the Fringe of Your Habit: Medieval Monasticism and Coastal Landscapes. *Perspectives in Landscape Archaeology*. H. Lewis and S. Semple, Eds. 66–77. Archaeopress, Oxford.

### CHAPTER 8

1. Westerdahl, C. (1992). The Maritime Cultural Landscape. *International Journal of Nautical Archaeology* **21**(1): 5–14.

   Westerdahl, C. (2011). The Maritime Cultural Landscape. In *The Oxford Handbook of Maritime Archaeology*. A. Catsambis, B. Ford, and D. Hamilton, Eds. 733–762. Oxford University Press, New York.

2. Bednarik, R.G. (2014). The Beginnings of Maritime Travel. *Advances in Anthropology* **4**: 209–221.

   Endicott, P., M. Metspalu, and T. Kivisild. (2007). Genetic Evidence on Modern Human Dispersals in South Asia: Y Chromosone and Mitochondrial DNA Perspectives: The World Through the Eyes of Two Haploid Genomes. In *The Evolution and History of Human Populations in South Asia.*, M.D. Petraglia and B. Allchin, Eds. 229–244. Springer, New York.

   Erlandson, J. (2010). Neptune's Children: The Evolution of Human Seafaring. In *The Global Origins of Seafaring*. A. Anderson, J. Barrett, and K. Boyle, Eds. 19–28. Oxbow Books, Oxford.

3. Aberg, A. and C. Lewis, Eds. (2000). *The Rising Tide, Archaeology and Coastal Landscapes*. Oxbow, Oxford.

   Flemming, N.C. (1971), *Cities in the Sea*. Doubleday, Garden City, NJ.

   Fulford, M., T. Champion, and A. Long, Eds. (1997). *England's Coastal Heritage*. English Heritage, London.

4. Ford, B. (2018). *The Shore Is a Bridge: The Maritime Cultural Landscape of Lake Ontario*. Texas A&M University Press, College Station.

5. Pieters, M., F. Verhaeghe, and G. Gevaert, Eds. (2006). *Fishery, Trade and Piracy: Fishermen and Fishermen's Settlements in and around the North Sea Area in the Middle Ages and Later*. Flemish Heritage Institute, Brussels.

6. Herteig, A.E. (1997). Early Landing Places. In *Studies in Maritime Archaeology*. Seán McGrail, Ed. 65–71, BAR British Series 256. Hedges, Oxford.

   Ilves, K. (2012). Do Ships Shape the Shore? An Analysis of the Credibility of Ship Archaeological Evidence for Landing Site Morphology in the Baltic Sea. *International Journal of Nautical Archaeology* **41**(1): 94–105.

7. Werner, W. (1997). The Largest Ship Trackway in Ancient Times: The Diolkos of the Isthmus of Corinth, Greece, and Early Attempts to Build a Canal. *International Journal of Nautical Archaeology* **26**(2): 98–119.

8. Clark, P., Ed. (2009). *Bronze Age Connections, Culture Contact in Prehistoric Europe*. Oxbow Books, Oxford.

   McGrail, S. (2014). *Early Ships and Seafaring: European Water Transport*. Pen and Sword, South Yorkshire.

   Wright, E. (1990). *The Ferriby Boats, Seacraft of the Bronze Age*. Routledge, New York.

9. Bass, G., Ed. (1996). *Ships and Shipwrecks of the Americas*. Thames and Hudson, New York.

10. Rogers, A. (2013). The Social Archaeology of Ports and Harbours. *Journal of Maritime Archaeology,* special issue **8**(2): 181–196.

11. Danish Institute at Athens (2017). Piraeus, the Zea Harbor Project. Danish Institute at Athens, Athens. Available at https://diathens.gr/en/aktiviteter/piraeus-the-zea-harbour-project.

Garland, R. (1987). *The Piraeus, From the Fifth to the First Century B.C.* Cornell University Press, Ithaca, NY.

Lovén, B. (2011). *The Ancient Harbours of the Piraeus. Volume I.1. The Zea Shipsheds. and Slipways: Architecture and Topography.* Danish Institute at Athens, Athens.

12. Hohfelder, R.L., C. Brandon, and J.P. Oleson (2007). Construction the Harbor of Caesarea Palaestina, Israel: New Evidence from the ROMACONS Field Campaign of October 2005. *International Journal of Nautical Archaeology* **36**(2): 409–415.

Raban, A., M. Atzy, B. Goodman, and Z. Gail (2009). *The Harbour of Sebastos (Caesarea Maritima) in its Roman Mediterranean Context.* BAR International Series 1930. Archaeopress, Oxford.

Raban, A., K.G. Holum (1996). *Caesarea Maritima, A Retrospective after Two Millennia.* E.J. Brill, New York.

Reinhardt, E.G. and A. Raban (1999). Destruction of Herod the Great's Harbor at Caesarea Maritima, Israel—Geoarchaeological Evidence. *Geology* **27**(9): 811–814.

13. Andersson, E.B., Ed. (1982). *Bryggen, The Hanseatic Settlement in Bergen.* Det Hanseatiske Museums, Bergen.

Herteig, A.E. (1959). The Excavation of "Bryggen," the Old Hanseatic Wharf in Bergen. *Medieval Archaeology* **3**(1): 177–186.

Trebbi, M. (2007). *Bryggen, The Heart of Bergen.* ARFO, Oslo.

UNESCO (2017). World Heritage Centre, The List, Bryggen. United Nations Educational, Scientific, and Cultural Organization, Paris. Available at http://whc.unesco.org/en/list/59/.

14. Marsden, P. (1994). *Ships of the Port of London, First to Eleventh Centuries AD.* English Heritage, London.

Milne, G. (1985). *The Roman Port of London.* B.T. Batsford, London.

Milne, G. (2003). *The Port of Medieval London.* Tempus, Mount Pleasant, SC.

Port of London Authority (2017). Thames Foreshore Access Including Metal Detecting, Searching and Digging. Port of London Authority, London. Available at https://www.pla.co.uk/Environment/Thames-foreshore-access-including-metal-detecting-searching-and-digging.

15. Delgado, J.P. (2002). The California Gold-Rush Ship *Niantic*. *Maritime Life and Tradition* **13**: 34–51.

Delgado, J.P. (2009). *Gold Rush Port, The Maritime Archaeology of San Francisco's Waterfront.* University of California Press, Berkeley.

Reid, S. (1999). The Ships of the San Francisco Gold Rush. *Sea History* **80**: 34–35.

16. Ford, B. (2013). The Reuse of Vessels as Harbor Structures: A Cross-Cultural Comparison. *Journal of Maritime Archaeology* **8**(2): 197–219.

Riess, W.C. (2014). *The Ship that Held Up Wall Street.* Texas A&M University Press, College Station.

17. Moser, J.D. (2011). Shipyard Archaeology. In *The Oxford Handbook of Maritime Archaeology*. A. Catsambis, B. Ford, and D. Hamilton, Eds. 834–855. Oxford University Press, New York.

18. Nitschke, J.L., S.R. Martin, and Y. Shalev. (2011). Between Carmel and the Sea: Tel Dor: The Late Periods. *Near Eastern Archaeology* **74**(3): 132–154.

Raban, A. (1987). The Harbor of the Sea Peoples at Dor. *Biblical Archaeologist* June: 118–126.

Stern, E. (2000). *Dor, Ruler of the Seas.* Israel Exploration Society, Jerusalem.

19. Gawronski, J. (2003). The Hogendijk Shipyard in Zaandam and the VOC Shipyard Oostenburg in Amsterdam. Examples of Recent Archaeological Slipway Research in the Netherlands. *Boats, Ships and Shipyards: Proceedings of the Ninth International Symposium on Boat and Ship Archaeology, Venice 2000.* Carlo Beltrame, Ed. 132–143, Oxbow Books, Oxford.

Goodburn, D., F. Meddens, S. Holden, and C. Phillpotts. (2011). Linking Land and Navy: Archaeological Investigations at the Site of the Woolwich Royal Dockyard, South-Eastern England. *International Journal of Nautical Archaeology* **40**(2): 306–327.

20. Church, S.K. (2010). Two Ming Dynasty Shipyards in Nanjing and their Infrastructure. *Shipwreck ASIA: Thematic Studies in East Asian Maritime Archaeology*. J. Kumura, Ed. 32–49. Maritime Archaeology Program, Adelaide.

    Nanjing Municipal Museum. (2006). *The Remains of the Treasure Shipyard: An Archaeological Report on Basin 6 of the Ming Dynasty Treasure Shipyard in Nanjing*. Cultural Relics Publishing House, Beijing.

21. Ford, B. (2002). Wooden Shipbuilding in Maryland Prior to the Mid-Nineteenth Century. *American Neptune* **62**(1): 69–90.

    Ford, B. (2007). Down by the Water's Edge: Modelling Shipyard Locations in Maryland, USA. *International Journal of Nautical Archaeology* **36**(1): 125–137.

    Stammers, M. (1999). Slipways and Steamchests: The Archaeology of 18th- and 19th-Centruy Wooden Merchant Shipyards in the United Kingdom. *International Journal of Nautical Archaeology* **28**(3): 253–264.

22. Thiesen, W.H. (2006). *Industrializing American Shipbuilding*. University Press of Florida, Gainesville.

23. Cavers, G. (2010). *Crannogs and Later Prehistoric Settlement in Western Scotland*. BAR British Series 510. Archeopress, Oxford.

    Fredengren, C. (2002). *Crannogs*. Wordwell, Bray.

    Henderson, J. and R. Sands. (2013). Irish and Scottish Crannogs. *Oxford Handbook of Wetland Archaeology*. F. Menotti and A. O'Sullivan, Eds. 269–282. Oxford University Press, New York.

    O'Sullivan, A. (1998). *The Archaeology of Lake Settlement in Ireland*. Royal Irish Academy, Dublin.

    Van de Noort, R. and A. O'Sullivan. (2006). *Rethinking Wetland Archaeology*. Duckworth, London.

24. Kehoe, A.B. (2017). *North America Before the European Invasions*. Routledge, New York.

    Pool, C.A. (2007). *Olmec Archaeology and Early Mesoamerica*. Cambridge University Press, New York.

25. Naylor, J. (2004). Access to International Trade in Middle Saxon England: A Case of Urban Over-Emphasis? *Close Encounters: Sea- and Riverborne Trade, Ports and Hinterlands, Ship Construction and navigation in Antiquity, the Middle Ages and in Modern Times*. BAR International Series 1283. Marinella Pasquinucci and Timm Weski, Eds. 139–148. Archeopress, Oxford.

**CHAPTER 9**

1. Ferreiro, L. (2007). *Ships and Science: The Birth of Naval Architecture in the Scientific Revolution, 1600–1800*. MIT Press, Cambridge.

    Finkel, I. (2014). *The Ark Before Noah: Decoding he Story of the Flood*. Doubleday, New York.

    Gallagher, R., and A. Islamov (2003). Early Man in Azerbaijan: When Ancient Stones Speak. *Azerbaijan International* **11**(1): 40–47.

    McGrail, S. (2014). *Early Ships and Seafaring: European Water Transport*. Pen and Sword Archaeology, Barnsley.

2. Beuker, door J.R. and M.J.L.Th. Niekus (1997). De Kano van Pesse—De Bijl Erin. Archeoforum. Available at http://www.archeoforum.nl/Pesse1.html.

    Greenhill, B. (1988). *The Evolution of the Wooden Ship*. Facts on File, New York.

    McGrail, S. (2014). *Early Ships and Seafaring: European Water Transport*. Pen and Sword Archaeology, Barnsley.

    McGrail, S., and M. Millet. (1985). The Hasholme Logboat. *Antiquity* **59**(226): 117–120.

3. Adney, E.T., and H. Chapelle. (1983). *The Bark Canoes and Skin Boats of North America*. Smithsonian Books, Washington, DC.

Gardiner, R., Ed. (1996). *The Earliest Ships: The Evolution of Boats into Ships*. Naval Institute Press, Annapolis, MD.

4. Patton, J. (2014). Considering the Wet Homelands of Indigenous Massachusetts. *Journal of Social Archaeology* **14**(1): 87–111.

Wheeler, R., J. Miller, R. McGee, D. Ruhl, B. Swann, and M. Memory. (2003). Archaic Period Canoes from Newnans Lake, Florida. *American Antiquity* **68**(3): 533–551.

5. Leshikar, M. (1996). The Earliest Watercraft: From Rafts to Viking Ships. *Ships and Shipwrecks of the Americas*. G. Bass, Ed. 13–32. Thames and Hudson, New York.

McGrail, S. (2004). *Boats of the World, From the Stone Age to Medieval Times*. Oxford University Press, New York.

McGrail, S. (2015). *Early Ships and Seafaring: Water Transport Beyond Europe*. Pen and Sword, Barnsley, UK.

6. Finkel, I. (2014). *The Ark Before Noah: Decoding the Story of the Flood*. Doubleday, New York.

7. McGrail, S. (2010). The Global Origins of Seagoing Water Transport. *The Global Origins of Seafaring*. A. Anderson, J. Barrett, and K. Boyle, Eds. 95–108. Oxbow Books, Oxford.

Wright, E. (1990). *The Ferriby Boats, Seacraft of the Bronze Age*. Routledge, New York.

8. Jenkins, N. (1980). *The Boat Beneath the Pyramid*. Thames and Hudson, London.

Johnstone, P. (1988). *Seacraft in Prehistory*. Routledge, London.

Lipke, P. (1984). *The Royal Ship of Cheops, a Retrospective Account of Discovery, Restoration and Reconstruction*. BAR International Series 225. National Maritime Museum, Greenwich.

Mark, S. (2009). The Construction of the Khufu I Vessel (c. 2566 BC): a Re-Evaluation. *International Journal of Nautical Archaeology* **38**(1): 133–152.

Ward, C. (2004). Boatbuilding in Ancient Egypt. *The Philosophy of Shipbuilding*, F. Hocker and C. Ward, Eds. 13–24. Texas A&M University Press, College Station.

Ward, C. and C. Zazzaro (2010). Evidence for Pharonic Seagoing Ships at Mersa/Wadi Gawasis, Egypt. *International Journal of Nautical Archaeology* **39**(1): 27–43.

9. Beltrame, C. (2000). *Sutiles Naves* of Roman Age, New Evidence and Technological Comparison with Pre-Roman Sewn Boats. *Down the River to the Sea*. J. Litwin, Ed. 91–96. Proceedings of the Eighth International Symposium Boat and Ship Archaeology, Gdańsk 1997. Polish Maritime Museum, Gdańsk.

Kahanov, Y. and P. Pomey. (2004). The Greek Sewn Shipbuilding Tradition and the Ma'agan Mikhael Ship: A Comparison with the Mediterranean Parallels from the Sixth to Fourth Centuries. *Mariner's Mirror* **90**(1): 6–28.

Linder, E. and Y. Kahanov (2003). *The Ma'agan Mikhael Ship: The Recovery of a 2400-year-old Merchantman, Final Report*. Israel Exploration Society and University of Haifa, Jerusalem.

Polzer, M. (2011). Early Shipbuilding in the Eastern Mediterranean. *Oxford Handbook of Maritime Archaeology*. A. Catsambis, B. Ford, and D. Hamilton, Eds. 349–378. Oxford University Press, New York.

Steffy, J.R. (1994). *Wooden Shipbuilding and the Interpretation of Shipwrecks*. Texas A&M University Press, College Station.

10. McCarthy, M. (2005). *Ships' Fastenings, From Sewn Boat to Steamship*. Texas A&M University Press, College Station.

Pomey, P., Y. Kahanov, and E. Rieth. (2012). Transition from Shell to Skeleton in Ancient Mediterranean Ship-Construction: Analysis, Problems, and Future Research. *International Journal of Nautical Archaeology* **41**(2): 235–314.

11. Pomey, P., Y. Kahanov, and E. Rieth. (2012). Transition from Shell to Skeleton in Ancient Mediterranean Ship-Construction: Analysis, Problems, and Future Research. *International Journal of Nautical Archaeology* **41**(2): 235–314.

12. Casson, L. (1996). Sailing Ships of the Ancient Mediterranean. *The Earliest Ships*. R. Gardiner, Ed. 39–51. Naval Institute Press, Annapolis, MD.

McGrail, S. (2004). *Boats of the World, From the Stone Age to Medieval Times*. Oxford University Press, New York.

13. Flecker, M. (2000). A 9th-century Arab or Indian Shipwreck in Indonesian Waters. *International Journal of Nautical Archaeology* **29**(2): 199–217

Hawkins, C. (1977). *The Dhow, an Illustrated History of the Dhow and Its World*. Nautical Publishing Company, Lymington, UK.

McGrail, S. (2015). *Early Ships and Seafaring: Water Transport Beyond Europe*. Pen and Sword, Barnsley, UK.

Ray, H.P. (2003). *The Archaeology of Seafaring in Ancient South Asia*. Cambridge University Press, Cambridge.

Shaikh, Z.S. Tripati, and V. Shinde. (2012). A Study of the Sewn-Plank Boats of Goa, India. *International Journal of Nautical Archaeology* **41**(1): 148–157.

14. Keith, M., Ed. (2016). *Site Formation Processes of Submerged Shipwrecks*, University Press of Florida, Gainesville.

Ray, H.P. (2003). *The Archaeology of Seafaring in Ancient South Asia*. Cambridge University Press, Cambridge.

15. Kimura, J. (2016). *Archaeology of East Asian Shipbuilding*. University Press of Florida, Gainesville.

Sasaki, R. (2011). A Survey of East Asian Shipbuilding Traditions during the Era of Chinese Maritime Expansion. *Oxford Handbook of Maritime Archaeology*. A. Catsambis, B. Ford, and D. Hamilton, Eds. 535–560. Oxford University Press, New York.

Van Tilburg, H.K. (2007). *Chinese Junks on the Pacific, Views from a Different Deck*. University Press of Florida, Gainesville.

16. Mott, L. (1991). The Development of the Rudder, AD 100–1660: A Technological Tale. Master's Thesis, Department of Anthropology, Texas A&M University, College Station.

Van Tilburg, H.K. (2007). *Chinese Junks on the Pacific, Views from a Different Deck*. University Press of Florida, Gainesville.

17. Van Tilburg, H.K. (2007). *Chinese Junks on the Pacific, Views from a Different Deck*. University Press of Florida, Gainesville.

18. Allaby, R., F. Friedlaender, F. Reed, K. Kidd, J. Kidd, G. Chambers, R. Lea, J.-H. Loo, G. Koki, J. Hodgson, D.A. Merriwether, J. Weber, and J. Friedlaender. (2010). Prehistoric Pacific Population Movements. *The Global Origins and Development of Seafaring*. A. Anderson, J. Barrett, and K. Boyle, Eds. 143–157. University of Cambridge, Cambridge.

Irwin, G. (2010). Pacific Voyaging and Settlement: Issues of Biogeography and Archaeology, Canoe Performance and Computer Simulation. *The Global Origins and Development of Seafaring*. A. Anderson, J. Barrett, and K. Boyle, Eds. 131–141. University of Cambridge, Cambridge.

19. Johns, D., G. Irwin, and Y. Sung (2014). An Early Sophisticated East Polynesian Voyaging Canoe Discovered on New Zealand's Coast. *PNAS: Proceedings of the National Academy of Sciences of the United States of America* **111**(41): 14728–14733.

20. Di Piazza, A. and E. Pearthree, Eds. (2008). *Canoes of the Grand Ocean*. BAR International Series 1802. Archaeopress, Oxford.

Feinberg, R. (1988). *Polynesian Seafaring and Navigation, Ocean Travel in Anutan Culture and Society*. Kent State University Press, Kent, OH.

McGrail, S. (2015). *Early Ships and Seafaring: Water Transport Beyond Europe*. Pen and Sword, Barnsley, UK.

21. Irwin, G. (2010). Pacific Voyaging and Settlement: Issues of Biogeography and Archaeology, Canoe Performance and Computer Simulation. *The Global Origins and Development of Seafaring*. A. Anderson, J. Barrett, and K. Boyle, Eds. 131–141. University of Cambridge, Cambridge.

McGrail, S. (2015). *Early Ships and Seafaring: Water Transport Beyond Europe*. Pen and Sword, Barnsley, UK.

22. Bennett, J., Ed. (2009). *Sailing into the Past, Learning from Replica Ships*. Naval Institute Press, Annapolis, MD.

Finney, B. (2003). *Sailing in the Wake of the Ancestors, Reviving Polynesian Voyaging*. Bishop Museum Press, Honolulu.

Finney, B. (1994). *Voyage of Rediscovery, A Cultural Odyssey through Polynesia*. University of California Press, Berkeley.

Polynesian Voyaging Society. (2017). Polynesian Voyaging Society. Polynesian Voyaging Society, Honolulu. Available at http://www.hokulea.com/.

23. Cunliffe, B. (2002). *The Extraordinary Voyage of Pytheas the Greek: The Man Who Discovered Britain*. Penguin, New York.

Marsden, P. (1994). *Ships of the Port of London, First to Eleventh Centuries AD*. English Heritage Archaeological Report 3. English Heritage, London.

24. Gardiner, R., Ed. (1996).*The Earliest Ships: The Evolution of Boats into Ships*. Naval Institute Press, Annapolis, MD.

McGrail, S. (2014). *Early Ships and Seafaring: European Water Transport*. Pen and Sword Archaeology, Barnsley, UK.

25. Crumlin-Pedersen, O. (1997). *Viking-Age Ships and Shipbuilding in Hedeby/Haithabu and Schleswig*. Ships and Boats of the North, 2. Viking Ship Museum, Roskilde, Denmark.

Crumlin-Pedersen, O. (2002). *The Skuldelev Ships 1: Topography, Archaeology, History, Conservation and Display*. Ships and Boats of the North, 4.1. Viking Ship Museum, Roskilde, Denmark.

Gardiner, R., Ed. (1996). *The Earliest Ships: The Evolution of Boats into Ships*. Naval Institute Press, Annapolis.

Viking Ship Museum (2017). The Five Ships. Viking Ship Museum, Roskilde. Available at http://www.vikingeskibsmuseet.dk/en/visit-the-museum/exhibitions/the-five-viking-ships/.

Williams, G. (2014). *The Viking Ship*. The British Museum Press, London.

26. Hocker, F. (2004). Bottom-Based Shipbuilding in Northwestern Europe. *The Philosophy of Shipbuilding: Conceptual Approaches to the Study of Wooden Ships*. F. Hocker and C. Ward, Eds. 65–93. Texas A&M University Press, College Station.

27. Gardiner, R., Ed. (1994) *Cogs, Caravels, and Galleons, The Sailing Ship 1000–1650*. Conway Maritime Press, London.

Hocker, F. (2004). Bottom-Based Shipbuilding in Northwestern Europe. I*The Philosophy of Shipbuilding: Conceptual Approaches to the Study of Wooden Ships*. F. Hocker and C. Ward, Eds. 65–93. Texas A&M University Press, College Station.

Hoffman, G., and P. Hoffman (2009). Sailing the Bremen Cog. *International Journal of Nautical Archaeology* **38**(2): 281–296.

Vermeersch, J., and K. Haneca (2015). Construction Features of Doel 1, a 14th-Century Cog found in Flanders. *International Journal of Nautical Archaeology* **44**(1): 111–131.

Zwick, D. (2013). Conceptual Evolution in Ancient Shipbuilding: An Attempt to Reinvigorate a Shunned Theoretical Framework. *Interpreting Shipwrecks: Maritime Archaeological Approaches*. Southampton Archaeology Monographs New Series No. 4. J. Adams and J. Rönnby, Eds. 46–72. Oxbow Books, Oxford.

28. Adams, J. (2013). *A Maritime Archaeology of Ships*. Oxbow Books, Oxford.

Adams, J. and J. Rönnby (2013). One of His Majesty's "*Beste Fraffwells*": The Wreck of an Early Carvel-built Ship at Franska Sternarna, Sweden. *International Journal of Nautical Archaeology* **42**(1): 103–117.

Gardiner, R., Ed. (1994). *Cogs, Caravels, and Galleons, The Sailing Ship 1000 – 1650*. Conway Maritime Press, London.

Hocker, F. (2004). Bottom-Based Shipbuilding in Northwestern Europe. *The Philosophy of Shipbuilding: Conceptual Approaches to the Study of Wooden Ships*. F. Hocker and C. Ward, Eds. 65–93. Texas A&M University Press, College Station.

29. Adams, J. (2013). *A Maritime Archaeology of Ships*. Oxbow Books, Oxford.

Hocker, F. (2004). Bottom-Based Shipbuilding in Northwestern Europe. *The Philosophy of Shipbuilding: Conceptual Approaches to the Study of Wooden Ships*. F. Hocker and C. Ward, Eds. 65–93. Texas A&M University Press, College Station.

Lemeé, C.P.P. (2006). *The Renaissance Shipwrecks from Christianshavn*. Ships and Boats of the North, Volume 6. Viking Ship Museum, Roskilde, Denmark.

Salisbury, C. (1961), The Woolwich Ship. *Mariner's Mirror* **47**(2): 81–90.

30. Alertz, U. (1995). The Naval Architecture and Oar Systems of Medieval and Later Galleys. *The Age of the Galley*. R. Gardiner, Ed. 142–162. Conway Maritime Press, London.

Bass, G., S. Mathews, J. R. Steffy, and F. van Doornick, Jr. (2004) *Serçe Limanı: An Eleventh Century Shipwreck*, Vol. 1. Texas A&M University Press, College Station.

Castro, F. (2005). *The Pepper Wreck: A Portuguese Indiaman the Mouth of the Tagus River*. Texas A&M University Press, College Station.

Palou, H., E. Reith, M. Izaguirre, A. Jover, X. Nieto, M. Pujol, X. Raurich, and C. Apestigui. (1998). *Excavacions Aequelógiques Subaquátiques a Cala Culip 2, Culip VI*. Museu d'Arqueologia da Catanlunya, Girona, Spain.

31. Ferreiro, L. (2007). *Ships and Science: The Birth of Naval Architecture in the Scientific Revolution, 1600–1800*. The MIT Press, Cambridge.

Lavery, B., Ed. (1986). *Deane's Doctrine of Naval Architecture, 1670*. Conway Maritime Press, London.

Thiesen, W. (2006). *Industrializing American Shipbuilding: The Transformation of Ship Design and Construction, 1820–1920*. University Press of Florida, Gainesville.

32. Crothers, W. (2000). *The American-Built Clipper Ship, 1850-1856*. International Marine, Camden, ME.

MacGregor, D. (1979). *Clipper Ships*. Argus Books, Watford, UK.

Royal Maritime Museum (2017). Cutty Sark. Royal Maritime Museum, Greenwich. Available at http://www.rmg.co.uk/cutty-sark.

Switzer, D. (2000). The Rescue and Preservation of the Only Existing American Clipper Ship. *Down the River to the Sea, Proceedings of the Eight International Symposium on Boat and Ship Archaeology, Gdańsk 1997*. J. Litwin, Ed. 197–200. Polish Maritime Museum, Gdańsk.

33. Crisman, K. (2011). The Archaeology of Steamships. *Oxford Handbook of Maritime Archaeology*. A. Catsambis, B. Ford, and D. Hamilton, Eds. 610–628. Oxford University Press, New York.

Crisman, K. (2014). The Western River Steamboat *Heroine*, 1832--1838, Oklahoma, USA: Construction. *International Journal of Nautical Archaeology* **43**(1): 128–150.

Nordevall, Eric. (2012). Eric Nordevall. Swedish Steamboat Association, Forsvik. Available at http://www.ericnordevall.se/en/.

Thiesen, W. (2006). *Industrializing American Shipbuilding: The Transformation of Ship Design and Construction, 1820–1920*. University Press of Florida, Gainesville.

34. Buchanan, A. (2006). *Brunel: The Life and Times of Isambard Kingdom Brunel*. Bloomsbury, London.

Gould, R. (2000). *Archaeology and the Social History of Ships*. Cambridge University Press, Cambridge.

Winklareth, R. (2000). *Naval Shipbuilders of the World from the Age of Sail to the Present Day*. Chatham Publishing, London.

35. Ransley, J. (2011). Maritime Communities and Traditions. *Oxford Handbook of Maritime Archaeology*. A. Catsambis, B. Ford, and D. Hamilton, Eds. 878–903. Oxford University Press, New York.

**CHAPTER 10**

1. McGrail, S. (2014). *Early Ships and Seafaring: European Water Transport*. Pen and Sword Archaeology, Barnsley, UK.

    Mounzer, G. (2015). The Odyssey Map. Available at https://www.thejournal.ie/homer-odyssey-geographical-locations-1213314-Dec2013/.

2. Casson, L. (1989). *The Periplus Maris Erythraei: Text with Introduction, Translation, and Commentary*. Princeton University Press, Princeton, NJ.

    Palsson, H., and P. Edwards. (2007). *The Book of Settlements:* Landnámabók. University of Manitoba Press, Manitoba.

3. Nicolai, R. (2014). A Critical Review of the Hypothesis of a Medieval Origin for Portolan Charts. University of Utrecht. Available at http://www.dart-europe.eu/full.php?id=1139867.

    Sandoval, C.R. (2008). Nautical Charts and Measurement Systems of the 17th Century. *Underwater and Maritime Archaeology in Latin America and the Caribbean*. M. Leshikar-Denton and P.L. Erreguerena, Eds. 91–102. Left Coast Press, Walnut Creek, CA.

4. Ball, D. (2017). Land, Ho! Maritime Navigation through the Early Nineteenth Century as Represented by the Mardi Gras Shipwreck. *Historical Archaeology* 51(3): 351–358.

    de Souza. P. (2001). *Seafaring and Civilization*. Profile Books, London.

    McGrail, S. (2014). *Early Ships and Seafaring: European Water Transport*. Penn and Sword, Barnsley, UK.

5. Ball, D. (2017). Land, Ho! Maritime Navigation through the Early Nineteenth Century as Represented by the Mardi Gras Shipwreck. *Historical Archaeology* 51(3): 351–358.

    Feinberg, R. (1988). *Polynesian Seafaring and Navigation: Ocean Travel in Anutan Culture and Society*. Kent State University Press, Kent, OH.

    McGrail, S. (2014). *Early Ships and Seafaring: European Water Transport*. Pen and Sword Archaeology, Barnsley, UK.

    McGrail, S. (2015). *Early Ships and Seafaring: Water Transport Beyond Europe*. Pen and Sword, Barnsley, UK.

    Morelle, R. (2017). Astrolabe: Shipwreck find Earliest Navigation Tool. BBC News. Available at http://www.bbc.com/news/science-environment-41724022.

6. Bruseth, J., Ed. (2014). La Belle, *The Ship That Changed History*. Bullock Texas State History Museum, Austin.

    Sobel, D. (1995). *Longitude: The True Story of a Lone Genius Who Solved the Greatest Scientific Problem of His Time*. Penguin, New York.

7. Corbin, A. (1999). *The Material Culture of Steamboat Passengers: Archaeological Evidence from the Missouri River*. Springer, New York.

    Redknap, M., Ed. (1997). *Artefacts from Wrecks: Dated Assemblages from the Late Middle Ages to the Industrial Revolution*. Oxbow Books, Oxford.

8. Gardiner, J., Ed. (2005). *Before the Mast: Life and Death aboard the* Mary Rose, *The Archaeology of the* Mary Rose, Volume 4. Mary Rose Trust, Portsmouth, UK.

9. Druett, J. (1998). *Hen Frigates: Wives of Merchant Captains Under Sail*. Simon and Schuster, New York.

    Druett, J. (2001) *Petticoat Whalers: Whaling Wives at Sea, 1820–1920*. University Press of New England, Lebanon.

    Druett, J. (2001). *She Captains: Heroines and Hellions of the Sea*. Simon and Schuster, New York.

    Mariners' Museum (2000). Women and the Sea. Available at https://www.marinersmuseum.org/sites/micro/women/intro/index.htm.

10. Bolster, W.J. (1997). *Black Jacks: African American Seamen in the Age of Sail*. Harvard University Press, Cambridge.

Linebaugh, P., and M. Rediker. (2000). *Many-Headed Hydra: Sailors, Slaves, Commoners, and the Hidden History of the Revolutionary Atlantic*. Beacon Press, Boston.

11. Tyng, C. (1999). *Before the Wind, The Memoir of an American Sea Captain, 1808–1833*. Viking, New York.

12. Casson, L. (1995). *Ships and Seamanship in the Ancient World*. Johns Hopkins University Press, Baltimore, MD.

Dana, R.H., Jr. (1997). *The Seaman's Friend, A Treatise on Practical Seamanship*. Dover, New York.

Harland, J. (2016). *Seamanship in the Age of Sail*. Naval Institute Press, Annapolis, MD.

13. Horrell, C. (2017). Analysis of the Mardi Gras Shipwreck Ship's Stove. *Historical Archaeology* **51**(3): 359–378.

Roberts, P., S. Weston, B. Wild, C. Boston, P. Ditchfield, A. Shortland, and A.M. Pollard. (2012). The Men of Nelson's Navy: A Comparative Stable Isotope Dietary Study of Late 18th Century and Early 19th Century Servicemen from Royal Naval Hospital Burial Grounds at Plymouth and Gosport, England. *American Journal of Physical Anthropology* **148**: 1–10.

Spalding, S. (2014). *Food at Sea: Shipboard Cuisine from Ancient to Modern Times*. Rowman and Littlefield, New York.

Tsai, G. (2017). Ship Biscuit and Salted Beef Project. Available at https://nauticalarch.org/category/ship-biscuit-and-salted-beef/.

14. Creighton, M. (1982). *Dogwatch and Liberty Days: Seafaring Life in the Nineteenth Century*. Peabody Museum of Salem, Salem, MA.
de Souza, P. (2001). *Seafaring and Civilization*. Profile Books, London.

15. Baron, J. (2009). Sailors' Scurvy Before and After James Lind—A Reassessment. *Nutrition Reviews* **67**(6): 315–332.

Brown, S. (2005). *Scurvy: How a Surgeon, a Mariner, and a Gentleman Solved the Greatest Medical Mystery of the Age of Sail*. St. Martin's Griffin, New York.

16. Boswell, J. (1785). *The Journal of a Tour of the Hebrides*. James Boswell, London. Available at http://www.gutenberg.org/ebooks/6018.

Burden, C. (2001). Medical Care for Seamen aboard Schooners, 1880–1930. *Nautical Research Journal* **46**(3): 164–167.

Druett, J. (2000). *Rough Medicine: Surgeons at Sea in the Age of Sail*. Routledge, New York.

Gardiner, J., Ed. (2005). *Before the Mast: Life and Death Aboard the* Mary Rose. Oxbow Books, Oxford.

17. Finlayson, R. (1824). *An Essay Addressed to the Captains of the Royal Navy, and Those of the Merchants' Service; On the Means of Preserving the Health of Their Crews with Directions for the Prevention of Dry Rot in Ships*. Thomas and George Underwood, London.

Springman, M.-J. (2000). Archaeological and Archival Indicators of Socio-Cultural Change on Board Ships in the 16th Century. *Down the River to the Sea: Proceedings of the Eight International Symposium on Boat and Ship Archaeology, Gdańsk 1997*. J. Litwin, Ed. 75–84. Polish Maritime Museum, Gdańsk.

18. Beck, H. (1973). *Folklore and the Sea*. Mystic Seaport, Mystic, CT.

Creighton, M. (1982). *Dogwatch and Liberty Days: Seafaring Life in the Nineteenth Century*. Peabody Museum of Salem, Salem, MA.

Gardiner, J., Ed. (2005). *Before the Mast: Life and Death aboard the* Mary Rose, *The Archaeology of the* Mary Rose, Volume 4. Mary Rose Trust, Portsmouth, UK.

Grego, J. (1891). *Royal Naval Exhibition, Humorous Art; The Social Aspects of Life in the Royal Navy*. Sampson Low, Marston, Searle, and Rivington, London.

Smith, R., Ed. (2018) *Florida's Lost Galleon: The Emanuel Point Shipwreck*. University of Florida Press, Gainesville.

19. Malinowski, B. (1948). *Magic, Science and Religion*. Doubleday, New York.

    Palmer, C. (1989). The Ritual Taboos of Fishermen: An Alternative Explanation. *Maritime Anthropological Studies* **2**(1): 59–68.

20. Atkins, C. (2009). More than a Hull: Religious Ritual and Sacred Space on Board the Ancient Ship. Master's Thesis, Department of Anthropology, Texas A&M University, College Station.

    Frost, H. (1995). An Anchor from Byblos in the National Museum. *National Museum News* (Lebanon) **2**: 23–26.

    Van de Noort, R. (2011). *North Sea Archaeologies: A Maritime Biography, 10,000 bc–ad 1500*. Oxford University Press, Oxford.

    Wachsmann, S. (1998). *Seagoing Ships and Seamanship in the Bronze Age Levant*. Chatham, London.

21. Beck, H. (1973). *Folklore and the Sea*. Mystic Seaport, Mystic, CT.

    Creighton, M. (1982). *Dogwatch and Liberty Days: Seafaring Life in the Nineteenth Century*. Peabody Museum of Salem, Salem, MA.

    Westerdahl, C. (2013). Odysseus and Sinbad as Metaphors. Some Crossdisciplinary Approaches to the Lore of the Seas. Årbok Norsk Maritimt Museum, Oslo.

22. Abrahams, R. (1974). *Deep the Water, Shallow the Shore*. University of Texas Press, Austin.

    Beck, H. (1973). *Folklore and the Sea*. Mystic Seaport, Mystic, CT.

    Hugill, S. (1961). *Shanties from the Seven Seas: Shipboard Work-songs and Songs Used as Work-songs from the Great Days of Sail*. Routledge, New York.

23. Lloyd, A.L. (1963). Reuben Ranzo. *Blow the Man Down* by A.L. Lloyd, E. MacColl, and H. H. Corbett. Topic Records, Uppingham.

24. Newman, S. (1998). Reading the Bodies of Early American Seafarers. *The William and Mary Quarterly*, 3rd Series, **55**(1): 59–82.

    Parry, A. (2006 [1933]). *Tattoo, Secrets of a Strange Art*. Dover Publications, Mineola, NY.

Tyng, C. (1999). *Before the Wind, The Memoir of an American Sea Captain, 1808–1833*. Viking, New York.

**CHAPTER 11**

1. Bard, K. and R. Fattovich. (2011). The Middle Kingdom Red Sea Harbor at Mersa/Wadi Gawasis. *Journal of the American Research Center in Egypt* **47**: 105–129.

2. Pulak, C. (1998). The Uluburun Shipwreck: An Overview. *International Journal of Nautical Archaeology* 27(3): 188–224.

    Pulak, C. (2008). The Uluburun Shipwreck and Late Bronze Age Trade. *Beyond Babylon: Art, Trade, and Diplomacy in the Second Millennium B.C.* J. Aruz, K. Benzel, and J. Evans, Eds. 288–305. Metropolitan Museum of Art, New York.

3. Moity, M., M. Rudel and A.-X. Wurst. (2003). *Master Seafarers: The Phoenicians and the Greeks*. Periplus, London.

    Polzer, M. (2014). The Bajo de la Campana Shipwreck and Colonial Trade in Spain. *Assyria to Iberia at the Dawn of the Classical Age*. J. Aruz, S. Graff, and Y. Rakic, Eds. 230–270. Metropolitan Museum of Art, New York.

4. Polzer, M. (2014). The Bajo de la Campana Shipwreck and Colonial Trade in Spain. *Assyria to Iberia at the Dawn of the Classical Age*. J. Aruz, S. Graff, and Y. Rakic, Eds. 230–270. Metropolitan Museum of Art, New York.

5. Roller, D. (2006). *Through the Pillars of Herakles: Greco-Roman Exploration of the Atlantic*. Routledge, New York.

6. Katzev, S.W. (2007). The Ancient Ship of Kyrenia, Beneath Cyprus Seas. *Great Moments in Greek Archaeology*. P. Valavanis and D. Hardy, Eds. 286–299. Oxford University Press, New York.

    Steffy, R.J. (1993). Ancient Ship Repair. *Tropis V: 5th International Symposium on Ship Construction in Antiquity Proceedings*. H. Tzalas, Ed. 395–408. Tropis, Athens.

7. Casson, L. (1994). *Travel in the Ancient World*. Johns Hopkins University Press, Baltimore, MD.

    Claridge, A. (1998). *Rome: An Oxford Archaeological Guide*. Oxford University Press, New York.

    de Souza, P. (2001). *Seafaring and Civilization*. Profile Books, London.

8. Marsden, P. (1994). *Ships of the Port of London: First to Eleventh Centuries AD*. English Heritage, London.

    Pomey, P., Y. Kahanov, and E. Rieth. (2012). Transition from Shell to Skeleton in Ancient Mediterranean Ship-Construction: Analysis, Problems, and Future Research. *International Journal of Nautical Archaeology* 41(2): 235–314.

    Tiboni, F. and S. Tusa. (2016). The Marausa Wreck, Sicily: Interim Report on a Boat Built in the Western Imperial Roman Tradition. *International Journal of Nautical Archaeology* 45(2): 239–252.

9. Beltrame, C., D. Gaddi, and S. Parizzi (2011). A Presumed Hydraulic Apparatus for the Transport of Live Fish, Found on the Roman Wreck at Grado, Italy. *International Journal of Nautical Archaeology* 40(2): 274–282.

    Wirsching, A. (2000). How the Obelisks Reached Rome: Evidence of Roman Double-Ships. *International Journal of Nautical Archaeology* 29(2): 273–283.

10. Sobecki, S. (2007). *The Sea and Medieval English Literature*. D.S. Brewer, Cambridge.

    Wooding, J. (2001). St Brendan's Boat: Dead Hides and the Living Sea in Columban and Related Hagiography. *Studies in Irish Hagiography: Saints and Scholars*. J. Carey, M. Herbert, and P. Ó Riain, Eds. 77–92. ISBS, Portland, OR.

11. Fitzhugh, W., and E. Ward. (2000). *Vikings: The North Atlantic Saga*. Smithsonian Institution Press, Washington, DC.

    Pringle, H. (19 October, 2012). Evidence of Viking Outpost found in Canada. *National Geographic News*. Available at news.nationalgeographic.com/news/2012/10/121019-viking-outpost-second-new-canada-science-sutherland/

12. Hussain, T. (2017). Why Did Vikings Have "Allah" Embroidered into Funeral Clothes? *BBC*. http://www.bbc.com/news/world-europe-41567391.

    Montgomery, J. (2000). Ibn Fadlān and the Rūsiyyah. *Journal of Arabic and Islamic Studies* 3: 1–25.

13. McGrail, S. (2015). *Early Ships and Seafaring: Water Transport Beyond Europe*. Pen and Sword, Barnsley, UK.

14. Burton, R. (2009). *The Seven Voyages of Sinbad the Sailor*. Digireads.com, New York.

    Gibb, H. (1994). *The Travels of Ibn Baṭṭūṭa*. Hakluyt Society, London.

    Marsden, W., Trans. (2008). *The Travels of Marco Polo the Venetian*. Alfred A. Knopf, New York.

15. Kimura, J. (2016). *Archaeology of East Asian Shipbuilding*. University Press of Florida, Gainesville.

    Miksic, J. (2013). *Singapore and the Silk Road of the Sea, 1300–1800*. National Museum of Singapore, Singapore.

    SEAArch. (2016). Maritime Silk Route. *SEAArch: The Southeast Asian Archaeology Newsblog*. Available at https://www.southeastasianarchaeology.com/tag/maritime-silk-route/.

16. Dreyer, E. (2007). *Zheng He, China and the Oceans in the Early Ming Dynasty, 1405–1433*. Pearson, New York.

17. Mearns, D., D. Parham, and B. Fohlich. (2016). A Portuguese East Indiaman from the 1502–1503 Fleet of Vasco da Gama off Al Hallaniyah Island, Oman: an interim report. *International Journal of Nautical Archaeology* 45(2): 331–351.

    Page, M. (2002). *The First Global Village: How Portugal Changed the World*. Casa Das Letras, Alfragide, Portugal.

18. Bass, G. (1996). *Ships and Shipwrecks of the Americas*. Thames and Hudson, New York.

Oertling, T. (2004). Characteristics of Fifteenth- and Sixteenth-Century Iberian Ships. *The Philosophy of Shipbuilding: Conceptual Approaches of the Study of Wooden Ships*. F. Hocker and C. Ward, Eds. 129–136. Texas A&M University Press, College Station.

Smith, R. (1993). *Vanguard of Empire: Ships of Exploration in the Age of Columbus*. Oxford University Press, New York.

19. Grenier, R., M-A. Bernier, and W. Stevens, Eds. (2007). *The Underwater Archaeology of Red Bay: Basque Shipbuilding and Whaling in the 16th Century*, 5 vols. Parks Canada, Ottawa.

20. Adams, J. (1985). *Sea Venture*: A Second Interim Report—Part 1. *International Journal of Nautical Archaeology* **14**(4): 275–299.

Bass, G. (1996). *Ships and Shipwrecks of the Americas*. Thames and Hudson, New York.

Bruseth, J., A. Borgens, B. Jones, and E. Ray, Eds. (2017). La Belle: *The Archaeology of a Seventeenth-Century Vessel of New World Colonization*. Texas A&M University Press, College Station.

Hall, J. (1996). A Seventeenth-Century Northern European Merchant Shipwreck in Monte Cristi Bay, Dominican Republic. PhD Dissertation, Department of Anthropology, Texas A&M University, College Station.

Patterson, M.L.R. (1988). The *Sea Venture*. *Mariner's Mirror* **74**(1): 37–48.

21. Ferris, N. (2011). *The Archaeology of Native-Lived Colonialism: Challenging History in the Great Lakes*. University of Arizona Press, Tucson.

Gosden, C. (2004). *Archaeology and Colonialism: Cultural Contact from 5000 BC to the Present*. Cambridge University Press, New York.

Stein, G., Ed. (2005). *The Archaeology of Colonial Encounters*. School of American Research Press, Santa Fe, NM.

22. van Duivendvoorde, W. (2015). *Dutch East India Company Shipbuilding: The Archaeological Study of* Batavia *and other Seventeenth-Century VOC Ships*. Texas A&M University Press, College Station.

23. Gibbs, M. (2003). The Archaeology of Crisis: Shipwreck Survivor Camps in Australia. *Historical Archaeology* **37**(1): 128–145.

24. Kahn, A. and J. Bouie. (2015). The Atlantic Slave Trade in Two Minutes. Available at http://www.slate.com/articles/life/the_history_of_american_slavery/2015/06/animated_interactive_of_the_history_of_the_atlantic_slave_trade.html.

Slave Wrecks Project. (2017). Slave Wrecks Project. Available at slavewrecksproject.org.

Trouvadore Project. (2008). Slave Ship Trouvadore. Available at slaveshiptrouvadore.org.

25. Svalesen, L. (2000). *The Slave Ship* Fredensborg. Indiana University Press, Bloomington.

26. Cook, G., R. Horlings, and A. Pietruszka. (2016). Maritime Archaeology and the Early Atlantic Trade: Research at Elmina, Ghana. *International Journal of Nautical Archaeology* **45**(2): 370–387.

DeCorse, C. (2001) *An Archaeology of Elmina*. Smithsonian Institution Press, Washington, DC.

DeCorse, C. (2008). Varied Pasts: History, Oral Tradition, and Archaeology on the Mina Coast. *Small Worlds: Method, Meaning, and Narrative in Microhistory*. J. Brooks, C. DeCorse, and J. Walton. 77–93. School for Advanced Research Press, Santa Fe, NM.

27. Callaway, E. (2016). Freedom in Exile. *Nature* **540**: 184–187.

28. Chapelle, H. (1967). *The Search for Speed Under Sail, 1700–1855*. W.W. Norton and Company, New York.

Crothers, W. (2000). *The American-Built Clipper Ship, 1850–1856*. International Marine, Camden, ME.

29. Faulkner, A. (1985). Archaeology of the Cod Fishery: Damariscove Island. *Historical Archaeology* **19**(2): 57–86.

Johnston, P. (1996). The End of the Age of Sail: Merchant Shipping in the Nineteenth Century. *Ships and Shipwrecks of the Americas*. G. Bass, Ed. 231–250. Thames and Hudson, New York.

Klippel, W. and J. Sichler (2004). North Atlantic Fishes in Inland Context: Pickled Mackerel (*Scomber scombrus*) in the Historic Period. *Historical Archaeology* **38**(4): 12–24.

Reitz, E. (2004)."Fishing Down the Food Web": A Case Study from St. Augustine, Florida, USA. *American Antiquity* **69**(1): 63–83.

30. Lawrence, S. and P. Davies (2011). *An Archaeology of Australia Since 1788*. Springer, New York.

31. Fitzhugh, W., A. Herzog, S. Perdikaris, and B. McLeod. (2011). Ship to Shore: Inuit, Early Europeans, and Maritime Landscapes in the Northern Gulf of St. Lawrence. *The Archaeology of Maritime Landscapes*. B. Ford, Ed. 99–128. Springer, New York.

Grenier, R., M.-A. Bernier, and W. Stevens, Eds. (2007). *The Underwater Archaeology of Red Bay: Basque Shipbuilding and Whaling in the 16th Century*, 5 vols. Parks Canada, Ottawa.

Lawrence, S., and P. Davies (2011). *An Archaeology of Australia Since 1788*. Springer, New York.

32. Bockstoce, J. (1986). *Whales, Ice, & Men: The History of Whaling in the Western Arctic*. University of Washington Press, Seattle.

Leavitt, J. (1973). *The* Charles W. Morgan. Mystic Seaport, Mystic, CT.

Mawar, G. (1999) *Ahab's Trade: The Saga of South Seas Whaling*. St. Martin's Press, New York.

Thanm K. (11 February 2011). Rare 1823 Wreck Found—Capt. Linked to "Moby-Dick," Cannibalism. National Geographic News. Available at https://news.nationalgeographic.com/news/2011/02/110211-two-brothers-whaling-ship-pollard-science-nantucket-noaa/.

33. Kunzig, R. (2014). Romans in France: An Ancient Wreck Tells of Romans in France. *National Geographic*. Available at http://ngm.nationalgeographic.com/2014/04/roman-boat/kunzig-text.

de Weerd, M. (1988). A Landlubber's View of Shipbuilding Procedure in the Celtic Barges of Zwammerdam, the Netherlands. *Local Boats,*

*Proceedings of the Fourth International Symposium on Boat and Ship Archaeology*. O.L. Filguerias, Ed. 35–51. Oxbow Books, Oxford.

34. Leshikar, M. (1996). The Earliest Watercraft: From Rafts to Viking Ships. *Ships and Shipwrecks of the Americas*. G. Bass, Ed. 13–32. Thames and Hudson, New York.

35. Wheeler, R. (1972). Waterways Open the New World, The North American Fur Trade. *A History of Seafaring Based on Underwater Archaeology*. G. Bass, Ed. 281–286. Walker and Company, New York.

36. de Fontaine, F.G. (1896). *Best Thoughts of Charles Dickens Arranged in Alphabetical Order*. G.W. Dillingham, New York.

Wagner, M. (2015). *The Wreck of the* America *in Southern Illinois: A Flatboat on the Ohio River*. Southern Illinois University Press, Carbondale.

37. Bélisle, J., and A. Lépine. (2003). La Sale de Machines du Vapeur *P.S. Lady Sherbrooke*. *Mer Et Monde, Questions d'archéologie Maritime*, C. Roy, Ed. Association des archéologues du Québec, Québec.

Corbin, A. (1999). *The Material Culture of Steamboat Passengers: Archaeological Evidence from the Missouri River*. Springer, New York.

Corbin, A., and B. Rodgers (2008). *The Steamboat* Montana *and the Opening of the West*. University Press of Florida, Gainesville.

Crisman, K. (2014). The Western River Steamboat *Heroine*, 1823–1838, Oklahoma, USA: Construction. *International Journal of Nautical Archaeology*. **43**(1): 128–150.

Kane, A. (2004). *The Western River Steamboat*. Texas A&M University Press, College Station.

38. Wade, G. (2005). The Zheng He Voyages: A Reassessment. *Journal of the Malaysian Branch of the Royal Asiatic Society* **78**(1): 37–58.

Watson, P. (12 September 2016). Ship Found in Arctic 168 years after doomed Northwest Passage attempt. *The Guardian*. Available at https://www.theguardian.com/world/2016/sep/12/hms-terror-wreck-found-arctic-nearly-170-years-northwest-passage-attempt.

**CHAPTER 12**

1. Wachsmann, S. (1998). *Seagoing Ships and Seamanship in the Bronze Age Levant*. Texas A&M University Press, College Station.

2. Polzer, M.E. (2014). Early Shipbuilding in the Eastern Mediterranean. *Oxford Handbook of Maritime Archaeology*. A. Catsambis, B. Ford, and D. Hamilton, Eds. 349–378. Oxford University Press, New York.

3. Catsambis, A. (2006). Before Antikythera: The First Underwater Archaeological Survey in Greece. *The International Journal of Nautical Archaeology* **35**(1): 104–107.

    Papalas, A.J. (1997). The Development of the Trireme. *The Mariner's Mirror* **83**(3): 259–271.

    Lolos, I. (2003). Ο Χρήστος Τσούντας στο Στενό της Σαλαμίνος, 1884: Η πρώτη οργανωμένη υποβρύχια αρχαιολογική έρευνα στην Ιστορία. *Enalia* **VII**:13–27.

    Lovém, B., and M. Schaldemose. (2012). *The Ancient Harbours of the Piraeus: The Zea Shipsheds and Slipways*. Monographs of the Danish Institute at Athens (15.1 & 15.2). Aarhus University Press, Aarhus.

4. Zachos, K.L. (2003). The Tropaeum of the Sea-battle of Actium at Nikopolis: Interim Report. *Journal of Roman Archaeology* **16**: 65–92.

5. Casson, L., and J. R. Steffy. (1991). *The Athlit Ram*. Texas A&M University Press, College Station.

6. Tusa, S., and J. Royal. (2012). The Landscape of the Naval Battle at the Egadi Islands (241 BC). *Journal of Roman Archaeology* **25**: 7–48.

7. Pryor, J.H., and E.M. Jeffreys. (2011). *The Age of the Dromon: The Byzantine Navy ca 500-1204*. Brill Academic Publishers, Leiden, The Netherlands.

8. Kocabaş, U. (2015). The Yenikapı Byzantine-Era Shipwrecks, Istanbul, Turkey: A Preliminary Report and Inventory of the 27 Wrecks Studied by Istanbul University. *The International Journal of Nautical Archaeology* **44**(1): 5–38.

    Pulak, C., R. Ingram, and M. Jones. (2015). Eight Byzantine Shipwrecks from the Theodosian Harbour Excavations at Yenikapı in Istanbul, Turkey: An Introduction. *The International Journal of Nautical Archaeology* **44**(1): 39–73.

9. Crumlin-Pedersen, O., and E. Bondesen, Eds. (2002). *The Skuldelev Ships I: Topography, Archaeology, History, Conservation and Display*. Viking Ship Museum, Roskilde, Denmark.

10. Delgado, J.P. (2008). *Khubilai Khan's Lost Fleet: In Search of a Legendary Armada*. University of California Press, Berkeley.

    Sasaki R.J. (2015). *The Origins of the Lost Fleet of the Mongol Empire*. Texas A&M University Press, College Station.

11. Beltrame, C., and R.G. Ridella, Eds. (2011). *Ships & Guns: The Sea Ordnance of Venice and Europe between the 15th and 17th centuries*. Oxbow Books, Oxford.

    Gardiner, R. (1995). *The Age of the Galley: Mediterranean Oared Vessels since Pre-Classical Times*. Conway Maritime Press, London.

    Parker, G. (2008). *The Cambridge Illustrated History of Warfare: The Triumph of the West*. Cambridge University Press, Cambridge.

12. Martin, C. (2011). Stowed or Mounted: The Spanish Armada of 1588 and the Strategic Logistics of Guns at Sea. In *Ships & Guns: The Sea Ordnance in Venice and Europe between the 15th and the 17th Centuries*. C. Beltrame and R. G. Ridella, Eds.. 85–97. Oxbow Books, Oxford.

13. Clarke, R., M. Dean, G. Hutchinson, S. McGrail, and J. Squirrell. (1993). Recent Work on the R. Hamble Wreck Near Bursledon, Hampshire. *The International Journal of Nautical Archaeology* **22**(1): 21–44.

    Friel, I. (1993). Henry V's *Grace Dieu* and the Wreck in the R. Hamble Near Bursledon, Hampshire. *The International Journal of Nautical Archaeology* **22**(1): 3–19.

    Parker, G. (2008). *The Cambridge Illustrated History of Warfare: The Triumph of the West*. Cambridge University Press. Cambridge.

14. Adams, J. (2013). *A Maritime Archaeology of Ships: Innovation and Social Change in Medieval and Early Modern Europe*. Oxbow Books, Oxford.

    Marsden, P. (2003). *Sealed by Time: The Loss and Recovery of the* Mary Rose. *The Archaeology of the* Mary Rose *Volume I*. Oxbow Books, Oxford.

15. Hocker, F. (2011). *Vasa*. Oxbow Books, Oxford.

16. Fraga, T. (2007). Santo Antonio de Tanná: Story and Reconstruction. Texas A&M University Master's Thesis, College Station.

    Piercy, R. (2005). The Tragedy of Santo Antonio de Tanna: Mombasa, Kenya. *Beneath the Seven Seas: Adventures with the Institute of Nautical Archaeology*. G.F. Bass, Ed. 172–179. Thames and Hudson, London.

17. Wilde-Ramsing, M.U. (2006). The Pirate Ship *Queen Anne's Revenge*. *X Marks the Spot: New Perspectives on Maritime History and Nautical Archaeology*. R.K. Skowronek and C.R. Ewen, Eds. 160–195. University Press of Florida, Gainesville.

18. Crisman, K.J. (2014). *Coffins of the Brave: Lake Shipwrecks of the War of 1812*. Texas A&M University Press, College Station.

19. Broadwater, J.D. (2012). *USS* Monitor: *A Historic Ship Completes Its Final Voyage*. Texas A&M University Press, College Station.

    National Oceanic and Atmospheric Administration (1998). *Charting a New Course for the* Monitor: *A Comprehensive, Long Range Preservation Plan with Options for Management, Stabilization, Preservation, Recovery, Conservation and Exhibition of Materials and Artifacts from the Monitor National Marine Sanctuary*. U.S. Department of Commerce, Washington, DC.

20. McClean, S. (2016). Historical Background. n H.L. Hunley *Recovery Operations*. R. Neyland and H. Brown, Eds. Naval History and Heritage Command, Washington, DC.

21. Neyland, R., and H.G. Brown, Eds. (2016). H.L. Hunley *Recovery Operations*. Naval History and Heritage Command, Washington, DC.

22. Neyland, R.S. (2014). Underwater Archaeology of the World Wars. *Oxford Handbook of Maritime Archaeology*. A. Catsambis, B. Ford, and D. Hamilton, Eds. 708–729. Oxford University Press, New York.

23. McCartney, I. (2017). *Jutland 1916: The Archaeology of a Naval Battlefield*. Conway, London.

24. Ballard, R., and R. Archbold (2007). *Robert Ballard's Guadalcanal*. Chartwell Books, Edison, NJ.

    Carrell, T., Ed. (1991). *Submerged Cultural Resources Assessment of Micronesia*. Southwest Cultural Resources Center Professional Papers No. 36. National Park Service, Santa Fe, NM.

    Delgado, J.P., D.J. Lenihan, and L.E. Murphy. (1991). *The Archaeology of the Atomic Bomb: A Submerged Cultural Resources Assessment of the Sunken Fleet of Operation Crossroads at Bikini and Kwajalein Atoll Lagoons*. Southwest Cultural Resources Center Professional Papers No. 37. National Park Service, Santa Fe, NM.

    Department of the Navy. (2008). *Archaeological Remote Sensing of Operation Neptune: The D-Day Landings at Omaha and Utah Beaches, Normandy, France*. Naval Historical Center Underwater Archaeology Branch, Washington, DC.

    Dresch, P., and J. McCarthy. (2012). *Scapa Flow Wreck Surveys: Archaeological Interpretation of Multibeam Data and Desk-Based Assessment* (REF 83680.04). Wessex Archaeology Limited, Salisbury, UK.

    McCartney, I. (2015). *The Maritime Archaeology of a Modern Conflict: Comparing the Archaeology of German Submarine Wrecks to the Historical Text*. Routledge, London.

25. Hulver, R. (2018). *A Grave Misfortune: The USS* Indianapolis *Tragedy*. Government Publishing Office, Washington, DC.

    Lenihan, D., J.P. Delgado, B. Dickinson, G. Cummins, S. Henderson, D.A. Martinez, and L.E. Murphy. (1990). *Submerged Cultural*

*Resources Study: USS* Arizona *Memorial and Pearl Harbor National Historic Landmark.* Southwest Cultural Resources Center Professional Papers No. 23. National Park Service, Santa Fe, NM.

26. Ballard, R.D., and R. Archbold. (2005). *The Lost Ships of Robert Ballard.* Thunder Bay Press, San Diego.

27. Coroneos, C., M. Carter, and C. Wilby. (2014). Relocation of United States Navy Consolidated PBY Catalina Wreckage: Final Report. Cosmos Archaeology PTY LTD. INPEX Ichthys LNG Project. Unpublished.

    Jung, S. (2001). Wings beneath the Sea: The Aviation Archaeology of Catalina Flying Boats in Darwin Harbour, Northern Territory. Master's Thesis. Northern Territory University (now Charles Darwin University), Darwin, NT.

28. Friedman, N. (2002). *U.S. Submarines through 1945: An Illustrated Design Theory.* Naval Institute Press, Annapolis, MD.

    Naval History and Heritage Command. (2015). *Dictionary of American Naval Fighting Ships* Nautilus. Available at https://www.history.navy.mil/research/histories/ship-histories/danfs/n/nautilus-ssn-571-iv.html.

**CHAPTER 13**

1. UNESCO (United Nations Educational, Scientific, and Cultural Organization). (1954). Convention for the Protection of Cultural Property in the Event of Armed Conflict. Available at http://unesdoc.unesco.org/images/0008/000824/082464mb.pdf.

    UNESCO. (1971). Records of the General Conference: Sixteenth Session Paris, 12 October to 14 November 1970. Available at http://unesdoc.unesco.org/images/0011/001140/114046e.pdf.

    UNESCO. (1972). Convention Concerning the Protection of the World Cultural and Natural Heritage. Available at http://whc.unesco.org/archive/convention-en.pdf.

    UNESCO. (2001). Convention on the Protection of the Underwater Cultural Heritage. Records of the General Conference: 31st Session Paris, 15 October to 3 November 2001. Available at http://unesdoc.unesco.org/images/0012/001246/124687e.pdf.

    UNESCO. (2017). Convention on the Protection of the Underwater Cultural Heritage (State Parties). Available at http://www.unesco.org/eri/la/convention.asp?KO=13520&language=E&order=alpha.

2. United Nations. (2018). Oceans & Seas. Available at https://sustainabledevelopment.un.org/topics/oceanandseas.

3. Koschtial, U. (2009) Beneath the Water, Heritage In Search of International Protection. *The UNESCO Courier* **2009**(1): 14–15.

4. UNESCO. (2017). Convention on the Protection of the Underwater Cultural Heritage (State Parties). Available at http://www.unesco.org/eri/la/convention.asp?KO=13520&language=E&order=alpha.

5. UNESCO. (2001). Convention on the Protection of the Underwater Cultural Heritage. Records of the General Conference: 31st Session Paris, 15 October to 3 November 2001. Available at http://unesdoc.unesco.org/images/0012/001246/124687e.pdf:51.

6. UNESCO. (2001). Records of the General Conference: 31st Session Paris, 15 October to 3 November 2001. Available at http://unesdoc.unesco.org/images/0012/001246/124687e.pdf: 58.

7. UNESCO. (2001). Convention on the Protection of the Underwater Cultural Heritage. Records of the General Conference: 31st Session Paris, 15 October to 3 November 2001. Available at http://unesdoc.unesco.org/images/0012/001246/124687e.pdf: 58–59.

8. UNESCO. (2001). Convention on the Protection of the Underwater Cultural Heritage. Records of the General Conference: 31st Session Paris, 15 October

to 3 November 2001. Available at http://unesdoc.unesco.org/images/0012/001246/124687e.pdf: 59.

9. UNESCO. (2001). Convention on the Protection of the Underwater Cultural Heritage. Records of the General Conference: 31st Session Paris, 15 October to 3 November 2001. Available at http://unesdoc.unesco.org/images/0012/001246/124687e.pdf: 60.

10. UNESCO. (2001). Convention on the Protection of the Underwater Cultural Heritage. Records of the General Conference: 31st Session Paris, 15 October to 3 November 2001. Available at http://unesdoc.unesco.org/images/0012/001246/124687e.pdf: 60–61.

#### CHAPTER 14

1. Surovell, T.A., J.L. Toohey, A.D. Myers, J.M. LaBelle, J.C.M. Ahern, and B. Reisig. (2017). The End of Archaeological Discovery. *American Antiquity* **82**(2): 288–230.

2. Advisory Council on Underwater Archaeology (ACUA). (2018). Organizations Providing Maritime Heritage Training to Recreational Divers. Available at https://acuaonline.org/get-involved/recreational-diver-heritage-education/.

3. Hambrecht, G., and M. Rockman. (2017). International Approaches to Climate Change and Cultural Heritage. *American Antiquity* **82**(4): 627–641.

   Florida Public Archaeology Network. (2017). Heritage Monitoring Scouts. Available at https://hms.fpan.us/

4. Bowens, A. (2009). *Underwater Archaeology: The NAS Guide to Principles and Practice,* second edition. Blackwell Publishing. Portsmouth, UK.

5. Catsambis, A., B. Ford, and J. Halligan. (2017). Maritime Archaeology. *Oxford Bibliography in Anthropology.* J. John Jackson, Ed. Oxford University Press, Oxford. Available at DOI: 10.1093/OBO/9780199766567-0176.

# INDEX